Food Preparation and Cooking

Levels 1 and 2

Roy Hayter

Hotel and Catering Training Company

HOTEL&
CATERING
TRAINING
COMPANY

MACMILLAN

First published 1992 by
THE MACMILLAN PRESS LTD
Houndmills, Basingstoke, Hampshire RG21 2XS
and London
Companies and representatives
throughout the world

ISBN 0–333–59161–5

Reprinted 1993

A catalogue record for this book is available from the
British Library

Typeset by Kate Jennings and Associates, London

Printed in Hong Kong

Contents

Section	Page	NVQ/SVQ units LEVEL 1	LEVEL 2
Acknowledgements	iv		
About this book	1		
Customer skills	3	G3 Deal with customers	
Safety and security	5	G1 Maintain a safe and secure working environment	as level 1
Hygiene	9	G2 Maintain a professional and hygienic appearance	as level 1
Cleaning procedures	15	1D12 Clean food production areas, equipment and utensils	2D12 Clean food production areas, equipment and utensils
Knife skills	21	1D10 Handle and maintain knives	2D10 Handle and maintain knives
Food handling and storage	25	1D11 Handle and store food	2D11 Accept and store food deliveries
Bread products	29	1D17 Prepare sandwiches, rolls and hot filled bread products	
Microwave	33	1D18 Microwave food	
Cooking for quick service	37	1D19 Deep fry food	
		1D20 Griddle, barbecue or grill foods	
		1D21 Prepare, cook and assemble food for quick service	
Vending	43	1C10 Clean and restock drinks machines/ equipment	
Meat and poultry	47	1D1 Prepare and cook meat and poultry dishes	2D1 Prepare and cook meat and poultry dishes
Fish	93	1D2 Prepare and cook fish dishes	2D2 Prepare and cook fish dishes
Shellfish	125		2D14 Prepare and cook shellfish dishes
Stocks, sauces and soups	135	1D4 Prepare and cook convenience stocks, sauces and soups	2D4 Prepare and cook stocks, sauces and soups
Fruit	149	1D14 Prepare and cook fruit	
Vegetables, rice and vegetable protein	155	1D13 Prepare and cook vegetables	2D18 Prepare and cook vegetable and rice dishes
		1D16 Prepare and cook rice	
		1D15 Prepare and cook vegetable protein dishes	
Pulses	179	1D5 Prepare and cook pulses	2D5 Prepare and cook pulse dishes
Pasta	183	1D6 Prepare and cook pasta dishes	2D6 Prepare and cook fresh pasta
Eggs and batters	189	1D3 Prepare and cook egg and batter dishes	2D3 Prepare and cook egg custard based desserts
Doughs	203	1D7 Prepare and cook dough products	2D7 Prepare and cook dough products
Pastry	215	1D8 Prepare and cook pastry dishes	2D8 Prepare and cook pastry dishes
Cakes and biscuits	237	1D9 Prepare, cook and decorate convenience cakes and biscuits	2D9 Prepare, cook and decorate cakes and biscuits
Cold presentation	259		2D13 Prepare food for cold presentation
Cook-chill	271		2D15 Cook-chill foods
Cook-freeze	275		2D16 Cook-freeze foods
Glossary	279		
Index	282		

Acknowledgements

The Hotel and Catering Training Company and The Macmillan Press gratefully acknowledge the contribution made to this book by the following:

Recipes
As acknowledged in the text, and Danny Stevenson

Advice with the text
Clive Finch, Visiting Professor, Thames Valley University

Photographic locations
Barclays Bank, London; Bournemouth University; E. Coaney & Co, Birmingham; Cranks Wholefoods, London; Gratte Brothers, Knebworth; John Layton & Co, London; Lewisham College, London; MEL Philips, Crawley; Oxford Brookes University

Loan of photographs
British Gas; The Flour Advisory Bureau; Forte; Impact Photos (page 37/Jeremey Nicholl; page 94/Roger Scruton; page 98/Barthelemy Claude); Little Chef; McDougalls Catering Services Ltd/Macalister Creative Services; Metropole Hotels; and Catherine Blackie (picture research)

Advice and help with the text, photographs and examples of documents
Rachel Lindner, Catering and Allied Services; Debbie Foster, Forte Heritage, and John Morris-Jones, Excelsior Forte Hotel, Heathrow; Gary Patchett, Metropole Hotels; Claire Wilson and Pam Frediani (coordinators and researchers)

Piloting/commenting on the text
Pam Rotherforth, Tim Neale and Philip Massey, Gardner Merchant; Pennie Munn, Tony Hall, Ian Pitt and Glen Forder, Basingstoke College of Technology; Peter Little, Graham Abbott and Dominic Harman, Brunel College of Technology, Bristol; Bernard Perry and Graham White, Westminster College, London; Susan Tukalo, June Barclay and Susan Brown, HCTC Scotland; Miles Holtby, Keith Adams and Alister Jones, HCTC Southern; Theo Guy, Richard Pelling, Gaynor Briggs and Christine Weeks, HCTC Western; Denise Johnson, Sarah Plows, Mark Fletcher, Helen Webb, Ian Burke and Pauline Crompton, HCTC Central; Kay Backham, Geraldine Barker, Katie Burgess, Ros Gillies and Judith Hogg, HCTC Coordinators; Melvyn Teare, HCTC Southern; Gill Pittard, HCTC Award-Making Division

Photographers
Richard Kirby, David Spears, Chris Browning, Ian Cameron, Keith Turnbull and Picture Link

Illustrators and artwork
Diana Beatty; also John Woodcock and Rob Shone; Ian Thompson (cover design); Stuart Reid (artwork for pages 1 and 2)

Illustrations, other material reproduced or drawn on in the text, and advice with the text
Asparagus Growers' Association; Automatic Vending Association of Great Britain and Derek Skinner; BBC *Vegetarian Good Food* and *Good Food*; Bloomsbury Publishing Ltd; Booker Fitch Food Services; British Chicken Information Service; The British Egg Information Service; British Food Information Service and Daphne MacCarthy; British Iceberg Growers' Association; The British Meat Information Service; British Sandwich Association; British Trades Alphabet, publishers of *GCSE Directions Cooking & Using Meat*; The Butter Council and Catherine Miller; *Caterer & Hotelkeeper* for extracts by Bob Gledhill (26.9.91) and from *The Bread Guide* by Michael Raffael; Craigmillar; Crypto Peerless; Danish Bacon and Meat Council; The Dutch Dairy Bureau; The Dutch Meat Board; Electricity Association and Jenny Webb; The Flour Advisory Bureau and Georgina Holloway; Food Focus, Food from Britain; The Fresh Fruit and Vegetable Information Bureau; M. Gilbert (Greenford) Ltd; Headline Book Publishing and Alfresco Leisure Publications; Kraft General Foods Food Service; Lucas Ingredients; Marlow Foods Ltd; McDougalls (RHM Foods Ltd) and Samantha Rutta, Jane Hildred, Anne Bullock; McDougalls Catering Foods Ltd and Alyson Stephenson, Catherine Nicholls; The Meat and Livestock Commission and Shirley Ascough, Keith Fisher; Merrychef Ltd and Verne George; Milk Marketing Board; MLC/Edu-Com Consultants; Mornflake Oats; National Dairy Council; Nestlé UK Ltd for recipes by Buitoni, Carnation, Crosse & Blackwell, Dufrais, Gale's, Herta, Nestlé and Sarsons, trade marks of Société des Produits Nestlé SA, Switzerland; New Zealand Meat Producers Board and Lamb Catering Advisory Service; Peerless Food Products; Pork and Bacon Promotion Council; Potato Marketing Board and Tony Reeve; Sainath Rao; Record Pasta, Pasta Foods; The Rice Bureau; Sankey Vending and Chris Gooch; Sea Fish Industry Authority; The Tandoori Clay Oven Company; The Tea Council; Vegetable Protein Association; The Vegetarian Catering Advisory Service and Mary Scott Morgan for extracts from *Checklist of vegetarian alternatives* published by HCIMA in *Hospitality*, October 1990; The Vegetarian Society and Judy McDonald

Other information sources drawn on in the text
Batchelors; Booker Belmont Wholesale and Don Greenwood; Brake Bros. Foodservice Ltd and Eileen Steinbock; British Gas; Brooke Bond Foods; The Cheeses of England & Wales Information Bureau; Cranbury Information Board; Four Square; Frozen Food Information Service; GFE Bartlett; HCIMA library; Hobart Still; Imperial Machines; Jeyes Cleaning Products; S. C. Johnson Professional; Kimberley-Clarke; Klix and Chris Jupp; Lever Industrial; Menumaster Inc; Microwave Association and Pratap Gadhvi; Moffat Appliances; Rowlett; Scotch Quality Beef and Lamb Association and Margaret Johnson; TMS Digital Thermometers; Universe Foods; Welsh Lamb Association and Nick Zalik; Wittenborg UK Ltd

About this book

This book will help you work towards the level 1 and/or level 2 NVQ/SVQ qualifications in *Food Preparation and Cooking*. All the core and optional units are covered in detail to give you the maximum choice of areas in which to develop your skills and competence.

The structure

The book is broken down into 25 sections. As you can see from the contents pages, most sections cover two NVQ/SVQ units, one from each level. Some deal with a unit which occurs at one level only, and two sections cover three closely related units for a particular level.

Finding your way within sections

Headings show clearly what is covered in any *double page opening* in the book. At the top:

- on the left-hand side is the *section title* and the *topics* being covered
- on the right-hand side, is the *number and title of the NVQ/SVQ unit* which the information relates to.

The book covers nutrition, healthy eating and certain cookery skills which at the moment do not directly relate to NVQ/SVQ requirements (but may be included in future revisions). These are put in boxes.

Range checklists

These are given at the end of each section. They will help you monitor your own progress. To avoid repetition, *laid down procedures* are not given each time. The following areas are always relevant:

- health and safety legislation
- food hygiene legislation
- establishment procedures.

What assessment for NVQ/SVQ is about

Your NVQ/SVQ assessor will concentrate on whether or not you can demonstrate a range of skills in the preparation and cooking of certain types of food. What is important is that you are competent in these skills, not how you have acquired them.

There is no one correct way of making fresh short pastry, for example, or a vinaigrette dressing. Where your workplace has laid down procedures designed to meet the needs of your customers, it is these which you should follow. That is why so many of the NVQ/SVQ performance criteria refer to *customer and dish requirements*. It will help to bear this in mind when you study the steps that are given throughout this book.

The contents guides are just that – a guide rather than a detailed list of what follows. They will help you see quickly how the information is organised in relation to key topics appearing in the NVQ/SVQ performance criteria and range statements.

On the first page of each section you will find a statement of the units and element titles which the section relates to.

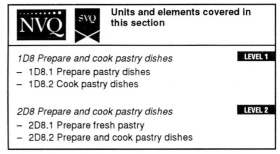

		Units and elements covered in this section

1D8 Prepare and cook pastry dishes — **LEVEL 1**
- 1D8.1 Prepare pastry dishes
- 1D8.2 Cook pastry dishes

2D8 Prepare and cook pastry dishes — **LEVEL 2**
- 2D8.1 Prepare fresh pastry
- 2D8.2 Prepare and cook pastry dishes

If a double page opening is to do with a level 1 unit only, there will be nothing in the lower space.

If it is to do with level 2 only, there will be nothing in the upper space.

If some of the text on a page relates only to level 1, or only to level 2, this is indicated by the appropriate symbol by the heading.

Preparation and finishing methods

Defrosting — **LEVEL 1**

Allow frozen pastry to thaw at room temperature while still in its wrapping. Alternatively thaw overnight in a refrigerator.

Mixing — **LEVEL 2**

Convenience pastry products carry their own instructions on the label. Follow these carefully to get the best

You will not be expected to learn huge amounts of facts to gain your NVQ/SVQ. As part of your assessment, you may be asked questions about work activities which your assessor is unable to see you doing in the workplace. You will also be questioned to check that you have the necessary *underpinning knowledge*, which in food preparation and cooking is largely concerned with hygiene.

ACTION and knowledge checks

These appear throughout the book to help you reinforce your understanding of the text, and to give you confidence in carrying out your workplace tasks. They also act as progress checks, so that you and your assessor have a better idea of what has been covered, and what has not.

To get the best value from the activities, discuss your completed work with a supervisor or manager at work, or a tutor from your college or training centre.

Recipes

Each section that deals with food commodities – meat and poultry, fish, fruit, vegetables, rice and so on – includes recipes to help you build up and demonstrate your competence across the NVQ/SVQ range for the units covered. The recipes are also intended to be interesting to do and appropriate for a wide cross-section of the industry's customers.

> Recipe writers vary in their approach to metric/imperial conversions. Often some rounding of numbers is acceptable, but on other occasions precision is essential. That is why, for example, you will sometimes see 225 g (8 oz), and on other occasions 200 g (8 oz). What is important is that you stick to either imperial measurements or metric measurements for any one recipe.

The principles of cookery

The approach in this book follows the organisation of the NVQ/SVQ standards in food preparation and cooking, which were arrived at after widespread consultation with industry. This means that the cooking processes of boiling, baking, steaming, deep frying, etc. are dealt with by type of food rather than as separate chapters.

Glossary and index

To make the text accessible to people working in all types of establishment, at all levels of the market, industry jargon is used as little as possible. Should you come across words you are not familiar with, they will be explained in the Glossary.

The index will also point you in the right direction if you can't find information where you expect it to be. Cheese, grains and nuts, for example, have been included where appropriate.

The KNOWLEDGE CHECKS and most of the ACTION panels provide space for you to write your answer below. With some ACTION panels space for an answer is not needed.

Suggested answers to the KNOWLEDGE CHECKS are given on a double page opening following the exercise. Avoid the temptation of looking at these first.

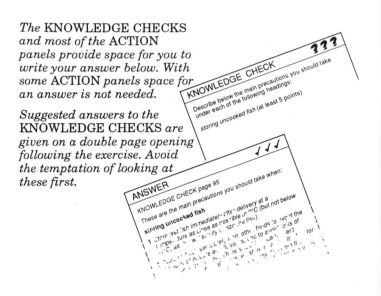

Key learning points link recipes with the NVQ/SVQ range statements.

> ### Red mullet in lettuce leaves
> *by British Iceberg Growers' Association*
>
> **Key learning points**
> » stuff and bake white fish
>
> **SERVES 6**
>
> 6   medium size red mullet, scaled,   6
>   gutted and cleaned
>   seasoning to taste

Tick off once you are confident you can meet the performance criteria for the stated food item, method, cooking process, etc. You should aim to cover the whole range, although your assessor only needs to observe your work in a specific number of areas.

NVQ SVQ RANGE CHECKLIST

LEVEL 1	LEVEL 2
1D2.1 Prepare fish for cooking	**2D2.1 Prepare fish for cooking**
prepare preprepared or convenience fish to be cooked by 3 of these methods	prepare
☐ grilling or barbecuing	☑ round fish
☐ steaming	☐ flat fish
☐ shallow frying	by 4 of these methods
☐ deep frying	☐ washing
using 1 of these methods	☐ trimming
☐ defrosting	☐ boning or filleting
☐ coating with flour or breadcrumbs or batter	☐ portioning
	☑ stuffing
	☐ skinning
1D2.2 Cook fish dishes	**2D2.2 Cook fish dishes**
cook prepared or convenience fish by 3 of these methods	cook
☐ deep frying	☐ white fish
☐ grilling or barbecuing	☐ oily fish
☐ shallow frying	by 4 of these methods
☐ steaming	☐ baking
	☐ grilling or barbecuing
	☐ shallow frying
	☐ steaming

In industry, you are most unlikely to find yourself cooking food for the same number of people every day. Adjusting recipe quantities up or down will therefore become second nature. For this reason, we have left the number of servings which each recipe makes as originally provided by the recipe writer.

> ### Quorn and rice ratatouille
> *by Crosse & Blackwell*
>
> **Key learning points**
> » skin, slice and chop vegetables
> » prepare risotto with long grain brown rice and Quorn
>
> **SERVES 4**
>
> 250 g   long grain brown rice, cooked   8 oz
> 30 ml   oil   2 tbsp
>   clove garlic, crushed and peeled
>   onion, sliced   8 oz

Introduction

If you are working in a fast food or quick service operation, you will probably have a lot of contact with customers. In other sorts of establishment, you may only meet customers when you are serving behind the carvery or buffet table.

It's possible that you have little direct contact with customers in your current job, but then who knows where your career might lead to? If you hope to be a head chef, or to have your own restaurant, you will be expected to leave the kitchen from time to time to talk to your customers.

The catering and hospitality industry would not exist without customers. And good hospitality means more than a meal, a drink and somewhere to sleep. It has a great deal to do with the attitude of staff. Helpful staff, polite staff, friendly staff – they make the difference between one place serving good food and another.

You should also consider how your attitude to your colleagues affects their dealings with customers. Everyone's enjoyment of what they do depends to a large extent on the sort of teamwork that exists. How much better the food you have prepared looks when it is served with care. How much nicer it is when restaurant staff pass on customers' compliments about the food, not just the complaints. How much easier the job is when everyone pulls their weight.

Different chefs have different approaches to teamwork and customer care. Some get the best out of their staff by creating a fairly hectic, noisy atmosphere, with a lot of pressure put on everyone. Others prefer the calmer approach. The fact remains that it is the more closely knit teams that get the customers coming back.

You have a very real role to play in this, whatever your personality, whatever stage you have reached in learning the skills of food preparation and cooking. Take on that role with enthusiasm and energy, and you will go far.

The range of customers in your workplace will depend on the type of establishment it is. In this staff restaurant of a city bank, there is quite a cross-section of ages and ethnic groups. Here every customer wants to enjoy a break from work, perhaps a chat with their colleagues, good food and friendly service from the catering staff.

Some customers will have special needs in terms of food – because they are on a diet, or have an allergy to certain types of food, or do not eat red meat, for example. Some customers will need understanding and patience from the catering staff, because they have a speech difficulty, for example, or restricted mobility.

Dealing with customers who want something different requires an understanding of their needs and a willingness to see things from their point of view. That is why the expression 'Put yourself in the customers' shoes' is repeated so often.

ACTION

Have some fun working through the questions overleaf. They're designed to introduce you to some of the key aspects of good customer skills.

Maintaining customer care

Give yourself marks out of 10 for the sort of impression you create with customers and work colleagues in the following areas:

- ☐ appearance
- ☐ personal hygiene
- ☐ posture (slouching deserves a low score)
- ☐ friendliness of your greeting
- ☐ warmth of your welcome
- ☐ going out of your way to be helpful to customers
- ☐ helping colleagues who are under pressure
- ☐ getting on with staff in other departments, e.g. restaurant, floor service (and this means staff generally, not those you particularly like)
- ☐ when answering the telephone
- ☐ remembering and using people's names
- ☐ dealing with children
- ☐ helping those with mobility or communication difficulties

If a customer asked you any of these questions, mark with a:

✓ those which you could answer helpfully

X those which you would be quite unable to help with

? those you couldn't provide the answer to yourself, but you would be able to direct the customer to someone who did have the answer

- ☐ how to get to the nearest motorway/main road
- ☐ how to get to the Post Office
- ☐ what dishes would be suitable for someone on a low fat diet
- ☐ whether the vegetable soup was made with meat stock, because they are vegetarian
- ☐ to tell them a bit more about the special of the day
- ☐ (if you work for a chain) where other restaurants/hotels in the group are located
- ☐ can they book a table in the restaurant for next week
- ☐ (if you work in a hotel) what the charge is for overnight accommodation
- ☐ what wine would go well with their fish dish

Complaints

How do you feel when you make a complaint? ✓ as appropriate.

- ☐ ready for a row
- ☐ nervous
- ☐ angry
- ☐ upset
- ☐ apologetic
- ☐ embarrassed
- ☐ inconvenienced
- ☐ hesitant

What reactions to your own complaints make you annoyed, angry or upset?

- ☐ no apology
- ☐ not listening
- ☐ blaming you
- ☐ passing the buck
- ☐ disinterest
- ☐ being fobbed off
- ☐ being kept waiting
- ☐ being interrupted

When people complain to you, how do you feel?

- ☐ frustrated
- ☐ guilty
- ☐ offended
- ☐ grateful
- ☐ sympathetic
- ☐ panicky
- ☐ put out
- ☐ helpless

What follows is the general procedure for handling complaints. Think back to the last occasion you dealt with a complaint from a customer. Rate your performance on each of the steps on a scale of 1 to 3: 3 you carried out the step *very well*, 2 your performance was *acceptable*, 1 you *failed* to follow the recommended procedure. Put your score in the box provided.

- ☐ Listen to the complaint until the customer has finished speaking. Do not interrupt.
- ☐ Apologise, but do not admit that you or the establishment are to blame.
- ☐ Do not make excuses or blame anyone else, especially the customer.
- ☐ Never argue, disagree or become aggressive.
- ☐ Keep calm and remain polite.
- ☐ Try to put the problem right yourself. If you cannot, get help from your supervisor or manager.
- ☐ Never offer something the establishment cannot provide.

- ☐ Thank the customer for bringing the matter to your attention.
- ☐ Check afterwards that the customer is satisfied with the action taken.
- ☐ Record the complaint according to the policies of your workplace, and make sure your supervisor knows.

Customer incidents

Think back to the last time you had to deal with a difficult problem at work. For example, a customer who was rude to you because you accidentally spilt some food over his or her sleeve.

How would you rate your performance in each of these areas – use a scale of 1 to 3 as above:

- ☐ dealing with the matter quickly
- ☐ being polite and friendly
- ☐ keeping calm
- ☐ not taking anger personally
- ☐ explaining to the customer what you can and cannot do, and why
- ☐ explaining to your supervisor what has happened

RANGE CHECKLIST

LEVEL 1

G3.1 Maintain customer care

2 of these groups of customers

- ☐ adults
- ☐ children
- ☐ those with mobility difficulties
- ☐ those with communication difficulties

G3.2 Deal with customer complaints

either of these types of complaints

- ☐ those which can be resolved within individual's authority
- ☐ those which cannot be resolved within individual's authority

G3.3 Deal with customer incidents

irregular or unplanned occurrences involving customers to include

- ☐ lost child
- ☐ spillages
- ☐ breakages
- ☐ lost property

Safety and security

Introduction

Everyone at work, from the most junior member of staff to the most senior director, is responsible for the health and safety of those around them.

The main piece of legislation covering health and safety at work is the *Health and Safety at Work Act, 1974*, or *HASAWA* for short. In summary, the Act and regulations made under the Act require *employers* to:

- ensure the building and the people in it are as safe as possible

- train staff in safe working practices and the use of equipment

- keep an accident book and provide first aid facilities

- provide equipment and tools with proper safeguards, and repair or replace worn or badly maintained equipment

- provide safe systems for the use, handling, storage and transport of materials such as cleaning agents, food and drink items

- take immediate action if any safety hazard is reported

- provide a written statement of policy describing the arrangements made for the health and safety of staff.

As an employee, you also have a duty under the law not to endanger your own health and safety, nor that of other people who may be affected by the way you work.

Contents guide

What to do in the event of a fire
1 Remain calm.
2 Walk, don't run.
3 Leave the building by the nearest safe route and exit. Do not use the lift. Do not stop to collect personal belongings.
4 Report to the person in charge at the assembly point outside.
5 Do not re-enter the building until you are told that it is safe to do so by the Senior Fire Officer or a manager in charge.

if you discover a fire first
- raise the alarm by operating the nearest fire alarm
- call for help using the procedure laid down in your workplace.

provided you do not put yourself or anyone else in danger
- make sure that colleagues and customers in your work area know there is a fire, and help them to escape
- attack the fire with the equipment provided
- switch off all electrical and gas appliances
- close all windows and the doors which will not be used during the evacuation

The combination oven pictured above shows a tray of plain steamed potatoes just ready for use. Note how the operator is using the door as a protection from escaping steam.

 **Units and elements covered in this section**

LEVEL 1	LEVEL 2

G1 Maintain a safe and secure working environment
- G1.1 Carry out procedures in the event of a fire
- G1.2 Carry out procedures on discovery of a suspicious item or package
- G1.3 Carry out procedures in the event of an accident
- G1.4 Maintain a safe environment for customers, staff and visitors
- G1.5 Maintain a secure environment for customers, staff and visitors

Safety first

Preventing falls

1 Walk, don't run.

2 Keep floor areas clean and dry. Spills or grease on the floor should be wiped up at once.

3 Do not allow flexes to trail across floors or food preparation surfaces.

4 Put up warning signs if cleaning floors or stairs.

5 Wear sensible non-slip shoes which cover and protect your toes, ideally with steel caps.

Preventing cuts

1 Clear up breakages immediately. If there is any possibility that broken pieces have fallen on to food lying nearby, this food should be disposed of.

2 Wrap up broken glass and china in paper or cardboard before putting it in a general-purpose waste bin. Ideally it should be put in a special bin, where there is no risk that it will cut through the plastic bag, or cut someone handling the rubbish at a later stage.

3 The lids from cans can be razor sharp. Cut the lid off entirely. Empty the can. Place the lid inside the empty can before putting it in the waste bin.

Preventing burns and scalds

1 Look after the uniform issued to you, and wear it as it is designed to be worn. Properly buttoned up, the double-fronted chef's jacket will protect you from burns. Keep the sleeves down so that your arms are also protected.

2 Do not leave metal spoons in boiling liquids.

3 Never leave pan handles over a flame, or protruding over the edge where they may be knocked. Do not reach over a lit gas burner — to get something from the other side of the stove, for example.

4 Take care not to stand directly in the path of the steam when removing lids from hot pans.

5 Always use dry oven cloths when lifting items in and out of the oven.

6 Be very careful when moving large pans of hot or boiling liquid. If the pan is too heavy for you to handle safely on your own, and there are two handles, get another person to take the other handle, or use a ladle to remove some of the contents to another pan.

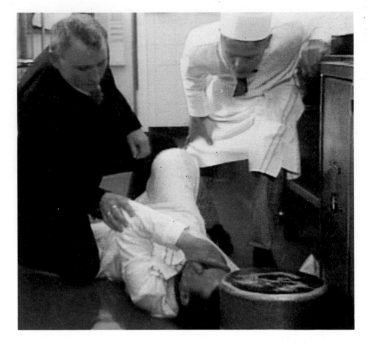

According to the most recent annual report by the Health and Safety Commission, trips and falls accounted for 35% of the accidents which took place on hotel and catering premises. Around 18% were caused by lifting heavy goods, and 15% from exposure to harmful substances such as cleaning agents.

In the year concerned, there were 2,229 reported injuries to hotel and catering staff, of which 1,858 led to three or more days off work, 369 were serious, and two resulted in death.

Seven customers and members of the public died from accidents on hotel and catering premises, and 467 had accidents.

The accident book

All accidents and illnesses at the workplace must by law be recorded in the accident book or on a suitable form. Details should include:

- date and time of incident
- full name and occupation of person involved
- nature of the injury or illness or dangerous occurrence
- place where the accident happened and a brief description of what happened
- names of any witnesses
- details of the person making the report, and time and date the report was made.

Example of an entry in the accident book

Daniel was slicing cabbage, his knife slipped and cut the top of his finger. Daniel went to hospital and the nail has now come completely off his finger. He will be off work for over 3 days.

Equipment

Many machines are dangerous if they are not operated properly. No person under the age of 18 may clean, lubricate or adjust any machinery if it exposes him or her to risk of injury from a moving part of that or any adjacent machine. No person may work at any machine specified on the list of *prescribed dangerous machines* (see box) unless he or she has been fully instructed as to the dangers arising in connection with it and a) has received sufficient training in work at the machine, or b) is under adequate supervision by a person who has a thorough knowledge and experience of the machine.

1 Always follow manufacturers' and workplace instructions when using equipment.

2 The blades of cutting machines are extremely sharp, so keep your hands well away from them even when they are not operating. When the machine has been turned off, wait for the blades to stop moving before you go near the machine.

3 Never use your hands to push food against a cutting or mincing blade. Slicers have a proper carriage to move the food with. A push stick should be used with mincers and a special long handled spoon with liquidisers. Take great care to prevent the spoon coming into contact with the blades, or both machine and spoon will be damaged.

4 Never operate machines if the safety guards are not in place.

5 Do not attempt to slice cucumbers, tomatoes, onions and similar small, unevenly shaped or slippery items in a machine. The carriage will not hold the food firmly enough.

6 Report any faults. Faulty equipment must display an 'out of order' notice.

7 Never overload electrical sockets.

8 Never use electrical equipment with wet hands. Do not use electrical equipment near sinks.

Lifting heavy weights

See also page 26.

1 If the object is too heavy, do not try to lift it without assistance from a colleague or by using a trolley or other lifting equipment.

2 Plan in advance how to lift and position the item.

3 Ensure that there is nothing in the way and that all doors are propped open. Give people plenty of warning about what you are doing.

4 Ensure that the eventual destination of the object is clear and that there is sufficient space.

5 To avoid confusion when lifting something with another person, agree in advance who should give the instructions and who will take the lead.

What to do in the event of an accident

If you are a trained first aider you will be able to take immediate action to help the casualty. If not, your priority should be to get urgent help from someone who can give first aid.

If the accident happens at a time when no first aider is on duty, you or your supervisor will need to get outside help without delay. Keep as calm as you can.

1 Use the nearest telephone.

2 Dial 999. No money is required.

3 When you get through, give the number of the telephone you are calling from so that the operator can call you back if necessary. Speak clearly.

4 Ask for the necessary service: ambulance, fire brigade or police.

5 Give the location of the accident.

6 State the nature of the accident or illness, the number of casualties, and as much detail of the injuries as possible.

7 Remain on the phone until the emergency service operator rings off – to be sure that you have given sufficient information.

While help is on its way, stay calm. Reassure the casualty kindly and confidently. Keep the casualty protected from the cold (but do not cover major burns).

Do not move the casualty unless absolutely necessary.

If the accident has been caused by an electric shock, break the contact by switching off the current at the plug or mains. Do not touch the casualty until the current has been switched off, or you will become a second victim.

Prescribed dangerous machines

Of those listed in the Prescribed Dangerous Machines Order, 1964, the following might be found in hotel and catering establishments:

- food mixing machines when used with attachments for mincing, slicing, chipping or any other cutting operation, or for crumbing
- machines with a circular saw blade, and bandsaws
- circular knife slicing machines
- potato chipping and vegetable slicing machines
- dough brakes and dough mixers
- pie and tart machines
- worm-type mincing machines
- rotary knife bowl-type chopping machines
- wrapping and packing machines.

ACTION

Remind yourself of the safety points for using deep fat fryers (pages 39 and 108) or microwave ovens (page 34). Then arrange to give a short talk, in the presence of your supervisor, to a colleague who is unfamiliar with using such equipment.

G1 Maintain a safe and secure working environment

Security

You may think that security is a subject more appropriate for front of house staff and those handling cash.

This is far from being the case. Substantial sums of money are tied up in food stocks. Then there's the question of your own belongings, and those of your colleagues. And if you are working in a quick service or fast food operation, you will have contact with customers, and may be expected to deal with lost property.

Thieves are often opportunist. That is, they do not plan a burglary, but seize the opportunity when it arises: a window left slightly open, a key carelessly dropped by a member of staff, deliveries left unattended, money left lying around.

1 Never leave keys in locks. Nor lying around or in supposedly safe places, such as the top drawer of the storekeeper's desk.

2 Never lend keys to anyone else.

3 Do not take valuables to work. If you have to, keep them safe in your locker while you are on duty. Keep lockers locked and the key in a safe place.

4 Put all equipment and materials in the correct place after use. Storage areas must always be kept locked when unattended.

5 Report anything belonging to you, colleagues, customers or the establishment which appears to be missing. This means taking the trouble to notice what is going on around you.

6 Respect workplace rules regarding, for example, taking personal handbags, shopping bags or baskets into work areas. Since these are favourite ways of removing stolen property from the premises, you will put yourself under suspicion.

7 The identity of contractors, sales representatives, tradespeople, local authority officials, meter readers and so on should be checked before they are allowed access to the building. In a large establishment, there will probably be a security officer who does this. All visitors and staff will be issued with an identity badge. In this case you should report anyone you see in the building who is not wearing a badge. Where appropriate, ask politely if you can help the person.

8 When customer's or colleague's property, such as coats, bags and umbrellas, is left behind, it should be handed in immediately to a supervisor. Attach a note to the lost property with details of where it was found, and the date and time. This will help identify the true owner.

9 When a claim is made for lost property, ask for a description of the item. If there is any doubt that the claim is genuine, or the lost property is a particularly valuable item, ask a manager to deal with the matter.

Dealing with a suspicious-looking item

1 If you see a suspicious-looking item which might be a bomb, do not touch it yourself or let colleagues or customers put themselves in possible danger.

2 Report the matter at once to a manager or someone in charge of security. Tell them calmly and accurately where the item is located, and why you think it is suspicious. They will get in touch with the emergency services.

3 Raise the alarm, if that is the procedure in your workplace, and help evacuate the building.

NVQ svq RANGE CHECKLIST

LEVEL 1		LEVEL 2

G1.1 Carry out procedures in the event of a fire

☐ all types of fire ☐

G1.2 Carry out procedures on discovery of a suspicious item or package

☐ all bags, packages and parcels which have been left unattended for no apparent reason ☐

G1.3 Carry our procedures in the event of an accident

☐ all accidents involving injury to customers, staff and visitors ☐

G1.4 Maintain a safe environment for customers, staff and visitors

☐ items, areas and incidents which threaten the safety of customers, staff and visitors (not fires or suspicious items or accidents) ☐

G1.5 Maintain a secure environment for customers, staff and visitors

in either of these staff areas

☐ work areas ☐
☐ staff facilities ☐

in 1 of these storage areas

☐ storerooms and cellars ☐
☐ store cupboards and cabinets ☐
☐ fridges and freezers ☐

in 1 of these customer areas

☐ private facilities for customers ☐
☐ public areas ☐

also

☐ lost property (not suspicious items or packages) ☐

Introduction

Whether you are working in a deluxe establishment, preparing the finest and most expensive foods, or in a small café offering a very limited range of basic dishes, there is one area where standards should be the same, and only the best. That area is hygiene.

Food not hygienically prepared is dangerous. It is harmful to health – food poisoning causes discomfort and illness, and in serious cases, death. It is also disastrous for business – even the best established reputation can be wiped out by the publicity resulting from a case of food poisoning, or a bad report by the Environmental Health Officer.

An awareness of these risks should be enough to convince everyone of the need for high standards. Yet reported incidents of food poisoning remain at very high levels. So much so, that in the last few years the government has introduced much tougher legislation.

Under the Food Safety Act 1990, a problem in your workplace could lead to:

- the premises being closed

- the proprietor or manager getting banned from running another food business

- unlimited fines and two years' imprisonment.

What you can do

Nearly all cases of food poisoning can be avoided if proper care is taken over:

- personal hygiene

- cleaning procedures

- stock rotation and not using food which has passed its use-by or best-before date

- preventing *cross-contamination* – the transfer of food poisoning bacteria from raw food to cooked food

- the temperatures at which food is stored and cooked, from the time it is delivered, until the time it is eaten.

Contents guide

NVQ **SVQ** **Units and elements covered in this section**

LEVEL 1	LEVEL 2

G2 Maintain a professional and hygienic appearance
– G2.1 Maintain a professional and hygienic appearance

Some tasks in the kitchen must involve touching food. This will not cause a problem if you always follow strict standards of personal hygiene. These need to become second nature, so that if there's a particular rush, hygiene is one area where you never take a short cut.

Remember that clean-looking hands are not necessarily clean. The smaller picture below was taken 2 hours after a 'clean' hand was placed on the photographer's glass plate. Imagine the damage that can occur if these numbers of bacteria were transferred to the chicken suprêmes being prepared on the left, and they were not cooked adequately.

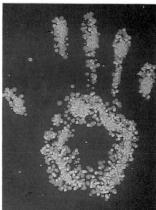

Food safety laws

The Food Safety Act 1990 places the responsibility for food safety on each link within the food production chain, from the farm to the final point of sale.

Under the Act 'food' refers to almost anything that is eaten, drunk or chewed. For instance, a cup of tea is regarded as food, and so is the water used to make the tea.

The legislation specifies the ways in which food fails to comply with the food safety requirements:

- if it is unfit for human consumption. Food would be unfit if, for example, it contained a cockroach

- if it is so contaminated that it would be unreasonable to expect it to be eaten or drunk in that state

- if it has been made harmful to health – by adding or removing something to or from it, by using unsuitable articles or substances for handling it, by subjecting it to an unsuitable process or treatment

- if it is not of the nature, substance or quality demanded by the purchaser – a steak pie which contains mostly vegetables with just one or two lumps of meat

- if it is falsely or misleadingly described or presented – canned soup served as 'fresh home-made'.

The Food Safety Act greatly strengthened the powers of enforcement officers– *Environmental Health Officers* (EHOs) (employed by local authorities), and trading standards officers. They may:

- enter food premises to investigate possible offences

- inspect premises, processes and records, copy any relevant records, take their own visual records such as still photographs and videos

- inspect food to see if it is safe

- take samples for investigation

- detain or seize suspect food in order to have it condemned.

Where there is an imminent risk of injury to health, the enforcement officer can close down premises immediately, without prior reference to a court.

Food is assumed to be for human consumption until the opposite is proved. If you were asked by an enforcement officer about an old container of food sitting at the back of the refrigerator, and which you had forgotten about until that moment, it would be no good claiming that it wasn't going to be served. Perhaps you would not have served it, but a colleague who was unaware of how long it had been there might do so.

The Food Safety Act also prepared the way for further legislation to keep pace with technological change.

Regulations made so far:

- permit the irradiation of food under licence (this process extends the storage life of the food). Irradiated food or dishes containing irradiated food must be clearly labelled at all stages, from transportation and storage, to sale and consumption

- require premises where food is stored, prepared or sold to be registered with the local authority.

A further provision will require anyone who handles food to have hygiene training.

The Food Hygiene Regulations

The Food Hygiene (General) Regulations 1970 ensure that food is protected from contamination by:

- raw and cooked food being kept separate during preparation

- during sales or delivery, open food being covered or effectively screened

- food handlers using hygienic work methods

- food handlers observing personal hygiene rules.

Storage temperatures for food

The *Food Hygiene (Amendment) Regulations 1990* and *1991* introduced a complex set of controls for storage temperatures of prepared foods. The rules and procedures in your workplace will take account of these, so what follows is a summary of the key points only.

1 All hot food must be kept above 63°C.
2 Soft cheeses, all cut cheeses, sandwiches/filled rolls/ similar bread products, and cooked products containing meat, fish, eggs, cheeses (or substitutes for these), cereals, pulses and vegetables must be kept at 5°C or colder. The same applies to smoked or cured fish, smoked or cured meat which has been cut or sliced after curing.
3 Desserts containing milk, cream cakes, prepared vegetable/fruit salads, cooked pies, pasties and sausage rolls into which nothing has been introduced after cooking, uncooked or partly cooked pastries and dough products containing meat or fish must be kept at 8°C or colder.

The same chilled storage temperatures apply to food in large delivery vehicles. Vehicles under 7.5 tonnes making local deliveries are allowed to operate to a standard of 8°C for all foods.

G2 Maintain a professional and hygienic appearance

Food poisoning

One of the reasons for cooking food, apart from making it more digestible and palatable, is to kill harmful microorganisms which may be present in the food.

The greatest danger is *food-poisoning bacteria*. There might be literally millions of these present on the food, yet they will be completely invisible. The food looks, smells and tastes perfectly normal.

The symptoms of food poisoning can start within an hour of eating harmful food, or as many as five days later. The commonest symptoms are stomach aches, vomiting and diarrhoea.

The bacteria responsible may have been:

- present on the food when it entered the kitchen – *salmonella* and *campylobacter*, for example, are found widely in the environment, in water, soil and sometimes therefore in raw foods such as poultry, meat and eggs

- spread from another food already contaminated – through poor food handling and storage

- carried by pets or pests, or by dust – through poor cleaning practices, inadequate supervision of the premises, badly designed premises or equipment, lack of maintenance, and so forth. Pests carry harmful bacteria, especially in the faeces and urine which are dropped on food as they eat. One mouse will shed about 70 droppings every day and as it has no effective bladder will dribble urine most of the time. One fly may be carrying as many as two million bacteria when it lands and vomits on food

- introduced by those handling the food – through poor personal hygiene practices. Like pests and pets, you carry bacteria on your skin and hair and in your mouth, nose and ears. Smoking, picking your nose or ears, or handling your hair can transfer bacteria to your hands, and from them to anything you touch. If you do not wash your hands properly after using the toilet, large numbers of bacteria will remain on them.

Conditions for growth of bacteria

Bacteria which cause food poisoning prefer a moist, warm environment which is not too acid, nor too alkaline. They generally prefer foods rich in protein, such as meat, milk or egg. Growth does not begin immediately, but once the bacteria have adapted to their environment, the number will double every 20 to 30 minutes.

Most food-poisoning bacteria prefer a temperature range of 20°C to 40°C – so kitchens are perfect for them! Some types will grow anywhere in the range 5°C to 63°C. This is known as the *temperature danger zone*.

Above 63°C most bacteria are rapidly killed. Below 5°C most types do not feed or multiply, but stay inactive.

There are exceptions. *Listeria monocytogenes* can grow to dangerous numbers in chilled stored foods. Certain bacteria protect themselves by forming spores at high temperatures. These are in effect dormant bacteria, like seeds they can withstand difficult conditions. Then, as soon as the environment is favourable, they germinate.

Staphylococcus (various strains) will produce spores if it has been allowed to multiply. It occurs in infected cuts, sores, boils and inflamed throat conditions, on normal healthy skin, especially on the face and hands and in the nasal passages.

Clostridium perfringens will also form spores. It occurs in the intestines of animals and many humans, also in raw meat and poultry, in water and in the soil.

Other dangers to food

Physical objects which find their way into food as a result of carelessness: pieces of jewellery, food packaging, plasters which have fallen off fingers etc.

Chemical contaminants: using copper or aluminium pans for cooking fruits, vinegar or other acidic foods.

Cleaning materials confused for food: because they have been stored in the wrong place, or in unlabelled containers, e.g. bleach in a lemonade bottle.

Food not properly prepared: kidney beans not boiled adequately, rhubarb leaves not trimmed off.

Moulds are small fungi. There are thousands of types of mould and certain kinds are used by the food industry – for example, in making cheese and bread (yeasts are fungi).

Very few moulds are actually poisonous, but they do spoil food. When moulds develop, the surface of the food becomes soft and moist, and the starches, sugar and porteins in the food are broken down and produce waste products. All this makes the food look unpleasant and taste musty.

Moulds are more likely to develop in moist conditions than in dry, which is why storage spaces should be dry and airy.

Personal hygiene

A checklist

1 Keep yourself clean and fresh. The body secretes moisture constantly through sweat glands located all over it. You will perspire more working under pressure in a hot environment. Sweat itself is virtually odourless and normally evaporates quickly. The smell comes from bacteria which live on the perspiration, especially in areas such as the underarms where it cannot evaporate freely. A daily bath or shower is the best protection.

2 Keep yourself healthy. A clear skin and complexion depend largely on adequate sleep, exercise and a balanced diet. You will enjoy your work more, and do a better job if you are not overtired.

3 Pay special attention to your hands. You depend on them for most tasks. The health of the people eating the food you have prepared depends on how clean you keep your hands. Your fingernails should be clean, trimmed and free of varnish.

4 Remove rings, bracelets, necklaces and earrings before going on duty. If you wear a wedding ring, this may be left on. Although it is important to know the time in a kitchen, it is best to rely on a clock rather than your watch which will trap food and dirt. There is also a risk you will damage your watch by getting it wet.

5 In food preparation areas, long flowing hair is not acceptable. It might get trapped in machinery and pieces of hair are likely to fall into food. There is usually a strict rule that hair must be kept in a net or covered by a hat. Whether or not this is the case, you will find that your hair (and this applies to beards and moustaches as well) absorbs smoke and food smells. Daily washing will keep it clean and in healthy condition.

6 You spend long hours on your feet. Wear comfortable shoes that will not slip, and which will provide protection against spills and dropped objects. Wash your feet every day, and keep your toe nails trimmed. Change socks daily.

7 Once you have changed into uniform, leave your outdoor clothing and footwear in the area set aside for this purpose. Don't take it with you into the kitchen. Respect your uniform. The traditional chef's outfit may not be particularly trendy but it's been found to do a good job. It provides protection against spills and hot equipment, and keeps away some of the heat of the kitchen.

8 Wash your hands thoroughly before touching food. Use plenty of hot water, and the soap and scrubbing brush which have been provided.

9 Dry your hands well after washing. Use the paper towels, hot air drier or roller towel provided – never a tea towel or kitchen cloth.

10 Do not wash food or food equipment in wash hand basins, and do not use food sinks for hand washing.

11 If you feel a sneeze coming, or you need to cough, turn away from any food. Hold a disposable paper tissue over your nose and mouth, and wash your hands afterwards.

12 Cover cuts, open sores and wounds with a waterproof dressing. Dressings for kitchen staff are often coloured blue so that if they do drop off they will be easily spotted.

13 Use a clean spoon for tasting food and wash it after use. Never taste food with your fingers.

14 Do not lick your fingers or touch your nose, mouth or hair.

15 Never smoke or spit in food handling areas.

16 Do not sit on work tables.

17 Report *any* illness or infection. Your supervisor will make the judgement of whether it is safe for you to work with food, or not. Don't put other people's health at risk, because you don't want to admit to feeling ill.

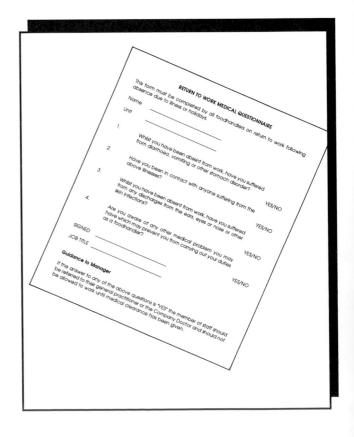

When to wash your hands
- after changing into uniform
- between one task and another
- when coming on duty or entering the kitchen
- after leaving the kitchen
- after handling raw food
- after going to the toilet
- after meal and rest breaks when you have been eating, drinking or smoking
- after handling waste or putting food in the dust bin
- after handling cleaning materials.

ACTION

Mark the thermometer below to show:
1. The critical temperature zone.
2. The temperature range at which most bacteria get killed.
3. The temperature range at which most bacteria lie dormant.
4. Storage temperature for frozen foods.

You have probably seen some diagrams showing cartoon-characters representing bacteria in various states of comfort and discomfort alongside the different temperatures.

Have a go yourself at making the vital messages of your diagram memorable.

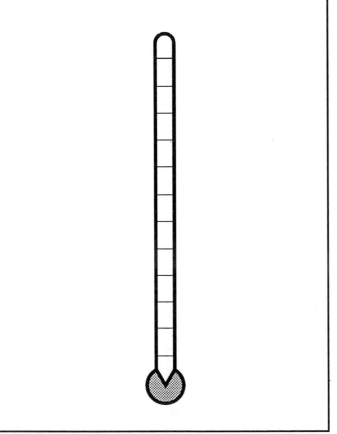

Good practice in the kitchen

Some of the following points are within your control. Others depend on management providing the appropriate resources. Whatever the facilities and equipment in your current workplace, if you are aware of the ideal situation, you will be able to make better use of what is available. You will also contribute more effectively to the effort of the whole team to improve standards.

1 Never allow utensils – including chopping boards, knives and slicing machines – which have been in contact with raw food to be used for cooked food, unless they have been thoroughly washed and sanitised.

2 Wherever possible, knives and chopping boards should be reserved for specific uses. This is much easier when a system of colour-coding is in operation, or the purpose of the equipment has been etched on to the surface by the manufacturer.

3 Keep raw foods well separated from cooked foods, and from foods which will not be cooked before serving. Raw meat and poultry should be stored in a different refrigerator from cooked meat and poultry, and from pâtés, milk, cheese, cream and so forth. If this is not possible, they should be on different shelves, cooked meat on the higher shelves, raw meat on the lower shelves. See *Food handling and storage*.

4 Where practicable, preprepared chilled and frozen foods should be stored separately from other chilled and frozen foods. Otherwise, opening and shutting the door to collect items in regular use will cause temperature variation.

5 Keep food at temperatures which are too low for rapid growth of bacteria, below 5°C, or too high, above 63°C.

6 Cook foods thoroughly, so that the temperature at the centre reaches 70°C or higher depending on the food, for a minimum of two minutes. Do not shorten the cooking times stated on food labels or in recipes. Make sure the oven is at the right temperature before starting.

7 Food which is to be thawed before cooking should be thawed safely (see page 26).

8 Cooked food should not be reheated more than once.

9 If food has to be in the critical temperature zone, this should be for as short a time as possible. So food should be served immediately after it has been cooked. If it has to be chilled, the cooling process should happen as fast as possible (within 90 minutes) and the food be refrigerated to prevent bacteria from reproducing. If food is reheated this should be done quickly and thoroughly, so that the temperature at the centre reaches at least 70°C. In some catering establishments a minimum core temperature of 75°C is laid down.

G2 Maintain a professional and hygienic appearance

10 Test that food is at a safe temperature by using a temperature probe. Always clean the probe before and after use, with a wipe of sanitising solution.

11 Keep waste bins properly covered and clean. Waste or refuse should not be allowed to remain in rooms where food is stored or handled for any longer than necessary.

12 Report any pests or signs of pests: droppings, footprints in dust or on food, gnaw marks, holes in sacks, or nesting sites.

13 Clear up spilt foods straight away.

14 Do not store cleaning materials where they might come into contact with food or drink.

15 Keep food which is displayed for sale, for example in self-service counters, covered or effectively screened from possible sources of contamination.

ACTION

Imagine that someone from head office has just carried out a health, hygiene and safety inspection.

Get together a group of your colleagues to discuss the following points which emerge from the report. One person in the group should play the role of manager, another the role of head chef, and so on.

The object of the meeting is to agree how these problems can be put right, and what should be done in future to prevent such problems going unreported. (They are all taken from an actual report.)

CHEF'S LOCKER ROOM

This was very untidy, with food debris, cigarette ends, clothing and uniforms scattered over the area.

The missing section of electric conduit and light covers require replacing.

REFRIGERATOR NO 4

The temperature recording charts are not being changed quickly enough.

More cleaning needs to be done in the corners.

DEEP FREEZE NO 5

The temperature recording chart indicates that the temperature is erratic on this deep freeze. Samples of food probed indicated minus 12°C.

MAIN LARDER

Much more cleaning attention requires to be paid beneath the sink and adjacent tabling, where there were thick accumulations of grease and food debris.

Soiled uniform whites require to be removed from the area.

Discarded linen cloths must not be used for cleaning down purposes, only disposable paper.

The refuse bin requires repair/replacement.

The most common causes of food poisoning

A study of food poisoning cases shows the causes to be, in descending order:

1 food prepared too far in advance
2 food stored or held at room temperature for too long
3 inadequate cooling/refrigeration
4 inadequate reheating
5 insufficient cooking
6 holding food too long in hot cupboards
7 cross-contamination
8 inadequate thawing.

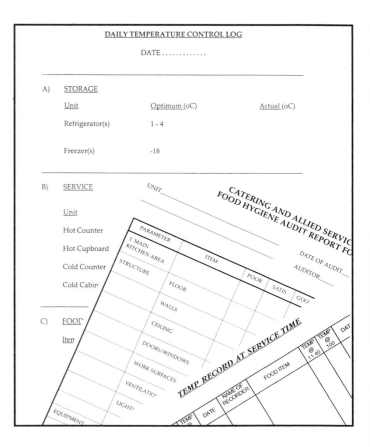

NVQ SVQ RANGE CHECKLIST

LEVEL 1   LEVEL 2

G2.1 Maintain a professional and hygienic appearance

laid down procedures in all relevant

☐   health and safety legislation   ☐
☐   food hygiene legislation   ☐
☐   establishment procedures   ☐

Food production areas

Areas where food and drink are prepared require the highest standards of hygiene. Generally a cleaning schedule is drawn up to make sure that every area and piece of equipment receive the attention they require. This may specify that the floor in the cold room and walk-in freezer is washed daily, while the walls and shelves are washed weekly.

1 Use cleaning equipment and procedures which will collect the dirt effectively, and not spread bacteria from one surface to another. Wet methods – mopping, scrubbing with hot detergent, and wiping with a damp cloth – followed by thorough rinsing, are generally best for kitchens.

2 Keep cleaning cloths separate from those used for other purposes – using a different colour will help. Cloths used for wiping a spill off the floor, for example, should never be used for cleaning food surfaces.

3 Display warning signs.

4 When high areas are being cleaned, use safety steps.

5 Wear protective gloves and protective clothing.

6 Change cleaning and rinsing solutions regularly. They will not do a proper job if you try to economise or, perhaps, to save yourself time. Rinsing water should be very hot.

7 Pay special attention to ledges, service pipes, ventilation grills, drainage and floor channels, where dirt and grease collect. Equipment which is on castors should be pulled out, so that you can clean the floor underneath properly.

8 Do not remove warning signs until floors are dry.

NVQ **SVQ** **Units and elements covered in this section**

1D12 Clean food production areas, equipment and utensils **LEVEL 1**
– 1D12.1 Clean food production areas
– 1D12.2 Clean food production equipment
– 1D12.3 Clean food production utensils

1D22 Clean and store crockery and cutlery
– 1D22.1 Clean crockery and cutlery
– 1D22.2 Store crockery and cutlery

2D12 Clean food production areas, equipment and utensils **LEVEL 2**
– 2D12.1 Clean food production areas
– 2D12.2 Clean food production equipment
– 2D12.3 Clean food production utensils

2D17 Clean cutting equipment
– 2D17.1 Clean cutting equipment

Contents guide

Cleaning agents

Water – the simplest cleaner of all. Applied under pressure it cleans hard surfaces such as the floors and walls in delivery areas. Water also rinses out dirt removed from a surface by another cleaning agent.

Soap – made from fats mixed with caustic soda. Soap can break up most dirt, but leaves a scum, so is unsuitable for general cleaning. Disinfectants are added to some liquid soaps for washing hands.

Detergents – made from chemicals mainly derived from petroleum. Mixed with water, they penetrate greasy surfaces. A body of dirt is broken up into fine particles which the detergent then coats, preventing the dirt from reforming and sticking to the surface again.

Neutral detergents – also called general-purpose detergents. Suitable for washing dishes, mopping floors and similar routine tasks.

Alkali detergents – also called hard surface cleaners. Used for heavier or more specialised tasks. They are corrosive and damage surfaces if not used with care.

Solvents – dissolve heavy grease and oil which water-based cleaners cannot cope with.

Abrasives – or scouring cleaners. Mostly used for cleaning enamel and ceramic surfaces including tiles. Abrasive powders are much coarser than liquids, creams and pastes, but all of them can damage surfaces.

Chemical disinfectants – will kill bacteria which survive the cleaning process. (Water at very high temperatures does the same job, but many pieces of equipment cannot be immersed in hot water.) They need time to kill the bacteria, and may be inactivated by waste food materials, by the fabric of cleaning cloths and by the materials of some surfaces.

Sanitisers – products designed both to clean and disinfect surfaces. Intended for 'clean-as-you-go' use, sanitisers do not replace the need for thorough washing, and where necessary the use of disinfectants. Powder sanitisers, dissolved in hot water, require a final rinse and are not suitable for use on certain metals. Liquid sanitisers are diluted before use. They must be left to dry, not rinsed off.

Wipes – products designed to provide a quick and convenient way of cleaning food temperature probes, small utensils and for wiping food preparation surfaces on a 'clean-as-you-go' basis. Use once only, then discard.

Food production equipment

Before starting, read the detailed cleaning instructions provided by the manufacturer or your workplace.

1 If you come across any faults in the equipment during cleaning, or something which needs maintenance, report this to your supervisor.

2 Generally, equipment should be turned off before you start cleaning, and allowed to cool. If the gas supply is turned off for cleaning, follow the correct procedure for re-igniting the pilot light.

3 A detergent solution is suitable for equipment or any part of the equipment which is not heavily engrained with burnt food, dirt and grease. This would generally apply to bains-marie and hot cupboards, steamers, the top and sides of bratt pans, the front of oven doors, and so on.

4 Pay particular attention to runners and sliding door channels. Where possible, remove shelves from ovens, hot cupboards and grills, and spill and drip trays from grills and hobs. They can be cleaned more thoroughly and conveniently in a large sink, and it will be possible to get at any food which has accumulated on shelf supports or under trays.

5 Don't overlook the legs, connecting gas and water supply pipes, nor the surrounding walls or floor.

6 Where necessary, use a degreasing agent and a scouring pad to remove heavy deposits.

7 Griddles need burnishing to keep a smooth, clean surface. They may also need greasing to prevent rust when not in use.

8 After cleaning, rinse with fresh, very hot water.

9 In some cases the kitchen will be hot enough for the equipment to air-dry quickly after rinsing (wet objects attract bacteria). Disposable paper towels are very effective, but take care that torn pieces of paper do not remain in the equipment. Towel drying is quick and efficient provided the towel is absolutely clean.

Using cleaning agents

1 Always wear protective clothing and protective gloves. Cleaning agents irritate and burn the skin. Goggles should be worn when using certain cleaning agents.

2 Always wash hands after doing any cleaning.

3 Dilute the product according to the manufacturer's/ workplace instructions. Use the right amount for the task.

4 Do not top up a cleaning solution, instead prepare a fresh one and dispose of the old solution.

5 Use the weaker agent first. Only if the dirt proves stubborn should you use a stronger agent.

6 Never mix products, because this may produce harmful gases.

7 Do not pierce an aerosol can, even if it appears to be empty. It may explode.

8 Do not make up disinfectant solutions until you are about to use them. They will lose effectiveness, in some cases after a few hours. Many disinfectants will taint food and these should not be used in food areas.

The manufacturer's instructions will explain

- dilution rates: too concentrated will damage surfaces and is wasteful, too dilute will not do the job properly
- how much time to give the cleaning agent to work
- how to rinse dirt and cleaning agent from the surface
- at what temperature the agent works best
- how to store the cleaning agent when not using it
- any safety warning such as to wear protective clothing
- how often to use the cleaning agent
- how to dispose of the used cleaning agent.

Storing cleaning agents

1 Keep away from foodstuffs.

2 Close all containers firmly after use.

3 Store containers upright.

4 Always store in a correctly labelled container.

5 Where products are bought in bulk, they should be decanted into clearly labelled containers with instructions on each for use.

6 Store in a well ventilated cupboard or room, away from fire risks.

Cleaning a deep fryer

1 Switch off and allow to cool fully.

2 Remove the wire baskets and wash them thoroughly in hot water and detergent.

3 Drain the oil, using the tap at the bottom of the fryer. Pour the oil through the special filter, taking care not to let it splash. You should never try and save time by filtering the oil while it is still hot. If some spills on to you, you could get a nasty burn. If you drain hot oil into a plastic bucket, the bucket will melt and the oil will spill everywhere, burning your feet.

4 Remove any debris in the empty fryer; hinged electric elements can be moved so that the bottom of the compartment can be cleaned.

5 Close the drain valve and fill the fryer with hot water and detergent (or follow instructions provided by the manufacturer of the fryer or cleaning agent). Boil the solution for a short time by setting the fryer at 100°C. Then switch off.

6 When the water and detergent solution is cool enough to work in safely, remove any build-up of oil from around the fryer, using a long-handled brush or soft abrasive pad. Wear gloves and do not move the abrasive pad so vigorously that the surface of the fryer is damaged.

7 Drain the washing solution out. Rinse well with clean water (three times is usually advised). Any trace of soap or detergent will make the fresh oil spoil rapidly.

8 Dry thoroughly with a soft cloth, close the outlet and refill with oil (fresh if necessary).

Cleaning food production utensils

After washing, pots and pans should be placed upside-down on racks (preferably of alloy or stainless steel), or if that is not possible on shelves.

Stainless steel Generally stainless steel requires the minimum of attention. Simply wash in diluted detergent or soapy water. Rinse and dry well. Avoid using bleaches, undiluted detergent and coarse abrasive cleaners as these can cause some staining.

Cast iron Do not wash. Use a dry cloth or absorbent kitchen paper and wipe firmly. Use salt as a scouring agent where necessary, or a little detergent and hot water. If an iron pan is washed by accident, warm it slightly, then give it a coating of oil and rub it with salt before use. Otherwise the food will stick to the pan's surface.

Copper Wash in hot water with detergent. Remove stuck-on food with a brush or soft cloth. Never use scourers or metal wool which damage the tin coating. Copper will retain its shine if polished from time to time with a good metal polish.

Aluminium Aluminium pans should be washed in hot water with detergent and scrubbed clean with a cloth or a hard bristle brush. Rinse thoroughly and dry. Never use washing/caustic soda or similar materials which react with the aluminium causing the surface to pit. Remove stains by boiling in a weak solution of vinegar and water. Do not put in a dishwasher.

From Gilma catalogue of Hotelware and Foodservice Products, *M. Gilbert (Greenford) Ltd.*

Above: *1) Colander, 2), 6) and 7) Various aluminium pans, 3) Bain-marie pan, 4) Sugar boiler, 5) Tin-lined copper saucepan, 8) Milk pan, 9) Double boiler, 10) Stainless steel pan, 11) Wire basket, 12) Perforated spoon, 13) Skimmer, 14) Ladle, 15) Wire scoop (pea ladle).*

1) Cast-iron frying pan, 2) Large frying pan, 3) Oval frying pan (for fish), 4) Non-stick frying pan, 5) Tin-lined copper flambé pan (for use in the restaurant), 6) Aluminium frying pan, 7) Cast-iron pancake pan, 8) Sauteuse, 9) and 10) Tin-lined copper sauté pans, 11) Aluminium sauté pan, 12) Palette knife, 13) Fish slice, 14) Griddle, 15) Aluminium omelette pan.

More about utensils

Plastics – generally can be washed in hot water with detergent. Rinse in very hot water and dry thoroughly afterwards. Avoid contact with heat, and soaking in water for long periods.

Wood – not often found in catering kitchens now, but you may still come across wooden rolling pins, pepper mills and similar equipment.

Never leave wood to soak in water, as this will cause it to split or warp. Simply wipe with a damp cloth and leave to dry. If food remains stuck on, scrape this off, wash briefly but thoroughly in hot soapy water, rinse and leave to dry away from direct heat.

Stainless steel utensils should be treated in the same way as stainless steel saucepans. Machine wash is preferable. If washing by hand, twin sinks should be used to ensure adequate rinsing. The rinsing water should be at a temperature of 75°C to 85°C.

Can openers should be washed after use. Otherwise any food caught on the opening mechanism may taint other food, and become a breeding ground for bacteria. Take hand-operated openers out of their socket, and scrub both the socket arm and the cutting head in the sink, using hot soapy water. Rinse with clean hot water and air dry.

A wide range of the small items of equipment found in professional kitchens is shown below.

1) and 2) Perforated spoons for draining food.

3) and 4) Metal spoons for portioning or serving.

5) Measuring jug – essential for accuracy.

6) Sieve – removing lumps in flours or liquids, draining foods and puréing soups and sauces.

7) Salt box – useful in a busy kitchen, where a small dispenser might easily get knocked over.

8) Grater with different sizes of serrated holes, the larger ones for hard vegetables like raw carrots, the smaller for finer jobs like grating lemon zest.

9) Ramekin made of ovenproof china, used for cooking and serving individual dishes like crème brulée.

10) Soufflé dish, made from ovenproof china (various sizes are available).

11) Funnel – for pouring liquids into jars and other containers with small openings.

12) *Sur le plat* dish – for cooking *oeufs sur le plat* (eggs baked in the oven or sometimes cooked on top of the stove, see page 200).

13) Oval pie dish – for cooking and serving sweet and savoury pies. Round dishes are generally used for sweet pies.

14) Fish slice – for handling small solid or semi-solid food items (not just fish).

15) Sauce ladle, with a lip for accurate pouring.

➙

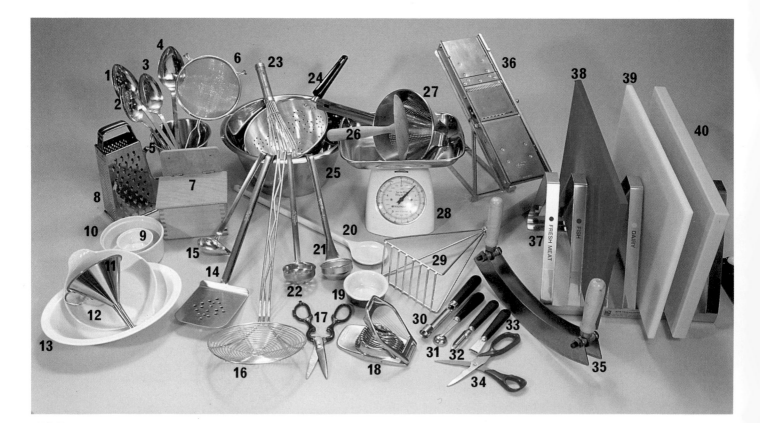

16) Spider – for scooping food out of a deep fat fryer or vegetables out of boiling water.

17) Poultry secateurs for cutting through (tender) bones/joints.

18) Egg slicer, fitted with fine wires to produce undamaged, whole slices.

19) Cocotte dish used for *oeuf en cocotte* (an egg dish that is baked in the oven).

20) Large spoon made of heat-resistant, durable plastic. This is better than a wooden spoon which might absorb and transfer food flavours and bacteria. Plastic spoons are best for stirring food in aluminium saucepans (metal spoons can cause discoloration).

21) Ladle – for handling liquids, testing pouring consistency, skimming impurities and fats off soups, sauces, stocks, stews and so forth.

22) Perforated ladle for handling small foods or finely cut items which need to be lifted clear of the cooking liquid.

23) Balloon whisk for beating air into cream or egg whites, or for thoroughly blending two or more liquids.

24) Colander for draining foods, e.g. pasta that has been boiled or salad vegetables after washing.

25) This type of stainless steel bowl is available in a wide range of sizes and is useful for mixing and storing food.

26) Wooden mushroom – for pounding purées, crushing brittle foods like peppercorns and forcing semi-liquids through sieves (using a liquidiser is easier!).

27) Conical strainer – for removing solids/lumps from liquids.

28) Small measuring/weighing scales. Scales are essential in any recipe where the success of the dish depends on accurate weighing of ingredients.

29) Masher for puréeing cooked potatoes, turnips, apples.

30) Corer for removing the centre (including the pips) from apples, pears and similar fruit.

31) Round scoop (*parisienne* cutter) for cutting balls out of melons, potatoes, carrots, etc. (illustration on page 151). Different sizes and oval shapes also available.

32) Peeler – for removing skin from vegetables and hard fruit like pears.

33) Zester – for removing the thin outer skin (not the pith) of lemons and other citrus fruits.

34) Kitchen scissors for general-purpose use.

35) Chopper with double blades (some have 3 or 4 blades) for chopping parsley (using a rocking action).

36) Mandolin for slicing (one blade produces a plain cut, the other a serrated cut).

37) Chopping board holder, colour-coded and labelled to indicate where particular boards should be kept, and what they should be used for.

38), 39) and 40) Colour-coded boards, blue for raw fish, white for dairy products and the thicker, turnip-coloured board for chopping vegetables. Red boards (not shown) are for raw meats.

Cutting equipment

LEVEL 2

It is against the law for anyone under 18 to clean power-driven or manual slicing or cutting machines (see page 7). If you are 18 or over, you should not attempt to clean these types of machine unless you have been instructed and trained, or are in the process of being trained and are working with a supervisor.

1 Turn the machine off at the plug or mains switch. Do not rely on the machine's control switch – you might accidentally knock it on during the cleaning.

2 Follow instructions on the machine for removing any parts that can be washed separately. Wash loose parts and attachments in a sink filled with hot water and detergent. Rinse in clean, very hot water.

3 Fill a cleaning bowl with a mild solution of warm water and the recommended detergent, and apply to the rest of the machine with a well wrung out cloth.

4 Avoid the use of harsh abrasive pads, which could damage the surfaces of the machine. A brush may come in useful for reaching recessed areas where food particles have accumulated.

5 Rinse carefully with clean, hot water.

6 Dry with a paper towel, or clean drying-up cloth. Mincing attachments, whisks and similar items which cannot be dried with a cloth should be allowed to air-dry.

7 Reassemble the machine carefully (making sure that your hands are clean).

8 Clean the areas underneath and around the machine.

ACTION

The *Control of Substances Hazardous to Health Regulations 1988*, COSHH for short, sets out measures to protect staff from any substances used at work, or arising from work activities that can harm their health. Cleaning agents which are toxic, harmful, irritant or corrosive fall into this category.

One of your employer's responsibilities under the Regulations is to carry out an assessment of the risks. Assume that you are asked to help with part of this task. Your job is to make a list of each of the cleaning agents used in your kitchen, and for each item note:

- possible harmful effects – study the labels and other information from the manufacturer
- where and how the substance is used or handled – you may need to ask your supervisor
- what precautions will prevent and control the risks – from the information on the label, and from your own knowledge of good cleaning procedures.

Discuss your completed list with your supervisor.

Crockery and cutlery

Industrial dishwashers work automatically, washing, rinsing and drying items. It should not be necessary to use a cloth at all. But if cutlery requires polishing, use a clean linen cloth.

1 Wear rubber gloves to protect your hands.

2 Scrape left-over food from plates, and empty the dregs from cups.

3 Sort items, so that plates, cups and cutlery are washed in their proper trays.

4 Remove from circulation any chipped, cracked, stained or broken items. They can cause injury and will harbour bacteria.

5 Pre-wash where necessary to remove encrusted dirt and grease.

6 Stack correctly in the baskets – to make sure items are washed thoroughly, and to prevent breakages and injury.

7 Use only the recommended detergent and rinsing solution. Read the labels carefully.

8 Do not stack plates, saucers and so forth for re-use, until they are properly dried.

Additional points for hand washing

1 Use two sinks. The first, for washing, should be filled with detergent and water at a temperature of at least 60°C. The second, for rinsing, should be filled with clean water (and possibly a rinsing agent) at a temperature of 75°C to 85°C to kill any bacteria. This is too hot for the hands, so use a basket to lower items and lift them out again.

2 Change detergent and rinsing water regularly.

3 Use nylon brushes or nylon scouring pads. Cloths are unsuitable because they might harbour bacteria. Steel wool or wire scouring pads will damage surfaces of crockery and cutlery.

NVQ **SVQ** **RANGE CHECKLIST**

LEVEL 1 **LEVEL 2**

1D12.1 Clean food production areas **2D12.1**

4 of these surfaces

☐ metal ☐
☐ wall tiles ☐
☐ painted ☐
☐ glass ☐
☐ floor tiles or vinyl or linoleum floor coverings ☐
laminated surfaces

- - - - - - - - - - - - - - - - - - - -

1D12.2 Clean food production equipment **2D12.2**

3 of these

☐ ovens ☐
☐ hobs and ranges ☐
☐ griddles or grills or salamanders ☐
☐ fryers ☐
☐ bain-marie or hotplates ☐

- - - - - - - - - - - - - - - - - - - -

1D12.3 Clean food production utensils **2D12.3**

6 of these utensils

☐ pots and pans ☐
☐ bowls or dishes or moulds ☐
☐ whisks ☐
☐ sieves or colanders or strainers ☐
☐ spoons or ladles or slices ☐
☐ graters ☐
☐ peelers or zesters or corers ☐
☐ can (tin) openers ☐

made of 4 of these materials

☐ stainless metal ☐
☐ coated metal ☐
☐ wooden ☐
☐ plastic ☐
☐ porcelain ☐
☐ earthenware ☐

LEVEL 1

1D22.1 Clean crockery and cutlery

cleaning by machine or by hand

☐ crockery
☐ cutlery

- - - - - - - - - - - - - - - - - - - -

1D22.2 Store crockery and cutlery

these items

☐ crockery
☐ cutlery

LEVEL 2

2D17.1 Clean cutting equipment

power-driven or manual machines as specified in the Prescribed Dangerous Machines Order, 1964, of 2 of these types

☐ mincing or chipping machines
☐ slicing machines
☐ rotary knife chopping machines
☐ mandolins

Introduction

Much of your work as a chef will depend on good knife skills. As with many aspects of working in a professional kitchen, success comes with an understanding of the basic rules and principles, and then plenty of practice.

Knife care and safety

1 When not in use, store your knives in a purpose-made case, wallet, box, knife block or on a magnetic rack. If you have to carry your knives from one area to another, put them away in their case first. Do not keep knives in a drawer, where they will knock together and get damaged edges.

2 When wiping a knife after use, keep the blade facing away from your hands and body. Wipe from the blunt to the sharp edge, so that you move in a direction away from your body.

3 Always wash knives thoroughly after you have finished a particular task. A quick wipe of the blade after cutting an onion and before slicing a tomato will leave the tomato tasting of onion. An even greater danger is that the knife will transfer harmful bacteria from uncooked to cooked food.

4 Generally knives should not be put in dishwashers. The jostling movement can damage the blade and cutting edge. Also the chemicals may cause pitting of the blade.

5 As necessary, clean knives from time to time during use. Don't let the handle get greasy when you are cutting a lot of meat, for example, otherwise the knife might slip and you will cut yourself.

6 Always keep knives sharp. A sharp knife will do the job more easily – you won't have to use a lot of pressure. A sharp knife is also less likely to slip.

7 Use the right knife for the right job, with the right chopping board. Follow the system in your workplace (e.g. colour coded equipment) for preventing cross-contamination between cooked and uncooked food.

8 Cut against the firm surface of a cutting board wherever practical. The board should not be in danger of slipping. It may help to put a damp cloth under the board.

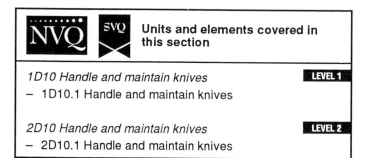

Poor knife techniques and untidy working practices are unfortunately responsible for many of the accidents which happen in kitchens. Consider one of the routine tasks, dicing vegetables. Your fingers act as a guide for the knife blade – a wrong position, or a moment's lack of concentration can easily lead to an accident.

1 Hold the knife firmly with the thumb on one side of the handle, the forefinger crooked on the other, and the remaining fingers curled around the handle.

2 With the other hand, hold the lengths of vegetable firmly, with your knuckles acting as a guide to the chopping/slicing motion.

3 Keep your thumb and finger tips well tucked away.

The photograph above shows the different steps involved in dicing vegetables (see page 162). By following these, you will soon become fast and accurate:

- the turnip has been trimmed so that it rests firmly on the board
- slices have then been cut
- these slices have been cut into long lengths like thick matchsticks
- finally, the lengths are cut into dice.

NVQ SVQ Units and elements covered in this section

1D10 Handle and maintain knives	LEVEL 1
– 1D10.1 Handle and maintain knives	

2D10 Handle and maintain knives	LEVEL 2
– 2D10.1 Handle and maintain knives	

Knife skills   *Handling knives*

Working methodically and safely

Good knife skills are part and parcel of working in an organised and efficient manner.

Before starting on a new task, set out only the tools and equipment you will need. Generally, only one knife should be in use at any one time. Keep the rest of your work area uncluttered.

Always pay full attention to the job you are doing, and work methodically:

- keep unprepared and prepared food quite separate
- establish a logical sequence, so that food is processed from left to right, or right to left.

A good example of this is peeling potatoes. Before you started learning catering, and you had to prepare a small quantity at home, you probably stood at the sink. One at a time you would take a potato out of the water, and trim it, letting the peelings fall into the sink water. The finished potato was then dropped into the same water so it did not discolour.

In large-scale catering, as you know, this approach would soon result in a sink full of peelings, peeled and unpeeled potatoes. Each time it would take longer to locate the next potato to peel. So it becomes much more sensible to spend a little time before starting, to organise space at two sinks, and use a large bowl (or three large bowls, one for the untrimmed potatoes, one for the trimmings, and one for the finished potatoes).

SAFETY ▲ ▲ ▲

NEVER walk around carrying a knife. If this is unavoidable, hold it close to the body with the point downwards, and the blunt edge facing in the direction you are walking.

NEVER leave knives near or hanging over the edge of a work surface. The safest position is where they won't be knocked by someone passing by.

NEVER leave knives on a work surface with the blade pointing upwards. Put the knife down so the blade lies flat against the work surface.

NEVER leave knives hidden in a pile of partly prepared food, or in a bowl or sink of water for washing later.

NEVER try to catch a knife if you drop it. Let it fall to the floor, then pick it up by the handle and wash it well.

NEVER use a knife with a loose handle.

ACTION

Study the photograph below and the list opposite of knives and small utensils. For each item:

- in the column headed *USE*, indicate whether it is used in your workplace frequently (F), sometimes (S), or never (N)
- in the column headed *EXP* (for *EXPERIENCE*), mark with a tick (✓) those items that you feel you can use confidently, and with a cross (X) those items that you have not had much or any practice with.

Agree with your supervisor which equipment you need to get more practised at using, and discuss how you can best do this. If you have worked through the checklist carefully, the areas for attention will be marked F or S in the *USE* column, and X in the *EXP* column.

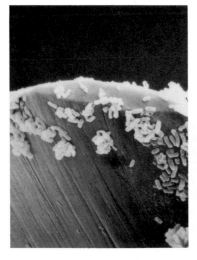

This knife blade looked clean, but under the microscope the bacteria still clinging to its surface are all too obvious.

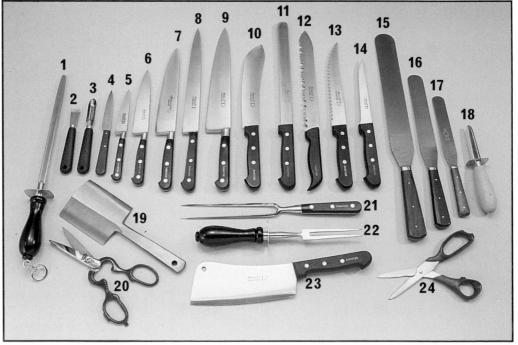

ACTION 23

	USE	EXP
1 *Steel* to sharpen knives – note the safety guard near the handle		
2 *Zester* for removing the fine outer skin from oranges, lemons, limes, etc.		
3 *Peeler* for peeling potatoes and other vegetables and fruit with a firm but thin skin. The sharp point is used for cutting out eyes from potatoes and small blemishes from other vegetables		
4 *Paring knife* with a thin, sharp and slightly flexible blade, useful for hand-held work, for example cutting an apple into segments, or trimming potatoes		
5 (also **6** and **7**) *Cook's knives* sometimes called *French cook's knives* or *professional cook's knives* of varying sizes. With firm blades and sharp points their uses include slicing, shredding or chopping vegetables, trimming and cutting meat		
8 *Filleting knife* with a thin, very flexible blade that makes it ideal for following the bones closely, as in filleting fish. The blade and point should be one of the sharpest knives in your set		
9 Large (and heavy) *cook's knife* used for chopping large items and also for tasks like chopping parsley when a rocking motion is used (see page 261). The wide blade is also useful for crushing garlic cloves		
10 *Butcher's steak knife* an example of a knife developed for a very specific use. The firm blade with its curved end makes it useful for slicing raw meat quickly		
11 *Carving knife* the long, thin, flexible blade makes it possible to slice meat thinly. Some chefs prefer to use a carving knife with a *scalloped* edge for cold meats, poultry, ham and smoked salmon. The hollows create a kind of vacuum, so that the food does not stick to the blade, and you get a cleaner cut. *Serrated* knives are ideal for crusty breads and cakes		
12 *Deep-freeze knife* with a serrated blade specially developed to cut through frozen meat. This knife is strictly for use when frozen meat has to be cut at short notice, so is not a particularly practical tool in a catering kitchen		
Saw edged cutting knives (not shown) the fine indentations along the cutting edge quickly penetrate the tough skin of tomatoes, citrus fruit, etc.		

	USE	EXP
13 *Bread knife* with a long thin blade and a serrated cutting edge		
14 *Boning knife* with a fine pointed razor-sharp tip. Most of the work is carried out towards the end of the point. The knife is held like a dagger. Because it has a strong, firm blade it will not bend or break under the considerable force that may have to be used. But this means that great care must be taken, because if the knife slips it could cause serious injury		
15 (also **16** and **17**) *Palette knives* of varying lengths and widths to shape smooth mixtures, or lift firm foods such as a burger. The blade is flexible, has a rounded end instead of a point, and is not sharp		
18 *Oyster knife* used to force open the shell of a fresh oyster, it has a short firm blade and a safety guard		
19 *Cutlet bat* for flattening pieces of raw meat, for example, veal escalopes and minute steaks		
20 *Poultry secateurs* for cutting through poultry bones. Some chefs prefer to use a knife to do this		
21 *Cook's fork* a particularly dangerous item with its long, sharp points. It is used for lifting roasted meats, although this needs to be done with great care to avoid piercing the meat, which would allow the juices to escape. In the case of a chicken, for example, you should insert the fork into the chest cavity and then lift		
22 *Carving fork* with a guard to protect the fingers from slipping into the way of the carving knife and short prongs to hold the meat firmly in place. Wherever possible, avoid piercing hot joints repeatedly with a fork. Some joints can be safely held by the bone, when the meat has been scraped off the bone before cooking, e.g. leg of lamb		
23 *Cleaver* or *chopper* found mainly in the butchery section of kitchens and used for chopping through large bones. The back of the chopper blade is used for cracking bones		
24 *Kitchen scissors* for cutting the fins and tails of fish (some chefs prefer to use a cook's knife for this job). Scissors are also used for more general tasks like cutting the string or the paper for a steamed pudding		

Buying your own knives

If you haven't already started, you will probably want to build up your own collection of knives. Good quality knives are expensive, but looked after well – and that's why it's better to have your own – they will make your job much easier and last a long time.

There is little point in trying to save money by buying knives intended for home cooks. You may also be tempted by claims that particular knives never require sharpening. Or by those that come in a storage scabbard which sharpens the blade each time it is withdrawn. Such knives are unlikely to last long in a professional kitchen and will not perform the job as efficiently.

The checklist on the previous page should have helped you identify what knives you would find it most useful to buy first. If you never do any boning, for example, there is not much point in buying a boning knife.

For a basic set you should start with the following:

- 6 cm (2½ inch) paring knife
- 14 cm (5½ inch) heavy cook's knife
- 23 cm (9 inch) or 26 cm (10 inch) heavy cook's knife
- vegetable peeler
- palette knife
- sharpening steel.

Points to look out for

1 Waterproof handle that will not be damaged when washed at very high temperatures. The traditional chef's knife has a black handle, but increasingly chefs prefer to use colour-coded equipment. So, for example, knives with a moulded plastic handle, coloured red, would only be used for preparing fresh meat. Some knives are permanently etched with the words *FRUIT / VEG*, for example.

2 Blade forged from one piece of steel, which runs right through the handle.

3 Blade held in the handle with a minimum of three retaining rivets, or a moulded handle. In less expensive knives, the blade is attached to the end of the handle and may snap off with heavy use. Poor quality knives also tend to swell when they are repeatedly submerged in water, and the handles eventually fall apart.

4 Knife should feel comfortable and balanced to hold.

5 Blade made of high carbon stainless steel. These will not rust or stain, nor will colour foods. You may come across chefs who prefer to use knives with carbon steel blades. While these are easier to sharpen than stainless steel, they tend to rust. They also stain certain foods such as onions and hard-boiled eggs.

Sharpening a knife using a steel

1 Hold the steel steady in one hand, pointing away from the body and downwards at a slight angle (or upwards if you find it easier).

2 Holding the knife with the sharp edge of the blade pointing away from you, sweep it along the steel. Start from the handle end of the steel and the handle end of the knife blade. Move the blade diagonally across and down the length of the steel until you reach the tip. Keep the blade of the knife at an angle of about 25° to the steel.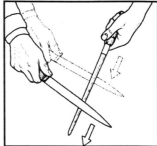

3 Repeat, using alternate sides of the steel.

4 Wipe the blade after sharpening, to remove any loose steel particles.

5 To test the blade is sharp, try cutting a soft tomato.

A knife should be sharpened little and often. Have your knives professionally reground every two years – more often in heavy use.

Some chefs prefer to move the knife blade towards the body. Others use a knife-sharpening machine or special block made of carborundum stone.

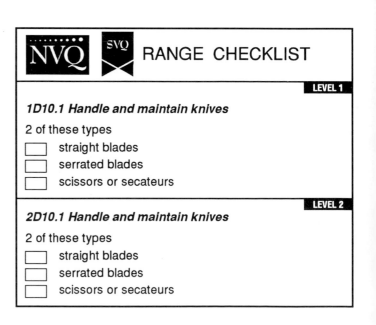

NVQ **SVQ** **RANGE CHECKLIST**

LEVEL 1

1D10.1 Handle and maintain knives

2 of these types

☐ straight blades
☐ serrated blades
☐ scissors or secateurs

LEVEL 2

2D10.1 Handle and maintain knives

2 of these types

☐ straight blades
☐ serrated blades
☐ scissors or secateurs

Introduction

The quality of the food that comes out of your kitchen depends on correct handling and storage. It is easy to overlook this, when so much skill and effort are required in the preparation, cooking and service stages. But kitchens cannot run well if the stores are chaotic, if food deliveries are left unchecked, or if food has to be thrown out because it has passed its use-by date.

Besides the common sense element of not wishing to serve food that might harm the people who eat it, the law on these matters is very strict. If the fault is yours, you could be in serious trouble, and so could your employer. (Food safety laws are summarised on page 10.)

Maintaining food stores

Obviously, the variety and extent of the storage areas, refrigerators and freezers in your kitchen will reflect its size and the style of operation. Nevertheless, there are some general rules which apply to food storage.

Security – in most catering establishments, the contents of the food stores represent a considerable sum of money. This means that they must be kept locked when there is no one in attendance, and the keys returned to the proper place. Often there will be specific times laid down for when food can be drawn from the stores.

General organisation – it should be easy to find items which are required, and to spot items which are running short. Similar things should be kept together. Once cartons or boxes have been broken into, the remaining contents should be taken out of the box. Do not pack refrigerators or freezers so tightly that the air cannot circulate.

Safety – the heavier items should be stored on the lower shelves. Shelves should be stacked so that there is no danger of items falling off.

Cleanliness – follow a regular cleaning schedule so that dirt does not build up. Report any signs of insects or vermin. Food should be stored away from the floor (on shelves or in bins), and kept covered.

At the correct temperature – refrigerators and freezers will generally have an external display so that you can see at a glance that the temperature is at the correct level. Get in the habit of checking this regularly, and if there is an automatic temperature recording chart, of observing that this is working properly. Report any problems to your supervisor, and do so without delay, otherwise the food may have to be thrown away.

Contents guide

All deliveries should be checked carefully against the original order, and the delivery documentation – for quantity and for quality.

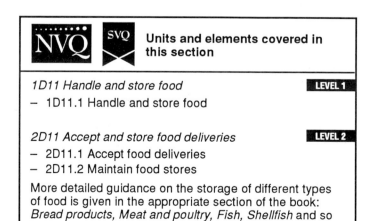

NVQ **SVQ** **Units and elements covered in this section**

1D11 Handle and store food **LEVEL 1**
– 1D11.1 Handle and store food

2D11 Accept and store food deliveries **LEVEL 2**
– 2D11.1 Accept food deliveries
– 2D11.2 Maintain food stores

More detailed guidance on the storage of different types of food is given in the appropriate section of the book: *Bread products, Meat and poultry, Fish, Shellfish* and so forth.

Storing deliveries

1 Move goods into their proper storage area immediately after delivery.

2 Transfer old stock to a position where it will be used before the new stock (*stock rotation*).

3 Generally, the packaging should not be removed from chilled and frozen convenience foods before storage. The packaging protects the food (frozen food may be quite brittle) from damage and problems such as freezer burn.

At what stage cartons, boxes and bags of bulk items like flour are emptied, will depend on the space available and stock levels. Do not leave boxes:

- stacked on the floor where they might get in someone's way. Food should be kept well above floor level
- part-filled.

Once a bag has been opened (of bulk granulated sugar, for example), the remaining contents should be transferred to a bin.

Collapse and dispose of empty boxes and cartons.

Thawing frozen food

For best results the thawing process should not be hurried.

1 Always try and keep a few days ahead in terms of what foods the kitchen will require defrosted. There will be a system in operation so that you do get sufficient notice – through function bookings lists, or through weekly requisitions, for example.

2 Check with the supplier's product information, or workplace instructions, on whether all or part of the packaging should be removed for defrosting. Poultry and meat are generally left in their original plastic wrapping, and a small hole made so that air can circulate more easily.

3 Transfer the food to a suitable refrigerator, thawing cabinet or cold room. The air temperature during defrosting should remain the same, and not lower than 0°C, nor higher than 5°C. This is to allow the ice crystals to break down slowly, without damage to structure of the food.

4 Follow the general rules for keeping different types of food separate (page 13). Raw meat should be defrosted in a separate fridge from dairy produce, and so forth.

5 In a general-purpose refrigerator or cold room, the food should be placed at the bottom.

6 For meat and poultry, use deep trays or containers which will catch the liquid that runs out during the thawing process.

7 Never refreeze food which has defrosted. Never return food to the freezer which has begun to defrost.

Thawing takes longer than you might initially think:

- 24 hours for small cuts of meat and joints, e.g. 1.35 kg (3 lb) chicken
- 36 to 48 hours for larger joints, e.g. 48 hours for a 3.2 kg (7 lb) turkey.

SAFETY △ △ △

Lifting a heavy object

The right way of lifting a heavy object is not, as many people think, to keep your back straight and stiff, while bending your knees.

If your muscles are tensed up and you get a sudden jar – because you have lost your balance, for example, or the object is heavier than you expected – you are much more likely to hurt yourself. Children and drunk adults rarely hurt themselves when they fall over, and that's because their muscles are relaxed.

The right method of lifting is something best learned from a qualified kinetic instructor. It involves training your mind, as well as practising various techniques. However, there are some general rules which you may find helpful to remember:

1 Keep your muscles relaxed.
2 Think about what you are going to do first, where the object has to be carried to, and check that the way is clear.
3 Get help if you think there is any chance that the object will be heavier than you can easily cope with.
4 Position your feet so that your body is well balanced as you move down to collect the object, and while lifting.
5 Position your hands carefully, one hand under the object to support its weight, the other ready to pull the box into the body as you move up. Use the palm of your hand, not just the finger tips.

The feet, the knees, the back, the hands and the head – all play a part in what is known as the fundamental kinetic lift *(illustrated here).*

Accepting food deliveries `LEVEL 2`

1 Check against your record of the order, and against the supplier's delivery note. Have you received the items that were ordered? Are the quantity and quality those which were specified? This will involve counting boxes, cartons and so forth, as well as examining the contents. Weigh fresh meat, fish, vegetables and other items sold by weight.

2 With a temperature probe, check the temperature of the outer layer of all chilled and frozen foods. Foods not in the acceptable temperature range should be rejected – for example, if cook-chill food is above 5°C. Check the requirements in your workplace. The regulations are complex (see page 10).

3 Fresh fish should be well iced. Fresh shellfish should be alive.

4 Check the packing is intact. Chilled and frozen foods should be labelled with the name of the company, description of the food, weight, product code, use-by date and ingredients list.

Rejecting goods

Any goods which do not correspond with what was ordered will in most cases have to be returned. This is best done at the time of delivery, but most suppliers will accept returned goods provided they are notified of the reason without delay.

Make sure that both you and the delivery person have a record of returned goods. This may be on both copies of the delivery note, on the order copy, or by asking the delivery person to make out a returns form or credit note. There has to be some means of making sure that returned goods are not subsequently paid for.

Stock control `LEVEL 2`

Procedures vary for keeping track of stock movement. In smaller establishments the emphasis is generally on ensuring that suppliers are paid for the goods accepted and no more. On the other hand, if the food gross profit results for the week or month are unsatisfactory, stock usage will be one of the areas investigated by management.

In bigger establishments, various forms, backed by a computerised system, will be used to monitor all aspects. This means that management know on a day-to-day basis such details as:

- what has been received, by type of commodity and by supplier

- the cost of all foods issued to the kitchen, by department

- what is left in stock, and its value

- the pattern of usage, so that minimum and maximum stock levels can be established, and adjusted as necessary.

A balance has to be struck between obtaining quantity discounts, the risk of stock deteriorating, and the amount of money tied up in stocks. You may have come across the expression *just in time* or *JIT*. For this to work, suppliers must be able to deliver at short notice, without charging premium prices.

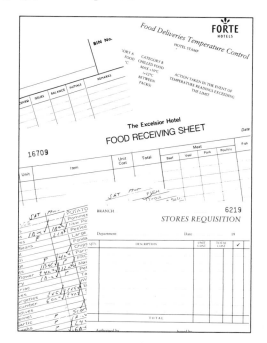

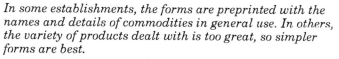

In some establishments, the forms are preprinted with the names and details of commodities in general use. In others, the variety of products dealt with is too great, so simpler forms are best.

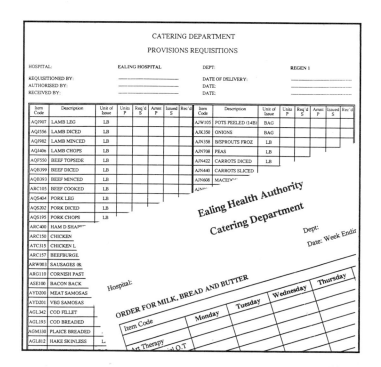

ACTION

What follows are reports on visits to two typical catering establishments.

1 Discuss what happened with your colleagues and supervisor. How do the procedures described compare with those in your workplace? In what respects are your own procedures better, and why do you think this?

2 With your supervisor's or tutor's help, arrange to make a similar visit yourself. If possible go to an establishment which is different from those you have experience of. Write up a brief report, and note any procedures which you think would be helpful in your own workplace.

Visit to BP Explorations, Stockley Park – a Catering and Allied Services unit

The storeman was not happy about the mushrooms – the chef had asked for 2nd class mushrooms for a specific purpose, but these were 'dustbin class'. The mushrooms were wrapped and set aside. The supplier was phoned and agreed to replace the mushrooms later that morning.

Use-by dates were checked. All salad, fruit and vegetables were examined for freshness and size – in particular those for the director's kitchen, as they were very expensive items. Milk pergals were examined for damage and leakages.

The storeman was not popular with all the delivery drivers as he was strict about checking temperatures. Gala Pie was tested, but not considered acceptable. Boned and rolled legs of pork

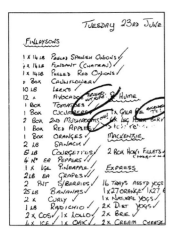

were probed. The print-out from the temperature probe was attached to the head chef's delivery list, as a record that foods were within the correct temperature range on arrival.

The storeman collapsed boxes, removed excess wrapping and wiped up spillages made during deliveries.

The storeman rotated stocks when putting away new supplies. He watched out for items used out of sequence, and tidied up broken boxes, etc. Stock levels were checked against menus. There was a display board in the dry stores, where chefs could write down items to be re-ordered.

Visit to the 850-bedroom Forte Excelsior Hotel, Heathrow

There was an emergency. 300 passengers from a delayed flight would be arriving later that morning. Lunch, possibly dinner, and breakfast needed to be planned and orders phoned through.

The head chef hurried in with his menus and emergency order for 35 lb fresh turkey, 2 legs of pork, 300 wings and breasts of chicken, 300 fresh rolls and 12 Canteloupe melons (for breakfast). (The hotel does not keep a large stock on the shelves, as Forte's suppliers are able to deliver quickly.)

08.30 A sous chef came in to find out if any Canteloupe melons had arrived. She was told they were on their way with the emergency delivery.

08.45 Two pallets of groceries arrived – completely covered in plastic wrapping. One pallet (65 cases of mineral water) was taken by a porter to the chill room. The storeman opened the grocery pallet, and checked the goods against the invoice. Returns were put aside for collection the next day, when a credit note would be issued by the driver. Eggs and butter went straight to the kitchen for the chef to check and store.

08.45 A waitress rushed in: 'Can I have some dark and tomato sauce for the breakfast meeting – they're using it so quickly'.

09.15 A chilled and frozen food delivery arrived. Temperature probe used – a frozen gâteau recorded minus 12.9°C (acceptable).

09.30 Fresh/frozen meat arrived – all items counted. Meat taken straight to kitchen to be examined and stored.

10.15 Fresh fish arrived. Inspected for quality, then sent to chilled storage. The very best quality was expected and certainly on this delivery it was.

Introduction

The UK is said to have the greatest range of breads in Western Europe. You can choose the shape – from cottage and bloomer, to cob and plait, and the flour – from wheatgerm and wholemeal, to soft-grain or stoneground. In addition there is a huge variety of rye breads, pittas and baguettes adopted from overseas, or novelty breads flavoured with herbs and spices.

Part-baked bread products can be finished on the premises to sell fresh and warm from the oven, with an enticing yeasty smell.

The large number of different breads available and an even bigger choice of fillings mean that it is possible to produce a huge range of sandwiches. But whatever the type being made it should be:

- fresh and appetising with a good flavour
- easy to handle and eat
- satisfying.

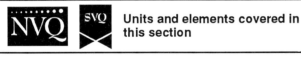

Units and elements covered in this section

1D17 Prepare sandwiches, rolls and hot filled bread products   **LEVEL 1**
- 1D17.1 Prepare sandwiches and rolls
- 1D17.2 Prepare hot filled bread products

For further information on the preparation of canapés, open sandwiches, presentation and garnishing, see *Cold presentation*.

'Sandwiches evolved from the piece of beef wedged between two slices of bread first ordered by the Earl of Sandwich in 1762 – to allow him to continue his card game.

'By the early Victorian era they had become dainty, feminine tit-bits, an essential part of formal afternoon teas. Chefs and cooks in the grand houses vied with each other to invent delicate fillings for wafer-thin sandwiches. Anyone who was anyone had a sandwich dedicated in his or her honour.'

Michael Raffael writing in *The Bread Guide, Caterer & Hotelkeeper.*

Quality and storage points: bread
- looks and smells fresh
- resilient when lightly pressed
- correct texture, colour and shape for the particular type of bread, e.g. hard crusts crisp but not tough.

Bread should be stored in a cool, well ventilated room. Do not refrigerate (this will only speed up the staling process).

Unwrapped bread should be covered with a clean tea towel or kitchen paper.

Bread which is still hot on delivery should be placed on a rack for the air to circulate and away from any cooked bread, otherwise condensation will occur.

As a general rule:
- white crust breads have the shortest shelf life
- brown breads keep better than their white equivalent. Seed breads and breads containing rye stay moist even after they have been part-sliced

- bread containing a little fat is more moist
- wholemeal loaves become more crumbly after a day
- enriched breads, teacakes and brioches are best eaten the day after baking
- the larger the loaf, the longer it stays fresh
- most sliced and wrapped breads, regardless of type, have the same shelf life.

Bread freezes well: uncut loaves, up to 2 months, cut loaves up to 1 month, crusty bread and rolls up to 2 weeks. The faster the freezing process, the better the end quality (slow freezing creates large ice crystals which damage the texture). Wrap the bread well to protect it from freezer burn.

Thaw at room temperature, still in wrapping. Large loaves will take about 4 hours, French sticks about 1 hour. After thawing, warm crusty breads and rolls for 5 to 10 minutes in an oven at 200°C.

Sliced bread can be toasted from frozen.

Preparation methods

Organise your work area before you start, so that you have everything to hand that you will need. For example:

on the left of your chopping board: stack of sliced bread

at the top: containers of spreadings, fillings and garnishes, arranged in the order in which they will be used

to the right: palette knife for spreading, sharp knives for cutting, spoons for fillings like mayonnaise, a damp cloth (or supply of disposable sanitising wipes) for cleaning the board down between operations

nearby: dustbin, refrigerator, washing facilities, any cooking equipment you will need to use.

Work in a logical sequence. For example:

1 Cream spreadings.

2 Prepare all your fillings: chopping, slicing, blending as necessary.

3 Slice the bread.

4 Spread all the bread.

5 Place the filling on to each bottom slice.

6 Cover with the top slice.

7 Stack rounds, so that you can slice through several layers at once.

8 Cut the sandwiches.

9 Garnish.

Slicing bread products

Make sure that the bread is sliced to the correct thickness for the style of sandwich you are preparing. For example, dainty tea sandwiches and rolled sandwiches served in a hotel or tea room need to be made with very thin slices, while a pub offering wholesome sandwiches as a lunch time snack should use thicker slices.

Lengths of French bread can be sliced in half lengthwise, leaving a hinge. Alternatively, make two parallel cuts running the length of the chunk.

Rolls can be treated similarly, or have their tops sliced off and replaced as a 'hat' on the filling.

Spreadings

Before fillings are put in sandwiches, the bread needs to be spread with butter, margarine, low-fat spread, mayonnaise, or a combination of these. This is to:

- provide flavour

- stop the bread from soaking up moisture from the filling. This has limited effect with fillings like cucumber and tomato. These are best made to order.

Butter can be salted or unsalted, and flavoured, for example, with mustard, horseradish, lemon, garlic, parsley or tarragon. Sweet flavourings (use with unsalted butter) include cinnamon, honey and orange.

Spreadings should be used soft so that they coat the bread smoothly and do not damage its surface. In most kitchens, butter will not take long to become soft. For reasons of hygiene, avoid leaving butter out overnight, or even for a few hours. A few seconds in the microwave on the defrost program will soften butter quickly.

Alternatively, cream the butter by mixing with a little milk: 30 ml milk (2 tbsp) to 225 g butter (8 oz).

For hand spreading, use a round-bladed or palette knife, with a smooth, sweeping movement. Take the spreading right to the edge of the slices.

Styles of sandwich

Simple – made with 2 slices of bread, with or without crusts.

Open faced – filling on 1 slice of bread.

Tea – small, made with 2 slices of bread, crusts trimmed off, light filling.

Club, triple or multi-deck – made with 3 or 4 slices of bread, one on top of the other and different fillings. Club sandwiches are usually made with toasted bread.

Rolled – 1 slice spread with filling and rolled up like a Swiss roll.

Pinwheel – rolled, then cut into circular shapes.

NUTRITION

Bread is low in fat and nutritious. It is a good source of fibre-rich starch, protein and some of the vitamins and minerals essential to good health.

For healthier sandwiches, use:

- thickly sliced bread
- low fat spreads and spread thinly
- lower fat cheeses
- lean meats, fish or skinless chicken
- low fat yogurt, lemon juice or other low fat dressings
- vegetables such as lettuce, carrots, celery and sweetcorn as good sources of fibre
- pulses, nuts, dried fruits.

> **Quantity guidelines**
>
> *from The Flour Advisory Bureau*
>
> A sandwich loaf 800 g (1¾ lb) yields 22 slices and requires 100 g (4 oz) creamed butter.
>
> Catering sandwich loaf 1600 g (3½ lb) yields 48 to 50 slices and requires 200 g creamed butter.
>
> Unsliced bloomer loaf yields 16 slices on average, and requires 100 g creamed butter.
>
> French stick 27 cm (20 inches) yields 20 slices or 5 chunks and requires about 150 g creamed butter.
>
> 24 bread rolls require 200 g creamed butter.

Fillings

Fillings can be sliced, puréed, creamed, flaked, chopped or grated and may need to be combined with a small amount of sauce of some sort. Hard-boiled eggs, for example, are usually chopped up and mixed with mayonnaise. The filling should be moist enough to balance the dryness of the bread.

Use creamy fillings for rolled sandwiches.

Choose two complementary fillings for double deckers.

There is enormous scope for being creative. But offering too wide a choice could waste time and money and confuse customers.

Toasted sandwiches

Toasted sandwiches can be made in a vertical slot toaster, under a standard grill, or with sealed edges in a contact grill. A point to remember is that fillings which become runny when heated – for instance, those with a sauce or sweet preserve base – are best prepared in a machine which seals the edges of the bread during cooking.

Ensure the butter and filling are evenly spread. Too little of either will result in uneven browning and burnt patches.

Overfull sandwiches will burst, making a mess of equipment and preparation areas, and spoiling the sandwich itself.

For sandwiches toasted under a grill or in a vertical slot toaster: butter two slices of bread and place the filling on the buttered side of one slice. Top with the second slice, buttered side inwards.

For sealed sandwiches: butter two slices of bread. Place the filling on the unbuttered side of one slice. Top with the second slice, buttered side uppermost.

Presentation

Try to arrange sandwiches so that the filling can be recognised. Small shapes can sometimes be stood upright, triangles can be arranged around the edge of a service plate.

Try a variety of shapes: squares, oblongs, triangles, rounds.

Combine white and brown bread for a chequered effect.

Attractive garnishes will add greatly to the visual appeal of the dish. Serve with a simple salad, or spear a cocktail stick through an appropriate garnish – for instance a stuffed olive, or a slice of fresh fruit – and secure this in the plated sandwich.

The many varieties of lettuce offer a choice of texture, colour and flavour.

Coloured napkins, an attractive plate of the correct size, polished knife and fork – all ideas that can turn a simple snack into something special.

If you are offering open sandwiches, your customers will probably require a knife and fork to eat them (the preparation of these is covered on page 263).

Preparing sandwiches in advance

In some establishments, sandwiches are prepared a little in advance of the time of service, and are then covered with an airtight wrapping, labelled and chilled for a short period – exactly how long will depend on both the bread and the filling.

Don't squash the sandwich into its wrapper, otherwise you will distort its shape and encourage sogginess.

HYGIENE

The very highest standards of hygiene are essential when preparing sandwiches – you can't rely on final cooking to kill any harmful bacteria. Remind yourself of the essential points covered earlier in the book in *Hygiene*.

Pay particular attention to the cleanliness of slicing and buttering machines, and their safe use (see page 7).

When prepared in advance, sandwiches, filled rolls and similar bread products which contain meat, fish, eggs (or substitutes for these), soft cheeses, or vegetables must be stored at 5°C or below – Food Hygiene Regulations, see page 10. The exception is if they are going to be served within 4 hours of the finish of preparation.

ACTION

Study the ideas on this page for fillings. In the box provided by each:

- tick (✔) those which are already available at your workplace
- cross (✗) those that you feel are definitely not appropriate
- rate the remaining ones on a scale of 1 to 3 in terms of how popular you think they would be with your customers. Use 3 for the most popular.

Discuss the outcome with your supervisor – what additions/ changes might be made to the range you offer, and what would be the selling price of new items?

Closed sandwiches, filled baps, stuffed pitta bread, rolls etc.

- [ ] prawn cocktail
- [ ] smoked mackerel with mayonnaise and horseradish
- [ ] egg and salami
- [ ] roast pork and apple sauce, or sage and onion stuffing, or onion relish
- [ ] chicken with yogurt and mint, or curried mayonnaise
- [ ] salmon with cucumber
- [ ] ox tongue with French mustard, or redcurrant jelly or mild pickle
- [ ] cream cheese with watercress and crispy bacon or dates and honey, or finely chopped walnuts
- [ ] crab with Worcestershire sauce and mustard
- [ ] brie with seedless green grapes and chopped walnuts
- [ ] crunchy peanut butter, bacon, sliced avocado
- [ ] sliced banana with lemon juice
- [ ] grated apple with lemon juice and sultanas
- [ ] turkey, Emmental cheese and bacon
- [ ] ham and pease pudding (a Yorkshire favourite)
- [ ] lean ham with mustard, sliced apple and celery
- [ ] salt beef with English mustard, sliced potato, radish and gherkins, grated carrot, mayonnaise
- [ ] liver sausage blended with Worcestershire sauce, chopped gherkins, chopped hard-boiled egg, mayonnaise

Some specialities

- [ ] Italian ciabatta bread – with salami, dolce latte, chopped tomato, garlic and oil
- [ ] Pan bagnat – baguette split open, doused with olive oil, rubbed with garlic and seasoned. Filled with spring onions, black olives, mild anchovy fillets, tomatoes, capsicums and often lettuce
- [ ] Arabian stuffed pitta – split, inside spread with a meat pâté, then stuffed with roughly chopped hard-boiled egg blended with olive oil, garlic, halved black olives
- [ ] Cumberland special – long roll cut twice lengthways. Sliced cooked Cumberland sausage in one cut, pickled red cabbage and chopped apple in the other

Hot sandwiches

- [ ] cheese and chutney and/or ham and/or salami
- [ ] sausage and mustard
- [ ] chicken and mango chutney
- [ ] cream cheese, prawns, chopped spring onion and/or bacon
- [ ] corned beef and sliced tomato
- [ ] grated cheese, apple, onion
- [ ] flaked tuna and tomato ketchup
- [ ] crispy roll, scooped out and filled with flaked tuna, cottage cheese, spring onion, parsley, bread-crumbs. Wrapped in kitchen foil and baked
- [ ] warmed muffin filled with flaked fish blended with soured cream
- [ ] ham on toast, with asparagus spears and grated cheese, grilled until the cheese melts

Some specialities

- [ ] Gulf Coast Poor Boys – Texan nickname for char-grilled, split baguettes topped with grilled shrimp and tartare sauce or white crabmeat and melted cheese
- [ ] Italian Hero sandwich – long crusty roll split lengthwise, filled with lightly fried onion and pepper slices and cooked spicy sausage
- [ ] Finnan egg – soft bap filled with flaked haddock, scrambled egg and freshly chopped parsley
- [ ] Bookmaker's sandwich – batted rump steak, grilled or fried and pressed between two thick crusts

of toasted or plain white bread

- [ ] Croque Monsieur – white bread sandwich with ham and cheese, lightly fried in olive oil
- [ ] Croque Madame – as above, but topped with a fried egg
- [ ] Doner kebab – warmed pitta bread filled with slices of hot lamb, also lettuce, chopped tomatoes, onion rings

Sealed sandwiches

- [ ] chopped (cooked) chicken and sweetcorn relish
- [ ] baked beans in tomato sauce, grilled bacon (chopped) and Worcestershire sauce
- [ ] sliced ham spread with sweet pickle
- [ ] grated apple, raisins, brown sugar and cinnamon
- [ ] cream cheese, strawberry jam
- [ ] cream cheese, thinly sliced banana

From The Flour Advisory Bureau, The Butter Information Council, The Tea Council.

NVQ | **SVQ** | RANGE CHECKLIST

LEVEL 1

1D17.1 Prepare sandwiches and rolls

with 5 of these fillings

- [ ] fats or pastes or spreads
- [ ] cooked meat or poultry or fish
- [ ] eggs
- [ ] salad or vegetables or fruit
- [ ] cheese
- [ ] sauces and dressings

using 6 of these preparation methods

- [ ] spreading
- [ ] slicing or chopping
- [ ] grating
- [ ] mixing
- [ ] mashing
- [ ] shelling
- [ ] peeling

for 2 of these

- [ ] sliced bread
- [ ] unsliced bread
- [ ] rolls or baps or baguettes or pitta bread

Introduction

Meals and snacks can be provided in just a few minutes with very little effort using microwave cooking. As well as being fast, energy-saving and versatile, microwave ovens are easy to operate. They often have a range of pre-set programs so that you do not even have to time the process.

With these advantages it is not surprising that commercial microwave ovens are now used in so many catering kitchens. These ovens are more robust than their domestic counterpart. They have to be. In a household, the microwave might be used three or four times a day. In a busy catering outlet, the pattern could easily be 2000 uses a day.

What happens

In microwave cooking, energy (not heat in the usual sense) is transferred to the food by electro-magnetic radiation. Microwaves pass into the food and make the water molecules vibrate, causing them to heat up very quickly.

The microwaves can penetrate only about 5 to 20 mm (¼ to ¾ inch) into the food. The rest of the cooking (towards the centre) takes place by conduction of heat from the outer layer.

The penetration depth depends on the water, fat, carbohydrate, protein and mineral content of the food.

Microwaving cooks by radiation, but the radiation is different from that involved in grilling. The inside of the microwave oven does not get hot as a grill does and the heating/cooking happens right through the food instead of being concentrated at its surface.

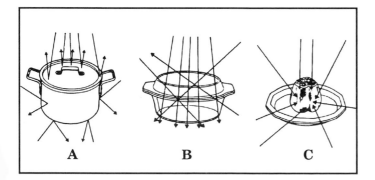

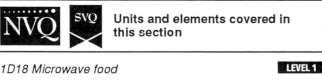

Units and elements covered in this section

1D18 Microwave food
LEVEL 1
- 1D18.1 Microwave food

Contents guide

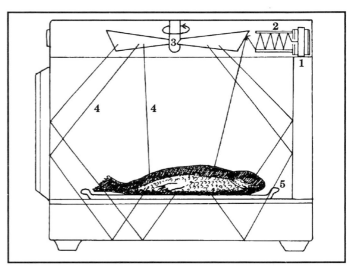

1) Magnetron (microwave generator), 2) Wave guide, 3) Circulating fan (stirrer), 4) Reflected and direct microwaves hitting food (all reflected off the stirrer), 5) Dish that microwaves can pass through.

Most microwave ovens operate at a frequency of exactly 2,450 MHz (a Megahertz is a million cycles per second). This frequency was chosen so that radar communications, which use the same band as microwaves, would not be disrupted.

A) Metal surfaces reflect microwaves. So metal saucepans and kitchen foil containers are not suitable for use in microwaving.

B) Glass and ceramic materials allow microwaves to pass through them without heating up, so they are good for use in microwave cooking.

C) All food contains some water. Microwaving moves the molecules about very rapidly, causing them to heat up through the food.

Each water molecule has a slightly positive electric charge at one end, and a slightly negative charge at the other. When an electro-magnetic field is created, the molecule lines itself up with the direction of the field. As soon as the field is reversed, the molecule turns round. This happens 5 billion times per second in a microwave oven.

The energy produced from the movement of the water molecules is transmitted to other molecules of protein, fat, etc., and the temperature of the food rises quickly.

When the microwave cooker is turned off, the water molecules take a moment to slow down and stop, giving a short extension to the cooking process – known as carry-over cooking.

Using a microwave oven

Some general points to remember:

1 Observe the standing times stated in recipes and package instructions. The effect of the microwaves on the food takes a few moments to stop, once the oven has been turned off.

2 Irregular shapes tend to heat unevenly, so try to make the shapes as regular as possible.

3 Cover most foods – but not breads and pastries – to trap the steam and encourage even heating. Use microwave-quality clingfilm, a lid or upturned plate.

4 Stir sauces, soups, stews and other thick liquids regularly to prevent them over-thickening at the outer edges, and to allow the heat to penetrate to the middle of the container. Remember to turn the microwave energy on again, once you have returned the food to the oven (if there is a pause setting, you will not need to do this).

5 The best way to check that the food has reached a safe temperature, 70°C to 75°C at the centre, is to use a temperature probe. Check every corner, and several points in the centre of large dishes.

6 When food is microwaved on a plate, the plate does not heat up. So once it is out of the oven the food will lose its heat fairly quickly. To get round this, transfer the food to a warm plate before service.

Microwave times

Always follow the manufacturer's (or workplace) instructions for the equipment you are using. Timing depends on the:

- maximum output power of the oven. This is expressed in terms of *output wattage*, for instance 1500 watts. The oven will be labelled with the output wattage

- particular setting you are using

- design of the oven: position of the fan and magnetron (and there may be more than one of these), also size of the inside of the oven cavity

- type of container used

- amount and location of the food within the oven – two jacket potatoes may take up to 50% longer to microwave than one

and on the food itself. Foods which are dense, such as meat, will take longer to microwave. On the other hand, a beefburger will cook in a shorter time and more successfully than a piece of steak of the same size. This is because the meat in the burger has been minced up. For the steak, the microwave heating pattern is complex. The result may be over-hot, shrunk gristle, less hot fat, and the lean meat undercooked.

SAFETY ▲▲▲

Do not operate a microwave oven without food or liquid inside. It can cause overheating of the components and damage the oven.

Allow steam to escape from covered foods by lifting the lid or clingfilm on the side furthest away from you.

Although the container itself will not be hot, the food inside can cause a nasty burn if handled incorrectly.

Food which has a skin or shell, e.g. tomatoes, potatoes, apples, peaches, egg yolks and whole trout, should be pricked or pierced before microwaving. Unless this is done the build-up of pressure inside as the water molecules turn to steam will cause the skin or shell to explode, and the food will splatter all over the inside of the oven. Never try to boil an egg in a microwave oven.

ACTION

You are working on the food counter in a pub. You have just come on duty to find that a new colleague of yours has prepared the plate of food shown below for reheating in the microwave.

Note the points you might make in such a situation, and if you feel it appropriate, draw your own illustration to support these learning messages.

Output wattage and microwaving times

The link between the output wattage of an oven and microwave times is illustrated by these examples from one of the leading manufacturers:

- to cook from raw a 50 g (9 oz) potato will take (at full power) 9 minutes in a 700 watt oven, compared with 4½ minutes in a 1500 watt oven

- to defrost a 1.6 kg (3½ lb) chicken in a 800 watt oven will take 40 minutes, compared with 24 minutes in a 1500 watt oven.

Defrosting

The defrost program of a microwave oven switches the microwave energy on and off in rapid bursts. Do not use a cooking or reheating program. Vegetables are best cooked straight from the freezer.

1 Keep food covered or wrapped in original packing if possible. Remove metal twist ties and pierce plastic pouches and boil-in-the-bag type products (unless package instructions state otherwise).

2 Brush off any visible ice crystals. Microwaves reflect away from ice.

3 Allow the food to rest after or between bursts of defrosting so the heat can equalise throughout.

4 Thoroughly stir liquids and dishes like stews after they have begun to defrost.

5 Do not attempt to defrost the food completely. Otherwise, there is a risk it will start to cook and dry out, while the centre remains frozen.

Microwaving is not recommended for defrosting large joints, or for large quantities of food. For these, use a refrigerator or rapid-thawing cabinet (see page 26).

Cooking

Because of its similarity to steaming, microwaves are ideal for most vegetables, for fruit and for fish. Not everyone agrees with this! Some people say that microwaved fish is rather rubbery.

Green vegetables keep their colour because they are cooked for such a short time. This speed, and the fact that only a little water is used, helps retain more vitamins than any other cooking method. In a test on broccoli and potato, the retention rate was 82% in a microwave, compared with 35% and 40% respectively when the vegetables were boiled in a saucepan (*Saunders and Bazalgette in* The Food Revolution).

Potatoes can be cooked either peeled or in their skins, but if a crisp skin is required as in baked potatoes, they should be finished off in a conventional oven.

The flavour of spices is intensified in microwaving. Use less than you would in ordinary cooking processes.

The key to successful microwave cooking lies in following instructions closely.

CHEF'S TIPS

Use boiling water for vegetables (unless you are cooking them in a little butter and lemon juice, like mushrooms). Add seasoning to the cooking liquid. Do not sprinkle salt directly on to the vegetables.

Scrambled eggs cook very quickly and are creamy and smooth. Do not attempt to boil or 'fry' an egg in a microwave.

For fish, use a little stock, wine, lemon juice or butter. Place the thickest part of fish steaks towards the edge of the dish. Take special care not to overcook.

Microwaves will cook but not tenderise meat, so they are better for quick casseroles than large joints.

Small joints or cubed poultry cook very successfully in sauces or liquids.

Rice and pasta need time to absorb cooking liquids, so there is little time advantage to be gained by microwave cooking.

Sauces and soups can be prepared quickly in a microwave without risk of lumps or burnt pans. Use little if any fat for the equivalent to the shallow frying stage in soups.

Courtesy of Merrychef's Catering Advisory Service

Regenerating (reheating frozen foods)

Provided you carefully follow the instructions on the label, microwaving is ideal for regenerating frozen preprepared foods. Some preprepared foods are not suitable nor intended for reheating in a microwave oven. This might be because they are packed in a kitchen foil container, or the dish will become soggy, for example.

It is quite likely that the microwave oven you are using has already been programmed for the different dishes you have to regenerate, so all you need to do is select the right program.

Where this is not the case, do check that the instructions are right for the output power of your microwave. If you are unsure, or there is some other problem, ask your supervisor for guidance.

A piece of kitchen paper placed under bread rolls, croissants and similar products will prevent them from become soggy.

Paper is also good for absorbing any excess fat or oil.

Do not regenerate the food until just before it is required. You cannot hold food hot in a microwave, as you might in a conventional oven.

If sweet pastries are to be sprinkled with sugar before service, do this after microwaving. The sugar will caramelise and may even burn if it is microwaved.

Looking after microwave ovens

1 Never tamper with any part of the oven, or attempt to remove the exterior casing.
2 Always close the cooker door gently.
3 Never cover the vent on the top (or side) of the oven.
4 Do not drape tea towels or other cloths over the oven. Do not be tempted to dry cloths in a microwave.
5 If you are the first to discover a fault, put an 'out of order' label on the oven and report the problem so that a service engineer can be called. Seals on the door which become damaged or loose must be replaced without delay.
6 Always follow the manufacturer's cleaning instructions.
7 Use a soft, soapy cloth to remove any spilt food inside the oven, rinse the oven surfaces with a clean cloth and finally polish them with a soft cloth. This cleaning routine should be followed regularly. If spills are not wiped up immediately after they have happened, the spilt food will absorb microwave energy and quickly burn.
8 Baked-on splashes can usually be loosened by boiling an open jug of water inside the oven. Do not use abrasives or a knife.
9 The seals around the door should be kept spotlessly clean. A build up of spilt food will prevent a tight seal being formed, and the effectiveness of the oven will be reduced.
10 The air filter, which is at the back or bottom front of most ovens, should be taken out and washed regularly with water and a mild detergent, dried and replaced.
11 Shields, which protect parts such as the stirrer, should also be cleaned with a mild detergent and water.
12 Abrasive cleaners should never be used – they will scratch the surface and reduce the effectiveness of the microwaves. Aerosol cleaners should also be avoided as they will get into the internal parts of the oven.

Suitable containers

Thermoplastic – check the label.

Paper plates and cups – provided they are moisture resistant and can stand high temperatures.

Oven-to-tableware.

Boil-in-the-bag pouches – as long as a hole is made in them to allow steam to escape.

China – provided it has no metallic decoration, e.g. a gilt rim. China dishes or pots should be fully glazed. An unglazed bottom will absorb water which in turn attracts microwave energy, so it is the pot not the food which is heated.

Other containers clearly labelled as suitable for microwave ovens.

Metal and foil

Containers made wholly or partially with metal, or decorated with gilt, may cause arcing if they are too close to the door or stainless steel walls of the inside of the oven. You may notice a crackling sound and a sort of sparking effect inside the oven. Arcing can damage oven components, and shatter the toughened glass door. Because metal reflects the microwaves, heating time will be longer, so that there is not much advantage in using metal containers in a microwave.

However, some manufacturers and microwave experts claim that metal containers can be used safely. The best course of action is to follow your workplace rules. Ask – don't try your own experiments to see what is or is not suitable.

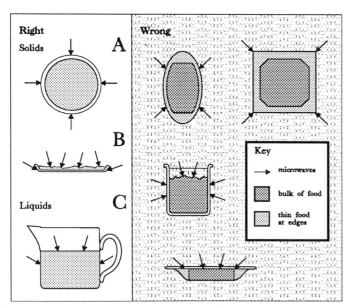

So that microwaves can penetrate the food evenly:

A) A plate with a narrow rim is better than a deep dish. Round shapes are good, and the larger and flatter the dish, the more surface area of food there will be for the microwaves to penetrate. Oval or square dishes will tend to have less food in their corners and this food will absorb too much of the energy, overheat and dry out before the food in the middle is thoroughly cooked.

B) A large shallow dish is better for solid foods than a small deep dish.

C) Liquids should be heated in a tall container such as a jug, rather than a low, shallow dish such as a soup plate. This makes handling easy and the liquid is less likely to spill over the top if it begins to boil.

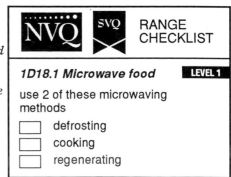

NVQ **SVQ** RANGE CHECKLIST

1D18.1 Microwave food **LEVEL 1**

use 2 of these microwaving methods

☐ defrosting
☐ cooking
☐ regenerating

Cooking for quick service

Introduction

Quick service – or to use an expression you will probably be more familiar with, fast food – has become a major sector of the catering and hospitality industry, and is still growing. This is because customers know what to expect, and are well satisfied with what they get: good quality food within a very short time of ordering.

The speed of the operation inevitably puts some pressure on the staff. Good teamwork helps them cope, as does a methodical, well ordered approach to each task.

Planning your work

Depending on your responsibilities, you will be allocated specific tasks and certain foods to prepare and cook during your shift.

1 Allow yourself enough time to keep to the standard expected.

2 Arrange your work area so that you have the space you need to work efficiently and correctly.

3 Avoid cluttering yourself up with things that you won't actually be needing for the task in hand. It's quite tempting, for example, to get everything you need out of the freezer or storeroom in one trip. But this will not make sense if as a result the food is kept at unsafe temperatures.

If you are involved in pre-opening tasks, how smoothly the rest of the session goes for you and your colleagues will obviously depend on the care you take. These tasks might include:

- turning the equipment on

- accepting and checking deliveries

- putting deliveries away in their correct storage places

- transferring foods from freezers to refrigerators to defrost

- checking that preparation (and service) equipment and utensils are clean and in the right place for use.

Contents guide

Cooking burgers on a rotary or conveyor-belt grill.

NVQ ⋈ **SVQ** **Units and elements covered in this section**

1D19 Deep fry food `LEVEL 1`

- 1D19.1 Deep fry food

1D20 Griddle, barbecue or grill foods

- 1D20.1 Griddle, barbecue or grill foods

1D21 Prepare, cook and assemble food for quick service

- 1D21.1 Prepare food and kitchen areas for quick service

- 1D21.2 Cook and assemble food products for quick service

For more information on deep frying, griddling, barbecuing and grilling, see the sections that describe the preparation and cooking of the various types of food, in particular *Meat and poultry* (pages 64–71) and *Fish* (pages 106–110).

Deep frying

The sort of foods you are likely to be deep frying in your workplace include fish, chicken pieces, chips, onion rings, possibly other vegetables, maybe also sweet products like fruit fritters and doughnuts.

How to get the best from deep frying

1   Check that you are using the right temperature (or program) for the food you are frying. The temperature for pre-cooking (blanching) chips, for example, is lower than that used for the final browning.

2   Do not attempt to fry large pieces of food which are still frozen, such as chicken portions. The food will end up overcooked on the outside, but undercooked inside. This, of course, is dangerous from a hygiene point of view. Chips can be fried straight from the freezer, but shake off excess ice crystals first.

3   Do make sure the food is dry before frying. Water and oil get along badly! Wet food is likely to make the hot oil spit everywhere, leading to nasty burns. Even a little water will cause the oil to froth dangerously. Excess moisture also shortens the life of the oil.

4   Always shake off excess breadcrumbs and drain battered food carefully before frying.

5   Do not place too much food in the oil at one time. This will cause the temperature of the oil to drop, which means the food will absorb more oil, spoiling its eating quality. An overloaded fryer is also likely to overflow, particularly when the food is first put in, and the oil froths up. The correct ratio is *one part food to six parts oil.*

6   Allow time for the heat to recover when you are frying frozen or chilled food. Temperature falls of 18°C to 28°C can occur when frozen pieces of food are immersed in hot oil.

7   Season foods after frying, not before, and do so well away from the oil. Salt and sugar, like water, are enemies of oil.

8   As the food cooks, being able to see small bubbles and the food quite clearly in the oil are good signs. Excessive bubbling and smoke rising from the surface are bad signs. When you first put the food in the oil, there may be some steam given off. This is nothing to worry about.

9   Skim food particles from the oil surface regularly. This will reduce the risk of them burning, spoiling the appearance of the food and the quality of the oil.

10   Keep an eye on the food so that it does not brown too much. If you are using a fryer with a timer, make sure the setting is correct for the particular task.

11   Food which floats on the surface of the oil should be turned over part-way through cooking, so that both sides get browned.

12   To avoid bits falling off in the oil, handle fragile foods and foods with loose coatings carefully.

13   Even if the food is not browning quickly enough, never set the thermostat above 205°C. Very high temperatures are dangerous, and cause the oil to spoil rapidly.

14   Drain food well after frying.

15   If, for some reason, the food has to be put in a hot cupboard to keep warm before serving, leave it uncovered. A cover will trap moisture and you will end up with a rather soggy result. If possible, time frying so that the food can be served immediately. It will taste much better that way.

An example of successful deep frying – the raw fish and chips have been attractively browned as well as cooked through by the end of the process.

This success is due to the coating, good quality frying oil and careful control of the cooking.

Looking after the oil

Regular filtering of the oil is probably the most important step. The experts recommend that this is done once a day, and the fryer wiped down thoroughly before the oil is replaced. Once a week the fryer should be thoroughly washed. (Some general points on cleaning deep fryers are given on page 16.)

Oils start to spoil from the moment they are heated up, and as soon as they are exposed to air – or, to be more precise, the oxygen in air. Deep frying oils are expensive commodities, so it makes sense to look after them by:

- turning the thermostat down, or putting the fryer on standby during slack periods. The recommended standby temperature is 93°C

- switching fryers off when you know they won't be used again (in accordance with your workplace instructions)

- using the correct utensils for handling food and filtering oil. The wrong ones, if they use iron or copper in their construction, will set up a chemical reaction which harms the oil.

Wherever possible, reduce exposure of oil to oxygen by:

- putting the lid on fryers as soon as you have finished using them

- not pouring from a great height when you are filling or topping up a fryer

- keeping the container as close to the tap as possible, when you drain oil for filtering.

Safety in deep frying

If oil gets too hot it will give off an unpleasant smoke that irritates the eyes, ears, nose and throat. If heating continues, the oil will burst into flames.

So deep frying is a potentially lethal operation, but by taking a number of commonsense precautions you can play your part in keeping the workplace and your colleagues and customers safe.

1 Never turn a fryer on when there is no oil in it. (Special rules apply to cleaning fryers.)

2 Never overfill fryers.

3 Do not leave fryers unattended while they are in use.

4 Never place a lid over the deep fryer when it is in use. (If you are using one of the special fryers that uses high pressure to reduce cooking time, this rule will not, of course, apply.)

5 Follow procedures for checking the accuracy of thermostats. Typically this will be done on a weekly basis, possibly more often in very busy establishments.

6 Allow oil to cool before draining.

7 Do not take shortcuts on workplace procedures for filtering the oil and cleaning the fryer.

8 Do not tamper with or move the fire-fighting equipment provided in your workplace.

9 Make sure you know what to do in the event of a fire.

10 If you are using a fat which is solid at room temperature for deep frying, it will need to be melted gently, at a temperature not higher than 130°C, before heating to frying temperature. Otherwise there is a risk that the fat nearest to the heat source will burn. Electrical elements may overheat, damaging the equipment.

Fires in deep fat fryers

If a deep fat fryer catches fire it is important to act quickly to prevent the fire spreading to other equipment and areas in the kitchen.

1 If you can reach the controls safely, turn off the fryer.

2 If it is safe to do so, place a lid over the burning oil. If not, spread a fire blanket over the fire. A fire blanket should be kept close to the fryer – it can smother the flames without catching fire itself and so starve the fire of oxygen.

3 If you have not already done so, turn off the electricity or gas supply to the fryer.

4 Report the fire to a supervisor.

5 If there is any sign that the fire is not completely under control, sound the fire alarm immediately. (Many kitchens have fire detection equipment that will automatically sound the alarm.)

6 If the fire seems to be under control, leave the blanket over the fryer for at least 15 minutes.

7 Never use sand, water or earth to extinguish a fat fire, because the burning oil will simply float on the water or spread over the surface of the earth or sand.

Remember that if the extractor system is not cleaned regularly, a deposit of fat will build up inside it and create a potential fire hazard.

In general, make sure that you know what the fire procedures are at your establishment so that you can act fast in an emergency (some basic steps are given on page 5).

Griddling, grilling and barbecuing

Burgers, steaks, sausages, tomatoes, fried eggs ... just some of the foods you are likely to be cooking by these methods.

How to get the best from griddling

Griddling is a variation of shallow frying, equivalent to using a very large frying pan.

1 Generally the less oil you use to grease the surface of the griddle, the better the food will taste. (Customers who want to cut down the amount of fat they eat will also appreciate this.) With bacon, for example, you may get away without adding any extra oil.

2 Use the correct oil for the griddle. This will probably be in a spray gun, for convenience. Do not use oil ladled out of the nearest deep fat fryer. This will mean topping up the fryer, which is probably more time-consuming than using the correct oil in the first place. The food you are griddling is also likely to pick up flavours of the foods which have been cooked in the fryer.

3 You may need to turn fried eggs over, if the customer wants them cooked on both sides – Americans call this 'over easy' (fried on one side only is 'sunny side up'). Most other foods will need to be turned halfway through cooking. Do this carefully using a palette knife, fish slice, or tongs, so that you do not spoil the final appearance of the food. Do not pierce the food with a fork as the juices will be lost.

4 Keep the griddle surface free of food debris by scraping it down regularly with the side of the palette knife or the special griddle scraper.

ACTION

Make a rough plan of your workplace (an example is given below) or college kitchen showing the locations of:

- all fire-fighting equipment, noting what type of fire each can be used against
- emergency exits
- fire alarm buttons
- telephones
- fire detectors
- switches for turning off the electrical power
- taps for turning off the gas supply.

How to get the best from grilling and barbecuing

There are various types of grill, the main difference being whether the heat source is above or below the food, or both. Food cooked on charcoal-type grills (picture on page 64) is often described as barbecued. The flavours and appearance are similar to food cooked out-of-doors on a real charcoal fire.

Grilling is a fast method of cooking, using very high temperatures. This means that the food needs careful attention to make sure it is cooked through to the inside, yet attractively browned on the outside.

If you are using a continuous grill, the speed of the machine will be set so that the food is cooked to exactly the right degree by the time the trays have completed their rotation.

With other equipment, it is a matter of experience, judgement and:

- making sure the grill is heated to the right temperature before you start cooking

- lightly brushing the grill bars with oil from time to time to prevent the food sticking

- keeping an eye on the food all the time

- turning it when necessary

- pushing the centre with food tongs to check how it is firming up – to get a better idea of when it is cooked through sufficiently.

Dry grilled food is not nice. You can help the food retain its precious juices by:

- always using tongs, a palette knife or fish slice to handle it. Do not pierce it with a fork

- judging the cooking speed so that you only have to turn the food once

- avoiding any delay between the time the food is cooked and its service.

Customers – and staff – at the Little Chef chain of roadside restaurants know exactly what standards to expect, thanks to the company's use of menus like this.

Cleaning equipment

See also *Cleaning procedures* (pages 15–20).

Griddles and grills should be cleaned down after use, and thoroughly cleaned once a week.

1 Allow the equipment to cool.
2 Wear protective gloves and a protective apron. If you are using an oven-cleaning agent to remove particularly heavy deposits, wear eye goggles.
3 Take removable parts of the equipment to wash in a sink filled with hot water and cleaning agent in the correct concentration. Depending on the model you are using, removable parts might be:
   for overhead grills/salamanders: grilling bars and branding trays, grease troughs, crumb trays, side racks
   for griddles: grease troughs.
4 Fill a bucket with fresh cleaning solution and use this to scrub all surfaces of the equipment, including the top and sides. Be careful not to flood the equipment and surrounding area.
5 Pay particular attention to crevices where dirt and grease can accumulate.
6 Use a degreasing agent and scouring pad where necessary to remove heavy deposits.
7 Rinse with clean, very hot water and air dry.
8 Support legs, shelves and supply pipes, as well as surrounding floor, should be cleaned weekly.

7am – 11am

The Breakfast Bar

The Early Starter Extra

15. **The Early Starter Extra**
Griddled Egg, Two Pork Sausages, Rasher of Back Bacon, Tomato and Fried Bread with an Orange Juice and Buttered Toast
£3.99

£3.99

10. **The Brunch Breakfast**
Two Griddled Eggs, Two Pork Sausages, Two Rashers of Back Bacon and Fried Sliced Potatoes
£3.99

Brunch Breakfast

£3.99

We're famous for our Breakfasts!

See our Big Choice Menu for an even bigger choice of Breakfasts

Z/92

Quick service

The equipment you are using and the methods of working laid down by your employers – these are all carefully planned and designed so that customers get consistently high quality products.

Nevertheless, the human touch remains all-important:

- you are likely to mess things up thoroughly if you forget to do something, or do not do something properly
- your colleagues will enjoy their work more and do a better job if you are helpful, cheerful and make a full contribution to the team effort
- your customers will come back – because the food is good, they get it quickly and the staff are friendly. There are plenty of other places that serve good food, but as you will know from your own experiences as a customer, they don't all have friendly staff.

Hygiene and safe working practices

Hygiene and safe working practices are important in all types of catering establishment. When customers can see you handling the food they are about to eat, you have to be particularly on guard. Things have to be kept tidy and equipment absolutely spotless all the time.

This is in contrast, perhaps, to catering kitchens which are quite separate from the serving area. They often look rather chaotic after the end of a busy service period.

General points to remember in quick service

1 Use any written or pictorial aids to keep to the company's quality standards and portion control.

2 Remember the customers are coming to your establishment because they know what to expect. That applies not just to quality, but also to how much they get – and this must be the same as everyone else gets, and what they got yesterday, and last week.

3 Pay constant attention to timings. You have to strike the balance – and it's not always easy – between having food ready so that people are not kept waiting, and the food spoiling because it has been kept hot for too long.

4 Carefully follow laid-down systems and procedures for monitoring how long food has been kept hot for, and rules for disposing of food that has passed its time limit. Alert your supervisor to any difficulties.

5 Keep fresh items refrigerated after preparation, if there is a delay before cooking/serving.

6 Keep food covered to prevent contamination and spoilage.

7 Dispose of waste in the correct bins. Keep bin lids closed.

8 Cook in batches of the appropriate quantity for service to continue uninterrupted.

9 Cook in batches to match the capacity of the cooking equipment. Attempting to fry too many pieces of fish at once will result in an unpleasant tasting, fat-saturated product. Overloading the grill will make it difficult to turn the food over. Turning the grill temperature up won't cook the food much faster either. It's very likely to lead to burning on the outside while the inside is undercooked.

10 Check that food is cooked through to the centre. Undercooked chicken is particularly dangerous because of the risk of salmonella poisoning (see page 11). A temperature probe inserted into the centre of the flesh should read 70°C or above (check your workplace instructions).

11 Keep raw food separate from cooked food at all stages. The exception is when you finally assemble the dish, adding a salad garnish, for example.

NVQ SVQ RANGE CHECKLIST

LEVEL 1

1D19.1 Deep fry food
[ ] preprepared or convenience

1D20.1 Griddle, barbecue or grill foods
[ ] preprepared or convenience foods

1D21.1 Prepare food and kitchen areas for quick service
[ ] preprepared or convenience food items

1D21.2 Cook and assemble food products for quick service
[ ] preprepared or convenience food items

NORTH EAST
INSTITUTE
OF FURTHER AND HIGHER
EDUCATION

ANTRIM CAMPUS

TYPING/WORD PROCESSING REQUIREMENTS

TYPE OF WORK	Typing recipes
DATE OF REQUEST	16/9/96
NAME	Jane Cardwell
SCHOOL	Soc Ed.
DATE REQUIRED	19/1/96

SPECIAL INSTRUCTIONS (if any)

Type recipes on separate sheets please.

P.154 Tropical Fruit Crumble. — A

P.232 Norfolk Pie. — B

P.230 Nutty savoury pastries. — C

P.89 Bacon - leek gratin — D

P.121 Fish bake — E

P.146, Scotch broth. — F.

FOR OFFICE USE ONLY

DATE RECEIVED ......16/9/96...... DATE COMPLETED 18/9/96.

TYPIST .....Aileen.....(AB/238.)....

Introduction

Most of us look on the vending machine as a modern invention. With five *billion* vended drinks dispensed each year from 200,000 machines in Britain, it is certainly a convenient and very popular one.

Yet the first record of a drinks machine was in 215 BC. Thanks to the ingenuity of a Greek mathematician, worshippers at the temples in Egypt could receive a measured quantity of holy water upon the drop of a coin.

Advances in technology have made drinks vending machines more sophisticated. They have become easier to maintain and clean. They offer a wider choice of products, and the quality can be as good as traditionally made drinks.

Significant advances have also been made in other forms of drinks dispensing equipment, those that you see, for example:

- behind the counter in fast food restaurants, for coffees, teas, fruit juice, cold fizzy drinks and milk shakes

- at self-service counters in motorway service areas, where you can select your own cup or pot of freshly brewed coffee, tea or chocolate.

Drinks machines

Premix – drink in bulk, ready to serve. For example, tea and coffee urns in a self-service staff restaurant, or fruit juice dispensers. The term premix is also sometimes applied to *in-cup* machines.

Postmix – the flavouring product is kept in concentrated liquid or powder form. At the press of the button, the ingredients are mixed in bowls by whippers, with hot water, iced still water, or for fizzy drinks, iced carbonated water. The drink is then delivered in a cup, at the point of service. It can include a freshbrew tea/coffee unit, cappuccino-style coffee, brand name soft drinks.

Fresh brew – uses leaf tea and/or ground coffee instead of instant products. The infusion process requires more time for the drink to be made, and even longer if the machine actually grinds the coffee beans before brewing. Most fresh brew vending machines will also offer postmix drinks made from instant ingredients, e.g. soup and hot chocolate.

In-cup – the required ingredients for each drink are already packed in the cup (in powdered form). The machine adds hot or cold water as required. The ingredients are kept fresh by the airtight stacking of the cups. Some machines have a bulk sugar canister to allow sugar to be added to taste.

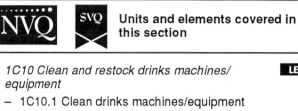

Units and elements covered in this section

1C10 Clean and restock drinks machines/equipment **LEVEL 1**
- 1C10.1 Clean drinks machines/equipment
- 1C10.2 Restock drinks machines/equipment

Sachets – dry ingredients (enough for one cup) sealed in a foil-type package. When a drink is selected, the sachet is emptied into the cup and hot water added, or the water directed through the sachet into the cup.

Coffee machines – of various types. *Pour 'n' serve* or *cona* units generally hold 12 cups. This means fresh coffee can be made at regular intervals to keep pace with demand. Where appropriate, customers can serve themselves.

Espresso machines rely on a high pressure boiler providing hot water and steam being 'expressed' through a small amount of coffee to produce one or two cups at a time. Some models grind the coffee beans as required, infuse the drink and dump the waste grouts and filter paper into a container within the machine. A steam jet and hot water supply mean that tea and other hot drinks can also be prepared.

Cold drinks machines – popular for milk, brand name soft drinks, mineral waters, fruit juices, as well as beers, wines and spirits. The machine stores the pre-packed cartons, cans or bottles, dispensing the selected item on demand.

Postmix dispense systems – concentrated syrups are piped to the point of dispense. When the tap is opened to pour the drink, the syrup mixes with water and carbon dioxide gas (from a cylinder) to make cola, tonic, lemonade, etc.

Cleaning

To protect the drinking quality of the product, machines require regular cleaning. In busy locations for equipment like conas, this may be several times a day. For vending machines, once a day is the normal routine.

Poor cleaning techniques can lead to blockages and machine breakdown. They might also cause contamination of the products, harming the health of your customers, and putting you and your employers at risk with the law (see *Hygiene,* pages 9–11).

General procedure

There are many makes of machine on the market, each different. The following points will support workplace training and help you follow manufacturer and workplace instructions.

Some operations are carried out only on a weekly basis, depending on the type of machine.

The first step is to collect all the cleaning materials you need:

- trolley, spare canisters and machine parts
- plastic buckets for washing removable equipment
- disposable cleaning cloths, sponges and disposable drying paper
- dusting brushes to clean surfaces, special brushes for nozzles and tubes. Check with the instructions – on some machines, special brushes must be used to avoid damaging surfaces
- detergent solution and sanitiser. Use the right one in the correct concentration. Replace by fresh solutions if you are cleaning several machines
- spray polish and cloths for cleaning the outside of the cabinet
- bin liners/rubbish bags for used filter papers, discarded cups, wrapping materials, etc.

Put on gloves to protect your hands, and an overall or uniform to protect your clothes.

Turn the machine off and remove the plug from the mains socket before starting to clean. Remember to switch on again before leaving the machine.

HYGIENE

- Are your hands clean?
- Are your overalls clean?
- Is your hair covered?
- Are all cuts, open sores etc. covered with a clean waterproof dressing?
- Do not smoke while cleaning or restocking.

SAFETY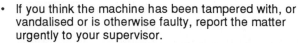

- If you think the machine has been tampered with, or vandalised or is otherwise faulty, report the matter urgently to your supervisor.
- Some vending machines should not be turned off when they are opened to clean or restock. The safety cut out switch comes into operation when you unlock the door. Check that this has in fact happened before you start the cleaning or restocking procedure.
- Never wipe electrical parts with a damp cloth.
- Handle CO_2 (carbon dioxide) cylinders carefully. (These are used in machines which dispense carbonated, i.e. fizzy, drinks). Full cylinders are usually stored strapped to the wall, empty cylinders lying flat and wedged so they will not roll.
- Use cleaning agents according to manufacturers' and workplace instructions.
- Never attempt to carry out any repairs for which you are not authorised.

Some of the drinks vended

Tea – instant or fresh brew

Coffee – instant, fresh brew or cappuccino-style, whipped or plain

Chocolate – whipped or plain

Meat extract drinks – e.g. Bovril

Soup – powdered, various flavours

Carbonated soft drinks – colas, lemon, orange, soda, etc.

Fruit juice – orange, apple, grapefruit, etc.

Types of cup used for vended drinks

Polystyrene – retains the heat of the drink, yet is cool enough to hold

Paper – cardboard lined with plastic. Inexpensive, but difficult to hold hot drinks

Plastic – light, inexpensive, but may become too hot to hold. Double wall cups are available

Most vended cups hold as much as a normal teacup: 175 ml (6 fl oz)

Vending machine suppliers and cup manufacturers are working on schemes for recycling used vended cups.

Premix machines

1   Empty the drinks container. You will usually have to measure and keep a record of any waste.

2   Wash the drinks container out with cleaning solution. Wash removable parts and, where necessary, soak in sanitising solution.

3   Rinse well. Air dry, or use disposable paper to remove moisture.

Postmix machines

1   Remove canisters ready to be refilled or replaced with spares. Cover dispense nozzle with cap, if supplied, to protect against spillages.

2   Dry-wipe all dust and powder spillages. Wet-wipe all areas of spillage and splash.

3   Remove for soaking in detergent /sanitising solution: mixing bowls, nozzles, troughs, whippers.

4   Replace parts with clean spares. Alternatively use the parts which have been soaked for at least 3 minutes.

5   Replace canisters.

6   Clean interior surfaces, cup station and chute.

7   Flush system with hot water from the machine.

8   Empty waste bucket and clean/replace. Check float or probe is in correct position, and working properly.

In-cup machines

1   Clean the cup station and transfer arm.

2   Weekly (usually): remove cup stacks. Clean and dry carousel columns. Replace cup stacks.

3   Wipe the water nozzle.

4   Remove waste tray, empty and clean in detergent/ sanitising solution. Dry before replacing.

The outside of machines

1   Clean and sanitise the delivery area for the products.

2   Wipe top, front and sides of machine.

3   Polish all exposed areas, particularly glass panels and doors to remove fingerprints.

4   Clean the area around the machine and ensure that the waste bin is empty.

Final checking

1   Close and lock door of vending machines.

2   Ensure that power is on.

3   Test drinks for quality, quantity and temperature. If required, check coin acceptance.

4   Check that indicator lights are working and that product descriptions/labels are correctly placed.

The outside of the machine is, of course, what customers see and notice most. It should be left looking sparkling.

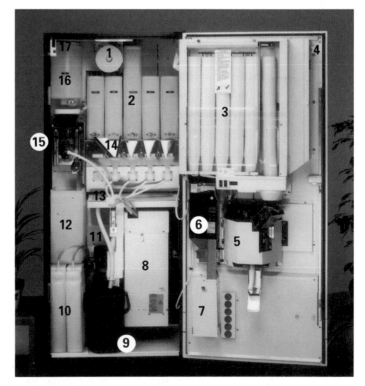

1) Brewer filter roll, 2) Instant ingredients canisters, 3) Cup magazine, 4) Audit switch and test vend switch, 5) Cup station, 6) Coin validator mechanism, 7) Cash box, 8) Refrigeration unit for cold drinks, 9) Waste bucket, 10) Syrup canisters, 11) CO_2 gas cylinder for carbonated drinks, 12) Brewer waste container, 13) Dispensing spouts, 14) Whipper units and mixing bowls, 15) Brewer unit, 16) Brewer ingredient canister (water heater is behind), 17) Door safety isolator switch.

Restocking

General procedure

1 Rotate stocks. Use stock on a first-in, first-out basis.

2 Do not use stock which has passed its use-by or best-before date.

3 Keep stocks in the correct conditions. For some items this will involve chilled storage.

4 When reloading with cups, avoid touching their rims. Some types of cups need to be loosened before they are stacked, otherwise they tend to stick together. Do not overload with cups, otherwise they can jam the machine.

5 Take care to put the right ingredients in canisters. For example, a non-dairy creamer is used for whitening coffee, and milk compound for tea.

6 After restocking postmix and fresh brew machines, test vend to check quality and temperature of drinks.

Premix machines

Fill dispenser to required stock level, with drink diluted/mixed as per instructions.

Coffee dispensers

1 Turn off machine. Empty and clean coffee pots.

2 Fill water containers to indicated level. (Not necessary if the machine is connected to the water supply.)

3 Insert fresh filter.

4 Add correct measure of coffee. For conas, the coffee is usually purchased in packets of the appropriate size.

5 Turn on machine when required for coffee service.

Start a new brew before the last pot is finished. Don't leave empty cona pots on the hotplate, or they will crack. If the machine is one where customers help themselves, you will need to keep an eye out for empty pots.

Postmix machines

1 For powdered drinks, lightly tap ingredients canisters to check stock levels and loosen ingredients. Place cover over dispense nozzle and remove to refill or replace. Check levels of liquid concentrates. Replace as required. Replace coffee/tea filter paper if machine has a freshbrew unit.

2 Check CO_2 cylinder pressure gauge. If low, close the cylinder valve and depressurise the circuit. Disconnect, and replace with new cylinder.

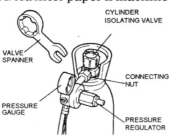

CYLINDER ISOLATING VALVE
VALVE SPANNER
CONNECTING NUT
PRESSURE GAUGE
PRESSURE REGULATOR

In-cup machines

1 Fill cup magazines. Make sure you put the cups in the correct position for the type of drink they contain. Do not force cups together as this could jam the separating mechanism.

2 Cover the top cup of each selection with the lid to provide an airtight seal, and protect the contents against contamination.

3 If the machine is a table-top model, not connected to the water supply, top up water tank to correct level.

Fault finding guide

No lights – machine switched off, door not closed, electrical fault.

Sold out sign shows – waste bucket full, no cups, cup turret/carousel not turning, disruption to mains water supply, ingredients canisters empty.

Cup delivery problems – cup carousel jammed, lack of cups, cups packed too tightly, wrong size (two different suppliers' cups used), cup chute wrongly assembled, cups fallen over in cup station, stabilising weight not in correct position.

Ingredient problem – canister not properly located, incorrect ingredients used or badly stored, blockage in system, water heating unit faulty, 'throw' adjustment required.

Condensation in machine – exhaust grill or steam extractor blocked.

Whippers leaking – incorrectly assembled, seal needs replacing.

Cold drinks warm – cooler not working.

Machine flooding – waste bucket float or switch not operating, waste bucket, pipes or housing not replaced correctly.

Carbonated drink problem – CO_2 cylinder empty, not turned on, not connected properly.

Fresh brew coffee/tea problem – filter needs cleaning or replacing, filter wiper jammed, canister not seated correctly, brewer unit not switched on.

NVQ **SVQ** RANGE CHECKLIST

LEVEL 1

1C10.1 Clean drinks machines/equipment

1C10.2 Restock drinks machines/equipment

1 of these types

☐	premix or postmix or fresh brew or in-cup vending machines	☐
☐	coffee machines	☐
☐	cold drinks machines	☐
☐	postmix dispense systems	☐

Introduction

For a great number of people, the focus of a really enjoyable meal is the meat or poultry dish.

Tastes have changed, of course. The traditional Sunday meal of roast beef and Yorkshire pudding is more likely to be roast chicken, a fish or pasta dish. Some people eat meat less often – besides the cost, they are concerned to reduce the amount of fat in their diet. For the same reason, other people will no longer eat red meat. And there are those who have stopped eating meat altogether – because of concern for the wellbeing of animals.

The meat industry has responded to these trends with generally leaner meat, and new butchery techniques that produce cuts and joints with no or very little visible fat. Caterers have changed their menus to include low-fat meat and poultry dishes, that are imaginative, appeal to today's customers, and are certainly as tasty as the rich classical dishes.

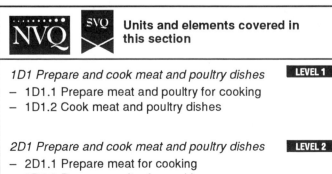

Units and elements covered in this section

1D1 Prepare and cook meat and poultry dishes **LEVEL 1**
- 1D1.1 Prepare meat and poultry for cooking
- 1D1.2 Cook meat and poultry dishes

2D1 Prepare and cook meat and poultry dishes **LEVEL 2**
- 2D1.1 Prepare meat for cooking
- 2D1.2 Prepare poultry for cooking
- 2D1.3 Cook meat and poultry dishes

Contents guide

Quality points

Preprepared or convenience meat and poultry
- packaging in good condition; cans not blown
- correctly labelled
- not beyond use-by date
- canned items not beyond best-before date

for frozen food
- no signs of freezer burn (dry white patches on the skin, caused by poor or lengthy storage)
- liquids released during defrosting not excessive

Beef
- smells fresh, not stale or sour (rancid), nor unpleasantly strong (high)
- outer fat layer even, smooth in texture, firm to the touch and creamy-white in colour (creamy-yellow for Scotch beef)
- outer surface of lean meat is purple/brown, with a smooth texture
- meat itself is bright red, without excessive fat or gristle
- fat flecks (called *marbling*) are visible in the prime cuts such as fillet or sirloin (photograph on page 53)

Lamb and mutton
- lean flesh of lamb firm, dull red, with fine texture or grain
- lamb bones porous, with slight bluish tinge
- mutton darker red and slightly coarser in texture
- fat evenly distributed, hard, brittle, flaky and clear white in colour

Pork
- the rind or skin smooth
- flesh lean, pale pink, firm, with little gristle
- fat white, firm, smooth and not excessive

Bacon
- no sign of stickiness
- thin, smooth, wrinkle-free rind
- white, smooth fat that is not excessive in proportion to the lean
- meat deep pink colour and firm

Ham
- fat firm, white and not excessive
- meat pink, moist but not sticky

Veal
- flesh pale pink and firm, not soft and flabby
- cut surfaces moist, not dry
- little fat covering, fat firm and pinkish
- bones pinkish white, porous, with small amounts of blood in their structure

Offal
- smell and colour not unusual or unpleasant (green or yellow staining is never a good sign)
- surface moist but not sticky

Chicken and turkey
- white skin (yellowish for corn-fed chickens)
- flesh firm to the touch, no stickiness on the skin
- legs and breast well fleshed
- breastbone flexible

The Meat and Livestock Commission is the central source of information on all matters relating to British meat.

PO Box 44, Winterhill House, Snowdon Drive, Milton Keynes MK6 1AX

Chicken

Whole birds range in weight from under 3 lb (1.35 kg) to around 7 lb (3.2 kg). They are available fresh, oven ready with or without giblets, or frozen.

Both fresh and frozen *chicken portions* come in a wide variety of different packs from single breasts, drumsticks or thighs to packs of mixed portions. Breasts and thighs are available skinless and boneless. There is an increasingly wide range of preprepared and convenience dishes in catering packs, from breadcrumbed portions and burgers to Chicken Kiev and Chicken Cordon Bleu.

Poussins are 4 to 6 week old chickens. They weigh about 1 lb (500 g) and usually serve one person.

Corn-fed chickens are reared on a diet of maize grain which gives the bird a distinctive yellow colour.

Storage

Uncooked meat and poultry should be kept well chilled (or frozen) from the time of delivery, up to the time of preparation and cooking. Unless this is done the food will spoil rapidly, and any harmful bacteria present will multiply to dangerous numbers. (See *Hygiene*.)

1 Frozen meat and poultry should be stored at −18°C or below. Some caterers specify −22°C.

2 Chilled meat and poultry should be stored between 0°C and 4°C. In recent years, the recommended temperature range has been lowered, so that some caterers specify 0°C, others (including the National Health Service) between −1°C and 1°C.

3 Fresh meat should always be kept apart from cooked food and from dairy products and similar foods which will not be cooked before service. (See *Food handling and storage* for general points.)

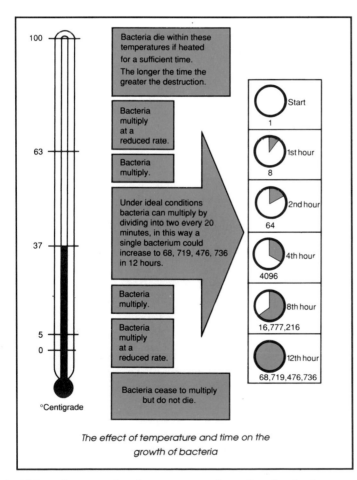

The effect of temperature and time on the growth of bacteria

Although contamination can start through unhygienic practices, some food is contaminated before it reaches the kitchen. Poultry is the cause of most reported cases of food poisoning, mainly through bacteria called salmonella, which chickens get exposed to during rearing. Salmonella can be destroyed with thorough cooking, making sure the heat reaches right to the centre of the bird or other meat.

Purchasing specifications

Many caterers specify in considerable detail the standard of meat they expect from their suppliers. Doing this:

- helps ensure that customers receive a consistent product of a certain standard
- cuts down the amount of preparation required, and wastage and loss arising from this preparation
- enables prices for the same product to be compared
- means that those responsible for receiving deliveries are able to recognise and check the standards required.

Details in specifications will cover such points as:

1 Country of origin.
2 Type of carcase including classification (this covers the *conformation,* i.e. shape of the carcase, and the fat cover).
3 Exact location of the cut.
4 Trim level.
5 Fat level. For mince and cubed/diced meat the *visual lean* (VL) content will be stated, e.g. VL 90 (which means 10% fat), or VL 80 (which means 20% fat).
6 Preparation (e.g. joint rolled and trimmed).
7 Weight, within certain tolerances.
8 Thickness, if appropriate.
9 Packaging. The type of packaging has a significant effect on the shelf-life of the meat. Vacuum packs give the longest shelf-life. For larger pieces of meat this can be up to 6 or 8 weeks, for steaks or chops up to 1 or 2 weeks.

Metropole Hotels

Meat Purchase Specification

LEG OF LAMB (BONELESS)

Carcase type To be derived from British lamb carcases, slaughtered within one year of birth.

Cut removal To be removed from the chump at a point no more than 1 inch below the round of the aitch bone.

Trim level Remove aitch bone and tail. Tunnel bone femur. Remove tibia, fibula and patella. Trim off ragged edges, discoloured tissues, connective tissue and cod fat.

Fat level External fat thickness not to exceed 3/8 inch at any point.

Preparation To be tied securely with 5 strings at even intervals.

Weight 3.5 to 5.5 lb.

Packaging To be interleaved with peach paper and packed in a waxed cardboard box. Four legs per box.

Storage To be stored at a temperature between 0°C and 2°C for a maturation period of 7 days prior to delivery.

Temperature on arrival To be delivered at a temperature between 0°C and 4°C.

Cuts of beef, lamb and pork

The carcase is prepared in individual joints and cuts to produce the best size and quality of meat for particular cooking purposes.

The names and details of many of these cuts vary from one part of the country to another. For example, the thick rib of beef is known as leg of mutton cut in Wales, East Anglia, West Midlands and the South. In Scotland the same cut has eight different names.

Cuts of meat which come from parts of the animal that do a lot of work – generally in the forequarter – need slow, moist cooking, such as stewing or braising.

Cuts which come from muscle areas not so heavily used by the animal – generally in the hindquarter – can be cooked by the faster, dry methods, such as grilling, roasting, shallow frying.

NUTRITION

Meat contains a large number of essential *minerals*. Liver and kidney are especially rich in iron and zinc, while beef and lamb are also good sources of these minerals.

Iron – helps the formation of red blood cells, the transfer and transport of oxygen. Not enough iron in the diet causes anaemia (main symptoms being tiredness and listlessness). A good intake is especially important for growing children, adolescents and pregnant women.

Zinc – essential for growth, healthy skin and sense of taste.

Meat, like fish, is a good source of the three major B *vitamins*: thiamin (vitamin B1), riboflavin (vitamin B2) and niacin (see page 94).

Liver, like oily fish, is a good source of vitamins A and D.

The *fat* content of meat depends on several factors including breed of animals, cut of meat and amount of trimming. For example, the percentage of total fat in the following roast meats is:

lean topside, no visible fat	4.4
topside with fat (88% lean)	12.0
lean leg of lamb, no visible fat	8.1
leg of lamb with fat (82% lean)	17.9
lean leg of pork	6.9
leg of pork with fat (76% lean)	19.8

Raw lean lamb contains 4.3% saturated fatty acids, 3.3% monounsaturated and 0.4% polyunsaturated. For beef and pork the proportions are, respectively: 1.9% and 2.8% saturated, 2.2% and 3.2% monounsaturated and 0.2% and 0.6% polyunsaturated. (*Source: Meat and Livestock Commission.*)

Beef

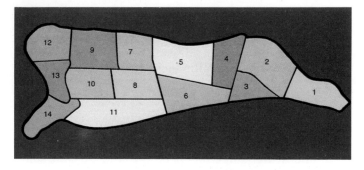

Hindleg (1) and **Shin (foreleg) (14)** or **hough** – sliced (for stews, casseroles, etc.) or minced.

Topside (2) and, underneath, **silverside**, or **round** and **rump**. Prepared as joints or steaks. Silverside is sometimes salted.

Thick flank (3) or **top rump** or **fleshy end** – prepared as joints or cut into steaks.

Rump (4) or **pope's eye** – cut into steaks.

Sirloin (5) – prepared as joints, with or without bone, with or without fillet. Also sliced into steaks.

Wing rib – rib end of the sirloin, prepared as joint with or without bones.

Fillet (attached to the internal surface of the carcase along the bones of the sirloin and rump) – trimmed whole, or cut into steaks.

Flank or **thin flank (6)** – boned and rolled as pot roast, lean meat used for mince, burgers, sausages, etc.

Forerib (7) or **rib roast** – the traditional cut of 'Roast beef of old England'. Sold on the bone, part-boned or boned and rolled. Also cut into steaks.

Thin ribs (8) and **thick ribs (10)** or **thick** and **thin runner** – usually boned and rolled, or sliced. Lean meat from the thin rib may be used for stewing beef, mince, etc.

Chuck and blade (9) or **shoulder** – divided into a number of different cuts and joints, including chuck steak.

Brisket (11) or **flank** – supplied on or off the bone, rolled, for braising, boiling or pot roasting.

Neck (12) or **sticking** and **clod (13)** or **gullet** – usually sliced or diced for stewing.

Traditional cuts of beef for grilling/shallow frying

Double entrecôte – boned out sirloin (no fillet), slice about 40 mm thick, 400 to 500 g

Entrecôte or *sirloin steak* – slices of the large 'eye' of the loin on the outside of the backbone, about 20 mm thick, 150 to 250 g

Entrecôte minute – flattened out/batted entrecôte, 150 to 200 g

Point steak – cut from triangular piece of rump, about 30 mm thick, 150 to 200 g

Rump steak – slices about 20 mm thick, 150 to 200 g

Côte à l'os – large rib steak (from whole sirloin, with fillet), 650 g (for two)

T-bone steak – consists of both 'eyes', sirloin and fillet, held together and separated by the backbone, 400 to 600 g (or larger for two)

Porterhouse steak – as T-bone, but cut further up sirloin (smaller piece of fillet), 400 to 600 g (or larger for two)

Chateaubriand – the head of the fillet, 400 to 500 g (for two)

Fillet steak – middle portion of fillet, 150 to 200 g

Tournedos – as fillet, usually tied into neat round shape, 150 to 200 g

Paillard – flattened out fillet, 150 to 200 g

Filet mignon/médaillons – slices from tail of fillet, 150 to 200 g

Veal

The location of these cuts is similar to beef.

Knuckle – sliced with or without bone for pie veal or stewing.

Thick flank – prepared as boneless steaks or escalopes.

Rump, topside, silverside – prepared as boneless steaks or escalopes.

Breast – bone-in joint or boneless rolled joint. Lean meat used as mince, stewing veal or pie veal.

Loin – bone-in joint, boneless rolled joint, bone-in cutlets or chops, slices of boneless steak or escalope. The fillet may be removed and prepared separately as slices of boneless steak or escalope.

Chuck – boned and rolled for roasting, or sliced as steak or escalope.

Neck, clod, shin – sliced or cubed for pies and casseroles.

Lamb

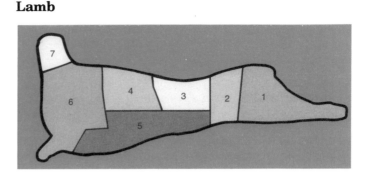

Leg (1) or **gigot** – prepared as whole leg, bone-in or partly boned, or part-leg (e.g. shank end or fillet end) when it may be boned, or sliced as steaks or gigot chops.

Chump (2) – prepared as boneless rolled joint, or as chump chops (bone-in or boneless).

Leg and chump provide a good sized roasting joint, when boned and rolled.

Loin (3) – prepared as a joint (bone-in) or as chops. Traditional loin chops have a small T-shaped bone. *Double loin chops* (also *Barnsley, crown* and *saddle chops*) are cut from an unsplit carcase. Also available are boneless *loin steaks*, heart shaped *valentine steaks* and *noisettes*.

Saddle is the unsplit carcase after removing the forequarters by a cut between the 12th and 13th rib, and also the legs. Usually supplied oven prepared, either bone in or boned and rolled.

Best end (4) or **single loin** – prepared as a bone-in joint or as cutlets. Lamb carcases may have 13 or 14 pairs of ribs, and this will affect the number of ribs in the joint.

What butchers sell as *loin chops* or *lamb chops* may come from either the loin or best end neck.

Rack is prepared from the best end, chined and trimmed, suitable as a joint or cutlets.

Crown of lamb – two best ends tied together to form a circle, with the eye of the meat on the outside.

Breast (5) or **flank** – bone-in or boneless joint, or sliced. More fat than most lamb cuts, so should be cooked on a rack. *Riblets* are short ribs for grilling or roasting.

Shoulder/middle neck (6)

Shoulder – economic joint for roasting or braising, cubed for stewing, cut into shoulder steaks, or minced.

Middle neck – cut from between the best end and scrag: used on the bone for casseroles.

Neck fillet – boneless, lean and tender, grill, barbecue or stir fry.

Scrag (7) or **neck** – for stewing.

Pork

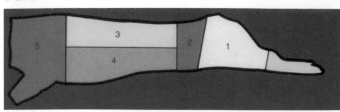

Leg (1) – bone-in, partly boned or boneless joint. Also prepared as escalopes or steaks, or cubed for kebabs and stir frys.

Chump (2) – bone-in or boneless joint, chump chops or steaks.

Loin (3) – prepared as joint, usually on the bone, as chops, with or without ribs, or with kidney, depending on what part they come from.

Fillet (tenderloin) – prepared from the loin, a prime piece of meat with little or no fat.

Loin and belly – roasting joint prepared from the whole loin and belly.

Belly (4) – bone-in or boneless joint, or sliced. Ribs removed from the belly and other joints are often used as barbecue *spare ribs*.

Shoulder (5) or **hand** – bone-in, partly boned, or boned and rolled whole, or sliced into steaks.

Bacon and ham

Most British bacon comes from a type of pig bred to produce a high proportion of lean meat. The body is basically divided into three: the *middle*, mostly sliced as rashers, either streaky or middlecut; *gammon* (the leg); and *shoulder*, for joints, steaks or rashers.

The meat is cured in brine (a salt solution), containing permitted preservatives which colour and flavour the meat. After maturing it is sold as *unsmoked* (green) bacon, or further processed to produce *smoked* bacon, with its darker colour and distinctive flavour.

Gammon is also sold cooked and cold as *ham*. Speciality hams are produced from whole legs, separated from the carcase before being cured and cooked by traditional methods.

Offal

Offal is a term used to cover:

- internal organs, such as brain, heart, tongue, sweetbreads (the pancreas), liver, kidneys and tripe

- parts of an animal that are left after the meat on the carcase has been removed, such as pig trotters, calves' feet and oxtail.

Offal such as oxtail and heart need longer, slower cooking such as braising or boiling. Liver and kidney need shorter cooking methods. Liver (cooked and minced) is the main ingredient of many types of pâté.

Liver (ox, calf, lamb, pork) – should have little if any smell, and an attractive colour, without tubes or dryness. Cut away any sinew, and remove the membrane.

Kidney (ox, calf, lamb, pork) – should have a deep red colour and smell fresh. If possible, keep kidneys in their suet until required. Cut away any tubes and fat and remove the skin.

Tongue (ox, lamb, pork) – must be clean, smell fresh, no excessive waste at the root end. Soak in cold water: for 24 hours if fresh, 4 to 6 hours if pickled. Remove any bone or gristle on the back of the tongue.

Brains (calf, lamb, pork) – soak in cold, salty water for 4 to 6 hours to remove any blood. Remove all the membrane, then re-wash.

Heart (ox, calf, lamb) – should look and smell fresh, and fat or tubes (which are trimmed off as the first stage of preparation) should not be excessive. Remove any clots of blood from the inside. Either slice, or if it is to be cooked whole, cut almost in half.

Sweetbreads (calf, lamb) – should be creamy white in colour, with a pleasant smell. Soak in cold, salty water for an hour or more to remove any visible blood, then wash thoroughly.

Tail (ox) – should have creamy-white fat and bright red flesh, with the tail segmented through the cartilage discs. Remove excess fat.

Tripe (ox) – usually bought cleaned, trimmed and partly cooked. Raw tripe must be boiled for 3 to 4 hours in salted water.

Some British speciality hams

York – cured with dry salt and lightly smoked. The meat is pale, with a mild, delicate flavour.

Cumberland – dry salted, with the addition of brown sugar.

Honey baked – baked with a coating of honey, or a mixture of honey, brown sugar and breadcrumbs.

Cumberland Royal – cured for a month in old ale, molasses, vinegar, salt and sugar, then matured for 3 months.

Cumbria Air Dried – herbs added during the curing process before it is air dried for a minimum of 12 months. Very thinly sliced and eaten uncooked (like Parma ham, the Italian speciality).

Hanging meat and ageing

The eating quality of meat depends on careful handling at the abattoir, where the animals are slaughtered, and on how the meat is stored until it is ready for sale. The aim is to have the meat at peak condition for eating when it is supplied to caterers or the general public.

When animals die, they go through a stage called *rigor mortis* when the muscles stiffen. Hanging up the meat before *rigor* sets in stretches the muscles so that when the stiffness has passed, the muscles will relax again, and the meat will not be tough.

The amount of time for *rigor* to pass varies – it is about a day for beef. During hanging, the temperature, airflow and humidity must be carefully controlled because bacteria can easily grow, and if the chilling is too rapid, the meat becomes tough.

Ageing is improving the flavour and tenderness of meat by extending the hanging period beyond the time necessary to cover *rigor mortis*. It is done under chilled conditions to allow certain changes to take place, but avoid excessive growth of bacteria. The benefits of ageing are most marked in beef and lamb, with 14 days considered the optimum time for choice cuts of beef, and 7 days for choice cuts of lamb.

Cuts for stewing, braising and boiling are not usually aged, since the process has little effect on tough connective tissue.

KNOWLEDGE CHECK ???

Describe below at least 3 main precautions you should take when preparing and storing uncooked meat and poultry, to prevent the growth and/or spread of harmful bacteria.

Answer on page 54.

Connective tissue and tenderness

Meat is the muscle of animals. Muscles are made up of many bundles of long fibres held together (and attached to the bone) by *connective tissue*.

The thickness of the fibres and the amount of connective tissue depend on the age of the animal and the amount of work a particular muscle does. Older animals and well-used muscles tend to produce coarser fibres and more connective tissue (as in tougher cuts of meat), but often the flavour is richer.

There are two types of connective tissue and they react differently when exposed to heat and moisture:

- *collagen*, white, the main constituent of tendons and the thin, membranous sheets surrounding the muscle fibres. It starts melting once the temperature reaches 60°C, slowly turning into a softer, jelly-like material: *gelatin*
- *elastin*, yellow, much tougher and forms cartilage (gristle). It is not much affected by heat and so stays tough and gristly, even after cooking.

The meat from young animals is generally finely fibred, with thin sheets of connective tissue (most of it in the form of collagen) separating the muscle fibres. On the whole, older and more exercised meat has more connective tissue, and a higher percentage of it is in the form of elastin. Also the collagen is tougher than in younger meat, and doesn't break down to gelatin so easily.

Marbling and tenderness

The rump steak in this photograph is *marbled*. In other words there is fat distributed through it. During cooking this melts, and runs through the meat tissue, lubricating it by helping separate the fibres which will eventually make it easier to cut and chew.

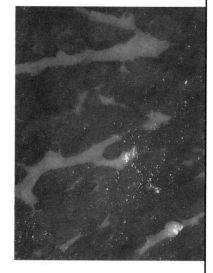

Marbling is particularly important in tender cuts of beef and lamb which are to be cooked quickly. If there is no internal fat these cuts tend to dry out and toughen during cooking.

Seam butchery

Seam butchery, popular elsewhere in Europe for many years, is a technique for separating out individual muscles by cutting through the natural seams between them. They can then be trimmed completely of fat. In many traditional British joints there are numerous muscles, and the fat between them is difficult or impossible to trim.

Seam butchery means less waste for the caterer, and more choice of cuts suitable for quick cooking methods.

Preparation methods

Defrosting   `LEVEL 1`

Meat and poultry must be completely defrosted before they are cooked. The only exceptions are preprepared foods like burgers, sometimes cooked from frozen.

In good time before it is required – up to 48 hours for a large joint – transfer the joint or bird to the refrigerator. Alternatively use a thawing cabinet. Fast defrosting can damage the food and increase fluid loss. (See page 26 for more details, and page 35 for defrosting using a microwave oven.)

Chickens and turkeys Remove giblets as soon as possible to speed up thawing. When defrosting is complete, the limbs should move easily. There should be no signs of ice crystals in the cavity.

Washing   `LEVEL 1`

Generally, the only occasion on which you will have to wash meat or poultry is when it has come into contact with blood during preparation, or for example, the intestines have broken inside the carcase of a bird during gutting.

Offal will usually require washing if you are having to prepare it yourself.

After washing, dry the food thoroughly with absorbent kitchen paper.

Seasoning   `LEVEL 1`

Seasoning – the addition of salt and white or black pepper – is considered to improve the flavour of food.

1 Use white not black pepper on foods which you want to keep an attractive white colour.

2 Add salt to roasts and grills after the meat has browned. Adding salt before cooking will attract the juices of the meat to the surface, and so slow down the browning reactions (which need high temperatures and dry heat).

3 Use freshly ground black pepper. It is more aromatic and flavourful than pre-ground.

NUTRITION

Unfortunately, a high salt intake can contribute to high blood pressure, and most people, according to government health advisors, eat too much salt.

For chefs, the difficulty is that unsalted food will appear rather tasteless to those that have got used to having salt on their food. On the other hand, the health of customers has to be considered – and they can, of course, add their own salt.

ANSWER   ✓✓✓

KNOWLEDGE CHECK page 53

Preparing and storing uncooked meat and poultry

Raw meat and poultry are quite likely to contain harmful bacteria even before they get into the kitchen. Fortunately this is not a problem when the food is thoroughly cooked and the proper precautions are taken. The following should remind you of what has already been mentioned earlier in the book in Hygiene:

1 *Where a colour coding system is in use, never allow chopping boards, knives etc. designated for handling raw food to come in contact with cooked food.*

2 *Otherwise, ensure that equipment is thoroughly washed and rinsed in very hot water and/or sanitised before it is used to handle cooked food.*

3 *At all times, keep raw foods well separated from cooked foods.*

4 *Wash hands thoroughly before and immediately after handling uncooked foods.*

5 *Where practicable, keep preparation of uncooked foods to specific areas of the kitchen.*

6 *Store uncooked food covered, at the correct temperature.*

7 *Defrost frozen food thoroughly before cooking, never refreeze once thawed.*

CHEF'S TIPS

Suggestions for reducing or replacing salt

with beef – horseradish, ginger, tomato, bay leaf, beer, black pepper, mustard

with chicken – lemon juice, garlic, paprika, parsley, orange juice, almonds

with fish – freshly ground pepper, lemon juice, paprika, parsley, orange juice, almonds

with pork – ginger, garlic, thyme, sage, apple, pineapple, cider

with lamb – mint, rosemary, basil, redcurrant, apricot, kidney beans, chilli powder, onion, tomato, vinaigrette

with potatoes – mint, parsley, onion

with rice – turmeric, saffron, onion, green pepper, cucumber, mint, vinegar, yogurt

with green beans – lemon juice, dill

with peas – mint, parsley

with cabbage – thyme, nutmeg, apple, apple juice

with carrots – parsley, cloves, tarragon, lemon juice

with tomatoes – basil, oregano, marjoram, vinaigrette

Skinning
LEVEL 2

Most of the meat you deal with will already have been skinned as part of the preparation by the supplier.

If you do have to skin a saddle or best end of lamb, for example, you will find that sometimes the skin pulls off quite easily. On other occasions, as with ham or gammon joints, it is a matter of lifting the skin away as you cut carefully through the layer of fat underneath.

Chicken breast and legs Gently pull the skin away, using the fingers. It should part quite easily from the flesh.

Liver If you are dealing with a whole liver from a calf, lamb, pig or ox, the thin skin or membrane (if present) will need to be removed before slicing. Gently pull away using the fingers and the tip of a small sharp knife. Take care not to cut the liver.

Lamb kidneys Remove the outer skin or membrane (if present) before cooking. Nick the membrane on the rounded side with the tip of a small sharp knife. Draw the skin back until it is only attached at the core. Cut a deep V-shape with scissors on either side of the core, so that you can remove the core and the skin together.

Trimming
LEVEL 2

Do this carefully so that you:

- improve the appearance of the cut or joint
- leave as much of the meat intact as possible
- remove as much gristle and sinew as possible
- leave an even thickness of fat (where fat is to be left). How much fat you trim off will depend on the type of meat, customer preference and the cooking process to be used.

Dicing
LEVEL 2

Meat and poultry are diced or cut into cubes for various types of casseroles, stews, curries, and dishes such as steak and kidney pie and pudding. The size of the finished piece will depend on the type of dish you are making and sometimes on the quality of the meat. For the sake of illustration, the following steps are based on cutting 25 mm (1 inch) cubes.

1 Trim off any visible fat or gristle.

2 Cut the meat into slices of the required thickness (e.g. 25 mm). With chicken breast and other small pieces of meat, this step is not necessary.

3 Cut these slices into strips (25 mm wide).

4 Cut these strips into pieces of the required size cube (25 × 25 × 25 mm).

Any fat or gristle which appears during slicing and cubing should be trimmed off, or at least avoided.

CHEF'S TIPS

To ease carving and give an attractive finish, the rind of pork should be scored in a neat criss-cross fashion: 3 mm deep incisions about 2 cm apart.

Although not for the health conscious – to make pork crackling really crispy, dry the rind then brush with oil and rub in coarsely ground sea salt. Don't cover or baste the joint during roasting. If necessary increase the oven heat in the last 15 minutes or so.

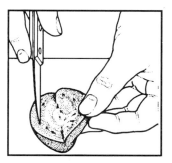

Preparing lamb's kidneys for grilling or barbecuing: 1) Skin and trim off the gristle (see text). 2) Slit through the bulging side of the core (but without cutting through the core) so that the kidney remains in one piece. 3) Open out and fix in this position with a small skewer.

An attractive way of preparing cocktail sausages for grilling. Hold the sausage at the centre, and use the finger and thumb of both hands gently to press the sausage meat away from the centre of the sausage. This needs to be done carefully otherwise you will burst the sausage. Twist the sausage in half. After cooking it can be split into two if required.

Diced ox kidney and beef thick flank for steak and kidney pudding.

Batting
LEVEL 2

Batting has a tenderising effect by breaking up the structure of the meat. It also speeds up cooking time, as the resulting piece is very thin.

1 From time to time dip the cutlet bat in water. This prevents the meat sticking to it. (Some chefs and butchers place a sheet of wet polythene between the meat and the cutlet bat, as this results in a smoother looking piece of meat.)

2 Use a regular motion, moving from the centre outwards, so that the thickness is reduced evenly.

Barding
LEVEL 2

This is used in roasting and braising to protect the outer layer of joints with no or insufficient surface fat. A thin layer or sheet of pork fat is placed (and usually tied) over the vulnerable surface. Bacon can also be used for added flavour.

During cooking the fat gradually melts, keeping the surface of the meat moist.

Marinating
LEVEL 2

Marinades are used to give a distinctive flavour to the finished dish. They can also tenderise, but this effect is not very great, as the acids in the liquid (which reduce toughness) can only get at the surface of the food. The acids may cause the colour of the meat to change. Red meat, for example, goes a browny-grey.

Depending on the style of dish, there is a wide choice of marinade ingredients: red or white wine, vinegar, brandy, beer, oil, yogurt, fresh fruit juices (lemon, lime, orange, pineapple, passion fruit, etc.), various herbs and spices.

The marinating time varies from 20 minutes or so, to several hours or even days. Too long and the surface of the meat becomes mushy.

Use a glass, china or stainless steel bowl (acids will damage plastic or aluminium containers). Ideally the marinade should fully cover the meat. If it does not, regularly turn the meat and spoon the marinade over.

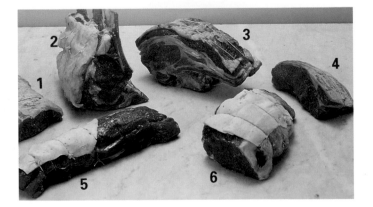

Stuffing
LEVEL 2

If a joint or bird is to be stuffed, this should be done before trussing or tying.

Place the stuffing so it will be securely held in place during cooking, and do not overstuff. When stuffing falls out of a joint during cooking, it becomes difficult to make good gravy from the pan juices.

For stuffed poultry dishes, either cook the stuffing separately, or place it in the neck cavity between the skin and the flesh of the breast. Never place stuffing in the chest cavity – this will stop the centre of the bird heating up sufficiently to kill harmful bacteria.

ACTION

Study the photograph at the foot of the page opposite, and highlight on the following list the names of those cuts which have been battened.

Beef: 1) Double entrecôte, 2) Entrecôte (or sirloin steak), 3) Entrecôte minute (or minute steak), 4) Tournedos, 5) Fillet steak, 6) Paillard (or escalope), 7) Médaillons, 8) Bâtons, 9) Filets mignons, 10) Rump, 11) Point steak

Veal: 12) Cutlet, 13) Chop, 14) Escalopes, 15) Piccatas

Pork: 16) Chop, 17) Cutlet

Lamb: 18) Cutlets, 19) Cutlets (trimmed), 20) Noisettes, 21) Rosettes, 22) Fillet

Offal: 23) Calf's liver, 24) Lamb's liver, 25) Lamb's kidney.

Cuts of beef prepared for roasting: 1) Sirloin (off the bone), 2) Wing rib, 3) Forerib, 4) Rump, 5) Fillet, 6) Topside. Note how the fillet and topside have been barded, and how the rib has been trimmed to leave the end of the bones clean.

Tying and rolling

For joints to keep a good shape during roasting, braising or boiling, it is best to tie them with string. (Often this will have been done by the butcher or supplier, either with string or using an elasticated net.)

If the joint has been stuffed or boned, tying is essential.

The aim is to keep the shape of the joint neat, and as uniform and natural looking as possible. This may mean surrounding the joint with just one or two lengths, or wrapping the string around at intervals of a few centimetres. The string will need to be kept quite tight, but not so tight it cuts into the flesh or squeezes out the stuffing.

1 Place a length of string around the centre of the joint. Pull tight and knot.

2 Then move outwards, tying fresh pieces of string at regular intervals to produce a well-shaped joint.

for grilling and shallow frying

When a neat round shape is required, tie once with string. For instance:

- tournedos (cut from the centre of beef fillet)
- rosettes of lamb (boned loin, cut into slices of 15 to 20 mm and surrounded by a flap of fat before tying).

Leg of lamb prepared for roasting and carving in view of the customers (e.g. at a buffet or carvery). The trimmed bone is covered with a paper frill just before service.

Various rolled and tied bacon joints, ready for boiling:
1) Smoked fore hock, 2) Smoked gammon, 3) Smoked collar,
4) Green collar, 5) Green gammon, 6) Green fore hock.

To roll bacon
1 Lay the rashers out flat on a chopping board.
2 Cut the rind off.
3 Form each rasher into a loose roll, starting from the narrow end.

Jointing (of chicken)

LEVEL 2

1 Remove the *wishbone* (see box below).

2 Remove the *winglets* by cutting down through the middle of the first joint from the chicken.

3 Remove the first *leg*. Pull the leg away from the carcase in the direction of the parson's nose, cutting through the skin as you do so. Carefully cut around the 'oyster' of flesh underneath the carcase so it comes away with the leg. When you reach the ball joint, pull the leg back firmly and cut through the joint. Repeat for the second leg.

4 Cut the legs in two through the middle joint, so that you have two *thigh pieces* and two *drumsticks*. Cut through the knuckle joint of the drumsticks to trim off the end of the leg.

5 Cut along the length of the breast bone and about halfway between the breast bone and the wing joint. The aim is to produce four equal-sized *breast portions*. Cut down through the flesh until you reach the wing joint. Cut through this.

6 Hold the chicken firmly by the parson's nose in an upright position, and using a heavy knife cut down between the carcase and the breast. (An illustration showing this step with a cooked bird appears on page 78.)

7 Cut the breast diagonally through the centre, using a firm pressing action with the knife so that you cut through the breast bone cleanly. The two pieces you make should be the same size.

Removing the wishbone

1 Lift open the flap of flesh at the neck end of the bird.
2 With the blade of a small knife, scrape down each side of the breast to expose both halves of the wishbone.
3 Slip the point of the knife behind the bone and cut down on both ends (one at a time) to free them.
4 Take hold of the freed ends, and carefully pull the wishbone up and away from the flesh, cutting it free.
5 When you reach the flat piece which joins the two halves, twist the wishbone to detach it completely.
6 Replace the flap of flesh.

ANSWER ✓✓✓

ACTION page 56

The following cuts are shown battened in the photograph: 3) Entrecôte minute (or minute steak), 6) Paillard (or escalope), 14) Veal escalopes, 15) Veal piccatas.

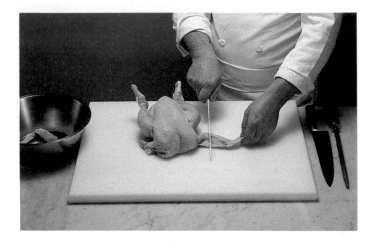

Step 2. Note how the winglet is held fully extended.

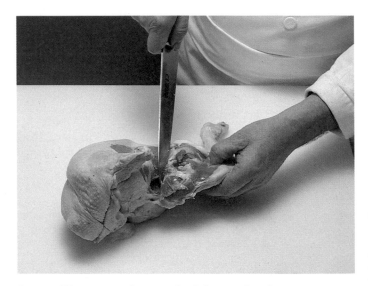

Step 3. The oyster of meat which lies under the carcase is particularly flavoursome. Unless you remove it with the leg it is likely to be wasted.

Step 5. Removing the second piece of breast. Although this means working cross-handed, it is the best position to judge where to make the cut.

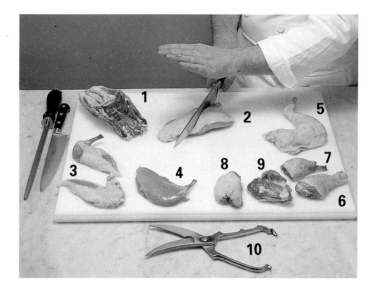

Jointing chicken. *1) The remaining half of the carcase after* step 6. *This is generally chopped into three equal pieces and cooked alongside the remainder of the chicken to add flavour (but not served). 2) Step 7 in action. 3) The first two cuts from the chicken breast (step 5). In the top sample the flesh has been scraped away from the bone (traditional practice for the best service). 4) Suprême (skinned). 5) Whole, untrimmed leg before step 4. 6) Drumstick and 7) with the flesh at the knuckle end scraped clean. 8) Thigh and 9) with the bone removed. 10) Poultry secateurs, sometimes used for jointing and trimming poultry.*

Preparing suprêmes (whole breast portions)

1 After removing the legs, remove the skin from the breast.
2 Carefully cut down the side of the breast bone using a filleting action so that all the flesh is removed from the carcase. Cut down through the wing joint to detach the suprême.

To improve the presentation, remove the sinew from the wing fillet so that it comes neatly away from the rest of the suprême. Cut the thick side of the suprême to form a pocket and insert the fillet in this. If required, lightly flatten the suprême with a cutlet bat.

Trussing *(2-string method)* **LEVEL 2**

Chickens and turkeys are trussed before roasting so that they cook more evenly (otherwise there is a danger that the legs and wings will stretch straight out from the bird, and cook too quickly). The appearance is also improved.

1 Thread the trussing needle with string.
2 With the bird resting breast side up, raise the legs, then press them both down firmly towards the front.
3 Pass the needle through the middle of one leg at the hinge between the drumstick and thigh joint, then go on pushing it through so that it comes out at the same point on the opposite leg.

4 Turn the bird over and with the needle pierce through the centre of one of the wing joints. (Large birds, such as the turkey here, are left with the winglet untrimmed. The string should go through the same place whether the winglet is trimmed off or not.)
5 Thread the needle through the neck flap, then through the second wing joint. The string will now be back at the side you started on.

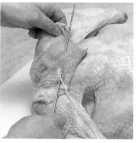

6 Slip the string out of the needle, and tighten the string so that the bird is forced into a neat shape. Knot the two ends of string together and trim off any spare.
7 Thread the needle with more string. Pushing the legs down this time, insert the needle through the bottom of the carcase (the parson's nose end). Pull the string through the body, back over the top of the legs, and then return to the point of entry. Tighten the string, knot the ends together and trim off any spare.

Roasting

`LEVELS 1 + 2`

Definition In roasting, food is cooked in an oven by dry heat at quite high temperatures. A small amount of fat or oil is used to stop the food drying out.

Meat, poultry and game are the items of food most commonly roasted, and certain vegetables.

Spit roasting can be a popular feature at large outdoor events. A whole ox, pig or lamb is cooked over an open fire.

How to get the best from roasting

For good results, you must follow carefully your workplace instructions about:

1 What roasting tray(s) and oven to use.

2 What temperature to set the oven at: for the start of cooking, and at various stages during cooking. Remember to allow time for the oven to reach the right temperature before you put the food in.

3 How long to roast the food for. With beef and lamb, this depends on whether the meat is to be served well done, medium or rare (for beef).

4 How to check the food is properly cooked, and at what stage this is best done.

5 How far in advance of service the food should be roasted. When the meat or poultry is to be served as a hot roast, it needs a short time to 'rest' before carving. But if the food is cooked too far in advance, it will dry out. There is also a risk that harmful bacteria will multiply and cause food poisoning.

6 When basting is required, once every 20 to 30 minutes is usually enough. Use the fat rather than the meat juices from the pan, otherwise the meat may not brown properly.

7 Chickens and turkeys should be turned over about mid-way through cooking, to allow both sides to colour. If the breast has not coloured sufficiently, sit the bird upright for the final stage. Avoid using any equipment that might accidentally puncture the skin, as this will lead to excessive fluid loss and toughening of the meat.

The role of fat in roasting

Fat plays a very important role in roasting by:

* preventing the surface of the food from drying out and becoming hard, so the roast looks and tastes good

* spreading through the food, helping make it more tender

* flavouring the food.

Most roasting joints have some fat of their own:

* on the surface – for example, on a leg of pork, or just under the skin of a chicken leg. Meat which has *external fat* is usually roasted fat-side up, so that the fat will run over the sides as it melts

* running through the structure of the meat itself. This *internal fat* may be blended in with the muscle fibres and hard to see, or readily visible as *marbling* (white specks against the more red colour of meat). It melts during cooking, helping to keep the meat moist.

If the food is likely to dry out during roasting because there is not enough fat naturally present, there are four main ways around the problem.

1 Adding fat to the roasting tray, and from time to time spooning this fat (and fat in the food which has melted) over the food: *basting*. The problem with this is that the oven door has to be opened each time. This lowers the temperature, so it takes longer to cook the food, and more gas or electricity is used, adding to costs. Basting is not usually necessary for joints which are covered by a layer of fat or if the fat is being kept to the minimum for health reasons.

2 Tying thin strips of fat over the vulnerable areas: *barding*.

3 Placing a piece of *kitchen foil* over unprotected areas of the food part-way through the cooking. The foil reflects the heat, but if the food is covered too soon, the foil will trap moisture against the surface and slow down or stop colour development.

4 Threading strips of fat just under the surface of the meat, and through the centre, using a special needle: *larding*. This is a specialised technique, used in some establishments for the best quality roast joints such as whole fillet, rump and cushion of veal.

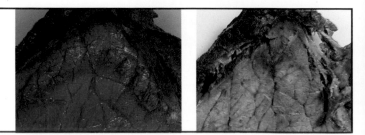

There are big differences in texture, colour and taste between rare and well-done beef. Usually when beef is cooked rare, a high temperature is used to produce a well-flavoured and browned crust, while leaving the inside cooked very little. Well-done beef is cooked using low-temperature roasting (after initial browning) so that there is time for the heat to penetrate and cook the meat thoroughly and evenly.

Roasting times and temperatures

Cooking time depends more on the size and shape of the cut than on the weight. Half a loin of pork takes about as long to roast as a whole loin. This is because even though it is only half the weight, the thickness is the same. So you should use temperature and weight charts only as a rough planning guide, not as a guarantee of when the meat will actually be done.

Remember also that:

- bones conduct heat faster than muscle, so a joint with a large bone through its centre will cook faster than one that has been boned and rolled

- ovens vary in efficiency. In old equipment, the heat circulation can be rather poor. If the oven is very full, or it has to be opened frequently, its efficiency will also be reduced

- in general-purpose ovens, the top of the oven is hotter than the bottom. Place roasts on the centre shelf whenever possible. If the oven is very full so the top or the bottom shelf has to be used, move items from the lower shelf up to the top shelf, and vice versa. Do this two or three times during the cooking.

The combination of high temperatures and dry heat gives roasts their characteristic golden brown surface colour and intensely flavoured crust. The higher the temperatures used in roasting, the quicker the surface of the food will colour. But high temperatures increase shrinkage and loss of juices.

1 A *combination of temperatures*: high (around 225°C) at the start of cooking (called *searing*), then reduced to 150°C to 170°C is very good for roasting large, not particularly tender cuts of meat (for example, rump). It is also ideal for joints that must be well cooked throughout, for example, pork and chicken.

2 *Low temperatures* (100°C to 150°C) for the entire cooking time are suitable for large turkeys where only a light surface colouring is desirable and thorough cooking is essential.

3 *Stuffed joints or poultry*, no matter what their size or tenderness, should be cooked at temperatures of around 165°C, although a higher temperature can be used at the start of cooking to brown the surface.

HYGIENE 👣 👣 👣

Temperatures below 165° C would take too long to heat meat which has been stuffed to a safe 70°C at the centre. This (together with the moistness) would present ideal conditions for any bacteria present in the stuffing or the centre of the meat to multiply rapidly and cause food poisoning. Higher temperatures used throughout roasting would mean that the joint was cooked before the internal temperature of the food had got high enough to kill any bacteria present.

Carry-over cooking

The internal temperature of a roast continues to rise for a short time after the food has been removed from the oven. This is because the outside of the roast is hotter than the inside and so the heat continues to be conducted through to the centre. This effect can raise the internal temperature by about 2°C for small roasts.

An average-sized roast should be removed from the oven when it is about 5°C to 7°C below the target internal temperature, and then allowed to stand.

The period of standing time depends on the size, thickness and surface area of the roast and the cooking temperature. For a medium-size, unstuffed chicken it is about 15 minutes, and for a large leg of pork it is about 30 minutes. Eventually, through experience, you will know how long to leave a particular roast before it is carved.

ACTION

On the next 3 occasions you have to roast a particular type of poultry or meat, record the details below. Ask your supervisor if you can carry out this activity for different sized joints, and whether the cooking temperatures can be varied slightly. Discuss your results with your supervisor.

Type of poultry or meat

Sample	1	2	3

Weight before cooking

Cooking time

Weight after cooking

Roasting temps used

if you have a temperature probe

Internal temp at finish of cooking

Standing time before portioning

Internal temp after standing

REMARKS

Checking when the roast is cooked

There are various methods that can be used to test when the roast is cooked. The most accurate (and hygienic) is to use a *temperature probe* to read the internal temperature of the roast.

1 Make sure that the probe is clean. Dip the point into a sanitising solution, or wipe with a special sanitising cloth.

2 Insert the probe into the centre of the joint. Keep it away from bones or layers of fat (which retain far more heat than the meat), otherwise it will give a higher reading than it should.

3 With a chicken or turkey, insert the probe into the fleshy part of the thigh, not the breast. This is because the thigh takes longer to cook.

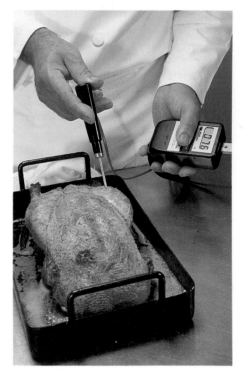

Using a hand-held temperature probe (a type of thermometer) to measure the internal temperature of a roast duck.

CHEF'S TIPS

When roasting a turkey, if the whole bird is being carved in the kitchen rather than in the presence of the customer, it is a good idea to cook the boned legs separately. Cooking time is reduced, and it will be much easier to carve neat rounds of meat (possibly with a centre of stuffing) that look more attractive than the odd-shaped cuts that come from carving the leg on the bird.

To prepare the turkey legs separately, remove them from the carcase, bone them and cut out all sinew and gristle. Bind the leg together with string (enclosing stuffing if required) to form a roll of meat and then roast it, or wrap each leg in a sheet of kitchen foil and bake in a dish with a little water (covering about a quarter the height of the rolled leg) in the same oven as the rest of the turkey. Cooking time: 1 hour.

Final internal roast temperatures

Chicken and turkey: 75°C

Pork: 85°C

Lamb well done: 82°C

Veal and well-done beef: 75°C to 80°C

Medium beef or lamb: 70°C to 75°C

Rare beef: 60°C

A second type of temperature probe is shown in this photograph.

Cooking the bird on its side means that the fat from the legs will run over the breast during cooking, helping to keep the breast moist.

The turkey is being cooked in a forced air convection oven. *The oven uses a fan to circulate the heat. This reduces cooking times by about a third. It improves browning: with such a lot of air movement, there is no chance for a layer of moisture (from juices evaporating off the meat) to build up round the meat* surface. *Lower temperatures can be used because the heat is distributed around the oven more efficiently. The faster cooking time and lower heat overall can reduce weight loss by 10 to 25%.*

The photograph on page 6 shows the same oven in use as a steamer. Another type of combination oven *can use a conventional heat source with microwave energy. The microwave part speeds up the cooking time needed for a roast, for example, and the convection part does the browning.*

Heat is transmitted more efficiently through metal than through air, and so the base of a roasting pan will be hotter than the air surrounding it.

There is a danger that with lean meat (like the boned sirloin of beef in this photograph), the base of the roast will fry on the floor of the pan, so it's a good idea to raise it off the base. This will cut down the amount of conducted heat reaching the roast and can be done by:

- using a metal rack called a *trivet*
- placing the roast on top of some roughly chopped vegetables, known as a *matignon* or *bed of roots*, which will also add flavour to the final gravy or sauce
- if the joint has been boned, the bones can be used as a base where they will both protect the roast and add flavour and colour to the gravy or sauce.

NUTRITION

Making roast meals healthier

Many people are careful for health reasons not to eat too much saturated fat. As meat that is roasted often has a fairly high fat content, and saturated fats are traditionally added, roast meals can be rather unhealthy. But it is possible to improve the situation:

1 Use only lean cuts of meat (e.g. beef rump).
2 Be especially careful to trim off excess fat before cooking.
3 Use a bed of bones, a trivet or a matignon (chopped vegetables), to raise the meat off the base of the pan, and keep it out of the pan drippings.
4 Brush a little polyunsaturated oil over the meat before roasting. Do not baste during cooking.
5 Use low roasting temperatures to prevent excessive moisture loss and shrinkage.
6 Before serving, remove the skin from chicken and turkey.
7 Make sure every bit of fat has been skimmed off the juices in the pan before you use them to make gravy.
8 Serve with high fibre, low fat foods such as pulses, fresh vegetables and fruit, salads, brown rice, wholemeal bread and pasta.

CHEF'S TIPS

by the Meat and Livestock Commission

Brush a joint with grated horseradish and mustard, or poke slivers of garlic into small cuts over the surface.

Spread the inside of a boned joint with garlic and herb soft cheese, roll up and tie.

Unlike sirloin, rib and rump roasting joints (which have a good degree of marbling), silverside and topside are very lean so require basting with the cooking fat during roasting. If braised or pot roasted, additional fat is unnecessary and the long, slow moist cooking tenderises the meat.

For a different gravy: drain off fat from roasting pan, and add some vegetable stock and wine or cider and a little cornflour to thicken. Bring to the boil and stir until reduced to the required consistency.

On the cooking top of this general-purpose oven are various sizes of aluminium roasting pans. Black roasting pans (on oven shelves) made of iron have the advantage that they do not reflect the heat, but absorb it. However they are more expensive. Copper roasting trays, more expensive still, are excellent conductors of heat and very strong.

Choosing the right-sized roasting pan is important: if it is too big, the juices that drain from the meat will fry on the base and burn, but it needs to be deep enough to catch the juices and fat running off the food as it cooks.

Grilling and barbecuing

Definition Grilling is a fast, dry method of cooking which uses the intense heat radiated by an electrical element, gas flame, or glowing charcoal. The heat source can be either above or below the food, or both.

When the process takes place out-of-doors, it is usually referred to as *barbecuing*. The heat source in this situation is usually glowing charcoal, a gas flame, or an open wood fire, positioned below the food.

Other foods are grilled, including fish, shellfish and vegetables. Overhead grills are used to brown *(gratinate* or *glaze)* a variety of sweet and savoury dishes.

How to get the best from grilling

There is a big difference between the speed of cooking:

- at the *surface* of the food – caused by infra-red heat radiation – essential to get the attractive surface browning that is characteristic of grilled food, and which creates such delicious flavours

- *inside* the food – caused by conduction of heat from the surface to the centre – a relatively slow process, but essential to cook the food.

It takes skill and practice to get the best combination of surface browning, while cooking the centre of the food to the degree of 'doneness' required.

1 Select meat and poultry that is tender, with a reasonable fat content.

2 Prepare the food in suitably sized pieces – thin slices or steaks are best – which are regular in shape.

3 Control the position of the food in relation to the heat source.

What you want to avoid, of course, is ending up with food that is:

- charred on the outside and under-cooked or even quite cold on the inside

- completely dried out, tough – even tender meat will toughen in these conditions – and burnt.

This selection of meat is being cooked on a simulated charcoal grill. During cooking, meat should be turned over carefully, using tongs rather than a fork to avoid piercing the surface of the meat (which would allow juices to escape). In this case, the bars of the grill have created an attractive pattern on the meat.

Shown above (clockwise from left) are: poussin (a whole bird, in this case, cut through the base and opened out), chateaubriand, gammon steak, pork fillet, entrecôte, lamb cutlets, chicken breast, pork chops, Barnsley chop, lamb's liver (being turned over), a second piece of liver, chump chop, fillet steak, large T-bone steak.

Simulated charcoal grills (also called char-broilers, char-grills, flame grills *or* lava-rock grills) *use gas or electricity to heat a bed of lava or man-made 'rocks' (sometimes made from ceramic substances), which radiate the heat upwards towards the food.*

Fat dripping from the food creates a certain amount of smoke which helps to flavour the food. Large models are usually free-standing (like the one shown), or floor-mounted, but there are also small models which are designed to be placed on a work surface.

This type of grill is less suitable for small items (unless skewered), as they are likely to fall through the bars.

Infra-red grills (gas or electric) operate at much higher temperatures than other types of grills. Cooking times are consequently shorter: sausages are cooked in around 6 minutes, chops in half that time, and toast takes about 50 seconds per side.

Continuous grills, which are used in many fast-food units, have a conveyor or belt that carries the food past the heat source so that there is a continuous sequence of raw food in, cooked food out.

Other points to watch when grilling

1 As grilling is such a fast process, preparation is especially important. It is easy to get into a muddle with trays of raw food waiting to be cooked, piles of plates or service dishes and bowls of garnish. The way that grill chefs keep track of different orders, especially when, for example, one customer wants a well-done steak, another two require medium steaks and a fourth has asked for a rare steak, is by being organised and methodical. For example, well done steaks in the centre, medium on the left, rare on the right.

2 Grills should be pre-heated: this could take as much as 15 to 20 minutes depending on the type of grill. Grills use a great deal of fuel, so they should be turned off whenever practicable.

3 Grill bars should be lightly brushed with oil before use to prevent food from sticking.

4 Small items (such as cocktail sausages) are best placed on a lightly oiled tray and cooked under an overhead grill. The disadvantage is that the food will sit in its own fat (released during cooking).

5 For neatness, or because tradition demands it, some cuts are tied with string before grilling (see page 57).

6 A really hot grill will produce an attractive criss-cross pattern of lines. If the grill is not fierce enough to do this, or does not have suitable grill trays, the food can be seared with a hot poker before being placed under the grill.

The electrical elements of this overhead grill or salamander are clearly visible. Gas is a popular alternative to electricity.

The grooves on the inside support the grill bars and allow the rack position to be adjusted. In some grills the grill tray (or brander) can be tilted so that the front is lower than the back – the food can be seen while cooking and items can be turned over without the tray being pulled out, otherwise a disadvantage of this type of grill. The cooking temperature can be varied according to the distance of the food from the heat source.

Overhead grills are usually situated at eye level, and are often part of a cooking range, above a work top or cooking surface. Some are fixed to the wall with brackets. Others form part of a special free-standing unit with racks and shelves below.

Some overhead grills have a special system of trays so that one can be loaded while another has food cooking on it. There are also models with open sides which can take awkwardly shaped items.

CHEF'S TIPS

When making kebabs, brush the skewers with oil before loading with the food. This will make it easier to remove the skewer once the food has been cooked and placed on the customer's plate.

When using a charcoal grill, a really aromatic effect can be created by sprinkling a few sprigs of rosemary or thyme on the grill towards the end of the cooking. Hickory chips and mesquite or similar aromatic woods will also create a tangy smoke.

NUTRITION

Choosing the correct oil or fat when grilling is important for health reasons. Ideally it should be low in saturated fat. The most suitable product to use is a polyunsaturated oil, such as corn oil, rape seed oil or soya oil. Olive oil is also suitable and has an excellent flavour but it is expensive.

If a butter flavour is required, use a mixture of clarified butter and a bland vegetable oil such as rape seed oil.

Avoid using animal fats such as lard or dripping, which are high in unsaturated fats and therefore unhealthy.

Loading the skewer for Kebabs Turkish style (page 86). During grilling the kebabs will be brushed with the marinade – the usual procedure for a grill dish involving marinating.

Guide to 'doneness' of steak
The photographs show fillet steak.

Rare or *blue* or *au bleu* – this should feel flabby when pressed with grilling tongs.

Underdone or *saignant* – when tested with grilling tongs, the flesh should spring back and there should be signs of red juices.

Medium or *à point* – this should feel firm and there should be slight traces of blood.

Well done or *bien cuit* – this should feel firm with no sign of blood. Note how the texture of the meat has altered in comparison with the rare steak.

How to get the best from barbecuing

In general, the procedures for barbecuing are similar to grilling (when the heat source is below the food).

1 Start cooking only when the barbecue has reached the right temperature. Real charcoal should look ash-grey in the light or have a red glow at night. There should never be any flames.

2 Gas-turbo barbecues, specially built for catering use, only take about 5 minutes to reach the right temperature. (A fan ensures the correct mixture of gas and air for fast and efficient heating. It also circulates cool air around the burner area, resulting in much lower external temperatures than the traditional barbecue.)

3 Turn meat over once only if possible, otherwise you will lose most of the juices into the fire.

4 Use tongs for turning food – spearing them with a fork means losing precious juices.

5 Baste food with its marinade sparingly. Otherwise a lot of marinade will drip into the fire, and is likely to cause excessive smoking and flaming.

6 Lean cuts, with all the fat trimmed off, are best. Fat dripping from the meat as it cooks is even more likely to cause flare-ups.

7 For kebabs, use flat skewers. The food tends to rotate on rounded skewers, making them difficult to turn over.

8 When the barbecue is out-of-doors, you may need to make special arrangements to store the food which is waiting to be cooked, and to keep cooked food hot if there is any delay before service. Make sure that a suitable fire extinguisher is handy. Store fuel and other flammable materials away from the cooking area.

One of the most important factors that decides how long food should be cooked is how thick it is. Both these pieces of pork have been grilled at the same temperature for the same length of time – although the thicker piece is burnt on the surface, it is still uncooked inside.

ACTION

You are just about to go home after a busy day in the kitchen, when your supervisor tells you that the grill chef won't be in the next day because of a family emergency. You are to take charge of the grill section for what is expected to be a busy lunch session.

Make some notes on the sort of things you can do to make the next day easier, using the headings suggested below, or your own if you prefer.

Familiarising yourself with the menu

Preparing garnishes

Preparation and cooking equipment

Service dishes

System for remembering orders

Tandoori cooking

`LEVELS 1 + 2`

Definition Tandoori cooking is an Indian method of cooking food in a clay oven. Meat, poultry and vegetables are put on long skewers which are placed in the oven. Nan bread is cooked on the inner oven wall.

Tandoor ovens cook by a combination of grilling, baking, barbecuing and roasting. No fat is used and temperatures are high, around 230°C.

The oven is shaped rather like the huge jar in which the thieves hid from Ali Baba. The original versions in the Punjab, a province in the north-west of India, were sunk neck-deep in the ground. While modern, above ground versions are heavily insulated on the outside, a good extraction system is needed to keep the kitchen from becoming unbearably hot.

How the oven works

The glowing charcoal at the bottom of the jar heats the sides of the tandoor to scorching point about half-way up, and to a hot glow for the rest, diminishing near the neck.

Charcoal is the traditional fuel and gives the authentic tandoori flavour. However, the oven takes 1 to 2 hours to heat up to the right temperature, longer if the oven is used infrequently. The temperature is then controlled by opening or shutting the small air vent at the side of the oven. Once cooking is finished, it is quite a messy business removing the ashes.

Gas-fired ovens have a heavy metal plate in the bottom, on which rests lava rock. They are more convenient to use, and cooking temperature can be controlled by turning the gas supply up or down.

Heavy-duty cast iron cookers of the type preferred by chefs in India are becoming available in the UK.

Cooking in a tandoor

1 Select meat and poultry that is tender, with a reasonable fat content.

2 Prepare the food in suitably sized pieces, regular in shape.

3 Place the food on the special long skewers. Use the thin skewers for chunks of meat and poultry, and for whole chickens. Use the slightly thicker skewers for minced kebabs.

4 Lower the skewers into the oven, the tips in the glowing but not flaming coals, the handle resting against the edges of the neck.

5 Keep an eye on the food, rotating the skewers from time to time, and changing their position if the surface is browning too quickly.

6 When required by the recipe, remove the food at intervals and baste with the marinade.

Tradition holds that a tandoor in regular use improves the flavour of anything cooked in it, for the heated clay itself releases a mellow fragrance that permeates the food. For tandoori chicken another important ingredient in the final taste is added by the particular kind of smoke that comes from the dripping of the marinade on to the hot coals.

Cooking nan bread

Nan bread is cooked in a few minutes in a tandoor (see page 212). The bread is placed against the side of the oven, where it is hot, but not scorching. The outward curved shape of the tandoor allows the greater part of the nan to hang loose over the heat, from the point at which it was attached to the inside. The weight of the dough pulls the nan into its characteristic tear-drop shape, and its elasticity keeps the nan from breaking off and falling into the coals.

SAFETY ▲▲▲

Take care not to touch the collar of the oven while lifting food in and out, or you are likely to give yourself a serious burn.

Allow the flames to subside after the oven has been ignited, and before opening the lid.

Use the ash pan for removing hot ashes from a charcoal tandoor. Empty the ashes into a metal drum. Cover with a lid and a soaking wet cloth. Stand in sink or outside if possible and pour over cold water until the ashes are cooled.

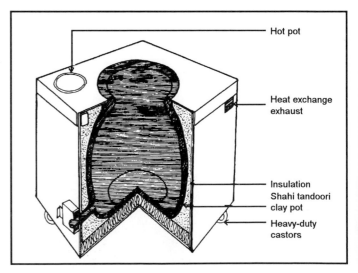

The clay pot of a tandoor oven is sealed on the inside before use by applying six coatings of a mixture of mustard oil, egg, spinach, jaggery sugar cane, salt and yogurt. These coatings are allowed to dry naturally before any heat is introduced.

Shallow frying

LEVELS 1 + 2

Definition In shallow frying the food is cooked on a hot, greased surface:

- the base of a suitable pan: for meat and poultry this is usually a general-purpose frying pan
- a solid cooking surface, such as a griddle. When this type of equipment is used the process is often called *griddling*.

The coating of oil (or fat) stops the food sticking (and burning). It also helps conduct heat to as much of the food's surface as possible.

Shallow frying is used as a first step in some braised and stewed dishes (see following pages), also stocks, sauces and soups (see that section).

Shallow frying (see appropriate sections) is also a popular method of cooking fish, shellfish, vegetables, vegetable protein and eggs.

Stir frying

Stir frying is a variation of shallow frying: cooking small pieces of food (very tender meat and poultry) quickly in the minimum amount of oil. The food is stirred constantly, usually in a *wok*: see page 165 for picture and more details of the process as it applies to vegetables.

Sautéing

Sautéing is tossing the food in the pan during cooking so that it cooks and browns on all sides. The name comes from the French for 'to jump'. Sometimes the food is described as sautéed even if it is too big to be tossed in the pan (sautéed chicken): this simply means it has been turned so that it is browned all over.

SAFETY

The first signs of burning fat before it bursts into flames are the blue smoke which appears just above its surface and an unpleasant smell of burning. Apart from being very dangerous, fat which is on the point of burning will ruin the flavour of the food.

Oil which spits or spills out of the pan during shallow frying may catch fire if it comes into contact with the gas flame or electrical element.

It is safer to bring serving dishes (previously warmed) to the pan, rather than to work the other way around.

Using a coating

Some foods will not brown and crisp satisfactorily unless they are first coated with flour, or a mixture of flour and beaten raw egg which is then covered with dried breadcrumbs, or a variation on these. For details on preparation methods, see page 104. Examples include: supreme of chicken, veal escalope and sliced liver.

Poor control of timing and temperatures in shallow frying leads to:

the food drying out

a burnt appearance and taste

uneven cooking

How to get the best from shallow frying

1 Make sure everything is ready before you start. As shallow frying is a fast cooking process, there may not be time later to collect anything you have forgotten.

2 Use the correct oil (or fat), following workplace or recipe instructions. Good proprietary-brand oils are expensive. Olive oil is too expensive to use on anything but special shallow fried dishes.

3 Use the minimum amount of oil. Some griddle chefs use a spray oil to give the lightest coating.

4 Allow the oil to reach the correct temperature before adding the food. Judging this is largely a matter of experience. Watch what happens when the food first comes into contact with the oil. If the oil is too cold, almost nothing will happen, while the right temperature usually produces a sizzling sound. If the oil is too hot, it will smoke (see Safety box on page 69, and also page 108).

5 When the oil has reached the right temperature, lower the food in gently so that the hot oil does not spit or splash.

6 Move the food around so that it cooks thoroughly without burning or sticking. Turn over or toss as stated in the recipe. If necessary, lower the temperature, or move the pan across the heat source during cooking to maintain an even spread of heat.

7 Choose the correct equipment – a palette knife or fish slice – for turning food over, and removing it from the pan. Do not pierce the food with a fork, as the juices will be lost.

Some of the most attractive effects of shallow frying – crisp outer surface and browning – come from the use of very high temperatures. Achieving this, while making sure that the inside of the food is properly cooked, is a skill that you will learn with care and practice. The dish illustrated is Chicken Maryland.

CHEF'S TIPS

Empty frying pans should never be left on a hot stove or over a lit gas burner. Even if there is no visible sign of damage the internal structure of the metal can be permanently affected. Cast iron, for example, can suddenly cause food to stick, no matter how many times it is re-seasoned. (See *page 17*.)

Red meats are ready to be turned when small drops of blood appear on the uncooked surface.

For improved colour (but not for the health conscious), add a knob of butter to the frying oil.

Religious beliefs and laws associated with meat

In the multi-ethnic and multi-cultural society that Britain has become, caterers need to take account of the many religious beliefs and laws that are associated with meat.

Jewish faith – Jews follow the custom and dietary laws set out in the Old Testament and the Talmud. Foods which fulfil this law are called Kosher foods. Meat must be ritually prepared by the traditional Jewish method of 'schechitah'. Forbidden foods include pork, offal, rabbit, eel and shellfish, as well as the hindquarters of animals.

Orthodox, very strict, Jews will not eat meat and dairy products at the same meal or use the same kitchen equipment in their preparation.

Hindu faith – Many Hindus are vegetarian, with the strictest refusing to eat meat, fish or eggs. Those who do eat meat will avoid beef, as the cow is considered a sacred animal.

Muslim faith – Muslims follow the rules laid down in the Qur'an. Permitted food is called 'halal'. Forbidden food, like pork and any other animals that are not ritually prepared for eating, are termed 'haram'.

Christian faith – Christians sometimes eat fish rather than meat on Fridays, particularly during Lent and on Good Friday.

Other religions like Sikh, Rastafarian and Seventh Day Adventists also have their own beliefs associated with eating meat.

From GCSE Directions Cooking & Using Meat *published by British Trades Alphabet in collaboration with Meat and Livestock Commission.*

Other points to watch when shallow frying

1 Where the decision is yours, use thin, tender cuts of meat or poultry.

2 Use the right type of pan (or griddle). In general, choose a frying pan with a thick, solid and perfectly flat base:

cast or *vitrified iron* and *stainless steel* are all suitable

tin-lined copper pans are excellent for food which is breadcrumbed, or finished in a sauce. The tin lining starts to melt at around 230°C (smoke point of the better oils) so they are not suitable for prolonged, high temperature frying (e.g. sauté potatoes)

catering-quality non-stick pans have the advantage that no or very little oil is necessary

sauteuse pans, with their sloping sides and wide surface area, should be used for dishes involving the reduction of a sauce

sauté pans – also *plat à sauter* – have straight, vertical sides. Despite their name, sauté pans are generally used for shallow frying meat that is too big to toss, or which is finished in a sauce.

3 If you are frying different-sized pieces of food, a jointed chicken for example, begin with the pieces that require the longest cooking time (thighs and drumsticks in this case).

4 For food which is only turned once during frying, cook the better-looking side first. It is easier to turn the food over without damage when it is only partly cooked, so the side cooked first generally looks best.

5 Time cooking so that the food does not need to be kept warm before service. If there is any delay, food which is in a sauce should be covered. Crisply finished items should be left uncovered or they will become soggy.

6 When the sauce is going to be made or finished in the pan, place the food to one side on a dish or tray and keep it warm. With some dishes, once the sauce is made, the food is returned to the pan, allowed to reheat in the sauce and then transferred to the serving dish. Be careful not to leave the food to stew in the sauce, spoiling its texture and flavour.

7 Food which is not reheated in the finished sauce can be placed on absorbent paper briefly after cooking to remove any excess oil.

If you are cooking for large numbers:

- fry in batches to suit the pan size. If you overfill the pan, it will be very difficult to turn the food and the temperature of the fat will drop too low

- after each batch is cooked, drain off any juices (these can be used later for the sauce) and remaining fat

- wipe the pan clean with absorbent paper

- put fresh oil in the pan, reheat, then cook the next batch.

The role of the oil (or fat)

Very little oil is needed for shallow frying, just enough to:

- prevent the food from sticking to the cooking surface

- prevent dry foods from burning by providing some moisture at the surface of the food

- enable the food to be moved during cooking, so that all its surfaces cook properly, or to be placed in a slightly cooler area of the pan or griddle to enable it to cook through to the centre

- ensure that heat is conducted to all parts of the food's surface even when an uneven shape means that some of it is not in direct contact with the cooking surface.

In some cases, for example, when a good quality non-stick surface is being used and quite fatty foods such as streaky bacon, pork and lamb chops are being shallow fried, no oil needs to be used. The food will release sufficient fat of its own to prevent sticking.

Which oil (or fat)?

Consider whether the oil (or fat) should contribute to the flavour of the food, as in some:

- Mediterranean-style dishes for which the recipe will state *olive oil*

- Chinese dishes which use *sesame oil* which has a strong nutty flavour, so use sparingly

- Indian and East African dishes which use *ghee* (from vegetable oils).

Otherwise, use mildly flavoured products. Here it is best to avoid those high in saturated fat, so good choices include *safflower, sunflower* and *proprietary blends* (with high smoke point, light, neutral flavour, labelled high in polyunsaturated fats).

Braising

LEVELS 1 + 2

Definition In braising, the food is partially covered with some kind of liquid which is kept at, or close to, boiling point.

There are various views about the details of the process, so that not all braised dishes share even the following characteristics.

1 Like roasting, braising uses whole joints or large cuts, but the long, slow, moist cooking means that the meat need not be prime quality. For this reason, beef topside, shoulder of veal and lamb are often braised. It is also used for celery, cabbage and other vegetables (see that section).

2 Like stewing, the liquids in which the food is cooked help keep it moist and add flavour. The cooking liquor forms the basis of the sauce which accompanies the food. Stock, demi-glace or jus lié, and wine are commonly used ingredients. Some braised meat and poultry dishes are marinated before cooking.

3 Many braised meat dishes rely for at least part of their taste on the flavours caused by browning. This is done before the liquid is added. The food is shallow fried or, for the larger joints especially, roasted for a short time in a very hot oven (230°C to 250°C). Sweetbreads, tongue and ham are generally braised 'white': no browning, white stock not brown.

4 During cooking, the joint of meat rests on a base of sliced or roughly chopped vegetables such as carrots, onions, leek and garlic – known sometimes as a *bed of roots*. This adds flavour and keeps the meat away from the very hot base of the cooking pan.

5 Cooking is started on top of the stove, and transferred to the oven after the liquid has come to the boil.

6 The cooking container is kept firmly closed for most, if not all, the cooking time.

SAFETY   ▲ ▲ ▲

When lifting a braising pan into or out of the oven, particularly if the pan is a large one, remove the lid first. You will then be able to keep an eye on the liquid inside and so should not be taken unawares by boiling hot liquid splashing out from under the lid.

If the pan is heavy, get someone to help you lift it out of the oven.

Always use thick, dry oven cloths to lift pans in and out of the oven, and to remove lids.

KNOWLEDGE CHECK   ???

Give 2 reasons why time and temperature are important when cooking meat and poultry dishes.

Answer on page 76.

This photograph shows some of the key features of braising: 1) chopped vegetables for the meat to sit on during cooking, 2) pan with a close fitting lid, 3) the practice of browning or searing the meat before the main cooking takes place (cushion of veal in this case), 4) ox tongue which has been blanched before cooking to remove impurities.

How to get the best from braising

1 Check that you have good quality stock, and, if the recipe requires, demi-glace or jus lié.

2 Other time-consuming activities you may have to do before braising can start, include:

larding or *barding* lean joints

trimming and tying up the meat so that it holds its shape during cooking and looks attractive to serve

marinating to add flavour

blanching to remove impurities from tongue, sweetbreads or ham (see page 77)

browning or *searing* the surface of the meat, and possibly the vegetable base.

3 Use base vegetables which will more or less keep their shape during cooking. Onions, carrots, leeks and celery are suitable. Avoid turnips and parsnips which would fall apart.

4 Choose an ovenproof cooking container with a tight fitting lid. The pan or pot should be just big enough for the food to fit in without touching the lid: otherwise the cooking liquid will not come up to the right level.

5 After bringing the cooking liquid to the boil on top of the stove, skim off any impurities or fat that rise to the surface (see page 74).

6 Check the food from time to time during cooking. You need to keep an eye on:

the quantity of the liquid. If it has reduced too much and there is a danger of the food drying out, add fresh stock or sauce (at boiling temperature)

the temperature. The liquid should not boil vigorously. If it does, reduce the oven temperature

the appearance of excess fat or impurities. These should be skimmed off and thrown away.

7 The sauce should be neither so thin that it runs off the food straight away, nor so thick that it clings to the surface. A good sauce will flow easily and evenly over the food, coating it evenly.

Glazing gives a very attractive appearance to joints of meat. The effect is partly created by the gelatin from the bones used in the stock:

1 As soon as the meat is cooked, remove from the cooking pan, place on a shallow dish or deep tray with some of the cooking liquid.

2 Return to the oven and baste frequently until the meat develops an attractive sheen or gloss: 15 to 30 minutes.

CHEF'S TIPS

Remove meats from their marinade about half an hour before cooking. Allow to drain, then dry thoroughly with absorbent kitchen paper or a clean cloth before browning. Damp meat will not brown properly.

If you are using rolled meat joints prepared by a butcher, check that they have been specially made for braising. Otherwise you may end up with a joint that carves poorly because it has been made up of pieces of meat.

Pot roasting

In pot roasting – also known by the French name *poêler* – the meat is cooked on a bed of chopped vegetables, with butter (or oil). The lid is kept closed during the first part of cooking, to trap the steam inside. This provides a moist heat.

Towards the end of cooking the lid is removed to allow the meat (cushion of veal in the photograph) to colour.

Stewing
`LEVELS 1 + 2`

Definition In the stewing process, pieces of food are gently simmered in a small amount of liquid. This liquid forms part of the finished dish and, with the help of other ingredients, contributes to the overall flavour.

The slow, gentle cooking is ideal for cooking tough cuts of meat and poultry. (Sometimes fish, or even fruit dishes, are described as stewed, although the cooking process has more in common with poaching or boiling.)

In stewing the cooking liquid is always thickened either:

- at the start of cooking, when a sauce is used, or a roux is made to thicken the liquid as it is added

- during cooking, by using ingredients such as potatoes which break down and thicken the liquid

- after the food has finished cooking.

CHEF'S TIPS

When making a large brown stew it is best to shallow fry the vegetables separately from the meat. Otherwise the juices released by the meat will make it difficult to brown the vegetables.

If the final sauce is too thin, strain it off into a second, clean saucepan. It can then be thickened without damaging or overcooking the main food item. Either boil rapidly to reduce, or add a thickening agent (see box opposite). Strain the corrected sauce back over the food (which should have been kept hot).

When cooked, meat should be easy to penetrate with a cocktail stick. The flesh on chicken joints or cutlets should come away from the bone easily.

How to get the best from stewing

1 The food needs to be stewed in small pieces, so it is only quite small food items that can be cooked whole, for example chicken legs.

2 If beans or lentils are being used in the stew, they may need to be soaked in advance, see *Pulses*.

3 Stews are usually begun on top of the stove and, once the cooking liquid has been brought to the boil, are covered with a tightly fitting lid and transferred to the oven. The more even, gentle heat of the oven produces a better (slower) speed of cooking, and reduces the risk of burning.

4 If cooking is continued on top of the stove, the stew needs to be stirred more frequently to make sure that food does not catch on the bottom of the pan and burn. The disadvantage of stirring is that it may cause the food to break up.

5 When vegetables contribute to the presentation (as well as the flavour) of the finished dish, add them to the stew in stages, so that they retain their shape and do not overcook.

Types of stew

There are a number of basic differences – of course, individual recipes give other variations.

Brown stews – meat (and any vegetables) browned by shallow frying, or briefly cooked in a very hot oven. Flour is then added to form a roux which will thicken the cooking liquid (brown stock).

Ragoût (from the French) – another name for a brown stew of beef.

Navarin – brown stew of mutton (or lamb), made with onions and, sometimes, potatoes, carrots, turnips and peas.

Frying meat in hot oil or placing it in a very hot oven enriches its colour and flavour. It used to be thought that these processes somehow sealed the meat, preventing the juices from escaping, but in fact this does not happen.

The onion and garlic in this photograph are being sweated: shallow fried very gently over a low heat without browning.

To skim the scum (impurities) and fat off a stew, carefully hold a ladle just beneath the surface of the liquid and move it forward and from side to side under the scum. Lift the ladle up and transfer the scum (with as little of the cooking liquid as possible) to another saucepan or bowl, so that it can be thrown away later.

Irish stew – white stew, made of stewing mutton or lamb, with potatoes, onions and other vegetables (see recipe on page 90).

White stews – made from white meats, such as chicken, veal, pork and lamb. There are two types:

blanquette – for tougher cuts of meat

- before stewing begins, impurities are removed by *blanching* (see page 77)
- vegetables are added to the stew raw, and on the whole used to provide flavour rather than colour
- liquid is thickened when the meat is almost cooked

fricassée – for better quality stewing meat such as chicken

- meat fried first, but extremely gently so that it does not brown (*sweating*)
- the cooking liquid (white stock) is thickened at the start of cooking, traditionally by making a roux.

Thickening a cooking liquid

The basic steps are:

1 Place a little of the thickening agent in a small bowl:
cornflour, arrowroot or waxy maize starch – use with cold water or cold stock
beurre manié – use equal quantities of flour and butter (no liquid)
fromage frais and flour – as beurre manié: the cheese gives a pleasant tangy flavour to the cooking liquid, and has a much lower fat content than butter (only 1 to 8%)
jaysee – use equal quantities of the cooking liquid and flour

2 Blend thoroughly so that you have a smooth paste.

3 Add the paste to the cooking liquid, a little at a time, and bring to the boil for a few minutes, stirring vigorously.

4 If the sauce is still too thin, repeat the process.

If using *egg yolk and cream* – called a *liaison* – to lighten the colour and add richness and flavour to a white stew, do so at the last minute. Allow the stew to reheat briefly, but not to boil, otherwise the sauce will curdle.

Thick yogurt, added at the last moment, will thicken a stew and provide a tangy flavour.

ACTION

Ask at your workplace if you can use a piece of stewing meat about 250 g (or you could buy a small amount).

1 Record the exact weight of the meat:

[_____] grammes

2 Trim off any fat and gristle and cut the meat into 20 to 25 mm cubes.

3 Work out and record:
a) weight of the cubes of meat:

[_____] grammes

b) weight of the bits you are unable to use:

[_____] grammes

c) cost per kilo of the cubes of meat (based on what the meat originally cost): [£ _____]

4 Divide the meat accurately into 2 portions. Using small saucepans with lids, and in each case ¼ litre of liquid:
a) place Portion A into boiling brown stock
b) place Portion B into cold water and bring to the boil

c) cover the saucepans with lids and transfer both of them to a moderate oven set at 180°C for 1 hour
d) strain off the cooking liquid

5 Record the weight of the portions of cooked meat:

Portion A [_____] grammes

Portion B [_____] grammes

6 Taste a sample of the liquid and cooked meat from each portion, and also note the appearance and texture:

Portion A

Portion B

7 Calculate and record the loss of weight for each sample: Portion A [_____] grammes

Portion B [_____] grammes

8 Calculate the cost per portion of the cooked meat:

Portion A [£ _____]

Portion B [£ _____]

Boiling

LEVEL 2

Definition Boiling is cooking in liquid at boiling point, that is when it is bubbling and giving off steam.

While the movement of the liquid (usually water or stock) can range from a rapid and vigorous bubbling action to a gentle simmering, the temperature remains constant (100°C for pure water boiled at sea level).

For meat and poultry, boiling is used:

- to remove impurities from, and cook joints which have been pickled or salted, such as silverside and brisket, gammon and ham

- cooking meat and poultry which is very flavoursome, but needs lengthy cooking in a moist environment, such as bacon hock or collar, leg of mutton, belly of pork and boiling fowls (old laying hens)

- remove impurities from and cook offal, such as oxtail, tongue (fresh or cured) and tripe (fresh or pickled)

- remove impurities from meat and some offal before braising or stewing – usually called *blanching*.

How to get the best from boiling

1 Joints should be of a fairly uniform shape, so that heat penetrates evenly through the meat during cooking.

2 Impurities that rise to the surface during the heating process should be skimmed off (if the liquid is not to be replaced). Otherwise they will make the liquid cloudy and unpleasantly flavoured.

The cooking process is started in cold water when it is important to remove excess salt, for example, from cured or pickled meat, or to remove undesirable substances like blood and fat from poor-quality meat.

After coming to the boil, the water is discarded, the meat rinsed under fresh cold water, returned to the (cleaned) pan which is refilled with cold water, and put back on the heat. This process, called *blanching* (see opposite), may be repeated for extremely salty food.

This photograph shows an attractive way of presenting Boiled leg of mutton with caper sauce. *Traditional British dishes have been enjoying something of a revival in recent years, as more customers appreciate the excellent flavours of some of these old recipes.*

CHEF'S TIPS

If you are boiling a joint of meat which will need a vegetable garnish or dumplings cooked in the same liquid, make sure you choose a big enough saucepan.

To test whether the meat is cooked, pierce it with a skewer or trussing needle. Hardly any pressure will be needed when the meat is cooked.

When you are boiling cured meats, and have brought the cold water to the boil with the meat in it, always taste the water. If it is very salty, replace it with fresh cold water and bring to the boil a second time.

ANSWER   ✓ ✓ ✓

KNOWLEDGE CHECK page 72

Time and temperature are important when cooking meat and poultry so the food is:

1 *Safe to eat: cooked to a sufficiently high temperature at the centre to kill harmful bacteria.*

2 *Enjoyable to eat: tender, cooked to the required degree of 'doneness', with the desired level of surface browning.*

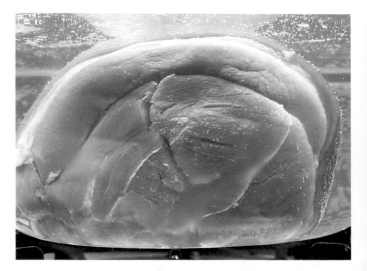

A gammon joint simmering in a special glass saucepan so you can see the gentle movement of the liquid.

Blanching meat and offal

1 Place in a suitable size saucepan and cover with cold water.

2 Bring to the boil and simmer for a short time (this will be stated in the recipe). You will usually see a scum form on the surface.

3 Remove the pan from the heat, carry carefully to a sink.

4 Position the pan under the cold water tap.

5 Turn the tap on and leave running until all the impurities have been washed away, and the cooking liquid has been replaced by cold, clear water. This stage is known as *refreshing*.

6 When there is a danger that the food will spill out into the sink, use a conical strainer to break the force of the water from the tap.

7 If the next stage is to boil the meat or offal to cook it, the pan should be washed out quickly, or exchanged for a clean one. Put the food back, cover with fresh cold water, add recipe ingredients and return to the heat.

HYGIENE 👣👣👣

Some bacteria produce spores which can survive even lengthy boiling. In the right conditions, the spores will germinate and the bacteria quickly start reproducing.

For this reason, boiled meats which are not going to be used straight away must be cooled rapidly and then stored in the refrigerator.

Steaming meat

The use of meat in steaming is usually restricted to steamed puddings. Meat which might otherwise be recommended for stewing can be used for this purpose: it should be cut into small chunks, placed in a pudding basin which has been lined with suet pastry and then steamed. Other ingredients are usually added to improve the flavour, as in a steak and mushroom pudding where chopped onion, mushrooms, chopped parsley, stock and seasoning would be included (see recipe on page 235).

Baking meat

When meat is baked, as opposed to roasted, something has to be done to stop the surfaces from drying out. There are many ways of doing this, the most common being:

• covering stewing-quality meat with a *pastry lid*, for example steak and kidney pie (the meat is cubed, and covered in stock to provide the moist conditions needed to make it tender)

• covering with a breadcrumb coating which enables tender pieces of turkey, chicken, pork and so forth to be baked in the oven (or grilled or shallow fried)

• enclosing with a batter, for instance *Toad-in-the-Hole*

• wrapping tender cuts in a paper bag, such as *suprême of chicken en papillotte* (meat is shallow fried briefly first)

• enclosing tender cuts with *pastry*, for example *leg of lamb en croûte*, or *fillet of beef Wellington,* a famous dish that is sometimes served at small banquets or private functions. With these types of dish, the meat has to be partially or completely cooked, then quickly chilled before wrapping in the pastry. The food is then returned to the oven and baked until the pastry has cooked and browned and the meat is thoroughly reheated.

ACTION

Prepare a poster to go on display in the staff changing room of a busy catering kitchen. The aim of the poster is to remind staff of the main contamination threats when preparing, cooking and storing meat and poultry dishes.

1 You may find it helpful to recall the most common causes of food poisoning – described earlier, in *Hygiene.*

2 A suggested theme for your poster is *The temptation in busy catering kitchens is to cut corners, but this is playing a dangerous game.*

3 Alternatively, decide for yourself the messages you will concentrate on. Remember, too many and your poster is likely to be ineffective.

Finishing and presenting

Portioning roast poultry

1 Remove legs and cut across the knee joints to divide each leg into a drumstick and a thigh. In some establishments, the next step is to remove the knuckles.

2 Remove winglets (if these have not already been removed before cooking).

3 Cut off each wing parallel to the breastbone and down through the wing joints. Ensure that four similar-sized portions will be produced from the wings and breast. *Optional*: trim off the knuckles from each wing.

4 Holding the bird upright (parson's nose upwards), chop down between the breast and carcase.

5 Cut any excess rib cage away from the breast and cut the breast in half. Alternatively, cut the two sides of the breast cleanly off the rib cage.

6 The aim of careful portioning is to give each person a piece of white meat (breast) and piece of dark (leg). Avoid putting two pieces of meat containing a lot of bone in one serving. The usual arrangement is for a portion to consist of either a thigh and a wing, or a drumstick and a piece of breast. A 1½ kg bird will provide four portions.

7 The meat of very large birds, such as turkeys, should be carved into thin slices. A serving will then usually include slices from the breast and slices from the leg.

8 If the carved meat is to be silver served to a number of people, or presented on a buffet, then it is helpful to keep each portion reasonably separate on the serving dish, and use the garnish to help identify each portion easily. Never overfill dishes, or pour too much gravy over the meat.

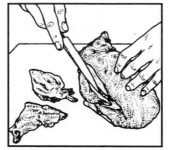
Step 1

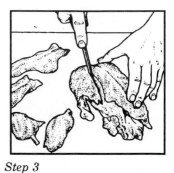
Step 3

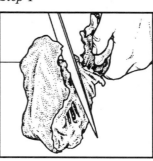
Step 4

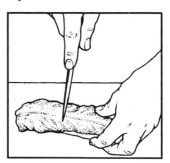
Step 5

These illustrations show a duck being carved. A chicken is carved in the same way. Alternatively, for duck and large roasting chickens, the legs can be prepared as already described, but the wing and the breast meat can be carved in slices, parallel to the length of the bird. The photograph shows this.

Traditional accompaniments for roasts

Beef Yorkshire pudding, roast gravy, horseradish sauce, watercress

Lamb Roast gravy, mint sauce or mint jelly, watercress

Mutton Roast gravy, white onion sauce, redcurrant jelly, watercress

Pork Sage and onion stuffing, roast gravy, apple sauce, watercress

Veal Parsley, thyme and lemon stuffing, roast gravy, watercress

Chicken Bread sauce, roast gravy, game chips, grilled bacon (*if stuffed*: parsley and thyme stuffing)

Turkey Chestnut stuffing, bread sauce, roast gravy, grilled chipolatas and bacon, cranberry sauce, watercress

Carving: general procedure

1 Select the correct knife and sharpen if necessary (see *Knife skills*).

2 Select a clean chopping board (yellow-coded for cooked meat). Wipe with a sanitiser.

3 Hold the joint firmly during carving, with a suitable fork. With legs and shoulders, it is sometimes easier and safer to hold the joint by the bone.

4 Where practical and comfortable, slice away from you, so that if the knife does slip there is less risk of cutting yourself.

5 Cut across the grain of the meat.

6 Let the knife do the work for you: use a gentle sawing action. If the knife is really sharp, as it should be, there is no need to push it hard.

Carving a leg of lamb or mutton

by The British Meat Information Service

1 With the meatier side of the leg uppermost, carve a narrow wedge-shaped piece of meat from the middle of the leg, right down to the bone.

2 Carve slices from either side of the first cut, slanting the knife to obtain larger slices.

3 For the underside, turn the joint over, remove any unwanted fat and carve in long horizontal slices.

Carving a shoulder of lamb

Boned

Carve into fairly thick slices, across the thickest part.

Not boned

1 Starting on the meatier side, carve a slice from the centre of the joint, cutting through to the bone in a V shape.

2 Cut slices from either side of the V, working outwards.

3 Carve the meat remaining at the top of the shank bone with short, vertical slices to the bone.

Carving best end of lamb

Cut right down between each cutlet bone. Serve two or three cutlets per portion.

Carving rib and sirloin of beef

Carve in the same direction as the rib bones in thin, even slices.

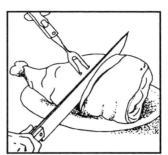

Leg: step 1

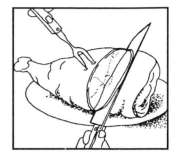

Leg: step 2

Leg: step 3

For a smaller leg, carve on the slant, towards the bone. Start at the shin end and work towards the thick part of the leg.

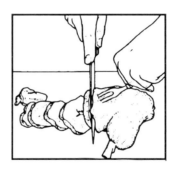

Carving a boned shoulder.

Carving beef wing rib and sirloin.

Before carving a rolled joint of meat, remove the string, then cut down through the meat in even slices.

Finishing and presenting grilled and shallow fried dishes

A colourful, appropriate garnish improves the presentation. Some garnishes also add flavour.

Respect traditional and workplace practice. If the dish is called by a certain name on the menu, then that is the garnish that must be used. Practise your own creative ideas at home, or on dishes where you have the discretion to use any suitable garnish:

1   Choose colours that contrast attractively with the other items being served.

2   Consider the huge range of healthy, vegetable garnishes: watercress, mustard and cress, grilled tomatoes, grilled mushrooms, parsley, lemon wedges, lettuce leaves, various boiled/steamed vegetables arranged in small bunches like bouquets of flowers.

3   Deep-fried potatoes are a popular garnish for steaks. They can be presented in various ways (see page 161): straw (cut into fine strips), chipped (very thinly sliced) or wafer (cut on a mandolin using a corrugated blade). French fried onions (onion rings dipped in milk and flour then deep fried) are also a popular garnish (page 173).

4   Use fat-rich garnishes with care. Butter, or butter blended with chopped parsley, shrimps, anchovy fillets or garlic, is the traditional garnish for many grilled and shallow fried dishes. Offer the garnish separately — it will keep firm if placed in a sauceboat with iced water — or check first that the customer does want it placed on the food.

Some traditional garnishes

Mirabeau Topped with anchovy fillets and olives, accompanied by watercress and anchovy butter.

Henry IV Watercress, parsley butter and deep fried Pont Neuf potatoes (sticks 40 mm long and 20 mm square).

Vert-pré Watercress, parsley butter and straw potatoes.

Maître d'Hôtel Watercress and parsley butter.

Caprice Fried bananas, lemon, parsley.

Américaine Watercress, grilled rashers of bacon, grilled tomato, French fried onions and straw potatoes.

This fillet steak is ready for service, cooked to the customer's requirements and garnished with watercress, straw potatoes, a grilled tomato and a decoratively prepared mushroom.

Note the use of colours in the garnish for the rump steak and among the ingredients for the kebab (recipe page 86). In this photograph the butter has been placed on the steak, but remember that some customers may not want to add extra fat to their food, so it is best offered separately.

Attractive or unusual serving dishes, where available, can do much to enhance the presentation of food.

Other presentation tips

When a *shallow fried dish* that requires sauce is prepared for large numbers, it is better to prepare the sauce in advance.

1 After the food has been cooked, drain off the fat from the pan, add a little stock, wine, spirit or just water (depending on the sauce).

2 Boil this up in the pan, stirring and scraping the bottom of the pan so that the thick juices left from the meat are dissolved.

3 Once the liquid has reduced by about half (or less if your sauce is too thick), strain into the hot sauce.

When serving *grilled or shallow fried meats*, such as veal or chicken, with a sauce, first pat the meat's surface with absorbent paper to remove any excess cooking fat. Otherwise the fat may form a line through the sauce and spoil the presentation.

Shallow fried meats which have been cooked in breadcrumbs must not be covered before service, or they will lose their crispness. For the same reason, any accompanying sauce should be offered in a sauceboat, not poured over the food.

If a *braised dish or stew*, for example, is to be presented to the customer in the container in which it was cooked, remove burn marks and other cooking stains by rubbing with a dampened cloth which has been dipped in salt.

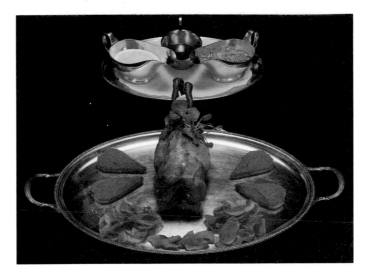

Remember the most simple garnishes are often the most effective.

Heart-shaped croûtons (as shown with this roast pheasant, where they have been covered with game farce, a type of pâté) also form an attractive garnish to stews and casseroles. The shaped piece of bread is fried in a little oil and/or butter until golden brown, then the point is dipped in chopped parsley.

ACTION

For two cuts of meat/poultry which are grilled or shallow fried in your workplace/college restaurant, create your own garnish as an alternative to the one currently used. If appropriate, come up with a new name for the dish.

Note your ideas below, so that you can discuss them with your assessor. If you have a chance, make up the garnish and photograph the dish as you see it presented.

Presentation of a fillet of beef with oysters poached in a red wine and pink peppercorn sauce in the Metropole Hotels group. The company's manual shows staff exactly how each dish should look when it reaches the customer.

Food Preparation and Cooking

Meat and poultry — Finishing and presenting concluded

ACTION

What follows is a list of some of the things that can go wrong in cooking meat and poultry.

Various suggestions are given for the possible reason/what could be done to correct the problem.

Work through the list, mark with a:

✓ those that you think are correct/ could cause the problem/will work

X those that are incorrect/would not cause the problem/will not work/ have nothing to do with the problem

? those that you think may be correct/may work/not sufficient information given.

Food not browning
- [ ] meat was marinaded
- [ ] food damp at the start of cooking
- [ ] a coating should have been used
- [ ] ingredients for stew were blanched
- [ ] roasting tray too full
- [ ] keep cooking
- [ ] put the frying pan under the grill
- [ ] red meat seasoned with salt before cooking
- [ ] baste the roast more often
- [ ] transfer the food to a microwave
- [ ] take some food out of the frying pan
- [ ] add more charcoal to the barbecue
- [ ] cover with kitchen foil
- [ ] move the grill tray closer to the heat
- [ ] turn the heat down
- [ ] drain the cooking juices out from the frying pan

Brown stew too pale
- [ ] add gravy browning
- [ ] turn heat up/increase oven temperature
- [ ] meat/vegetables not browned properly before adding liquid ingredients
- [ ] add wine
- [ ] add demi-glace
- [ ] white stock used

White stew light brown
- [ ] vegetables sweated
- [ ] roux overcooked
- [ ] brown stock used
- [ ] add beurre manié

- [ ] blend in a little fromage blanc or quark

Food undercooked
- [ ] grill/oven not prewarmed
- [ ] food not adequately defrosted
- [ ] temperature probe was touching bone
- [ ] roasting time based on weight of joint
- [ ] stir fry dish cooked in sauté pan
- [ ] continue cooking
- [ ] turn the heat up
- [ ] baste with marinade
- [ ] transfer to the microwave oven
- [ ] transfer shallow fried dish to oven

(Hot) sauce too thin
- [ ] too much flour used for roux
- [ ] add gelatin
- [ ] use a jayzee
- [ ] boil vigorously
- [ ] add egg yolks and boil
- [ ] add cornflour and serve immediately
- [ ] use arrowroot

Oil in pan starts to smoke
- [ ] turn the heat down and continue cooking
- [ ] wrong type of oil or fat is being used
- [ ] add some fresh oil and carry on cooking
- [ ] pour off the smoking oil and replace with fresh oil

Food tough and dry
- [ ] cooked too quickly
- [ ] cooked too slowly
- [ ] cooked at too high a temperature
- [ ] quality chosen not suitable for the cooking process
- [ ] meat was pierced by a fork while cooking
- [ ] recipe cooking guide incorrect
- [ ] delay in serving the food after cooking
- [ ] temperature probe was touching bone
- [ ] delay in serving the food after carving or portioning
- [ ] roasts basted regularly
- [ ] meat/poultry should not have been barded before cooking
- [ ] roast turkey cooked resting on its side
- [ ] serve with a sauce

Food looks and/or tastes burnt
- [ ] stew stirred regularly during cooking

- [ ] cooked at too high a temperature
- [ ] food not properly trimmed, tied up or trussed
- [ ] cooking container on the bottom shelf of a conventional gas oven
- [ ] thickening roux in a stew cooked for a few minutes
- [ ] flaring up during cooking on a barbecue grill
- [ ] add cream or yogurt

Meat distorted/misshapen
- [ ] roast was tied/trussed
- [ ] poor quality meat was used
- [ ] meat not trimmed properly

Food broken up
- [ ] constant stirring during stir fry cooking
- [ ] badly handled during and after cooking
- [ ] overcooked
- [ ] meat cut too small
- [ ] meat tough
- [ ] add more sauce

Food which should be crisp is soggy
- [ ] kept hot for short time after cooking
- [ ] not covered before service
- [ ] oil not hot enough
- [ ] cooking temperature too high

Sautéed meat or poultry resembles stew
- [ ] cooking not finished in sauce
- [ ] food left resting in warm sauce for too long

Stew is greasy
- [ ] butter used for browning stage
- [ ] meat not trimmed adequately
- [ ] fat skimmed off during cooking
- [ ] stew standing for long time before service

Marinated meat uneven or unpleasant colour
- [ ] meat entirely covered by marinade
- [ ] meat not turned regularly in the marinade
- [ ] aluminium basin used to hold the marinating food

Serving dish looks crowded
- [ ] remove some of the garnish
- [ ] reduce the portion size
- [ ] transfer everything to a larger serving dish

Food looks lost on serving dish
- [ ] transfer to a smaller serving dish
- [ ] use additional garnish
- [ ] add some more food to the dish

Roast turkey with chestnut stuffing

Key learning points
» prepare chestnut stuffing
» roast turkey
» make roast gravy
» prepare and cook rolls of bacon and chipolata sausages

SERVES 20

1 × 7 kg	turkey, trussed	1 × 15 ½ lb
25 ml	oil	1 fl oz
	salt to taste	

Stuffing

50 g	margarine or butter	2 oz
175 g	onion, finely chopped	6 oz
225 g	white breadcrumbs	8 oz
75 g	chopped suet	3 oz
450 g	fresh chestnuts	1 lb
225 g	pork sausage meat	8 oz
2	eggs	2
15 ml	mixed dried herbs	1 tbsp
	seasoning to taste	

Garnish and accompaniments

2	bunches washed watercress	2
20	chipolata sausages	20
20	rashers of bacon, rolled	20
1 litre	brown stock to make gravy	2 pt
575 ml	bread sauce (page 144)	1 pt
575 ml	cranberry sauce (page 145)	1 pt

1 Place the turkey in a roasting tray on its side. Season lightly if desired. Brush with oil, and place in an oven at 165°C.

2 Cook until lightly coloured, basting from time to time. Turn the bird over on to its other side and continue cooking.

3 When both sides are coloured, turn the turkey breast-side up and complete the cooking. A general guide for the cooking time is 30 to 40 minutes per kilogram, which in this case would work out at 3½ to 4 hours. A temperature probe inserted into the thickest part of the thigh should record a minimum of 75°C.

4 Transfer the turkey to a clean tray, with the vent of the bird up so that any steam can easily escape. Leave in a warm place while you make the gravy.

5 Grill the chipolatas and the bacon.

6 Remove the string, and carve the leg and breast into neat slices.

7 Arrange the slices attractively on warm serving dishes, along with the stuffing, chipolatas and bacon rolls. Coat with a little of the hot gravy, add watercress and serve immediately, accompanied by gravy, hot bread sauce and cranberry sauce.

Stuffing

1 Slit the skin of the chestnuts once on the domed side. Place them (on a baking tray in a little water) in a hot oven for 8 to 10 minutes. Cool slightly, then peel and roughly chop.

2 Cook the onions gently in the fat for 2 to 3 minutes. Add the herbs and cook for a further 2 minutes. Allow to cool in a large bowl, then mix in the breadcrumbs, suet, chestnuts, sausage meat, seasoning and eggs.

3 Shape the stuffing into a thick sausage, about 50 mm in diameter and wrap in lightly oiled greaseproof paper. Cook in a low-pressure steamer for about 1 hour.

Alternatively: divide the stuffing into 40 half-portions. Cut the rashers of bacon into two halves. Place a ball of stuffing towards the thicker end of the rasher, and roll the bacon round the stuffing. Place on a lightly oiled tray and cook in the oven with the turkey for 30 to 40 minutes.

Gravy

1 Carefully pour off the fat from the roasting tray, leaving behind the sediment and any juices.

2 Sprinkle with salt, and heat on top of the stove until the sediment sticks to the bottom of the tray.

3 Pour off any remaining fat. Add the stock, bring to the boil and simmer for 2 to 3 minutes, stirring until the sediment has dissolved.

4 Strain into a clean saucepan. Skim off any fat which rises to the surface. Reheat. Check seasoning and serve.

Roast saddle of lamb with apricot and ginger stuffing
by the New Zealand Lamb Catering Advisory Service

Key learning points
» prepare apricot stuffing
» stuff and roll a boned joint of meat
» roast boned saddle of lamb

SERVES 6 to 8

1.4 kg	boneless saddle of lamb	3 lb
	oil for basting	
	salt to taste	
8	apricot halves (garnish)	8

Stuffing

175 g	dried apricots, soaked for 4 hours	6 oz
100 g	fresh breadcrumbs	4 oz
50 g	onion, finely chopped	2 oz
10 ml	fresh ginger, finely chopped	2 tsp
	seasoning to taste	
1	egg, beaten lightly	1

1 Drain the apricots, chop into small pieces.

2 Thoroughly combine the stuffing ingredients. Lay along the centre of the saddle and carefully roll the meat to enclose the stuffing. Secure with string.

3 Place the saddle in a roasting tray, brush with oil. Season with salt if required.

4 Roast in a preheated oven at 200°C for about 10 minutes, then turn the heat down to 170°C. Cook for a further 70 to 90 minutes to serve pink (medium-done). The final internal temperature should be 70°C to 75°C.

5 Carve and decorate with apricot halves.

Roasting – cooking times *by Meat and Livestock Commission*

Beef – rare	20 minutes per 450 g/1 lb plus 20 minutes
Beef – medium	25 minutes per 450 g/1 lb plus 25 minutes
Beef – well done	30 minutes per 450 g/1 lb plus 30 minutes
Pork – well done	35 minutes per 450 g/1 lb plus 35 minutes
Lamb – medium	25 minutes per 450 g/1 lb plus 25 minutes
Lamb – well done	30 minutes per 450 g/1 lb plus 30 minutes

Joints weighing less than 1.25 kg (2½ lb) may need 5 minutes per 450 g/1 lb extra cooking time.

Braised gammon in mushroom sauce
by Pork and Bacon Promotion Council and others

Key learning points
» make a roux
» braise gammon

SERVES 10

1.25 kg	gammon joint (boneless)	2½ lb
575 ml	brown stock (hot)	1 pt
50 g	margarine	2 oz
25 g	tomato paste	1 oz
100 g	button mushrooms, sliced	4 oz
25 g	flour	1 oz
50 g	onion, finely chopped	2 oz
	seasoning to taste	

1 In the braising pan which you will be using to cook the meat, shallow fry the onion and mushrooms.

2 Add the flour, stirring in thoroughly. Allow to cook for a few minutes, stirring all the time. This is making a roux (see page 143).

3 Add the tomato paste and mix well.

4 Gradually add the hot stock, stirring thoroughly with each addition until you get a smooth paste.

5 When all the stock has been added (by this time the sauce will be fairly thin), bring to the boil and season.

6 Place the gammon in the sauce, baste well with the sauce, cover the pan and transfer to the oven at about 180°C for 70 minutes or so. Baste from time to time with the sauce.

7 When cooked, allow the gammon to rest for 10 minutes.

8 Carve into neat slices and arrange on the warm serving dish. Surround by the sauce. Offer remaining sauce in a sauceboat.

Leg of lamb pot roast *Pierna de cordero de Rioja*
by the New Zealand Lamb Catering Advisory Service

Key learning points
» prepare a variation of braising/stewing/pot roasting
» boil pulses

Pilgrims passed through the Rioja region on their way to visit the shrine of St James, patron saint of Spain. In medieval times, a local man built a paved road, a bridge and an inn where pilgrims could rest and enjoy the Rioja wine and a meal made from the renowned beans of the region.

SERVES 10

1.5 kg	leg of lamb, boned and rolled	3 lb
	seasoning to taste	
50 ml	olive oil	2 fl oz
4	cloves garlic, peeled, cut into slivers	4
20	shallots, peeled and trimmed	20
5	large carrots, peeled and cubed	5
575 ml	lamb or chicken stock	1 pt
250 g	white beans, soaked for 12 hours	9 oz
50 g	onion, sliced	2 oz
1	bay leaf	1

1 Rub the leg of lamb all over with salt and pepper.

2 Brown the lamb in hot oil in a large pan, adding the garlic, shallots and carrots and browning those also.

3 Pour in the stock, bring to the boil and simmer for 1½ hours.

4 While the meat is cooking, cook the beans in a separate pot with plenty of water, the onion and bay leaf. Bring to the boil, cover and simmer for 1 hour, adding a little salt when the beans are half cooked.

5 Drain the beans, and add them to the lamb. Cook for a further 20 minutes.

6 To serve, remove the lamb and slice. Arrange the slices on the serving dish, garnish with the beans, carrots and shallots and pour over some of the gravy.

Roast beef with mustard and black peppercorn crust
by Meat and Livestock Commission

Key learning points
» roast beef
» enhance the presentation and flavour of roast meat by baking with a crust during the last stage of cooking

SERVES 4 to 6

900 g–1.35 kg	beef topside	2–3 lb
15 ml	black peppercorns, crushed	1 tbsp
45 ml	English mustard	3 tbsp
30 ml	fresh parsley, chopped	2 tbsp
5 ml	oil	1 tsp
25 g	breadcrumbs	1 oz

1 Press the crushed black peppercorns all over the surface of the joint, and place on a trivet in a roasting tin. Roast at 180°C for the calculated time (see previous page for table of roasting times).

2 Remove joint from the oven 15 minutes before the end of cooking. Spread the mustard over the surface. Mix the breadcrumbs with the oil and parsley, and press on to the mustard.

3 Return to the oven for the final 15 minutes until the breadcrumbs are golden.

4 Allow the joint to stand for 10 minutes before carving.

Chicken tikka irani
by Sainath Rao

Key learning points
» prepare a marinade
» cook chicken in a tandoor

SERVES 2

500 g	chicken breasts, boned and skinned, cut into chunks	1 lb 2 oz
200 ml	yogurt	7 fl oz
30 ml	single cream	2 tbsp
30 ml	oil	2 tbsp
15 ml	lemon juice	1 tbsp
3 ml	garlic paste	½ tsp
3 ml	white pepper powder	½ tsp
	pinch green cardamom powder	
10 ml	salt	2 tsp

1 Mix all ingredients of the marinade together in a bowl. Add the chicken pieces and stir well. Cover and place in the refrigerator for at least 4 hours.

2 Drain the chicken. Place the pieces slightly apart from each other on the thicker tandoor skewer.

3 Place the loaded skewers into the hot tandoor vertically. Replace the oven lid. At 2 minute intervals, until the chicken is cooked (about 4 to 5 minutes), turn the skewers. Towards the end of cooking, brush with oil or butter to get a crustier finish.

Lamb mince kebabs
by Sainath Rao

Key learning points
» prepare kebabs with mince
» cook kebabs in a tandoor

SERVES 2

500 g	lamb mince	1 lb 2 oz
5 ml	green chilli, chopped	1 tsp
5 ml	fresh coriander leaves, chopped	1 tsp
10 ml	salt	2 tsp
50 g	butter	2 oz
	mixed spices powder (Garam Masala)	

1 Mix all the ingredients together in a bowl and divide into about 8 equal portions.

2 Roll each portion in the palm of your hand. Then pat around a thick tandoor skewer so they join up forming a long, evenly shaped tube about 5 mm thickness, surrounding the skewer.

From time to time dip your fingers into cold water so the mince sticks to the skewer not to your fingers.

3 Insert the skewer into a hot tandoor, put the lid on and cook until done. Rotate rods during cooking (3 to 10 minutes).

Barbecue spare ribs of pork Chinese style

Key learning points
» prepare a marinade
» grill or barbecue spare ribs of pork

SERVES 10

3 kg	spare ribs of pork (trimmed and in sections of 4 or 5 ribs)	6 lb
10	wedges or halves of lemon (garnish)	10

Marinade

100 ml	oil	4 fl oz
200 g	onions, roughly chopped	8 oz
8	cloves of garlic, crushed and peeled	8
2	small chilli peppers (flesh only)	2
50 g	spring onions, trimmed	2 oz
20 g	root ginger	¾ oz
175 g	honey	6 oz
225 ml	soy sauce	8 fl oz
125 ml	sherry	4 fl oz
125 ml	vinegar	4 fl oz
50 ml	lemon juice	2 fl oz
10 g	lemon zest	½ oz
	seasoning to taste	

1 Liquidise the marinade ingredients to a smooth, thick liquid. Pour into a large glass, porcelain or stainless steel bowl.

2 Cut through the bottom of each rib and up between the ribs, taking care to leave them joined at the top.

3 Place the ribs in the marinade and thoroughly baste.

4 Cover and keep chilled for 4 to 6 hours. Two or three times during this period, turn the ribs over in the marinade and baste them.

5 Remove the ribs from the marinade and drain.

6 Grill until brown on both sides and fully cooked, about 15 to 20 minutes. Turn the ribs over when half-done and baste them with the marinade during cooking.

7 Cut into single ribs and place on a warm serving dish. Garnish with the lemon. Serve at once.

Mexican burgers
by Meat and Livestock Commission

Key learning points
» prepare burgers from minced meat
» make a savoury sauce
» grill or barbecue burgers

SERVES 6

450 g	lean minced meat	1 lb
1	small onion, finely chopped	1
1	clove garlic, crushed and peeled	1
½ each	small red and green pepper, seeded and finely chopped	½ each
5–10 ml	chilli powder	1–2 tsp
15 ml	tomato ketchup	1 tbsp
50 g	Bulgar or cracked wheat	2 oz
	seasoning to taste	
1	egg, size 3, beaten	1
	plain flour, to shape burgers	
	oil for cooking	

Sauce

1 × 227 g	can tomatoes, chopped	1 × 8 oz
15 ml	clear honey	1 tbsp
	tabasco sauce, dash	
4	spring onions, trimmed and chopped	4

1 Soak the Bulgar or cracked wheat for 10 minutes in boiling water (enough to cover). Drain well.

2 In a large bowl mix together all the ingredients for the burgers until thoroughly combined.

3 Place in a refrigerator, chill for 15 minutes.

4 With lightly floured hands, divide mixture into 6 portions, and shape into burgers.

5 Brush the burgers with a little oil and grill or barbecue for 6 to 8 minutes each side.

6 Meanwhile make the sauce. Combine all the ingredients in a saucepan, bring to the boil and simmer for 10 minutes until reduced slightly.

7 Place the burgers on warm serving dishes, garnish as you wish, and serve accompanied by the sauce.

Rump steak maître d'hôtel

Key learning points
- » grill steak
- » make parsley (maître d'hôtel) butter

SERVES 1

1 x 225 g	rump steak	1 x 8 oz
	seasoning to taste	
	oil	
	few sprigs watercress (garnish)	
Parsley butter		*makes 50 g (2 oz)*
50 g	butter	2 oz
	squeeze of lemon juice	
	chopped parsley, good pinch	
	cayenne pepper, pinch	

1 Lightly brush each side of the steak with oil. Season with pepper (if required). Oil the grill bars.

2 Grill the steak until it has developed a good colour on one side. Turn over and continue to cook until done to the required degree. If the meat is drying out, brush with a little oil. When cooked, season with salt (if required).

3 Place on a warm serving dish and decorate with watercress. Accompany by a slice of parsley butter placed in a sauceboat with iced water so that it remains firm.

Parsley butter

1 Mix the butter with a fork until soft. Add the lemon juice, parsley and cayenne pepper and thoroughly mix together.

2 Place the mixture on a sheet of dampened greaseproof paper. Roll it to form a neat sausage shape about 25 mm in diameter. Put in refrigerator to harden.

3 For service, remove the paper and cut the roll into thin rounds about 3 mm thick.

Spicy yogurt chicken
by British Chicken Information Service

Key learning points
- » prepare a spicy coating for a grilled chicken dish
- » grill quarters of chicken

Accompany by boiled rice, a mixed salad, pickles and Indian bread.

SERVES 4

4	chicken quarters	4
175 ml	natural yogurt	6 fl oz
1	small lemon for the rind and juice	1
10 ml	medium curry paste	2 tsp
15 ml	sesame seeds	1 tbsp

1 Remove the skin from the chicken and slash the flesh at intervals with a sharp knife.

2 Mix together the yogurt, finely grated rind of the lemon, juice of the lemon and curry paste.

3 Spread this mixture evenly over the chicken and place on a foil-lined grillpan or baking sheet.

4 Grill the chicken under a moderate heat until golden brown on both sides and thoroughly cooked: about 15 minutes or so. Turn the chicken half-way through cooking and when nearly cooked, sprinkle with sesame seeds. Serve at once.

Bacon stir fry
by Pork and Bacon Promotion Council and others

Key learning point
- » stir fry bacon

SERVES 10

900 g	diced streaky bacon	2 lb
50 g	sliced onion	2 oz
225 g	sweetcorn kernels	8 oz
225 g	beansprouts	8 oz
30 ml	oil	2 tbsp
25 g	ground ginger	1 oz
	grated rind of 1 orange	

1 Fry the bacon until crisp, remove to a warm serving dish, and keep warm.

2 Fry the onions and beansprouts in oil. Add the sweetcorn, ginger and orange.

3 Quickly toss all the ingredients together and serve at once.

Kebabs Turkish style

Key learning points
- » prepare a marinade
- » grill or barbecue lamb kebabs

SERVES 4

500 g	cubed lean lamb (40 mm x 10 mm)	1¼ lb
12–16	onion pieces (about 40 mm long)	12–16
12–16	red pepper (40 mm squares)	12–16
12–16	green pepper (40 mm squares)	12–16
12–16	whole mushrooms (stalks removed)	12–16
8	fresh (or dried) bay leaves	8
Marinade		
25 g	onion, roughly chopped	1 oz
2.5 ml	grated lemon zest	½ tsp
15 ml	coriander leaves, chopped	1 tbsp
25 ml	oil	1 fl oz
150 ml	natural yogurt	5 fl oz
1	clove garlic, crushed and peeled	1
	squeeze lemon juice	
	seasoning to taste	

1 Thoroughly mix or liquidise the ingredients for the marinade.

2 Place the lamb in a glass, porcelain or stainless steel bowl. Pour over the marinade. Cover and place in a refrigerator for about 6 hours. (Stir the lamb two or three times during this period.)

3 Remove the lamb from the marinade. Thread the pieces of food neatly on the skewer, so that you build up a repeating pattern of the various ingredients until the skewer is full/all the ingredients have been used. The pattern might be: onion, bayleaf, meat, red pepper, mushroom, meat, green pepper, then start on the next skewer. When all four skewers have been partly filled in this way, return to the first and start again. Ideally by the time you have finished each skewer will be equally full, with a similar arrangement of ingredients.

4 Brush over the surfaces of the kebabs with the marinade.

5 Grill the kebabs. Turn as required and brush with marinade.

6 Place on the warm service dish. Serve at once.

Marinated walnut chicken breasts
by The British Iceberg Growers' Association

Key learning points
» prepare a marinade
» barbecue or grill chicken

SERVES 4

4	chicken breasts, skinned and boned	4
120 ml	walnut oil	4 fl oz
1	lemon, squeezed for juice	1
2	cloves garlic, crushed and peeled	2
30 ml	fresh tarragon, chopped	2 tbsp
5 ml	grated orange rind	1 tsp
	seasoning to taste	
50 g	walnuts, roughly chopped	2 oz
30 ml	medium dry sherry	2 tbsp
½	iceberg lettuce, roughly chopped	½
2	fresh peaches or nectarines, halved, stoned and sliced	2
	sprigs fresh tarragon (garnish)	

1 Put the chicken breasts into a shallow dish. Spike each one 3 or 4 times at regular intervals with the tip of a sharp knife (to allow the marinade to permeate the chicken).

2 Mix half the oil with the lemon juice, sherry, garlic, chopped tarragon, orange rind, seasoning and half the walnuts. Spoon this over the chicken, cover and chill for at least 4 hours.

3 Drain the chicken breasts, and thread each on to a skewer lengthways. Barbecue over a moderate heat for 8 to 10 minutes, or grill for 12 minutes.

4 Meanwhile, pour the marinade into a saucepan, add the remaining oil and bring to the boil. Keep warm.

5 Toss the lettuce with the peach slices and arrange on the serving dish. Immediately arrange the spiked chicken breasts on top, spoon over the hot dressing, garnish with the sprigs of tarragon, remaining walnuts and serve.

Pork steaks with lemon and chive sauce
by Meat and Livestock Commission

Key learning points
» prepare a marinade
» grill or barbecue pork
Limes can be used instead of lemons.

SERVES 4

4 × 175--200 g	pork steaks	4 × 6–7 oz
120 ml	white wine	8 tbsp
30 ml	oil	2 tbsp
30 ml	lemon juice	2 tbsp
	seasoning to taste	
2	bay leaves	2

Sauce

1	lemon, for grated rind and juice	1
25 g	chives, chopped	1 oz
10 ml	cornflour	2 tsp
125 ml	single cream	4 fl oz
	seasoning to taste	

1 Mix all the marinade ingredients together, add the pork steaks, cover and refrigerate for 1 to 2 hours.

2 Drain the steaks, and grill for 7 to 8 minutes on each side, depending on thickness.

3 Meanwhile, blend the cornflour with a little cream. Put in a saucepan with the other sauce ingredients. Heat gently, stirring continuously until the sauce thickens. Pour over the pork and serve.

Veal escalopes in cider sauce with Viennese cabbage
by Dufrais

Key learning points
» shallow fry veal (or pork)
» cook red cabbage in Viennese style
» make an accompanying sauce and finish with cream

SERVES 4

60 ml	grapeseed oil	4 tbsp
2	medium onions, 1 sliced, 1 chopped	2
450 g	red cabbage, shredded	1 lb
50 g	brown sugar	2 oz
75 ml	cider vinegar	5 tbsp
4	veal or pork escalopes	4
1	eating apple, peeled and sliced (optional)	1
15 ml	wholegrain mustard	1 tbsp
150 ml	double or single cream	5 fl oz
	seasoning to taste	

1 In a large saucepan, heat 30 ml (2 tbsp) oil and soften sliced onion. Add cabbage, sugar, 30 ml vinegar and 60 ml water. Stir well, cover and gently simmer for 35 to 40 minutes.

2 Meanwhile, heat 15 ml (1 tbsp) oil in a large frying pan. Fry veal escalopes for 2 to 3 minutes on each side, pork for 4 to 6 minutes. Remove from pan and keep hot. Add remaining oil and chopped onion to the pan and cook for 3 to 4 minutes. Add apple, remaining vinegar and mustard. Cook for 5 minutes or until the apple is soft.

3 Stir in cream and season well. Replace escalopes, heat through and serve with the cabbage.

Chicken breasts with walnut pesto
by British Chicken Information Service

Key learning points
» stuff chicken breasts
» shallow fry chicken

SERVES 6

6	chicken breasts, skinned	6
2	cloves garlic, peeled	2
90 ml	fresh basil, chopped	6 tbsp
60 ml	fresh parsley, chopped	4 tbsp
50 g	Parmesan cheese, grated	2 oz
50 g	walnuts, chopped	2 oz
90 ml	olive oil	6 tbsp
	ground black pepper	
30 ml	wholemeal flour	2 tbsp

1 For the pesto: place garlic, basil, parsley, walnuts, Parmesan and half the oil in a food processor and blend for a few seconds until finely chopped.

2 Cut a slit through one side of each chicken breast to open out like a pocket. Fill this pocket with the pesto mixture.

3 Mix a little pepper into the flour, then toss the chicken in this to coat lightly. Shake off excess.

4 Heat remaining oil in a pan and fry the chicken gently for 12 to 15 minutes, or until cooked. Turn once during cooking. Serve immediately.

Chicken Maryland

Key learning points
» coat chicken suprêmes with breadcrumbs
» prepare and cook sweetcorn pancakes
» shallow fry chicken

SERVES 4

4 x 100 g	suprêmes of chicken, skin removed, and trimmed	4 × 4 oz
30 ml	oil	1 fl oz
	knob of butter	
1 or 2	eggs beaten with a little water	1 or 2
50 g	flour (seasoned)	2 oz
50 g	breadcrumbs	2 oz

Garnish

2	bananas	2
4	rashers streaky bacon, rind removed	4
4	small tomatoes	4
4	croquette potatoes or straw potatoes (optional)	4
125 ml	horseradish sauce	4 fl oz
4	sprigs parsley	4

Sweetcorn pancakes

100 g	cooked sweetcorn kernels	4 oz
25 ml	egg (about ½ egg)	1 fl oz
25 g	flour	1 oz
25 ml	oil for frying	1 fl oz
	seasoning to taste	

1 Coat the suprêmes with flour, beaten egg and breadcrumbs. (See page 96 for more detailed instructions.)

2 Make a criss-cross design on the suprêmes by pressing with the edge of a palette knife.

3 Prepare the sweetcorn pancakes: mix together the sweetcorn, egg and seasoning, add the flour and mix again.

4 Prepare the tomatoes for grilling: remove the stalk and make a small cross-shaped cut through the skin only in the top.

5 Heat the oil and butter in a frying pan. Place the suprêmes in, presentation side down. Fry until a good colour has developed and the chicken is half cooked. Turn over and complete the cooking (about 15 minutes in total).

6 Set the suprêmes aside on a tray, resting on a sheet of absorbent paper. Keep hot while you cook the garnish:

bacon rashers and *tomatoes*: grill

bananas: peel, cut in half lengthways,

coat with flour and shallow fry in butter and/or oil until golden brown on both sides, or grill

pancakes: neatly spoon the mixture into hot oil in a preheated pan, so that it forms small rounds about 5 mm thick. Shallow fry to a golden brown on both sides. Drain well

croquette potatoes: deep fry

parsley: deep fry until crisp.

7 Place the cooked suprêmes on a warm service dish, then nearly arrange the garnish around them (see photograph on page 70). Serve accompanied by the horseradish sauce.

Liver and onions

Key learning points
» coat liver with flour to shallow fry
» shallow fry liver
» prepare a Lyonnaise sauce

SERVES 20

2½ kg	thinly sliced lamb's or calf's liver	5½ lb
225 g	flour, seasoned	8 oz
120 ml	oil for frying	4 fl oz
	chopped parsley (garnish)	

Lyonnaise sauce

100 g	oil or butter	4 oz
550 g	onions, sliced	1 lb 4 oz
120 ml	vinegar	4 fl oz
120 ml	white wine	4 fl oz
1¼ litre	demi-glace or jus lié (page 143)	2½ pt

1 Melt the fat in a saucepan or sauté pan. Add the onions and shallow fry until light brown.

2 Add the vinegar and wine. Boil rapidly until the liquid has reduced by two-thirds.

3 Add the demi-glace and simmer for 2 to 3 minutes until the sauce is well blended. If it seems too thin to coat the liver evenly, reduce further. Skim if required and check seasoning.

4 Coat the liver with the seasoned flour, shake off any excess flour, then fry quickly on each side, keeping slightly underdone.

5 Remove the liver from the pan and place on absorbent paper to drain thoroughly. Transfer to warm serving dish(es). Coat with the hot sauce. Sprinkle with parsley and serve.

Stir fried beef and vegetables in oyster sauce

Key learning points
» stir fry meat or poultry (or vegetarian alternative)
» prepare an oyster sauce

SERVES 4

450 g	tail of fillet of beef, or rump steak cut into thin strips 50 mm long	1 lb
100 g	onion, finely sliced	4 oz
100 g	carrot cut into 30 to 40 mm thin strips	4 oz
50 g	beansprouts	2 oz
50 g	sliced bamboo shoots	2 oz
45 ml	oyster sauce	3 tbsp
15 ml	soy sauce	1 tbsp
45 ml	dry sherry	3 tbsp
60 ml	vegetable oil	4 tbsp
¼ tsp	ground ginger	¼ tsp
	clove of garlic, crushed and peeled	
	caster sugar, pinch	
	salt and white pepper, pinch	
50 g	cornflour	2 oz

1 Place the carrot strips in boiling water for about 20 seconds, then cool them in running water and drain.

2 Season the meat to taste with salt, pepper and ginger.

3 Heat the oil in a medium-sized wok or frying pan. Add the onion and garlic and fry for 20 seconds stirring all the time.

4 Dust the beef with the cornflour. Shake off any surplus then add to the pan and fry for 1 minute, stirring all the time.

5 Add the carrots, beansprouts and bamboo shoots and continue frying and stirring for another minute or so. Keep the beef underdone.

6 Pour off any surplus oil, then return the pan to the heat, add the oyster sauce, soy sauce, sherry and sugar.

7 Continue cooking and stirring for another 30 seconds to warm the sauce through, then immediately transfer to a warm service dish and serve.

Sautéed kidneys with peppers
by Dufrais

Key learning points
» shallow fry kidneys
» prepare a sautéed dish with sauce
Accompany by triangles of toast.

SERVES 4

10–12	lambs' kidneys, skinned, cored and quartered or halved	10–12
25 g	flour, seasoned	1 oz
45 ml	olive oil	3 tbsp
1	large onion, finely chopped	1
1	clove garlic, crushed and peeled	1
200 ml	red Bistro Chef or red wine	7 fl oz
50 ml	beef stock	2 fl oz
1	bay leaf	1
100 g	red pepper, deseeded and sliced	4 oz
45 ml	fresh parsley, chopped	3 tbsp

1 Heat the oil in a large frying pan. Fry the onion and garlic until golden. Add the kidneys which you have coated in seasoned flour. Cook, stirring, for 1 to 2 minutes. Gradually stir in the Bistro Chef and stock. Add the red pepper and bay leaf. Simmer, uncovered, for about 10 minutes.

2 Remove the bay leaf, stir in the parsley and serve.

Moussaka
by Meat and Livestock Commission

Key learning points
» use a combination of cooking processes with minced lamb
» prepare aubergines

SERVES 4

450 g	minced lamb	1 lb
2	medium-sized aubergines, sliced	2
1	onion, finely sliced	1
1 × 397 g	can chopped tomatoes	1 × 14 oz
15 ml	tomato purée	1 tbsp
2.5 ml	ground cinnamon	½ tsp
2.5 ml	ground nutmeg	½ tsp
	bay leaf, sprig thyme and 3 or 4 parsley stalks	
	black pepper	
575 ml	mornay sauce (page 143), warmed and 1 egg added just before use	1 pt

1 Layer the aubergine slices in a colander and sprinkle each layer with salt. Leave to stand for 20 minutes. Rinse thoroughly and dry on kitchen paper. (This process will remove the bitter taste that aubergines sometimes have.)

2 Place mince in a saucepan over a low heat. When the fat starts to run out, increase heat and add the onion. Fry for 3 minutes. Add the tomatoes, purée, cinnamon, nutmeg, herbs and pepper. Bring to the boil and simmer, uncovered, for 15 to 20 minutes or until slightly reduced.

3 Place the aubergines in boiling water for 1 to 2 minutes to blanch. Drain and place on absorbent kitchen paper to dry.

4 In an ovenproof dish, layer the meat and aubergines alternately, finishing with the aubergines. Check the seasoning of the mornay sauce and pour over the top of the aubergines. Bake for 15 to 20 minutes at 180°C until golden. Stand for about 5 minutes before serving to allow the layers to set slightly.

Chilli-con-carne
by Meat and Livestock Commission

Key learning point
» make a beef stew with pulses
For a milder chilli, omit fresh chilli, or reduce amount of chilli powder. Serve with brown rice. Can also be used as a filling for jacket potatoes.

SERVES 4

450 g	braising steak, cubed	1 lb
30 ml	vegetable oil	2 tbsp
1	large onion, finely chopped	1
1	clove garlic, crushed and peeled	1
30 ml	malt vinegar	2 tbsp
	seasoning to taste	
5 ml	dried oregano	1 tsp
5 ml	chilli powder	1 tsp
1	fresh green chilli, deseeded and finely chopped	1
30 ml	tomato purée	2 tbsp
150 ml	beef stock	5 fl oz
1 × 397 g	can chopped tomatoes	1 × 14 oz
1 × 397 g	can red kidney beans, drained and rinsed	1 × 14 oz

1 Heat oil in large pan and fry onion and garlic until softened. Add beef and cook until well browned.

2 Add the remaining ingredients with the exception of the kidney beans. Bring to the boil, cover and simmer for about 90 minutes or until meat is tender and sauce has become rich and thick.

3 Add kidney beans and continue cooking for 15 minutes. Serve.

Bacon and leek gratin
by Potato Marketing Board

Key learning point
» use a combination of cooking processes with bacon
From *Catering for the Elderly*, a booklet of recipes for use in residential homes.

SERVES 10

450 g	bacon, derinded and chopped	1 lb
450 g	leeks, trimmed and sliced	1 lb
1 × 397 g	can chopped tomatoes	1 × 14 oz
15 ml	cornflour	1 tbsp
150 ml	water or stock	5 fl oz
900 g	potatoes, peeled and sliced	2 lb
50 g	grated cheese	2 oz
	seasoning to taste	

1 Fry the bacon and leeks together for 10 minutes. Add the tomatoes and continue to cook for 5 minutes. Season. Dissolve cornflour with the water or stock and add to the pan.

2 Meanwhile, boil the sliced potatoes for a few minutes. Drain.

3 Lay half the potatoes on the base of a lightly oiled 25 cm (10 inch) ovenproof dish. Place the bacon mixture on top and finish off with another layer of potatoes. Sprinkle the cheese on top.

4 Put in the oven to bake at 200°C for 30 minutes or until the potatoes are cooked and the cheese is browned. Serve.

Lancashire hot pot

by Gary Rhodes, The Greenhouse Restaurant, Mayfair, London. Published by Caterer & Hotelkeeper, 18 April 1991

Key learning points
» sweat vegetables without colouring
» cook a traditional English dish by a modern method

SERVES 4

4	thick, lean lamb chump chops	4
4	potatoes, peeled and cut into round slices about 2 mm thick	4
2 each	carrots, sticks of celery, onions, finely diced	2 each
1	leek, finely diced	1
½	clove garlic, crushed and peeled	½
2	sprigs fresh rosemary	2
575 ml	reduced, dark lamb stock	1 pt
	chopped parsley, sprinkling	
50 to 75 g	butter	2 to 3 oz
	seasoning to taste	

1 If required, clarify the lamb fat. Trim excess fat off the chops, and render – that is, melt – it down with a touch of water. Allow to gently heat until the fat is golden brown in colour. Cool, then strain through a clean cloth or very fine strainer.

2 Shallow fry the chops to brown them on both sides. Use a little of the butter, or preferably lamb fat. Place in a casserole.

3 Shallow fry the sliced potato in the butter (or lamb fat) with some rosemary. Place to one side.

4 Gently cook the vegetables, garlic and more of the rosemary in a little butter. Spoon on to the top of each chop. Arrange the sliced potatoes on top in a neat pattern.

5 Pour the reduced stock over the chops and place on the stove. Allow to simmer, then transfer to a medium-hot oven (180°C) for 35 to 40 minutes or so.

6 When cooked, remove the lamb, keeping the vegetables and potatoes on top.

7 Pour off the liquid, reduce if needed. Add one or two knobs of butter for a rich texture. Taste for seasoning. Plate the four chops and, if the potato has not coloured enough, lightly brush with butter and put under the grill.

8 Pour the liquid over, garnish with chopped parsley and serve.

Irish stew

Key learning points
» blanch and refresh meat
» make a traditional stew using mutton or lamb

SERVES 30

4½ kg	20 mm cubes of stewing mutton or lamb	10 lb
3 kg	potatoes, finely sliced or potato trimmings left over from another dish	6½ lb
750 g each	onion, white leeks, celery, finely sliced	26 oz each
450 g	white cabbage, finely sliced	1 lb
	white mutton stock or water to cover	
	seasoning to taste	
	bay leaf, sprig of thyme	

Garnish

675 g	potatoes cut in to 20 mm cubes, or small balls, or barrel shapes	1½ lb
450 g	button onions, peeled	1 lb
	chopped parsley	

1 Place the meat in a saucepan, cover with cold water, and bring to the boil.

2 Refresh the meat under cold running water until all the scum has washed away. Drain the meat.

3 Place the meat into a clean saucepan and cover with the cold stock or water. Bring to the boil, skimming off any scum as it forms. Wipe around the sides of the saucepan if impurities collect there.

4 Add the potato, onion, celery, leek, cabbage and seasoning. Cover with a lid and transfer to a medium oven at 180°C. From time to time, remove the stew from the oven and skim off any fat or impurities. The vegetables should break up during this stage, so that the stew thickens.

5 When the meat is almost cooked, after about 1¼ hours, add the button onions.

6 Cook for 10 minutes, add the shaped potatoes and cook for a further 15 minutes or so. The aim is for the meat and garnish to be cooked at more or less the same time.

7 Check the seasoning. Transfer the stew to a warm serving dish and sprinkle with chopped parsley.

Veal blanquette

Key learning points
» blanch and refresh meat
» make a white stew (blanquette) using veal
» make a roux

SERVES 4

500 g	stewing veal cut into cubes of about 20 mm	1¼ lb
575 ml	white veal stock	1 pt
1	carrot	1
1	onion clouté (bay leaf fixed to the onion with a clove)	1
25 g	margarine or butter	1 oz
25 g	flour	1 oz
125 ml	cream	4 fl oz
	salt and white pepper to taste	
	pinch of chopped parsley (optional)	

1 Place the meat in a saucepan, cover it with cold water and bring to the boil.

2 Refresh the meat under cold running water until all the scum has washed away. Drain the meat.

3 Place the meat into a clean saucepan and cover with the cold stock. Add the carrot and the onion clouté. Bring to the boil.

4 Cover with a lid, and transfer to the oven to slowly simmer until almost cooked: about 1 hour at 180°C. Add stock and skim as necessary during cooking.

5 Melt the fat in a separate saucepan, add the flour and mix together. Cook for 3 to 4 minutes without developing any colour.

6 Drain off the cooking liquid from the meat and vegetables. Discard the vegetables and herbs and place the meat in a clean saucepan. Keep it warm to one side of the stove.

7 Add the cooking liquid to the roux a little at a time, stirring in thoroughly. Simmer for 8 to 10 minutes.

8 Strain the sauce over the meat and bring back to the boil. Simmer for 5 to 10 minutes to complete the cooking of the meat.

9 Blend in the cream, adjust the seasoning and transfer to a warm serving dish. Sprinkle with parsley (if required) and serve.

Boiled leg of mutton with caper sauce

Key learning points
» boil leg of mutton
» prepare an attractive vegetable garnish, involving different cooking times for individual ingredients

SERVES 10 to 15

3½ kg	leg of mutton prepared for boiling with aitch bone removed, excess fat trimmed, knuckle end trimmed to leave clean bone, and tied to keep its shape	7 ¾ lb
450 g	small onions, peeled	1 lb
450 g	small carrots, topped, tailed and peeled or scraped clean	1 lb
450 g	swedes or turnips, cut into neat pieces	1 lb
450 g	celery	1 lb
450 g	small leeks	1 lb
	parsley, thyme and bay leaf	
	cold white stock or water to cover	
	seasoning to taste	
	chopped parsley (optional)	
575 ml	caper sauce (page 144)	1 pt

1 Place the leg into a saucepan (big enough to hold the vegetables that will be added later). Cover with cold stock or water, add seasoning and bring to the boil.

2 Skim off any scum. Wipe clean the sides of the pan.

3 Simmer the meat for 1½ hours. Skim and top up with additional liquid as necessary.

4 Complete preparations of the garnish:

onions and *carrots*: keep whole, as with very small turnips when available

swedes (and large turnips): cut into large neat pieces, not bigger than the onions

celery: trim the root end, and remove any stalks that are past their best. Wash thoroughly, then tie string round it if individual stalks are likely to come loose during cooking

leeks: trim and remove spoiled leaves. Cut a slit lengthwise, starting just above the root end (the leek will fall apart if it is cut fully in half). Wash thoroughly, then tie them together in a bundle.

5 After the meat has cooked for about 1½ hours, add the herbs and celery and cook for about 40 minutes more.

6 Add the carrots, onions and swede or turnip and cook for 10 minutes.

7 Add the leeks last of all, and simmer until all the vegetables and meat are cooked, another 15 minutes or so.

8 Transfer the leg to a suitable metal tray, remove the string, and keep warm, ready for carving.

9 Remove the vegetable garnish, cut the string from the celery and leek:

celery: divide into portions about the same size as the carrots

leeks: cut completely through the root end, neatly fold over to form lengths slightly shorter than the carrots.

10 Neatly arrange the vegetable garnish around the leg, for presentation to the customers (see photograph on page 76). Alternatively carve the meat, and arrange one piece of each of the vegetables by each portion of meat.

Spiced lamb with onions *Dopiazah*
by the New Zealand Lamb Catering Advisory Service

Key learning point
» make a lamb curry
This is a traditional regional dish from the southernmost tip of India

Variation: add 2 tbsp caster sugar and 2 tbsp wine vinegar at stage 3.

SERVES 10

1.35 kg	lean shoulder of lamb, diced	3 lb
175 g	oil	6 oz
175 g	unsalted butter	6 oz
2 kg	onions, sliced	4 lb
20 ml	ground cumin	4 tsp
10 ml	ground fenugreek	2 tsp
30 ml	ground turmeric	2 tbsp
20 ml	garam masala	4 tsp
6	fresh green chillies, deseeded and chopped	6
575 ml	water	1 pt
	salt to taste	

1 Cook the onions in the butter and oil until soft. Set half the onions aside. Add the spices to the remaining onions, and fry for 3 minutes.

2 Add the chillies, then the lamb and brown evenly.

3 Pour on the water, bring to the boil. Reduce heat and simmer for 1 hour, or until the meat is tender.

4 Add the reserved onions and continue cooking until excess liquid evaporates and the curry is fairly dry. Season with salt.

Paprika beef with wholemeal dumplings
by McDougalls (*RHM Foods*)

Key learning point
» make a beef stew with wholemeal dumplings

SERVES 4

450 g	stewing steak, cubed	1 lb
30 ml	oil	2 tbsp
1	red pepper, sliced	1
1	onion, chopped	1
15 ml	paprika	1 tbsp
275 ml	stock	½ pt
	salt	

Dumplings

175 g	wholemeal flour	6 oz
15 ml	baking powder	1 tbsp
75 g	suet	3 oz
	salt	
	cold water to mix	

1 Fry beef in oil until browned. Add peppers and onion, frying until soft. Stir in paprika, stock and salt. Bring to the boil.

2 Turn into an ovenproof casserole dish. Cover and place in oven for 1½ to 2 hours at 180°C, or until almost cooked.

3 Mix all the dumpling ingredients together with sufficient cold water to make a firm dough. Shape into 8 balls and place in the casserole. Simmer for a further 20 minutes. Serve.

Boiled silverside of beef and dumplings

Key learning points
» soak cured meat to remove excess salt
» boil silverside of beef
» prepare and cook dumplings

SERVES 4

600 g	cured silverside	1 lb 5 oz
4 each	small carrots and small onions	4 each
	cold white stock or water to cover	
	bouquet garni	
	chopped parsley (optional)	
100 g	suet pastry (see page 228)	4 oz

1 Soak the beef in cold water for 24 hours to remove excess salt.

2 Discard the soaking water and place the beef into a suitably sized saucepan. Cover with cold stock or water and bring to the boil. Skim if a scum forms.

3 Add the bouquet garni and allow the liquid to simmer until almost cooked (about 1½ hours).

4 Add the carrots and onions and simmer for 10 to 15 minutes more.

5 Roll the pieces of suet pastry between your (floured) hands to form dumplings.

6 Add the dumplings to the cooking liquor and simmer until cooked: a further 15 to 20 minutes.

7 Remove the beef from the pan, allow to cool slightly, then carve.

8 Garnish with the carrots, onions and dumplings and coat with a little of the cooking liquor. Sprinkle some parsley over the dumplings or onions if desired. Serve a sauceboat of the cooking liquor separately if required.

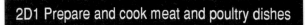

NVQ SVQ RANGE CHECKLIST

LEVEL 1

1D1.1 Prepare meat and poultry for cooking

prepare preprepared or convenience meat and poultry of these types
- [ ] beef or lamb or pork or bacon
- [ ] chicken or turkey

using 1 of these preparation methods
- [ ] defrosting
- [ ] washing
- [ ] seasoning

to prepare for 3 of these cooking methods
- [ ] roasting
- [ ] grilling or barbecuing or tandoori cooking
- [ ] shallow frying or griddling or stir frying
- [ ] braising or stewing
- [ ] steaming

1D1.2 Cook meat and poultry dishes

of these types
- [ ] beef or lamb or pork or bacon
- [ ] chicken or turkey

by 3 of these methods
- [ ] roasting
- [ ] grilling or barbecuing or tandoori cooking
- [ ] shallow frying or griddling or stir frying
- [ ] braising or stewing

LEVEL 2

2D1.1 Prepare meat for cooking

of 2 of these types
- [ ] beef or veal
- [ ] lamb or mutton
- [ ] pork or bacon
- [ ] offal

by 4 of these preparation methods
- [ ] trimming
- [ ] dicing
- [ ] trussing or tying
- [ ] rolling
- [ ] stuffing
- [ ] batting
- [ ] barding

2D1.2 prepare poultry for cooking

prepare chicken or turkey by 5 of these methods
- [ ] washing
- [ ] skinning
- [ ] trimming
- [ ] jointing
- [ ] trussing or tying
- [ ] batting
- [ ] barding
- [ ] dicing
- [ ] marinating

2D1.3 Cook meat and poultry dishes

of 3 of these types
- [ ] beef
- [ ] lamb or mutton
- [ ] pork or veal
- [ ] bacon or gammon
- [ ] offal
- [ ] chicken or turkey

by 3 of these methods
- [ ] roasting
- [ ] grilling or barbecuing or tandoori cooking
- [ ] shallow frying or griddling or stir frying
- [ ] braising or stewing
- [ ] boiling

Introduction

The public's taste for fish has grown during the past decade – and the signs are that the trend will continue. While fried fish and chips are likely to remain Britain's favourite, many people are becoming more adventurous in the varieties of fish they are willing to try, and in the ways in which the fish is cooked.

Travel abroad has been a big factor in this trend. So has the influence of the various ethnic communities.

Pollution and depletion of fish stocks have seen some varieties such as cod and herring become more difficult to obtain and therefore more expensive. On the other hand, commercial fish farming has meant that trout and salmon are no longer luxury items – yet many people (incorrectly) regard them as being difficult to cook.

Types of fish

Fish are sometimes divided up according to their condition when purchased:

– frozen

– canned

– smoked

– 'wet': meaning fresh as opposed to salted

and sometimes by where they come from:

– sea, or freshwater

– farmed or wild (for salmon)

– exotic (imported from all corners of the world: examples include snapper, shark, parrotfish and tuna).

Freshwater fish are sometimes divided into river and lake fish.

But perhaps the most useful way of classifying fish for caterers is:

– by their shape, whether they are *flat* or *round*

– by the general characteristics of their flesh, whether they are *white* or *oily*.

Flat fish, such as sole and plaice, are filleted in a different way from round fish such as cod, hake, whiting, salmon and herring. The reason is quite simply to get the best-sized fillets in the easiest way.

The flesh of the last two examples, salmon and herring, has a different and easily detectable characteristic. It is oily – there is more fat in its flesh than in white fish. Other oily fish are mackerel, tuna, anchovy and sardine, quite different in flavour and taste from white fish such as turbot and halibut.

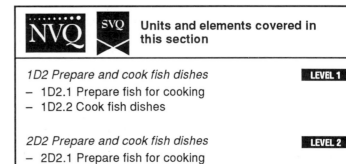

	Units and elements covered in this section
1D2 Prepare and cook fish dishes	**LEVEL 1**
– 1D2.1 Prepare fish for cooking	
– 1D2.2 Cook fish dishes	
2D2 Prepare and cook fish dishes	**LEVEL 2**
– 2D2.1 Prepare fish for cooking	
– 2D2.2 Cook fish dishes	

Quality points

Preprepared or convenience fish
– packaging in good condition
– correctly labelled
– not passed its use-by date
– to required specification

for fillets of wet fish
– flesh white and translucent
– flesh firm not ragged or gaping
– neat, well-trimmed fillets
– no smell of ammonia or sour odours
– no areas of discoloration
– no bruising or blood clots

for frozen fish
– the packaging and food should feel completely firm with no sign of thawing
– no dull, white patches: a sign of freezer burn caused by poor or over-lengthy storage
– no small white ice crystals: these suggest the fish has started to thaw and been re-frozen
– there should be little fluid loss when thawing
– once thawed, the fish flesh should feel firm. Gaping (flesh breaking up into its natural layers) was thought to be a result of poor handling and storage. The Ministry of Agriculture, Fisheries and Food, Dory Research Station advises that this is a natural occurrence – a sign of well fed fish, and can be particularly pronounced with round fish.

Whole wet fish
– bright skin with a good sheen
– scales firmly attached
– eyes bright, clear and full
– gills, if present, are bright red underneath, when lifted
– flesh is firm and springy to the touch: after pressing with a finger, the dent should flatten out quickly

In general, *avoid* fish with:
– dull or slimy skin
– damaged skin
– sunken, cloudy eyes
– sour, unpleasant smell (however, skate sometimes smells slightly of ammonia until cooked)

A trawler at sea.

NUTRITION

Fish is high in protein (needed for the growth and replacement of body tissue), and in certain vitamins and minerals. These include:

thiamin – which controls the release of energy from glucose in the diet

riboflavin – needed for proper functioning of muscles

niacin – necessary for healthy skin

calcium – essential for healthy bones and teeth. Canned fish is a good source (because the soft bones are normally eaten)

iodine – constituent of thyroid hormones, which regulate many body processes.

Oily fish are good sources of *vitamin A*, necessary for vision in dim light, and for the protective mucous membranes, e.g. in the nose and throat, to work properly, and of *vitamin D*, which helps calcium to be absorbed.

The *fat* content of white fish flesh is very low (under 2%). For oily fish, the amount is between 0.5 and 20%, depending on the variety and season of the year. These are mostly polyunsaturated fatty acids, including the group known as *Omega 3*. These have been shown to have a lowering effect on blood fats. This decreases the chance of blood vessels clogging up with cholesterol. Omega 3 can also help to make blood less 'sticky', so that it flows more easily around the body. This reduces the likelihood of a heart attack.

Smoked fish quality checklist
– no discoloration
– a fresh, glossy appearance
– bright and clean surface, with no smuts caused by the smoking process
– a pleasant, smoky smell

Cooking fish

by Sea Fish Industry Authority

Fish is naturally tender. The connective tissue readily softens and dissolves, so it cooks quickly and is easily digested.

Fish consists of short bundles of muscle fibres separated by a thin layer of connective tissue.

When fish is cooked the muscle fibres (*collagen*) alter their structure and coagulate to form the characteristic firm flakes of fish (shown in the photograph).

The small amount of connective tissue (*myocommas*) is easily broken down and converted to gelatin at a lower temperature than meat. It is important not to overcook fish, which will result in a tough, dry texture due to the hardening of the muscle fibres.

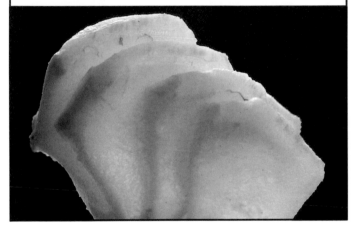

SEAFISH

The Sea Fish Industry Authority is the UK's central source of information on all matters relating to sea fish, cookery and nutrition.

Sea Fisheries House, 18–19 Logie Mill, Beaverbank Office Park, Logie Green Road, Edinburgh EH7 4HG

KNOWLEDGE CHECK ???

Describe below the main precautions you should take under each of the following headings:

storing uncooked fish (at least 5 points)

preparing uncooked fish (at least 2 points)

Answer on page 98.

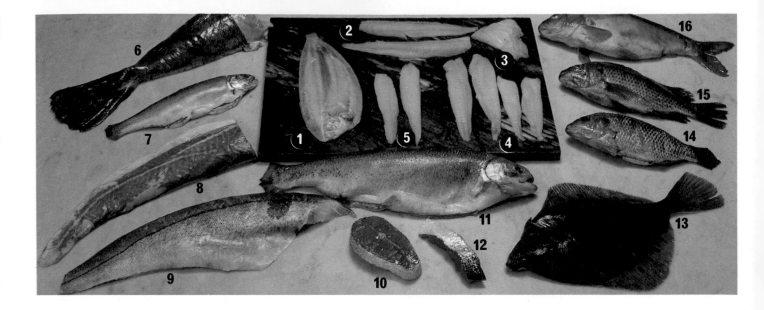

White fish, flat

Lemon sole (1) trimmed and skinned and **Fillets of lemon sole (5)** soft textured, more in common with plaice than Dover sole. May to Feb

Dover sole very fine flavour, expensive. May to Feb

Plaice (13) and **fillets of plaice (4)** mild, soft flesh. May to Feb

Skate only the wings are eaten, succulent flesh. Slight ammonia smell disappears during cooking. May to Feb

Flounder thick flounder can be poached like turbot, a thin one should be cooked like sole. March to Nov

Turbot one of the finest sea foods, firm flesh, delicate in flavour, very expensive. April to Feb

Halibut flavour almost as good as turbot. Less expensive. June to March

Dab flesh soft and fragile. Sept to May

Brill sweet, delicate flesh, softer than turbot. June to Feb

Megrim lends itself well to cooking with strong flavours. May to March

Witch best grilled or fried, but also poaches well. Good with zesty flavours like orange and lemon or something spicy such as ginger. May to Feb

White fish, round

Fillets of whiting (2) delicate flavour, good for lighter dishes like mousses and for steaming, poaching or frying. June to Feb

Monkfish (6) (or **angler**) firm, very white flesh, regarded by many to be as succulent as lobster. All year

Cod (8) and **suprême of cod (3)** succulent, large flaked flesh. June to Feb

Haddock (9) light, firm texture, good keeping qualities. May to Feb. Cold smoked as smoked haddock fillets, golden cutlets and Finnan haddock. Hot smoked as Arbroath smokies

Grey mullet (14) prepared **(15)** unprepared. Firm, white flesh, delicate flavour. Sept to Feb

Red mullet distinctive flavour, between shrimp and sole. May to Nov

Bass delicately flavoured, milky flesh. Aug to March

John Dory firm, delicate, excellently flavoured flesh, an extraordinarily ugly fish. All year

Coley very versatile, can be used for soups, pies, fish cakes and casseroles. Slightly off-white coloured flesh – turns white on cooking. Aug to Feb

Ling baked or fried goes well with stronger tasting vegetables like leeks or peppers. Sept to July

Huss good for soups, stews and kebabs, and frying as steak or goujons, firm flesh and no bones, other than the big one down the centre, which can be easily removed. All year

Pollack somewhat short on flavour, best with sauce, or in fish cakes and pies. May to Sept

Hake delicate taste contrasts well with stronger flavours like curry sauce, red wine or tomato sauce. June to March

Red sea bream rather coarse but juicy flesh, and pleasant taste that suits fairly strong accompanying flavours. June to Feb

Red gurnard very ugly appearance, quite sweet flesh, excellent in soups. July to Feb

Conger eel long, sharp bones, good for soups, mousselines and terrines. March to Oct

Oily seawater fish

Anchovy delicate flavour, delicious grilled or fried. June to Dec

Herring tasty fish, rich in protein, fat, iodine and vitamins A and D. Strong smell while cooking. May to Dec. Cold smoked as kippers, bloaters, red herring. Hot smoked as buckling

Mackerel firm, richly flavoured, very oily and rich in vitamins. All year. Hot smoked (occasionally cold)

Pilchard/Sardine delicious fried, grilled or barbecued. Small young pilchards are known as sardines. Jan, Feb, April, Nov, Dec

Sprat very oily, grill or shallow fry. Inexpensive. Oct to March

Tuna firm, meaty eating. Very close-grained, rather unattractive, flesh improves during cooking. All year

Small sprats, herring or mackerel are often sold as whitebait

Freshwater fish

Trout (7) familiar and delicious fish

Darne (10) of salmon and **suprême of salmon (12)** known as the king of fish. Much of it is now farmed

Salmon trout (11) combines the succulent texture of trout with the colour and flavour of salmon

Carp (16) often stuffed and baked

ACTION   97

Use this page to make your own seasonal chart for fish. All the information you need is on the page opposite (except that in the chart the names of fish are all in alphabetical order).

By shading (with a pencil or highlighter pen) the months when each variety is in season, you will end up with a chart similar to the one on page 126 for shellfish.

	January	February	March	April	May	June	July	August	September	October	November	December
White fish, flat												
Brill												
Dab												
Dover sole												
Flounder												
Halibut												
Lemon sole												
Megrim												
Plaice												
Skate												
Turbot												
Witch												
White fish, round												
Bass												
Cod												
Coley												
Conger eel												
Grey mullet												
Haddock												
Hake												
Huss												
John Dory												
Ling												
Monkfish												
Pollack												
Red gurnard												
Red mullet												
Red sea bream												
Whiting												
Oily seawater fish												
Anchovy												
Herring												
Mackerel												
Pilchard/Sardine												
Sprat												
Tuna												

Preparation methods

Defrosting   LEVEL 1

1. Time thawing carefully, so that the fish is ready just when it is needed.

2. Use a thawing cabinet if possible, or the defrost setting on a microwave oven. Alternatively, place on a tray in a refrigerator and thaw for 12 hours.

3. Once the fish begins to thaw it must be treated as fresh wet fish.

Some preprepared frozen fish portions should be cooked without defrosting. Check the package or workplace instructions.

Never:

- freeze any fish which has been previously frozen.

- thaw fish in water – it makes the fish soggy, difficult to cook and unappetising.

Fish are supported by the water they swim in. This means their muscles have relatively little work to do, and do not need large amounts of oxygen. For this reason, fish flesh has much less of the protein called myoglobin than the leg meat of a turkey, for example, which has to do a lot more work. The amount of myoglobin affects the colour of the flesh – so most fish flesh is white, whereas most meat is dark.

CHEF'S TIPS

Thawing times for frozen fillets may be reduced by separating the fillets.

A 50 mm frozen block of fillets will take about 10 hours to thaw at 7°C.

ANSWER   ✓✓✓

KNOWLEDGE CHECK page 95

These are the main precautions you should take when:

storing uncooked fish

1. *Store wet fish immediately after delivery at a temperature as close as possible to 0°C (but not below −1°C, as this will slowly freeze the fish).*

2. *Store wet fish separately from other foods to avoid the transfer of odours and flavours, and to avoid risks of cross-contamination. There should be ice present around the fish at all times. A fish refrigerator is ideal for this. It is purpose made to collect any drips from the crushed ice in which the fish is stored. Drawers, plastic boxes or other containers used to hold the fish must have drain holes.*

3. *Store whole, filleted and portioned fish separately to avoid contamination risks.*

4. *Keep different types of fish apart.*

5. *Smoked fillets should not be allowed to come into direct contact with ice, as this will cause the colour to leach out.*

6. *Use wet fish as soon as possible after delivery, ideally within a day.*

7. *Do not store preprepared, convenience or frozen fish beyond its use-by date, and rotate stocks.*

8. *Store frozen fish at −18°C or colder.*

Ready to eat cooked fish, such as smoked mackerel, should be stored on the shelves above raw fish and other raw foodstuffs to avoid cross-contamination.

preparing uncooked fish

1. *Use equipment which is reserved for preparing uncooked fish. If this is not possible, thoroughly wash and sanitise equipment before use.*

2. *Work well away from areas where cooked food or raw meat is being handled.*

3. *Keep your preparation area clean, wash your hands, chopping boards, knives and so forth regularly.*

There is further information in the section on Hygiene.

Washing LEVEL 2

Fresh fish should be washed thoroughly under cold, running water:

- before preparing
- during preparation if necessary, for instance when scaling
- after removing the intestines
- after scaling.

Trimming LEVEL 2

For fish which is to be served whole, it is usual to trim the fins, and in some cases, the head. (Trimming is also an integral part of the procedure for filleting.)

To trim the fins

Use a pair of fish scissors, cutting against the natural lie of the fins.

Alternatively, a cook's knife will remove them quickly:

- with the fish firmly on the board, fan out the fins with the back of the knife point, then use the (sharp) cutting edge to remove them.

With the head left on

1 Open the gill slits and using scissors or a knife cut away the gills: they are usually attached firmly at both ends.

2 Remove the eyes, using the point of a sharp knife or peeler.

To remove the head

For a round fish, cut it off just below the gills.

For a flat fish, cut from both sides of the head towards the body, forming a V-shaped cut.

Scaling

This can make quite a mess, with scales shooting everywhere, so do it carefully and in a part of the kitchen where it will be easy to clear up thoroughly afterwards.

1 Use a firm-bladed knife, ideally a cook's knife.
2 If you have not had much experience, it is advisable to use the back of the knife blade. This will reduce the risk of accidentally damaging the skin of the fish.
3 Hold the knife at a slight angle and scrape the scales from tail to head, so that the knife is lifting the scales up and away from the body.
4 While doing this, hold the fish firmly by the tail.

Gutting (removing the intestines)

Take care to avoid puncturing the internal organs or damaging the flesh. Hold the fish so that you are cutting away from yourself. Then if the knife does slip you are less likely to have an injury.

Sometimes the roe is saved to add flavour to the accompanying sauce.

from a round fish

1 Make a slit along the belly from below the head, to extend two-thirds the length of the fish.
2 Using your fingers or the handle of a spoon, pull out and discard the internal organs. Scrape or wash away any dark membrane (looks like black skin) from inside the cavity. Also scrape away any congealed blood lying along the back bone.

from a flat fish

1 Make a semi-circular slit behind the head on the darker side of the fish.
2 With your fingers, or the handle of a spoon, gently pull out all the internal organs.
3 Any roe remaining further up the fish can be carefully squeezed out without having to slit the pocket open further.

After gutting, thoroughly wash the inside of the fish under cold running water. There should be no trace of blood left.

Boning and filleting   `LEVEL 2`

A filleting knife, with its flexible blade, is ideal for this task.

Do not be too discouraged if on your first attempts you leave some flesh on the backbone. With experience, you will get good, even shaped fillets, with smooth surfaces, and the bone left really clean.

There is no need to trim off the tail or fins before you fillet fish. They should not get in the way, and they can be discarded with the carcase (or used to make fish stock).

Filleting a flat fish

Larger fish are normally prepared as four fillets, two from each side. This is sometimes called *quarter-cutting*.

1 Place the fish on the chopping board, dark side up, with the tail end nearest you.

2 Starting at the head, make a cut down the centre line of the fish, through to the bone.

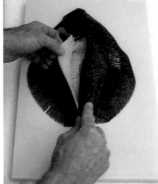

3 Work the blade of the knife into the cut, and gently lift the flesh up. Keeping the knife blade as close to the bones as possible, and using a light stroking movement, gradually free the fillet from the backbone.

4 Turn the fish around, so that the head is facing you, and remove the second fillet.

5 Turn the fish over to get two more fillets.

Small flat fish – up to 450 g (1 lb) or so – are usually cut into two fillets only, one from each side. This is known as *cross-cutting*, and there is a picture overleaf of the finished fillet.

1 Lay the fish on the board, head facing you.

2 Insert a knife into the flesh at one corner near the head, with the blade facing away from you. With a sawing movement work the knife blade across and down the backbone, to free the fillet.

3 Turn the fish over and remove the other fillet in the same way.

Filleting a round fish

A round fish has only two fillets, one on each side.

Some chefs find it easier to remove the head first, and to trim the fins.

1 Lay the fish on one side on a chopping board.

2 Working from the head towards the tail, cut down the backbone using the knife blade to feel along the rib bones. Lift the fillet away as you cut, so you can better control the action of the knife.

3 Turn the fish over, and repeat steps 1 and 2 to remove the second fillet.

Boning a round fish – butterfly fillets

This is suitable for very fresh mackerel, herring, sardines, trout and sprats. Once the fish has been gutted, trimmed and cleaned:

1 Split the fish along the full length on the underside.

2 Open the body out, and place on a chopping board with the skin uppermost.

3 Using your thumbs or the heel of your hand, press firmly along the back of the fish to help release the backbone from the flesh.

4 Turn the fish over and ease the backbone away from the flesh, starting at the head and working towards the tail.

Boning a round fish for stuffing

After the scales, gills and intestines have been removed, and the fish trimmed:

1 Lengthen the opening along the belly to expose the backbone, ribs and flesh of the fish.

2 Work down the length of the fish, freeing the flesh from the ribs. If the rib bones are fairly big, they can be freed one at a time, and snapped off at the backbone. With a small-boned fish the operation becomes more fiddly.

3 Sever the backbone at the head, then work towards the tail, freeing the backbone. With some fish, this can be done fairly easily using your fingers. Otherwise scissors or a sharp knife will help.

4 Cut the backbone free when you reach the tail.

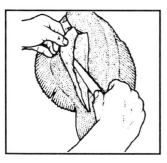

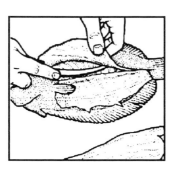

Filleting a flat fish.

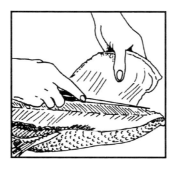

Filleting a round fish.

Butterfly fillets.

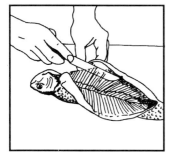

Boning a round fish for stuffing.

ACTION

1 Visit some fish suppliers in your area, including, if possible, a good fishmonger or market stall holder specialising in fresh fish, a large supermarket, and a frozen food centre.

2 Make notes on the various types of fish you see, and their prices.

3 From your notes, sort the different fish into their main types.

4 For each type, list below the names and prices of a few examples which you have not often come across.

5 On your list, highlight two types of fish not currently offered on the menu at your workplace/college, but which you think would be popular with the customers.

Skinning

LEVEL 2

Your fingers play an important role in skinning whole flat fish. For skinning fillets a medium-sized cook's knife is probably the best choice, but some chefs prefer to use a filleting knife.

Flat fish

Whole lemon sole, plaice and flounder are skinned from head to tail.

1 With the point of a knife, loosen the skin from around the head.

2 Work your thumb carefully between the skin and the flesh.

3 When enough skin has been worked loose to get a good grip:

   press the palm of one hand firmly on the head/skinned area of the fish, to hold the fish firmly

   tightly grip the flap of skin using the fingers of your other hand, and pull to tear the skin away.

Dover sole

Whole Dover sole is skinned in a different way from other whole flat fish.

1 Cut across the skin at the tail.

2 Scrape away enough skin from the flesh to get a good fingerhold.

3 Hold the tail firmly with one hand.

4 Gripping the skin with the fingers of your other hand, pull the skin away towards the head.

Skinning a fillet

1 Place the fillet on the chopping board, skin down.

2 Cut through the flesh to the skin at the tail end.

3 With one hand, hold the fillet firmly by the tail end.

4 With the other hand, hold the blade at a slight angle and, using a sawing movement, push the knife down and forwards at the same time.

5 The aim is to keep the blade as close to the skin as possible, yet not cut through it. If you do cut through the skin, try and correct the situation quickly, because it can be quite difficult to cut away any bits of skin that are left on the fillet.

Skinning a Dover sole.

Skinning a cross-cut fillet.

Note how the knife is kept pressed firmly down.

CHEF'S TIPS

If you have trouble getting a good grip of fish as you skin or trim it, dip your fingers in salt.

Portioning

The amount of fish you allow per serving will depend on the policy at your establishment, the menu and the customers.

	Portions per kg
For steaks and other large cuts, allow 150 to 200 g per portion.	
As a rough guide, this is the yield of prepared fish:	
cod, haddock – on the bone	6
plaice, turbot, brill, halibut – on the bone	4
cod and plaice fillet	8
whitebait	8–10
salmon – with head and bone	5

	One fish weighing
As a rough guide, allow the following per portion:	
herring, mackerel, whiting – whole	180–200 g
trout – whole	180–200 g
sole – main dish	250–300 g

Stuffing

Round fish are often stuffed. The space remaining in the belly, once the fish has been gutted and cleaned, is ideal for holding a stuffing. The flavours will spread deliciously through the flesh as the fish cooks.

Provided you do not attempt to overstuff the fish, there is not usually any problem with stuffing falling out during cooking.

Fillets of fish can also be stuffed: place a small amount of stuffing in the centre of the fillet and roll up.

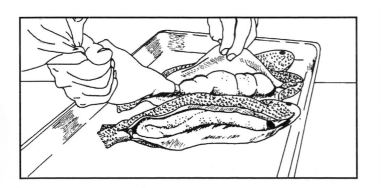

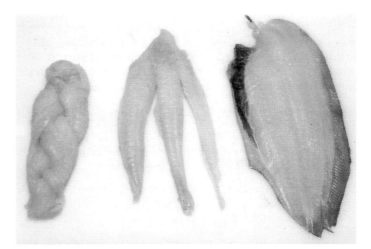

How to prepare plaited fillets. *1) Skin the fillet, 2) Cut into 3 strips, almost to the top of the fillet, but just left joined, 3) Plait these lengths together.*

Cutting salmon darnes or steaks.

Preparing goujons.

Traditional cuts of fish

Délice – trimmed fillet, folded in two.

Paupiette – small fillet rolled into a cylindrical shape. Often filled with stuffing.

Goujon – thin strip 60 to 80 mm long and 15 mm thick, usually cut at an angle across the fillet, in order to get the correct length. Some chefs prefer thinner goujons (5 mm).

Goujonnettes – smaller version of goujons, not often seen now.

Suprême – fillet from large fish, cut into slices at an angle of about 45°.

Darne – slice from a round fish, cut through the bone.

Tronçon – slice from large flat fish, cut through the bone.

Côtelette – tronçon cut in half.

For some of these terms there is no better name in English – so you will often find *goujon* and *suprême* used in combination with the English name for the fish, e.g. *goujons of plaice.*

The equivalent English term for cuts of fish through the bone, i.e. *darne* and *tronçon*, is cutlet or steak.

Coating

LEVELS 1 + 2

Check workplace instructions or the recipe. Many traditional recipes call for particular coatings. For example, fried fish Orly style (see page 118) is coated with batter and served with tomato sauce.

The type of coating used should complement the size and texture of the fish.

1 Use trays with reasonably deep sides, or large bowls to hold the various coating ingredients.

2 Arrange your preparation area so that you only have what is required, and can work in a strict sequence from uncoated to coated food.

3 If the coating requires two or three processes, you will find it much easier to work with a colleague. For example, if the coating is flour, beaten egg then breadcrumbs:

person A coats one piece of fish at a time with flour, then places the pieces in the beaten egg mixture

person B lifts the pieces out of the egg one at a time, and applies the breadcrumb coating.

4 If teamwork is not practical, you should follow a similar sequence to avoid getting a build up of flour, egg and breadcrumbs on your fingers:

flour a number of pieces and place them in the egg

lift them out of the egg and place in the breadcrumbs

wipe your hands dry before breadcrumbing each batch.

5 Do not put too much of any coating on the food. Shake off excess flour and breadcrumbs. Let excess egg wash and batter run off.

6 Generally, coatings should not be applied to the food until just before cooking. Breadcrumb-coated fish can be prepared some hours in advance, provided the fish is kept properly chilled:

lay the coated pieces of fish slightly spaced apart on trays, and cover with greaseproof paper before refrigerating

do not put more than two or three layers on each tray, otherwise the bottom layer will get squashed under the weight

for the same reason, the trays should not be stacked.

CHEF'S TIPS

If you are coating food with breadcrumbs, and have to do so without any help, use one hand to flour the food and place it in the beaten egg, and the other hand to lift it out of the egg and coat with breadcrumbs.

ACTION

Prepare 4 small pieces of fish for deep frying: **Samples A, B, C** and **D**.

Stage 1: cooking samples A and B

1 Coat both pieces in a batter of your choice (a recipe is given on page 118).

2 Deep fry them at a temperature of 180°C until cooked (3 to 6 minutes). Drain them.

3 Cover **A** with an upturned plate or kitchen foil. Leave **B** uncovered.

4 Place both pieces in a hot cupboard.

Stage 2: 15 minutes or so later, cooking samples C and D

5 Coat **C** in the batter (as 1 above).

6 Coat **D** in milk and flour only.

7 Deep fry both pieces (as 2 above).

8 Now compare the taste, texture and colour of all 4 pieces of fish.

9 Note your comments below, and what you think the reasons are for any differences.

Sample A

Sample B

Sample C

Sample D

Why a coating and which one?

Fish is coated:

- to achieve a brown, crisp surface after cooking – fish does not contain enough sugar or starch to brown and crisp on its own, even at the high temperatures reached in deep frying, shallow frying or grilling

- to help hold its shape and texture during cooking – most fish has quite delicate flesh, which will dry out in intense heat, and quickly begin to fall apart

- to seal the surface – thus reducing moisture loss during cooking. In deep frying, a coating will also reduce the amount of fat absorbed by the fish.

There are three basic groups of coating.

Flour

Traditionally, white flour is used, seasoned with salt and pepper to add flavour.

For *grilling* and *shallow frying*, the fish is lightly coated in flour immediately before cooking. The flour will stick quite easily to the moist (but not wet) surface of the fish.

For *deep frying*, the fish is dipped in milk before being coated with flour. This forms a thicker coating. The disadvantage of this type of coating is that flour particles are left in the oil, causing it to spoil quickly.

Breadcrumbs

The fish needs preparation in some way so that the crumbs will stick:

- brushed with oil or melted butter, then breadcrumbed – for *grilling* or *shallow frying*

- lightly coated with flour (which can be seasoned if required), then dipped in *egg wash* (raw egg, beaten with a little water or milk), then in breadcrumbs – for *deep frying* or *shallow frying*.

Batter

Batter is a popular coating that suits the deep frying process particularly well. The fish is coated in flour first, so that the batter will stay on during cooking.

Batter is made of flour, a liquid such as water or milk, and yeast, baking powder or beaten egg white to give a lighter texture.

Other ingredients to add extra flavour or improve the final texture can be used. For example, whole eggs (for texture and flavour) or beer (for flavour) might be used in place of some of the liquid content. Oil is sometimes used as part of the liquid to produce a softer texture.

The batter for Japanese *tempura* dishes is made by whisking iced water with egg yolks until frothy, then adding plain flour to make a smooth batter.

Some terms

Breaded, panéd, English style and *pané à l'anglaise* – coated with breadcrumbs before frying.

Battered – coated with batter (sometimes called *pâté à frire*).

Floured, French style and *à la française* – moistened with milk and then coated with flour before frying.

Fried fish Orly style (batter coating).

Whitebait would be totally dominated by a traditional batter coating, so flour is more appropriate.

CHEF'S TIPS

For a healthier finished dish, use:

- freshly ground black pepper only, or herbs and spices of your choice, but not salt
- wholemeal flour/brown breadcrumbs
- in place of flour/breadcrumb coatings, use oatmeal, barley or crushed breakfast cereals such as bran flakes
- polyunsaturated oil.

Deep frying   `LEVELS 1 + 2`

Definition Deep frying is cooking food by entirely submerging it in very hot oil (or fat).

The aim is to get a crisp, brown surface, and to enhance the flavour of the food. Achieving this, while making sure that the food is adequately cooked all the way through, depends on four main points.

1 Careful selection and preparation of the food

Choose quite small, evenly shaped pieces of food, that need only a short cooking time to make them tender.

Not suitable are:

- large pieces of food – by the time the centre has cooked, the surface will be overcooked

- very small pieces of food – after frying, there will be hardly any soft centre, just a crispy surface

- food which is not even in shape – the thin parts will overcook before the thicker parts are done

- food which is not firm – it will fall apart in the hot fat

- food with a high fat content, such as mackerel, tuna and salmon – it will taste unacceptably greasy after it has absorbed still more fat from deep frying.

2 Using a suitable coating

Fish will not develop an attractive colour or texture unless it is first coated with, for example, batter or breadcrumbs. A coating also:

- adds flavour

- helps the food hold its shape during cooking

- reduces moisture loss

- prevents the food absorbing too much oil.

3 Using a suitable oil (or fat)

The purpose of the oil in deep frying is to bring heat into contact with as much of the surface of the food as possible at one time, at a temperature high enough to brown and crisp the surface. This means the oil must:

- be able to reach the high cooking temperatures – frying temperatures for fish are in the range 170°C to 182°C. Dripping, for example, is not suitable because it will start smoking at around 163°C

- enhance the flavour of the food – oil that has been used too often, or not looked after properly, will develop quite strong off-flavours that get passed on to the food

- be cost effective to use in a catering situation – as your supervisor will undoubtedly have told you, oil is expensive. Proprietary brands are specially manufactured to have improved stability, with antioxidants to improve storage life, and antifoaming agents to extend frying life.

High quality oils:

- will produce an attractive finish to the food

- there will be minimum absorption into the food – leaving tastier food and a longer lasting oil

- will be high in polyunsaturates and low in saturates.

4 Controlling the cooking

The deep fryer will have a thermostat to allow you to set the cooking temperature. It may also have a timer, and, if you are working with one of the more advanced deep fryers, the frying basket will automatically lift out of the oil after the pre-set time. What is important is that you:

- keep an eye on the food, so that it does not brown too much

- turn food which floats on the surface of the oil, so that both sides are browned

- do not place too much food in the oil at one time: this will cause the temperature of the oil to drop. The general rule is that the ratio of food to oil should be no more than one to six

- allow time for the heat to recover when frying frozen or chilled food – temperature falls of 18°C to 28°C can occur when frozen fish pieces are immersed in hot oil

- never heat oil above 205°C, or it will spoil rapidly

- do not leave the fryer set at a high temperature when it is not in use. If necessary, ask whether you should turn the fryer off, or set it on stand-by, reducing the temperature to about 93°C.

Foods that are low in fat will always absorb some oil during frying. The potato on the left of this photograph has been treated with a fat dye, so that you can see exactly how much has been taken in. About 10% has been absorbed – the fat absorption of potato chips is usually in the order 5 to 6%, but cooking them at 10°C below the recommended temperature will increase the amount absorbed to around 30%.

More about fats and oils

Caterers have a choice of three types of frying medium, which can be grouped according to their appearance at room temperature:

solid – such as palm oil, lard, dripping, proprietary brands, which have to be dug out of their carton. Except for unrefined dripping, most are very stable. Solid frying fats must be melted gently, at a temperature not higher than 130°C, before heating to frying temperature. Otherwise, they might burn before they melt

liquid – easier to handle because they can be poured. The most stable, such as groundnut and corn oils, are generally the most expensive

fluid – proprietary brands designed to offer the best combination of qualities: pourable, so they do not need special melting before heating to frying temperature, and generally more stable than normal vegetable oil blends.

Note how:

1   The fish has been evenly coated and is not dripping with excess batter.

2   The tray holding the remaining pieces of fish is being kept well away from the oil.

3   A spider is to hand, so that the fish can be removed the moment it is cooked.

The frying life of oils and fats

Oils and fats start to deteriorate as soon as they are exposed to air. They spoil more quickly at high temperatures and in the presence of water:

– becoming darker in colour and thickening
– frothing, particularly when wet foods are fried
– smoking more readily
– coating the sides of the fryer with a sticky, dark brown gum that is difficult to remove

and food fried in oil which has deteriorated becomes:

– more discoloured, and patchy in colour
– poorer in flavour
– greasier in texture
– unpleasant smelling.

The steps recommending for looking after oils and fats (on page 39) are based on:

• keeping the oil free of loose particles of food – these burn and cause smoking. Drain fryers regularly, clean out before refilling with the filtered oil
• seasoning after cooking – salt speeds up deterioration
• reducing the exposure to oxygen – keep fryers covered when not in use, never pour oils from a great height, when filtering oil reduce the free fall to the minimum and return to the fryer quickly
• avoiding contact with metals such as copper, brass and iron – use stainless steel equipment for handling food
• replacing the antioxidants by topping up with fresh oil or fat – if the frying process is not busy, or the food being cooked does not absorb much oil, it is better to choose a more stable (and probably more expensive) frying medium
• keeping oil which is in use as busy as possible – never heat three fryers, when two will do. Oil begins to break down as soon as it is heated, however good it is
• not mixing different brands of oils – they each have different qualities. To mix them may cause variations in taste and colour, or even burning.

Note how the electric elements of the fryer at the right of the picture are positioned above the funnel-shaped bottom, so that any loose particles of food will slip down into the cooler oil below the heating element.

A variety of baskets to hold small items of food are shown: round, square or oblong to suit the shape of the fryer, and deep enough to reach just above the heat source.

The long handled round and flat spoons made of wire are called spiders and are used to lift and turn larger items of food including any food which has been coated with batter (the batter would stick to a basket).

Fine mesh skimmers are also available to remove small particles of food floating on the surface or suspended in the oil.

SAFETY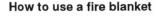

Safety precautions for deep frying

adapted from Wesson, The Guide to Good Frying Management, Kraft General Foods

When using an oil heated to high temperatures, you should always exercise the greatest care in the kitchen. Hot oil is a potential hazard – so follow these simple rules to ensure your kitchen runs smoothly.

DON'T
- overfill the fryer with oil
- overheat the oil – if it starts smoking, switch off heat immediately, and tell your supervisor
- leave fryers unattended while in use
- attempt to extinguish a fryer fire with water or sand.

DO
- follow the correct procedure for filtering and changing oil.

DO MAKE SURE YOU KNOW

what to do in the event of a fire, in particular:
- when and how to sound the fire alarm
- who should be told of the fire, and how they can be contacted quickly
- how to use a fire blanket
- what fire extinguisher to use for a fire involving oil or fat, where it is kept, and how to use it
- where the switches are to turn off the electricity and/or gas to the fryer.

How to use a fire blanket

1 Lift the blanket high with both hands, arms extended upwards. This action will protect your body from the heat and flames.
2 Taking care, drop the blanket over the flames in a movement away from your body.
3 If a person's clothes are on fire, wrap the blanket around the burning area, keeping the victim's nose and mouth open to the air so that he or she can still breathe.
4 Take care that the blanket does not flap, thus fanning the flames.

How to check the thermostat on a deep fryer

adapted from Wesson, The Guide to Good Frying Management, Kraft General Foods

1 Set the thermostat at a normal frying temperature of about 175°C.
2 Using an oil thermometer, record the temperature of the oil when the heat cuts off. This should be higher than the thermostat setting – by about 2.5 to 8°C.
   Example A: 182°C
   Example B: 180°C
3 Record the temperature at which the heat switches on again.
   Example A: 170°C
   Example B: 163°C
4 Add the two temperatures together and divide by two. This figure should be within 2.5°C of the thermostat setting. If the gap is any larger your thermostat should be serviced, re-set or replaced.

   Example A: $182 + 170 = \dfrac{352}{2} = 176°C$ *OK*

   Example B: $180 + 163 = \dfrac{343}{2} = 171.5°C$ *needs service*

Left: *fresh oil.*

Right: *oil that has deteriorated*

This fish has broken up into small pieces because it was handled too much during cooking. Delicate items cooked in baskets can also be damaged by over-vigorous shaking.

Main reasons for deterioration of oil
1 Over-use.
2 Inadequate filtering or skimming.
3 Presence of traces of detergent after cleaning.
4 Overheating.
5 Holding oil at operating temperature when it is not in use.
6 Not covered when cool.
7 Failure to top up oil with new oil after use.
8 Constant frying of wet foods.
9 Salt or sugar falling off food into oil.

Oil that foams and darkens, as it has done here, is dangerous to use and will spoil any food cooked in it.

To prevent this happening, oil should be drained off and filtered daily.

ACTION

Refer back to the notes you made on your visits to local fish suppliers – *ACTION* on page 101. Imagine that you have been asked to advise on new menus to be introduced at two different types of catering establishment:
- the main student restaurant at a large college
- a small ethnic restaurant, opening up soon in your area (choose any appropriate nationality).

In each case the new menu is to include one fish dish that is deep fried and one that is shallow fried. That means you must come up with 4 new menu items in all, each one with a short description that will make the dish sound interesting to the rather different groups of people choosing from the new menu.

Student restaurant

1 *Deep fried dish*

Description

2 *Shallow fried dish*

Description

Ethnic restaurant

3 *Deep fried dish*

Description

4 *Shallow fried dish*

Description

Grilling and barbecuing

LEVELS 1 + 2

Grilling is a fast, dry method of cookery which uses the intense heat radiated by an electrical element, gas flame, or glowing charcoal.

The heat source may be:

- above the food – as in an overhead grill or salamander
- below the food – as in a barbecue or simulated charcoal grill
- above and below the food – as in some infra-red grills.

Grilling is suitable for many whole fish – small to medium-size, and cuts – especially steaks, cutlets, and when cubed and skewered as a kebab. Because fish is so tender, fillets need particularly careful handling if grilled.

Many other types of food are grilled, and in *Meat and poultry* the process is described in more detail (page 64).

General points to remember when grilling fish

1 Whole fish (gutted and trimmed) should be scored before grilling. Make two or three short parallel cuts through the skin on each side of the thickest part of the fish. By allowing the heat to penetrate, this stops the outside of the fish from becoming dry before the inside is fully cooked. It also removes any danger of the skin splitting open of its own accord, which can look unattractive.

2 Some fish, like plaice and sole, have black skin. This should be removed entirely. White skin is often left on because it can look quite appetising when cooked.

3 Grill the presentation side last (see box on page 112). (If you cooked it first, the appearance might be spoilt when you turn the fish over.)

4 White fish, fillets and cuts must be basted or moistened during cooking to stop them from drying out.

5 Fish such as herring and mackerel, which are protected by natural oils, may not require frequent basting during grilling.

6 Where possible, use a special wire fish holder or tray to make handling easier.

7 Oil the holder (or the grill bars if you are not using a holder or tray), to stop the fish from sticking.

8 Whole fish and thick cuts should be turned part way through cooking, so that they cook evenly throughout.

CHEF'S TIPS

When barbecuing, place the fish on branches of rosemary, fennel or dill. You can also stuff the cavities with herbs. Alternatively, wrap in kitchen foil with herbs or in vine leaves.

Trays *(shown left)* are ideal for grilling fish and delicate or small foods (for example, mushrooms and tomatoes) under an overhead grill.

Fish grilling wires *(shown right)* make it possible to turn the fish over easily, without risking damage to the flesh and can be used on overhead grills or charcoal grills.

ACTION

Once again refer back to the notes you made when visiting the fish suppliers in your area.

Choose two types of fish that you think would be popular as grilled dishes at your workplace/college.

In the space below write down the name of the dish, and a short description as it might appear on the menu.

Try and be as original as possible with your suggestions, so you are not copying ideas you described in the earlier activity, or dishes which are already on the menu.

1 *Dish*

Description

2 *Dish*

Description

Steaming   `LEVEL 1`

Definition Steaming is cooking food by steam.

In its simplest application, the steam is produced by boiling water in a saucepan. The fish is placed on a tray or plate, supported above the level of the boiling water by a rack or stand. The lid is kept on the saucepan, so that the fish is surrounded by steam.

In a catering situation, steaming is normally done in a steamer. For fish, this will usually be an atmospheric or low-pressure steamer, or a pressureless convection steamer.

Steaming offers caterers the benefits of easy, quick preparation and cooking. There is little loss of flavour or colour, and the fish retains many of its nutrients.

Steaming is suitable for fillets of white fish, and for various cuts (but not the small ones). Small whole fish can also be steamed.

Oily fish is not usually steamed.

General points to remember when steaming fish

1 Before cooking, lightly moisten the fish with a little fish stock, lemon juice, milk or water (or follow specific recipe instructions). Season to taste with salt and white pepper (not black pepper which will look unappetising against the white background of the cooked fish).

2 Cook for a short time only.

3 Prepare sauces separately.

ACTION

As a companion to the one you prepared in *Meat and poultry*, draw up a poster which will remind busy catering staff of the main contamination threats when preparing, cooking and storing fish dishes.

Before finalising your ideas, discuss the project with a number of people. You may find that they do not readily think of fish in connection with food poisoning. This is because fish that has gone 'bad' usually smells and tastes so unpleasant that there is no hesitation in throwing it away. For this reason, your poster must be particularly thought-provoking.

Right: *steamed halibut cutlet.*

Left: *steamed fillet of plaice.*

A simple garnish works best for a dish of this sort. Note that the lemon pieces have been carefully prepared.

The segment *has been trimmed at both ends, and at the centre, to remove excess white pith.*

The serrated lemon half *has been cut from a whole lemon by working around it with the end of a small cook's knife.*

Any visible pips have been prised out with the tip of the knife blade.

Shallow frying

`LEVELS 1 + 2`

In shallow frying the fish is cooked in a little oil or fat at quite high temperatures, using a frying pan (or similar equipment).

Many other types of food are shallow fried, see particularly *Meat and poultry*, page 69.

General points to remember when shallow frying fish

1 Use the minimum amount of oil/fat. The idea is not to deep fry the fish.

2 Preheat the oil/fat to ensure that it is very hot.

3 Do not allow the oil/fat to smoke. This is not only dangerous, but will cause the outside of the fish to burn.

4 Cook the presentation side of the fish first (see box).

5 Fry over a high heat to start with. This helps brown the fish, and will set a breadcrumb coating, helping to seal in the flavour.

6 Reduce the heat to continue cooking larger cuts and pieces of fish.

7 Between batches of cooking, change the oil or fat, and wipe the pan clean with absorbent kitchen paper. This will make sure you don't get a build up of tiny burnt pieces of food (from the coating, for example).

8 Do not overfill the pan. Allow yourself space to turn the fish over easily.

9 Serve the food as soon as possible after cooking. Do not cover fish which has been coated, otherwise it will become soggy.

One of the attractive effects of shallow frying is the crisp brown surface it creates. These goujons of plaice have been coated with breadcrumbs.

Presentation side

This is the side which will give the better appearance after cooking:

for whole flat fish (when the white skin is usually left on, while the black skin is removed) – the unskinned side

for fillets – the side which was nearest the bone

for whole round fish and for other cuts of fish (e.g. steaks, cutlets, goujons) – the side that looks best is usually the side cooked first.

The traditional French way to cook fish for shallow frying is to pass the fish through seasoned flour, shaking off any surplus. When cooked, fish prepared in this way is described as being in the meunière *style or* à la meunière. *Literally translated, this means in the style of the miller's wife.*

It is thought that a miller's wife picked up a fish with floury hands and discovered that the flour-coated parts cooked the best.

Stir frying fish: general procedure

1 Cut the fillets of fish into thin strips.
2 Toss for a few minutes over high heat, using a wok or large frying pan, and very little oil.
3 Add vegetables, and cook for a few minutes longer.
4 Season and serve at once.

Which oil or fat in shallow frying?

If you do not have specific instructions about what oil or fat to use, consider the following points:

- products with a bland taste will least affect the delicate flavour of the fish. Rapeseed/colza oil, with its slightly bitter flavour, is therefore not usually suitable

- some dishes depend for much of their flavour on using some butter, or, as in the recipe for sea bass on page 119, a particular type of oil

- butter on its own is not satisfactory because it will burn. A mixture of oil and butter overcomes this disadvantage. Alternatively clarified butter can be used

- polyunsaturated fats are more healthy than saturated fats which are thought to contribute to heart disease. Check the label before choosing a particular product.

You should also consider the cost of the product:

- butter and olive oil, with their fine flavours, are among the more expensive choices

- virgin olive oil, which comes from the first pressing, is very flavoursome, but particularly expensive

- grapeseed oil is aromatic, high in polyunsaturated fats, low in saturated fats, but expensive

- sunflower and safflower oils have a light, fairly neutral flavour, a high proportion of polyunsaturated fats, high smoke point, and low proportion of saturated fats. They are quite economical

- corn oil is also economical, but has quite a strong frying smell, and its flavour is better suited for salad dressings and mayonnaise

- palm oil is economical and has a high smoke point, but a high proportion of saturated fats.

Baking

In baking, food is cooked by the mainly dry heat inside an oven.

Unlike pastry goods, potatoes and other foods which are commonly baked, fish requires some protection from the direct heat of the oven. This is done in one or both the following ways:

by helping the fish retain moisture

The fish is baked in an enclosed container, typically:

- an ovenproof dish, with the lid on
- a foil parcel
- a paper parcel (*en papillote*).

A coating of breadcrumbs or oatmeal, for example, works in a similar way.

by adding moisture

Ways of doing this include:

- brushing the fish with oil or butter before cooking
- marinating the fish before cooking
- basting the fish during cooking with a small quantity of wine, fish stock, cream or marinade
- stuffing whole fish, cutlets and rolled fillets with a moist mixture, such as lemon, parsley and thyme stuffing.

Liquids that form part of the cooking process will, as these examples indicate, add flavour to the fish. After cooking, the remaining liquid is usually served with the fish, or used to make the accompanying sauce.

Clarifying butter

1 Melt the butter over a very low heat.
2 Skim off the foam. Allow to stand for about 10 minutes, so that the milk solids separate from the liquid.
3 Ladle off the clear yellow liquid into a clean bowl – some chefs take the added precaution of straining it at the same time, using a very fine strainer. Take care to leave the residue undisturbed in the bottom of the pan.
4 Use at once or store chilled.

Poaching

`LEVEL 2`

Definition Poaching is a method of cooking food gently in not quite boiling liquid.

Because of the gentle nature of the cooking, poaching is a favourite way of cooking most varieties of fish, and in particular those with a more delicate flavour or texture.

The cooking liquid contributes to the taste of the finished dish, either by giving flavour to the food, or by forming the basis of an accompanying sauce, or both. Spices, herbs, salt, pepper, lemon juice, wine, vinegar, chopped onions or shallots, and sliced mushrooms are some of the ingredients that can be used.

The food is either completely or partially covered by the cooking liquid. These techniques have their own names and particular characteristics: *deep poaching* and *shallow poaching*. Some chefs and recipes have developed variations on these two styles, but to take proper account of these would mean inserting the words 'usually' or 'generally' in every statement made on these pages!

Deep poaching

Used for whole fish – as big as will fit into the largest fish kettle you have available – and large cuts of fish. The size of the piece means that there is little danger of the fish falling apart during cooking. It also results in an attractive finished product for presentation at a special meal, or display on a buffet table.

Only one item of food is poached in the fish kettle at a time. When two or three whole salmon are to be deep poached, for example, they would be cooked in separate fish kettles, or one after the other, in freshly prepared cooking liquid. Such an arrangement would clearly not be suitable for poached fish which is to be served hot at a banquet, for example.

1   The fish is completely covered by the poaching liquid.

2   The skin is left on for cooking. This provides additional protection.

3   The starting temperature is hot for cuts. This keeps the overall cooking time to the minimum (always important with tender foods). For whole fish it is cold, otherwise the flesh will shrink suddenly and unevenly, causing distortion. (So-called blue trout is the main exception.)

4   Poaching is done on top of the stove.

5   The liquid contributes flavour to the food during cooking. Sometimes a little is served with the finished dish. Otherwise it is discarded.

Fish kettles of various different sizes specially designed for poaching whole round fish, such as salmon. The lids fit tightly. A perforated drainer fits into the bottom of the kettle and has handles that will reach above the surface of the cooking liquid on either side. This is useful for removing the cooked fish.

Fish kettles are made of stainless steel, aluminium or tin-lined copper. For poaching whole turbot, a diamond shaped kettle is used, but these are not often seen now.

A vinegar court-bouillon which will complement the flavour of salmon, trout, or skate, for example. The ingredients – water, onion, carrot, celery, leek, parsley, bay leaf, thyme, peppercorns, salt and vinegar – are brought to the boil and simmered for 15 to 20 minutes (recipe on page 127). Some chefs omit the celery and leek.

The court-bouillon can be made either in the fish kettle, or separately in a saucepan allowing it to be strained into the fish kettle when cooked. This second method has the advantage of keeping the fish free of the vegetable ingredients which would need to be removed later.

Either way, the court-bouillon is allowed to get cold before the fish is added.

Shallow poaching

Used for thin or fragile cuts of fish which would break up if they were deep poached.

As many pieces of fish as will fit comfortably in the saucepan can be cooked at the same time. The pieces should be kept slightly apart, so that the poaching liquid heats up evenly, and the fish can be removed without damage when it is cooked.

For large quantities, poaching can be done in a deep tray.

So that the uncovered portion of the food does not dry out, and the heat distribution is as even as possible, the food is covered with a piece of greaseproof paper and often a lid as well. The paper is buttered or oiled to prevent it sticking to the food. And to avoid the risk of the edges burning in the oven, the paper is shaped to fit neatly inside the container (see page 225).

There are many opinions as to exactly what covering to use. Some chefs use kitchen foil, but others say that kitchen foil should be avoided because it will make any wine used in the poaching liquid discolour, and the chemicals in some greaseproof paper may give the food a disagreeable flavour. Sometimes buttered brown paper is used. So there is no easy answer, and you should always check on what method is preferred in your workplace.

1 The liquid level comes about two-thirds of the way up the food.

2 Most cuts of fish can be cooked, as well as small whole fish.

3 Because the small amount of liquid used will heat up quickly from cold, there is no need to preheat it.

4 Cooking is started in a saucepan on top of the stove. When the liquid has reached the right temperature (just under boiling point), the poaching process can be continued in the oven for more even heating.

5 Some of the cooking liquid is served with the food, or it is incorporated into the accompanying sauce.

Cooking the sauce

When the liquid used in poaching forms the basis of a thickened sauce, the sauce will usually have to be cooked separately so that it can be boiled.

This is because the temperature in poaching is not high enough to cook any starch used to thicken the sauce properly.

How to get the best from poaching

1 Fresh fish, if scaly, should be scaled before deep poaching. For shallow poaching the skin is removed (unless it is easier to remove it after cooking).

2 Frozen fish must be defrosted before poaching (with the possible exception of small cuts). This will avoid uneven cooking, which can lead to a risk of food poisoning.

3 Prepare the poaching liquid in advance for deep poaching, so that it has time to cool.

4 When cooking for large numbers, some preparation can be done in advance of shallow poaching. The cooking containers can be lined with the base of chopped vegetable, the pieces of fish placed on top, the whole thing covered and placed in the cold room a few hours before cooking needs to start.

5 In deep poaching, the fish is often allowed to cool in the cooking liquid. This helps the flavours to develop more fully, and to keep the fish moist. Cooling must take place as quickly as possible for reasons of hygiene. Place the kettle in a cool room, or in a sink with cold water, which must be regularly replaced until the cooking liquid has cooled. The fish is then removed, carefully drained and placed in the refrigerator.

HYGIENE

Poaching temperatures (see page 11) will allow the survival of certain types of bacteria. So it is important that any poached food spends as little time as possible in a warm environment:

- decorations for a hot poached dish should be prepared in advance as far as possible, and kept simple
- poached dishes to be served cold, on a buffet, for example, should be chilled quickly after cooking
- decoration work on a cold poached dish should be done in a very cool room, with the food resting on a bed of ice. Work as fast as possible. Often a simple bold design will be just as appealing, and much more hygienic, as a complicated one that might take hours
- when decorating by hand, take particular care to keep your hands scrupulously clean.

Finishing and presenting

There are a number of ways of testing whether or not the fish is cooked. Choose the method that is least likely to damage the appearance of the finished dish:

- press gently with the back of a teaspoon. It should give under the pressure and not spring back. If it springs back as if you were pressing a sponge, the fish is not yet cooked

- insert a cocktail stick or skewer into the thickest part of the flesh. There should be little resistance

- cooked fish flesh loses its translucent appearance and becomes opaque. This is particularly easy to see on white fillets.

If the fish breaks up, it is overcooked.

When fish is cooked correctly, it can be easily taken off the bone.

Deep fried fish

Immediately after frying, place the cooked fish on a tra lined with absorbent kitchen paper. This will he remove excess oil.

Season foods well away from the fryer.

When the fish is to be presented to the customer on a serving dish (that is, not plated in the kitchen), line the dish with a dish paper.

Poached fish

Careful draining is important whether the food is served hot or cold, as any cooking liquid left on the food will spoil the appearance of the sauce. Take great care in handling the food while draining because it may easily fall apart.

When reducing the liquid after removing fish which has been shallow poached, shake the pan gently from time to time and stir the liquid to prevent burning.

> **To prepare a decorative lemon**
>
> See photograph opposite.
> 1 Cut a whole lemon in half through the middle so that you cut across the segments.
> 2 Cut a sliver of peel almost all the way round the cut edge.
> 3 Tie the length of peel into a loose knot.

To remove the skin before service

from steaks or cutlets

1 Catch one end of the skin with the prong of a fork.
2 Twist the fork around to roll up the loosened skin.
3 Alternatively the skin can be carefully cut off with a knife.

from a whole cooked fish

1 Use a palette or filleting knife and your finger to carefully lift the skin off.
2 Gently scrape away any brown surface or skin remaining on the flesh.
3 Remove the base of any fins along the back and belly.

To remove the centre bones from steaks

1 Insert the sharp point of a small knife firmly into the middle of each bone.
2 Carefully pull outwards.
3 If the fish is not properly cooked, the bones will not come free, and you will need to cook the fish for a few minutes longer.

Garnishes

Simple garnishes which work well with fish dishes include:

- parsley
- watercress
- fresh herbs such as dill and fennel

and with deep fried dishes:

- deep fried parsley
- salad arrangement, e.g. lettuce, slices or shapes of cucumber, quarters or slices of tomato
- pickled vegetables, e.g. cucumber, gherkins.

If there are no specific recipe or workplace instructions for garnishing a particular dish, and you have to make up your own garnish, choose items that will provide between them, and with the fish, a good balance and contrast of:

- colour
- flavour
- texture.

CHEF'S TIPS

If you are adding butter to enrich the sauce, do this at the last minute and do not allow the sauce to boil again, otherwise the butter fat will separate out and float to the surface, producing an unattractive effect.

If whitebait are kept in iced water until they are about to be coated and cooked, they are easier to handle than they otherwise would be.

Place food coated with breadcrumbs in the oil with the best side down. Breadcrumbs that come loose will float in the oil and burn, and then settle on the side of the food that will eventually be face down on the serving dish.

Dry fish before passing through flour. This ensures that the coating is even and reduces the risk of the flour becoming sticky.

Dealing with the unexpected

Fish cooks quickly – only fast action can prevent a difficulty from becoming a disaster. For instance:

- if the surface is not browning sufficiently in grilling or shallow frying, you can increase the heat. With deep or shallow frying, you can try cooking less food at one time
- if a poaching liquid has begun to boil, you should immediately turn the heat down
- if a sauce is too thick or too thin, you should correct it before pouring over the food, or serving (see page 75)
- if there is a delay in serving a hot poached, steamed or baked fish dish, and there is a danger the fish will dry out, cover with a piece of greaseproof paper and place in a hot cupboard. Don't add the sauce until the last moment.

Learning from your mistakes

... and avoiding similar problems in the future.

Fish is tasteless

- poor quality or badly stored fish was used

Fish is dry and has a poor appearance

- overcooked
- cooking temperatures too high
- not adequately coated for frying or grilling
- black skin of flat fish not removed before cooking
- surplus coating not removed before cooking
- badly handled during or after cooking

Poached fish has a tough, rubbery texture

- temperature of cooking liquid too high, causing the flesh to toughen and shrink

Poached, baked or steamed fish sticks to the cooking utensil (or to the covering paper)

- surfaces not prepared properly. They should be lightly brushed with oil or rubbed with butter or margarine

Sauce watery, running off the fish

- fish not drained properly after poaching or shallow frying
- sauce too thin

Cream in sauce separates

- cooking liquid reduced too much after the cream has been added. To avoid this, shake the pan gently, or stir from time to time while reducing the sauce to ensure an even reduction

Steamed fish unpleasantly flavoured

- steamer not properly cleaned after being used to cook strongly-flavoured food

This photograph is used in the Metropole Hotels group to set the company's standard for presentation of suprême of salmon with cucumber and caviar sauce.

Deep fried cod in batter

Key learning points
» make yeast batter
» coat fish with batter
» deep fry round, white fish

The fish can be marinated for 20 to 30 minutes before coating to add flavour. For the marinade, use the juice of 1½ lemons, 250 ml oil, 6 g chopped parsley and 60 g finely chopped spring onions or shallots.

It can also be served with a tomato sauce (page 144), and the dish is then called *Orly style*.

SERVES 10

10 × 175 g	suprêmes of cod fillet	10 × 6 oz
10	lemon wedges	10
	parsley sprigs	
	plain flour, seasoned if required	

Batter

400 g	strong flour	14 oz
10 g	caster sugar	¼ oz
20 g	compressed yeast (fresh)	¾ oz
500 ml	milk (or water)	18 fl oz
	pinch salt	

1 Sieve together the flour, sugar and salt for the batter into a large bowl.

2 Warm the milk to 40°C.

3 Mix the yeast with a little of the milk and add this mixture to the flour. Whisk in the remaining milk to produce a smooth batter. Cover and leave to ferment in a warm place for 1 hour.

4 One at a time, coat the suprêmes with the seasoned plain flour (shaking off any excess), then with the batter (draw the fish gently over the side of the bowl to remove any surplus batter).

5 Deep fry at 180°C until crisp and golden brown (3 to 6 minutes). Turn the fish with a spider when necessary.

6 Drain well. Place on a warm serving dish lined with a dish paper. Decorate with the lemon and plain or deep fried parsley, and serve. Do not cover.

Deep fried goujons of plaice with tartare sauce

Key learning points
» breadcrumb fish
» deep fry flat white fish

SERVES 2

4 × 75 g	plaice fillets cut into goujons	4 × 3 oz
2	lemon wedges	2
2	sprigs parsley	2
	tartare sauce (page 145)	
50 g	flour, seasoned if required	2 oz
1	egg beaten with little milk	1
50 g	breadcrumbs	2 oz

1 One at a time, lightly coat the goujons with the flour, beaten egg and breadcrumbs. Shake off any excess.

2 Roll each goujon lightly between the palms of your hands to neaten the shape.

3 Place the goujons into a frying basket, then deep fry at 185°C until crisp and golden brown (about 2 minutes).

4 Drain well, then place on a warm serving dish lined with a dish paper. Decorate with the lemon wedges and plain parsley (or deep fried). Do not cover. Serve at once, accompanied with the tartare sauce.

Sprats boursin
by Sea Fish Industry Authority

Key learning points
» stuff sprats with cream cheese
» breadcrumb fish
» deep fry sprats (oily fish)

SERVES 4

450 g	sprats, boned	1 lb
125 g	Boursin cream cheese	5 oz
	flour for dusting	
2	eggs, beaten with little water	2
	breadcrumbs for coating	
	seasoning to taste	

1 Season the sprats. Spread the insides with the cream cheese. Fold over to reshape the sprat.

2 Dust in flour. Dip in beaten egg. Coat in breadcrumbs.

3 Deep fry at 180°C for 4 minutes.

4 Drain and serve at once.

Crispy whitebait
by Sea Fish Industry Authority

Key learning point
» deep fry oily fish

SERVES 4 to 6

900 g	whitebait, fresh or defrosted	2 lb
50–100 g	seasoned flour	2–4 oz
5 ml	cayenne pepper	1 tsp
15 ml	fresh parsley, chopped	1 tbsp
	lemon wedges (garnish)	

1 Carefully rinse and dry the whitebait. Coat with seasoned flour (this should be done immediately before frying).

2 Deep fry at 180°C for about 2 minutes, or until crisp. Drain on absorbent kitchen paper.

3 Serve immediately sprinkled with parsley and cayenne pepper and garnished with lemon wedges.

Battered witch fingers
by Sea Fish Industry Authority

Key learning points
» prepare a simple batter
» deep fry white fish

This recipe is also suitable for megrim, dab, whiting and plaice.

Serve with a selection of relishes or dips.

MAKES 18 to 24 fingers

450 g	witch fillets, fresh or defrosted, skinned, and cut into strips	1 lb
	seasoned flour	
1	egg yolk	1
225 ml	iced water	8 fl oz
100 g	self-raising flour	4 oz

1 Place the egg yolk into a bowl and pour in the iced water. Mix together, then add the flour and stir for about 10 seconds. The batter does not need to be smooth.

2 Coat the strips of fish in the seasoned flour, then in the batter, shaking off any excess.

3 Deep fry at 170°C for a few minutes, until golden brown.

4 Drain on absorbent kitchen paper. Serve immediately.

Fillets of sole meunière

Key learning points
» flour fish
» shallow fry flat, white fish
» make beurre noisette

SERVES 1

2 × 75 g	fillets of sole	2 × 3 oz
12 g	butter	½ oz
5 ml	oil	1 tsp
	flour, seasoned if required	

For finishing

25 g	butter	1 oz
3	slices peeled lemon	3
	squeeze of lemon juice	
	fresh parsley, chopped	

1 In a suitable frying pan, heat the oil, then add the butter.

2 Lightly coat both sides of the fillets in the seasoned flour, shake off any surplus and place the fish into the pan, presentation side downwards.

3 Fry the fish until it has turned golden brown, then carefully turn it over. Continue frying until cooked. A small fillet will take 3 to 5 minutes in all.

4 Remove the fillets from the pan and arrange them in a warm serving dish, presentation side upwards. Decorate with the lemon slices and a sprinkling of chopped parsley.

5 Place the butter into a clean, hot frying pan, shake the pan until the butter has turned an even golden brown colour, then add the squeeze of lemon juice. This will cause the butter to froth. Immediately pour this mixture (called *beurre noisette*) over the fish and serve at once.

Fillet of sea bass with black olives
by Rory Kennedy, Hanbury Manor, Hertfordshire. Published by Caterer & Hotelkeeper, 26 September 1991

Key learning points
» shallow fry sea bass
» prepare a simple, but finely flavoured sauce and garnish

SERVES 4

4 × 100 g	sea bass fillets	4 × 4 oz
400 g	new potatoes	14 oz
12 g	garlic purée	½ oz
50 ml	virgin olive oil	2 fl oz
30 ml	fresh dill, chopped	2 tbsp
	seasoning to taste	

Sauce

200 ml	virgin olive oil	7 fl oz
1	lemon, for juice	1
2	beef tomatoes peeled, deseeded and chopped	2
100 g	black olives, stoned and chopped	4 oz
30 ml	fresh dill, chopped	2 tbsp
	seasoning to taste	

Prepare the potatoes

1 Steam the potatoes in their skins.

2 When cooked and still warm, peel and lightly crush with a fork.

3 Add a little of the olive oil (warmed), the garlic purée and dill. Season.

4 Cover and keep warm while you are cooking the fish.

Cook the fish

1 Season well.

2 Sauté in the olive oil, ensuring the top is cooked golden brown.

Make the sauce

1 Warm the olive oil with the olives. Season with salt, pepper and lemon juice.

2 At the last moment, add the dill and tomato.

To serve (plated in the kitchen)

1 Place a large tablespoon of the crushed potato in the centre of each plate.

2 For each serving, spoon 2 or 3 tablespoons of the sauce around the potato.

3 Place the cooked fish on the potato base and serve immediately.

Asparagus and trout stir fry
by The Asparagus Growers' Association

Key learning point
» stir fry vegetables and trout

SERVES 4

10 ml	cornflour	2 tsp
5 ml	soy sauce	1 tsp
55 ml	oil	3½ tbsp
400 g	trout fillets, cut into 25 mm wide strips	14 oz
1	clove garlic, crushed and peeled	1
	25 mm piece fresh root ginger, very finely chopped	
500 g	fresh asparagus, cut into thin diagonal slices	1 lb 2 oz
2	small carrots, thinly sliced with serrated edge	2
2	courgettes, cut into matchsticks	2
30 ml	chicken stock	2 tbsp
175 g	fresh beansprouts	6 oz

1 Mix together cornflour, soy sauce and 10 ml oil. Stir in trout and mix until evenly coated.

2 Heat 30 ml oil in a wok or large frying pan. Add trout and gently stir fry for about 2 minutes. Transfer trout to a clean dish and keep warm.

3 Add remaining oil to pan. Add garlic and ginger and stir fry for 30 seconds.

4 Add asparagus, carrots and courgettes and stir fry for another 30 seconds.

5 Add chicken stock and cook, stirring frequently for 3 to 4 minutes.

6 Stir in beansprouts and cook for a minute.

7 Return trout to pan, and stir fry just to heat through. Serve at once.

Grilled salmon steaks

Key learning points
» flour fish
» grill oily fish (or white fish)

This method is suitable for *small whole fish*, e.g. herrings, trout, sardines, *whole flat fish*, e.g. lemon or Dover sole, *fillets* e.g. plaice, and *steaks*, e.g. halibut.

SERVES 4

4 × 225 g	salmon steaks	4 × 8 oz
Coating		
50 g	flour, seasoned if required	2 oz
50 g	oil or melted butter	2 oz
	seasoning to taste	
Garnish		
4	lemon wedges or halves	4
8	slices parsley butter (page 86)	8
	sprigs of parsley	

1 Coat the fish with the seasoned flour. Shake off any surplus, then brush lightly with oil or melted butter.

2 Grill until the fish develops a good colour. Turn over when half-cooked (after about 6 minutes) and continue grilling until the fish is cooked (about another 6 minutes). Brush with more oil or melted butter if the fish starts to dry out.

3 Arrange the steaks on a warm serving dish. Decorate with the parsley and lemon. Serve accompanied by slices of parsley butter (placed in a sauceboat or dish with iced water).

Grilled mackerel with gooseberry sauce

Key learning points
» flour fish
» grill or barbecue oily fish

SERVES 1

1 × 350 g	whole mackerel (prepared)	1 × 12 oz
Coating		
25 g	flour, seasoned if required	1 oz
25 g	oil or butter	1 oz
	seasoning to taste	
Garnish		
1	lemon wedge or half	1
	branch parsley	
	gooseberry sauce (page 145)	

1 Make 4 or 5 short cuts across the back of the fish, taking care to cut only just through the skin.

2 Lightly coat the fish with the flour. Shake off any surplus then brush with melted butter or oil.

3 Grill or barbecue the mackerel for about 8 minutes on each side. When the fish is cooked, the flesh should yield when pressed, with no sign of sponginess.

4 Place the fish on a warm service dish, then decorate with the lemon and parsley. Accompany by the gooseberry sauce.

Tandoori fish fillets
by Sea Fish Industry Authority

Key learning points
» prepare a simple marinade for fish
» grill and present a marinated fish dish
If you are using frozen fillets, increase cooking time to 10 to 15 minutes
Accompany with yellow rice and a crisp green salad.

SERVES 4

4 × 150 g	fillets of white fish	4 × 6 oz
140 ml	natural yogurt	5 fl oz
15–30 ml	prepared tandoori mix	1–2 tbsp
15 ml	oil	1 tbsp
15 ml	lemon juice	1 tbsp
	salt to taste	

1 Blend together the yogurt, tandoori mix and oil.

2 Arrange the fish fillets in a shallow ovenproof dish. (The fish will be cooked in the same dish.) Sprinkle with lemon juice, season with salt and coat well with tandoori mixture.

3 Cover and refrigerate for 30 minutes.

4 Pour off excess tandoori mixture from the fish fillets. Place the dish under the grill and cook for 7 to 10 minutes, basting with tandoori mixture and turning halfway through cooking. (If you are using frozen fillets, increase cooking time to 10 to 15 minutes.)

5 Serve at once.

Tandoori fish skewers
by Potato Marketing Board

Key learning point
» prepare variation on tandoori fish fillets

SERVES 4

900 g	firm white fish, skinned and cut into 24 large pieces	2 lb
30 ml	tandoori paste	2 tbsp
30 ml	natural yogurt	2 tbsp
24	small new potatoes, well scrubbed and cooked	24
½	cucumber, cut into 24 thick chunks	½
10 ml	vegetable oil	2 tsp
5 ml	barbecue seasoning	1 tsp
	lemon wedges (garnish)	

1 Place the fish in a shallow dish. Mix the tandoori paste with yogurt and pour over the fish. Leave to marinate overnight in the refrigerator.

2 Drain the fish. Fill the skewers with alternate layers of fish, potatoes and cucumber.

3 Lightly brush with oil, sprinkle with barbecue seasoning and grill or barbecue for 10 minutes, turning once. Serve immediately.

Sole fillets with lemon herb butter
by The Butter Council

Key learning point
» grill white fish

For the butter, follow the same procedure as parsley butter (page 86). For the quantity in the recipe below use 15 ml (1 tbsp) lemon juice, 15 ml parsley and 5 ml fresh or dried tarragon.

SERVES 4

4 × 150 g	fillets of sole	4 × 6 oz
75 g	lemon, parsley and tarragon butter	3 oz
	seasoning to taste	

1 Place one slice of butter on to each fillet, season and grill for about 8 minutes until cooked.

2 Serve at once accompanied by more herb butter in a sauceboat with iced water.

Fisherman's pie
by Sea Fish Industry Authority

Key learning point
» make a pie with smoked and white fish and bake

SERVES 4

225 g	smoked fish fillets skinned and cubed (e.g. smoked cod or haddock)	8 oz
225 g	white fish fillets skinned and cubed (e.g. cod, coley or whiting)	8 oz
50 g	frozen peas	2 oz
280 ml	béchamel sauce (page 143)	½ pt
450 g	mashed potato	1 lb
25 g	butter or margarine	1 oz

1 Lightly mix together the fish and peas. Place in a medium-sized ovenproof dish.

2 Pour over white sauce.

3 Top with mashed potato. Pipe with a star tube or spread with a palette knife and decorate surface by making a pattern with the prongs of a fork.

4 Dot with the butter or margarine. Bake at 190°C for 40 to 45 minutes until potato is golden brown.

Cheesy baked cod steaks
by Sea Fish Industry Authority

Key learning point
» bake white fish

SERVES 4

4 × 175 g	cod steaks (fresh or frozen)	4 × 6 oz
	knob of butter or margarine	
15 ml	Worcestershire sauce	1 tbsp
1	small packet plain potato crisps	1
50 g	grated cheese (e.g. Cheddar)	2 oz

1 Arrange fish in an ovenproof dish. Dot with butter or margarine. Sprinkle with Worcestershire sauce.

2 Bake for 10 minutes at 200°C (frozen steaks: 15 minutes).

3 Crush crisps and mix with cheese. Sprinkle over fish and bake for a further 10 minutes or so: the crisps will brown quickly.

Fillets of plaice with watercress, leek and vermouth
by Craigmillar/Meadowland

Key learning points
» bake white fish
» thicken a sauce by liquidising
For information on Meadowland, see page 182.

SERVES 8

8 × 150 g	fillets of plaice	8 × 6 oz
50 ml	vermouth	2 fl oz
	seasoning to taste	
50 g	margarine	2 oz
30 g	watercress	½ bunch
2	shallots, finely chopped	2
125 g	mushrooms, chopped	4 oz
6	baby leeks, sliced	6
150 ml	fish stock	¼ pt
150 ml	Meadowland	¼ pt

1 Season the fish. Roll up and place in a shallow ovenproof dish. Sprinkle 10 ml (2 tsp) vermouth over the fish. Cover tightly and bake at 180°C for 20 to 25 minutes.

2 Meanwhile gently fry the watercress, shallots, mushrooms and leeks in the margarine. Add vermouth and boil until reduced. Stir in the stock. Liquidise until smooth.

3 Return sauce to the pan, add Meadowland and reheat but do not boil. Check seasoning.

4 Drain cooked fish, arrange on warm serving dish and pour sauce over. Garnish with watercress and serve.

Bacon haddie
by Pork and Bacon Promotion Council and others

Key learning point
» bake smoked haddock
Can be offered as an alternative on a breakfast buffet.

SERVES 10

10	slices smoked bacon	10
675 g	smoked haddock (cooked)	1½ lb
500 ml	béchamel sauce (page 143)	1 pt

1 Wrap haddock in bacon and place in ovenproof dish. Coat with sauce and bake at 180°C for 30 minutes.

2 Garnish with sprigs of fresh parsley and serve.

Steamed fish

Key learning point
» steam fish
Any small cut of fish or small whole fish can be cooked in this way.

SERVES 20

20 × 150 g	fish fillets, skinned	20 × 6 oz
	fish stock, milk or water	
	seasoning to taste	
20	lemon pieces/wedges and sprigs of parsley (garnish)	20

1 Lightly oil the base of a suitable cooking dish or steamer tray. Place the fish in it, spaced slightly apart. Season and moisten with a little fish stock.

2 Cover with a lid and steam in an atmospheric or low-pressure steamer for 15 to 20 minutes (check timing with instructions for the equipment).

3 To serve, coat the fish with a little of the cooking liquid and garnish (see photograph on page 111).

Two fish bake
by Dufrais

Key learning point
» bake white and smoked fish
In the mornay sauce recipe (page 143), use Bistro Chef/white wine in place of some of the milk.

SERVES 4

675 g	potatoes, cooked and diced	1½ lb
350 g each	cod fillet and smoked haddock fillet, skinned and cubed	12 oz each
575 ml	mornay sauce *packet*	1 pt
60 ml	parsley, freshly chopped	4 tbsp
25 g	~~Gruyère~~ Cheddar cheese, grated	1 oz

1 Place the fish in an ovenproof dish. Mix the sauce with the chopped parsley and pour over the fish. Top with diced potato and reserved cheese. Bake for 25 minutes at 200°C.

2 Garnish with flat leafed parsley.

Poached fillets of sole Bréval style

Key learning points
» poach flat white fish
» make a sauce incorporating the poaching liquid
» thicken a sauce by reduction

SERVES 4

8 × 75 g	fillets of sole	8 × 3 oz
5 g	butter	¼ oz
25 g	shallot or onion, finely chopped	1 oz
100 g	white mushrooms, sliced	4 oz
225 g	tomatoes, peeled, deseeded and chopped	8 oz
	little parsley, chopped	
50 ml	dry white wine	2 fl oz
150 ml	fish stock	6 fl oz
	squeeze lemon juice	
350 ml	fish velouté	12 fl oz
50 ml	whipping or double cream, lightly whipped	2 fl oz

1 Butter the base of a suitable dish or pan. Add the shallots, mushrooms, tomato and some of the chopped parsley.

2 Fold the fillets of sole neatly into two, and place them on the base you have just formed. Sprinkle with chopped parsley. Add the wine, lemon juice and enough fish stock to bring the liquid to two-thirds the height of the fillets.

3 Cover with buttered greaseproof paper, put the lid on the pan, and place the pan over the heat.

4 Bring almost to the boil, then continue cooking in a moderate oven (175°C) for about 6 minutes.

5 When cooked, carefully remove the fillets. Transfer them to a suitable dish or tray, cover with the cooking paper and place in a warm oven or hot cupboard.

6 Boil the liquid remaining in the cooking pan vigorously until it has reduced to a small amount, and become quite thick.

7 Add the fish velouté and return to the boil.

8 Remove the sauce from the heat and lightly fold the whipped cream through it.

9 Adjust seasoning, then pour a little of the sauce into the serving dish, so that it evenly coats the base.

10 Arrange the fillets in pairs on the dish, then coat them with the remaining sauce. Avoid flooding the fillets: it should be possible to see their shape.

11 Place the dish under a preheated grill to lightly brown the surface of the sauce. Serve at once.

Fillets of sole with butter sauce
by Dufrais

Key learning point
» poach white fish

SERVES 4

12	quarter fillets of lemon sole, skinned and rolled	12
150 ml	fish stock	¼ pt
15 ml	white wine vinegar	1 tbsp
50 g	butter	2 oz
2.5 ml	fennel seeds	½ tsp
6	anchovy fillets, chopped	6
1	large spring onion, trimmed and finely diced	1
15 ml	fresh parsley, chopped	1 tbsp
	paprika to taste	
	fresh fennel (garnish)	

1 Poach the fish fillets in the fish stock with 5 ml wine vinegar for 7 to 8 minutes until firm and white. Drain and keep warm.

2 Melt the butter and shallow fry the fennel seeds until the butter is golden. Add the anchovy, onion and remaining vinegar and boil rapidly for a few minutes. Add the parsley and season with paprika.

3 Pour the sauce over the fish, garnish with fresh fennel and serve.

Fish and pasta creole
by Sea Fish Industry Authority

Key learning points
» poach white fish
» cook a fish dish with pasta

SERVES 20

100 g	butter	4 oz
1–2	cloves garlic, crushed and peeled	1–2
10 sticks	(1 head) celery, washed and diced	10 sticks
1½ litre	fish stock	2½ pt
900 g	sweetcorn (frozen or tinned)	2 lb
3–3½ kg	coley or monkfish fillets, cubed	7½ lb
1	bay leaf	1
450 g	macaroni	1 lb
4 × A2½ cans	whole tomatoes	4 × A2½ cans
	seasoning to taste	
	fresh parsley, chopped (garnish)	

1 Melt the butter in a large saucepan and lightly fry the garlic and celery.

2 Add the stock, sweetcorn, fish, bay leaf and macaroni. Season and gently simmer for 10 to 12 minutes until the fish and macaroni are tender.

3 Add tomatoes (drained). Reheat briefly, adjust seasoning. Remove bayleaf.

4 Serve hot, decorated with chopped parsley.

Smoked haddock kedgeree

Key learning points
» poach smoked fish
» remove skin and bones from cooked fish, and flake fish

Kedgeree can be made the same way with salmon, or a combination of two or three types of fish.

SERVES 10

350 g	long grain rice, cooked	14 oz
1 kg	smoked haddock	2½ lb
5	hard-boiled eggs	5
150 g	margarine or butter	6 oz
	chopped parsley (optional)	
1 litre	fish stock or water	2 pt
	seasoning to taste	
500 ml	curry sauce (page 144)	1 pt

1 Lightly butter or oil the sides and base of a suitable pan. Place the fish in the pan, and barely cover with fish stock or water. Cover with a circle of buttered greaseproof paper, and the saucepan lid.

2 On top of the stove, bring almost to the boil. Cook slowly over low heat on top of the stove or transfer to a moderate oven.

3 When cooked (about 10 minutes) drain the fish. After cooling sufficiently, remove the bones and skin. Flake the fish and place it aside in a bowl.

4 Cut the egg whites into small dice and chop the yolks roughly.

5 Heat the butter or margarine in a large sauteuse and add the fish, eggs and rice. Toss the ingredients together and allow to reheat thoroughly. Check the seasoning.

6 Neatly arrange the kedgeree in a warm service dish and sprinkle with chopped parsley. Accompany with curry sauce.

Poached salmon steaks with sherry mayonnaise
by Dufrais

Key learning points
» poach oily fish
» make a variation on mayonnaise (page 265)

This dish can also be served cold.

SERVES 4

15 ml	sherry vinegar	1 tbsp
2.5 ml	French mustard	½ tsp
15 ml	pasteurised egg yolk (1 yolk)	1 tbsp
	pinch of sugar, salt and freshly milled black pepper	
150 ml	oil	¼ pt
4 × 150 g	salmon steaks	4 × 6 oz
150 ml	fish stock	¼ pt
15 ml	sherry vinegar	1 tbsp

1 Place the egg yolk, sugar, salt, pepper and mustard in a small bowl. Beat in the vinegar. Beat in the oil a drop at a time until thick and creamy.

2 Poach the salmon in the fish stock and vinegar for about 15 minutes. Drain and serve with the sauce.

Herring and yogurt salad
by Sea Fish Industry Authority

Key learning points
» poach oily fish
» prepare rollmops

SERVES 2 to 4

4 × 150 g	whole herrings, boned	4 × 6 oz
1	medium sized onion, sliced finely	1
6	whole black peppercorns	6
140 ml	tarragon vinegar	5 fl oz
140 ml	fish stock	5 fl oz
140 ml	natural yogurt	5 fl oz
1	eating apple, sliced and dipped in lemon juice to keep colour	1

1 Roll the herrings up from head to tail, and secure with a cocktail stick. Place in a shallow ovenproof dish. Cover with the onion, seasonings, tarragon vinegar and stock. Poach in the oven at 160°C for 30 minutes.

2 Remove from the oven and chill.

3 When chilled, carefully lift out the rollmops and arrange on a serving dish. Strain the liquid.

4 Blend a little of the liquid with the yogurt. Pour over the fish. Decorate with the sliced apple.

Quick fish pâté
by The Butter Council

Key learning point
» prepare simple smoked fish pâté

SERVES 4

225 g	smoked mackerel	8 oz
25 g	butter	1 oz
10 ml	horseradish sauce	2 tsp
15 ml	fresh parsley, chopped	1 tbsp
30 ml	natural yogurt	2 tbsp
10 ml	lemon juice	2 tsp
	freshly ground black pepper	

1 Remove skin and bones from the fish. Place in a bowl and mash with a fork.

2 Melt the butter over a very low heat, so it does not separate. Immediately mix into the fish. Add horseradish, parsley, yogurt and lemon juice. Beat well. Season with pepper.

3 Spoon into dishes, cover and chill.

Salmon mousse
by Dufrais

Key learning point
» prepare a cold mousse

Use fresh, cooked salmon if preferred.

SERVES 4 to 6

275 ml	béchamel sauce (page 143)	½ pt
	seasoning to taste	
10 ml	gelatin	2 tsp
50 ml	cold water	2 fl oz
1 × 212 g	can salmon, drained, skin and bones removed	1 × 7½ oz
60 ml	white Bistro Chef/white wine	4 tbsp
5 ml	dried chervil	1 tsp
140 ml	whipping cream, lightly whipped	¼ pt

1 Sprinkle the gelatin over cold water. Make up to 150 ml (¼ pt) with boiling water and stir until dissolved. Cool then mix into the béchamel.

2 Mash the salmon with the Bistro Chef and chervil. Season. Stir into the béchamel. Fold in the cream.

3 Pour into oiled moulds and place in the refrigerator for 2 to 3 hours to set.

4 When required, turn out of the moulds (see page 266). Decorate with a twist of lemon and parsley.

Red mullet in lettuce leaves
by British Iceberg Growers' Association

Key learning point
» stuff and bake white fish

SERVES 6

6	medium size red mullet, scaled, gutted and cleaned	6
	seasoning to taste	
50 g	Chevre cheese, crumbled	2 oz
15 ml	grated lemon rind	1 tbsp
5 ml	Pesto sauce	1 tsp
30 ml	iceberg lettuce, finely chopped	2 tbsp
12	iceberg lettuce leaves	12
225 ml	dry white wine	8 fl oz
100 g	iceberg lettuce, coarsely chopped	4 oz
½	avocado, peeled and roughly chopped	½
	fresh basil (garnish)	

1 Season the mullet inside and out.

2 Mix the Chevre cheese with the lemon rind, Pesto, finely chopped lettuce and seasoning. Stuff the cavity of the fish with this mixture.

3 Boil the lettuce leaves for 1 minute, and chill immediately under cold running water. Drain thoroughly.

4 Wrap each stuffed mullet in 2 lettuce leaves and place side by side in an ovenproof dish. Spoon the wine over the fish and cover with foil.

5 Bake at 180°C for 30 to 35 minutes, until the mullet are just tender. Lift the mullet on to the serving dish and keep warm.

6 Pour the cooking juices into a liquidiser, add the coarsely chopped lettuce and avocado. Blend until smooth. Reheat.

7 Serve the mullet garnished with basil and accompanied by the sauce.

Steamed trout
by Sarson's

Key learning point
» stuff and steam trout in the Oriental style

The fish can be steamed over a pan of boiling water. Place in a colander or on a plate, and cover with kitchen foil and the saucepan lid.

SERVES 2

15 ml	grapeseed oil	1 tbsp
1	small onion, finely chopped	1
50 g	mushrooms, finely chopped	2 oz
25 g	cashew nuts, toasted and roughly chopped	1 oz
60 ml	Sukiyaki sauce	4 tbsp
25 g	fresh breadcrumbs	1 oz
15 ml	fresh parsley, chopped	1 tbsp
2 × 225 g	trout, scaled, gutted and washed	2 × 8 oz
4	individual Chinese leaves	4
25 g each	carrot and celery, cut into matchsticks	1 oz each

1 Fry the onion in the oil until soft. Add mushrooms, cashew nuts and 30 ml Sukiyaki sauce and cook for 1 minute.

2 Remove from heat and mix in breadcrumbs and parsley. Stuff the cavity of the trout with this mixture.

3 Lay out 2 large sheets of greaseproof paper. Place 2 Chinese leaves on each. Lay the fish on top. Pour 15 ml Sukiyaki sauce over the fish, sprinkle over the carrot and celery.

4 Bring up the sides of the paper to make a parcel enclosing the fish. Place on a perforated tray in a low-pressure steamer and steam for 20 to 30 minutes.

5 Carefully unwrap the greaseproof paper, remove the fish and serve at once.

NVQ SVQ RANGE CHECKLIST

LEVEL 1

1D2.1 Prepare fish for cooking

prepare preprepared or convenience fish to be cooked by 3 of these methods

☐ grilling or barbecuing
☐ steaming
☐ shallow frying
☐ deep frying

using 1 of these methods

☐ defrosting
☐ coating with flour or breadcrumbs or batter

1D2.2 Cook fish dishes

cook preprepared or convenience fish by 3 of these methods

☐ deep frying
☐ grilling or barbecuing
☐ shallow frying
☐ steaming

LEVEL 2

2D2.1 Prepare fish for cooking

prepare

☐ round fish
☐ flat fish

by 4 of these methods

☐ washing
☐ trimming
☐ boning or filleting
☐ portioning
☐ stuffing
☐ skinning

2D2.2 Cook fish dishes

cook

☐ white fish
☐ oily fish

by 3 of these methods

☐ baking
☐ grilling or barbecuing
☐ shallow frying
☐ deep frying
☐ poaching

Shellfish

Introduction

British caterers have a choice of some of the finest shellfish in the world. To make sure that the customer gets the best possible product, shellfish should be bought alive, or very recently cooked from a reliable supplier, and then served as soon as possible.

Many types of shellfish can be bought frozen or canned. These products are very useful, especially if the fish is to be mixed with other ingredients.

An increasing number of ready-prepared shellfish dishes are also available.

Types of shellfish

Shellfish are divided into those with:

- jointed legs and a tough outer layer or shell covering the body, such as brown crab, spider crab, crawfish, lobsters, prawns and shrimps – *crustaceans*

- soft bodies and a shell they retreat into, such as cockles, clams, mussels, oysters, scallops, whelks and winkles – *molluscs*.

Contents guide

Units and elements covered in this section

2D14 Prepare and cook shellfish dishes   LEVEL 2
– 2D14.1 Prepare and cook shellfish dishes

1) and 3) Crabs, 2) Crawfish (spiny lobster), 4) Mussels, 5) King prawns, 6) Prawns, 7) Scampi (Dublin Bay prawns or langoustines), 8) Lobster. All cooked, except for the mussels.

Quality points

Shellfish is best purchased *live* from a reliable supplier or direct from a wholesale market or port where the catch is freshly landed. This is the only way to guarantee freshness.

They should be packed and sold in moist, cool conditions, when they will survive for some time out of water:

- crustaceans will show signs of life by obvious movement
- the shells of molluscs should be tightly closed or shut rapidly when tapped. If the shells are open or close slowly then it is likely that the creatures are dead or dying and the flesh is deteriorating, so they should not be used.

for live shellfish

- fresh salty sea smell
- clear, fresh colour
- a heavy and full sound when tapped lightly
- no claws missing on crabs and lobsters
- lobster tails spring back into place after being uncurled. Lobster claws should be bound with elastic bands on delivery to prevent injury through fighting
- lobsters are fairly heavy in proportion to size
- hen crabs and lobsters have broader tails and more flesh than cock lobsters
- crab claws are large and fairly heavy

for cooked shellfish

- shells are intact: if cracked the meat texture may have been damaged by water seepage during cooking
- soft crab or lobster shells which feel light could indicate a newly grown shell. This temporarily spoils their eating quality
- shrimps and prawns are even-sized, not too small and firm to the touch
- liquid in cooked crab and lobsters, caused by the shrinking of the flesh from the shell, could indicate overcooking
- there should be no signs of discoloration, nor unpleasant smells indicating spoilage.

	Jan	Feb	Mar	Apr	May	Jun	Jul	Aug	Sep	Oct	Nov	Dec
Crustaceans												
Crab				▨	▨	▨	▨	▨	▨	▨	▨	▨
Crawfish				▨	▨	▨	▨	▨	▨	▨	▨	▨
Crayfish	▨	▨	▨							▨	▨	▨
Lobster				▨	▨	▨	▨	▨	▨			
Prawns		▨	▨	▨	▨	▨	▨	▨	▨	▨	▨	▨
Scampi		▨	▨	▨	▨	▨	▨	▨	▨	▨	▨	▨
Shrimps		▨	▨	▨	▨	▨	▨	▨	▨	▨	▨	▨
Molluscs												
Cockles					▨	▨	▨	▨	▨	▨	▨	▨
Mussels	▨	▨	▨						▨	▨	▨	▨
Oysters	▨	▨	▨	▨					▨	▨	▨	▨
Scallops	▨	▨	▨							▨	▨	▨
Whelks		▨	▨	▨	▨	▨	▨	▨				
Winkles			▨	▨	▨	▨	▨	▨	▨	▨		

▨ *When shellfish are at their best.*

Storage

The greatest care must be taken in storing and handling shellfish. Their fine eating quality depends on absolute freshness.

Shellfish which has been allowed to deteriorate is likely to cause severe illness if eaten.

Never freeze shellfish which might have been frozen before – which could be the case with bought-in cooked shellfish.

of live shellfish

1 Store at a temperature between 2°C and 10°C.
2 Keep in its packaging to avoid moisture loss.
3 Ensure that all live shellfish remain moist.
4 Molluscs should be kept in a container embedded in ice. The round side of the shell should face downwards to help collect and retain the natural juices.
5 Check regularly to make sure the shellfish are still alive. Reject any dead or dying specimens.

of cooked shellfish

1 Cooked shellfish should be stored covered, at between 0°C and 4°C.
2 Cooked products must not come into contact with uncooked food of any sort.
3 Frozen shellfish should be defrosted overnight in a refrigerator. Use within 12 hours.

Preparation and cooking methods: introduction

Shellfish has a delicate flavour. This means that many customers prefer their shellfish cooked plainly, or with very light accompaniments.

Crustaceans can be boiled in salted water or in a court-bouillon (see below) in which the acid has a tenderising effect. The shells help the flesh to keep its shape and protect it from damage, but great care should be taken not to overcook the shellfish, or it will become tough.

Boiling is the usual cooking method for crustaceans that are going to be served cold. Using the shell to present the finished dish gives an attractive presentation. But because it is so difficult to clean the shell hygienically many chefs prefer to use a shell-shaped china dish.

Boiling – or blanching – is also often used to pre-cook shellfish that is going to be cooked by another method, such as grilling or shallow frying.

Mussels and whelks are the only molluscs that are usually boiled. Other molluscs, such as scallops, are more often poached, grilled or shallow fried.

Vinegar court-bouillon for cooking shellfish

MAKES 1 litre (2 pt)

1 litre	water	2 pt
50 g each	onion and carrot, sliced	2 oz each
25 g each	celery and leek, sliced (optional)	1 oz each
50 ml	white wine vinegar	2 fl oz
	salt	

sprig of thyme, bay leaf, few parsley stalks

1 Place all the ingredients into a saucepan. Bring to the boil and simmer for about 20 minutes.
2 Add the shellfish, and return to the boil. Simmer until the shellfish is cooked. Cooking times depend on size, and are shorter when the fish is left to cool in the court-bouillon (these times given in brackets). Here is a rough guide:
scampi tails (in their shells): 5 to 6 minutes (4 to 5 minutes)
lobster and *crab*:
medium size (750 g/1½ lb): 20 to 25 minutes (15 to 20 minutes)
large (1¼ kg / 2¾ lb): 35 to 40 minutes (30 to 35 minutes)

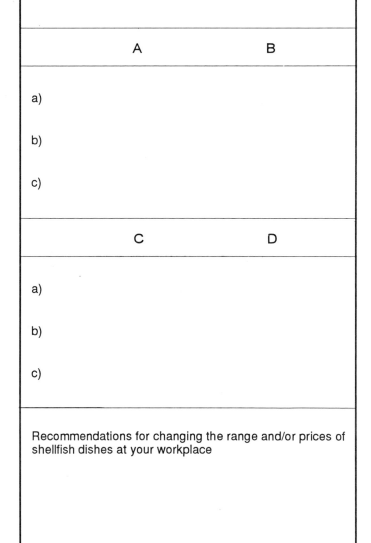

ACTION 127

Carry out a survey of the menus of some of the local restaurants and hotels in your area. You will find this exercise more helpful if you concentrate on those establishments which might be thought to compete with the one where you work. Briefly summarise your results in the format suggested below, then discuss them with your supervisor.

Restaurant/hotel: A   B   C   D

Total no. of items on menu

No. of items with shellfish

Name and price of 3 most expensive shellfish dishes at each establishment

	A	B
a)		
b)		
c)		

	C	D
a)		
b)		
c)		

Recommendations for changing the range and/or prices of shellfish dishes at your workplace

Crab

The brown crab is the easiest to find in British shops. The velvet crab and spider crab, also found around the coast of Britain, are mostly sent to Europe where they are very much prized.

Cock crabs are larger than hens and have bigger claws. During the summer months, the hen's shell is lined with delicious pink coral.

There are two types of meat in a crab:

- *white*, found in the legs and claws

- *brown*, found in the body, which has the stronger flavour of the two types, and is creamy in texture.

Crab is usually boiled in a court-bouillon (see previous page). It may then be eaten cold as a first course, or with a salad as a main course or meal, or the meat is used in a wide range of recipes.

Removing the flesh from a cooked crab

1 Holding the crab upside down, remove the claws one at a time. Twist sharply and pull, so that the claws become detached as close to the crab's body as possible.

2 Twist the smaller part of each claw back on itself, so it breaks off from the larger section (with the pincer).

3 Crack open the claw pieces by hitting sharply with the back of a knife or a cleaver. Alternatively, use a saw.

4 Remove the meat from each claw piece. The handle of a teaspoon comes in useful at this stage, especially for getting the meat out of the pincers. Alternatively, use the point of a skewer.

5 Take care to free the meat of every bit of splintered shell. Place this, the *white meat*, aside in a clean dish.

6 Holding the crab steady, grip the soft undershell firmly and pull open. If the mouth has not come away, press it down with your thumbs until it breaks cleanly with a click. (In the photograph, the mouth has come away with the undershell: the chef demonstrator's thumb marks the position.)

Step 1

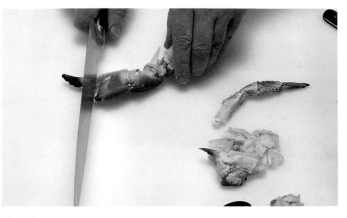

Step 3

Step 5

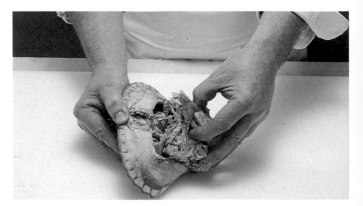

Step 6

7 Pull off and discard the gills (*dead man's fingers*). Scrape into a second bowl any *brown meat* clinging to this part of the crab.

8 Remove the hard piece of sac behind the eyes and discard.

9 With a spoon (held in the usual way this time), scrape out all the soft yellowish-brown meat and any coral meat from inside the crab shell. Put this with other brown meat.

10 Wash the shell very thoroughly, then break open by carefully pressing the outside of the shell along the natural line.

11 Rewash the shell and allow to dry.

Dressing the crab

To dress one crab, about 1 kg uncooked weight, serving 1 person as a main course, you will need:

1	hard-boiled egg	1
50–75 ml	mayonnaise	2–3 fl oz
15–30 ml	fresh white breadcrumbs	1–2 tbsp
	parsley, freshly chopped	

1 Finely chop or sieve the egg yolk and egg white, and keep separate.

2 Force the brown meat through a sieve. Then mix with enough breadcrumbs and mayonnaise to form a paste. Check the seasoning.

3 Place the paste into both sides of the shell and smooth the surface with a palette knife.

4 Arrange the white meat in the centre, then decorate over the top with lines of sieved egg yolk, sieved egg white and chopped parsley.

Some chefs present dressed crab with the white meat arranged at either side, and the dark meat in the centre. Another method is to arrange the white and brown meat in rows.

Anchovies can be arranged in a criss-cross fashion down the centre of the crab, with a slice of stuffed olive placed between. Capers can also be used in the arrangement.

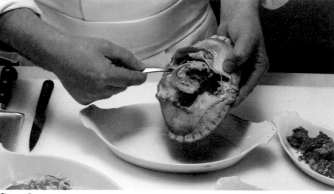

Step 7

Step 9

Step 10

Brown crab

Spider crab

Dressing the crab

Lobster, crawfish and crayfish

Lobsters and their cousins the crawfish are regarded as the most delectable of all shellfish, rare and very expensive to buy.

Most of the lobsters sold in Britain's shops have already been cooked, however many caterers prefer to buy them live. They can then be cooked in a number of ways:

- boiled whole in salted water with a little vinegar for 15 to 25 minutes according to size. Alternatively use a court-bouillon for all the cooking, or part of the cooking (after boiling for 5 minutes in salted water). During cooking their colour changes from deep blue to scarlet

- split in half, and grilled. Alternatively, flesh removed, chopped and grilled or shallow fried

- a combination of processes. The lobster is cooked initially by boiling or steaming. The flesh is removed, chopped and then shallow fried or sautéed. Usually it is combined with a sauce before being grilled or gratinated to brown.

Crawfish is slightly paler than lobster when cooked. It has no claws. The tail meat is well flavoured, although it can sometimes be coarse. It is prepared and cooked in a similar way to lobster.

Crayfish is the only edible freshwater shellfish. It is smaller than a lobster, and comparatively sweet fleshed. It is normally cooked whole, after gutting. To do this, take hold of the middle tail flap, twist to dislocate from the shell, then pull carefully. The gut should come away in one piece.

Preparing lobster

1 Twist and pull off the claws and legs or pincers.

2 Crack open the claws and legs with the back of a heavy knife (see crab, page 128). Remove the flesh and set aside in a clean bowl. Discard the blade of cartilage in the centre of the claw meat.

3 Split the lobster body in half using a large knife:

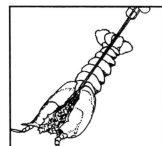

draw the knife through the head from the shoulder up towards the eye;

reinsert the knife and draw it in the opposite direction, cutting down to and right through the tip of the tail;

pull the halves apart to expose the flesh.

4 Discard the white gills or sac, which you will find in the top of the head.

5 Pull out and discard the intestinal canal (dark-coloured thread), which runs down the middle of the tail flesh. The end of a teaspoon may help you catch hold of it.

6 Scrape out the creamy white head meat with a teaspoon, also the greenish liver, or tomalley. These are very flavourful for adding to sauces or soups.

7 Remove and discard the feathery gills situated in cavities either side of the body, between the creamy white head meat and the small legs.

8 Remove the tail flesh. This should pull away easily in one piece, with the red skin-like coating intact. Place with the meat from the claws.

If you have got time, it is possible to use the meat out of the little legs. Break off at each joint first, and squeeze from the bottom upwards.

Dressed lobster meat is sometimes presented with the legs and claws in place.

Oysters Pollution of much of the sea has made top quality oysters difficult to obtain. Indeed some chefs will no longer serve oysters in the form they are considered best – raw. For cooked dishes requiring oysters, they use canned or frozen ones.

When oysters are to be eaten raw, they should not be prepared until the very last moment, in order to retain their sea-fresh flavour and juices. Hold the oyster firmly in one hand, with a cloth. With the other hand force the blade of an oyster knife between the two shells, and twist to prise the shells apart. Ask the fishmonger to give you a demonstration!

Discard the flat shell. Without allowing the juices to spill, slip the knife blade under the oyster to free it. Serve on a bed of crushed ice.

Scallops Usually sold open and cleaned, attached to the flat shell, or on their own. They are delicious poached, grilled or shallow fried. They become rubbery if overcooked. If poaching, detach the orange roe and cook for a shorter time.

Winkles and whelks Can be used in paella or fish soups and stews, or eaten on their own. Steam for a few moments, extract from their shells with a pin or small fork, then sprinkle with lemon juice, butter and black pepper. Also popular ready-cooked, when they are eaten cold with vinegar, brown bread and butter. Whelks, the larger of the two, are normally sliced lengthways. They can be breadcrumbed and fried.

Cockles Usually bought bottled in brine or vinegar (but this tends to mask their flavour).

Shrimps and prawns

Shrimps are the smallest crustacean found in British waters, and are pink or brown when cooked. Prawns are slightly larger. The names are often used interchangeably.

Only the tail of shrimps and prawns is edible. If purchased fresh (not common), they are cooked by boiling in salted water for a minute or two. Alternatively, they can be shallow fried, grilled, or cooked in combination with an enormous variety of ingredients for paella, seafood soup, mousses, soufflés, kebabs, fish stews and so forth.

Scampi

Also called *Dublin Bay prawns, Norway lobsters* or *langoustines*, scampi are regarded by many as the most handsome of the crustaceans. They are like small lobsters with elongated claws, and retain their attractive peach and coral colours after cooking.

Usually only the tail is eaten, as there is not enough meat in the head or claws to warrant the effort of picking it out.

Scampi can be cooked in a court-bouillon, shallow fried, or grilled. Much of the scampi sold to caterers has been peeled and coated with breadcrumbs, ready for deep frying.

Mussels

Mussels cling to the seabed or hang from rocks or ropes. Their shells range in colour from blue-black to golden tortoiseshell. They take about two years to reach maturity, and have an excellent, slightly sweet flavour.

Mussels produce a surprising quantity of moisture as they cook, so you only need a small amount of liquid to cook them. They are usually boiled (see pages 132 and 133) in a heavy pan over a high heat for just as long as it takes for their shells to open – a matter of minutes. Over-cooked mussels tend to be rubbery.

Preparing mussels

Simply scrub them under a cold tap – scraping off any barnacles, and pull away the wiry 'beard' which sprouts between each shell.

Peeling prawns (and shrimps)

1 Straighten the prawn out and pull off the whole head with a twisting movement.
2 Holding the prawn upside down, insert your fingers under the legs and pull the shell apart to expose the pink flesh.
3 With the fingers of one hand, take a firm hold of the exposed flesh at the head end. With the other hand, pinch the tail to release pressure.
4 Pull the body and shell apart.

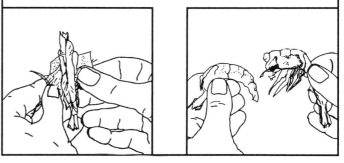

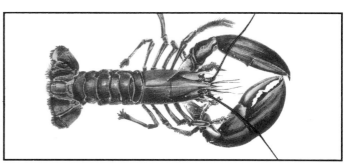

Uncooked lobster.

Uncooked crawfish.

Mussels will open during cooking.

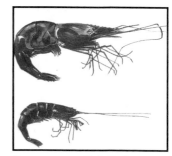

Prawns are slightly larger than shrimps.

Hot crab starter
by Sea Fish Industry Authority

Key learning point
» prepare and grill avocado stuffed with shellfish

SERVES 10

350 g	mixed crabmeat, fresh or defrosted	12 oz
225 g	low fat cream cheese	8 oz
30 ml	tomato purée	2 tbsp
	seasoning to taste	
	tabasco	
5	avocados, halved and stoned	5
½	lemon, juice of	½
5	rashers streaky bacon	5

1 Mix together the crabmeat, cream cheese, tomato purée, seasoning and a few drops of tabasco.

2 Carefully scoop out centres of avocados without damaging the skin. Place skins to one side.

3 Roughly chop avocado, mix with lemon juice, and fold into crabmeat mixture.

4 Divide mixture between the avocado shells, filling until rounded.

5 Top with a rasher of bacon, and grill under a medium heat for about 10 minutes, or until the crab mixture has warmed through and the bacon is crisp.

Garlic potted prawns
by The Butter Council

Key learning points
» prepare a classic cold starter using prawns
» use butter to set a cold dish

SERVES 4

225 g	peeled cooked prawns	8 oz
50 g	butter	2 oz
1	clove garlic, crushed and peeled	1
	seasoning to taste	
15 ml	fresh parsley, chopped	1 tbsp

1 Dry the prawns on kitchen paper and place in individual pots. Season.

2 Melt the butter in a saucepan. Add the garlic and fry for 1 minute, then add the parsley.

3 Pour over the prawns and chill thoroughly before serving.

Stuffed mushrooms (with crab)
by Sea Fish Industry Authority

Key learning point
» stuff mushrooms with a shellfish mixture and grill

SERVES 4

225 g	white crabmeat	8 oz
8	medium sized mushrooms	8
50 g	low fat soft cheese	2 oz
15 ml	chopped chives	1 tbsp
50 g	wholemeal breadcrumbs	2 oz
	seasoning to taste	

1 Rinse mushrooms and pat dry.

2 Remove stalks and chop finely. Stir in crabmeat, cheese, seasoning and chives.

3 Divide mixture between mushrooms. Sprinkle with breadcrumbs.

4 Place under medium grill and cook for 10 to 15 minutes until golden brown.

Moules marinière
by Sea Fish Industry Authority

Key learning point
» boil mussels

Traditional French style for serving mussels. Serve with French bread.

SERVES 4

2 kg	fresh mussels, washed and scrubbed	4 lbs
25 g	butter or margarine	1 oz
1	onion, chopped finely	1
1	clove garlic, crushed and peeled	1
280 ml	dry white wine, or stock	½ pt
30 ml	lemon juice	2 tbsp
3	bay leaves	3
45 ml	fresh parsley, chopped	3 tbsp
	seasoning to taste	

1 Melt the butter or margarine in a large saucepan and lightly fry the onions and garlic, until onions are soft and transparent.

2 Add the liquids, bay leaves and seasonings and bring to the boil. Add the mussels all at once, cover and cook over a high heat, shaking the pan occasionally to ensure even cooking.

3 When all the mussels have opened (and discard any that have not) transfer to a heated serving dish, reserving the liquid.

4 Return the liquid to the heat and boil rapidly until reduced by half, stir in the parsley and season to taste.

5 Pour the sauce over the mussels, before serving.

Seafood kebabs
by Sea Fish Industry Authority

Key learning points
» grill or barbecue a kebab with prawns and fresh scallops
» prepare and use a marinade for shellfish

Variation: shallow fry the prepared peppers in oil for a few minutes before assembling the kebabs.

Serve with wholemeal pitta bread or brown rice.

SERVES 4

8	fresh scallops	8
8	whole prawns	8
1 each	red and yellow pepper, large	1 each
Marinade		
150 ml	sunflower oil	5 fl oz
5 ml	fennel seeds	1 tsp
10 ml	fresh marjoram, chopped	2 tsp
10 ml	fresh thyme, chopped	2 tsp
2	bay leaves	2
½	lemon, juice of	½
	seasoning to taste	

1 Slice the scallops in half.

2 Using a cocktail or small pastry cutter, cut 8 circles from each pepper.

3 In sequence, so that the ingredients provide attractive contrasts of colour and texture, thread the scallops, peppers and whole prawns on to 4 skewers. You should begin and end with a piece of pepper, so that the fish is firmly anchored on to the skewer.

4 Thoroughly blend the marinade ingredients together (shaking them in a screw-top jar is a good way to do this).

5 Pour the marinade over the kebabs, cover and leave in a refrigerator for 1 to 2 hours.

6 Grill or barbecue the kebabs for 5 to 10 minutes, turning once.

Moules à la bordelaise
by Sea Fish Industry Authority

Key learning points
» prepare and cook a traditional seafood dish of mussels
» boil mussels
» gratinate the mussels to brown

SERVES 4

2 litre	fresh mussels, washed and scrubbed	4 pt
125 ml	dry white wine	4 fl oz
25 g	butter	1 oz
1	medium onion, finely chopped	1
1	clove garlic, crushed and peeled	1
450 g	fresh tomatoes, peeled, deseeded and chopped	1 lb
45 ml	fresh parsley, chopped	3 tbsp
½	lemon, rind of	½
	seasoning to taste	
75 g	fresh brown breadcrumbs	3 oz
	melted butter	

1 Place the mussels and wine in a large pan, cover and boil vigorously until they have opened.

2 Strain the mussels and remove empty half shells. Reserve the cooking liquid.

3 Melt the butter and fry the garlic and onion for 2 minutes. Add the tomato, parsley, lemon and seasoning. Stir in the cooking liquid. Simmer until the tomato is cooked.

4 Arrange the mussels in a suitable heatproof dish (a gratiné dish, for example). Pour over the sauce (which should be quite thin), and sprinkle with breadcrumbs.

5 Dribble a little melted butter over the top and pop under a moderate grill until golden brown. Serve immediately.

Lobster theodore
by Sea Fish Industry Authority

Key learning points
» prepare cooked lobster and combine with recipe ingredients
» grill lobster
This recipe is also suitable for crawfish and crayfish.

SERVES 2

1 × 625 g	lobster, cooked	1 × 1 lb 6 oz
1	clove garlic, crushed and peeled	1
25 g	butter	1 oz
	seasoning to taste	
15 ml	grated Parmesan cheese	1 tbsp
5 ml	dry mustard powder	1 tsp
25 g	fresh breadcrumbs	1 oz

1 Cut the lobster in half and remove the meat (see page 130 for detailed steps). Slice, then add to the meat from the claws, the liver and any red coral (roe).

2 Clean out the shell halves carefully.

3 Mix the lobster meat with the butter (which should be softened first), garlic and seasoning. Divide between the shell halves.

4 Grill for 5 minutes. The lobster should be quite close to the grill (80 mm or so) so that the cooking is quick.

5 Meanwhile mix the cheese and mustard with the breadcrumbs. Place on top of the lobster, and return to the grill until a crispy golden topping has formed. Serve immediately.

King prawn tempura
by Sarson's

Key learning points
» prepare a tempura-style batter
» deep fry prawns
Serve with Sukiyaki sauce.

SERVES 4

2	egg yolks, size 3	2
400 ml	ice cold water	14 fl oz
225 g	plain flour, sifted	8 oz
16	king prawns, uncooked	16
	1 small aubergine, 2 courgettes, 1 red pepper, chopped into bite-size pieces	
225 g	mushrooms	8 oz
100 g	baby corn	4 oz

1 Peel each prawn, except for the last tail segment. Remove the vein that lies along the tail flesh. Make a straight incision on the underside of the prawn at the head end to prevent the prawn curling when cooked.

2 Whisk egg yolks and water until frothy. Add flour and whisk to a smooth batter.

3 Dip the prawns and vegetables in the batter and deep fry at 177°C for a few minutes until golden brown. Serve at once.

Honey sesame prawns
by Dufrais

Key learning point
» deep fry prawns
Serve with nutty vegetable stir fry (see page 172).

SERVES 4

15 ml	sesame oil	1 tbsp
6	spring onions, trimmed and finely chopped	6
5 ml	root ginger, grated	1 tsp
125 ml	water	4 fl oz
600 ml	light soy sauce	4 tbsp
15 ml	lemon juice	1 tbsp
60 ml	clear honey	4 tbsp
5 ml	sweet chilli sauce	1 tsp
45 ml	cornflour	3 tbsp
15 ml	water	1 tbsp
680 g	whole prawns	1½ lb
25 g	toasted sesame seeds	1 oz

1 Heat the sesame oil in a large pan and lightly fry the onions and ginger.

2 Add 125 ml water, soy sauce, lemon juice, honey and chilli sauce. Bring to the boil.

3 Mix together 10 ml cornflour and 15 ml water, add to the sauce, whisking continuously. Reduce heat.

4 Toss prawns in the remaining cornflour and deep fry at 177°C for a few minutes until golden. Drain on kitchen paper.

5 Quickly mix the prawns with the hot sauce, add the sesame seeds and serve at once.

Stir fried fish
by Sea Fish Industry Authority

Key learning points
» stir fry fish and shellfish
» adapt a stir fried recipe according to availability of ingredients

SERVES 4

450 g	prepared fish or shellfish e.g. white crabmeat, squid (sliced)	1 lb
30 ml	sunflower oil	2 tbsp
	freshly ground black pepper to taste	

suggestions for crab

4	sticks celery, finely sliced	4
1	large red pepper, deseeded and sliced	1
50 g	mushrooms, sliced	2 oz
10–15 ml	soy sauce	2–3 tsp

suggestions for squid

2	cloves garlic, crushed and peeled	2
½	fresh chilli, deseeded and finely sliced	½
1	bunch spring onions, trimmed and sliced	1
2	carrots, sliced	2
100 g	beansprouts	4 oz
150 ml	fish stock	5 fl oz
15 ml	soy sauce	1 tbsp
5 ml	cornflour	1 tsp
50 g	roasted peanuts	2 oz

1 Heat the oil in a large wok or large, deep frying pan.

for crab

2 Add all the vegetables, and stir fry for 2 to 3 minutes.

3 Add the crabmeat, soy sauce and pepper, and cook for another 2 to 3 minutes until heated through.

for squid

2 Fry the garlic and chilli for 1 minute.

3 Add the sliced squid. Stirring continuously, cook for 2 minutes.

4 Stir in the onions, carrots and beansprouts. Cook for a further 2 minutes.

5 Pour in the stock and soy sauce blended with the cornflour.

6 Cook over a high heat, stirring until the sauce thickens. Add peanuts, seasoning and serve immediately.

Nutty paella
by Dufrais

Key learning points
» poach prawns
» cook risotto rice

SERVES 2 to 3

30 ml	walnut oil	2 tbsp
1	medium onion, finely chopped	1
100 g	cleaned calamari, uncooked, sliced in rings	4 oz
5 ml	turmeric	1 tsp
175 g	risotto rice	6 oz
575 ml	fish stock	1 pt
100 g	shelled prawns	4 oz
100 g	frozen petits pois	4 oz
1 × 105 g	can smoked oysters, drained	1 × 3.7 oz
30 ml	garlic wine vinegar	2 tbp
75 g	cashew nuts, toasted	3 oz

1 Heat the oil in a large frying pan. Add onion, calamari, turmeric and rice, and fry for 1 to 2 minutes.

2 Add fish stock, cover and cook, stirring occasionally, for 15 minutes.

3 Add prawns, peas, smoked oysters and vinegar. Cook for a further 4 to 5 minutes.

4 Mix in cashew nuts and serve.

Hot shellfish stew
by Sea Fish Industry Authority

Key learning points
» boil shellfish
» prepare and cook a shellfish stew
Accompany with pasta and French bread.

SERVES 4

900 g	mixed prepared shellfish, e.g. prawns, scallops, mussels, squid	2 lb
10 ml	oil	2 tsp
1	large onion, chopped	1
2	cloves garlic, crushed and peeled	2
1 × 400 g	can chopped tomatoes	1 × 14 oz
30 ml	tomato purée	2 tbsp
150 ml	red wine or fish stock	5 fl oz
30–45 ml	chilli and garlic sauce	2–3 tbsp
1 each	red and green pepper, diced	1 each
	seasoning to taste	
	chopped parsley (optional)	

1 Heat the oil in a large pan and cook the onion and garlic until the onion is soft and transparent.

2 Stir in the tomatoes, tomato purée, red wine, chilli and garlic sauce, and peppers.

3 Bring to the boil and simmer for about 15 minutes until the peppers are cooked.

4 Add the shellfish, simmer for a further 3 to 5 minutes until cooked.

5 Season, garnish with parsley and serve immediately.

NVQ **SVQ** RANGE CHECKLIST

LEVEL 2

2D14.1 Prepare and cook shellfish dishes

for 2 of these types
☐ crab
☐ crayfish or crawfish or lobster
☐ prawns or shrimps or scampi
☐ mussels

cooking by 2 of these methods
☐ grilling or barbecuing
☐ shallow frying or stir frying or deep frying
☐ boiling or poaching or blanching

Introduction

A few years ago, you would find in most kitchens a bubbling stockpot, containing a great variety of bones and vegetables. Often this would be left to simmer for days, with the addition from time to time of vegetable trimmings, bones left over after roasts had been carved, and so forth. A good stockpot, it was said, was the only way to make an acceptable sauce or soup.

Now, because of increased awareness of hygiene, the use of fresh stock has been banned in a great many kitchens. Where it is used, there are strict rules about how long it can be kept for, and in what conditions.

Some consider the use of convenience sauces and soups unprofessional. Others accept that they have a role in situations where budgets are very restricted.

The quality and range of convenience products have improved enormously. Some can be used as they are. Others provide the base for a sauce or soup, so you still have plenty of scope for providing your own touch.

Units and elements covered in this section

1D4 Prepare and cook convenience stocks, sauces and soups   LEVEL 1

– 1D4.1 Prepare and cook convenience stocks, sauces and soups

2D4 Prepare and cook stocks, sauces and soups   LEVEL 2

– 2D4.1 Prepare and cook stocks
– 2D4.2 Prepare and cook sauces
– 2D4.3 Prepare and cook soups

Contents guide

A selection of fresh herbs used in the preparation and garnishing of stocks, sauces and soups: 1) Sage, 2) Flat-leaved parsley, 3) Curly-leaved parsley, 4) Coriander, 5) Dill, 6) Chervil, 7) Thyme, 8) Chives, 9) Marjoram, 10) Basil, 11) Mint, 12) Tarragon, 13) Rosemary, 14) Bay leaf.

Using convenience stocks, sauces and soups

LEVEL 1

These are available:

- ready-to-use in cans, jars, cartons or special sachets
- in concentrated liquid form, requiring the addition of water or milk
- in granular or dried powder form or as cubes, to be blended with the recipe liquid, or mixed with water.

Some products can be kept at room temperature, and have a long shelf-life. Frozen products also have quite a long shelf-life, and some chilled products last up to 16 days. In all cases, you should be guided by the storage instructions on the packet and the use-by or best-before date. Any products that have passed the stated date should not be used, but reported to your supervisor.

Before use, you should also check that the packaging is in good condition. Damaged goods should not be used.

General points to remember using convenience products

1 Before reducing convenience stocks, or a sauce or soup made with them, check the taste. For example, some products contain quite a lot of salt, and any reduction will result in a dish that is too salty.

2 For concentrated products, it is better to use rather less than the amount stated in the instructions on the packet. If necessary you can then add a little more. Most chefs consider convenience stocks too powerful to be used in the amount that is recommended.

3 For stocks and base sauces, choose the flavour that is most appropriate for the dish you are making. For example, fish stock or fish velouté to make a sauce to accompany poached fish, vegetable stock or a product approved by the Vegetarian Society (and carrying its V logo) for any dish described on the menu as suitable for vegetarians.

Some terms you may come across on convenience stocks

fonds de légumes – vegetable stock

fonds blanc de volaille – white chicken stock

fonds brun clair – clear brown stock

fumet de crustacés – shellfish stock

fumet de poisson – fish stock

jus de veau lié – thickened veal stock

HYGIENE

All food becomes a danger to health if food poisoning bacteria are allowed to multiply. Convenience stocks, sauces and soups are no exception, so you should take all the usual precautions when handling them:

- with concentrated products, make up only as much as you need at the time
- if you do make too much, cool the remaining liquid as fast as possible – one way of doing this is to put the saucepan in a sink filled with cold water – and then place it in the refrigerator. Reheat thoroughly before use. Do not reheat left over products more than once
- if you use only part of a carton of convenience sauce or soup, transfer the remainder to a clean bowl, cover with clingfilm and place in the refrigerator
- use convenience products on a first-in, first-out basis. In other words, use the older stock first (provided it has not gone beyond the use-by date).

CHEF'S TIPS

Some slightly more elaborate ideas for improving the presentation of convenience soups (see also Action box opposite):

1 Addition of finely diced cooked meat, poultry, rice, pulses, pasta or vegetables to match the flavour of the soup, for example:
   chopped fresh spinach leaves on cream of spinach
   tiny onion rings on white onion soup
   small circles of sliced ham on golden pea and ham soup.

2 Addition of prawns, cubes of fish, smoked oysters, etc. to match the flavour of fish soups.

3 Croûtes on French onion soup: slices of French bread baked in the oven until they are thoroughly dried out and lightly browned, topped with grated Gruyère or Parmesan cheese and browned under a hot grill just before serving. For added flavour, rub with garlic after baking. For added richness, baste with a little olive oil half way through baking, and before grilling.

4 Adapting the soup by, for example:
   adding cooked rice and basil to tomato soup for a hearty winter soup
   adding Stilton to white onion soup for a seasonal soup over the Christmas period.

Double cream may be frozen in cubes (see page 238) in an ice tray to add to sauces and soups.

Hard cheese (e.g. Cheddar and Cheshire) can be grated and then frozen. Use straight from the freezer for adding to sauces and soups. Freeze in small quantities (up to 450 g/1 lb). Wrap in kitchen foil, then in a freezer bag and seal.

ACTION

1 Make a list below of the main convenience stocks, sauces and soups used in your workplace. Put yourself in the position of having to explain to a new colleague how each product is used, and particular points to remember – for example, use in a certain concentration, or bring to the boil with chopped vegetables to add flavour. Note these points below.

Convenience stocks

Convenience sauces

Convenience soups

2 Now consider each of the following ideas for improving the presentation of convenience soups. For each of the suggestions, name one soup that this would be suitable for, e.g. *dash of brandy – lobster bisque*

1 *sprinkling of chopped fresh chives*

2 *sprinkling of chopped fresh chervil*

3 *sprinkling of chopped fresh mint*

4 *pinch of paprika*

5 *some picked watercress leaves*

6 *swirl of cream*

7 *swirl of yogurt*

8 *swirl of crème fraîche*

9 *dash of sherry*

10 *dash of red wine*

11 *dash of dry white wine or dry white vermouth*

12 *dash of brandy*

13 *sprinkling of croûtons*

14 *a few cubes of ice (a chilled soup)*

15 *spoonful of lumpfish roe (mock caviar)*

16 *slice of parsley butter stirred in at the last moment*

17 *helping of game chips*

18 *toasted croûte (slice from French stick) of bread, floated on soup, sprinkled with grated cheese, oil or butter, then browned under the grill*

3 Now describe one idea of your own for improving the presentation of a popular convenience soup.

Preparation of fresh stocks, sauces and soups

LEVEL 2

The quality of the stock will only be as good as its ingredients. While there is no need to use perfectly shaped carrots, for example, it is important that the carrots are fresh. If you use vegetables which are bruised or beginning to rot, the stock will develop unpleasant flavours (see pages 158–9).

Some general rules

1 Vegetables should be thoroughly washed. Trim off and discard any bruised or damaged pieces.

2 Bones for meat, poultry and fish stocks should look and smell fresh.

3 There is nothing to be gained by cooking a stock for longer than the stated recipe time (see page 140). Once the ingredients have been cooked, there is no more flavour to be extracted from them, and further cooking is likely to turn the stock sour.

Use of bones

1 Meat trimmings, and the bones from freshly roasted joints will considerably enhance the flavour of the stock, and add colour. Pork and ham bones – and, in the opinion of some chefs, lamb bones – are too strong for a general-purpose stock.

2 Chicken giblets can be added to stock: the neck, the gizzard (membrane removed, gizzard cut into pieces) and the heart (outer membrane and fat removed, heart opened and any blood clots removed). Chicken wings are ideal for stock, and using the whole of a boiling fowl will make excellent stock.

Use of vegetables

1 For brown stock, the vegetables (and the bones if they are small and easy to handle) can be browned by shallow frying in a little hot fat. This may be more convenient than browning them in the oven.

2 For vegetable stocks it is important to chop all the vegetables up quite small so their flavour can be extracted quickly – 20 to 30 minutes for the simmering stage will avoid the dangers of any vegetables turning sour and developing unpleasant off-flavours.

3 Good use can be made of clean vegetable trimmings by adding them to stockpots, particularly the stalks of mushrooms, the skins and seeds of tomatoes, the trimmings of celery, leeks, carrots and onions.

4 Parsnips, cabbage, Brussels sprouts, swedes, turnips and cauliflower have strong flavours. Only use when their flavour is specifically required, and then simmer for no longer than 30 minutes.

HYGIENE

Good catering practices should avoid use of stockpots altogether, according to the chief Environmental Health Officer (EHO) at the Department of Health – quoted in *Caterer & Hotelkeeper*, 26 September 1991. The article, written by Bob Gledhill, continues:

The main problem is the time it takes stock to cool down before it can be refrigerated. In the few hours it could take to cool, it will pass through temperature bands that encourage maximum bacterial growth.

If the stock is properly reheated most of the bacteria will be killed, but some of the most virulent are resistant to temperatures of up to 100°C and will survive.

"The main risk in a stockpot is *Clostridium perfringens*. That is the sort of organism which has been found in a number of institutional outbreaks of food poisoning, associated with gravies, stews, curries and sauces, simply because of the reheating factor", explains Mike Jacob, chief EHO at the Department of Health.

"From a food hygiene point of view the use of a stockpot is not one of the best practices, particularly if you don't maintain a fairly high temperature. To have a stockpot which is continually on the go or being reheated and cooled down is inconsistent with our normal advice that you use something once or only reheat it once at the very most," he says.

Another problem with liquid stocks is the temptation to keep them for long periods after production, which encourages further bacterial growth, even with refrigeration. There is no obvious way to detect contamination of stock other than via its smell and taste, by which time the liquid could be in a dangerous state.

It is difficult to judge how EHOs will evaluate stock making in the light of food safety legislation, but it is possible that short-life stocks may escape a government clamp down if they are kept very hot and are used immediately.

A simple fish stock which is cooked for a quarter of an hour and used immediately may be acceptable, as with other short-cooking stocks such as chicken.

It is the rich beef and veal stocks which are the most likely to be outlawed.

Institutional kitchens have been the first to phase out stockpots, both on health and cost grounds. Large hotel groups are certainly looking at the issue. They would prefer to instruct chefs not to use traditional stockpots than have any health risk that would reverberate throughout the group.

CHEF'S TIPS

When stocks are being made for a specific purpose, they can be given a more individual flavour. The choice of bones will obviously have a considerable effect on the underlying flavour – chicken, beef, veal, lamb, game, fish and so forth. Interesting flavours can be added by using: fresh tarragon and chervil, garlic, tomato purée, juniper berries and sage (to game stock) and wine (but red wine should be used only in dark-coloured stocks).

5 Starchy vegetables (e.g. potatoes) should never be added to stock. They will cloud the liquid.

Removing fat and impurities

1 Stocks containing meat, and therefore some fat, should never be boiled vigorously because the fat will break up into such tiny globules that it will be almost impossible to remove effectively.

2 Once as much fat as possible has been skimmed off the top of a stock, any that remains can be soaked up by floating a piece of clean kitchen paper on the top for a few seconds and then removing it. When stocks are chilled, any remaining fat will solidify on the surface and can be easily removed before reheating.

Seasoning

Do not add salt to stocks. If you do, the stock will taste very salty by the time it has reduced.

Chilling stock

If stock is not to be used directly after it has been made, or some stock is left over, it must be chilled as quickly as possible, and then stored in the refrigerator or cold room. A blast chiller is ideal for this purpose (see page 273), but not many kitchens have this type of (very expensive) equipment.

Do not put hot stock in a refrigerator. The hot liquid will cause condensation, so that water runs off the surfaces and drips on food. There is also a danger that the temperature inside the refrigerator will go up.

1 Stand the stockpot or saucepan in a deep sink and run cold water around it. Many sinks have a special device that will keep the water level below the rim of the cooling stock.

2 Do not cover the stockpot with a lid during cooling as this will slow down the cooling process.

3 Once the stock has cooled, transfer it immediately to the refrigerator or cold room.

Using chilled stock

Before using chilled stock it should be boiled at some stage. In many recipes this will occur as part of the preparation of the dish. If not, you should boil the stock before it is added to the recipe ingredients (see Hygiene box on opposite page).

To skim stock

1 Push the scum to one side of the pot using the outside of the ladle.

2 Move the lip of the ladle just under the surface of the liquid and scoop up the scum. Take care not to remove the good liquid at the same time.

ACTION

On the next few occasions you make stock, and it has to be chilled after cooking, record the details below. Then discuss with your supervisor how you can reduce chilling times even further.

Type of stock	Quantity made	Chilling method	Chilling time

Meat, poultry or game stock (white and brown)

MAKES 5 litre (10 pt)

2 kg	raw bones (beef, lamb, veal, chicken, game)	4½ lb
225 g each	onion, carrots	8 oz each
50 g each	celery, leeks	2 oz each
5 litre	cold water	10 pt

sprigs of thyme, bay leaf, and parsley stalks and peppercorns

1 Break up or saw into small pieces any large bones that will not fit easily into the stockpot. Remove any fat and any marrow in the centre of beef bones.

For white stocks

2a Cover the bones with cold water. Bring to the boil, simmer for a few minutes, pour off the cooking water and wash off the bones in cold running water.

2b Place the blanched bones, the vegetables (prepared but left whole) and the herbs into the stockpot.

For brown stocks

2a Put the bones in a roasting tray and place in a hot oven at 200°C.

2b Roughly chop the prepared vegetables. Then after the bones have been in the oven for 15 to 20 minutes and have turned a light brown colour, put the chopped vegetables in the oven with them.

2c When the bones have turned a darker brown and the vegetables have also browned (another 10 to 15 minutes), remove from the oven. Drain off the fat, then transfer to the stockpot.

2d Pour off the fat from the roasting tray. Then put a little cold water into the tray and bring it to the boil on top of the stove, scraping the bottom and sides of the pan so that the residue left by the bones and vegetables is dissolved in the water. Add this to the stockpot with the herbs.

For white and brown stocks

3 Add the water and bring to the boil.

4 Skim off any surface fat and impurities that rise to the surface. Slowly simmer lamb and mutton stock 1 hour, beef 3 to 4 hours, poultry and veal 2 to 3 hours, feathered game 3 hours. Skim as required.

5 During cooking, regularly skim off any impurities that rise to the surface.

6 When the stock is ready, strain it off into a clean container.

Fish stock

MAKES 5 litre (10 pt)

2 kg	white fish bones (haddock, whiting, sole, turbot)	4½ lb
275 g	onions, finely sliced	10 oz
50 ml	lemon juice (1 large lemon)	2 fl oz
5 litre	cold water	10 pt
5	peppercorns (optional)	5
2	bay leaves	2

parsley stalks

1 Place all the ingredients in a stockpot or saucepan. Alternatively (see photograph caption on opposite page, top right) gently cook the fishbones and onions in a little butter before adding the water.

2 Bring to the boil and skim off any impurities.

3 Simmer for about 20 minutes. Skim as required.

4 Strain into a clean container.

Vegetable stock

MAKES 5 litre (10 pt)

1 kg	onion, chopped quite small	2 lb
675 g	carrots, chopped quite small	1½ lb
5 litre	cold water	10 pt
350 g each	leeks and celery, chopped quite small	12 oz each

sprig of thyme, bay leaf and parsley stalks

Additional ingredients as available/preferred

tomato trimmings, mushroom trimmings, celeriac, asparagus, sweetcorn, watercress, swede, turnip, cabbage, garlic, marjoram

1 Place all the ingredients into the stockpot, and bring to the boil.

2 Simmer slowly until the vegetables are cooked, 20 to 30 minutes.

3 Strain into a clean container.

> If you have only a small selection of fresh vegetables, a good vegetable extract can be added, preferably one with a low salt/sodium content.

The ingredients for a white stock. Because marrow has a high fat content, it has been removed from the centre of the raw bones. The vegetables (carrot, leek, onion, celery) are left whole. In the background are some bones which have been blanched and are now ready for cooking. Parsley stalks, bay leaf and whole peppercorns are also added to the stock, but never salt, which should be added in the final stages of the preparation of dishes in which stock has been used.

Brown stocks use the same herbs and vegetables as white stocks. The difference is that the bones and roughly chopped vegetables are browned before being added to the water. In the background of this picture are the browned ingredients.

The tin-lined copper stockpots shown above have a tap at the base which makes it very easy to drain off the stock once it has been cooked. Because copper utensils are so expensive, many kitchens use aluminium or stainless steel stockpots (left).

A steam-jacketed kettle (right) is ideal for making large quantities of stock. The tap on the right is for adding water, the tap on the bottom left for draining off the stock.

Making fish stock is an excellent way of using up what is left over when fish has been filleted.

Butter is also shown in the photograph (on the tray with the plaice carcases), because traditionally the fishbones and onions are sweated in butter before the water is added to enrich the flavour of the stock. This stage would be left out for a low-fat meal. You would also leave out the fat if the stock was being used for fish aspic. The fat would make the liquid rather cloudy, spoiling the appearance of cold dishes.

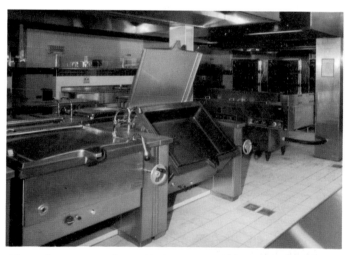

Above: bratt pan, also called tilting pan or skillet. Ideal for combined cooking processes, such as shallow frying and stewing, or for browning bones and vegetables and then adding water to make stock. The speed of cooking can be controlled.

Right: a tilting steam-jacketed kettle. The source of heat (steam circulating in the double jacket) is all round the food, rather than from the base only, as in a conventional stockpot.

Fresh sauces

Most sauces (but there are some exceptions like gravy, see page 83) are thickened in one of the following ways.

1 At the start of cooking by making a roux

A roux is a blend of flour and fat (usually in equal quantities) cooked together for a few minutes to make a white roux (pale yellow colour and soft texture), or for slightly longer to make a brown roux (brown colour). The recipe liquid is then added, a little at a time.

2 By reduction of the liquid

For this to work, the original stock must have quite a lot of natural gelatin (from the bones). The advantage of this method is that the use of fat can be avoided.

3 As a result of the ingredients breaking down

Apples, redcurrants, cranberries and so forth, when cooked for long enough, will turn into a mush. For a smoother sauce, they can be puréed – either forced through a sieve, or blended in a food processor.

4 By the use of egg yolks

This method is used for hollandaise (page 145), mayonnaise (page 265) and egg custard sauces (page 201).

5 After cooking by adding a thickening agent

These all contain starch, so the effect is similar to using a roux. Cornflour, arrowroot, fécule (potato flour), gram flour, and plain flour can all be used. The danger is that lumps will form, so cornflour and arrowroot, for example, are blended first with a little cold water or some of the recipe liquid. Flour can be mixed with butter to form beurre manié. This type of thickener is often used for stews, and you will find more details on page 75.

6 After cooking by adding cream, egg yolks, yogurt etc.

These also add richness and flavour to the sauce. The choice includes crème fraîche, thick yogurt, fromage frais and quark (which will not curdle if boiled). If cream is first blended with egg yolk (to form a liaison), the thickening effect is greater.

7 By using a thick base sauce

These fall into four groups:

- béchamel (white sauce), which with the addition of the appropriate ingredients makes anchovy, egg, onion, parsley, mustard, mornay sauces, etc.

- velouté, like béchamel, but uses stock not milk

- espagnole or basic brown sauce, served as a sauce in its own right, or makes other sauces such as Italienne

demi-glace, concentrated form of espagnole, the foundation for many classical sauces including chasseur (shallots, mushrooms, tomato, white wine), diable (shallots, vinegar, white wine, crushed peppercorns), piquante (sauce diable with gherkins, capers, parsley, chives, tarragon and chervil).

Fresh soups

Soups are traditionally divided into a number of categories, and these help explain how they are cooked.

Bisque A thick, smooth fish soup, made from crab and lobster, for example, which has been puréed. Sometimes cream and brandy are added just before service and the soup is decorated with small cubes of the cooked fish.

Broths Plain-boiled soups served as they are cooked, with chopped vegetables and often barley, rice or pulses.

Consommé Clear soup based on good quality stock, clarified during cooking by the use of egg whites and garnished in many different ways, e.g. royale, a dice of savoury egg custard. Some consommés are served cold, when they set as a soft jelly.

Cream A thick soup to which cream is traditionally added. Generally cream soups start with a roux. Low-fat yogurt is sometimes used to give a similar creamy texture, and slightly sharp flavour.

Purée A thick soup with vegetables and/or pulses puréed in a food processor or forced through a sieve. For example, lentil soup, potato soup.

Some soups have names which do not indicate how or of what they are made. For example, bouillabaisse, a type of fish stew, minestrone, made with a variety of vegetables and pasta, potage, unsieved soup with vegetables, Vichyssoise and borscht.

CHEF'S TIPS

Using a metal spoon for stirring in a metal pan can cause discoloration of the sauce, stock or soup (especially if an aluminium pan is used). A plastic spoon is best.

Many chefs use a spatula when making a roux (as in the photograph on the opposite page). The shape of the blade (with straight edges) makes it easier to keep food from sticking to the bottom of the pan and burning.

There are a number of ways of preventing a skin forming on a sauce when it is cooling:

- place small pieces of butter on the surface, or brush over with melted butter
- rest a circle of greaseproof paper over the surface
- float over the surface a thin film of milk, stock or water (as appropriate, depending on what liquid has been used in the sauce).

Before browning a dish with a sauce under the grill or in the oven, test a small sample on the back of a fireproof saucer or dish to see that it browns satisfactorily.

Basic brown sauce *Sauce espagnole*

MAKES 1 litre (2 pt)

75 g	white fat or dripping	3 oz
60 g	flour	2½ oz
100 g each	onion and carrots, roughly chopped	4 oz each
50 g each	celery and leek, roughly chopped	2 oz each
25 g	tomato purée	1 oz
1.4 litre	brown stock (hot)	2½ pt

sprig of thyme, ½ bay leaf and parsley stalks

1 Melt 50 g (2 oz) of the fat in a saucepan, mix in the flour.

2 Cook over a medium heat for 8 to 10 minutes, stirring continuously to avoid burning, until the mixture has turned a good even brown colour. This is to make a *brown roux*.

3 Allow to cool slightly, then mix in the tomato purée.

4 Return to the heat, add the hot stock, a little at a time, stirring until smooth after each addition.

5 Skim off any fat or impurities that rise to the surface. Add the herbs.

6 Shallow fry the vegetables in the remaining fat until lightly browned.

7 Add the vegetables to the sauce and continue cooking for about 4 hours. During cooking, skim frequently. Top up with additional stock if the sauce thickens too much (when it may start to burn at the bottom).

8 Strain the sauce into a clean saucepan or bowl and use it immediately, or chill until required.

Demi-glace

MAKES 1 litre (2 pt)

1 litre	basic brown sauce	2 pt
1 litre	brown stock	2 pt

1 Bring the brown sauce to the boil.

2 Add the brown stock (which may be hot or cold) and return the liquid to the boil, simmering until it has reduced by half. Skim off any fat or impurities that rise to the surface during cooking and stir occasionally.

3 Strain and use immediately or chill until required.

Jus lié

MAKES ½ litre (1 pt)

½ litre	brown veal, poultry or beef stock or combination	1 pt
12 g	tomato purée	½ oz
sprig of thyme, ¼ bay leaf and parsley stalks		
12 g	arrowroot or cornflour	½ oz
25 ml	cold water	1 fl oz

1 Boil the stock and add the herbs and tomato purée.

2 Mix the arrowroot and cold water well, and stir into the stock. Reboil and simmer for 30 minutes.

3 Strain the jus lié into a clean saucepan or bowl. Use immediately, or chill until required.

Velouté

MAKES 1 litre (2 pt)

100 g	margarine or butter	4 oz
100 g	flour	4 oz
1 litre	meat, poultry or fish stock (hot) as required	2 pt

1 Melt the fat in a saucepan, add the flour and mix together. Cook over a low heat for 4 to 5 minutes to make a *fawn roux* (sandy colour).

2 Slowly blend in the hot stock, bring to the boil and simmer for 1 hour. Skim off any fat or impurities that rise to the surface.

3 Strain. Use immediately or chill until required.

Béchamel/Mornay sauce

MAKES 900 ml (1½ pt)

75 g	margarine or butter	3 oz
75 g	flour	3 oz
900 ml	milk	1½ pt
1	onion, with bay leaf attached to it by a clove (*onion clouté*)	1
seasoning to taste		

For mornay sauce

75 g	grated cheese (Gruyère and an equal amount of Parmesan, or a similar hard cheese to taste)	3 oz

1 In a saucepan, gently warm the milk with the onion clouté for 5 to 8 minutes. This is known as *infusing*.

2 Melt the fat in a second saucepan, add the flour and mix. Cook over a low heat for 4 to 5 minutes making sure that the mixture does not change colour. This is making a *white roux*.

3 Remove the onion from the milk and set aside. Slowly blend the hot milk into the roux, stirring till smooth with each addition of milk.

4 Return the onion clouté to the sauce and bring to the boil. Reduce the heat and simmer gently for 20 minutes. Skim off any fat or impurities that rise to the surface.

5 Discard the onion. Strain the sauce.

6 Check seasoning and consistency – the sauce should be creamy and smooth enough to pour.

7 You have now made *béchamel sauce*. To turn it into *mornay sauce*, add the grated cheese, and stir until thoroughly blended.

Preparing a brown roux.

Caper sauce

Key learning point
» make roux-based sauce

MAKES 500 ml (1 pt)

50 g	margarine, butter or oil	2 oz
50 g	flour	2 oz
500 ml	mutton stock (hot) or cooking liquor from boiled mutton (see page 91)	1 pt
50 g	capers	2 oz
	seasoning to taste	

1 Melt the fat. Mix in the flour, then cook over a low heat for 4 to 5 minutes without over-colouring (a fawn roux).

2 Blend in a little at a time of the hot stock or cooking liquor. Bring to the boil, then simmer for 60 minutes.

3 Strain. Add the capers, check seasoning.

Curry sauce

Key learning point
» make flour-thickened sauce

MAKES 500 ml (1 pt)

50 g	margarine, butter or oil	2 oz
100 g	onion, finely chopped	4 oz
1	clove garlic, crushed and peeled	1
10 g	curry powder	½ oz
50 g	flour	2 oz
10 g	tomato purée	½ oz
575 ml	brown stock (hot)	1 pt
10 g	desiccated coconut	½ oz
10 g	sultanas	½ oz
25 g	mango chutney	1 oz
50 g	cooking apple, peeled, finely chopped	2 oz

1 Cook the onion and garlic in the fat until soft but not coloured. Add the curry powder and cook for a minute or so. Mix in the flour and cook over a low heat for 2 to 3 minutes.

2 Mix in the tomato purée. Allow to cool slightly, then slowly blend in the hot stock, and return to the heat. Simmer for 15 minutes. Skim as required.

3 Add the apple, sultanas, chutney and coconut. Simmer for a further 20 minutes. Check seasoning. Strain or liquidise for a smooth sauce.

Tomato sauce

Key learning point
» make flour-thickened sauce

MAKES 1 litre (2 pt)

100 g	margarine, butter or oil	4 oz
100 g	flour	4 oz
100 g each	carrots and onion, roughly chopped	4 oz each
50 g each	celery and leek, roughly chopped	2 oz each
1	clove garlic, crushed and peeled	1
	bay leaf, sprig thyme and 3 or 4 parsley stalks	
50 g	streaky bacon, cut into 1 cm pieces	2 oz
100 g	tomato purée	4 oz
1 litre	white stock (hot)	2 pt
	seasoning to taste	

1 Melt the fat. Add the bacon and vegetables and cook without allowing to colour for 6 to 8 minutes.

2 Mix in the flour and cook over a low heat for about 4 minutes, stirring regularly so it does not burn.

3 Mix in the tomato purée. Allow to cool slightly, then slowly blend in the hot stock. Bring to the boil and simmer for about 1 hour. Stir occasionally. Skim as required. Top up with additional stock if it gets very thick.

4 Strain the sauce or liquidise. Check consistency (should be similar to that of double cream) and season to taste.

Bread sauce

Key learning point
» make starch-thickened sauce

MAKES 500 ml (1 pint)

575 ml	milk	1 pt
1	small onion clouté (bay leaf fixed to it by a clove)	1
60 g	white breadcrumbs	2½ oz
20 g	butter	¾ oz
	salt and white pepper to taste	

1 Place the milk and studded onion into a saucepan and bring to the boil. Cover with a lid and leave on a very low heat to allow the milk to infuse.

2 After 15 minutes remove the onion. Mix in breadcrumbs. Simmer for 2 to 3 minutes (uncovered) until thick.

3 Season, mix in the butter and serve.

Bolognaise sauce

Key learning point
» make demi-glace based sauce

MAKES about 350 ml (14 fl oz)

10 g	margarine, butter or oil	½ oz
50 g	onion, finely chopped	2 oz
4	cloves garlic, crushed and peeled	4
175 g	minced beef	6 oz
10 g	tomato purée	½ oz
225 ml	demi-glace or jus lié	8 fl oz
100 m	brown stock	4 fl oz
	seasoning to taste	

1 Melt the fat, add the onion and garlic and cook for 2 to 3 minutes. Add the beef and continue frying until lightly browned, 8 to 12 minutes.

2 Add the tomato purée, demi-glace and stock and bring to the boil. Simmer gently for about 45 minutes. Skim as required. Stir occasionally and top up with additional stock if the mixture gets too thick. The mixture should just reach a pouring consistency. Adjust seasoning if necessary.

Sauce italienne

Key learning point
» make espagnole-based sauce

MAKES 250 ml (½ pint)

5 g	butter, margarine or oil	¼ oz
25 g	shallots or onion, finely chopped	1 oz
50 g	mushrooms, roughly chopped	2 oz
275 g	tomatoes, skinned, deseeded and chopped	10 oz
225 ml	jus lié or demi-glace	8 fl oz
25 g	cooked ham, diced	1 oz
15 ml	good pinch of fines herbs, chopped	1 tbsp
	seasoning to taste	

1 Shallow fry the shallots (or onions) until lightly coloured (in either a saucepan or a sauteuse).

2 Add the mushrooms and continue frying for 3 to 4 minutes.

3 Add the chopped tomato and brown sauce. Bring to the boil, then simmer.

4 Add the ham and the herbs to the simmering sauce, which should be the consistency of double cream at this stage. Adjust seasoning if necessary.

Tartare sauce

Key learning point
» make egg-based sauce

MAKES 100 ml (4 fl oz)

125 ml	mayonnaise (see page 265)	4 fl oz
30 g	gherkins	1 oz
15 g	capers	½ oz
	pinch fresh parsley	

Roughly chop the gherkins and capers and mix through the mayonnaise with parsley.

Hollandaise sauce

Key learning point
» make egg-based sauce

Alternative: reduce the vinegar with some crushed peppercorns before step 2. Then add to the egg yolks with about 20 ml of cold water. Strain the finished sauce through a piece of muslin before use.

SERVES 8 to 10

25 ml	white wine vinegar	1 fl oz
2	egg yolks	2
275 g	butter	10 oz
	squeeze lemon juice	
salt, pepper and pinch cayenne pepper to taste		

1 Melt the butter over a gentle heat and allow it to become clear.

2 Place the vinegar and egg yolks into a small sauteuse. Place this in a larger saucepan containing water at just below boiling point (a *bain-marie*).

3 Over a very low heat, whisk until the mixture reaches the *ribbon stage*, that is fluffy and stiff enough to show whisk marks. (At this stage it is known as a *sabayon*.) The mixture will scramble if it gets too hot, so it may be necessary to remove it from the heat occasionally.

4 Take off the heat and slowly whisk in the butter, but not any milky residue.

5 Season and whisk through the lemon juice. Place into a clean bowl and keep warm in another bowl of warm water until required for service.

Hollandaise will separate if kept too long. In all events, it should be used within an hour or two, because of the risk of food poisoning.

Cranberry sauce

Key learning point
» make fruit-based sauce (puréed if wished)

MAKES 500 ml (1 pint)

350 g	cranberries, stalks removed	12 oz
75 g	sugar	3 oz
225 ml	water	8 fl oz

1 Place the cranberries into a tin-lined or stainless steel saucepan, add sugar and water. Bring to the boil, then simmer until the fruit becomes a soft pulp (5 to 8 minutes).

2 Serve hot or cold. Liquidise for a smooth sauce.

Melba sauce

Key learning point
» make fruit purée sauce

SERVES 4

225 g	raspberries	8 oz
50 g	sugar	2 oz
50 ml	water	2 fl oz

1 Place the ingredients into a saucepan and bring to the boil. Simmer for 5 minutes then pass through a fine strainer.

2 Cool. Store chilled until required.

Gooseberry sauce

Key learning point
» make fruit sauce (puréed if wished)

SERVES 4 to 5

175 g	gooseberries, topped and tailed	6 oz
25 g	sugar	1 oz
50 ml	water	2 fl oz
	squeeze of lemon juice (optional)	

1 Place the gooseberries into a saucepan with the sugar, lemon juice and water. Bring to the boil then slowly simmer until the fruit has turned into a soft pulp. Stir occasionally.

2 Liquidise for a smooth sauce, or serve as a pulp.

3 Reheat, and add more sugar if necessary.

Butterscotch sauce

Key learning point
» make caramel-based sauce

An unlined copper pan is best for making caramel. Aluminium pans tend to develop tiny irregularities in the surface. Undissolved sugar crystals get trapped in these, causing the sugar mixture to re-crystallise.

A more precise method of knowing when the sugar has reached the right stage is to use a sugar thermometer (step 4).

SERVES 4

100 g	granulated sugar	4 oz
50 ml	water	2 fl oz
100 ml	double cream	4 fl oz

1 Bring the sugar and water to the boil over a low heat. Stir occasionally so all the sugar crystals are dissolved. Wipe down the sides of the pan with a clean brush dipped in water to remove splashes of sugar.

2 Then boil the mixture quickly. Do not stir. Do not shake the pan.

3 When the mixture has turned a golden brown colour take the pan off the heat. Whisk the cream through the mixture, dribbling it in a little at a time.

4 Allow to cool. Stir before use. If the sauce is too thick, add a little more cream.

Scotch broth

Key learning point
» make broth

SERVES 4 to 5

1 litre	white stock	2 pt
25 g	pearl barley, washed	1 oz
50 g each	onion, carrot and turnip, finely chopped	2 oz each
25 g each	celery and leek, finely chopped	1 oz each
	chopped parsley (optional garnish)	
	salt and white pepper to taste	

1 Bring the stock to the boil. Add the washed barley, and simmer for about 1 hour. Top up with stock as required.

2 Add the onion, carrot, turnip and celery. Simmer for 10 to 15 minutes.

3 Add the leeks then simmer until all the vegetables are cooked, another 10 to 15 minutes.

4 Skim off any fat, check seasoning.

Vichyssoise

Key learning point
» make puréed soup

SERVES 4 to 5

15 g	margarine or butter	½ oz
75 g	onion, roughly chopped	3 oz
225 g	leek (white part only), roughly chopped	8 oz
350 g	potato, roughly chopped	12 oz
850 ml	white chicken stock	1½ pt
	sprig of thyme and ½ bay leaf	
	seasoning to taste	

To garnish

125 ml	whipping cream, lightly whipped or thick yogurt	4 fl oz
	chopped chives and parsley	

1 Cook the onions and leeks in the fat until soft but not brown.

2 Add the stock and bring to the boil. Add the potatoes and herbs. Simmer until cooked, about 30 minutes. Stir occasionally. Skim as necessary.

3 Remove the bay leaf and thyme. Liquidise. Add a little more chicken stock if it is too thick. Quickly chill.

4 To serve, fold the cream or yogurt through the soup. Sprinkle with the chives and parsley.

Mid-winter parsnip soup
by Sonia Stevenson, published in Caterer & Hotelkeeper, *30 January 1992*

Key learning point
» make puréed soup

SERVES 6

450 g	parsnips, peeled, cored and chopped	1 lb
100 g	butter	4 oz
¼	onion, chopped	¼
10 ml	mild curry powder	2 tsp
6	cardamoms	6
1½ litre	brown stock (hot)	3 pt
	seasoning to taste	

To garnish

150 ml	whipping cream, lightly whipped	5 fl oz
	chives, freshly chopped	

1 Cook the parsnip and onion gently in the butter for 15 minutes, without colouring.

2 Add the curry powder and seeds from the cardamoms. Cook for a further 5 minutes.

3 Add stock and seasoning, then simmer until cooked, about 30 minutes.

4 Liquidise. Reheat.

5 Adjust seasoning and thickness to taste. Serve with a swirl of cream and sprinkle of chives.

Cream of mushroom soup
by The British Egg Information Service

Key learning point
» make low-fat variation on cream soup, enriched with egg yolk

SERVES 4

150 g	button mushrooms	5 oz
50 g	polyunsaturated margarine	2 oz
15 ml	brown or white plain flour	1 tbsp
300 ml	chicken stock (hot)	½ pt
575 ml	skimmed milk (hot)	1 pt
	seasoning to taste	

To finish

30 ml	low fat yogurt	2 tbsp
2	egg yolks	2
	parsley, freshly chopped	

1 Coarsely chop the mushrooms into even-sized pieces for a chunky soup, or slice finely.

2 In a heavy-based saucepan, melt the margarine and add the mushrooms. Stir for 1 to 2 minutes over a gentle heat without browning.

3 Take off the heat and stir in the flour. Return to the heat and cook for about 1 minute. Slowly pour in the hot chicken stock, then the hot milk, stirring well with each addition to get a smooth consistency.

4 Bring to the boil, then simmer for about 10 minutes, covered.

5 Blend together the yogurt and egg yolks until evenly mixed.

6 Take the soup off the heat and stir in the yogurt mixture. Season to taste. Serve at once, with a sprinkling of chopped parsley.

Tomato and haricot bean soup
by The Fresh Fruit and Vegetable Information Bureau

Key learning point
» make puréed soup with pulses

SERVES 4

100 g	haricot beans, soaked for 12 hours	4 oz
100 g	streaky bacon, chopped	4 oz
1	medium onion, finely chopped	1
2	sticks celery, chopped	2
450 g	tomatoes, skinned, deseeded and chopped	1 lb
1	clove garlic, crushed and peeled	1
1 litre	beef stock	2 pt
30 ml	tomato purée	2 tbsp
	seasoning to taste	
30 ml	fresh parsley, chopped	2 tbsp

1 Fry the bacon gently to extract the fat, add the onion and celery and cook in the bacon fat for 2 to 3 minutes.

2 Add the remaining ingredients apart from the parsley, and simmer gently until the beans are tender, about 60 minutes.

3 Blend or liquidise until smooth. Return to the pan, add parsley and heat through to serve.

Lettuce soup with mushrooms
by Roy Ackerman, published in The Chef's Apprentice, *Headline Book Publishing in association with Alfresco Leisure Publications*

Key learning point
» make pureed soup

SERVES 4

100 g	butter	4 oz
100 g	onion, chopped	4 oz
½	clove garlic, crushed and chopped	½
225 g	potatoes, chopped small	8 oz
1½ litre	chicken stock (hot)	2½ pt
	1 sprig thyme, 3 to 4 parsley stalks	
1	lettuce	1
100 g	button mushrooms, sliced	4 oz
	seasoning to taste	
	chives or parsley, freshly chopped (to garnish)	

1 Melt half the butter in a saucepan, add the onion, garlic and potato and cook gently for 3 to 4 minutes, without browning.

2 Add the stock and bring to the boil. Add the thyme, parsley stalks and seasoning, and simmer for 15 minutes.

3 Choose a few leaves from the heart of the lettuce, finely shred and set aside for garnishing the soup. Add the remaining lettuce leaves to the soup, and simmer for a further 10 minutes.

4 Remove the herb sprigs, and liquidise the soup until smooth. Reheat.

5 Meanwhile, gently cook the mushrooms in the remaining butter. Add the mushrooms to the soup, with the shredded lettuce, chopped chives or parsley, and serve at once.

Mussel and pasta soup
by Sea Fish Industry Authority

Key learning point
» make a fish soup

SERVES 4

900 g	mussels, washed and debearded	2 lb
	(alternatively, use 450 g of frozen mussel meat)	
15 ml	oil	1 tbsp
1	large onion, finely sliced	1
10 ml	garlic sauce	1 dsp
4	sticks celery, diced	4
225 g	carrots, finely chopped	8 oz
1¼ litre	fish or vegetable stock	2 pt
1 × 425 g	can chick peas, drained	1 × 15 oz
100 g	pasta shells	4 oz
	seasoning to taste	

1 Heat the oil in a large saucepan. Cook the onion gently until it is soft and transparent.

2 Stir in the garlic sauce, celery and carrots, and cook for a further 3 to 4 minutes.

3 Add the stock and chick peas, cover and simmer until the vegetables are tender.

4 Stir in the pasta shells and continue to simmer until almost cooked.

5 Add the mussels to the soup, cover and cook for 5 to 6 minutes, or until the mussel shells have opened. (Discard any that have not.)

6 Season and serve immediately, with chunks of crusty bread.

Creole soup
by Dufrais

Key learning point
» make a broth-type soup

SERVES 6

30 ml	sesame oil	2 tbsp
1	large onion, chopped	1
3	cloves garlic, crushed	3
15 ml	sweet chilli sauce	1 tbsp
350 g	tomatoes, diced	12 oz
1 each	red and green pepper, diced	1 each
575 ml	tomato juice	1 pt
575 ml	chicken stock	1 pt
45 ml	cider vinegar	3 tbsp
100 g	cucumber, diced	4 oz
150 ml	soured cream	5 fl oz
	paprika	
	seasoning to taste	

1 Heat oil in a large pan and soften onion and garlic. Add all remaining ingredients, except vinegar and cucumber. Simmer for 20 to 30 minutes.

2 Remove from heat and add vinegar and cucumber. Serve with soured cream and paprika.

Watercress and yogurt soup
by The Fresh Fruit and Vegetable Information Bureau

» make puréed soup

SERVES 1 to 2

1	bunch watercress	1
1	clove garlic, crushed and peeled	1
½	lemon, grated rind and juice	½
5 ml	honey	1 tsp
150 ml	chicken stock	5 fl oz
150 ml	natural yogurt	5 fl oz
	seasoning to taste	

1 Put the watercress leaves in a saucepan with the garlic, lemon rind and juice, honey and stock. Bring to the boil and simmer for 10 minutes.

2 Blend in a liquidiser with the yogurt. Season.

3 Serve well chilled with a few leaves of watercress floating on the surface.

Gazpacho
by Dufrais

Key learning point
» make a cold soup (puréed)

SERVES 6

1	onion, chopped	1
1	cucumber, peeled and chopped	1
1	red pepper, seeds removed and chopped	1
1	clove garlic, peeled and crushed	1
450 g	ripe tomatoes, seeds removed and chopped	1
15 ml	basil or parsley, chopped	1 tbsp
45 ml	red wine vinegar	3 tbsp
275 ml	vegetable stock	½ pt
575 ml	tomato juice	1 pt
	seasoning to taste	
	basil leaves (to garnish)	

finely chopped vegetables such as red and green pepper, cucumber, onion and tomato, and small fried croûtons of bread (alternative garnish)

1 Purée together all the ingredients except the tomato juice.

2 Stir in the tomato juice. Season to taste.

3 Cover and chill.

4 Serve garnished with ice cubes and basil leaves, or selection of chopped vegetables and croûtons.

Chinese hot and sour soup
by Dufrais

Key learning point
» make a broth-type soup thickened with cornflour

SERVES 4

850 ml	chicken stock	1½ pt
50 g	lean bacon or gammon cut into thin strips	2 oz
50 g	mushrooms, cut into thin strips	2 oz
25 g	cooked pork or chicken, cut into thin strips	1 oz
25 g	bamboo shoots, cut into thin strips	1 oz
25 g	prawns	1 oz
25 g	peas	1 oz
2	spring onions, trimmed and finely chopped	2
30 ml	soy sauce	2 tbsp
10 ml	cornflour	2 tsp
45 ml	garlic wine vinegar	3 tbsp
	seasoning to taste	
1	egg, beaten	1

1 Simmer the stock, bacon and mushrooms, covered, for 15 minutes. Add the pork, bamboo shoots, prawns, peas and onions.

2 Mix the soy sauce with the cornflour and stir into the soup with the wine vinegar. Simmer gently for 5 minutes.

3 Season, stir in beaten egg and serve.

Russian borscht
by Dufrais

Key learning point
» make a broth

SERVES 4 to 6

30 ml	sherry vinegar	2 tbsp
100 g	lean braising steak, cut into strips	4 oz
100 g	white cabbage, finely shredded	4 oz
2	sticks celery, thinly sliced	2
1	medium leek, thinly sliced	1
1 each	medium turnip and potato, grated	1 each
225 g	raw beetroot, grated	8 oz
1½ litre	beef stock	2½ pt
225 g	can tomatoes	8 oz
150 ml	soured cream	¼ pt
15 ml	chopped dill	1 tbsp
	seasoning to taste	

1 Place all the ingredients together in a large saucepan, except the soured cream and dill.

2 Bring slowly to the boil, reduce heat, cover and simmer for 45 to 60 minutes, or until the meat is tender.

3 Adjust seasoning to taste and serve topped with soured cream and dill.

NVQ SVQ RANGE CHECKLIST

LEVEL 1

1D4.1 Prepare and cook convenience stocks, sauces and soups

preparing at least 4 of these products
- [ ] dried soups
- [ ] canned (tinned) soups
- [ ] condensed soups
- [ ] stock cubes
- [ ] dried sauces
- [ ] canned(tinned)/jars/cartons of sauce

using at least 2 of these preparation methods
- [ ] reconstitution with boiling water
- [ ] reconstitution with cold water
- [ ] reconstitution with milk

LEVEL 2

2D4.1 Prepare and cook stocks

making at least 2 types
- [ ] meat or poultry or game
- [ ] fish
- [ ] vegetable

2D4.2 Prepare and cook sauces

making at least 3 of these
- [ ] roux sauce
- [ ] starch thickened sauce
- [ ] egg based sauce
- [ ] meat or poultry or vegetable gravy

2D4.3 Prepare and cook soups
making each of these types
- [ ] cream
- [ ] broth
- [ ] purée

Introduction

When is fruit ready to eat? Some fruits have to ripen before they are picked, for example, oranges, grapefruit and lemons which are firm and not easily damaged by handling, and strawberries, raspberries and grapes which have to be very carefully packed and handled to avoid damage.

Others, for example, melons and peaches, are often transported and then sold when they are still unripe to avoid bruising. For such fruits there are two options:

- buy under-ripe and store until ripe
- pick out the most ripe items.

Generally, if a fruit feels soft when squeezed very gently in the hand it is a sign of ripeness – although it could mean that you are not the first to try that particular piece of fruit! This technique can be used for pears, peaches, plums, apricots, mangoes and kiwi fruit. When testing avocados, in some varieties the large central pip can also be heard rattling if the avocado is ripe.

Judging the ripeness of hard-skinned fruit like melons requires more experience and knowledge of the variety – some tips overleaf.

NVQ **SVQ** **Units and elements covered in this section**

1D14 Prepare and cook fruit **LEVEL 1**
- 1D14.1 Prepare fruit for hot and cold dishes
- 1D14.2 Cook fruit dishes

Colourful displays at markets like this are tempting, so you need to know what you are looking for in terms of ripeness and quality.

1) Plums, 2) Golden Delicious apples, 3) Red Delicious apple, 4) Lemons, 5) Grapefruit, 6) Pears, 7) Oranges, 8) Pineapple, 9) Honeydew melon, 10) Bananas, 11) Canteloupe melon, 12) Peach, 13) Grapes, 14) Pink grapefruit, 15) Galia melon, 16) Strawberries, 17) Kiwi fruit. Sprigs of mint (foreground) provide an attractive green decorative touch to bowls of fruit.

Quality points

Preprepared fruit

- packaging in good condition and correctly labelled
- not passed use-by or best-before date

Fresh fruit

- no blemishes or discoloration
- no signs of bruising, decay or insect damage
- good colour, size and shape, and a fresh appearance with no sign of wilting or ageing
- uniform size and shape. A wide variation of sizes in any one box is a sign of poor grading (or none at all). The quality may not be inferior as a result, but unevenly sized items will spoil the appearance of salads and fruit displays, make portion control very difficult and add considerably to preparation time when the food is to be cut up
- clean, although with freshly picked local farm produce or organically grown items, the presence of a little soil is acceptable

Quality grades

There are four quality grades within EC regulations:

Extra class – specially selected produce of excellent quality. Not always available in large quantities

Class I – first class fruit with no important defects

Class II – good quality fruit with some minor blemishes

Class III – lower quality produce. This grade is not used if there is sufficient Class I or II fruit to meet demand.

Berries or soft fruits – blackberries, blueberries, cranberries, blackcurrants, redcurrants, gooseberries, loganberries, raspberries, strawberries and cape gooseberries. Best used within 24 hours of purchase. Remove any cellophane wrapping and discard damaged or bruised fruit. Store chilled and do not wash until required. Cooking gooseberries can be kept chilled for up to 3 days.

Hard fruit – apples, pears. Popular varieties of apple are: Cox's Orange Pippin (crisp, juicy and semi-sweet – British), Bramley's Seedlings (excellent for cooking – British), Granny Smith (green skinned, crisp and juicy – mostly imported from South Africa) and Golden Delicious (colour from green to yellow when ripe – mostly imported from France). Store apples chilled.

Pear varieties include Bartlett, Beurré Hardy, Comice and Conference. Usually purchased under-ripe and can be kept in that condition for up to 2 weeks if chilled. To ripen, put in a warm place until there is slight softening near the stalk. When ripe, use within 2 to 3 days.

Stone fruits – cherries, damsons, plums, apricots, greengages, peaches and nectarines. Use ripe fruit on day of purchase. Unripe fruit will ripen quickly at room temperature.

Citrus fruits – oranges, blood oranges, lemons, limes, grapefruit, mandarins, clementines, tangerines and satsumas. Will keep in a cool place for up to a week. Do not refrigerate.

Tropical and other fruits

Avocados will ripen at room temperature in 2 to 3 days. Store ripe fruit in a cool place.

Bananas – ripen green-tipped bananas in a warm room. Never put bananas in the refrigerator as this destroys their colour and flavour.

Dates can be kept for several days in the refrigerator.

Fresh figs are very fragile. Use on day of purchase.

Grapes are best kept chilled when not wanted for immediate use.

Kiwi fruit will ripen at room temperature.

Pineapples should be eaten within 24 hours of purchase. Under-ripe fruit will ripen within 2 to 3 days at room temperature.

Rhubarb – keep in the bottom of the refrigerator, and use within 3 days of purchase.

CHEF'S TIPS

Canteloupes (including Charentais and Ogen varieties) and *honeydew melons* should give slightly at the firm touch of a finger particularly at the blossom end (the opposite end to the stalk). They should also smell sweet and flowery. Generally, the heavier the melon is for its size, the riper and juicier it will be, but if juice can be heard sloshing around inside it is a sign that the melon is mushy and over-ripe.

Watermelons should produce a deep resonant sound when tapped. If they are not yet ripe, the sound will be somewhat metallic. Too ripe and they will sound hollow.

Pineapples are ripe when a leaf can be pulled out easily, or the leafy top moves from side to side with a little pressure. Some varieties turn yellow as they ripen. The smell becomes more fragrant.

SAFETY

The leaves of rhubarb are highly poisonous. Trim off carefully and discard.

Preparing fruit

To preserve the quality and vitamin content, do not wash or prepare until required. Peel hard fruit as thinly as possible.

Bananas and apples discolour very rapidly after peeling or cutting. Submerge in water with a little lemon juice added. Or brush with lemon juice.

When serving fresh, remove from the refrigerator about an hour before. This helps develop the flavour.

Preparing a fruit salad

Fruit pips which are big enough to cause discomfort should be removed. This includes grapes, but there are some pips, as in pomegranates and passion fruit, that cannot be removed without wasting a great deal of flesh.

Provided it is not too chewy, the skin may be left on grapes and on apples to provide extra colour and texture.

Opinions differ regarding apples and bananas. Some prefer them added at the last moment, so that they are as firm as possible. Others like them to have softened slightly. But don't put them in too soon or they will turn to mush.

Tinned fruit must be drained carefully or the salad will become watery and sloppy, and possibly too sweet if the fruit has been packed in syrup.

Blanching – that is submerging the fruit in very hot water for 10 to 20 seconds – will make it easier to peel peaches, apricots and similar fruit.

To cut citrus fruit into segments: 1) Peel the fruit, cutting just beneath the pith.

A parisienne cutter makes it quite easy to produce attractive melon balls.

Push the cutter well into the flesh of the fruit, working it from side to side so that it cuts around the fruit, rather than squeezing it. Make the cuts as close to each other as you can, without spoiling the uniformity of their shape.

2) Cut out each segment individually, by cutting down towards the centre on both sides of the membrane.

Dried fruits

Drying – reducing the water content of tissue to the point that very few microbes can grow in it – is one of the oldest methods of food preservation. Prunes, raisins and dates are still dried in the sun in many parts of the world, but forced hot-air drying is now widely used.

Dried fruits should be soaked before cooking to replace the water content efficiently. Cover in water at about 80°C and leave for 2 hours. This produces a better texture and flavour than soaking for 12 hours in cold water, the usual practice.

Dried fruits can be used in desserts and salads. Apricots (which are very high in dietary fibre), prunes, bananas, dates, figs, raisins and sultanas are popular in their dried form. Some dried fruits, for example cherries and crystallised fruits (also called candied fruits), are used to decorate and flavour desserts.

1) Prunes, 2) Figs, 3) Pears, 4) Dates, 5) Apricots, 6) Apples, 7) Peaches.

Cooking fruit

Cooked fruit dishes range from baked apples, stewed rhubarb and pineapple fritters (deep fried) to pies, flans, mousses, purées and classic favourites like *Peach Melba* and *Pear Belle Hélène* (combinations of poached fruit and ice cream).

Fruit is easily overcooked. For a summer pudding, for example, the fruit is only cooked for 2 or 3 minutes (recipe on page 154). Cooking times for poaching or stewing apple depend on the variety of apple, but 5 to 10 minutes are likely to be sufficient.

For these reasons, you should:

* follow recipe instructions carefully

* check cooking progress after about two-thirds of the recommended time has elapsed, and at regular intervals until the fruit is cooked. With many fruits you can see when it is adequately cooked – apple, for example, will have visibly softened and changed to a more opaque colour. With others, you may need to prod the fruit gently with a cocktail stick.

If the fruit is being poached or stewed, it is usually left to cool in the cooking liquid. In these situations, you should remove the fruit from the heat before cooking has completed.

If you are stewing fruit, you will not need much liquid, because the fruit will release its own juices.

A circle of greaseproof paper – a cartouche – laid on the surface of fruit while it is being poached will stop the fruit floating above the surface of the cooking liquid (see page 225 on how to cut a neat circle). Without the paper, the fruit would cook unevenly and the presentation would be spoilt.

CHEF'S TIPS

If you have been using salt in the water to stop fruit from discolouring before it is deep fried, rinse the fruit before use and dry thoroughly in absorbent kitchen paper.

For a deliciously different flavour, add a little elderflower to the poaching liquid when cooking gooseberries.

For pears, recommended additions include wine, cider, honey and ginger.

Limes can be used in the same way, or as an alternative to lemons. As the flavour is stronger, use about one-third less than you would of lemon. To obtain maximum juice, warm the lime a little, roll firmly on a work surface, then squeeze.

To make segmenting citrus fruit easier, place the fruit in the freezer for 30 minutes beforehand. This will firm up the flesh.

Add a little lemon juice to blueberries when poaching. It will help bring out the full taste of the fruit (which can be somewhat bland).

NUTRITION

As well as providing good natural roughage, fruit is an excellent source of vitamins and minerals.

Apricots, melons and peaches are good sources of *vitamin A* (essential for healthy eyes and skin).

Blackcurrants and kiwi fruit are very high in *vitamin C* (essential for maintaining healthy connective tissue). Good supplies are present in all citrus fruit, gooseberries, raspberries and strawberries. About one-third of the vitamin C in the average diet comes from fruit.

Iron (important for oxygen transport and transfer in the blood) is found in avocados, blackcurrants, passion fruit and raspberries.

Rhubarb and lemons contain a great deal of *calcium* (essential for healthy bones and teeth). Also found in blackberries, blackcurrants, oranges and raspberries.

Tangy lemon and apricot mousse
by Gales/Nestlé

Key learning points
» prepare dish with citrus fruits, purée fruit
» use powdered gelatin

SERVES 4

1 × 420 g	can apricot halves	1 × 14.8 oz
	in natural juice, drained, retaining juice	
1 × 11 g	sachet powdered gelatin	1 × 0.4 oz
60 ml	lemon curd	4 tbsp
½	orange, grated rind	½
150 ml	whipping cream, lightly whipped	5 fl oz
	strips of orange and lemon rind (to decorate)	

1 Place 60 ml (4 tbsp) of the juice from the apricots into a small bowl. Sprinkle over the gelatin and leave to stand for 10 minutes.

2 Meanwhile, liquidise the apricot halves with 60 ml (4 tbsp) of the juice, the lemon curd and lemon rind, to make a smooth purée. Pour into a large mixing bowl.

3 Stand the bowl of gelatin in a pan of very warm water. Stir occasionally until the gelatin has just melted, but not become hot. Immediately fold into the apricot mixture with the whipped cream.

4 Spoon into serving dishes and chill for at least 1 hour. Decorate with strips of orange and lemon rind.

Baked almond custard with raspberry coulis
by Coleen Hobson for The Vegetarian Society

Key learning points
» purée soft fruit
» prepare a vegetarian dish using soya milk

SERVES 4

175 g	finely ground almonds	6 oz
30–45 ml	Cointreau or Drambuie	2–3 tbsp
50 g	creamed coconut, grated (optional)	2 oz
	pinch orange rind	
1	orange, juice of	1
45 ml	maple syrup	3 tbsp
425 ml	concentrated unsweetened soya milk	¾ pt
450 g	raspberries, fresh or frozen	1 lb
	maple syrup to taste (for sweetening coulis)	

1 Blend the almonds, liqueur, coconut, orange juice and rind, maple syrup and soya milk until smooth and creamy.

2 Pour into a greased 850 ml (1½ pt) ovenproof dish, then put into a deep-sided baking tray with some water in the bottom. Bake at 180°C for 1 hour. Cool, then chill.

3 Press the raspberries through a sieve until the seeds remain. Sweeten to taste with the maple syrup.

4 To serve, place 1 or 2 ice cream scoops of the baked mixture on the serving place. Surround with the raspberry coulis.

Apple beignets
by The Dutch Dairy Bureau

Key learning points
» make an egg batter
» deep fry apples
The Dutch traditionally celebrate New Year's Eve by drinking punch and eating apple beignets.

SERVES 28 as a party dish

4	cooking apples, peeled, cored, cut into rings	4
100 g	self-raising flour	4 oz
	pinch of salt	
1	egg, beaten lightly	1
125 ml	milk	5 fl oz
	icing sugar to dust	

1 For the batter, sift together the flour and salt. Make a well in the centre, put the egg and milk into this, and gradually beat in.

2 Rinse the apples, and dry well on absorbent kitchen paper. Dip each ring into the batter and deep fry for 2 to 3 minutes at 177°C, until golden brown.

3 Drain on absorbent kitchen paper. Sprinkle with icing sugar and serve immediately.

Peach Melba

Key learning point
» poach a stone fruit

SERVES 4

2	large peaches, skinned and halved	2
575 ml	water	1 pt
225 g	sugar	8 oz
½	lemon, juice of	½
225 ml	Melba sauce (page 145)	8 fl oz
225 ml	vanilla ice-cream (4 medium scoops)	8 fl oz
	Chantilly cream (page 251)	

1 In a small saucepan bring the water, sugar and lemon juice to the boil. Simmer until the sugar has dissolved.

2 Place the peach halves in the syrup. Cover with a circle of greaseproof paper and poach until cooked. The liquid should be very hot but not boiling. Cooking time varies considerably depending on the ripeness of the fruit; 8 to 10 minutes would be a general guide.

3 Allow the peaches to cool in the syrup. Chill until required.

4 For service, portion the ice-cream into individual serving dishes (e.g. coupes). Drain the peaches, then place one half on each serving of ice-cream.

5 Coat with Melba sauce and decorate with piped rosettes of Chantilly cream.

Pears with butterscotch sauce

Key learning point
» poach soft fruit

SERVES 4

4	medium pears, peeled, stalk left attached	4
575 ml	poaching syrup (see Peach Melba, step 1)	1 pt
225 ml	butterscotch sauce (page 145)	8 fl oz

1 Trim the bottoms so that the pears will sit upright.

2 and 3 Poaching as for Peach Melba.

4 For service, drain the pears. Arrange in a dish and coat with butterscotch sauce.

Apple and hazelnut layers
by Booker Fitch Food Services

Key learning point
» prepare a baked apple dish

SERVES 6 to 8

900 g	cooking apples	2 lb
2	thinly pared strips of lemon rind	2
50 g	butter	2 oz
100 g	no sugar added apricot jam	4 oz
225 g	hazelnuts, finely ground	8 oz
225 g	Danish rye bread, made into crumbs	8 oz
45 ml	no sugar added mixed berry jam	3 tbsp
150 ml	whipping cream	5 fl oz
100 g	low fat soft cheese	4 oz
	angelica and hazelnuts (to garnish)	

1 Core and chop the apples, without peeling. Put into a saucepan with the lemon rind, half the butter and the apricot jam. Cover and cook gently for 15 minutes or until the fruit becomes a soft pulp.

2 Rub the fruit through a fine sieve. Cool completely.

3 Fry the crumbs in the remaining butter until crisp. Add the ground hazelnuts and berry jam. Cool completely.

4 Put one-third of the crumb mixture into a 850 ml (30 fl oz) soufflé dish (or other high-sided dish). Put in half the apple purée, another third of the crumbs, remaining purée and remaining crumbs. Chill for at least 1 hour.

5 Whip the cream and beat in the cheese. Pile on top of the chilled pudding. Decorate with angelica and hazelnuts and serve.

Summer pudding
by The Fresh Fruit and Vegetable Information Bureau

Key learning point
» prepare a pudding with soft fruits

SERVES 6

8 to 10	thin slices of white bread	8 to 10
450 g	raspberries	1 lb
225 g	redcurrants, trimmed	8 oz
225 g	blackcurrants	8 oz
225 g	granulated sugar	8 oz

1 Grease the base and sides of a 1 litre (2 pt) soufflé type dish. (A pudding dish will probably be too deep, with the result that the pudding collapses.)

2 Simmer the fruit with the sugar in a covered pan for 2 to 3 minutes, until the juices flow from the fruit.

3 Remove the crusts from the bread, and line the base and sides of the dish. Top with half the fruit mixture. Cover with a layer of bread and then the remaining fruit. Finally add a layer of bread.

4 Put a plate over the top and weight it down gently so that the fruit and bread are pressed together. You should see some of the juice come to the top of the bread. Chill for at least 6 hours.

5 Unmould carefully on to a serving dish and serve with cream.

Tropical fruit crumble

Key learning point
» prepare a baked fruit dish with apricots and passion fruit

SERVES 2

75 g	wholemeal flour	3 oz
50 g	unsweetened muesli	2 oz
1.25 ml	baking powder	¼ tsp
40 g	butter	1½ oz
25 g	soft brown sugar	1 oz
1 × 425 g	can apricot halves in natural juice, drained, reserving 45 ml (3 tbsp) juice	1 × 15 oz
1	passion fruit	1

1 Place flour, muesli and baking powder in a bowl, rub in butter and add sugar.

2 Arrange apricots in a 575 ml (1 pt) ovenproof dish. Cut passion fruit in half, scoop out pulp and spoon over apricots with reserved fruit juice.

3 Cover fruit with the muesli topping. Bake at 200°C for 20 to 30 minutes.

4 Serve hot or cold by itself or with natural yogurt or soured cream.

Spiced orange segments
by The Fresh Fruit and Vegetable Information Bureau

Key learning point
» prepare citrus fruit dessert

SERVES 4 to 6

100 g	sugar	4 oz
150 ml	water	5 fl oz
275 ml	red wine	½ pt
2	cloves	2
1	cinnamon stick	1
1	lemon slice	1
5	oranges, cut into segments	5

1 Dissolve the sugar in the water and red wine. Bring to the boil, and add the cloves, cinnamon and lemon. Simmer for 5 minutes.

2 Strain the hot sauce over the orange segments. Cool and chill.

3 Serve with soured cream.

NVQ **SVQ** RANGE CHECKLIST

1D14.1 Prepare fruit for hot and cold dishes

preparing 2 of these types of fruit
- [ ] hard fruit
- [ ] citrus fruit
- [ ] stone fruit
- [ ] soft fruit

using 4 of these methods
- [ ] peeling or skinning
- [ ] chopping or shredding or cutting
- [ ] slicing
- [ ] trimming
- [ ] grating

1D14.2 Cook fruit dishes

cooking 2 of the types of fruit listed above by 3 of these methods
- [ ] baking   [ ] deep frying
- [ ] boiling   [ ] steaming
- [ ] braising or stewing or poaching

Introduction

This is an area of catering which has perhaps changed more than any other in the last decade.

Thanks to modern methods of storage and transportation, caterers can get most vegetables fresh throughout the year. And alongside the familiar varieties is a huge array of exotic produce from all corners of the world.

Technology has also improved the quality and choice of convenience vegetables. Those that are frozen are processed within hours of being harvested, so that quality and nutritional content are very high. A wide and varied range of preprepared fresh vegetables and ready-made dishes extend the huge choice already offered by canned, frozen and dehydrated products.

Not many years ago, people thought in terms of two types of rice: long grain – for plain boiled or savoury dishes, and short grain – for milk puddings and sweet dishes. With dozens of speciality rices now readily available in the UK, and the more popular of these also sold partly or fully cooked, this distinction has become redundant.

Views have changed on the best methods of cooking vegetables. There was an easy rule to remember: vegetables which grow under the ground get started off in cold water, others in boiling water. But starting cooking in cold water is no longer considered good practice, in view of the harm caused to the nutritional value of the food.

More people are becoming vegetarian. Some of these still like the taste and texture of meat. Others want nothing to do with meat but want a protein-rich, convenient food to add interest to vegetables and pulses. Yet others want to limit their meat intake, by avoiding those cuts and dishes which have a high saturated fat content.

To meet this growing market, many millions of pounds have been spent in developing high quality, vegetable protein products. After TVP had been hailed on a 1960s *Tomorrow's World* programme on BBC as 'the new wonder food', many people were disappointed to find that it didn't actually taste very good. With the improvements to vegetable protein products since then, the stigma has been successfully shaken off. For instance, Quorn (pronounced *kworn*), one of the leading brands, enjoys an upmarket, healthy image.

Contents guide

Units and elements covered in this section

1D13 Prepare and cook vegetables `LEVEL 1`
- 1D13.1 Prepare vegetables for hot and cold dishes
- 1D13.2 Cook vegetable dishes

1D15 Prepare and cook vegetable protein dishes
- 1D15.1 Prepare and cook vegetable protein dishes

1D16 Prepare and cook rice
- 1D16.1 Prepare and cook rice

2D18 Prepare and cook vegetable and rice dishes `LEVEL 2`
- 2D18.1 Prepare vegetable dishes
- 2D18.2 Cook and finish vegetable dishes
- 2D18.3 Prepare and cook rice dishes

Quality points: vegetables

Convenience vegetables

– not passed use-by or best-before date

– packaging in good condition

Storing frozen vegetables

1 Rotate stock. New deliveries of frozen food should be stored so that they are used after current stocks have been exhausted.

2 Follow instructions on the packet. Pay particular attention to the storage time. For frozen vegetables stored at −18°C or below, this varies between 3 and 12 months.

3 Frozen vegetables should not be defrosted before cooking. This will avoid loss of water-soluble vitamins and colour, and possible damage to the texture that can happen during thawing.

Fresh vegetables, general quality points

– clean, no soil. Some soil may be acceptable on new potatoes and on organic and locally grown produce

– compact and crisp

– good colour

– no bruising or cuts

– no signs of blight or disease, insect or pest damage

– no blemishes

Storing fresh vegetables, general points

Disease and bruising are quickly passed on when vegetables are left packed tightly together in bags, sacks or boxes.

1 Store in a cool dry place, preferably on racks so that air can circulate freely around each vegetable. Some vegetables are best stored in a refrigerator, preferably one reserved for keeping vegetables, or in salad drawers in a general-purpose refrigerator.

2 Always separate blemished from perfect produce.

3 Root vegetables should stay fresh for 5 to 6 days.

4 Green vegetables should be bought fresh daily if possible, or at least every 2 to 3 days. Remove from polybags, or punch holes for ventilation. Loosen or remove clingfilm.

Types of vegetable

The terms vegetable and fruit mean different things to different people. Vegetables are generally thought of as savoury, while fruits are thought of as being sweet (with a few exceptions like the lemon).

But strictly speaking, many of the best known vegetables are in fact fruits: tomatoes and aubergines, cucumbers, peppers, courgettes, marrows and pumpkins.

So a more useful way of classifying vegetables is to think in terms of what part of the plant is eaten: *roots, tubers, bulbs, leaves, flower heads, fruit, stems, légumes (or seeds)* and *fungi*.

Some of the frozen vegetables available to caterers: 1) Diced mixed peppers, 2) Brussels sprouts, 3) Sliced green beans, 4) Broccoli, 5) Cauliflower, 6) Leaf spinach, 7) Corn on the cob, 8) Peas, 9) Sweetcorn.

Spoilage

The flavour and texture of most vegetables start to deteriorate from the moment they are picked. The cells go on using up food even though the plant has been cut off from food and water. Peas lose up to 40% of their sugar in 6 hours at room temperature. Broccoli and asparagus go on using sugar to make tough woody fibres.

If the vegetables dry out or wilt, the water loss from the cells will leave concentrated substances that may start to eat away at the cell walls. Damage to the cell walls can mean that enzymes will destroy vitamin C, develop off-flavours and cause discoloration.

Mould spores quickly spread from mouldy foods to good foods.

If vegetables are sealed off from air, in a plastic bag, for example, alcohol builds up in them and eventually causes cell damage.

Roots *The root anchors the plant to the ground, and carries moisture and nutrients to the rest of the plant. Carrots and turnips are examples.*

Tubers *A tuber is an underground stem, which carries nutrients from the roots to the rest of the plant. Potatoes are tubers.*

Bulbs *Bulbs, e.g. onions and leeks, are leaf bases swollen with water and carbohydrate stored for the next year's growth.*

Leaves *In a process called photosynthesis, leaves use sunlight to produce food (in the form of sugar) plus oxygen. Cabbage, spinach, watercress and lettuce are leaves.*

Flower heads *Left to grow they would eventually develop male pollen and female ovules, to produce seeds. Cauliflower and broccoli are examples.*

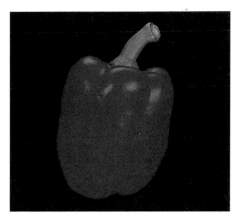

Fruit *When animals eat the fruit, its seeds pass straight through the digestive system, and get scattered far and wide. Peppers and tomatoes are examples.*

Stems *When sold, fennel and celery usually have the roots trimmed, but some of the leaves are left on. Asparagus is a stem with the bud.*

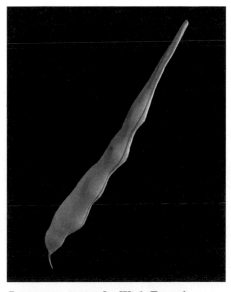

Legumes *or* **seeds** *With French beans, the seeds are eaten complete with their seed case. With haricot beans and garden peas, only the seeds are eaten.*

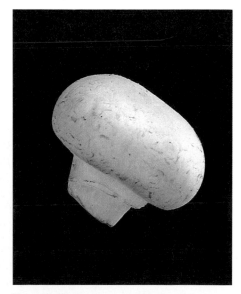

Fungi *These are almost the only vegetable foodstuff that does not derive from a green plant. Mushrooms, truffles and morels are fungi.*

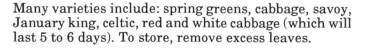
More about fresh vegetables

Unless otherwise stated, the general quality and storage guidelines (see page 156) apply. Points for preparation, where relevant, are given below for the more unusual vegetables, otherwise see pages 160–3.

Artichokes: Globe – leaves stiff, with slight bloom. Avoid those with fully opened leaves or fuzzy, miscoloured centres. Few centimetres of stalk attached.

Artichokes: Jerusalem – really misshapen samples are difficult to peel.

Asparagus spears – even size and thickness, with tight buds, only the base of the stem is woody. Colour is green, white or violet. The straighter the shoot and the more compact the tip, the better the quality. Store in a cool, humid place.

Aubergines – glossy, smooth skin, firm. The shape is not critical – either long or round. Store in a cool place or salad drawer of refrigerator. To remove the bitter taste, sprinkle all cut surfaces with salt after preparation. Leave for 20 minutes. Rinse thoroughly and dry on kitchen paper.

Baby sweetcorn – firm, bright yellow colour. Remove protective husks (if any). Cook whole.

Bean sprouts – crisp, with fat juicy stems which measure 40 to 65 mm (1½ to 2½ inches). Use on day of purchase. Rinse and drain well before use.

Beans – firm, crisp pods, which should snap easily.

Beetroot – firm. Store in a cool, dry, airy place. *Cooked beetroot* – rich bright red colour, skins rub off easily. Store in the refrigerator for up to 3 days.

Broccoli or **Purple sprouting** – bright green, firm. Shoots snap easily. Avoid woody stalks.

Brussels sprouts – good even colour, tightly packed leaves, white stalked base. Use on day of purchase.

Cabbage – firm body, crisp, bright looking leaves.

Many varieties include: spring greens, cabbage, savoy, January king, celtic, red and white cabbage (which will last 5 to 6 days). To store, remove excess leaves.

Carrots – hard to the touch, should snap easily. Store in cool, dark place, or refrigerator.

Cauliflower – white with crisp green outer leaves.

Celeriac – firm, feels heavy for its size. Best are medium in size with smooth outside. Peel and sprinkle with lemon juice to prevent discoloration.

Celery – regular shaped stalks, greenish-white or green depending on variety. Remove excess leaves before storing in the refrigerator. Best left in its plastic sleeve.

Chayote or **Christophine** – inside flesh white and firm. Very delicate flavour between vegetable marrow and cucumber. Peel and remove stone.

Chicory or **Endive** – conical shape, crisp, white leaves tipped with yellow, packed tightly. Trim base. Wash thoroughly.

Chilli pepper – the long thin variety is very hot, the shorter variety milder. Like onions, chillies give off a vapour when cut, which might give a tingling sensation to skin and throat. It is most important to wash your hands after handling chillies because eyes can become very painful if rubbed afterwards.

Courgettes – firm, with smooth skins. Refrigerate.

Cucumber – stalk end firm. Store in cool place or refrigerate. Leave shrink wrapping on until use.

Doody (or *dudi*) or **Bottle gourd** – one type long, the other round. Cream to pale green colour when at their best. Remove centre seeds before cooking.

Eddoes – brown, hairy skin. Use as potatoes.

Fennel – well-rounded, pale green or white. Trim leafy top stems close to the root. Feathery leaves can be added to the cooking liquid for extra flavour or finely chopped for a garnish.

Left photograph:
1) Potatoes (old), 2) Celeriac, 3) Swede,
4) Eddoes, 5) Kohlrabi, 6) Leeks,
7) Carrots, 8) Turnips, 9) Jerusalem
artichokes, 10) Salsify, 11) Parsnips,
12) Onions, 13) Shallots, 14) Potatoes
(new).

Right photograph:
1) White cabbage, 2) Cauliflower,
3) Savoy cabbage, 4) Spaghetti marrow,
5) Spring greens, 6) Butternut squash,
7) Broccoli, 8) Celery, 9) Asparagus,
10) Globe artichoke, 11) Chayote,
12) Fennel, 13) Doody (bottle gourd),
14) Runner beans, 15) Baby sweetcorn,
16) Spinach, 17) Mangetout,
18) Courgettes, 19) French beans.

Garlic – plump, firm cloves. Avoid those with green shoots. Store in airy, dry place.

Ginger – roundish, with kidney-shaped and finger-like nobbles. Skin light reddish-brown.

Kohlrabi – choose young ones, the size of an orange. White, very light green or purple in colour. Very young samples are good in salads: trim leafy top and root base, scrub thoroughly in cold running water, peel thickly.

Leeks – firm, white bulbs, bright green unwilted leaves which have been trimmed. Avoid any which have had the base of the root removed, as these will deteriorate quickly. Keep cool or store in refrigerator.

Lettuce – avoid any that are drooping or wilting. Varieties include cos, round, iceberg, Webbs wonder, little gem, oakleaf, lollo rosso. Store in refrigerator.

Mangetout or **Sugar peas** – bright green pods, juicy. Row of little peas down one side just visible.

Marrows – avoid those larger than 20 cm (8 inches) as these may be watery and bitter.

Mushrooms – many varieties. Button (buds that have not opened), and cups (larger, showing gills) should have clean firm, white caps and fleshy stems. Flats: opened with full flavour and dark colour. Mushrooms dry out quickly, so use on day of purchase.

Okra – small, firm, slightly underripe and bright looking. Cut away the conical cap from the stalk end but do not expose the seeds and sticky juices inside. Before cooking, soak for 1 hour in vinegar and water (125 ml/4 fl oz vinegar to ½ litre/1 pt water), drain and dry gently to preserve the shape. This removes the gluey juices.

Onions – firm, no green shoots or black/brown marks. Keep in cool, dry, dark place.

Parsnips – fresh, white roots with few whiskers and nobbles. Should snap easily. No brown patches.

Peas in the pod – bright, firm, plump.

Peppers or **Capsicums** – firm. Colours range from green and red, to white, yellow and deep purple. Before use, remove the inside seeds and membrane.

Potatoes – good shape. Avoid greening or scuffed skins, deep eyes and new shoots. Keep in cool, dry, dark atmosphere, away from strong-smelling foods. If the skin has turned green, potatoes should be thrown away, or at the very least heavily peeled.

Radishes – firm and smooth. Any leaves should appear fresh. Store in refrigerator.

Salsify – regular-shaped, with fresh grey-green leaves. Handle gently to avoid damaging.

Shallots – dry and sound.

Spinach – stalks tender. Avoid flowering shoots and yellow leaves.

Swedes – avoid over-large ones, and those which look knobbly or have side roots.

Sweet potato – avoid cut or scratched samples. Wash gently to avoid damaging the skin.

Sweetcorn – kernels pale, golden yellow, leaves green and firm. A fingernail stuck into the husk should result in a milky liquid oozing out. Store in refrigerator.

Tomatoes – firm for use in salads, grilling, etc. Keep in refrigerator. Soft ones may be acceptable for making sauces, soup, etc., and should be used at once — chilling will only make them softer. Green and hard tomatoes will ripen in 2 to 3 days in a sunny room.

Turnips – firm, with smooth skin that is white, pale green or violet.

Watercress – dark green. Remove discoloured or wilted leaves and store in a perforated polythene bag or closed salad drawer. Refresh in cold water before using.

ACTION

Visit a selection of vegetable markets, greengrocers and supermarkets in your area. Make a list of the unusual vegetables you see, and tick them off against the details on these pages. For those not described here, find out as much as you can from the greengrocer about their quality points and preparation.

Preparing fresh vegetables

Protect the vitamin content of vegetables at all stages:

- don't prepare vegetables until you need them
- use a sharp knife
- only peel vegetables when absolutely necessary – most of the nutritional content lies close to the skin
- don't soak vegetables in cold water after you have prepared them (except for potatoes)
- prepare (and cook) them as close to service as possible.

Cutting French fries/chips

For French fries prepared in the classical way, the lengths of potatoes are cut very precisely. As you will note from the photograph (*top left*), this means trimming the potato quite severely. However, the trimmings can be used to make vichyssoise soup, for example.

1 Cut off the round edges of the potatoes to make squared off chunks.

2 Cut the chunks into slices 40 mm (1½ inch) long and 10 mm thick.

3 Cut the slices into sticks about 10 mm thick. This should produce sticks which are approximately 40 × 40 × 10 mm.

Preparing mushrooms

There is no need to peel cultivated mushrooms, nor do they usually need washing.

To slice, cut through the cap and stem to form slices in an umbrella shape. For a sturdier shape, cut in half and then in quarters.

In top establishments, the stems are usually pulled off or cut level with the cap.

Preparing leeks

As grit and mud can penetrate the layers of the leek, it is essential that they are washed carefully.

1 Trim off the green part and roots (taking care not to cut into the leaf bases). Remove any old outer leaves.

2 Cut once down the length of the leek, almost to the base – or, if necessary, twice, so that you are effectively cutting most of the leek into quarters. Fan out the leaves and wash under cold running water.

French fries, step 1.

French fries, step 2.

Cutting onion rings.

Quarters and slices of mushroom.

Trimming potatoes into barrel shapes for château *potatoes: 1) Cut off the top and bottom. 2) Holding the potato by the ends you have just cut, cut even slices from bottom to top, working your way around the potato, and retaining an oval shape to the potato. Ideally you should end up with a potato that has 6 or 8 sides, of even width, without having to remove too much of the potato.*

Preparing leeks.

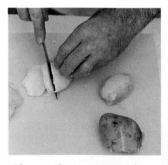

Above: *these potatoes have been boiled (or steamed) with their skins on, peeled while warm, then sliced about 5 mm thick for sautéing.*

Left: *for braising or boiling, trim and tie the celery as shown. After cooking, cut in half, then fold over. (Recipe on page 173.)*

Cuts of potato for deep frying

Many styles of cut and shaped potatoes are still known by their French names.

The square and rectangle shaped pieces are: *Pont Neuf* (1), square batons 40 mm long and 20 mm thick, *cubes* or *bataille* (2), 15 mm squares, *chips/French fries* or *frîtes* (3), sticks 40 mm long and 10 mm thick.

Very decorative cuts requiring quite a lot of skill are: *spiral* or *Bénédictine* (4) and (5), coiled strips 20 mm wide and 2 mm thick, *chain* or *en chaînes* (6), interlocking links about 7 mm wide and 2 mm thick.

Other decorative cuts, less time-consuming to do are: *thick matchsticks* or *mignonettes* (7), 40 mm long and 5 mm thick, *straw* or *pailles* (8), fine strips, *fine straw* or *chiffonette* (9), very fine strips, *star* or *étoile* (10), cubes cut into stars, *wafer* or *gaufrettes* (11), thin slices cut in a trellis pattern, *collerette* (12), thin rounds with grooved edges, *woodchip* or *copeaux* (13), thin lengths of varying widths cut like woodchips, *matchstick* or *allumettes* (14), thick sticks 40 mm long, 2 mm thick.

Varieties of potatoes: deep frying and roasting

Floury varieties of potatoes are less suitable for deep frying than varieties like Désirée, Maris Piper, Pentland Crown and Romano which will retain a firmer texture. Evenly shaped potatoes are best for cutting into shapes because there should be less wastage from trimming. Trimmings can be used in a soup.

Most varieties of potato roast well (although new potatoes are not often roasted). They should be:

- not too small, otherwise they are likely to dry out
- evenly shaped, so the minimum amount of trimming and handling is required
- of similar size so that they all cook at the same rate.

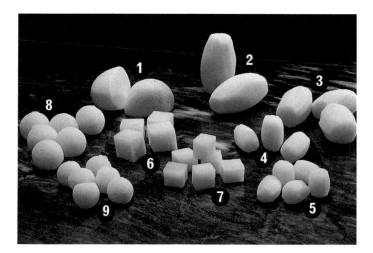

Cuts of potato for roasting

For plain roasting, large potatoes tend to be cut in half (1) or roughly trimmed to an even shape (2).

Special cuts include the barrel-shapes, made using a small turning knife: *château* (3) which should be 55 to 60 mm long, *cocotte* (4) 40 to 45 mm long and *olivette* (5) 20 mm long, which can also be made using a special spoon with an olive-shaped bowl.

Cube shapes are *pavée* (6), which should measure 20 mm and *parmentier* (7), 10 mm.

Ball shapes are *parisienne* (8), which are made using special spoons like small ice-cream scoops and should be 30 mm in diameter, and *noisette* (9), 25 mm in diameter.

Dicing vegetables

1 Cut lengthwise into slices about 3 mm thick. (This step is not necessary for celery.)

2 Cut lengthwise again to form sticks. Once you become practised, you can pile two or three slices on top of each other and cut through the pile in one go.

3 Gather a pile of sticks, turning them so they are in a comfortable position to cut. Slice through the sticks, forming small dice of equal size (3 mm).

Finely chopping onion

1 Clean and peel the onion.

2 Trim the root end carefully (if you trim off too much the onion will fall apart).

3 Cut the onion in half from top to bottom and place each half flat side down on the chopping board.

4 Slice the onion towards the root end (without cutting through the base so that the onion is still just held together). The size of these slices decides how big the dice will be.

5 Cut a series of vertical slices towards the root (again not cutting through the base).

6 Now cut across the onion at right angles to form dice. If some of the dice are too big (this tends to happen with the slices that come from the curved outer edges), chop them smaller on the board.

Preparing chopped tomato flesh (concassé)

1 Remove the stalks, then place the tomatoes in boiling water for 10 to 16 seconds (depending on ripeness) to loosen the skin.

2 Cool immediately under cold running water.

3 Remove the skins. This should be fairly easy, if you have kept the tomatoes in the boiling water for the right length of time.

4 Cut the tomatoes in half. With a teaspoon, scoop out the seeds. These can be used in stock or soup.

5 Chop the flesh into medium-sized cubes.

Preparing tomatoes for grilling and salads

Wash and remove stalk. For grilling, baking, salads and garnishes, cut in half. If required use zig-zag cut (see page 265), or for salads, cut into quarters or slice.

Alternatively, leave whole for grilling:

• with the tip of a knife, cut out the eye (where the stalk was attached)

• make an X-shaped cut in the top of the tomato just deep enough to penetrate the skin.

Sometimes, tomatoes are also skinned before grilling, follow steps 1 to 3 above.

Dicing vegetables, step 1.

Dicing, step 2.

Dicing, step 3.

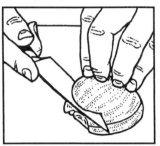

Chopping an onion, step 4.

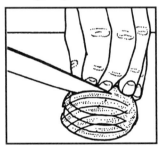

Onion, step 5.

Onion, step 6.

Cutting triangular shapes.

For some recipes, such as Irish stew (see page 90), the vegetables can be cut into shapes known as paysanne: *small squares, rounds or triangles, as shown in the photograph. If they are added towards the end of the cooking process, they will improve the overall presentation of the dish.*

Slicing aubergines

Peel, slice thickly, sprinkle with salt and leave to stand for 30 to 60 minutes. Wash, then dry with kitchen paper.

For grilling, score the top of each slice.

Lettuce

1 Separate the leaves. With most round lettuces there is a quick way of doing this: take firm hold of the core, twist it and pull it out. If possible, avoid cutting (rather than tearing) lettuce leaves as they bruise and discolour easily. If a knife has to be used, for example, to shred the lettuce, use one with a stainless steel blade to reduce the risk of browning.

2 Wash the leaves carefully, then drain thoroughly. With iceberg varieties it is a good idea to run water into the hole left by the core. The lettuce can then be turned upside down to drain.

Cucumber (for salad)

1 Peel thinly. For a decorative edge, cut shallow, V-shaped grooves out of the skin down the length of the cucumber.

2 Slice thinly. It is quite common to draw out some of the excess water from the cucumber before serving. To do this, sprinkle the slices with salt and set aside for 30 minutes. Then wash the slices quickly under cold running water and allow to drain thoroughly.

Chicory (for salad)

1 Remove any wilted leaves.

2 Trim the stems just short of the bottom of the leaves so that the leaves do not fall apart.

3 Wash thoroughly, then drain.

4 Cut the chicory into quarters along the length, or trim off the remainder of the stem and break into separate leaves.

Why salads spoil

Crisp textures and bright colours are the mark of a good salad. They can be spoilt by:

- loss of moisture – though if the problem is not too bad, rinsing in cold water and chilling will restore crispness
- too much moisture – if the salad vegetables are not drained properly after washing they will be waterlogged
- lack of circulating air. Make sure salad vegetables are not packed too tightly
- being cut up too far in advance or being bruised, which will create dark marks. Chilling slows down this process as does the presence of an acid such as lemon juice. Cooking has the same effect, though this is obviously not a method that can be used for salads using raw ingredients. A few salads can be made using blanched ingredients, e.g. celeriac.

Other vegetable preparation points

Broad beans – shell.

Brussels sprouts – cut away any loose outer leaves. It should not be necessary to cut a cross in the base.

Carrots – remove wispy tails, and trim off stalk end. Only peel older carrots.

Cauliflower – if cooking whole, cut out the centre of the core from the stalk using a sharp knife or apple corer. This speeds up cooking.

Celery – remove any damaged stalks. For cooking whole: trim the root end and remove any blemishes with a peeler or small knife. Alternatively break off stalks individually and slice or cut into pieces.

Courgettes and marrows – top and tail. As preferred, cut into lengths, slices, or half along length and stuff.

French beans – top and tail.

Garlic – pull off required cloves, smash with the flat of a heavy knife, discard the skin and chop as finely as you require. Or peel and put through a garlic squeezer.

Mangetout – top and tail.

Parsnips – peel thinly, and remove the hard inner core of large parsnips as they may be woody.

Peas – shell.

Potatoes – remove any eyes, or new roots. Peeling should usually be thin, because most of the nutrients lie just beneath the skin.

Runner beans – top and tail, or slice at an angle.

Salsify – blanch after washing to make peeling easier. Like *celeriac*, it should then be left in cold water with the addition of a little lemon juice to prevent discolouring before cooking.

Spinach – cut off the large stalks, or tear them out.

Spring onions – trim off the root end, and the green stalk to leave the bulb and a short piece of white stem about 5 to 7 cm (2 to 2¾ inches) long.

Swedes and turnips – peel young ones thinly, older ones more thickly.

Sweetcorn – gently tear away the outer leaves from the top down to the base, rub and pull away the long silks. Chop off the ends.

Preparing stuffed cabbage for braising. The cabbage and ball of stuffing are enclosed in an outer leaf, wrapped in a cloth and squeezed firmly to produce a good even shape. (Recipe on page 175.)

Cooking vegetables

The cooking of potatoes is dealt with in more detail overleaf.

Boiling

Boiling is perhaps the most used method of cooking vegetables. The cooking liquid is in contact with the whole of the food's surface, and so heat transfer is quick and efficient.

A short cooking time is important because it means less vitamin C is lost. Other general rules are:

1 Use the minimum amount of water.

2 Bring the water to the boil before adding vegetables.

3 Keep the lid on the pot during cooking.

4 Lift the lid from time to time during cooking to allow any volatile acids (such as those created during the cooking of cauliflower, broccoli or Brussels sprouts) to escape.

5 Keep liquid movement to a gentle simmering action, to avoid damaging the vegetables.

6 When a glazed effect is required, for example, with carrots, turnips or button onions, increase the speed of cooking in the final stages. The aim is to evaporate off the remaining water, leaving the butter and sugar used in the recipe to coat the vegetables.

7 For cooking bulb vegetables whole, e.g. onions and leeks, trim the root end but take care not to remove completely as this helps to hold the vegetable together.

8 Leaf vegetables, e.g. Brussels sprouts, spinach and lettuce, tend to be rather delicate and are easily overcooked. Spinach, especially, will go limp very fast when cooked, and lose colour and nutritional value.

9 Flower vegetables, e.g. cauliflower and broccoli, are quite difficult to cook because the stalk tends to be tough and the flower is very delicate. If the stalk is tough it should be trimmed off, or the vegetable divided into florets. It is a common mistake to cook the stalk until it is edible and end up overcooking the delicate flower.

Poaching

Poaching is not usually used as a method of cooking vegetables. It is too slow and not hot enough for green and root vegetables.

However, mushrooms, tomatoes, onions and shallots are used in many poaching recipes to provide a base for other foods and to add flavour either to the main dish or to the accompanying sauce.

Steaming

Steaming has several advantages as a cooking method for vegetables:

- cooking is very fast, particularly in pressureless convection steamers and high pressure steamers. This means the vegetables can be cooked immediately before they are served, even from a frozen state

- two or more vegetables can be cooked at the same time, without cross-flavouring (transfer of flavours)

- the food is still and does not roll around as it does in a boiling liquid, so it is less likely to break up

- fewer of the water-soluble vitamins B and C are lost

- loss of vitamins through contact with air is also reduced, especially in pressureless convection and high-pressure steamers

- colour retention is good, especially for green vegetables

- cooking times can be calculated precisely, so the food is less likely to be overcooked. Many steamers can be set to stop cooking automatically at the required time.

Blanching

Blanching is mainly used to:

- partly cook vegetables before baking, roasting, braising or stir frying, for example. This does reduce cooking time, but the main reason is usually to get a better finished product. For example, blanching celery and cabbage stops the finished dish getting a somewhat bitter flavour

- make it easier to peel tomatoes

- make it easier to shape cabbage and lettuce which is to be braised, so that the final presentation is appetising, and, where appropriate, a stuffing can be enclosed

- shorten the pre-service cooking time of vegetables so as to avoid holding them for a long time in a bain-marie or hot cupboard.

Blanching always involves a second stage, called *refreshing*. This is to stop the vegetables cooking. Where the purpose of blanching is to shorten pre-service cooking time, then a third stage is involved, *reheating*.

1 Place the vegetables for a short time in a small amount of boiling water. How long depends on the purpose of blanching and the degree to which the vegetable should be cooked. For skinning tomatoes, 10 to 16 seconds are generally sufficient to loosen the skin. For celery and cabbage which is to be braised, about 10 minutes are long enough to draw out the bitterness.

2 As soon as the vegetables are sufficiently cooked, either plunge into cold water, or run cold water into the saucepan through a sieve. The sieve will break up the force of the water. It also prevents the vegetables from washing over the edge of the pan, a particular problem with peas and other small items.

3 To reheat vegetables for service, either plunge into boiling water or use a microwave oven.

Stewing

Most vegetables can be stewed in their own right to make tasty main course casseroles, vegetable curries and so forth. Vegetables are also used to add flavour to meat, poultry and fish stews.

Pay careful attention to:

- special preparation steps. For example, sprinkling salt on aubergines, leaving for 20 minutes or so, then washing – in order to extract some of the bitterness and excess moisture
- initial cooking. For example, whether the vegetables are to be browned by frying over a fairly high heat, or cooked more gently so that they do not change colour
- stages at which different vegetables are added. Obviously it does not take as long to cook frozen peas as it does button onions, so the onions should be almost cooked before the peas are added.

Braising

Braised vegetables gain extra flavour from the cooking liquid. It is best for vegetables which do not turn into a mush when cooked for a long time, such as cabbage, lettuce, celery, onions, leeks, fennel and chicory.

Baking

Mostly used for potatoes, and sometimes for tomatoes. The skin provides a natural protection from the dry heat.

Roasting

Potatoes and parsnips are traditional accompaniments to the British roast meal. Sweet potatoes are sometimes roasted, as are onions and Jerusalem artichokes.

Grilling and barbecuing

Tomatoes and mushrooms are perhaps the most popular grilled vegetables, although peppers, courgettes and aubergines are also good. They should be brushed lightly with oil or butter before cooking. Other vegetables are likely to dry up in the intense heat.

Shallow frying

Most vegetables can be shallow fried. Mushrooms, onions, tomatoes, aubergines, courgettes and peppers are commonly cooked by this method. Or, like leeks, carrots and celery, they are shallow fried as a first step before stewing, roasting or braising, or making a soup. Potatoes are usually boiled or steamed first.

Other vegetables, such as French beans and sprouts, are sometimes quickly fried or sautéed (tossed) in butter just before service. The vegetables have to be boiled or steamed first.

Stir frying

As stir frying is such a fast method of cooking, and the vegetables are usually eaten quite crisp, it is a good method of conserving vitamins. For best results, prepare the vegetables just before cooking, and serve at once.

Deep frying

Potatoes, onions (as rings), aubergines and courgettes (as round slices or pieces), and mushrooms are deep fried from raw. Japanese style *tempura* dishes are raw vegetables such as aubergines, broccoli, cauliflower, green peppers, mushrooms and spring onions, which are dipped in batter and then deep fried. (See the description for prawns cooked by this method on page 133.)

SAFETY ⚠ ⚠ ⚠

When you are boiling large quantities of potatoes, carry them to the stove in an empty pot, then add boiling water from another saucepan. If you add the potatoes to the boiling water, it is easy to splash and burn yourself.

Shown in the wok: red, green and yellow peppers, water chestnuts, mushrooms, bamboo shoots, bean sprouts, baby corn, carrots, celery, onions and garlic.

These vegetables have been sweated, which means very gently shallow fried without browning. The pan was covered to make sure that no browning could happen.

Roasting potatoes

1 Peel and wash the potatoes.

2 Cut into even-sized pieces, leaving small potatoes whole, and cutting larger ones to a similar size. Or trim to form barrel shapes, see page 160.

3 Keep the potatoes in cold water until required.

4 Thoroughly drain. Season lightly with the salt if required, then place in a hot oven at 200°C to 220°C.

5 Cook the potatoes until golden brown on top.

6 Turn them over and continue cooking until the potatoes are done and all surfaces are crisp and golden brown. This will take 45 to 60 minutes.

Alternatives

Before roasting:

• boil in water for a short time (*parboil*)

• shallow fry in the fat in the roasting tray for 3 to 4 minutes.

For a healthier result:

• do not parboil or shallow fry

• brush lightly with polyunsaturated oil and place on a flat baking sheet

• do not turn while roasting.

Deep frying potatoes

See also pages 160 and 161 for preparing different cuts.

1 Wash freshly prepared potatoes thoroughly to remove as much surface starch as possible. Otherwise, the pieces of potato tend to stick together during cooking.

2 Drain and dry well just before cooking. Water will cause the fat to foam.

3 Place in a frying basket and deep fry at 170°C to 190°C until crisp and brown (4 to 5 minutes for chips).

4 Shake the frying basket occasionally to release any steam and ensure that the potatoes do not stick together.

5 Serve immediately. Do not cover.

Potatoes do not stay crisp for long after deep frying. When cooking large quantities, a two-stage approach is usually more practical:

• deep fry at 160°C to 170°C, so that they soften but do not brown (4 to 6 minutes for chips). This is often referred to as *blanching*

• thoroughly drain, place in single layers on trays and keep chilled until required (but preferably not more than 4 to 6 hours)

• complete cooking at 185°C to 190°C (2 to 3 minutes for chips).

Potato varieties

There are many varieties of potato, each with a different texture. Some (usually new) are 'waxy' and others (usually old-crop) are 'floury'. See also page 161.

for boiling

Early varieties (June to July) – Home Guard, Arran Comet, Ulster Sceptre, Maris Bard, Pentland Javelin, Alcmaria and Premiere.

Second earlies (August to March) – Wilja and Estima.

Main crop varieties (September to May) – Désirée, Maris Piper, Cara and Romano.

for creaming, mashing or puréeing – floury varieties, particularly Pentland Squire, Désirée and King Edward.

for baking – floury varieties, particularly King Edward, Pentland Dell, Pentland Squire. Also: Wilja, Estima, Désirée, Maris Piper, Cara and Romano.

Some classical potato dishes

There are hundreds, perhaps thousands of different ways of cooking potatoes. Here are a few of the classical dishes that are not mentioned elsewhere in this section:

Duchesse – puréed, enriched with butter or margarine and egg yolks, piped in swirls/pyramid shapes, baked until golden brown

Croquette – duchesse mixture, cylinder or cork-shaped, coated in flour, beaten egg and breadcrumbs, deep fried

Almond – duchesse mixture, shaped into small rounds or medallions, coated with flour, beaten egg and chopped almonds, deep fried

Marquise – duchesse mixture piped into small baskets, browned in the oven or under the grill, hollow filled with hot chopped tomato (concassé)

Berny – as Almond, with addition of finely chopped truffle, and shaped like an apricot

Boulangère – layered dish of thinly sliced potato and onion, covered with stock and baked

Lyonnaise – as sautéed potato, with thinly sliced sautéed onion (sometimes fried at the same time as the potatoes)

NUTRITION

Cut chips thickly to reduce the amount of oil they absorb in relation to their size. Instead of blanching them first in oil, try boiling them until just cooked, and then deep fry to brown and crisp.

Think before you salt. Many customers are trying to cut down their salt intake for health reasons. If they are not, and particularly like the taste of salt, they can always add their own.

For a healthier alternative, keep the skin on sautéed potatoes.

Baking potatoes

1 Thoroughly wash the potatoes (you may need to scrub them) and remove any blemishes.

2 Wipe the potatoes dry, then pierce them in 3 or 4 places with the prongs of a fork. This will allow the steam to escape and avoid the danger of bursting.

3 Sprinkle a thin layer of cooking salt on a baking tray, then place the potatoes on it. The salt prevents the potatoes scorching where they touch the tray, but is not necessary if they are being cooked on open rack shelves. If a soft skin is required, rub the potato with oil before cooking.

4 Bake the potatoes in a moderate oven at 200°C until tender. This will take 1 to 1½ hours. To test, place one of the potatoes in a clean towel and squeeze lightly. You should feel the inside giving way.

5 Brush off any salt from the surfaces of the potatoes.

6 Cut a deep cross in the tops and place them on a warm serving dish. Garnish as required (many suggestions are given on page 176).

Sautéing potatoes

1 Wash and scrub the potatoes. Do not peel.

2 Place them in boiling water and simmer until just cooked but still firm. Alternatively, steam.

3 Drain and allow to cool, then peel the skins as soon as the potatoes can be held comfortably. (It is more difficult to peel them when they are cold.)

4 Cut the potatoes into slices about 5 mm (¼ inch) thick.

5 Heat the oil in a large frying pan which should, if possible, hold all the potatoes at one time. Otherwise fry in batches and keep warm on a tray. Use just enough oil to cover the base of the pan.

6 Add the potatoes and cook quickly until they are an attractive golden brown on both sides. Turn them over carefully with a fish slice or spatula, or shake the pan to toss.

7 Allow to drain briefly in a colander. Season to taste. Sprinkle with parsley if required, and serve immediately.

ACTION

Try some of the different ways of roasting potatoes. Either do this as a separate exercise using 5 potatoes, or treat one potato differently from the main batch on the next 5 occasions you are roasting some. Stick to the one variety of potato.

Invite some colleagues to form a tasting panel and comment on the taste, texture and appearance of each finished product.

Record their conclusions below, with your general views on whether the result justifies changing your method of roasting potatoes.

Here are the variations:

1 Boil the potato for a few minutes in water, drain thoroughly, then roast it.

2 Before roasting, shallow fry to lightly brown the outside of the potato.

3 Place the potato on a flat cooking tray with very low sides. Brush the potato with oil only at the start of roasting. Use the minimum amount of oil and do not turn the potato during cooking.

4 Use a higher (or lower) oven temperature.

5 Do not use seasoning.

Rice

Drawn extensively from Rice for all Seasons *published by The Rice Bureau.*

Regular long grain white rice has a subtle flavour which complements both rich and delicate sauces. Milled to remove the husk and bran layer, the grain is slim and four to five times as long as it is wide. On cooking, the grains separate to give an attractive fluffy effect.

Easy-cook long grain white rice (parboiled or pre-fluffed rice) offers a fuller flavour. Unlike regular rice which is milled direct from the field, it is steamed under pressure before milling. The process hardens the grain, reducing the possibility of over-cooking. It also helps retain much of the natural vitamin and mineral content present in the milled layers. The golden colour of the uncooked rice turns to white on cooking.

Brown long grain rice (wholegrain rice) has a distinctly nutty flavour. It undergoes only minimal milling which removes the husk but retains the bran layer and thus more of the vitamins, minerals and fibre. Also available in easy-cook form.

Basmati rice is very long grained and has a fragrant flavour and aroma. Grown in the foothills of the Himalayas it is sometimes described as the prince of rice. It is used in Indian dishes such as biryani and pilau rice. Easy-cook and brown basmati are also available.

Jasmine rice (Thai fragrant rice) is another aromatic rice, although its flavour is slightly less pronounced than that of basmati. Originating in Thailand it differs from other long grain rices in that it has a soft and slightly sticky texture when cooked. This rice is good with both Chinese and south-east Asian food.

Risotto rice (Arborio rice) is a medium grain rice. It originates in Italy, and has given its name to the dish risotto, in which it is used. Risotto rice absorbs up to five times its weight in liquid. During cooking, starch is released to give the creamy texture characteristic of the classic risotto.

Pudding rice typically comes from Italy and is the one to use for puddings and sweets. The grains are short, tubby and chalky in appearance and cling together on cooking.

Wild rice is not true rice at all, but an aquatic grass. The grains are long and slim and range in colour from dark brown to black. It is grown in the USA and Canada where it was the traditional food of the American Indians. It is often mixed with other types of rice such as white or brown long grain and basmati for its visual appeal.

Glutinous rice (sweet or sticky rice) is actually gluten-free, like all rice. Its round, pearl-like grain turns sticky when cooked and it tastes slightly sweet.

Storing rice

1 Store in a cool, dry place.

2 Once opened, transfer to an air-tight container.

3 Do not use beyond the best-before date.

4 Store frozen and convenience rice according to the package instructions.

Gluten allergies

Rice is gluten-free and a very useful food for coeliacs and others who are allergic to gluten.

Grains

The term *grain* is used to describe the seedlike fruit of those types of grasses which are grown for eating. They are a valuable source of protein, dietary fibre and vitamins (especially the B vitamins).

Grains can be used as rice substitutes (bulghur, barley and buckwheat), in stuffings, casseroles, soups, to make rissoles, and for baked products.

Barley – whole grain barley, or scotch barley has only part of the indigestible husk removed. Pear barley has all of it removed and is then polished. Also available as flakes and flour.

Bulghur – boiled wheat which has been dried to a paste and then ground up. (Some people misleadingly call it cracked wheat.)

Buckwheat – roasted or unroasted, also as flour and noodles.

Corn or *maize* – gluten-free, available as cornmeal and cornflour.

Millet – gluten-free, flakes and flour.

Oats – whole, flakes, rolled oats.

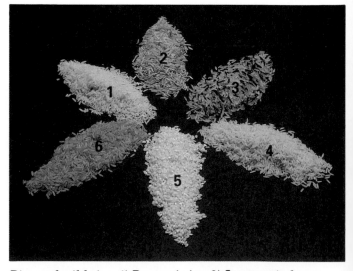

Rice and wild rice. 1) Basmati rice, 2) Long grain brown rice, 3) Wild rice mixed with brown rice, 4) Long grain Patna rice, 5) Short grain pudding rice, 6) Long grain brown rice.

CHEF'S TIPS

Advice from The Rice Bureau

The best way to ensure beautifully fluffy rice is to use the *absorption method*. Simple and easy, this method also retains all the nutritional goodness of rice. Nothing is lost into the water.

1 Allow 50 g (2 oz) rice per person and cook in double the amount of liquid by volume (see below).
2 Put rice, water and salt to taste into a saucepan and bring to the boil. Stir once and lower the heat to simmer.
3 Cover and cook for the length of time recommended below. Avoid the temptation to lift the lid during cooking.
4 Serve within 10 minutes of cooking, or the rice grains will start to stick together in the pan.

As risotto rice requires much more attention during cooking, do check recipe or packet instructions.

Alternatively

Place the rice, water and salt in a casserole dish, cover and place in the oven at 180°C. Cook for the recommended length of time, or until the rice is tender and all the liquid has been absorbed.

	Quantity of rice g	Quantity of water ml	Cooking times (minutes)	
			Stove top	**Oven**
Long grain	250	500	15	40
Long grain easy-cook	250	550	18	45
Basmati	250	450	10	35
Basmati easy-cook	250	600	12	40
Long grain brown	250	625	35	75
Basmati brown	250	600	25	50
Jasmine	250	450	10	35
Wild	250	750	45	100
Med. grain (risotto)	250	1 litre	30	–

For long grain brown easy-cook, check package instructions. General recommendation is:

	250	650	30	70

For short grain (pudding rice), lower oven temperature to 150°C, and use water, not milk:

	50	600	40	120

For convenience rices, check package instructions.

For different flavours, use fruit juices, wine, cider, or combinations of these in place of the recipe water.

ACTION

With your supervisor's permission, carry out the following evaluation.

1 Choose 3 different types of rice which might make suitable alternatives for the range of dishes currently served in your workplace.
2 If possible, include in your sample both an easy-cook, and a frozen, cooked product.
3 Ask a few colleagues to form a tasting panel, and give you their verdict on the appearance, texture and flavour of your dishes.
4 Work out the portion costs, and compare these to the costs of products currently used. Comment on the implications for selling prices and profitability. How do preparation and cooking times compare with current products?
5 Summarise your findings and recommendations below.

Rice A

Rice B

Rice C

Vegetable protein

Vegetable protein products are low in fat and high in protein. They are generally suitable for vegetarian dishes, and as meat substitutes.

Tofu

Tofu is soybean curd. Not many years ago, the only types available were the Morinaga, imported from Japan, and home-made tofu bought at Chinese stores. The choice from wholefood suppliers has expanded considerably, ranging from very soft to quite firm in texture, and including smoked.

The protein value of tofu is as high as chicken. High in essential amino acids, which most grains lack, tofu also boosts the protein value of the foods it is served with. For example, stir fried tofu and vegetables, with a grain like rice, millet buckwheat or couscous, is a wholesome meal, richer than it would seem. A tofu mixture in a wholemeal sandwich or pitta bread is a good combination.

Tofu has a fairly bland taste.

1 The very soft types can be used at once for puddings, when you need a smooth, thick sauce, or drained and left for a day before cutting.

2 Mashed up, it can be used in cheesecake, ice-cream or blended with soft fruits.

3 Thinly sliced smoked tofu makes a tasty first course served with sliced avocado and a fruit like mango or pawpaw, and dressed with a lime vinaigrette.

4 Squares of tofu marinaded in soy sauce with grated ginger and chopped spring onion can be grilled as kebabs, or used in stir fries.

5 To help the flavour of the marinade become absorbed, lightly score the cubes of tofu. Alternatively, rub the tofu with herbs and spices.

6 Tofu pieces, rolled in breadcrumbs or dipped in batter, can be fried. The coating should be flavoured for best results.

Tempeh

Tempeh is made from soya beans that have been injected with a special fungus and left to ferment. The distinctive black specks are similar in nature to the blue veins in some cheese, and do no harm.

Tempeh is chewy and has its own flavour. It is high in protein, and free from gluten and salt.

Textured vegetable protein (TVP)

TVP is basically a dried foam made from soya flour. The flour which is left behind after the oil has been extracted is mixed with water to form a dough. This is heated under pressure, and then forced through a small nozzle. The fall in pressure causes the TVP to expand as it leaves the nozzle. The resulting texture is rather like sponge. It is then cut into chunks or flakes, ground up to form mince or powder, sometimes flavoured to resemble meat, and sold in this dried form.

TVP is high in protein and dietary fibre, very low in fat and in saturated fat.

Different qualities of TVP are available, for use:

• in place of some of the meat in pies, casseroles and dishes such as spaghetti bolognaise (on its own, this type has a rather beany texture and aftertaste)

• as a binding and filler in sausages and burgers

• as a meat alternative in casseroles, stews, pies, burgers, soups, curries

• to add texture and interest to vegetable and fruit dishes.

The better quality (and more expensive) products have been processed to remove the soluble carbohydrate from the soya flour. This is responsible for a not-very-pleasant beany taste and an unfortunate social side effect, flatulence.

A good quality product will have a bland taste, meat-like texture and no side effects. It readily takes up the flavours of accompanying ingredients and sauces.

Different types of vegetarianism

Semi or *demi vegetarians* – exclude red meat or all meat, but fish and other animal products are still eaten. Some also exclude poultry.

Lacto-ovo-vegetarians – exclude all meat, fish and poultry. Milk, milk products and eggs are still consumed.

Lacto-vegetarians – exclude all meat, fish, poultry and eggs. Milk and milk products are still consumed.

Vegans – consume no foods of animal origin. Diets comprise vegetables, vegetable oils, cereals, nuts, fruit and seeds.

Fruitarian – an extreme form of veganism, which excludes all foods of animal origin but also pulses and cereals. Diets comprise mainly raw and dried fruit, nuts, honey and olive oil.

Definitions from Nutrition and Vegetarianism *published by the National Dairy Council.*

Wheatpro

Wheatpro, from Lucas Ingredients, has similar characteristics to top quality TVP products. The raw material in this case is gluten, obtained by washing away other water-soluble proteins and starches from wheat flour.

Catering suppliers may sell preprepared products made from Wheatpro, for example burgers. Convenience vegetarian and vegetable dishes may also include Wheatpro.

1 Wheatpro mixes for burgers, pastry rolls and pies should be stored in dry, well ventilated conditions, away from sunlight and strong odours. Do not store for more than 6 months.

2 Follow instructions on the packaging for mixing and cooking.

3 Once reconstituted, Wheatpro should be handled and stored as fresh meat.

Quorn

Quorn is available from catering suppliers and supermarkets. With a mild savoury taste and firm but tender texture, it can be used in place of meat or fish in most recipes for stir fries, grills, casseroles, stews, quiches and similar dishes, including those which are microwaved.

Quorn is high in protein and dietary fibre, and low in fat. It is suitable for meat eaters and vegetarians alike, but not for vegans as it contains a small quantity of egg white.

1 Quorn is already cooked, so the recipe cooking time should be reduced when you are using it in place of meat or fish. The aim is to allow the different ingredients to blend together and develop the sauce flavour, and for the dish to be heated through to the right temperature. Between 4 and 15 minutes will usually be long enough for the Quorn to do this.

2 Quorn readily picks up the flavours of other ingredients with which it is cooked. When using strong flavours such as garlic, wine, lemon and herbs, reduce the recipe quantities by about half. Reduce marinating time to 30 minutes.

3 To grill Quorn, brush each piece with a little oil or a glaze to prevent it drying out.

4 Store Quorn in the refrigerator, and use before the date indicated on the packet. Quorn freezes very successfully, and will keep in the freezer for up to 3 months. To thaw, place the Quorn in a refrigerator for 12 hours. Use within 24 hours of thawing.

5 Quorn can be cooked straight from the freezer, by adding it to the recipe sauce, and allowing to heat through for 10 to 15 minutes.

6 As a guide, 225 to 350 g (8 to 12 oz) of Quorn will serve 4 people, depending on the recipe.

Checklist of vegetarian alternatives

by Mary Scott Morgan, writing in Hospitality, *published by HCIMA*

NEVER SUITABLE

meat, fish, poultry – use nuts, pulses, grains, seeds, manufactured foods like nutmeat, TVP, tofu, tempeh

meat stock, e.g. in sauces, stock cubes – make your own vegetable stock, or use vegetable stock flavourings

animal rennet used in making most cheese, whey, fromage frais and some margarines – use products labelled suitable for vegetarians

animal fats and oils, e.g. suet and lard – use vegetable oils, butter (usually acceptable)

gelatin or aspic – use agar agar

OFTEN UNSUITABLE

eggs and by-products (for vegans) – if eggs are acceptable, use free-range

egg by-products – check ingredients list

Quorn is a registered trade name. Its generic name, *mycoprotein*, was agreed by the Ministry of Agriculture, Fisheries and Food, when it was approved for sale in 1985.

Quorn is vegetable in origin, a distant relative of the mushroom. Although it occurs naturally in the soil, very precise conditions have to be created for its production in commercial quantities.

Nutty vegetable stir fry
by Sarsons

Key learning points
» shred vegetables
» stir fry leaf vegetables
» make a dish suitable for vegetarians

SERVES 4 to 6

30 ml	untoasted sesame oil	2 tbsp
350 g	red cabbage, shredded	12 oz
175 g	fresh spinach, shredded	6 oz
225 g	fresh beansprouts	8 oz
50 g	pine nuts	2 oz
45 ml	soy sauce	3 tbsp

Heat oil in a wok, then stir fry cabbage for 2 minutes. Add spinach and beansprouts, cook for a further 2 minutes. Add pine nuts and soy sauce, cook for a final 2 minutes.

Potato skins with guacamole
by Dufrais

Key learning points
» bake potatoes
» scoop out potato skins
» make guacamole

SERVES 4

3	large potatoes	3
2	medium avocados	2
½	small onion, finely chopped	½
1	tomato, peeled, deseeded, roughly chopped	1
20 ml	garlic wine vinegar	4 tsp
15 ml	natural yogurt	1 tbsp
30 ml	mayonnaise	2 tbsp
	seasoning to taste	
45 ml	sesame oil	3 tbsp

1 Place potatoes on a baking sheet and bake for 1½ hours at 200°C.

2 Meanwhile prepare the guacamole. Place flesh of avocado and all ingredients except sesame oil in a bowl and mash together. Cover and chill.

3 Cut potatoes lengthways into quarters, scoop out most of the flesh, leaving about 5 mm (¼ inch).

4 Place potato skins on a baking sheet, brush with sesame oil and lightly sprinkle with salt. Return to the oven and bake at 230°C for 10 minutes, or until crisp.

5 Serve with guacamole.

Vegetarian kebabs with apple and mint rice
by Crosse & Blackwell

Key learning points
» decoratively slice vegetables
» prepare cold dish with long grain brown rice, carrot and cucumber
» make a dish suitable for vegetarians

SERVES 4

225 ml	fresh apple juice	8 fl oz
175 g	small closed cup mushrooms	6 oz
1	green apple, cored and chopped	1
15 ml	lemon juice	1 tbsp
350 g	long grain brown rice, cooked	12 oz
10 ml	mint, freshly chopped	2 tsp
1	carrot, cut into 75 mm (3 inch) lengths	1
75 mm	piece of cucumber, thinly sliced lengthways	3 inch
100 g	Edam cheese, cubed	4 oz

1 Marinade mushrooms in the apple juice for 3 hours. Stir occasionally.

2 Coat apple in lemon juice, then stir into rice with the mint. Chill.

3 Using a peeler, pare long, wide strips of carrot. Roll up and thread on to wooden skewers, alternating with curls of cucumber, the mushrooms and cheese. Serve with the rice.

Mushrooms in the Greek style
by Dufrais

Key learning points
» chop and skin vegetables
» prepare cold mushroom dish
» make a dish suitable for vegetarians

SERVES 4

30 ml	vegetable oil	2 tbsp
1	medium onion, chopped	1
1	clove garlic, crushed and peeled	1
30 ml	tomato purée	2 tbsp
275 ml	red Bistro Chef or red wine	½ pt
	bouquet garni	
5 ml	ground coriander	1 tsp
5 ml	sugar	1 tsp
450 g	button mushrooms	1 lb
225 g	tomatoes, skinned and quartered	8 oz
	fresh coriander (to garnish)	
	seasoning to taste	

1 Heat the oil in a frying pan. Fry the onion and garlic for 5 minutes. Stir in tomato purée, Bistro Chef, bouquet garni, coriander and sugar. Season.

2 Add mushrooms and tomatoes, cook gently, uncovered for about 10 minutes. Remove bouquet garni. Place in clean bowl and chill well. Garnish with coriander.

Creamy Quorn casserole
by Marlow Foods

Key learning points
» chop and slice vegetables
» shallow fry vegetable protein
» make a dish suitable for vegetarians

SERVES 4

30 ml	vegetable oil	2 tbsp
250 g	Quorn	9 oz
1	small onion, chopped	1
100 g	mushrooms, sliced	4 oz
1 × 198 g	can sweetcorn	1 × 7 oz
275 ml	vegetable stock	½ pt
30 ml	dry white wine	2 tbsp
30 ml	wholegrain mustard	2 tbsp
2.5 ml	ground cumin	½ tsp
50 g	full fat soft cheese	2 oz
15 ml	cornflour	1 tbsp
	seasoning to taste	
30 ml	half fat cream	2 tbsp

1 Heat the oil in a large saucepan. Fry the Quorn and onion, cooking until the onion softens.

2 Add the mushrooms, fry for another 3 minutes. Add the sweetcorn, stock, wine, mustard, cumin and cheese. Bring to the boil, stirring continuously.

3 Blend the cornflour with a little water. Add to the Quorn mixture, stirring until the sauce thickens. Season.

4 Remove from the heat and stir in the cream. Serve with wholegrain rice.

Vegetable medley
by The Dutch Dairy Bureau

Key learning points
» peel and finely slice vegetables
» shallow fry mixed vegetables
» make a dish suitable for vegetarians

SERVES 4

50 g	unsalted butter	2 oz
1 kg	potatoes, finely sliced	2 lb
225 g	onions, finely sliced	8 oz
275 g	Gouda cheese, coarsely grated	10 oz
1 each	red and green pepper, deseeded and chopped	1 each
	black pepper	

1   Melt butter in a frying pan. Place the potatoes, onions, cheese and peppers in alternate layers, seasoning well between each layer. Finish with a layer of cheese.

2   Cover with a piece of foil, cook over a gentle heat for 35 to 40 minutes.

Simple beefless hash
by Linda McCartney, in Home Cooking (Bloomsbury Publishing, 1989)

Key learning points
» dice/chop vegetables
» prepare a dish with textured vegetable protein

SERVES 4

350 g	potatoes, diced	12 oz
25 g	butter or margarine	1 oz
1	large onion, chopped	1
1	clove garlic, crushed and peeled	1
10 ml	mixed herbs	2 tsp
15 ml	vegetable extract	1 tbsp
1 × 126 g	packet TVP chunks	1 × 4½ oz
350 ml	vegetable stock or water	12 fl oz
30 ml	tomato purée	2 tbsp
	seasoning to taste	

1   Boil the diced potato for 1 minute. Drain.

2   Fry the onion and garlic in the butter until soft. Add the herbs, then the diced potato and cook for 2 to 3 minutes. Add the vegetable extract and TVP. Stir for a few minutes.

3   Stir in the vegetable stock, tomato purée and seasoning. Cover and simmer for 15 minutes, adding a little extra stock if necessary to make a thick sauce.

Quorn and rice ratatouille
by Crosse & Blackwell

Key learning points
» skin, slice and chop vegetables
» prepare risotto with long grain brown rice and Quorn
» make a dish suitable for vegetarians

SERVES 4

225 g	long grain brown rice, cooked	8 oz
30 ml	oil	2 tbsp
1	large onion, chopped	1
2	cloves garlic, crushed and peeled	2
225 g	aubergine, sliced	8 oz
1	red pepper, deseeded and sliced	1
350 g	courgette, sliced	12 oz
10 ml each	fresh sage and thyme, chopped	2 tsp each
15 ml	lemon juice	1 tbsp
30 ml	stock	2 tbsp
3	tomatoes, skinned, deseeded and chopped	3
30 ml	tomato purée	2 tbsp
1 × 250 g	packet Quorn	1 × 9 oz
	seasoning to taste	

1   Heat oil and cook onion and garlic until soft. Stir in aubergine, red pepper, courgettes, herbs, lemon juice and stock. Cover and cook gently for about 15 minutes. Stir occasionally.

2   Stir in tomatoes, tomato purée and Quorn, cover and cook for 10 minutes. Stir in rice, seasoning and heat through.

French fried onions

Key learning points
» slice onions
» coat onions and deep fry

SERVES 10

1 kg	onions, finely sliced as rings (page 160)	2 lb
275 ml	milk	10 fl oz
225 g	flour, seasoned	8 oz

1   Soak the rings briefly in milk then drain them and coat them with flour. Shake off any loose flour.

2   Place the onion rings in a frying basket and deep fry at 185°C until crisp and golden brown. During frying, lightly shake the frying basket to ensure that the rings are not sticking together.

3   Drain well. Lightly season with salt and serve immediately.

Braised celery

Key learning points
» chop vegetables
» braise celery and prepare accompanying sauce using jus lié

As an alternative to adding jus lié in step 6, thicken the stock with a little cornflour or arrowroot, colour slightly with gravy browning.

SERVES 10

5	small heads of celery	5
850 ml	brown stock	1½ pt
225 ml	jus lié	½ pt
5	thin slices of fat bacon (optional)	5
	sprig of thyme, 1 bay leaf and parsley stalks	
	chopped parsley (optional)	
100 g each	onions and carrots, roughly chopped	4 oz each
50 g	leeks, roughly chopped	2 oz

1   After preparing, cut each head of celery to a length of about 150 mm (6 inches). Secure neatly with string.

2   Place celery in boiling water, simmer for about 10 minutes. Drain.

3   In a small braising pan (or saucepan with lid), rest the blanched celery on top of the onion, carrot and leek. Cover each celery head with a slice of bacon (if required).

4   Pour in the stock up to two-thirds the height of the celery. Add the thyme, bay leaf and parsley stalks. Cover with greased greaseproof paper and lid, then bring almost to the boil.

5   Braise in the oven at 200°C until tender, 1½ to 2 hours.

6   Put the celery (and bacon) aside in a warm oven or hot cupboard, covered. Boil the cooking liquor until it has reduced to half. Add the jus lié. Reboil, simmer for 2 to 3 minutes. Strain into a clean pan. Skim off any fat and check seasoning.

7   Remove the string from the celery and cut each head in half lengthways. Neatly fold each head across its length. (Photograph on page 160.)

8   Place the celery in a warm serving dish, check that it is still hot, then coat with the sauce. If required, sprinkle with parsley.

173

Cauliflower cheese Dutch style
by The Dutch Dairy Bureau

Key learning points
» make roux-based white sauce
» boil cauliflower

SERVES 4

1	large cauliflower, cut into florets	1
25 g	unsalted butter	1 oz
25 g	plain flour	1 oz
275 ml	skimmed milk (hot)	½ pt
175 g	Edam cheese, finely grated	6 oz
175 g	back bacon, grilled, then cut into pieces	6 oz
1	small onion, cut into rings	1
	chives, freshly chopped (to garnish)	
	paprika, pinch (to garnish)	

1 Cook the cauliflower florets in boiling water until just tender, about 15 minutes.

2 Meanwhile, melt the butter in a saucepan, add the flour and cook for 3 to 4 minutes. Gradually add the milk, stirring smooth after each addition. Add cheese and onion rings.

3 Place cauliflower and bacon in serving dish. Pour over cheese sauce. Garnish with chives and paprika, and serve.

Vegeburgers
by Crosse & Blackwell

Key learning points
» purée beans and nuts, slice vegetables
» bake a dish with long grain rice, carrots and onion
» make a dish suitable for vegetarians

SERVES 4

100 g	baked beans	4 oz
100 g	unsalted nuts	4 oz
100 g	carrots, sliced	4 oz
1	small onion, chopped	1
15 ml	corn oil	1 tbsp
30 ml	tomato chutney	2 tbsp
175 g	long grain rice, cooked	6 oz
45 ml	wholemeal flour	3 tbsp
	lettuce, stuffed olives, gherkins, tomato, cucumber, carrot (to garnish)	

1 Place the beans and nuts into a processor and blend well.

2 Fry the carrots and onion in hot oil until golden and soft.

3 Remove from the heat and thoroughly mix in the puréed beans, then the tomato chutney and rice.

4 Using a little flour, shape the mixture into 4 burgers.

5 Bake in oven at 190°C until golden brown.

6 Garnish each burger with lettuce leaf, olives, gherkin, slice or quarter of tomato, slice of cucumber and slice of carrot.

Egg and potato croquettes
by The British Egg Information Service

Key learning points
» mould croquettes, coat and shallow fry
» make a dish suitable for vegetarians

SERVES 4

450–575 g	cooked mashed potatoes	1–1½ lb
	seasoning to taste	
2	eggs, hard-boiled, shelled and roughly chopped	2
2	eggs, 1 to bind mixture, 1 beaten for coating	2
25 g	butter	1 oz
75 g	Cheddar cheese, grated	3 oz
100–175 g	fresh white or brown breadcrumbs	4–6 oz
	little soya oil for shallow frying	

1 Mix well the potato, hard-boiled eggs, butter, cheese, seasoning and 1 egg to bind.

2 Divide the mixture into 8 even-sized pieces. With lightly floured hands, form mixture into round croquettes. Coat with the second egg (beaten lightly) and roll in the breadcrumbs.

3 Fry in oil until light golden brown, turning once.

4 Drain well and serve hot.

Paella (seafood rice)
by Carnation

Key learning points
» cook risotto rice
» cook mussels, prawns and white fish
Saffron will give this dish an attractive yellow colour, but it is very expensive.
Change the fish as desired, e.g. replace mussels with increased quantity of cod.

SERVES 10

30 ml	oil	2 tbsp
2	garlic, crushed and peeled	2
2	medium onions, sliced	2
60 ml	tomato purée	4 tbsp
450 g	risotto rice	1 lb
850 ml	vegetable stock	1½ pt
15 ml	turmeric	1 tbsp
	seasoning to taste	
15 ml	paprika	1 tbsp
1 × 397 g	can chopped tomatoes	1 × 14 oz
75 g	coconut milk powder	3 oz
1 × 397 g	can evaporated milk	1 × 14 oz
225 g	cooked chicken, sliced	8 oz
100 g	smoked mackerel, flaked	4 oz
450 g	cooked, peeled prawns	1 lb
450 g	fresh, live mussels, cleaned (see page 131)	1 lb
225 g	fresh cod, diced	8 oz
60 ml	fresh parsley, chopped	4 tbsp

1 Heat oil in a very large non-stick pan. Fry garlic and onions for 5 minutes. Stir in tomato purée and rice.

2 Add stock, spices, seasonings and tomatoes, simmer for 10 minutes, stirring occasionally.

3 Blend coconut milk powder with evaporated milk, add to the pan and heat for a further 5 minutes.

4 Add chicken, mackerel, prawns, mussels, cod and parsley. Heat until mussels have opened and cod and rice are thoroughly cooked, about 10 minutes. Serve at once.

Aubergine and courgette risotto
by Dufrais

Key learning points
» dice and shallow fry vegetables
» prepare risotto
» make a dish suitable for vegetarians

SERVES 4

350 g	aubergine, trimmed and diced	12 oz
10 ml	salt	2 tsp
45 ml	vegetable oil	3 tbsp
2	small onions, roughly chopped	2
1	clove garlic, crushed and peeled	1
5 ml	dried sage	1 tsp
275 g	arborio (risotto) rice	10 oz
475 ml	vegetable stock	18 fl oz
1 × 230 g	can chopped tomatoes	1 × 8 oz
15 ml	caster sugar	1 tbsp
225 g	courgettes, diced	8 oz
200 ml	red Bistro Chef or red wine	7 fl oz
	sprig of fresh sage (to garnish)	

1 Sprinkle the prepared aubergine with salt. Leave to stand for about 30 minutes. Rinse well and dry with kitchen paper.

2 Heat the oil in a large frying pan. Fry the onions, garlic and sage until soft. Add the aubergine and continue cooking for a few minutes. Stir in the rice, stock, tomatoes and sugar.

3 Cover and simmer for 12 minutes, stirring occasionally.

4 Add the courgettes and red Bistro Chef or wine. Cook for 4 to 6 minutes, covered, or until tender.

5 Serve garnished with fresh sage.

Braised rice

Key learning point
» braise long grain rice
For extra flavour, a bay leaf may be added to the rice before it is put in the oven. Remove before service.

SERVES 20

550 g	long grain rice	1¼ lb
100 g	margarine or butter	4 oz
275 g	shallots or onions, finely chopped	10 oz
1 litre	chicken or vegetable stock	2 pt
	seasoning to taste	

1 Melt half the fat in a sauteuse or plat à sauter. Add the shallots and cook gently until soft, but not coloured. Add the rice and cook for about 3 minutes, stirring frequently. Stir in the stock and bring to the boil.

2 Cover with a circle of greased greaseproof paper, then put the lid on and transfer to a hot oven at 230°C for about 15 minutes. The rice should have absorbed all the stock.

3 Stir the remaining margarine or butter through the rice with a fork. Check seasoning and serve as soon as possible.

Stuffed cabbage leaves
by The Rice Bureau

Key learning point
» cook and stuff cabbage with long grain rice
As a variation, in place of the cabbage, use vine leaves. Blanch the vine leaves for 1 minute (step 4), drain, then place on absorbent kitchen paper dull side upwards.

SERVES 10 to 20

30 ml	olive oil	2 tbsp
1	onion, finely chopped	1
1	clove garlic, crushed and peeled	1
75 g	long grain rice	3 oz
175 g	minced pork	6 oz
175 ml	stock or water	6 fl oz
	pinch salt	
20	small cabbage leaves	20
15 ml	lemon juice	1 tbsp
	seasoning to taste	
150 ml	tomato juice	5 fl oz

1 Heat the oil and fry the onion and garlic until tender. Add the rice and pork and cook for 5 minutes.

2 Pour on the stock, add salt. Bring to the boil and stir. Cover and simmer for 15 minutes, or until rice is tender and liquid absorbed.

3 Remove from pan and allow to cool.

4 Meanwhile, blanch the cabbage leaves in boiling salted water for 5 to 10 minutes. Drain thoroughly.

5 Add lemon juice and seasoning to rice mixture. Place a spoonful of rice mixture in the centre of each cabbage leaf, fold and roll up tightly.

6 Place in a casserole, packed tightly, then pour on the tomato juice. Cover and bake in oven at 180°C for 45 minutes.

Peach meringue pudding
by The Rice Bureau

Key learning points
» cook short grain rice
» make meringue

SERVES 8

75 g	short grain rice	3 oz
575 ml	milk	1 pt
125 g	caster sugar	5 oz
2.5 ml	ground nutmeg	½ tsp
2	eggs, size 4, separated	2
40 ml	raspberry conserve	8 tsp
4	ripe peaches, halved and stones removed	4

1 Place rice, milk, nutmeg and 25 g (1 oz) of the caster sugar in a saucepan. Bring to the boil, then simmer very gently, stirring frequently, until the rice is cooked and most of the milk absorbed, about 25 minutes.

2 Beat the egg yolks into the rice, then pour the mixture into a glass soufflé dish.

3 Place a little raspberry conserve in each peach half. Arrange the peaches against the outside of the dish, so the conserve can be seen through the side of the dish.

4 Whisk the egg white until stiff. Whisk in half the remaining sugar, then fold in the rest. Spoon meringue over the rice and peaches.

5 Bake at 190°C for about 5 minutes. Serve hot, or leave to cool then chill before serving.

Turkey stir fry
by The Rice Bureau

Key learning point
» stir fry long grain brown rice

SERVES 4

350 g	turkey breast, thinly sliced	12 oz
60 ml	sunflower oil	4 tbsp
15 ml	sesame seeds	1 tbsp
1	red pepper, deseeded and sliced	1
4	spring onions, trimmed and chopped	4
200 g	baby corn	7 oz
100 g	mangetout	4 oz
675 g	long grain brown rice, cooked	1½ lb

1 Place a wok or heavy-based frying pan over a high heat, add half the oil and fry the turkey for 3 to 4 minutes, stirring continuously. Remove from the pan and keep warm.

2 Place the remaining oil in the pan and stir fry the sesame seeds, pepper and spring onions for 4 minutes.

3 Add the baby corn and mangetout, stir fry for a further 3 minutes. Add the rice and cook for a further 1 to 2 minutes.

4 Combine with the turkey, and serve.

Potato, cheese and onion pie
by The Fresh Fruit and Vegetable Information Bureau

Key learning points
» slice vegetables
» bake potato and onions in stock

SERVES 4

1	medium onion, thinly sliced	1
15 ml	vegetable oil	1 tbsp
3	large potatoes	3
2	leeks	2
100 g	curd cheese	4 oz
30 ml	chives, freshly chopped	2 tbsp
6	tomatoes, skinned, deseeded and chopped	6
1	clove garlic, crushed and peeled	1
	seasoning to taste	
60 ml	chicken stock	4 tbsp
30 ml	Parmesan cheese, grated	2 tbsp

1 Boil the potatoes in their skins for 10 minutes. Peel and thinly slice.

2 Slice the leeks into rings, then boil for 3 minutes.

3 Fry the onion gently in the oil.

4 Layer the onion, potato and leeks in an ovenproof dish with small knobs of cheese between each layer.

5 Mix the chives, tomatoes, garlic, seasoning and chicken stock together. Spoon over the potato mixture. Sprinkle with Parmesan cheese.

6 Bake at 190°C for 25 minutes. Serve hot with a salad.

Salsify au gratin
by The Fresh Fruit and Vegetable Information Bureau

Key learning point
» prepare and cook an unusual vegetable

SERVES 3 to 4

450 g	young salsify roots, scrubbed thoroughly	1 lb
275 ml	béchamel (page 143)	½ pt
3	large tomatoes, skinned, deseeded and chopped	3
100 g	grated cheese	4 oz
	pinch ground nutmeg	
	seasoning to taste	

1 Cook the salsify in boiling water for 15 minutes until tender.

2 Drain thoroughly. Peel when cool enough to handle. Place in a greased ovenproof dish.

3 Season the béchamel, mix with the nutmeg, chopped tomatoes and half the cheese. Pour over the salsify. Sprinkle the remaining cheese over the top.

4 Bake at 190°C for about 15 minutes, or until brown. Serve.

Fillings for baked jacket potatoes – Cooking instructions on page 167.

Simple fillings

sour cream and chives

grated Cheddar or Cheshire

chicken in curry sauce

chopped egg and sweetcorn relish

baked beans and ham

cheese, tomato and onion

prawns in cocktail sauce

chilli con carne

coleslaw and cheese

tuna and egg mayonnaise

scrambled egg and bacon

ratatouille and cheese

Specialities

Tuna salad – flaked tuna, diced cucumber, chopped tomato, finely chopped spring onion

Curried mushroom – chopped onion fried quickly in oil or butter, curry powder added, then sliced mushrooms and cooked until soft

Fisherman's delight – smoked mackerel fillets, flaked and mixed with sweetcorn, peas and mayonnaise

Beachcomber – prawns and diced crab sticks combined together with marie-rose sauce (mayonnaise, tomato ketchup, Worcestershire sauce)

Derbyshire – sage Derby cheese, grated and mixed with sliced mushrooms and diced bacon and fried

Waistliner – cottage cheese, diced red pepper and sweetcorn

The Cheshire cat – grated Cheshire cheese, diced apple, mustard and a little butter

Festive filling – cooked chopped turkey and apple, with cranberry sauce

Trawler pots – smoked mackerel fillets, flaked and mandarin orange segments blended with mayonnaise

Arabian night – chilli con carne, mango chutney, sultanas, chopped walnuts

Tropicana – cooked diced chicken, sour cream and cubes of fresh mango

Ideas by the Potato Marketing Board.

Spinach and egg ramekin
by The Fresh Fruit and Vegetable Information Bureau

Key learning points
» use moulds to shape food
» bake eggs
» make a dish suitable for vegetarians

SERVES 6

25 g	butter or margarine	1 oz
225 g	spinach, cooked and chopped	8 oz
1	small onion, chopped	1
100 g	Cheddar cheese, grated	4 oz
6	eggs	6
150 ml	double cream	5 fl oz
1	clove garlic, crushed and peeled	1
	seasoning to taste	

1 Melt the butter in a pan and fry the onion until soft. Place in a bowl with the spinach and mix. Add seasoning.

2 Put equal amounts of this mixture into 6 greased ramekins. Break an egg on to each spinach base.

3 Add the garlic to the cream, stir well and pour over the top of the eggs. Sprinkle grated cheese over.

4 Stand ramekins in a roasting tin half filled with boiling water, and bake in the oven at 180°C for 15 to 20 minutes until the eggs are cooked. Serve immediately.

Asparagus and sun-dried tomato risotto
by Angela Dwyer, Wilds Restaurant, Fulham, London, published by Caterer & Hotelkeeper *in* Chef, May 1991

Key learning points
» boil asparagus
» cook a risotto dish
» make a dish suitable for vegetarians

SERVES 4

¾ kg	asparagus	1½ lb
575 ml	water	1 pt
1	small red onion, diced	1
50 g	unsalted butter	2 oz
225 g	risotto rice	8 oz
50 g	sun-dried tomatoes	2 oz
45 to 60 ml	fresh basil, chopped	3 to 4 tbsp
	grated Parmesan cheese and seasoning to taste	

1 Peel asparagus and cook in boiling salted water for a few minutes until just tender. Cool in iced water.

2 Chop asparagus into 20 mm (1 inch) pieces. Roughly chop sun-dried tomatoes. Put aside.

3 Heat half the butter in a stainless steel pan (preferably), and fry the onion. Add rice and cook until it turns opaque.

4 Add seasoning and start adding the water, a little at a time. Simmer gently. Cook until the rice is al dente. Stir often.

5 Correct seasoning, and mix in the rest of the butter, the tomatoes and asparagus, and some Parmesan.

6 Serve at once, garnish with the basil and some more Parmesan.

Stuffed onions
by The Fresh Fruit and Vegetable Information Bureau

Key learning point
» stuff and bake onions

SERVES 4

4	large onions	4
50 g	fresh breadcrumbs	2 oz
15 ml	chopped herbs	1 tbsp
	seasoning to taste	
150 g	chopped bacon or ham	5 oz
1	egg, beaten (to bind)	1
	butter to glaze	
150 ml	stock	5 fl oz

1 Peel the onions and boil for 6 to 8 minutes. Drain.

2 When cool enough to handle, carefully hollow out some of the centre of the onions. Chop this and mix with fresh breadcrumbs, chopped herbs, seasoning, bacon or ham, and the egg to bind.

3 Press the stuffing into the hollowed out onions.

4 Place the onions in a lightly greased ovenproof dish. Brush with a little melted butter. Spoon some stock over to a depth of 10 mm (¼ inch). Cover with kitchen foil.

5 Bake at 190°C for 45 minutes. Baste once or twice during cooking.

6 Serve hot.

Stuffed aubergine boats
by The Fresh Fruit and Vegetable Information Bureau

Key learning points
» bake aubergine with brown rice
» pipe stuffing mixture

SERVES 4

2	medium aubergines, cut in half	2
30 ml	sunflower or soya oil	2 tbsp
1	onion, chopped	1
225 g	chicken or turkey livers, chopped	8 oz
45 to 60 ml	fresh parsley, chopped	3 to 4 tbsp
2.5 ml	lemon rind, finely grated	½ tsp
1	clove garlic, crushed and peeled	1
1 large tomato, skinned, deseeded and chopped		1
175 g	brown rice, cooked	6 oz
	seasoning to taste	
30 ml	grated cheese	2 tbsp
4	twists of lemon	4

1 Scoop out and chop the flesh from the aubergines to within 15 mm (¾ inch) from the edge.

2 Blanch the aubergine shells in very hot water for 2 minutes. Drain well.

3 Heat the oil and fry the aubergine flesh and onion until soft. Add the livers and cook for 3 to 4 minutes. Stir in the parsley, lemon rind, garlic, chopped tomato and rice. Season.

4 Pipe or spoon this mixture into the aubergine shells.

5 Place on a greased baking tray, cover with tin foil and bake at 200°C for 15 to 20 minutes.

6 Serve hot with a sprinkling of cheese and lemon twist on each half.

177

NVQ SVQ RANGE CHECKLIST

1D13.1 Prepare vegetables for hot and cold dishes
using 4 of these preparation methods

- [ ] peel or skin or shell
- [ ] chop or shred or cut
- [ ] slice
- [ ] trim
- [ ] grate

to prepare 5 of these types of vegetable

- [ ] roots
- [ ] tubers
- [ ] bulbs
- [ ] leaves
- [ ] flower heads
- [ ] stems
- [ ] fungi
- [ ] vegetable fruit (tomatoes)

for these dishes

- [ ] salads and hot or cold starters
- [ ] hot vegetable dishes

1D13.2 Cook vegetable dishes
cooking prepared or convenience vegetables of 5 of the types listed above, by 5 of these cooking methods

- [ ] roasting
- [ ] grilling
- [ ] boiling
- [ ] steaming
- [ ] baking
- [ ] shallow frying or griddling or stir frying
- [ ] braising or stewing or poaching
- [ ] deep frying

1D16.1 Prepare and cook rice
preparing and cooking 2 of these rices

- [ ] brown rice
- [ ] long grain or Basmati rice
- [ ] short grain or Italian rice

by 2 of these methods

- [ ] boiling
- [ ] baking or braising
- [ ] steaming

1D15.1 Prepare and cook vegetable protein dishes
prepare and cook 2 of these types

- [ ] reconstituted textured vegetable protein (TVP)
- [ ] tempeh
- [ ] tofu
- [ ] Quorn

by 3 of these cooking processes

- [ ] grilling or barbecuing
- [ ] boiling
- [ ] shallow frying or stir frying
- [ ] braising or stewing

2D18.1 Prepare vegetable dishes
using 2 of these preparation methods

- [ ] puréeing
- [ ] stuffing
- [ ] use of moulds

to prepare 6 of these types of vegetable

- [ ] roots
- [ ] tubers
- [ ] bulbs
- [ ] leaves
- [ ] flower heads
- [ ] stems
- [ ] fungi
- [ ] vegetable fruit (tomatoes)
- [ ] legumes
- [ ] frozen/convenience
- [ ] vegetable protein

2D18.2 Cook and finish vegetable dishes
cooking prepared or convenience vegetables of 6 of the types listed above, by 6 of these cooking methods

- [ ] roasting
- [ ] grilling
- [ ] boiling
- [ ] steaming
- [ ] browning
- [ ] baking
- [ ] shallow frying or griddling or stir frying
- [ ] braising or stewing or poaching
- [ ] deep frying

and finishing by 4 of these methods

- [ ] glazing
- [ ] coating
- [ ] colouring
- [ ] using hot sauces
- [ ] using cold sauces
- [ ] garnishing
- [ ] piping

2D18.3 Prepare and cook rice dishes
using 2 of these types of rice

- [ ] brown rice
- [ ] long grain or Basmati rice
- [ ] short grain or Italian rice

to make 3 of these dishes

- [ ] boiled rice
- [ ] rice pilau/pilaff
- [ ] risotto
- [ ] mixed fried rice/stir fried
- [ ] steamed rice

LEVEL 1

LEVEL 2

Introduction

Pulse is a collective name for about 20 different varieties of beans, peas and lentils:

Aduki – strong, sweet, slightly nutty flavour, from China.

Black-eye beans – more easily digested than most other pulses, from USA.

Black kidney beans – large, shiny bean, may be used as a substitute for red kidney beans, from China.

Brown lentils – retain shape well during cooking, from Canada.

Butter beans – large white, flat kidney-shaped beans, from USA.

Cannelini beans – small white kidney beans, make a good substitute for haricot beans, from Italy.

Chick peas – small, round and golden brown, from Turkey.

Flageolet – considered to be the finest of all pulses since they are harvested when young and very small. Mainly from Argentina.

Haricot beans – also known as *navy beans*, the dried seeds of French beans, creamy white, used as baked beans, from North America.

Contents guide

Lentils – come in a range of colours. Split lentils are inclined to break up if overcooked.

Marrowfat peas – any of several varieties of pea plant that have large seeds.

Mung beans – often used as sprouting beans, moss green, from Thailand. Have a sweetish flavour and hold their shape well.

Pinto beans – speckled pink colour, a variety of kidney beans, from USA.

Red kidney beans – mealy textured beans, from USA.

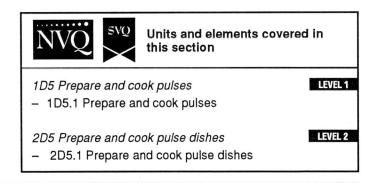

NVQ SVQ Units and elements covered in this section

1D5 Prepare and cook pulses — **LEVEL 1**
- 1D5.1 Prepare and cook pulses

2D5 Prepare and cook pulse dishes — **LEVEL 2**
- 2D5.1 Prepare and cook pulse dishes

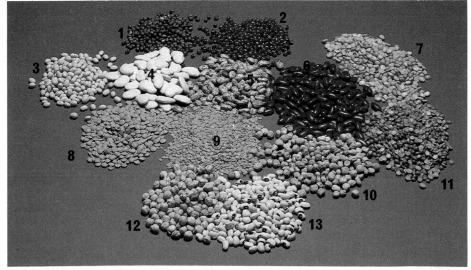

1) *Mung beans,* 2) *Aduki beans,*
3) *Haricot beans,* 4) *Butter beans,*
5) *Pinto beans,* 6) *Red kidney beans,*
7) *Yellow split peas,* 8) *Green lentils,*
9) *Red split lentils,* 10) *Marrowfat peas,* 11) *Green split peas,* 12) *Chick peas,* 13) *Black-eye beans.*

Quality and storage points

Store in airtight containers away from direct sunlight.

Although dried pulses keep well for long periods, it is best to eat them as fresh as possible. Old pulses take longer to cook and are more difficult to digest.

Do not use if they are beyond the best-before date.

Cooking pulses

Pulses can be eaten on their own as a vegetable course, or in stews, soups, casseroles, burgers, kebabs, salads and pancakes. Boiling is the principal method of cooking pulses, followed by the appropriate method for the particular dish, e.g. baking.

Soaking pulses

Pulses cook faster and more easily when they have been soaked.

Check a day in advance what the instructions are for soaking, since soaking for up to 12 hours is often recommended, and 3 to 4 hours is quite normal.

Red lentils and split peas do not need soaking.

Always throw away the soaking water, and rinse the pulses before cooking in fresh water.

If the pulses have started to smell rotten and ferment – which might happen if they have been soaked for too long, or in a warm place – then they should not be used.

Boiling pulses

Generally, pulses should be boiled rapidly for the first 10 minutes of cooking (see Safety box).

If using salt, do not add to the cooking water until the end of the cooking time. Otherwise the salt will make the pulses tough.

Do not add bicarbonate of soda to the boiling water. Although it is said to soften the pulses during cooking, it destroys the B vitamins.

Cooking times for pulses, even for the same variety, vary considerably. At regular intervals during the second half of the recommended recipe cooking time, remove a few pulses and test.

If you find you haven't got time to soak and cook pulses, it would be better to use a canned variety. Check with your supervisor.

Using canned pulses

Canning does not affect the protein content of pulses, but sometimes salt or sugar is added. It is best to drain the beans well before use, and if necessary to rinse them.

NUTRITION

Pulses are low in fat and highly nutritious. They are a very good source of fibre, protein, vitamin B and minerals.

The high protein content of pulses makes them an increasingly popular alternative to meat. As pulses are low in some essential amino acids, they need to be eaten with a cereal such as rice or wholemeal bread, or nuts or seeds to make a balanced, healthy diet. Meals for vegetarians should take this into account.

SAFETY

Red kidney beans contain toxic substances which cause acute *gastroenteritis* (inflammation of the stomach and intestines) and even death. To get rid of the toxins, you have to discard the soaking water and then boil the beans rapidly in an uncovered saucepan for the first 10 minutes of cooking. They can then be simmered until soft.

It is a good general rule to boil all dried pulses fast for 10 minutes or so before simmering.

ACTION

Complete the table below to show the recommended soaking time and cooking time for different pulses. For those pulses used in your workplace, you should find details on the packet. Otherwise visit a local health food shop, or good supermarket, and study the information on the packets.

	Soaking time (minutes)	Cooking time (minutes)
Aduki		
Black-eye beans		
Black kidney beans		
Brown lentils		
Butter beans		
Cannelini beans		
Chick peas		
Flageolet		
Haricot beans		
Lentils		
Marrowfat peas		
Mung beans		
Pinto beans		
Red kidney beans		

Calabrian lamb and vegetable stew
by New Zealand Lamb Catering Advisory Service

Key learning point
» make a stew with lamb, pulses and pasta
This dish originates in Calabria, the region which forms the 'toe' of Italy.

SERVES 10

1.35 kg	lean, diced shoulder of lamb	3 lb
75 g	red kidney beans	3 oz
75 g	navy beans	3 oz
75 g	chick peas	3 oz
75 g	lentils	3 oz
100 ml	olive oil	4 fl oz
225 g	bacon, chopped	8 oz
225 g	carrots, chopped	8 oz
450 g	onion, chopped	1 lb
1	clove garlic, crushed and peeled	1
2.1 litre	light stock	3½ pt
½	small green cabbage, shredded, boiled for 1 minute, cooled and drained	½
100 g	mushrooms, sliced	4 oz
225 g	farfalle, or other small pasta	8 oz
100 g	grated Parmesan or Pecorino cheese	4 oz
	seasoning to taste	

1 If using dried beans, soak for 12 hours, then bring to the boil and simmer for 1½ hours. If using the canned variety, simply rinse and set aside.

2 Fry the lamb and bacon in the hot oil, add the carrots, onion and garlic and cook for 5 minutes.

3 Pour in the stock, bring to the boil, then simmer gently for 1 hour.

4 Add the drained beans, mushrooms and cabbage. Stir well and bring back to the boil.

5 Put in the pasta, stir well to disperse evenly, and simmer for 15 minutes, or until pasta is cooked. Season to taste.

6 Serve sprinkled with the grated cheese.

Curried peas
by Chris Hardisty for The Vegetarian Society

Key learning point
» make curry with split peas
Serve on a bed of rice and garnish with banana slices.

SERVES 2

100 g	split peas, soaked for 2 hours	4 oz
1	small onion, finely sliced	1
1	small carrot, diced	1
15 ml	vegetable oil	1 tbsp
10 ml	flour	1 dstsp
10 ml	curry powder	1 dstsp
1	small apple, diced	1
	small handful sultanas	
75 ml	milk or soya milk	3 fl oz
	pinch salt	

1 Drain the peas, cover with fresh water and bring to the boil. Simmer for 30 minutes until soft.

2 Meanwhile, gently fry the onion and carrot in the oil until softened.

3 Drain the peas, reserving the cooking liquid. Add the peas to the onion and carrot, together with the flour, curry powder, apple and sultanas and cook for a minute or two.

4 Slowly add the milk, then 275 ml (10 fl oz) of the reserved cooking liquid and stir until thickened. Season and simmer for 20 minutes. Stir occasionally.

5 Garnish and serve.

Lentil savoury
by The Vegetarian Society

Key learning points
» boil lentils
» make a casserole-type dish with lentils

SERVES 4

175 g	red lentils	6 oz
2.5 ml each	basil and mixed herbs	½ tsp
50 g	margarine	2 oz
2	onions, chopped	2
30 ml	tomato purée	2 tbsp
	seasoning to taste	
1 × 340 g	can tomatoes	1 × 14 oz
5 ml	brown sugar	1 tsp
175 g	vegetarian Cheddar cheese, sliced	6 oz
150 ml	soured cream	5 fl oz
	seasoning to taste	

1 Place lentils in a pan with enough water to cover them. Add herbs and simmer until tender, about 50 minutes. Drain.

2 In a saucepan, fry the onion in the margarine until soft. Add the lentils, tomato purée, tomatoes and sugar. Season. Simmer for 15 minutes.

3 Pour into a greased ovenproof dish. Cover with cheese and cream. Bake for 5 to 10 minutes at 180°C until the cheese has melted. Serve at once.

Masoor dhal
by The Vegetarian Society

Key learning point
» make red lentil casserole

SERVES 4

225 g	red split lentils, soaked in hot water for 1 to 2 hours, then drained	8 oz
5 ml each	cumin seeds and poppy seeds	1 tsp each
10 ml	coriander seeds	2 tsp
6	whole cloves	6
1	piece cinnamon, 5 cm (2 inches) long	1
4	green cardamom pods	4
4	black peppercorns	4
2.5 ml	chilli powder	½ tsp
5 ml	turmeric	1 tsp
30 ml	ghee (clarified butter, see page 113)	2 tbsp
2	onions, chopped	2
4	cloves garlic, crushed and peeled	4
50 g	creamed coconut, grated	2 oz
	seasoning to taste	

1 Cook the spices (cumin, poppy, coriander, cloves, cinnamon, cardamon, peppercorns, chilli and turmeric) in a heavy-based frying pan without oil for a few minutes. Grind until smooth in a coffee grinder or food blender.

2 Heat the ghee, and fry half the quantity of spices for 2 minutes. Add the onion and garlic, and cook for another 2 minutes.

3 Add the lentils and 1 pint of fresh water. Simmer, covered for 50 minutes. Give the contents of the pan a good stir and add the other half of the spices. Cook for another 10 minutes.

4 Add the creamed coconut and seasoning. Serve hot.

Red bean patties
by Sarah Maxwell in BBC Good Food

Key learning point
» make patties/burgers with pulses and shallow or deep fry

SERVES 2

1 × 225 g	can red kidney beans, drained	1 × 8 oz
50 g	flour	2 oz
1	egg, beaten	1
50 g	wholemeal breadcrumbs	2 oz
1	small onion, chopped	1
15 ml	fresh parsley, chopped	1 tbsp
1	clove garlic, crushed and peeled	1
2.5 ml	ground coriander	½ tsp
2.5 ml	ground cumin	½ tsp
	seasoning to taste	

1 Mash or purée all the ingredients (but not the flour) together until almost smooth.

2 Divide into 4 balls, roll lightly in the flour and press into a patty or burger shape.

3 Shallow fry until crisp and lightly browned, or deep fry at 190°C for 3 to 5 minutes.

Vegetarian seekh kebabs
by Sara Lewis in BBC Good Food

Key learning point
» make kebabs with pulses and grill or barbecue

SERVES 4

1	small onion, finely chopped	1
50 g	blanched almonds, chopped	2 oz
2	cloves garlic, crushed and peeled	2
60 ml	sunflower oil	4 tbsp
	generous pinch chilli powder, ground cinnamon and grated nutmeg	
1 × 397 g	can red kidney beans, drained	1 × 14 oz
50 g	fresh breadcrumbs	2 oz
30 ml	fresh coriander leaves	2 tbsp
1	egg yolk	1
15 ml	sesame seeds (garnish)	1 tbsp

Tomato relish

350 g	tomatoes, skinned, deseeded and chopped	12 oz
½	small onion	½
30 ml	fresh coriander leaves	2 tbsp
5 ml	tomato purée	1 tsp
2.5 ml	sugar	½ tsp
	seasoning to taste	

1 Fry the onion, almonds and garlic in a little of the oil until softened. Add spices and cook for 1 minute.

2 Liquidise or purée this mixture with the remaining ingredients until smooth. Divide into 8 portions, and shape each one around a skewer (or 2 per longer skewer), to form thick cigar-shaped kebabs.

3 Brush the kebabs with oil and grill for 4 minutes. Turn, brush with oil, sprinkle with sesame seeds and cook for 4 minutes more until browned.

4 Meanwhile liquidise or purée all the relish ingredients together. Serve with the hot kebabs.

Bean and vegetable goulash
by Craigmillar/Meadowland

Key learning points
» make a stew with various vegetables, red kidney beans and flageolets, thickened with cornflour
» make a dish suitable for vegetarians

Meadowland, for the garnish, is a blend of buttermilk and vegetable fat.
Use freshly cooked beans, if preferred.

SERVES 5

15 ml	olive oil	1 tbsp
100 g	small button onions	4 oz
4	sticks celery, sliced thickly	4
4	small courgettes, sliced thickly	4
1	clove garlic, crushed and peeled	1
2	carrots, thickly sliced	2
50 g	baby sweetcorn	2 oz
1 × 397 g	can chopped tomatoes	1 × 14 oz
275 ml	vegetable stock	½ pt
15 ml	paprika	1 tbsp
2.5 ml	caraway seeds	½ tsp
	seasoning to taste	
15 ml	cornflour	1 tbsp
30 ml	water	2 tbsp
1 × 425 g	can red kidney beans, drained	1 × 15 oz
1 × 410 g	can flageolet beans, drained	1 × 14.4 oz
15 ml	lemon juice	1 tbsp
150 ml	lightly whipped Meadowland (to garnish)	5 fl oz
	paprika (to garnish)	

1 Heat the oil and fry the vegetables until lightly brown. Add the tomatoes, stock, paprika, caraway seeds and seasoning.

2 Bring to the boil. Cover and simmer for about 20 minutes, until vegetables are just tender.

3 Blend together the cornflour and water. Stir into the vegetable mixture. Add beans and lemon juice. Cover and simmer a further 10 to 15 minutes until heated through.

4 To serve, lightly swirl in the Meadowland and sprinkle with paprika.

NVQ **SVQ** **RANGE CHECKLIST**

LEVEL 1

1D5.1 Prepare and cook pulses

boil 1 of these

- [ ] beans
- [ ] peas
- [ ] lentils

LEVEL 2

2D5.1 Prepare and cook pulse dishes

use 2 of these cooking processes

- [ ] stewing or casseroling
- [ ] grilling or barbecuing
- [ ] baking
- [ ] shallow frying or stir frying

to make 2 of these dishes

- [ ] loaf or bake
- [ ] casserole or curry
- [ ] rissoles or burgers

from 1 of these pulses

- [ ] beans
- [ ] peas
- [ ] lentils

Introduction

Pasta comes in over 200 different shapes, with more than 600 names for these shapes. It can be sauced, stuffed, layered and baked. There is virtually no limit to the combinations that are possible with vegetables, seafood, pulses, cheeses and meats.

The basic ingredients of pasta are flour and water. Wheat flours are usually used for home-made pastas and commercially-made flat noodles. *Durum wheat semolina* – made from the larger pieces of endosperm sifted out during the milling process (see page 204) – is used for commercially-made pastas. It gives the pasta its rich amber colour and prevents it from losing shape and becoming mushy in cooking.

Some types of pasta also use oil or egg. Egg pasta is a darker yellow colour.

Green pasta is traditionally made by adding spinach to the mix, red pasta by adding tomato. More recent introductions are black pasta, coloured with squid-ink, and tricoloured pasta – packed to give a mixture of green, red and white (*tricolore*) pieces. Wholewheat pasta is also available.

Generally fresh and frozen pasta has whole egg in it, giving it a softer, smoother texture which goes well with cream and lighter tasting sauces. These products offer a considerable choice, particularly for stuffed pasta shapes and filled pasta dishes.

In its dried form, pasta keeps well – up to 12 months generally. Fresh products can also have a long storage life – up to 60 days for those sold in controlled atmosphere packages. Frozen pasta will keep well under proper storage conditions.

Contents guide

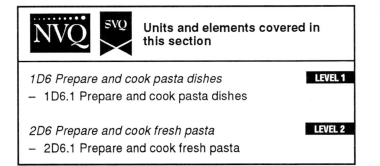

NVQ SVQ	**Units and elements covered in this section**

1D6 Prepare and cook pasta dishes **LEVEL 1**
– 1D6.1 Prepare and cook pasta dishes

2D6 Prepare and cook fresh pasta **LEVEL 2**
– 2D6.1 Prepare and cook fresh pasta

1) *Vermicelli,* 2) *Lasagne,* 3) *Green tagliatelle,*
4) *Tagliatelle,* 5) *Cannelloni,* 6) *Green and white lasagne,*
7) *Wholewheat spaghetti,* 8) *Spaghetti,* 9) *Green spaghetti,*
10) *Pastine,* 11) *Pasta shells,* 12) *Spaghettini,* 13) *Short macaroni,* 14) *Tortellini,* 15) *Alphabet shapes*

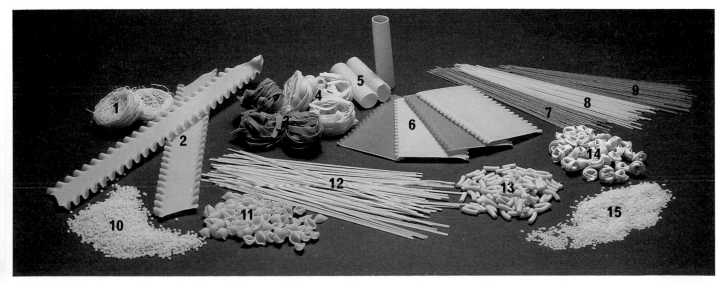

Cooking pasta

LEVELS 1 + 2

As a general guide, the longer, thin and flat varieties, such as spaghetti and fettuccine, are more suitable for the thinner sauces, while pasta shapes such as conchiglie and penne are ideal for the thicker sauces which find their way into the holes and folds.

1 Most frozen pastas do not require defrosting before cooking.

2 Good quality dried pasta will double in size and almost treble in weight when cooked. As a guideline, allow 55 to 85 g (2 to 3 oz) of pasta per person, depending on the thickness and richness of the accompanying sauce.

3 Always use a large saucepan containing plenty of fast boiling water and a little salt. You will need 1 to 1½ litres (2 to 3 pints) of water for every 225 g (8 oz) dry pasta.

4 Once you have emptied the pasta into the boiling water, stir it occasionally with a plastic spoon. Good quality pasta should not then stick.

5 Many things can affect the required cooking time. Read the packet instructions carefully, but use your own judgement and test the pasta at regular intervals during cooking. The aim is to serve it tender, but still firm.

6 Filled pastas such as tortellini and ravioli should stand for a minute or two before draining. Otherwise pasta should be drained and tossed as soon as it's cooked. And don't drain it too well. A little water remaining from the cooking helps the pasta absorb the sauce.

CHEF'S TIPS

In its dried form, pasta keeps well – up to 12 months generally. Fresh products can also have a long storage life – up to 60 days for those sold in controlled atmosphere packages. Frozen pasta will keep well under proper storage conditions.

Dried pasta is regarded as the best for straight and simple shapes. It has a firm texture and goes well with the heavier sauces. For people who like their pasta *al dente*, dried pasta cooks up best. An Italian expression, *al dente* translates as 'to the tooth', meaning the food offers slight resistance when bitten into.

NUTRITION

Pasta is low in fat, high in fibre, and a good source of protein.

Pasta contains complex carbohydrates, which the body digests slowly, providing a gradual release of energy.

Pasta Top 10

Compiled by *Caterer & Hotelkeeper*.

1 *Spaghetti* – and its cousins, *spaghettini* and *spaghettoni*.
2 *Lasagne* and *lasagne verdi* (green).
3 *Fusilli* – spirals or twists, red, white and green varieties.
4 *Maccheroni* – macaroni.
5 *Tortellini* – stuffed pasta shapes, also called tortelloni and tortelli.
6 *Tagliatelle* – white or green.
7 *Conchiglie* – shells.
8 *Penne* – quills/small hollow tubes.
9 *Fettuccine* – the Roman type of tagliatelle. The two differ only slightly, fettuccine being a little narrower and thicker than the traditional tagliatelle.
10 *Cappelletti* – shaped like peaked hats and stuffed.

Also popular are:

Bucatini – slightly thicker than spaghetti.

Fiocchetti or *farfalle* – bows or butterflies.

Rigatoni – fluted, curved, hollow tubes.

Ravioli – small squares, stuffed.

Gnocchi – dumplings made from semolina paste, sometimes potato, sometimes a choux pastry mix. Used to garnish soup, served alone with cheese or with a sauce. Strictly speaking, this is not a pasta.

Fine egg noodles – made with wheat flour and egg, these are probably the most commonly used Oriental noodles, often sold in compressed squares.

ACTION

Ask your supervisor to help you contact various pasta suppliers to get details of their current range of products, including dried, fresh and frozen pasta.

1 From the information you receive, decide on 2 or 3 new pasta dishes which might be popular with customers, either as specialities of the day, or as permanent menu items.

2 For each of these dishes, write a brief description below that would be suitable for the menu.

3 With the help of your supervisor, work out how much the dish would cost to produce, and what the selling price would need to be.

Preparing fresh pasta

As with the main types of pastry and cakes, many chefs have their own favourite recipe for basic pasta dough. For example, some prefer to use a strong flour, others a general-purpose flour. A marble surface is best for rolling and shaping the pasta.

If you are using a machine to do the mixing, as well as the shaping and cutting, there will be specific instructions to follow.

Shaping pasta dough by hand

1 Rest the dough in a cool place, covered, for 30 to 45 minutes before using.

2 Divide the dough into manageable amounts for rolling (two for the quantity in the recipe overleaf).

3 For dusting the dough during rolling, use a strong flour. Rice flour or semolina also work well.

4 With your hands, flatten the ball of dough slightly to form a thick oblong about 25 mm (1 inch) thick. The aim, as you roll the dough, is to turn this into a paper thin rectangle.

5 Start at the end of the oblong near you, and roll the dough out lengthwise away from yourself. Stop rolling within 25 mm or so of the far edge.

6 Turn the dough through 90° and roll across its width.

7 Repeat, turning and rolling the dough until it is very thin. As necessary, dust the top lightly with flour. If the dough begins to stick to the board, lift it and sprinkle some flour under it.

8 When you have got the right thickness, sprinkle the surface of the dough with flour. Leave it to rest and dry out for 30 minutes or so before cutting. (Some chefs omit this step.)

for lasagne

Cut the sheets of dough into smaller rectangles. Choose a size that gives you pieces of similar dimensions, and no odd trimmings, say 150 × 75 mm (6 × 3 inches).

Assembling a lasagne dish. The style shown here is bolognaise (recipe overleaf).

for noodles

Cut into ribbon-like strips about 5 mm wide. A quick way of doing this is to roll the floured rectangle of dough over on itself from the long side, like a Swiss roll. Then cut a series of strips and unroll.

The length of the noodles should be roughly the same, but exactly how long is a matter of opinion. Preferences vary from 25 to 80 cm.

for cannelloni

1 Cut into squares about 6 × 6 cm (2½ × 2½ inches).

2 Boil vigorously in salted water for 5 to 10 minutes until tender. When adding to the water, stir to make sure the pasta pieces do not stick together.

3 Refresh under cold running water. Drain well.

4 Lay out side by side on a work surface, or slightly dampened cloth.

5 Pipe or spoon a small amount of the chosen filling on the bottom third of each pasta square. Roll up to enclose the stuffing.

6 Arrange the stuffed pasta in a greased baking dish, side by side. Cover with the recipe sauce and bake as instructed.

for tortellini

1 With a pastry cutter, make 50 mm (2 inch) circles.

2 Brush the edges with beaten egg. Spoon or pipe a small amount of filling on top.

3 Fold each circle over in half, to enclose the filling. Gently press the moistened edges together.

4 Wrap each half circle of dough around your finger and press the ends together, to form a ring.

for ravioli

You require two rectangles of dough, of similar size.

1 Brush one sheet with beaten egg. Place a small mound of the filling every 50 mm (2 inches) across and down the pasta, to form a pattern rather like a chessboard.

2 Carefully spread the second sheet of pasta on top. Press down firmly around each mound of filling, starting at the centre of the rectangle and working outwards so that you do not leave air pockets.

3 With a ravioli cutter, pastry wheel or small, sharp knife, cut the pasta into squares along the lines between the mounds of filling.

4 Separate on to a well floured tray, and leave to dry in a cool place for 20 to 30 minutes before cooking.

Basic egg pasta dough

Key learning point
» prepare basic egg pasta dough

Can be used for freshly-made lasagne, noodles, cannelloni, tortellini, ravioli and other pasta shapes.

MAKES 350 g (12 oz)

175 g	plain flour	6 oz
1	egg	1
1	egg white	1
12.5 ml	olive oil	2½ tsp
1	level tsp salt	1
	few drops water	

1 Put the flour into a large mixing bowl or in a heap on a pastry board. Make a well in the centre and add the egg, egg white, oil and salt.

2 Mix together with your fingers until the dough can be gathered into a rough ball. Moisten any remaining dry bits of flour with drops of water and press them into the ball.

3 Knead the dough on a floured board, working in a little extra flour if the dough seems sticky. After about 10 minutes the dough should be smooth, shiny and elastic.

4 Cover the dough and put it in a cool place to rest for 30 to 45 minutes.

Spaghetti Italian style

Key learning points
» use convenience or preprepared pasta
» noodles, ravioli and tortellini can be cooked and served in a similar way

Parmesan cheese is the traditional accompaniment to many pasta dishes. Prepared grated Parmesan is an acceptable and less expensive alternative to grating your own.

SERVES 10

500 g	spaghetti	1 lb 2 oz
100 g	butter	4 oz
100 g	Parmesan cheese, freshly grated	4 oz
	salt and freshly milled black pepper to taste	

1 Place the spaghetti in a large saucepan containing about 5 litres (10 pints) of boiling salted water. Stir to separate the spaghetti.

2 Return to the boil (with a fairly vigorous bubbling movement). Cook for 12 to 15 minutes, stirring occasionally.

3 When it is cooked, drain the spaghetti in a colander. If it is sticky, wash or rinse it with very hot water and drain again.

4 Melt the butter in a sauteuse and heat until foaming, being careful not to let it burn.

5 Add the drained spaghetti and toss to coat thoroughly in butter. Also add half the Parmesan and season with the milled pepper.

6 Place the spaghetti on a serving dish. The remaining cheese can be sprinkled over the top of the spaghetti, or offered separately.

Lasagne bolognaise

Key learning points
» use convenience or preprepared pasta
» prepare pasta dish with meat filling
» use green, white or wholewheat pasta

Some chefs start by putting a drop of béchamel sauce in the base of the dish (step 4). Another variation is to use the béchamel for the top layer only.

SERVES 2

100 g	lasagne	4 oz
400 ml	bolognaise sauce (page 144)	14 fl oz
175 ml	béchamel sauce (page 143)	7 fl oz
25 ml	cream	1 fl oz
40 g	Parmesan cheese, freshly grated	2 oz
	nutmeg, salt and freshly milled black pepper to taste	

1 Boil the lasagne fairly vigorously in plenty of salted water. Stir from time to time to prevent the pieces from sticking together.

2 When cooked (12 to 15 minutes), refresh the lasagne under cold running water and drain thoroughly.

3 Mix the cream through the béchamel (white) sauce and season with nutmeg.

4 Place a layer of lasagne in the base of a greased ovenproof dish. Coat with a layer of bolognaise sauce and sprinkle this with Parmesan. Cover with a layer of lasagne, coat this with the béchamel, and sprinkle with Parmesan. Repeat the pattern two or three times until you have filled the dish. Finish with a top layer of cream sauce and Parmesan.

5 Bake at 200°C for 25 to 30 minutes until golden brown and thoroughly reheated. Serve at once.

Spiced courgette and pasta pot

Key learning points
» make a baked pasta dish, suitable for vegetarians or those on low-fat diets
» use egg as setting agent

SERVES 10

275 g	wholemeal macaroni	10 oz
10 ml	polyunsaturated oil	2 tsp
550 g	onions, finely chopped	1¼ lb
4	cloves garlic, crushed and peeled	4
1.25 kg	courgettes, sliced into rounds	2½ lb
175 g each	green and red peppers, sliced	6 oz each
550 g	button mushrooms	1¼ lb
5 g	chilli pepper to taste	¼ oz
10 g each	ground cumin and paprika	½ oz each
275 g	haricot beans, cooked	10 oz
7	eggs	7
425 ml	low-fat natural yogurt	15 fl oz
600 ml	skimmed milk	1 pt
	seasoning to taste	
	fresh parsley, chopped (to garnish)	

1 Place the macaroni into boiling salted water. Return to the boil, then simmer for 12 to 15 minutes, stirring from time to time.

2 When the macaroni is cooked, immediately cool under cold running water. Drain thoroughly.

3 Heat the oil in a large frying pan, add the onions and garlic, and cook until soft but not coloured, about 4 minutes. Add the courgettes, peppers, mushrooms and spices, and fry until the vegetables are lightly cooked. Lightly mix in the haricot beans and macaroni.

4 Place this mixture into a greased casserole dish or portion-size ovenproof dishes.

5 Whisk together the eggs, yogurt, milk and seasoning until well combined. Pour over the vegetables and pasta, just to cover them. Add a little more after the mixture has soaked through.

6 Bake until lightly set, about 20 minutes at 200°C. Serve with a sprinkling of chopped parsley.

Sukiyaki vegetable noodles
by Sarsons

Key learning points
» use convenience egg noodles
» stir fry vegetables
» make a dish suitable for vegetarians

SERVES 4 to 6

150 g	fine egg noodles	5 oz
30 ml	sesame oil	2 tbsp
50 g	spring onions, trimmed and finely chopped	2 oz
100 g	baby corn, sliced into thin rings	4 oz
½	red pepper, diced small	½
100 g	button mushrooms, sliced	4 oz
60 ml	Sukiyaki sauce	4 tbsp
15 ml	clear honey	1 tbsp

1 Cook noodles according to packet instructions, drain and mix in 15 ml of the oil.

2 Meanwhile, heat remaining oil in a wok and stir fry onions, corn and pepper for 2 minutes. Add mushrooms and cook for 1 minute.

3 Add drained noodles, Sukiyaki sauce and honey. Stir fry until warmed through.

Farfalle all'amatriciana
by Buitoni

Key learning points
» use convenience pasta bows
» make a dish suitable for vegetarians

Alternative pasta shapes: *Conchiglie* (shells), *Eliche* (twists), *Eliche tricolore* (red, white and green twists).

Served by the locals of Amatrice, in central Italy, at a feast on the first Sunday after the August holiday of Ferragosta.

SERVES 3 to 4

15 ml	olive oil	1 tbsp
1	medium onion, sliced into rings	1
100 g	back bacon, chopped	4 oz
150 ml	dry white wine	5 fl oz
1 × 425 g	can chopped tomatoes	1 × 15 oz
5 ml	fresh basil, roughly chopped	1 tsp
	seasoning to taste	
350 g	farfalle (bows)	12 oz
75 g	Parmesan cheese, freshly grated	3 oz

1 Heat the oil in a large pan. Add the onion and cook for 4 to 5 minutes until transparent. Add the bacon and cook for a further 3 to 4 minutes.

2 Add the wine, tomatoes, basil and seasoning. Bring to the boil and simmer for 10 to 15 minutes.

3 Cook the pasta in boiling salted water as directed on the packet. Drain well, toss in the hot sauce, sprinkle with Parmesan cheese and serve.

Spaghetti alla carbonara
by Dufrais

Key learning points
» use convenience or preprepared pasta
» make dish with bacon and Parmesan cheese

Variations: 1) use wholewheat spaghetti, 2) reduce quantity of oil, 3) use no oil and dry fry the bacon, 4) omit wine, 5) add cream. If omitting wine or reducing quantity of oil, do not reduce at step 2. If adding cream, do this at step 4 with the eggs, and cook for 1 minute after combining mixture and before serving.

Reputed to have been a favourite dish of the Roman carbonari (charcoal burners).

SERVES 4

350 g	spaghetti	12 oz
45 ml	olive oil	3 tbsp
1	medium onion, chopped	1
6	rashers of smoked bacon, derinded and chopped	6
100 ml	white Bistro Chef, or white wine	4 fl oz
4	eggs, size 2	4
75 g	Parmesan cheese, freshly grated	3 oz
30 ml	parsley, freshly chopped	2 tbsp
1	garlic clove, crushed and peeled	1
	seasoning to taste	

1 Drop the spaghetti into plenty of rapidly boiling salted water. Allow it to curl around the pan as it softens. Boil for 8 to 10 minutes until tender.

2 Meanwhile, fry the onion and bacon in the oil for 4 minutes until golden brown. Add Bistro Chef or white wine and boil until most of the liquid has evaporated.

3 Beat the eggs with the Parmesan, parsley and garlic. Season.

4 Drain the spaghetti. Immediately, stir in the beaten eggs, onion and bacon, so that the heat from the spaghetti cooks the egg. Serve accompanied with more Parmesan.

Lasagne con vegetali
by Buitoni

Key learning points
» prepare a baked pasta dish
» make a dish suitable for vegetarians
» use white or wholewheat lasagne

SERVES 4 to 6

15 ml	olive oil	1 tbsp
2	onions, finely chopped	2
2 each	red and green peppers, deseeded and chopped	2 each
1 × 425 g	can chopped tomatoes	1 × 15 oz
1	clove garlic, crushed and peeled	1
60 ml	tomato purée	4 tbsp
10 ml	fresh basil, chopped	2 tsp
	seasoning to taste	
9 sheets	lasagne verdi	9 sheets
275 ml	mornay (cheese) sauce (page 143)	½ pt
40 g	Gruyère cheese, grated	1½ oz

1 Heat the oil and fry the onions and peppers for 4 to 5 minutes until softened. Add the tomatoes, garlic, tomato purée, basil and seasoning. Cover and simmer for 30 minutes.

2 Spoon a little of the cooked vegetables into a 28 × 17 cm (11 × 6¾ inches) rectangular ovenproof dish and add a layer of lasagne, without overlapping.

3 Continue with alternate layers of lasagne and vegetables, finishing with a layer of lasagne. Spread the mornay sauce over the top and sprinkle with the Gruyère.

4 Bake for 25 to 30 minutes at 180°C. Serve with a mixed salad.

Cannelloni con spinaci e mandorle
by Buitoni

Key learning points
» prepare stuffed pasta dish, baked
» make a dish suitable for vegetarians

SERVES 6

350 g	fresh spinach, blanched, chopped finely	12 oz
30 ml	olive oil	2 tbsp
1	large onion, finely chopped	1
1	clove garlic, crushed and peeled	1
1	green pepper, deseeded and finely chopped	1
50 g	ground almonds	2 oz
25 g	whole almonds, finely chopped	1
2.5 ml	nutmeg	½ tsp
20 ml	fresh oregano, chopped	4 tsp
150 ml	vegetable stock	5 fl oz
	seasoning to taste	
12	cannelloni tubes	12

for the sauce

1	medium onion, finely chopped	1
1 × 425 g	can chopped tomatoes	1 × 15 oz
5 ml	sugar	1 tsp
75 g	Mozzarella cheese, grated	3 oz

1 Heat 15 ml (1 tbsp) oil in a large saucepan and fry the onion, garlic and pepper for 3 to 4 minutes until soft. Add the spinach, almonds, nutmeg, 10 ml (2 tsp) oregano, stock and seasoning. Cook for a further 2 to 3 minutes.

2 Fill the cannelloni with this mixture and place in a lightly greased shallow ovenproof dish.

3 Heat the remaining oil in a large saucepan and fry the onion for 4 to 5 minutes until browned. Add the tomato, remaining oregano and sugar. Bring to the boil and simmer for 5 minutes.

4 Pour this sauce over the cannelloni. Top with Mozzarella and bake for 30 to 35 minutes at 200°C. Serve immediately.

Fettuccine con i carciofi
by Buitoni

Key learning points
» use convenience green pasta
» prepare a velouté-based dish

SERVES 4

225 g	fettuccine verdi	8 oz
280 ml	chicken velouté (page 143) or use half milk/half stock in recipe	½ pt
45 ml	dry white wine	3 tbsp
100 g	back bacon, chopped and grilled	4 oz
1 × 397 g	can artichoke hearts, cut into halves	1 × 14 oz
	seasoning to taste	
30 ml	fresh parsley, chopped	2 tbsp

1 Cook the pasta in boiling salted water, as directed on the packet.

2 Meanwhile, bring the velouté to the boil, add the wine, bacon, artichoke hearts and seasoning. Drain the pasta and toss in the sauce.

3 Sprinkle with parsley and serve.

Chicken and corn tagliatelle
by Record Pasta

Key learning points
» prepare a white pasta dish
» make a roux-based sauce

SERVES 4

50 g	margarine	2 oz
1	green pepper, chopped	1
3	sticks celery, chopped	3
50 g	flour	2 oz
575 ml	hot milk	1 pt
	seasoning to taste	
1 × 312 g	can sweetcorn	1 × 11 oz
350 g	diced cooked chicken	12 oz
225–350 g	tagliatelle	8–12 oz
50 g	cheese, grated	2 oz

1 Melt the margarine in a pan, add the pepper and celery, and cook for a few minutes without colouring.

2 Mix in the flour and cook for 1 minute. Gradually stir in the hot milk. Bring to the boil, then add the sweetcorn and chicken. Season and simmer for 5 minutes.

3 Meanwhile cook the pasta as directed on the packet. Drain and either combine with the chicken mixture or serve separately, with a little grated cheese sprinkled on top.

NVQ **SVQ** **RANGE CHECKLIST**

LEVEL 1

1D6.1 Prepare and cook pasta dishes

2 of these pasta dishes
- [ ] lasagne or cannelloni
- [ ] noodles or spaghetti
- [ ] stuffed pasta
- [ ] pasta shapes

made from
- [ ] dried or fresh or convenience chilled pasta
- [ ] white or green or wholewheat

LEVEL 2

2D6.1 Prepare and cook fresh pasta

by hand or by pasta shaping and cutting machine, make 3 of these shapes
- [ ] lasagne
- [ ] cannelloni
- [ ] noodles
- [ ] stuffed pasta
- [ ] pasta shapes

and prepare and cook 3 of these
- [ ] white pasta
- [ ] green or red pasta
- [ ] wholewheat pasta
- [ ] vegetable or meat fillings

Introduction

Eggs are one of the most versatile ingredients in cooking, and one of the most widely used. On their own, they are a favourite breakfast dish, or a quickly prepared and nutritious meal for later in the day. With the addition of a few simple ingredients, eggs also make a classic start or finish to a more elaborate lunch or dinner.

In the kitchen, you will find eggs used to perform a surprising number of quite different tasks. Those you are likely to encounter include:

setting the mixture in a flan or quiche lorraine, so that what begins as a runny liquid becomes a firm, but not hard mass. The same sort of thing happens when the mixture for a crème caramel is baked. In this case it is firm enough to be turned out after cooking

thickening an egg custard – of the type used to make a fresh egg custard to serve with stewed fruit, for example, or in the making of an ice cream. Great care must be taken not to overcook the mixture, otherwise you end up with a lumpy, unpleasant result. If badly overcooked, you will get a scrambled egg type mixture

raising a sponge cake – so that you get a light, airy texture. The egg whites are beaten so that they greatly increase in volume, trapping millions of small bubbles of air. These expand in the heat of the oven. A similar, more dramatic effect is achieved in a soufflé. The drawback with soufflés of this type is that they start collapsing as soon as they come out the oven

lightening sweet and savoury mousses – this also uses the ability of the egg whites to trap air when beaten. These are often quite rich, with fruit purée, cream, sugar, etc. in the recipe. Some chocolate mousses are made lighter by using beaten egg white

binding together mixtures – egg yolks are used in some stuffings, to bind the breadcrumbs, herbs and other ingredients. When a coating of flour, beaten egg and breadcrumbs is given to fish or meat, it is the egg which helps the coating to stick to the food and firm up during cooking

enriching a mixture – egg yolks are used in some pastries to give a richer tasting product, and to put the final touches to sauces. When used in this way in sauces, the sauce must not be overheated otherwise the egg begins to set

glazing the surface of many baked pastry products – in other words, giving them an attractive shiny appearance after baking. Beaten egg (egg wash is its other name when used in this way) will help seal two layers of pastry together.

A rather more specialised use of eggs is to *clarify* a mixture. You will see this happen when fresh aspic (a sort of savoury jelly) or consommé (a clear soup) is made. Egg white is mixed into the minced meat and finely chopped vegetables before the stock is added. As the mixture cooks, the egg white collects together the meat and vegetables, leaving a clear liquid.

In many cases, eggs fulfil a number of these functions at the same time. In pancakes and fritter batters, for example, they provide texture and flavour. In Yorkshire pudding and toad-in-the-hole, they also provide lightness.

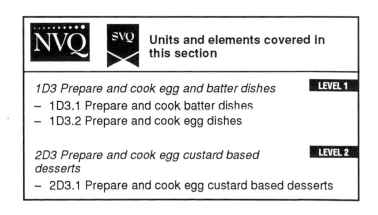

NVQ SVQ Units and elements covered in this section

1D3 Prepare and cook egg and batter dishes   **LEVEL 1**
- 1D3.1 Prepare and cook batter dishes
- 1D3.2 Prepare and cook egg dishes

2D3 Prepare and cook egg custard based desserts   **LEVEL 2**
- 2D3.1 Prepare and cook egg custard based desserts

Quality points

Eggs

- eggs are class A (see box on opposite page)
- not passed use-by date
- packaging gives the information required by EC regulations. This includes: grade, size of eggs, name and address of those responsible for packing.

There are strict controls over the use of the terms *free range* and *barn eggs*. For example, free range birds must have continuous daytime access to open-air runs which are mainly covered with vegetation and with a maximum stocking density of 1000 hens per hectare (395 hens per acre). The hen houses (for night time) must have a maximum stocking density of 7 birds per square metre of floor space. The type of floor covering is also specified.

A fresh egg has a very thick white. During storage, the natural ageing process causes the white to become more and more runny, so it is possible to tell quite easily if eggs are not fresh, by the consistency of the white when they are cracked open. In stored eggs, the membrane that surrounds the yolk is weakened so the yolk breaks very easily.

Convenience batter mixes

- packaging in good condition
- not passed use-by date
- stored in cool, dry conditions, in a closed, pest- and rodent-proof container

Storage of eggs

1 Store in a refrigerator. Storage in a cool room is no longer recommended, in view of the risk of the eggs becoming contaminated with salmonella. Another reason for keeping eggs chilled is to protect their freshness.

2 Keep the eggs in their original boxes or trays. If this is not practicable, transfer to egg trays, the pointed end of the egg facing downwards. This will reduce the risk of breakages, and reduce loss of contents by evaporation through the porous shell. Do not store eggs loose in bowls, as this can result in cracks.

3 Keep eggs away from strong-smelling foods – eggs pick up foreign flavours and tastes quite easily if unprotected. When eggs are washed (rarely necessary) this removes the natural protective coating.

4 Whole eggs out of their shells must be kept refrigerated and covered, and should be used within two days. Egg whites will keep in a refrigerator for several days, and freeze well. Egg yolks dry out quickly, so moisten them with a little water, cover

A collection of frozen, chilled and thawed pasteurised egg products: egg yolks, whites and beaten whole eggs.

The pasteurisation process kills most of the harmful bacteria that may be present in raw egg. They are therefore particularly suitable for dishes in which the egg is not cooked: mayonnaise (which uses raw egg yolk), sorbets and some sweet mousses (which use beaten egg white).

Egg boxes marked with the Lion trade mark comply with current standards of hygiene, enforced by the British government. There is no similar quality assurance for imported eggs.

them tightly and store chilled. Do not keep for longer than a day. Alternatively, mix with a little sugar or salt (½ tsp per 3 egg yolks) and freeze. This mixture can be used for glazing, egg wash, binding burgers, etc.

5 Hard-boiled eggs for salads, decorating food etc. should be kept well chilled, in a place where they will not be confused with raw eggs. Do not store with uncooked foods.

Handling and storing pasteurised eggs

1 Read the instructions on the packaging.

2 Defrost frozen products for 12 hours in a refrigerator before use.

3 Never refreeze defrosted products, or freeze chilled products.

4 Always use the contents of a container within 48 hours of defrosting and/or opening, or before the use-by date.

NUTRITION

A single large egg provides about 11% of the recommended daily intake of proteins for adults. Eggs contain 11% fat (all in the yolk), of which 63% is unsaturated. They are a good source of vitamins A, B1 (thiamin), B2 (riboflavin), B12 and D, and of iron and calcium (see pages 50 and 94).

Although some people think of brown eggs as more healthy than white eggs, this is actually untrue. The colour of the egg shell depends on the breed of the hen and does not affect the nutritional value of the egg.

Neither is the colour of the egg yolk an indication of its nutritional value. The variation in yolk colour arises from the natural process of transfer of pigments from the hen's food. A diet of maize meal, or less costly cereals with grassmeal added, will result in a natural deep yolk colour.

HYGIENE

1 Make sure that hands, preparation surfaces, utensils and containers are clean when handling eggs.
2 Never use cracked or dirty eggs.
3 Wash your hands after handling eggs, and before handling other food.
4 Use pasteurised egg in recipes where the egg is used raw or partly cooked.
5 Serve egg dishes as soon as possible after preparation. If the dish is not going to be eaten immediately, chill quickly and keep in the refrigerator.
6 Do not serve lightly cooked eggs to anyone who is ill or feeling unwell, pregnant women, babies and infants, and the elderly.

ACTION

Arrange with your supervisor (or do this at home) to put aside a selection of eggs at intervals of one week for the next 4 weeks. Explain that you want to see how they are affected by ageing.

The sample eggs must be labelled *NOT FOR CONSUMPTION* and kept apart from other foodstuffs. Keep them in a cool room.

The suggested sample is:

A 2 eggs to be kept for 4 weeks

B 2 eggs put aside one week later to be kept for 3 weeks

C 2 eggs put aside 2 weeks later to be kept for 1 week

D 2 absolutely fresh eggs for day of test.

Put a brine solution (575 ml/1 pint cold water to 2 tbsp salt) in a deep glass bowl, or better still a large spaghetti jar. Carefully drop in the sample eggs, starting with the two freshest; they should lie on their side on the bottom of the bowl. Continue with the other samples. Very stale eggs will float on the top of the brine solution.

Dry the eggs, then break them one by one on a tray or other suitable flat surface. Note the state of the egg white and the egg yolk.

As this egg is very fresh and has been carefully cooked, the yolk is a nice round shape and there is no discoloration.

How eggs are graded

Shortly after they are laid, chicken eggs are graded according to their size and according to the thickness of the egg white and the strength of the membrane or skin enclosing the egg yolk.

In the testing process, the egg is held in front of an especially strong light source. In a top quality egg, the white is clear and so thick that the yolk is held firmly in place in the centre of the egg, even when it is shaken, and the yolk is only just visible as a grey shadow.

If the egg is of poor quality and the yolk is not held in the centre of the egg, it will cast a clear, dark shadow wherever it is nearest the shell.

Sizes of eggs

Most recipes, unless they state otherwise, use size 3 eggs. These weigh between 60 and 65 g.

There are seven egg sizes altogether, from size 1 which weighs 70 g and over, to size 7 weighing under 45 g. Sizes 2 to 6 are in bands of 5 g.

Classes of eggs

Class A – naturally clean, fresh eggs, internally perfect with shells intact.

Class B – downgraded from A for one or more reasons, e.g. size of the air gap, the yolk has become relatively immobile, the white has become gelatinous, refrigerated or preserved before sale.

Class C – not available for sale in shops. Used in food and other manufacturing.

Cooking eggs

LEVEL 1

There are six simple methods of cooking eggs by themselves: boiling, baking, poaching, frying, scrambling and as an omelette.

You will have been served boiled eggs so runny that some of the white remains transparent, scrambled eggs which are almost solid, fried eggs that are rubbery. This is because cooking has not been properly controlled.

When heat is applied to an egg, the egg starts changing from its naturally fluid state. This is because the proteins in the egg start to set or *coagulate*.

Take the boiled egg as an example. If the temperature of the water is too high (100°C rather than the recommended 96°C), there is a tendency for the white to become very firm, while the yolk remains too soft. Four degrees may not seem a lot, but it is sufficient for the rate at which the heat penetrates the egg to get out of balance.

Some points to remember when cooking eggs

1   Take the eggs you require out of the refrigerator 20 to 30 minutes before use. This will give them time to come up to room temperature, and they will cook better.

2   When making scrambled egg or an omelette, add salt (if required) at the last moment before cooking. Salt in contact with the beaten egg mixture for too long will result in a rather runny, watery end product.

Boiled eggs

• Whether the egg is soft or hard-boiled depends on the temperature reached inside the egg. The longer the egg remains in the water (which should be just off the boil at 96°C), the more heat will reach the yolk.

• Over-cooking causes a greenish-black discoloration on the surface of a hard-cooked yolk. This is due to the formation of iron sulphide – which happens when hydrogen sulphide from the egg white mixes with iron from the yolk. If hard-boiled eggs are to be served or used cold, stop the cooking quickly by putting the eggs under cold running water.

• If an egg does crack during boiling, sprinkle a little salt on the crack. Salt in the boiling water will also help.

• For boiling a number of eggs at the same time, put the eggs in a wire basket, then lower into the water – just as you would chips into the deep fryer.

• Soft-boiled eggs are considered a health risk, because the temperature is not high enough to kill any salmonella bacteria which may be present.

There are two methods of boiling eggs.

Method 1

1   Lower eggs into simmering water, covering them completely.

2   Bring water back to simmering point and time:

	Soft-boiled	Hard-boiled
Sizes 2 and 3	4 minutes	12 minutes
Sizes 4 and 5	3 minutes	10 minutes

Method 2

1   Lower eggs into cold water, cover them completely.

for soft-boiled eggs

2   Bring water to a rolling boil.

3   Remove saucepan from heat and leave eggs to stand in the water for the following times:

sizes 2 and 3, 3 minutes

sizes 4 and 5, 2 minutes

for hard-boiled eggs

2   Bring water to the boil, turn down heat and simmer gently for the following times:

sizes 2 and 3, 10 minutes

sizes 4 and 5, 8 minutes

Baked eggs

One of the simplest ways of cooking eggs is to bake or *shirr* them in the attractive little dishes designed specifically for the purpose.

An egg *en cocotte* is baked in a ramekin with sides high enough to protect the egg from direct heat. An egg *sur le plat* is baked on a flatter dish (see photograph on page 194).

At their simplest, baked eggs are cooked in buttered dishes with a little salt and pepper (sprinkled under the eggs so as not to spot their surface). Some cream may be added. Often a garnish is placed at the bottom of the ramekin (e.g. herbs, chopped ham, chopped cooked mushrooms), or by the side of eggs *sur le plat* (e.g. sausages and tomato sauce for Bercy style).

Oeufs en cocotte

1   Rub butter around the sides and bottom of individual cocotte or ramekin dishes. Sprinkle with seasoning. Add any flavourings or base ingredients.

2   Break an egg into each dish. If required, top each egg yolk with a small knob of butter or a little cream.

3 Cover the dish with kitchen foil to prevent the surface drying in the heat. Alternatively, leave the eggs uncovered to form a shiny skin *en mirou*.

4 Bake at 160°C for 5 to 8 minutes, depending on the firmness required. Test by gently shaking the ramekins.

Poached eggs

You may have come across poached eggs which have been cooked in a poaching pan. This looks like a frying pan in shape, and works like a double saucepan. The eggs sit in little hollows or moulds above the level of the boiling water. The lid of the pan is kept on during cooking. Because there is no direct contact between the egg and the water, this is not true poaching.

The traditional way of poaching eggs is to break the egg into simmering water. A little white vinegar in the water will help the egg to keep an attractive shape (see photographs and Action).

• Use absolutely fresh eggs – as an egg ages it becomes more watery, and the white will spread out in the water rather than staying in an attractive shape.

• If you are poaching only one or two eggs, you can get the white to wrap around the yolk by stirring the water before you add the eggs.

• Some recipes suggest that the action of boiling water will cause the egg white to wrap around the yolk. However the convection currents are strong enough just below boiling point to produce this wrapping effect.

Method for poaching eggs

1 Pour about 4 cm (1½ inches) of water into a shallow-sided pan (a plat à sauter or sauté pan is ideal) and heat.

2 When the water has started to simmer, break each egg into a small bowl and slip it over the rim into the water.

3 Keep the heat low and poach the eggs for 2 to 3 minutes.

4 Use a slotted draining spoon to remove the eggs and serve immediately.

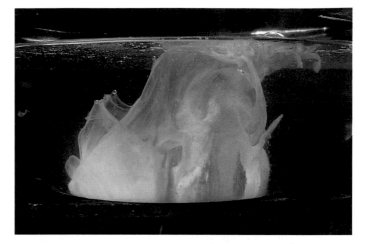

Neatness of shape in a poached egg is a test of the chef's skill.

Note how the egg is being slid gently into the simmering water using a small bowl. A deep saucer or cup will do just as well.

These poached eggs (see next page also) are being prepared in advance of service, for finishing and presenting as Eggs florentine As soon as they are cooked, the eggs are transferred to the bowl of iced water (right edge of picture).

ACTION

1 Take 2 eggs from the same box (so that you can assume they are both equally fresh).
2 Bring half a litre of water to the boil in each of two saucepans. Then turn the heat down until there are no bubbles rising.
3 Add a teaspoonful of vinegar to one of the saucepans.
4 Carefully crack an egg into each pan.
5 Record your results after 3 minutes when the eggs are cooked.

Effect of adding vinegar to egg-poaching water

Poached eggs florentine in preparation. The ball of cooked spinach (shown right) is flattened slightly, the cooked egg placed on top, then covered with mornay sauce. (More information on previous page, recipe on page 200.)

Fried eggs (shallow fried/pan fried eggs)

A little oil, butter or margarine is used to stop the egg sticking to the pan and to add flavour.

A moderate heat is better than a high heat, which tends to cause the white of the egg to become leathery, and to shrink and become brown at the edges.

1 Heat a little oil – or butter and oil – in a frying pan. When the oil is hot but not sizzling, break the eggs, one at a time, into the pan. Do not overfill the pan, or you will find it difficult to remove the eggs without damaging the yolk. Alternatively cook on a griddle.

2 Cook eggs gently over a moderate heat. As the egg white begins to set, spoon oil over the surface to ensure even cooking and to set the yolk to a translucent film. This is for *sunny side up*, to use the American expression. If the eggs are turned over halfway through cooking so that the yolk is in direct contact with the heat of the pan, this is *over easy*.

3 When egg is set to the desired level, lift out carefully with a perforated slice, allowing any excess oil to drain off.

Scrambled eggs

1 Break the eggs into a bowl and beat well with a fork to combine yolks and white. Season to taste.

2 Melt a little butter or margarine in a heavy saucepan over a gentle heat. As soon as the fat melts, pour in the eggs.

3 Keeping the heat low, stir when large creamy flakes start to form. Too much heat will dry the flakes, too much stirring will break them up.

4 When softly set, remove from heat. Serve immediately.

Omelettes

The whole eggs are whisked (a little cold water may be added to lighten the mixture) and then heated in a pan. As the egg begins to set, it is moved quickly with a fork to allow more of the liquid egg to come into contact with the pan base. Stirring and heating holds the cooked egg together. A high heat is needed – the only time high heat should be used for cooking eggs.

Too little heat will give a rather unevenly cooked omelette. Too much stirring prevents the omelette base from browning. Cooking for too long dries up the egg. Pan size is crucial, as too few eggs in a large pan produce a pancake-like result.

There are three types of omelette (recipes on page 199):

Folded omelette – filling spread across the middle before folding over to serve. Also called *French omelette*.

Flat omelette – various cooked foods such as onion, peppers, bacon and potatoes are cooked in the pan with the egg, and the omelette is served flat. Also called *Spanish omelette* or *tortilla* (in Spain and Mexico), or *frittata* (in Italy).

Soufflé omelette – egg white whisked separately to give added lightness and fluffiness to the mixture.

Making a folded omelette – drawing the cooked egg from the edge of the pan inwards so that the liquid egg runs through to cook on the base of the pan. In the foreground is a finished omelette. Note its colour and shape: thick in the centre, tapered at both ends.

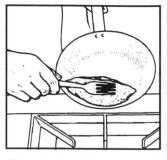

The omelette is folded in from both ends. Here the first fold is made. | *The sloping side of the omelette pan is a help in making the final fold.*

Cooking egg custard

The two basic ingredients of an egg custard are whole eggs and milk.

For a savoury egg custard – to make a quiche, for example – seasoning will be added.

When the custard is being used to make a dessert dish, or as a sauce to accompany stewed fruit, for example, sugar will be added. Other flavourings include cinnamon and nutmeg.

When a fairly thick custard is required to line the base of a fruit flan, for example, or to fill choux pastry buns, flour is beaten into the eggs and sugar, before the addition of the hot milk. The mixture must then be brought to the boil to cook the starch in the flour. This mixture is called *pastry cream* or *crème pâtissière*.

Basic steps for making egg custard

1 Lightly beat the eggs in a bowl with the seasoning or sugar.

2 Gradually beat in the hot milk.

3 Pour the egg and milk mixture into a clean saucepan over a low heat. Stir gently and often, so that the custard cooks to a creamy but not frothy consistency. On no account let the custard overcook, otherwise lumps will form.

Milk and beaten egg are a fairly thick liquid when raw. Heat changes the mixture to a firmer consistency, able to keep its shape, even when cut into a small cube. This strength comes mainly from the setting or coagulation of the egg proteins.

During heating, various proteins in the egg all join up to form a kind of network that traps small pockets of liquid. If the mixture is overheated, some of the liquid starts to be squeezed out and a rubbery texture is produced, or the mixture curdles, with solid lumps floating in the wrung-out liquid.

CHEF'S TIPS

Most egg custards are made from whole eggs. For a richer flavour and softer texture, use a higher proportion of egg yolks to egg whites.

For an even richer mixture, substitute cream for some of the milk in the recipe. *Crème brûlée*, one of the finest dishes of this type, uses no milk at all, just cream.

A vanilla pod may be soaked in the hot milk before it is added to the eggs for a delicate flavour. Alternatively use vanilla sugar. This is easy to make: fill a jar with caster sugar and push 2 or 3 vanilla pods into it. Leave for a few weeks, topping up as necessary until the pods have lost their flavour.

Add a tiny amount of cornflour or potato flour to *crème anglaise* (a light egg custard sauce) if you want to reduce the risk of the egg mixture overheating.

This type of egg custard thickens as it cools. To judge when to remove it from the heat, dip a spoon into the custard. When ready, the custard will coat the back of the spoon, and if you run your finger through the coating, it should show a clean line.

To test whether a baked custard is cooked sufficiently, pierce the centre (the last part to cook) with the tip of a knife. It should come out cleanly. Another test is to shake the dish gently. The centre of the custard should wobble like a jelly.

The egg custard has thickened sufficiently to coat the back of the spoon, and form 'ribbons' when lifted. Note that the saucepan is sitting in a larger pan of water, so that the heat is as gentle as possible. The bigger saucepan is acting as a bain-marie.

ACTION

1 Make 4 egg custard mixtures varying the ingredients as follows:

   A 1 egg + 175 ml (6 fl oz) milk

   B 1 egg + 175 ml milk + ½ tsp salt

   C 2 eggs + 175 ml milk

   D 2 eggs + 175 ml water.

2 In each case, warm the liquid slightly before whisking it into the egg(s).

3 Add salt in B, then pour the 4 batches of mixture into 4 small heat-proof dishes (glass if possible).

4 Label the dishes, place them in a baking tray half-full of cold water and bake in an oven at 150°C.

5 After 15 minutes, turn the oven up to 200°C.

6 Time how long it takes each mixture to set and how much longer for each to curdle (or set solid with large air bubbles).

7 Note down your results and record your comments below on the texture and taste of all 4 mixtures.

	Time to set	Time to curdle	Texture and taste
A			
B			
C			
D			

8 Discuss with your tutor or supervisor why the mixtures have taken different times to set, and what could be done to avoid curdling/overcooking when making egg custards. Make some notes below.

Cooking batters

There are three basic types of egg batter:

- for making pancakes

- for covering fruit (and vegetables) which is to be deep fried – the batter protects the fruit from the hot oil, in the same way that batters protect fish which is deep fried (see page 104)

- for making Yorkshire pudding, a traditional accompaniment to roast beef and also used to make dishes like toad-in-the-hole (sausages in a Yorkshire pudding batter).

Pancakes

The mixture should be thick enough to spread across the base of the pan – like double cream as opposed to single cream.

The mixture should be allowed to rest before cooking. This allows the flour particles to expand in the liquid and ensures a tender, light result.

Pancakes can be made in advance and reheated as required. They freeze well. Layer each one between greaseproof paper so they can be removed individually when required.

Batters

Batters should be thick enough to coat the food evenly, and provide protection from the hot oil, but not so thick that they overwhelm the texture or flavour of the food they are enclosing.

Basic batters (egg, flour, seasoning, milk or water) should be rested before cooking (see above).

Those that rely for their lightness on beaten egg white, or yeast, should be cooked as quickly as possible after the egg white has been folded in or the yeast has fermented.

Fruits to be frittered (i.e. coated in batter and deep fried) should be in thin slices or small pieces. Shake off excess batter and drop food into hot fat. Drain well after cooking.

Yorkshire pudding batter

To trap the air and help the Yorkshire pudding to rise, the cooking fat and oven must be very hot. (Some people are tempted to use self-raising flour in place of plain flour, but this causes the mixture to expand too much, so that it collapses a short time after leaving the oven.)

Fruit fritters
by McDougalls (RHM Foods)

Key learning points
» prepare batter using beaten egg white
» deep fry fruit
Recipes for a yeast batter and plain batter are on page 118.

SERVES 4

8	pieces of fruit of your choice, e.g. whole or halved bananas, rings of pineapple, rings of apple	8

Batter

100 g	plain flour	4 oz
	pinch of salt	
15 ml	oil	1 tbsp
150 ml	warm water	5 fl oz
1	egg white	1
	flour to coat fruit	
	icing or caster sugar for glaze	

1 For the batter, mix flour, salt and oil with warm water to form a smooth paste.

2 Whisk the egg white until stiff and carefully fold into batter mixture.

3 Coat the fruit pieces in the flour, then the batter.

4 Deep fry at 180°C for a few minutes, or until lightly browned. Remove and place on absorbent kitchen paper so any excess oil is soaked up.

5 Dust the tops with sugar, then place under an overhead grill until the sugar has melted, forming an attractive golden brown glaze.

Yorkshire pudding

Key learning point
» prepare a roasted batter dish

SERVES 10 to 12

225 g	plain or strong flour	8 oz
2	eggs (size 3)	2
575 ml	milk	1 pt
	pinch of salt and pepper	
	oil	

1 Sieve the flour, salt and pepper together into a mixing bowl. Make a well in the centre. Add the eggs, half of the milk and whisk until the mixture is smooth and thick. Then whisk in the remaining milk to form a smooth thin batter. Strain into clean bowl.

2 Cover and allow to rest for about an hour.

3 Place a little oil in the baking tins (or tray), enough to cover the base of the tins to a depth of about 3 mm.

4 Put the greased tins in the oven at 200°C to become very hot (about 10 minutes). Take them out of the oven and fill to the top with batter. Return to the oven and bake until fully risen and brown: 25 to 30 minutes.

5 Turn the puddings upside down in their moulds (this removes the fat from the centres) and replace in the oven for a further 10 minutes.

6 When cooked, lift carefully out of the tin or moulds, allowing any fat to drain away. Serve at once.

Cheesy vegetable bake
by McDougalls (RHM Foods)

Key learning points
» prepare a basic batter
» prepare a baked batter dish suitable for vegetarians

SERVES 4

100 g	broccoli, florets	4 oz
100 g	courgettes, sliced	4 oz
150 g	cauliflower, florets	5 oz
75 g	cheese, grated	3 oz
5 ml	mustard powder	1 tsp

Batter

100 g	plain or strong white flour	4 oz
	pinch salt	
1	egg, size 4	1
275 ml	milk, or half-milk half-water	½ pt

1 Mix flour and salt. Make a well in the centre of the mixture. Drop in the egg and a little milk. Beat well and stir in the remaining milk.

2 Grease a 15 × 30 cm (6 × 12 inch) ovenproof dish.

3 Cook the broccoli, courgettes and cauliflower in simmering water for 3 to 4 minutes. Drain well, place in dish and sprinkle with cheese and mustard.

4 Pour batter over the vegetables and bake for 30 to 35 minutes at 220°C until well risen and golden.

To mix batters, make a well in the centre of the flour, then add the egg and some of the milk. How much milk is added will depend on the size of the bowl you are using. The idea is not to flood the whole of the surface of the flour.

Starting from the middle, gradually incorporate the flour into the liquid.

Lemon pancakes *Crêpes au citron*

Key learning points
» prepare a pancake batter
» shallow fry pancakes
» toss or turn pancakes

For alternative pancake fillings, any of the suggestions for vol-au-vents on page 230 are suitable.

For banana and cinnamon pancakes: combine whipped cream with a pinch of cinnamon. Fill pancakes with sliced bananas and the whipped cream mixture, and scatter with a little soft brown sugar.

SERVES 4

75 g	plain flour	3 oz
1	egg	1
225 ml	milk	8 fl oz
15 g	butter	½ oz
30 ml	oil for cooking	2 tbsp
50 g	caster sugar	2 oz
4	lemon segments	4
	pinch of salt	

1 Sieve together the flour and salt. Make a well in the centre. Add the egg and half the milk. Whisk to a smooth thick batter, starting from the centre and working outwards gradually incorporating all the flour. Whisk in the remaining milk to produce a thin batter. Strain into clean bowl.

2 Melt the butter and blend it in. Cover the mixture and put it aside in a cool place to rest for about 1 hour.

3 Heat the pancake pan and add a little oil. When hot, pour off the surplus oil, then pour in enough batter to cover the bottom of the pan, tilting the pan to ensure that the batter spreads evenly across it.

4 Cook the batter quickly until it turns golden brown. Toss the crêpe or turn it over with a palette knife and cook the other side.

5 Turn the crêpe out on to a warm plate, then cover with an upturned plate and keep hot in a warm oven or hot cupboard.

6 Repeat the procedure, piling the pancakes one on top of the other between the plates, until you have produced 12 small crêpes (3 per portion). The pancakes should not stick together, but if they start to do so, place a small square of greaseproof paper between each one.

7 Sprinkle each crêpe with caster sugar then fold in half and half again to form a triangular shape.

8 Place the crêpes on a hot serving dish, in one long row or 4 small rows, each slightly overlapping the next. Sprinkle with caster sugar and garnish with the lemon.

Learning from your mistakes

Pancakes stick to pan/griddle

1 The equipment was dirty: it should be thoroughly wiped with absorbent paper before the next pancake is cooked.

2 The equipment was cleaned incorrectly, e.g. washed in water. If this has happened, switch to another pan so that the one which sticks can be prepared properly again (see page 17).

3 Too much or too little oil was used in the pan.

4 The pancake mixture was too light. In this case the rest of the mixture can be improved by adding in a little more flour, either by blending it in with a liquidiser or by hand whisking (and then straining it before use to remove any lumps).

Tossing the pancake.

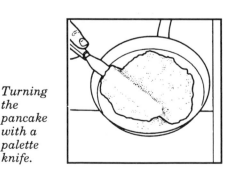

Turning the pancake with a palette knife.

Apple and raisin pancakes with rum butter sauce
by The Butter Council

Key learning points
» prepare a pancake batter
» shallow fry pancakes
» prepare rich filling and sauce

SERVES 4

100 g	plain flour	4 oz
	pinch of salt	
5 ml	finely grated lemon rind	1 tsp
1	egg	1
275 ml	milk	½ pt
75 g	butter	3 oz
225 g	cooking apples, peeled, cored and sliced	8 oz
25 g	raisins	1 oz
50 g	brown sugar	2 oz
15 ml	rum or brandy	1 tbsp
15 ml	lemon juice	1 tbsp

1 Sift the flour into a bowl, add the salt, lemon rind, egg and milk, and whisk together to make a smooth batter.

2 Using a tiny knob of butter for each, make 8 small pancakes and keep warm in a low oven (steps 3 to 6 as in lemon pancakes).

3 Cook the apples with the raisins in a little water until soft.

4 Melt the remaining butter and sugar together in a saucepan and stir well. Add the brandy and lemon juice.

5 Divide the apple mixture between the pancakes and roll up or fold into triangles. Place on warm serving dishes, pour over the sauce and serve.

Folded omelette
by The British Egg Information Service

Key learning point
» make a folded omelette

SERVES 1

3	eggs	3
15 ml	cold water	1 tbsp
	seasoning to taste	
15 g	butter or margarine	½ oz

1 Heat a 15 to 18 cm (6 to 7 inch) omelette pan gently. Break eggs into a bowl, add water, seasoning and beat lightly with a fork to break up whites and yolks.

2 Place fat in pan and turn up heat until the fat is sizzling but not brown. Pour in egg mixture.

3 With a fork or spatula, draw cooked egg from the edge of the pan inwards so that the liquid egg runs through to cook on pan base.

4 While the top is still runny, fold over a third of the omelette away from the pan handle. Add chosen filling.

5 Grip the handle of the pan underneath – with palm uppermost – and shake omelette to the edge of the pan away from handle.

6 Tip it over in three folds on to a warm serving plate. Serve immediately.

Fillings for a folded omelette

Cheese Scatter 25 g (1 oz) grated Cheddar or Cheshire cheese over the omelette just before folding.

Parmesan Mix 15 g (½ oz) grated Parmesan through the beaten egg, then proceed as recipe.

Ham Mix 50 g (2 oz) cooked ham (cut into small even-sized dice) through the beaten egg, then proceed as basic recipe.

Mushroom Shallow fry 25 g (1 oz) sliced mushroom in butter, mix through the beaten egg and proceed as basic recipe. Or cook the mushrooms in the pan, add the egg and continue cooking.

Peppers and onion Gently fry 25 g sliced red pepper and 25 g sliced onion in butter until softened. Add beaten egg with 1 tbsp of single cream, chopped chives, then proceed as basic recipe.

Flat omelette
by The British Egg Information Service

Key learning point
» make a flat omelette

Most vegetables can be used to add flavour and interest to a flat omelette. Here are a few suggestions:
- thinly sliced green and red peppers added with the onion
- 1 clove crushed garlic added to potato
- chopped tomato and cooked rice instead of potato
- finely diced cooked ham and good pinch chopped parsley (*Fermière omelette*)

SERVES 2

15 ml	olive or vegetable oil	1 tbsp
100 g	onion, finely chopped	4 oz
175 g	potato, cooked, diced	6 oz
4	eggs	4
20 ml	cold water	4 tsp
	seasoning to taste	

1 Heat oil in a 15 to 18 cm (6 to 7 inch) omelette pan. Add onion and cook slowly until soft.

2 Add diced potato and heat through.

3 Beat the eggs, water and seasoning together in a basin, with a fork.

4 When the onion mixture is hot, pour in the egg and cook, drawing egg from edge of pan inwards, so that the liquid egg runs through to cook on the pan base.

5 While the top is slightly runny, place pan under a hot grill until the top is just set. Do not fold the omelette, but slide it out flat.

Soufflé omelette (sweet with savoury variation)
by The British Egg Information Service

Key learning point
» make a soufflé omelette

Suggested fillings

Sweet: warmed jam, fruit purée, pie fillings or fresh fruits.

Savoury: substitute salt and pepper for the sugar when mixing eggs and use grated cheese, chopped cooked mushrooms or ham for fillings.

SERVES 2

2	eggs	2
10 ml	cold water	2 tsp
15 g	caster sugar	½ oz
15 g	butter or margarine	½ oz
	icing sugar to dust	

1 Put 15 to 18 cm (6 to 7 inch) omelette pan over low heat to get hot.

2 Separate eggs. Whisk yolks, water and caster sugar together until pale and creamy. Whisk egg whites until just stiff. Fold white into yolk mixture.

3 Melt fat in pan. Spread in egg mixture. Cook without moving until bottom is set and a pale golden brown.

4 Place omelette under hot grill until top is set or put in oven at 200°C (providing you are using an omelette pan with a heat-proof handle).

5 Place filling of your choice over half the omelette. Fold in half and slide on to a warm plate. Dust top with icing sugar. Serve at once.

Raspberry soufflé omelette
by The Butter Council

Key learning points
» make dessert soufflé omelette
» dust with icing sugar and sear with skewer to decorate

SERVES 1

100 g	frozen raspberries	4 oz
25 g	caster sugar	1 oz
10 ml	arrowroot or cornflour mixed with a little water	2 tsp
2	eggs, separated	2
15 g	butter, preferably unsalted	½ oz
	icing sugar, to serve	

1 Put the raspberries in a saucepan with half the sugar and two tablespoons of water. Heat very gently, then thicken with a little arrowroot or cornflour.

2 Whisk the egg whites until stiff, then fold in the beaten yolks and remaining caster sugar.

3 Heat the butter in an omelette pan, add the eggs and cook for about 2 minutes until the base is set.

4 Flash under a hot grill to cook the top.

5 Turn out on to a warm plate, fill with raspberries and fold over. Sift icing sugar over the top, and sear with a red hot skewer to form a criss-cross pattern. Serve immediately.

Eggs florentine

Key learning points
» poach eggs
» grill assembled dish to brown

SERVES 10

10	fresh eggs (size 1 or 2), poached in advance and chilled	10
1¼ kg	spinach	3 lb
50 g	margarine or butter	2 oz
850 ml	mornay sauce (page 143)	1½ pt
50 g	Parmesan cheese, grated	2 oz
	seasoning to taste	

1 Cook the spinach in a small quantity of boiling salted water (covered) for 3 to 5 minutes.

2 Cool the spinach under cold running water, drain thoroughly in a conical strainer or sieve. Squeeze dry and form into balls, one ball per portion.

3 Heat the margarine or butter in a sauteuse until it foams. Add the spinach and heat gently. Season to taste.

4 Meanwhile, heat the eggs in a saucepan of very hot (but not boiling) salted water for about 1 minute. Drain thoroughly.

5 Neatly arrange the hot spinach on the serving dishes. Place an egg on top. Coat with the hot mornay sauce, sprinkle with Parmesan and, if required, melted butter.

6 Put each dish under the grill until the surface of the sauce turns golden brown. Serve immediately.

Double bacon breakfast
by Pork and Bacon Promotion Council and others

Key learning point
» make a baked egg dish

SERVES 10

675 g	back bacon rashers	1½ lb
350 g	cooked back bacon (crisp) cut into strips	¾ lb
10	eggs	10
275 g	butter	10 oz
	seasoning to taste	
5	tomatoes	5

1 Beat eggs and season.

2 Place cooked bacon strips in well-greased dishes. Pour egg mixture over bacon, and bake for 15 minutes at 200°C.

3 Serve surrounded by the freshly grilled bacon rashers and tomatoes.

Shirred eggs Bercy style

Key learning point
» prepare baked egg dish

SERVES 6

6	eggs	6
15 g	butter	¾ oz
6	chipolata sausages, twisted in two (page 55) and grilled	6
150 ml	tomato sauce, hot (page 144)	5 fl oz
	seasoning to taste	

1 Smear the butter over the inside bases of 6 *sur le plat* dishes and season lightly.

2 Break an egg into each dish.

3 Place the egg dishes over a gentle heat (a solid top cooking surface is best) until the whites are lightly set.

4 Transfer to the centre shelf of a moderate oven, 170°C to 190°C, and cook until the whites are set, and the yolks soft (3 to 5 minutes) or hard (5 to 8 minutes), according to customer requirements.

5 Place one chipolata sausage on each dish, and coat with tomato sauce.

Carrot and coriander quiche
by Mary Gwynn in BBC Vegetarian Good Food

Key learning points
» prepare short pastry with wholemeal flour and oatmeal
» fill a flan with a vegetable and fromage frais mix, set with eggs
» make a dish suitable for vegetarians

As a variation, use parsley in place of coriander.

SERVES 6

150 g	wholemeal flour	5 oz
25 g	toasted fine oatmeal	1 oz
75 g	butter or polyunsaturated margarine	3 oz
4	eggs, beaten	4
275 g	fromage frais	10 oz
15 ml	olive oil	1 tbsp
1	small onion, chopped	1
450 g	carrot, grated	1 lb
60 ml	fresh coriander, chopped	4 tbsp
	seasoning to taste	

1 Mix the flour and oatmeal together. Rub in the butter until the mixture resembles fine breadcrumbs. Mix to a soft dough with 4 or 5 tbsp of cold water. Cover and chill for 15 minutes.

2 Roll out the pastry and use to line a 20 cm (8 inch) deep loose-bottomed flan tin. Prick the base and bake the pastry case blind for 10 minutes at 190°C.

3 Beat the eggs with the fromage frais. Heat the oil in a pan and cook the onion until softened. Stir in the grated carrot, coriander and seasoning. Spread over the pastry base and pour over the egg mixture.

4 Bake for about 40 minutes.

Egg custard sauce *Crème anglaise*

Key learning points
» make a thin egg custard suitable for use in trifles, and to accompany various desserts
» thicken custard using cornflour (or potato flour)

MAKES 850 ml (1½ pt)

575 ml	milk	1 pt
4	egg yolks	4
25 g	caster sugar	1 oz
5 ml	cornflour	1 tsp
	few drops vanilla essence	

1 Heat the milk until it is just beginning to form a skin.

2 Put the egg yolks, sugar, cornflour and vanilla essence in a basin, beat thoroughly. Pour a little hot milk into this, beat well, then add a little more hot milk, continuing to beat.

3 Pour this mixture into the saucepan containing the remainder of the milk. Stir continuously over a very gentle heat until the custard is thick enough to coat the back of the spoon. On no account let it boil, or it will curdle.

4 Serve hot. Alternatively, chill until required.

Baked egg custard
by The British Egg Information Service

Key learning point
» bake rich egg custard

SERVES 4

575 ml	milk, warmed until it 'steams'	1 pt
3	eggs, beaten together	3
25 g	caster sugar	1 oz
	few drops vanilla essence and/or a little freshly grated nutmeg	

1 Whisk the eggs and sugar lightly in a bowl. Gradually stir in the hot milk.

2 Pour the mixture through a conical strainer into a 900 ml (1½ pint) very lightly buttered ovenproof dish. Add the essence or sprinkle on the nutmeg.

3 Stand the dish in a roasting tin in the oven, filled with warm water to come half-way up the sides of the dish. Like the type of bain-marie used on top of the stove, and in hot cupboards, the water gives a gentler heating.

4 Bake at 160°C for about 45 to 50 minutes, or until just set and firm to the touch. Serve hot or cold.

Pastry cream *Crème pâtissière*
by McDougalls (RHM Foods)

Key learning points
» prepare thickened egg custard suitable for base of fruit flans and tartlets

A variation on this recipe uses (for 275 ml/ ½ pt milk and the given amount of sugar) 1½ egg yolks and 25 g/1 oz plain flour.

MAKES 425 ml (¾ pt)

1	egg, size 4, separated	1
1	egg yolk	1
50 g	caster sugar	2 oz
30 ml	plain flour	2 tbsp
30 ml	cornflour	2 tbsp
275 ml	milk	½ pt
	vanilla essence	

1 Blend the egg yolks and sugar until thick and creamy.

2 Beat in the flour, cornflour and a little cold milk to make a smooth paste.

3 Heat the remaining milk in a saucepan until almost boiling, and slowly pour on to the egg mixture, stirring continuously.

4 Rinse out the saucepan with cold water (this stops burning of any milk left on the side of the pan). Return the mixture to it, and stir over a low heat until simmering. Remove from heat.

5 Beat the egg white until stiff and fold into mixture. Add vanilla essence to taste.

6 Allow to cool before using.

Crème caramel

Key learning points
» make caramel
» bake rich egg custard

SERVES 20

Caramel

450 g	granulated sugar	1 lb
200 ml	cold water	7 fl oz
150 ml	hot water	5 fl oz

Egg custard

1½ litre	milk	2½ pt
500 ml	eggs (about 10 or 11)	17½ fl oz
150 g	caster sugar	5 oz
5 ml	vanilla essence	1 tsp

1 Place the sugar and cold water into a sugar boiling pan.

2 Bring to the boil and continue boiling until golden brown. This will take about 8 minutes and the syrup will suddenly start changing colour, so be careful not to let it burn. During cooking, remove any splashes from the sides of the pan with a clean brush dipped in water.

3 Remove the pan from the heat and dip into cold water for 5 seconds – this will stop further cooking.

4 Carefully add the hot water and gently shake the pan so that the water combines with the caramel. The water will cause the caramel to bubble violently so keep your wrists and arms well covered.

5 Pour the hot caramel into 20 dariole moulds and allow to cool and set.

Egg custard

1 Warm the milk in a saucepan.

2 Whisk together the eggs, sugar and vanilla essence. Pour the milk on the egg mixture, whisk together.

3 Place the moulds into a deep oven tray. Strain the custard, then pour it into the moulds. Add enough cold water to half fill the tray.

4 Place in the oven at 160°C and cook until set, which will take 1 to 1½ hours. Alternatively, cook in a bain-marie with hot water for 45 minutes.

5 Remove the moulds from the tray, allow to cool, then place in a refrigerator to chill.

6 To serve: loosen the edges of the custard by gently pressing around the rim of the mould with the fingers and lightly shake the mould to free the custard at the sides. Turn out on to the cold serving dish. Pour over any caramel remaining in the moulds.

Vanilla ice cream (French style)

Key learning points

» prepare ice cream using egg custard

» use a digital thermometer to check temperature

» use an ice-cream making machine

This recipe is demonstrated by Danny Stevenson in the HCTC video *Foodcraft 11: Desserts*.

MAKES 1¼ litres (2½ pt)

715 ml	milk	1¼ pt
4	egg yolks (from size 3 eggs)	4
125 g	caster sugar	5 oz
5 ml	vanilla essence	1 tsp
275 ml	cream	½ pt

1 Lightly whisk together the egg yolks and sugar, using a mixing bowl large enough to hold the milk (step 2).

2 Place the milk in a saucepan, heat until it is very hot, but not boiling, then pour it on to the yolks and sugar, whisking the mixture as you do so.

3 Transfer the mixture to a clean pan and place over a low heat. Stir the mixture constantly until it reaches a temperature of 80°C. Hold it at this temperature for a minimum of 15 seconds. The mixture must not boil or overcook, otherwise it will curdle (this stage happens very soon after it has thickened).

4 Place the pan in a cool place or in a sink partly filled with cold water. The egg custard should be cooled as quickly as possible and in all events the freezing stage (step 6) should be completed within 90 minutes of the pan being removed from the heat.

5 Mix in the vanilla essence and cream.

6 Pour the mixture into an ice-cream making machine and freeze. During this stage of freezing the ice-cream mixture will trap air and expand in volume by between 50 and 75%. This is known as *overrun*.

7 Once it is ready, the ice cream should be removed, placed in a container which can be sealed tightly and stored in an ice-cream conservator or freezer.

Autumn fruit trifle
by Peter Gladwin, Party Ingredients, Nine Elms, London

Key learning points

» prepare modern variation on classical dish

» combine seasonal fruits for contrast of colours and flavours.

As an alternative to Beaumes-de-Venise use a sweet dessert wine, or sherry.

The making of this dish is demonstrated by Peter Gladwin in the HCTC video *Foodcraft 11: Desserts*.

SERVES 6

450 g	sponge cake (e.g. Génoise)	1 lb
225 g	raspberry jam	8 oz
275 ml	double cream	½ pt
125 ml	Muscat-de-Beaumes-de-Venise	4 fl oz
675 g	autumn fruits: plums (at least 3), blackberries, raspberries, blueberries, grapes	1½ lb
100 g	sugar	4 oz
575 ml	fresh egg custard	1 pt

1 Select an attractive glass bowl. Place a small piece of the sponge in the base (as a support for the plum decoration in step 2).

2 Cut around the plums to form discs. Put aside the ends. Place the best pieces in fairly widely spaced rows up the sides of the serving dish.

3 Roughly chop the remainder of the plums, and remove the stones. Place them in a saucepan with a little water and the sugar. Bring to the boil, stirring continuously. Turn the heat off, then gently stir in the blueberries and raspberries (to cook in the residual heat).

4 Line the sides of the bowl (between the rows of plum discs) with slices of sponge (spread with jam on the side that faces into the centre of the bowl). Carefully lift these aside, and trickle custard down the side of the dish, between the sponge and the glass surface. Try to avoid the custard running in front of the plum discs.

5 Pour the Beaumes-de-Venise wine over the sponge.

6 Assemble the centre of trifle with alternating layers of sponge (spread with jam), stewed fruit and custard, ending up with a layer of custard.

7 Whip the cream. Spread some of it over the surface of the trifle. Then pipe parallel rows across the surface.

8 Slice the bottom off the grapes, and cut carefully up from this to remove the pips.

9 Fill the space between the rows of cream with blackberries and grapes (alternating).

RANGE CHECKLIST

LEVEL 1

1D3.1 Prepare and cook batter dishes

prepare preprepared or convenience batter of one of these types

☐ pancake mixtures

☐ Yorkshire pudding mixtures

☐ coating mixtures

and cook by 2 of these methods

☐ shallow frying

☐ deep frying

☐ roasting

- - - - - - - - - - - - - - - - - -

1D3.2 Prepare and cook egg dishes

using fresh hens' eggs or liquid pasteurised eggs, prepare and cook 4 of these

☐ scrambled eggs

☐ omelette

☐ poached eggs

☐ fried eggs

☐ hard boiled eggs

LEVEL 2

2D3.1 Prepare and cook egg custard based desserts

using fresh hens' eggs or liquid pasteurised eggs, prepare and cook 3 of these desserts

☐ trifle

☐ baked egg custard desserts

☐ crème caramel

☐ pâtissière cream

Introduction

The simplest kind of bread, flat bread, is just a baked dough of flour and water. This is sometimes called unleavened bread, meaning that it has not risen. Leavened or raised breads are the kind that most people are familiar with, and enjoy regularly. They have had yeast and usually some salt added to the dough to give lightness and flavour.

There are hundreds, perhaps even thousands, of variations on the basic recipe: milk can be used instead of water, fat can be added, or sugar, spices, currants, eggs or even yogurt. These involve a fairly lengthy process before baking can begin, of mixing, fermenting (when the yeast does its work by producing carbon dioxide), knocking back and further proving. To cut down this time, most of the bread sold in shops and supermarkets has been made using special mixing equipment and flour improvers. These help the dough to rise, producing a lighter, softer loaf. The most widely used improver is ascorbic acid (vitamin C).

For any type of bread, especially those using yeast, the final texture is extremely important. For the yeast to develop the best texture, great care has to be taken that the right ingredients are combined, and treated in the right way.

The main aims, as far as the yeast is concerned, are to make sure that it ferments without producing a sour taste or an unpleasant smell and that the gas pockets produced by the yeast are the same fairly small size, with the best chance of staying trapped in the dough, and evenly distributed through it.

Some breads

In the richer countries of the world there is now a vast range of foods that can broadly be described as bread:

- white, brown and wholemeal, black rye, malt, sour dough, soda and softgrain
- traditional and modern loaf shapes such as: sliced, split tin, plait, bloomer, cob, farmhouse, coburg, Vienna, Danish
- rolls in all shapes, sizes and recipes: crumpets, muffins, fruit loaf, buns, pykelets
- continental and imported products, such as: French baguettes, croissants, brioches, Dutch farm bread, Greek daktyla and pitta breads, Eastern European cholla (or challa) and bagels, American soft grain hoagies, Arabic bread and Westphalian wheat and rye farmbread.

Just some of the many types of bread now available.

Contents guide

Units and elements covered in this section

1D7 Prepare and cook dough products `LEVEL 1`
- 1D7.1 Prepare dough products for cooking
- 1D7.2 Cook dough products

2D7 Prepare and cook dough products `LEVEL 2`
- 2D7.1 Prepare dough products for cooking
- 2D7.2 Cook dough products

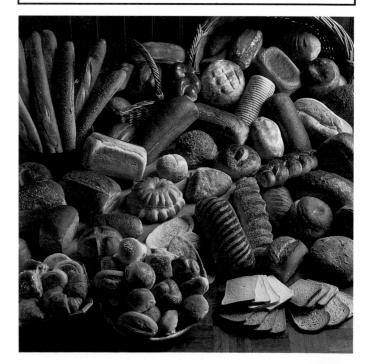

Quality points

Using convenience or prepierared products

– packaging in good condition

– correctly labelled

– not beyond use-by or best-before date

Check the package instructions: some products can be baked straight from the freezer, others require defrosting, and others proving. Generally:

• frozen unbaked doughs, rolls or buns should be put in the refrigerator to defrost over several hours, then left in a warm room or proving oven

• frozen baked goods should be put in a warm room to defrost quickly.

Yeast

There are many different types of yeast, from brewer's yeast, which is used in making beer, to the sort of wild yeast that you can see as a dull, pale mauve powder on black grapes. The type of yeast that is used in baking is available in two main forms: compressed and dried. Fast action easy-blend yeasts are also available. These are specially formulated so that doughs made from them only need to rise once.

Compressed (or fresh) yeast

– almost odourless (hint of sweet fruitiness)

– firm, plastic texture

– creamy colour

– dissolves easily in water, without forming lumps

A sour, unpleasant smell, sticky texture and browning on the surface are all signs that the yeast is dying or dead.

The yeast will die at temperatures above 50°C. Salt also destroys yeast, and should never be in direct contact with it.

The ideal storage temperature for yeast is between 4°C and 6°C. It should be kept in its original packaging, or wrapped in kitchen foil, coloured film or waxed paper to protect it from the light. Under these conditions it will keep for some weeks, but it is better to order smaller quantities, more often, so that long storage is unnecessary.

Compressed yeast can be frozen, and will keep quite well for several months. Freeze in small quantities, for example, enough for one batch of baking. Defrost for 12 hours in a refrigerator.

Dried yeast

This will keep for several months if stored in a moisture-free sealed container, in a cool, dry place. Before use, dissolve in warm water, following carefully the instructions on the packet. It is particularly important to get the temperature of the water right. If it is too high or too low, the yeast is likely to lose most of its fermenting power.

NUTRITION

by the Flour Advisory Bureau

Wheat grain is made up of four components. The starchy *endosperm* makes up the largest part (82%) and contains about 10% protein. The outer *bran* layers (8%) are the main source of fibre, and the intermediate layer called *aleurone* (7%) is rich in protein, minerals and vitamins. The remainder is the *wheatgerm* (3%) which contains protein, oil and vitamins.

Wholegrain or wholewheat flour – as the name suggests – contains 100% of the cleaned wheat grain. Brown flour contains about 85% of the wheat grain, while white flour contains about 75%.

In white flour, most of the bran and wheatgerm is removed during the refining process. This leaves the starchy endosperm, but still as much fibre – 3.4% – as raw white cabbage on a weight-for-weight basis.

The softened grains added to white flour to make soft-grain white bread increase the fibre content by 30%. Brown flour contains 6.8% and wholemeal flour 9.6% – that's more than stewed prunes or baked beans.

Because much of the vitamin and mineral content of the flour is contained in the bran and wheatgerm, white flours are fortified with iron and B vitamins.

A prescribed level of calcium is also added to all flour with the exception of self-raising and wholemeal.

Types of flour

A wide variety of white and brown flours is available. Recent and popular introductions include:

- *soft grain* – white bread flours with added softened kibbled grains, e.g. Champion, Mighty White
- traditional *wheatgerm* – with extra wheat germ added, e.g. Hovis, Vitbe, Turog
- *malted wheatgrain* – brown flour with added malted grains, e.g. Granary, Harvester, Countryman
- *bran enriched* – brown or wholemeal flour with added bran, e.g. HiBran, Hifibre Wholemeal
- *organic* – milled from a wheat grown and processed naturally without the use of chemicals.

Today, most flour is produced by roller milling. After thorough cleaning, the wheat grains pass through a succession of rollers and sieves to be separated into their various components. These are then kept apart, for the production of white flour, or blended back together to produce wholemeal and brown flours.

White flour comes in various strengths according to how much protein the flour contains and therefore how much gluten it will make (see also page 239).

Strong or *hard flours* are suitable for bread because they develop a lot of gluten. Normally 11 to 12% of their weight is protein, and up to 15% for North American wheat. Strong white flour is creamy white, feels slightly coarse when rubbed between the fingers and if squeezed into a lump will quickly fall apart again.

Stoneground bread is made by the traditional process. The grain is fed between two millstones, the top one revolving, crushing the grain and pushing it outwards. As it passes across the stone, the grain gets more and more finely ground, eventually to become flour.

Other cereals such as oats, barley, maize and rye can be ground to produce flour (see page 168). They are usually used in combination with wheat flour to introduce their own distinctive flavours.

Storing flour

Plain flour has a shelf-life of 4 to 6 months, wholemeal and brown flours of 2 to 3 months.

1 Keep flour in a cool, dry room.
2 Store away from the floor on shelves, or in special flour bins (these will usually be on wheels so they can be moved easily to clean).
3 Once a packet or bag has been opened, transfer the contents to a bin, preferably with moulded corners for easy cleaning. The container must be cleaned with detergent, rinsed and allowed to air dry thoroughly before filling with a new batch of flour.
4 Label bins to indicate the type of flour they contain, and the date by which it must be used (from the best-before date printed on the original packaging).

ACTION

Identify the name of each of the various breads shown in the illustration, and write them down in the space provided.

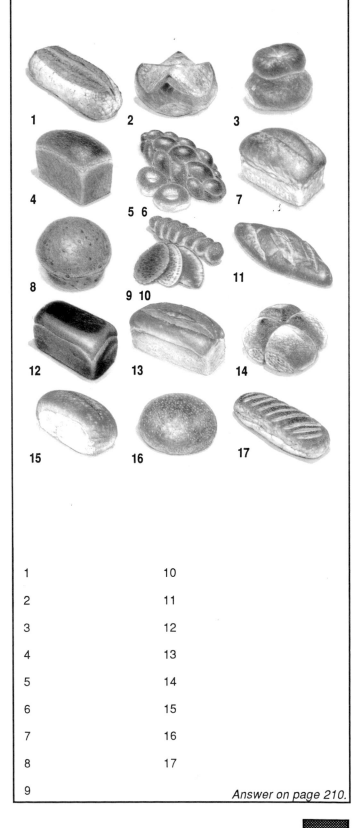

1	10
2	11
3	12
4	13
5	14
6	15
7	16
8	17
9	

Answer on page 210.

Preparing yeast dough   `LEVEL 2`

The preparation and cooking of yeast doughs breaks down into distinct steps or stages. With some products, particularly those which use fast-action yeast, only one mixing stage and only one proving stage are necessary.

1 Initial mixing

After the yeast, liquid and flour have been quickly blended together, the dough is mixed vigorously, often with the hands. This is called *kneading* and is continued until the dough has a shiny surface and is no longer sticky to the touch.

What is happening is that the gas pockets (that started forming as soon as the first mixture was made) are being squeezed and split up into more, smaller pockets, and the gluten is being developed.

Any fats or sugar included in the mixture will slow down gluten development, and the dough will have to be kneaded longer than would otherwise be necessary.

If you have access to a mixer with a dough hook, this will take the hard work out of this stage. Follow workplace instructions – working with a small amount of dough is much more successful than attempting a large batch all at once.

2 Fermentation (or initial proving)

For this stage, the dough is set aside (covered) to ferment. The recipe will indicate what temperature the dough needs to be at so that the yeast will ferment properly and continue to produce gases. During this stage, the gas pockets will stretch the dough to its limit – usually to double its size.

3 Knocking back (or kneading)

At the end of the fermentation stage, the dough is knocked back to its original size.

This divides the gas pockets once again, which improves the texture as well as taking the strain off the dough, and allows the dough to cool down (heat is produced by fermentation).

4 Weighing (or scaling) and dividing

Next, the dough is placed on a baking sheet or in a baking tin. For rolls, buns or pizzas, or for large mixes making several loaves, the dough has to be divided up – all but the most experienced bakers do this by weighing each portion.

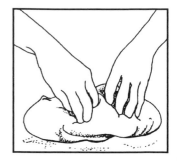

Kneading – work the dough by folding it with the palms of your hands.

Keep folding and pushing down to get some air in the dough, and to develop the gluten to give it elasticity.

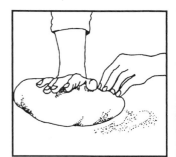

The dough should be divided by weight. Don't risk doing this by eye, because, as the dough is expanding all the time, it is difficult to judge. Check the accuracy of scales regularly – even a small discrepancy in the ingredients can spoil the end result.

5 Proving

The last fermentation stage before baking is called proving. It allows the yeast to produce gas, enlarging the many pockets that have now been created in the dough. These will expand during baking to leave a closely knit structure of holes in the cooked product. During proving the dough should double in size.

Some other points to remember when preparing doughs

1 The temperature of the liquid in the dough is very important – too hot or too cold and the yeast will not work. To obtain a hand-hot temperature, mix together 275 ml (½ pint) boiling water with 575 ml (1 pint) cold, and measure the recipe water from this mixture.

2 Salt plays three important roles in yeast doughs, besides adding flavour. It strengthens the gluten, helps colour the crust, and slows down the staling process once the product is cooked. However it does slow down the action of the yeast, so too much salt may mean that the dough does not rise properly. If you are concerned about using salt on health grounds, use low sodium salt instead.

3 Kneading should be done in a warm place, free from draughts.

4 While proving, the surface of the dough should be covered with oiled polythene to keep it moist, and to prevent a skin forming. Covering the dough also protects it from dust (and that includes bacteria).

5 To test whether the dough has expanded to its fullest extent, press it: it should not spring back.

6 If the bread tins are cold, warm them slightly before putting the dough in.

7 Always brush tins with white cooking fat so that bread won't stick.

ACTION

The various items of machinery used in the mixing and shaping of dough products are potentially dangerous. Make a list below of some of the accidents which might happen from using these machines without proper care.

Some of the other terms you might come across in baking breads

Bulk fermented dough – another term for the dough-making process described on these pages.

No-time dough – when the fermentation process is speeded up by the addition of improvers (see page 203), and the dough is given a longer, more vigorous mixing by machine.

Ferment and dough – used less often now that high activity yeasts and improvers are available. The process is used for doughs which contain quite a lot of fat and sugar. In the first stage, the yeast is blended to a thin batter and fermented with about 20% of the recipe's flour and all of the water. Once this has *dropped back* (the ferment rises so much that it can no longer support its own bulk and drops back), it is blended with the other recipe ingredients to form a dough.

Retardation – stopping or arresting the fermentation process part-way through by chilling the dough. Final proving can then take place as convenient, so ensuring a fresher product.

Dough enrichment – adding fat, milk or egg yolk to increase the food value, add to the flavour, and produce a softer product which lasts longer before going stale.

HYGIENE

Keep your hands scrupulously clean when hand-mixing dough. The stickiness of the dough will draw out any dirt left under your fingernails, or engrained on your skin.

Wash bread-making equipment such as scales, mixing bowls, dough hooks, sieves, scrapers and work surfaces, after every use.

The product will reach a sufficiently high temperature during baking to kill most harmful bacteria, but it would be unwise to rely on this. An Environmental Health Officer (EHO) would certainly not accept such an excuse for poor hygiene practices, and is likely to issue a warning, or for serious offences a notice of improvement (see page 10).

Baking yeast doughs `LEVELS 1 + 2`

The recipe should give an exact oven temperature, but as a general rule it should be set between 200°C and 245°C for ordinary doughs and 175°C to 195°C for sweetened doughs (this lower temperature prevents the surface browning before the inside has set).

How long baking takes depends on the ingredients used and the size of the product.

During baking the pockets of gas created by the yeast during proving expand as they heat up, and the yeast has a final burst of activity (sometimes called *oven spring*). This is why the last stage of knocking back (see step 3 on page 206) is important in recipes using compressed yeast – if the dough has been left stretched as far as it would go, it might burst at this stage.

Once the centre of the dough has reached about 60°C, the yeast is killed, the starch in the flour begins to gelatinise (how much will depend on the water content) and the gluten proteins coagulate. Both of these actions firm up the structure of the dough and the final stage then occurs: surface browning and crust formation.

Breads are often sprayed with steam during the first 10 minutes or so of baking to produce a hard, glossy brown crust. Glazing will also help the surface to brown.

Points to remember when baking doughs

1 If you are using a conventional oven, the heat may vary by as much as 20°C from shelf to shelf. With such equipment the best position is centre for bread loaves, and just above centre for rolls.

2 For a *soft* crust, dust the dough with flour before baking. Wrap in a cloth when baked. For a *crisp* crust, brush with milk. Alternatively, use salted water (in the proportions 2 teaspoons salt to 2 tablespoons water). For a *golden crust*, brush with egg beaten with a little milk. Brushing with warmed honey or a sugar syrup will give a sticky finish. For the sugar syrup the proportions are: 2 tablespoons of sugar to the same amount of water.

3 Allow room for the dough to expand in the oven, by not positioning directly under another shelf.

4 When a golden brown crust has formed it usually means that the bread is cooked. Loaves and rolls should sound hollow when tapped: if they sound dense and feel heavy, it means that the inside is uncooked.

Cooling

After baking, yeast products should be removed from the baking containers as soon as possible and allowed to cool on racks, with plenty of space around them so that air can circulate.

When bread leaves the oven its surface is very dry and hot – over 200°C – while the interior is moist and only about 93°C.

As the bread cools the moisture works its way out and the temperature evens out. Although the starch solidifies as the temperature goes down, it still lets air and gases through it. This is just as well because the gas left in pockets starts to get smaller and air has to get in to fill the holes – otherwise the bread would collapse.

CHEF'S TIPS

There are many ways of adding interest, variety and extra fibre and vitamins to bread and rolls. After glazing and before baking, lightly sprinkle the surface with one of the following:

- poppy, caraway, celery or fennel seeds
- sesame seeds – a favourite on the soft rolls used with hamburgers
- cracked wheat, barley or wheat flakes, wheat germ, oatmeal or crushed cornflakes.

The tops of white bread loaves can be cut decoratively. Using a very sharp knife, slash the surface of the dough just before proving.

Wholemeal breads should not be slashed. The dough is too fragile and would collapse.

Developing a crust

Most types of bread have to be helped if a hard crust is wanted. Because bread does not contain very much liquid, the starch in the flour cannot absorb the amount of moisture it needs to gelatinise completely (see page 245). To solve this problem, the air in the oven is made moist – by placing a pan of hot water at the bottom of the oven, or injecting steam into the oven, or lightly spraying the surface of the bread with water during the first stage of cooking. As a result, a thin layer of completely gelatinised starch forms on the surface, and then dries out to become brown and crusty.

Kitchens in which dough products are prepared in large quantities on a regular basis will usually have a dedicated dough mixer of the type shown here.

Some baking disasters! Texture too coarse and open for the type of bread (left), *too dense* (centre), *uneven with large holes* (right). *Crust under-developed* (back).

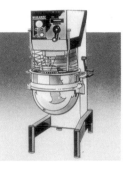

In the smaller operation, a mixer which can make fillings and toppings as well as mixing dough offers greater flexibility.

The shelves in this large rack oven rotate during cooking to provide an even heat.

Specialist ovens like this one (above) are in fact made up of a number of separate ovens stacked one on top of the other. Each oven has its own temperature control and usually a timer. As each oven is quite small from top to bottom, there is very little disturbance of the hot air each time the door is opened or shut.

A proving oven (right) allows the fermentation stage of yeast products to be accurately controlled. The dough is protected from draughts, the oven can be set at exactly the right temperature and humidity, and there is usually a timer.

Learning from your mistakes

Texture coarse and open
- too much yeast
- too little salt
- dough undermixed
- proving time too long

Texture too dense
- wrong flour used
- too much salt
- too little yeast, or yeast killed by too much heat
- dough undermixed
- proving occurred at too low a temperature or for too short a time
- egg or fat has curdled
- oven too hot
- oven conditions too dry

Texture uneven with large holes
- wrong flour used
- too little salt
- dough undermixed
- proving time too long
- baking container too large
- oven temperature too low

Crust too thick
- too little sugar
- oven too hot
- oven conditions too moist

Crust underdeveloped
- oven temperature too low
- oven conditions too dry

Crust cracked
- too little sugar
- dough allowed to dry out while rising
- baking container too small
- oven too hot

Traditional bread and rolls
by McDougalls (RHM Foods)

Key learning points
» make traditional bread products using flour of your choice
» use fast action dried yeast

MAKES 2 × ½ kg (1 lb) loaves or 16 to 20 rolls

675 g	flour: strong white or plain 100% wholemeal	1½ lb
10 ml	salt	2 tsp
25 g	lard or vegetable fat	1 oz
1	sachet fast action dried yeast	1
425 ml	warm water	¾ pt

1 Mix together the flour and salt, rub in fat, then stir in dried yeast.

2 Add the water and mix to a dough.

3 Turn out on to a lightly floured surface and knead for 10 minutes.

4 Divide and shape the dough, as required, and place in greased tins.

5 Cover with oiled polythene and leave in a warm place until doubled in size.

6 Uncover and bake in an oven preheated to 230°C: ½ kg (1 lb) loaves approximately 25 minutes, 1 kg (2 lb) loaf approximately 35 minutes, rolls approximately 15 minutes.

Granary muffins
by The Butter Council

Key learning point
» make variation on basic dough, with butter and eggs

MAKES 8 to 10

450 g	brown malted flour	1 lb
5 ml	salt	1 tsp
1	sachet fast action dried yeast	1
40 g	butter, melted	1½ oz
1	egg, size 3, beaten	1
275 ml	milk, warmed	½ pt

1 Mix the flour, salt and yeast in a large bowl. Add butter, egg and milk, and mix to a dough.

2 Turn on to a floured board and knead for 5 minutes or until smooth and elastic.

3 Return to mixing bowl, cover loosely with oiled polythene and allow to rest in a warm place for 10 minutes. Roll out to 1 cm (½ inch) thickness, cut into 8 cm (4 inch) rounds and place on a lightly greased baking sheet. Cover loosely with polythene and leave in a warm place for about 30 minutes or until doubled in size.

4 Bake in a preheated oven at 220°C for 15 minutes until golden. Serve warm, split and buttered, or split, toasted and buttered.

Garlic and herb bread
by McDougalls (RHM Foods)

Key learning points
» make speciality bread
» plait bread dough

The photograph on page 103 shows plaited fillets of fish – the technique is the same for dough.

MAKES 10 slices

450 g	strong white flour	1 lb
10 ml	salt	2 tsp
15 g	lard	½ oz
10 ml	mixed dried herbs	2 tsp
1	sachet fast action dried yeast	1
2	cloves garlic, crushed and peeled	2
275 ml	hand hot water	½ pt
	beaten egg to glaze	
	poppy seeds	

1 Grease baking sheet. Have ready a sheet of lightly oiled polythene.

2 Mix flour and salt, rub in fat, and stir in herbs, dried yeast and garlic. Add water and mix well. Turn on to a floured board and knead for 10 minutes until smooth.

3 Divide the dough into 3 pieces. Form each into a sausage shape, pinch ends together and form into a plait. Place on a greased baking tray, cover with oiled polythene and leave in a warm place until doubled in size.

4 Glaze with beaten egg, sprinkle with poppy seeds and bake for about 30 minutes at 200°C.

CHEF'S TIPS

The *fast action yeast* specified in many of these recipes has been specially developed to reduce the amount of time and effort required to produce a good textured product:

• dough made with it only needs to rise once
• it does not need to be diluted in water before mixing with the flour.

If you are using normal compressed yeast, the recipe should be adjusted:

1 Allow 15 g (½ oz) fresh yeast for quantities up to 450 g (1 lb), and 25 g (1 oz) for quantities up to 1½ kg (3 lb).

2 Blend the fresh yeast into the warm liquid from the recipe and leave to stand until the surface froths, about 10 minutes.

3 Make up dough as normal, knead well, cover lightly with oiled polythene and leave in a warm place to double in size.

4 Knead again, shape as required, cover, allow to rise again, and cook as for recipe.

For *dried yeasts,* follow instructions on packet for rehydrating. Doughs made with dried yeast must be kneaded and left to rise twice.

ANSWER ✓✓✓

ACTION page 205.

1) Danish, 2) Coburg, 3) Cottage, 4) Tin loaf, 5) Bagels (with holes) and 6) Cholla, 7) Farmhouse, 8) Pan cob, 9) Pittas (in front) and 10) Daktyla, 11) Vienna, 12) Sandwich loaf, 13) Split tin, 14) Soda bread, 15) Batch, 16) Cob, 17) Bloomer.

Pitta bread
by McDougalls (RHM Foods)

Key learning point
» prepare speciality bread using flour of your choice

MAKES 8 to 10

450 g	flour: strong white, plain brown or plain 100% wholemeal	1 lb
5 ml	salt	1 tsp
1	sachet fast action dried yeast	1
300 ml	warm water	½ pt

1 Mix the flour and salt, stir in the yeast.

2 Add water and mix to a dough. Knead for 10 minutes or until smooth.

3 Divide dough into 8 to 10 pieces. Roll each piece into an oval shape and place on a greased baking tray.

4 Brush with oil or water and place under a hot grill for 2 minutes, or until golden, on both sides.

Garlic bread
by McDougalls Catering Foods

Key learning point
» make speciality bread using convenience pizza mix

SERVES 10

450 g	pizza base mix	1 lb
350 ml	water	12 fl oz
6	cloves garlic, crushed and peeled	6
50 g	butter, melted	2 oz
25 g	fresh parsley, chopped	1 oz

1 Make up the pizza mix as directed on the packet. Add half the garlic.

2 Divide into 10 dough balls. Roll into shapes as for pitta bread and score the top with a knife.

3 Place on a baking sheet and bake at 200°C for 6 to 10 minutes.

4 Add remaining garlic and parsley to melted butter, and brush over hot garlic bread. Serve immediately.

Orange sunbread

Key learning points
» use fresh or dried yeast
» make yeast batter and combine with dough
» make decorative shape

SERVES 6 to 8

Yeast batter

15 g (½ oz) fresh yeast *or* 10 ml (2 tsp) dried yeast

5 ml	sugar	1 tsp
225 ml	milk, warmed	8 fl oz
100 g	strong white flour	4 oz

Dough

350 g	strong white flour	12 oz
50 g	butter	2 oz
5 ml	salt	1 tsp
50 g	currants	2 oz
1	grated rind and juice of orange	1
1	egg, beaten	1
1	extra beaten egg for glazing	1

Icing

100 g	icing sugar, sieved	4 oz
1	orange, grated rind and juice	1
25 g	currants	1 oz

1 For the batter: stir fresh or dried yeast and sugar into milk. If using dried yeast, leave to stand for 5 minutes. Mix in flour and leave until frothy for about 20 minutes.

2 For the dough: rub butter into the flour. Stir in salt, currants and orange rind.

3 Combine the batter and dough mixtures with the beaten egg and orange juice. Mix to a soft dough.

4 Turn out on to floured surface and knead dough with extra flour for about 10 minutes until smooth, soft and no longer sticky.

5 Leave to rise in an oiled polythene bag until it doubles in size.

6 When risen, remove from bag and knead for 5 minutes. Place on baking tray and:

a) roll into a 25 cm (10 inch) round approximately 2.5 cm (1 inch) thick

b) cut through dough 2.5 cm (1 inch) from centre (of the sun) to the outside edge, leaving 5 cm (2 inch) between cuts (the sun rays)

c) twist each portion to the right twice

d) fit a 23 cm (9 inch) plain flan ring over the dough, adjusting the dough to fit the ring (so the sun rays are curved)

e) if making 2 small sunbreads, cut dough in half and follow above method using 2 × 18 cm (7 inch) flan rings.

7 Brush with beaten egg to glaze, and leave to rise in a warm place for about 20 minutes or until double in size. Bake at 220°C for 20 to 30 minutes for small sunbreads, 30 to 40 minutes for the large sunbread, until golden brown and the base sounds hollow when tapped. Leave to cool.

8 Mix icing sugar, orange rind and juice together. Pour over top of sunbread allowing icing to trickle down the sides. Sprinkle with currants.

Tandoori roti
by Sainath Rao

Key learning point
» make an unleavened bread using a tandoor oven

Roti is the Indian word for bread. See page 68 for more details of tandoori cooking.

MAKES 8

225 g	wholewheat flour	8 oz
5 ml	salt	1 tsp
50 g	butter	2 oz
	warm water	

1 Add all the ingredients and sufficient water to make a pliable dough. Keep aside in a warm place for at least 2 hours.

2 Knead dough well again, divide into 8 balls and press each ball into a circle with the palm of your hand.

3 Using the special pad, press each circle of dough on to the inner wall of the tandoor and cook until done (a few minutes).

Nan bread
by Sainath Rao

Key learning point
» make a leavened bread using a tandoor oven

Nan or *naan* is the general term for long, flat, roughly oval pieces of slightly leavened dough, baked in a tandoor oven – see page 68.

SERVES 4

550 g	plain flour	20 oz
5 ml	baking powder	1 tsp
10 ml	salt	2 tsp
45 ml	oil	3 tbsp
150 ml	water	5 fl oz
125 ml	milk	4 fl oz

1 Mix all ingredients together in a bowl and knead until a soft dough is formed.

2 Cover with a wet cloth. Leave for 12 hours in a warm place.

3 The next day divide the dough into 8 equal portions. Roll each portion into a ball and flatten it on a table top into a circle, keeping it as even as possible.

4 Either place each circle of dough on the palm of your hand and quickly press against the inside of the tandoor (near the top), or use the special pad.

5 Cook for a few minutes until done, and remove using the two skewers provided with tandoors.

Oaten bread and rolls
by Mornflake Oats

Key learning points
» use dried yeast
» make a dough with oats

MAKES 2 loaves or 12 rolls

450 g	strong plain flour	1 lb
10 ml	salt	2 tsp
225 g	oats	8 oz
15 ml	dried yeast	1 tbsp
10 ml	sugar	2 tsp
	water to mix	
	beaten egg to glaze	

1 Mix together the sifted flour, salt and oats.

2 Measure yeast and sugar into a measuring jug and fill up to 425 ml (¾ pt) with hand-hot water. Stir well and leave in a warm place for about 10 minutes until frothy.

3 Stir yeast mixture into flour, etc. to give a soft dough. Knead on a floured surface for 5 minutes until smooth and elastic. Place in a floured bowl and cover lightly with greased polythene. Prove until double in size.

4 Knead the dough again and shape.

For loaves

5 Halve the dough and shape each piece to fit into a greased 850 ml (1½ pt) loaf tin. Cover and prove until double in size. Brush with beaten egg and bake at 230°C for 20 minutes, then at 190°C for a further 45 minutes, or until the loaf sounds hollow when tapped.

For rolls

5 Shape dough into 12 rounded rolls and make a 1 cm (½ inch) cut across the top of each. Arrange on two greased baking sheets. Cover and prove until doubled in size. Brush with beaten egg and bake at 230°C for 10 to 15 minutes, or until they sound hollow when tapped.

6 Cool the loaves/rolls on a wire rack. Serve the same day.

Wholemeal Chelsea buns
by McDougalls (RHM Foods)

Key learning points
» make an enriched dough for buns
» make a sugar glaze

MAKES 16 slices

450 g	wholemeal flour	1 lb
5 ml	salt	1 tsp
50 g	margarine	2 oz
50 g	soft brown sugar	2 oz
1	sachet fast action dried yeast	1
150 ml	milk, warmed	5 fl oz
2	eggs, size 3, beaten	2
Filling		
25 g	butter or margarine, melted	1 oz
50 g	soft brown sugar	2 oz
5 ml	cinnamon	1 tsp
50 g	dried apricots, finely chopped	2 oz
50 g	dates, finely chopped	2 oz
25 g	almonds, finely chopped	1 oz
Sugar glaze		
30 ml each	milk, sugar, water	2 tbsp each

1 For the dough, rub the margarine into the flour and salt. Stir in sugar and yeast. Add milk and eggs, mix well and knead on a floured surface for 10 minutes until smooth.

2 Place dough in a bowl, cover with lightly oiled polythene and leave in a warm place until doubled in size (50 to 60 minutes).

3 Roll out the dough to a 35 cm (14 inch) square and brush with the melted butter. Mix together the sugar, cinnamon, apricots, dates and almonds and sprinkle over the dough. Roll up Swiss roll style (see page 248) and cut into 16 slices.

4 Arrange cut side down on a greased baking tray. Cover and leave in a warm place until double in size. Bake at 200°C for 25 minutes.

5 Meanwhile heat the milk, sugar and water for the glaze until the sugar has dissolved. Simmer for 2 minutes. Brush over the buns while they are still hot. Remove to a wire rack and cool.

Marguerita pizza
by McDougalls Catering Foods

Key learning points
» make pizza using convenience pizza mix
» top with alternative fillings of your choice

MAKES 30 cm (12 inch) pizza

350 g	pizza base mix	12 oz
250 ml	water	9 fl oz
175 g	chopped tomatoes (drained and thickened)	6 oz
175 g	Mozzarella cheese (sliced into fingers)	6 oz
15 ml	basil	1 tbsp

1 Make up the pizza base mix as directed on the packet.

2 Press into a 30 cm (12 inch) pizza tin (or shape into a circle of this size).

3 Prick base with fork.

4 Top with tomatoes.

5 Arrange Mozzarella cheese and sprinkle on basil.

6 Bake at 200°C for 6 to 8 minutes.

Pizza romana

Key learning point
» make fresh pizza dough

SERVES 10

Pizza dough

675 g	plain (soft) flour	1½ lb
5 ml	salt	1 tsp
75 ml	oil	3 fl oz
30 g	compressed yeast (fresh)	1¼ oz
400 ml	cold water at 18°C	14 fl oz

Topping

100 g	onions, finely chopped	4 oz
1	clove of garlic, peeled and crushed	1
50 ml	oil	2 fl oz
1 × 900 g	can chopped tomatoes	1 × 2 lb
25 g	tomato purée	1 oz
5 ml	fresh oregano, chopped	1 tsp
10 ml	fresh basil, chopped	2 tsp
20	anchovy fillets	20
150 g	Mozzarella cheese	6 oz
100 g	Parmesan cheese, grated	4 oz
	seasoning to taste	
	oil for brushing over the pizza bases	

1 Prepare the topping:

a) gently shallow fry the onions and garlic in the oil without browning for 2 to 3 minutes

b) add the oregano and basil and cook for a further 2 minutes

c) add the tinned tomatoes and tomato purée and simmer until the mixture becomes quite thick (about 20 minutes)

d) check the seasoning, then allow the mixture to cool

e) cut the anchovy fillets in half lengthways

f) cut the Mozzarella into pieces.

2 Prepare the dough:

a) sieve the flour and salt together into a mixing bowl

b) make a hollow in the centre and add the oil

c) place the yeast into a small bowl, add some of the water, mix until combined, then add the yeast and water mixture to the flour

d) add most of the remaining water and mix together until a smooth, pliable, soft dough is produced. Add the remainder of the water if the dough is too stiff to work easily

e) cover and set aside for 15 minutes at room temperature (this will allow the yeast to ferment).

3 Divide the dough into 10 pieces of equal weight, then mould these into balls.

4 Roll out the balls of dough into thin rounds and place them on greased baking trays.

5 Lightly brush over the surfaces of the dough bases with oil.

6 Add the topping, leaving a 10 mm border uncovered round each base.

7 Decorate the topping with the anchovy fillets, then add the Mozzarella and Parmesan.

8 Allow the pizzas to sit at room temperature for 30 to 40 minutes.

9 Bake at 225°C until cooked, about 15 to 20 minutes.

Pizza topping ideas *by McDougalls Catering Foods*

Marguerita Mozzarella cheese, tomato

Mushroom Mushroom, Mozzarella, tomato

Seafood special Tuna, calamari, mussels, prawns, anchovies, olives, tomato, Mozzarella

Giardinera Tomato, Mozzarella, mushroom, onion, peppers, sweetcorn

American Mozzarella, tomato, pepperoni, sausage

Mexican Mozzarella, tomato, pepperoni, hot chilli, peppers

Sunnyside up Ham, pepperoni, egg, capers, olives, Mozzarella, tomato

Quattro formaggio Tomato, four cheeses

Chilli Chilli con carne, Mozzarella, tomato

Hawaiian Mozzarella, tomato, pineapple, ham, chicken

Tuna fish and banana Tuna, banana, Mozzarella, tomato, oregano

Vegetarian Tomato, green and red peppers, sweetcorn, mushrooms, onions, fresh herbs, Mozzarella

Jamaican hot Pepperoni, chilli, spinach, tuna, tomato, Mozzarella

Toscana Ham, olives, mushroom, Mozzarella, tomato, basil

Garlic inferno Tomato, garlic, hot chilli peppers, onion, creamed garlic, Mozzarella

Jam doughnuts

Key learning points
» prepare a bun dough using compressed yeast
» deep fry doughnuts

SERVES 18

550 g	strong flour	1¼ lb
5 g	salt	¼ oz
75 g	caster sugar	3 oz
75 g	margarine or butter	3 oz
1	egg (size 3)	1
25 g	compressed yeast (fresh)	1 oz
225 ml	water (tepid)	8 fl oz
225 g	raspberry jam	8 oz
	caster sugar flavoured with a pinch of cinnamon	

1 Sieve together the flour, salt and sugar into a mixing bowl.

2 Cut the margarine or butter into small pieces and rub lightly into the flour to achieve a fine breadcrumb-like consistency.

3 Break up the yeast in a small bowl, and mix with some of the water.

4 Add the yeast (now dissolved in water) and egg to the dry ingredients.

5 Add most of the remaining water (keeping a small quantity to one side to correct consistency later if necessary).

6 Knead thoroughly until a smooth, pliable dough which does not stick to the fingers is produced (known as a clear dough).

7 Cover the dough with oiled polythene, and leave to ferment for about 45 minutes at 27°C. (For best results, use a prover.) During this time, the dough should roughly double in size.

8 Work the dough thoroughly by pressing firmly down on to it with the knuckles of both hands and folding it two or three times (known as knocking back).

9 Recover the dough, and allow to ferment for a further 15 minutes at the same temperature as before.

10 Work the dough again, then divide it into at least 18 pieces, each weighing 40 g (1¾ oz).

11 With your hands, roll these pieces on a lightly floured work surface until they are round and even.

12 Make a small hole in the centre of each ball with the tip of a finger dipped in flour.

13 Insert a little raspberry jam into the hole using a piping bag with a fine nozzle. Dampen the edges of the hole with a little water, then draw the dough over to close the hole and to produce a good seal.

14 Place the doughnuts on a well-oiled baking tray then leave them to prove until double in size: 30 to 40 minutes. On this occasion a little steam should be let into the prover. The proving temperature should be 27°C.

15 When the doughnuts have proved, carefully lift from the tray and deep fry them at 180°C until golden brown. This will take about 6 minutes. Half-way through the cooking time, turn the doughnuts over with a spider.

16 When cooking is completed, remove the doughnuts from the oil and drain them thoroughly.

17 Roll the doughnuts in the cinnamon sugar and serve warm or cold, on a serving dish lined with a doily.

The finished doughnuts.

Introduction

Making good pastry is not simply a matter of following recipes. You need to have a certain lightness of touch, and to become familiar with the basic techniques and rules that form the foundation of successful pastry making. Then it's a matter of practice, patience and more practice.

There is now a wide range of convenience pastry products for caterers to choose from. Used properly, these ensure consistently high standards for the customer. They also provide a good introduction to the techniques of handling pastry, so that when you are ready or have to make your own pastry, you will learn more quickly how to get the best results.

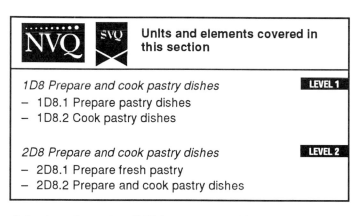

Units and elements covered in this section

1D8 Prepare and cook pastry dishes **LEVEL 1**
- 1D8.1 Prepare pastry dishes
- 1D8.2 Cook pastry dishes

2D8 Prepare and cook pastry dishes **LEVEL 2**
- 2D8.1 Prepare fresh pastry
- 2D8.2 Prepare and cook pastry dishes

Contents guide

Selection of pastries: 1) Vol-au-vents and bouchées (puff), 2) Spotted dick (suet), 3) Game pie (hot water), 4) Apple pie (sweet short), 5) Steak and kidney pudding (suet), 6) Gâteau Pithivier (puff), 7) Quiche (short), 8) Lemon meringue flan (sweet short), 9) Apple strudel (strudel), 10) Cornish pasty (short), 11) Sausage roll (puff).

Quality points

Prepared and convenience products
- packaging in good condition
- correctly labelled
- not passed its use-by date

Flour
- original packaging in good condition if unopened
- not passed best-before date on packaging
- stored in cool conditions in a clean rodent-proof container with a tight fitting lid
- no sign of infestation by pests

Fat
- not passed use-by date
- stored chilled, in a suitable container or wrapped
- stored away from strong-smelling foods

What contributes to the texture of pastry

Fats have a tenderising effect in pastry as a result of 'shortening' or cutting up the gluten. This is why fats used in baking are known as shortening agents. Gluten is an elastic type substance made when gliadin and glutenin (two of the proteins present in flour) are mixed with a liquid – see page 245.

The effect can be seen most clearly in rough puff pastry. Small pieces of fat are deliberately left not entirely mixed with the flour. During baking, the fat creates a flaky effect by splitting the gluten into layers.

Air makes an important contribution to pastry texture. Trapped in the mixture, the air expands as it is heated.

Water is a simple but very effective raising agent. When heated it turns to steam and expands to around 1600 times its original volume.

Butter (1) is popular in baking because of its rich flavour. However, it is relatively expensive and its low melting point makes it difficult to blend evenly with the flour in pastry-making. Concentrated butter, which has had most of the moisture, milk solids and salts removed, is firmer in texture and therefore better in baking. The recipe will need adjusting.

Margarine (2) is a little easier to handle than butter, but *Soft margarine (3)* is not good for pastry-making because it is too soft to be rubbed into flour. The only way round this is to blend it with about a third of the flour, add the liquid and then gradually add the rest of the flour.

Pastry margarine (4) which has a higher melting point than ordinary margarine is ideal for puff pastry, but with short pastry tends to result in a tough product.

Compound white fats (5) and (6) are widely used by caterers. They are made from vegetable oils, treated in a special way to raise the melting point above room temperature, so that they are suitable for pastry and bread-making.

High ratio fats (7) are specially made so that they take up a greater amount of liquid and sugar than ordinary fats. They cream easily and are used with high-ratio flours in some recipes for sponge cakes (see page 239).

Lard (8) was once highly valued for savoury pie crusts, because of its flavour and the flaky quality it produces. Nowadays it is less popular with customers.

Suet (left photograph) is the layer of fat that forms around the kidneys of the ox. In its unprepared state it is hard and solid. The papery skin and connective tissue should be removed and the suet chopped finely or shredded in a mincer. A little flour is usually added to prevent the fragments sticking together.

Suet helps give cooked pastry a crumbly texture. This is because the solid fragments melt during the cooking and the steam that is left causes expansion.

Suet gives pastry a characteristic flavour and texture. Because it melts at a temperature a little higher than normal body temperature, it causes a slight clinging sensation in the mouth.

Preparation and finishing methods

Defrosting `LEVEL 1`

Allow frozen pastry to thaw at room temperature while still in its wrapping. Alternatively thaw for 10 to 12 hours in a refrigerator.

Mixing `LEVEL 2`

Convenience pastry products carry their own instructions on the label. Follow these carefully to get the best results.

The detailed procedures for mixing fresh pastry are explained later in this section. The general aim for *short* and *sweet short pastry* is to handle the mixture as little as possible. Some of the other rules for these pastries are:

1 If you have taken the fat straight out of the refrigerator, allow it to warm up slightly (to room temperature), so that it is soft and pliable, but not so soft that it becomes oily during the mixing.

2 Use the tips of your fingers, held well above the surface, so that the flour falls back into the bowl, and incorporates as much air as possible. By using the tips of your fingers, you also keep the fat away from the warmth of your hands as much as possible.

3 You should end up with a sandy-textured mixture rather like breadcrumbs. There should be no loose flour left.

4 Do not mix any more than necessary. The pastry will get another chance to blend together when it is rolled.

Machine-mixing

Hand-mixing is just as quick as machine-mixing and it is better for small quantities of short pastry because it is easier to avoid over-mixing. If you have increased the quantities by a large amount, or find it easier to use a machine, make sure you blend at low speed using the pastry beater.

When using a machine, you should also adjust the recipe method. For example, for short pastry:

- the fat can be left in large chunks
- the fat is blended with half the flour
- then the water is added, followed by the remainder of the flour, and mixed to a smooth dough.

Resting (relaxing) `LEVELS 1 + 2`

Fresh pastry mixtures should be rested in a cold room or refrigerator:

- before and after rolling
- between rolling where repeated rolling is necessary, as in puff pastry
- before cutting or shaping
- before baking.

Resting gives the starch in the flour time to absorb the liquids more evenly. It also helps the fat firm up so the pastry keeps a better texture, shapes and cuts more easily, and shrinks less when cooking.

While the pastry is resting, or if it is to be kept aside for a while before use, it should be properly protected against contamination. Covering also helps prevent a skin forming. Therefore:

- transfer firm mixtures to a food-quality plastic bag
- put loose mixtures, such as short pastry before it is rolled, in a clean bowl, and cover with clingfilm.

Alternatively firm or loose mixtures can be kept in a bowl or on a tray. A bowl with a tight fitting lid is ideal, otherwise cover with a suitable size plate (when there is no danger of it being knocked off and broken). A sheet of slightly dampened greaseproof paper, or a dampened clean tea towel, are other ways of protecting the surface of the pastry from drying out.

With hand-mixing there is a danger that the warmth of the hands will melt the fat. Particles of cool fat should remain in the mixture until it is baked so that when they melt a flaky texture is left. If the fat does melt during mixing, the final result will be dense. This is one reason for resting the pastry in a refrigerator.

Rolling
`LEVELS 1 + 2`

1 First shape the pastry dough with your knuckles to a small version of the shape you intend to roll it. This cuts down waste, and reduces the amount of rolling required.

2 Use a firm even stroke, with equal pressure over the length of the rolling pin. Keep your fingers well clear of the pastry.

3 Stop rolling just short of the edge. If you roll over the edge, the pastry will not keep an even thickness.

4 Roll the pastry in one direction only: away from your body. Turn the pastry rather than rolling in all sorts of different directions as this will distort it.

5 As soon as there is any danger of the pastry sticking, sprinkle flour over the surface of the rolling pin. Lift the pastry up with the rolling pin, sprinkle the work surface with flour and put the pastry back. It is usually turned at this stage. Some chefs also sprinkle flour over the surface of the pastry. If you find this helps, be careful not to use too much.

6 Use a flour dredger to dust surfaces. Too much extra flour will only make the pastry hard.

7 If, in spite of flouring, the dough starts sticking too much, and becomes unmanageable, transfer to a tray or bowl, cover and place in the refrigerator for 10 to 15 minutes to recover.

8 If you have chilled the dough for longer than 30 minutes, allow it to stand for a few minutes at room temperature to soften slightly before rolling again.

9 When the shape begins to get too elongated, lift the pastry up with the rolling pin, sprinkle the work surface with flour and put the pastry back, turned slightly, so that you continue to roll away from you.

Note how the rolling pin is being held, with the fingers well clear of the pastry.

Kneading, folding and relaxing
`LEVEL 2`

The special lightness of puff and rough puff pastry is created by using two types of dough: one mostly flour, the other mostly fat.

1 The fat is *kneaded* until it has a similar consistency to the flour dough.

2 The two mixtures are combined, then repeatedly *folded* so that the end result consists of many layers of the flour dough separated by the fat mixture. During cooking the fat melts into the flour, leaving a pocket or layer of air.

3 Regularly during the mixing and folding process, the pastry must be covered and chilled, so that the fat has a chance to firm up again. This is called *relaxing*.

CHEF'S TIPS

If you have hot hands, hold your wrists under a running cold tap for a few minutes before starting to mix or handle pastry.

Cutting and shaping LEVELS 1 + 2

1 To lift the rolled pastry on to the baking tray, flan ring, or whatever, partly wrap it around the floured rolling pin. Alternatively, fold the pastry in half, and if necessary in half again. Lift by hand, place in position, unfold.

2 Pastry should be cut cleanly. This is particularly important for puff and flaky pastry, so that you free the layers, and the pastry rises neatly during baking.

3 Use a pastry cutter (a metal one is best) when you require a particular shape. Dip the edge of the cutter in flour. Press the cutter into the dough firmly, don't twist. For cutting puff pastry shapes and vol-au-vents, some chefs prefer to dip the cutter in hot oil, others to grease it lightly with pastry margarine/white fat.

4 After you have cut shapes for pie tops, the top ring for a vol-au-vent or bouchée, turn the pastry over. The underside (which was next to the work surface) is smooth and the pastry will rise evenly.

5 Keep trimmings for making decorations. Trimmings of puff pastry can be used for cheese straws or fleurons and other dishes where it is not so important for the pastry to rise evenly. Pile them one on top of the other rather than crushing into a ball.

To line a flan case

1 Roll the pastry into a ball. Lightly flatten the ball to form a round shape.

2 Roll it out into a round, 3 to 4 mm thick and larger than the flan ring. To check the size, place the ring on top of the pastry. Trim off ragged edges and excess, so that the pastry forms a neat circle bigger than the flan ring by an amount equal to the depth of the sides of the ring, plus an allowance.

3 Place the ring on a floured baking tray. Lift the pastry on to the ring.

4 Work the edges of the pastry gently down the inside of the ring, so that you avoid stretching the pastry, yet make sure that the sides are well covered.

5 Trim the top by rolling the rolling pin across the top of the ring. Put the trimmings aside.

6 Lightly press up the top edges of the pastry, making sure they are even, and just higher than the top of the flan ring. At this stage, you can decorate the edges, by crimping between your fingers or using a pastry wheel.

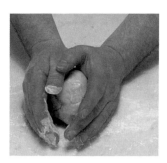

Shape the pastry dough to a small version of the shape you intend to roll.

Push the pastry gently, but firmly into the edges of the flan ring, so that the sides are evenly and well covered.

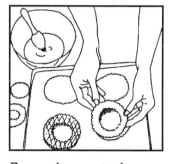

For a vol-au-vent, place a ring of pastry on to a base of the same size (brushed with beaten egg so the two stick together).

To shape dumplings, roll a little of the mixture between the palms of your hands (floured so the dough will not stick).

To prepare vol-au-vents and bouchées

1 Roll out puff pastry into a sheet about 5 mm thick.

2 Cut into rounds using a fluted pastry cutter for the size required: 75 to 80 mm diameter for vol-au-vents and 35 to 40 mm for bouchées. Cut twice as many rounds as you require vol-au-vents/bouchées.

3 For half the rounds: using a smaller pastry cutter (45 mm for vol-au-vents, 20 mm for bouchées) with plain edges, cut out and remove the centre of the ring. The centres can be set aside for use in another recipe, or baked separately to form lids. They will cook quickly.

4 Spread the solid circles out on the work surface or baking tray. Brush each with beaten egg.

5 Place a ring of pastry carefully on top of each circle. Press all round so that it sticks to the bottom layer.

6 Brush the ring with egg. Do not let the egg run down the sides, otherwise the pastry will rise unevenly.

7 Allow to rest for 10 to 20 minutes before baking.

For simpler vol-au-vents and bouchées, use just one layer of pastry. Brush with egg. To form the lid, cut an incision into the surface of the pastry, using a lightly greased plain cutter of smaller diameter. After baking, cut off and remove the lid. Discard the mushy dough from the inside.

To fill pasties

1 Pile the filling down the centre of the circle of pastry.

2 Brush the edge with beaten egg.

3 Bring both edges of the pastry upwards so that they meet over the top of the filling. Press together to seal.

4 Make a series of pinches along the top to create an attractive wavy edge.

To wrap fruit in a pastry case for baking

1 Cut the pastry into a round, square, or triangle large enough to enclose the fruit.

2 Place the fruit in the centre of the triangle.

3 Dampen the edges of the pastry with beaten egg.

4 One side at a time, lift the corners of the pastry up over the top of the fruit.

5 Pinch the edges of the pastry together to seal.

To make pastry leaves

1 Cut out pieces of pastry in the shape of a leaf.

2 Mark veins on the leaf with the back of the knife.

3 Pinch one end to form a leaf shape.

To make a pastry rose

1 Cut three pastry circles in decreasing sizes.

2 Place one on top of the other with the smallest circle on the top.

3 Draw circles together into a ball and pinch to seal.

4 Turn the ball upside down, so that the side you have pinched is at the bottom, and the smooth, rounded side is uppermost.

5 Cut a cross through the top.

6 Open out the pastry layers, one at a time to form the petals of the rose.

To make twisted cheese straws

1 Roll out puff pastry to a thickness of 3 to 5 mm, and forming a large rectangle as wide as you want the cheese straws to be long (say, 200 mm × 500 mm).

2 Brush with beaten egg, sprinkle with cheese and paprika as specified in the recipe.

3 Fold over so the rectangle is half its original width (100 mm × 500 mm).

4 Cut strips about 10 mm wide. (You should get 50.)

5 Unfold the strips (which will measure 10 mm × 200 mm). Holding each end of the strip, roll forwards with one hand, and backwards with the other. The strip will be twisted like a corkscrew.

Pasties (see page 232 for recipe).

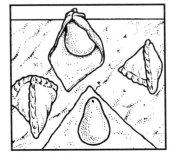

Fruit in pastry (see page 234 for recipe).

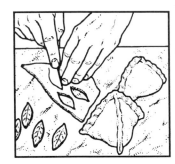

Pastry leaves.

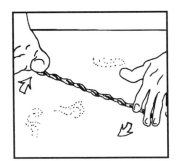

Cheese straws.

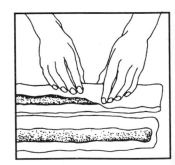

Sausage rolls (see page 230 for recipe).

Decorative shapes can be made quite easily if you have a variety of pastry cutters.

Crimping the rim of the pastry as shown here is one way to enhance the presentation of pies.

To line a pudding basin with suet pastry

1 Roll out about three-quarters of the pastry 8 to 10 mm thick, in a circle big enough to line the basin. You can probably judge this by eye, but if you want to make sure, measure what size the pastry needs to be by experimenting with a circle of greaseproof paper. Allow for the pastry to overlap the sides of the basin.

2 With the rolling pin, lift the pastry up.

3 Press the pastry into the basin to make sure no air gaps are left at the bottom or along the sides. Leave the edges overlapping the side of the basin for the time being.

4 Almost fill the basin with the mixture.

5 Dampen the edges of the pastry with a little stock or water.

6 Roll out the remaining pastry into a circle.

7 Cover the top of the pudding. Seal the edges. Trim off the excess pastry.

To wrap a pudding for steaming in a basin

1 Cover pudding with a circle of lightly greased greaseproof paper, folded in the middle with a pleat about 25 mm wide, to allow for expansion during cooking.

2 Over the greaseproof paper place a pudding cloth (such as an old, clean tea towel or table napkin), also pleated in the middle.

3 Twist a piece of string twice round the basin below the rim and tie the paper and cloth securely.

4 Tie the opposite ends of the pudding cloth together. This makes a convenient handle for lifting the pudding in and out of the steamer.

Lining a basin with suet pastry.

The lid should be firmly sealed.

Tying the ends of the cloth makes it easier to handle the pudding.

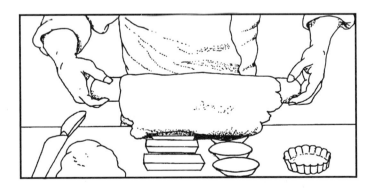

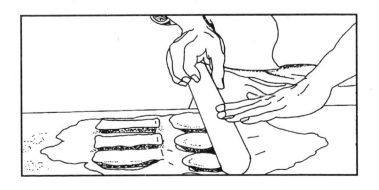

These illustrations (adapted from La Methode *by Jacques Pépin) show a quick way of lining pastry boats, tartlet and patty tins of various shapes and sizes. 1) Place the tins quite close together. 2) Drape the pastry over the top. 3) Gently push the pastry into each container. Use a piece of dough dipped in flour to do this. 4) Trim the dough by rolling over the top of the moulds. Finish by pressing with your fingers.*

Glazing
LEVEL 2

Pastry is glazed to give it an attractive brown surface after baking. Egg beaten with a little milk gives the richest glaze. Water can be used in place of milk.

The addition of milk or water makes it easier to use the *egg wash*, as it is called by many chefs, and means it goes further. However egg can be used on its own, provided it is well beaten.

Milk used on its own does help brown the surface, but not as well as egg.

1 Brush just before baking, so pastry does not get soggy.

2 With puff pastry and rough puff pastry, do not let the glaze run down the sides. If it does it will set in the oven and seal the pastry layers together.

Dessert pies can be brushed with lightly beaten egg white and sprinkled with caster sugar.

Glazing cooked dishes

Flans and tarts filled or decorated with fruit are glazed to give the fruit an attractive, shiny finish, and stop it discolouring. There is quite a choice of glazings including:

Fruit juice or syrup thickened with arrowroot

Arrowroot is better than cornflour for thickening a glaze, because it sets to a more transparent jelly.

1 Use 1 rounded teaspoon per 150 ml fruit juice (¼ pint).

2 In a saucepan, dilute the arrowroot with a little of the juice. Stir in the rest of the juice and bring to the boil, stirring all the time, so the mixture thickens evenly.

3 Draw off the heat and spoon the glaze over tart or flan while hot. An arrowroot glaze thickens and clears immediately, so quickly draw off heat as soon as it comes to the boil, otherwise air bubbles will get trapped in the liquid.

Fruit jelly

This can be a convenience product, or made from a suitable recipe. Use complementary flavours, such as lemon or lime with banana.

1 Dissolve jelly, as directed on packet.

2 Stir over a bowl of iced water until jelly begins to thicken and show signs of setting.

3 Spoon over fruit. Work fast, as the jelly will set quite quickly.

4 Chill until firm.

Fruit jam or jelly

Popular choices include apricot jam, apple jam or jelly, redcurrant jelly or similar. Extra thickening is usually unnecessary because the jam or jelly will return to its original consistency once it has chilled.

1 Warm the jam with a little water, lemon juice or brandy, depending on recipe.

2 Strain if you are using a jam with bits of fruit or pips in it.

3 Use warm.

Adding sugar makes a lighter glaze, but the mixture will need re-cooking.

Dusting
LEVELS 1 + 2

Dusting means coating a surface with a light, even coat of a fine powdery substance such as flour or caster sugar.

In pastry-making the rolling pin, and whatever surface is being used to roll the pastry on, have to be dusted with flour from time to time to prevent the pastry sticking. Before cooking, the baking tray may be dusted for the same reason.

The surface of the pastry dish is sometimes dusted with caster or icing sugar:

• before baking to give a glaze

• after baking to give a decorative finish.

Flour can be quite evenly dusted by hand, especially with experience. Throw a small amount over the surface with a quick flick of your wrist.

A sifter is preferred by some chefs.

For dusting caster or icing sugar, it is best to use a sieve. Place a few spoons of sugar in the sieve, then gently shake over the surface of the food.

Preparing the baking tray

It is best to use a white fat such as pastry margarine for greasing containers. Butter or yellow margarine will stick or even burn (because of the milk solids in butter and the water in yellow margarine).

Brush or rub the fat over the whole surface.

Dust with flour, where the recipe specifies. Tip the tray in all directions to spread the flour evenly. Give a bang to the back of the sheet to shake off excess flour: the finished coating should be light and uniform.

For puff and rough puff pastry items, the baking tray should be dampened with cold water after greasing. This helps prevent the pastry burning on the underside in the very hot oven.

Filling

LEVELS 1 + 2

For fillings that are cooked in the pastry, there is always a danger that the filling and/or juices will leak out during cooking.

1 Follow the recipe instructions carefully with regard to the amount of filling.

2 Check whether the ingredients will increase in volume during cooking. Dishes involving liquid will create steam. You will need to allow room for expansion in these situations. A small hole cut in the top of a steak and kidney or fruit pie will allow steam to escape.

3 Use minimum liquid in a covered fruit pie to avoid the contents bubbling out. For a pie serving six people or so, only 2 to 3 tablespoons of water will be needed. The fruit will supply extra juices.

4 With a double crust fruit pie (that is, the top and bottom of the pie is made of pastry), a good seal around the rim is essential to hold in pie juices. Dampen only the bottom crust with beaten egg, and press together firmly (it can be more difficult to form a good seal if both edges are dampened).

5 In a covered fruit pie, start and end with a layer of fruit. Sugar (if required) should go on the intermediate layers, not directly under the crust (which would make the pastry soggy).

6 With products like flans and quiches which are put in the oven to bake with an egg custard or other fairly liquid filling, you need a steady hand to avoid spills as you transfer the food to the oven. One way around the problem is to place the prepared pastry case on its baking tray on the oven rack, then slowly pour in the filling from a jug.

Piping

LEVEL 2

Piping is a very decorative way of finishing pastries. How to fill and use a piping bag is covered in detail on page 246.

How to fill and use a piping bag is covered in detail on page 246.

ACTION

If you need to, get some practice at using a piping bag.

Then arrange to teach the skill to a small group of your friends who don't know much about working in a professional kitchen. Ask your supervisor's help in devising a way of making your demonstration effective, yet fun.

HYGIENE

You might not think hygiene particularly relevant in relation to pastry making. But consider for a moment what would happen if:

- the piping bag used to decorate a fruit flan with cream was not cleaned properly after it had been used the previous day
- a meat pastie is left in the heated display cabinet after service, and although the cabinet is turned off it is a warm summer evening. The following day the pie is reheated in the cabinet and in due course sold to a customer
- the knife used to dice cooked chicken for the vol-au-vents had been previously used for trimming some raw meat, and was simply wiped clean with a wet cloth.

To avoid these dangers, you need to pay careful attention to how pastry products are stored, and for what period of time (both will depend on the type of pastry and the filling). You should also make sure that there is no danger of cross-contamination at any stage in handling pastry products, but particularly after they have been cooked.

Note how the piping bag is held. One hand is guiding the direction of the nozzle, the other is holding the top tight so the contents don't get squeezed out, at the same time applying sufficient pressure for the contents to emerge from the piping nozzle smoothly and continuously.

Preparing fresh pastry `LEVEL 2`

Sweet and savoury pastries are made with a wide range of different textures which are achieved by varying the ingredients and methods of combining them.

Sweet and savoury short pastry must have very little gluten development, but a little needs to take place to hold the pastry together. So:

- use a soft flour (it will develop less gluten than a plain or hard flour)
- blend the flour thoroughly (but lightly) with the fat
- use the minimum amount of liquid
- mix as little as possible.

The small quantity of liquid also means that not very much of the starch can gelatinise, so the flakes of pastry are dry and crisp. This texture is however more difficult to achieve in a quiche, because of the liquid used in the filling.

Puff pastry has to be very light. This is achieved by using a strong flour, an equal quantity of fat and an elaborate mixing and rolling process. In the end the pastry is made up of somewhere between 80 and 240 alternating layers of fat and dough. As the pastry is baked the water in the dough turns to steam and puffs the separate layers of fat apart. Eventually the fat melts and is absorbed by the dough layers as they set, leaving layers of air in the finished product.

Fresh suet pastry is generally steamed not baked. This is because suet needs quite a long time and moist heat to melt into the surrounding mixture.

General points to remember

1 Always use accurate equipment for weighing solid ingredients, and for measuring liquids.

2 A very hot oven – 200°C to 220°C – is essential for baking puff and rough puff. It forces the pastry to rise in layers. The heat also enables the flour to absorb the fat as it melts: too cool an oven, and you'll find the fat runs all over the baking sheet.

3 There is a tendency for the pastry case of a quiche lorraine (or similar dish in which the pastry is cooked at the same time as the custard) to remain slightly soggy. To help overcome this problem, use a thin black baking tray. This sort of tray will not reflect the heat, but instead transfer it more efficiently to the pastry case, so offsetting the cooling of the custard. Also, if possible, use an oven which can be regulated to produce substantial bottom heat to cook the pastry from beneath.

4 Short and puff pastries can be prepared in advance. Place in an airtight container, or cover the bowl with clingfilm, and keep in the refrigerator for up to 3 days.

5 Prepared pastry can be stored for longer if frozen.

Baking blind, step 4.

Baking blind

To avoid the pastry or tart case becoming soggy after it has been filled with fruit, pastry cream or a similar filling, it is baked empty first. This is known as *baking blind*.

The base of the pastry will tend to rise during cooking, so not leaving much room for the filling. To stop this happening:

1 Line the flan ring with pastry.

2 Prick the base of the pastry all over with a fork.

3 Line the pastry case with a circle of greaseproof paper, large enough to extend beyond the sides slightly.

4 Fill the shell with dry beans, rice, small metal balls made for this purpose, or any heavy, dry ingredient.

5 Bake at 200°C until the pastry is set, about 20 minutes.

6 Remove the beans and paper.

7 Carefully lift the flan ring off the pastry.

8 Continue baking the flan case until it is evenly coloured, a further 10 minutes. Some chefs brush the pastry base with beaten egg before returning to the oven, as an added precaution.

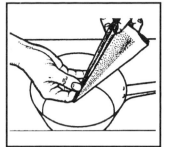

To make a circle of greaseproof paper

1 Fold a square or oblong sheet of greaseproof paper into half, then half again.

2 Fold again, diagonally, to form a triangle.

3 Repeat the folding two or three times until a narrow dart shape has been formed.

4 Place the point of the dart over the centre of the saucepan, flan ring or dish, and mark where the paper should be trimmed. If you want the circle of paper to:

fit exactly inside the saucepan, flan ring or dish, mark it at the point it meets the edge

overlap the edge, or cover the sides of a flan ring, for example, allow a few centimetres or so extra, according to the depth of the flan ring, or the amount of overlap required.

5 With scissors or a knife, trim the paper to this mark.

6 Open out to form a circle.

Baking blind, step 7.

ACTION

1 Measure out 30 g (1½ oz) of arrowroot and the same amount of cornflour. Dilute each with about 50 ml (2 fl oz) of cold water.

2 Pour ½ litre (1 pint) of water into each of 2 saucepans. Bring both to the boil, add the diluted arrowroot to one, the cornflour to the other.

3 Reboil both for 1 minute, take off the heat.

4 Make notes below about the consistency and colour. Then cool both solutions, and note how their consistency and colour have changed.

	Hot	Cooled
Cornflour		
Arrowroot		

5 On the basis of your observations, also note which of the two thickeners you would use for each of the following and what you would use as an alternative if you had neither arrowroot nor cornflour available

	a) *Thickener*	b) *Alternative*
stew too thin		
fruit syrup glaze		

Short pastry

MAKES 450 g (1 lb)

300 g	plain (soft) flour	10 oz
150 g	butter, margarine or white fat	5 oz
50 ml	water	2 fl oz

pinch salt

1 Sieve the flour to incorporate air and remove any lumps.

2 Cut the fat into small lumps ready to add to the flour.

3 Dissolve the salt in the water.

4 Place the flour in a bowl. Add the fat to it and rub together gently so that the fat is evenly blended into the flour.

5 Make a hollow in the centre of the pastry, and pour the cold water into it. Blend carefully, working from the centre outwards until the mixture just holds together.

6 Cover the bowl of pastry with clingfilm, and place it in a refrigerator to rest for at least 30 minutes before use.

Sweet short pastry

MAKES 350 g (12 oz)

225 g	plain (soft) flour	8 oz
100 g	butter or margarine	4 oz
50 g	caster sugar	2 oz
½	egg (size 3)	½
pinch	grated lemon zest (optional)	pinch

1 Sieve the flour to remove any lumps.

2 Let the butter or margarine soften slightly and then cut into small pieces.

3 Blend the fat lightly into the flour to produce a sandy texture.

4 If you have to use a whole egg, beat it lightly first so that half can be measured off. Mix this half with the sugar and lemon zest.

5 Add the egg and sugar mixture to the fat and flour, and mix to a smooth dough. Rest before using.

Puff pastry

MAKES 550 g (1 lb 4 oz)

225 g	strong flour	8 oz
225 g	pastry margarine	8 oz
150 ml	cold water	5 fl oz

pinch salt

pinch cream of tartar or few drops lemon juice

1 Sieve together the flour and salt and cream of tartar. (Cream of tartar or lemon juice helps make the dough more elastic, so there is less risk of the fat oozing out between the layers of dough.)

2 Rub in 50 g of the margarine.

3 Add the water (and lemon juice, if using). Mix to a smooth dough. Cover and leave in a cool place or refrigerator to rest for half an hour or so.

Method A – star or French method

4 Meanwhile, knead the rest of the margarine until it is the same consistency as the dough, and form into a square cake shape. If the fat is too cold, it will break and crumble and push through the dough during rolling. If it is too warm, it will run out from between the layers.

5 Make a criss-cross cut in the top of the rested dough. Roll or spread out with your hands the four sections of the dough, to make a large four-leafed clover shape. The centre of the clover should be about four times thicker than the leaves.

6 Place the prepared margarine in the centre of the clover. Bring the four leaves up and over the margarine, to enclose it totally.

Method B – English method

4 Roll the margarine mixture into a rectangle about 10 mm thick.

5 Roll the dough mixture into a rectangle about 10 mm wider than the margarine mixture and slightly more than three times as long.

6 Place the margarine mixture in the centre of the dough, and fold the dough over from both ends, to enclose the margarine completely. Gently press the open ends with a rolling pin to seal.

Recipe continues

7 Roll the dough into a rectangle. Roll gently, without pressing down too hard and leave quite thick at this stage – 10 mm or so. Transfer to a tray, cover and place in the refrigerator to rest for about 10 minutes.

8   Roll the dough to form a larger rectangle about three times as long as it is wide. This way you can fold the pastry in three (step 9) and end up with a neat square shape.

9   Take one end of the dough and fold it back on itself to a point about two-thirds up the rectangle. Fold the other end over on top of this, so that you end up with a square of dough consisting of three layers. Before folding over the pastry, brush any excess flour off the surfaces that will meet. (Unless you do this, dry flour will be caught between the surfaces, and the end product will be rather dry and tough.)

10 At this stage you have made what is called a *single turn*.

11 Transfer to a tray, cover and place in the refrigerator to rest for 30 minutes or so.

12 With the open ends of the dough facing towards and away from you, roll the dough to form a rectangle of similar size to step 9. Once again fold both ends over to the centre. This is the second turn. Rest as before.

13 Repeat step 10 until you have carried out a total of 5 or 6 turns. Rest the dough after the fourth turn. If the dough has become very elastic and difficult to work, stop after 5 turns. To keep track of how many turns you have given the pastry, mark it with the appropriate number of pinches before putting aside to rest.

14 Allow to rest before using.

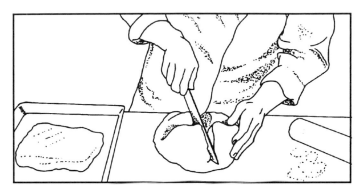

Puff pastry, step A5.

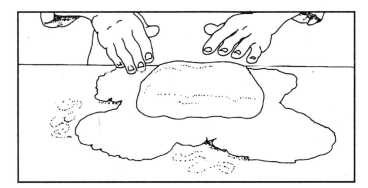

Puff pastry, step A6.

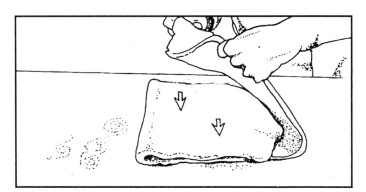

Puff pastry, step 9 – making a single turn.

CHEF'S TIPS

To get a richer puff pastry, replace up to 50 g (2 oz) of the pastry margarine with an equal weight of butter.

Traditional recipes for puff pastry use butter only. This gives a delicious, rich texture and fragrance to the finished product. But because butter melts at a lower temperature than pastry margarine, it is more difficult to make a puff pastry this way successfully.

If using butter, mix it with some of the flour before folding in.

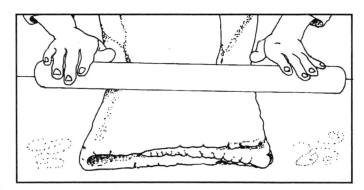

Puff pastry, step 10.

Rough puff pastry

MAKES 350 g (14 oz)

225 g	strong flour	8 oz
175 g	pastry margarine, margarine or butter	6 oz
125 ml	cold water	5 fl oz
	pinch salt	

pinch cream of tartar or squeeze lemon juice

1 Sieve the flour and salt and cream of tartar.

2 Cut the chilled fat into small cubes about 15 mm, and lightly mix into the flour, so that the pieces of fat do not break up.

3 Add the water (and lemon juice). Mix to a fairly stiff dough without breaking up the lumps of fat. Gather the dough into a ball, then transfer to a floured board.

4 Roll into a rectangle. Give one single turn (as described in step 9 of puff pastry). Transfer to a tray, cover and allow to rest in a refrigerator for about half an hour.

5 Give 3 more turns, allowing to rest between each.

6 Allow to rest before using.

Suet pastry

MAKES 900 g (2 lb)

450 g	plain flour	1 lb
25 g	baking powder	1 oz
225 g	chopped beef suet	8 oz
300 ml	cold water	10 fl oz
	pinch salt	

1 Sieve the flour, baking powder and salt into a bowl.

2 Add the suet and thoroughly mix the ingredients together.

3 Add the water and lightly mix to form a paste.

NUTRITION 🖋🖋🖋

To increase the fibre content of short pastry, replace half the white flour by wholemeal.

For a healthier alternative to traditional suet pastry, replace the suet with an oil high in polyunsaturates, such as sunflower, corn or soya. For the quantity given in the recipe on this page:

• use 125 ml oil (4 fl oz)
• reduce the water in the recipe to 175 ml (just under 6 fl oz).

Left: *pastry which has shrunk.*

Back: *pastry which has become soggy.*

Right: *pastry which has become greasy and shrunk.*

Learning from your mistakes

Product has shrunk
– too much liquid
– too little fat
– dough overmixed
– dough not allowed to rest

Product is soggy
– too much liquid
– temperature too low

Product is greasy
– too much fat used
– temperature too low

Texture solid and dense
– wrong sort of flour
– too much liquid
– too little fat
– dough overmixed
– oven temperature too low
– wrong position in oven

Texture tough and chewy
– wrong sort of flour
– too much liquid used
– too little fat used
– dough overmixed
– dough not allowed to rest
– oven temperature too low

Shape is uneven
– dough overmixed
– oven temperature too low
– wrong position in oven

Product looks too pale
– temperature too low

Product looks too dark
– oven temperature too high
– cooked for too long

*Above: Fish plait
(recipe page 231)*

*Right: Norfolk pie
(page 232)*

Choux pastry

MAKES 12 ECLAIRS OR 8 CHOUX BUNS
OR 16 SWEET PROFITEROLES

150 ml	water	5 fl oz
100 g	butter or margarine	4 oz
125 g	strong flour	5 oz
4 eggs	beaten lightly	4 eggs
	pinch sugar	

1 Sieve the flour and sugar.
2 Place the water and fat in a small saucepan and bring to the boil.
3 Add all the flour in one go and mix thoroughly.
4 Stir over a low heat for about 1 minute. The mixture should leave the sides of the saucepan cleanly.
5 Allow to cool for a few minutes. (If the mixture is too hot for the next stage, the egg will start cooking too soon.)
6 Add the beaten egg at little at a time, mixing the paste vigorously. Scrape down the bowl occasionally to ensure even mixing.
7 Continue adding the egg until you get a soft consistency: the mixture should just be able to hold its shape when piped.
8 Place the mixture into a piping bag with a plain nozzle of the appropriate diameter. There are no set rules, but here are some guidelines, using a 10 mm plain nozzle:
   10 mm diameter for profiteroles
   60 mm length for éclairs
   25 mm diameter for choux buns
9 Pipe on to a greased baking sheet.
10 Bake at 200°C to 220°C until crisp and golden brown, about 25 to 30 minutes.

Choux pastry, step 3, shooting in the flour.

Choux pastry, step 4. If the mixture does not leave the sides of the saucepan cleanly, you have probably got the quantities wrong.

Choux pastry, step 6. When the sides of the pan become clean again, as shown, the mixture is ready for more egg to be added.

Sausage rolls

Key learning points
» use preprepared puff pastry/or a convenience product with sausage meat

MAKES 8 to 12 ROLLS

225 g	puff pastry	8 oz
275 g	sausage meat	10 oz
	or vegetarian sausage meat	
	beaten egg	

1 Roll out the pastry into a rectangle 16 to 20 cm wide and 2 to 3 mm thick. Cut this in half to form two long strips 8 to 10 cm wide.

2 Roll the sausage meat into a long rope shape, about 20 mm thick. Lightly flour your hands, so that the meat does not stick to them.

3 Place the meat along the centre of each strip of pastry. Brush both edges of the pastry with the beaten egg.

4 Lift the pastry up and over the meat, so that the two moistened edges meet. Press the edges firmly together. If required pinch together, or decorate with the back of a knife.

5 Cut the pastry rolls into equal lengths of 5 to 8 cm. Brush with egg to glaze. Place on lightly greased baking tray. Cut 2 or 3 slits across the top of each roll for the steam to escape.

6 Allow to rest for 10 to 15 minutes. Bake at 220°C for about 20 minutes, until browned and fully cooked.

Vol-au-vent fillings see page 219

by McDougalls Catering Foods

Tuna and sweetcorn Mix equal quantity flaked tuna and sweetcorn with sufficient mayonnaise to bind. Season.

Mushroom Gently fry sliced mushrooms in butter. Bind with white sauce. Add soy sauce and seasoning to taste.

Seafood Mix together flaked white fish with prawns, lemon juice, paprika, and bind with white sauce.

Tomato and mushroom Gently fry thinly sliced tomatoes and mushrooms in butter. Bind with white sauce.

Curried chicken Mix cold cooked, chopped chicken with small amount of curry powder and white sauce.

Hartig Boterletter (savoury butter letter)

by The Dutch Dairy Bureau

Key learning points
» roll, cut and shape puff pastry
» bake and serve a traditional Dutch dish

SERVES 2 to 4

225 g	puff pastry	8 oz
75 g	Gouda grated	3 oz
30 ml	tomato chutney/pickle	2 tbsp
10 ml	mixed herbs	2 tsp
1	eating apple, cored and finely chopped	1
	seasoning to taste	
1	egg, beaten lightly with little water	1
12 g	flaked almonds	½ oz

1 Roll out the pastry into a long rectangle about 15 × 50 cm (6 × 18 inches).

2 Spread the chutney or pickle over all the pastry, except for: a strip of 3 to 4 cm along one of the long sides (to seal the pastry later) and a narrow strip at both short ends (so that they too can be sealed).

3 Sprinkle the grated Gouda, herbs and chopped apple over the chutney.

4 Brush with beaten egg the strip along the long edge that you have left uncovered.

5 Starting with the long edge that has been covered with the mixture, carefully roll the pastry up (in the same way as you would a Swiss roll), right up to the strip which has been brushed with egg. Press along this edge firmly, so that the pastry is sealed.

6 Brush the open ends of the 'sausage' with the beaten egg, and fold the pastry edges underneath to seal.

7 Shape the roll into the initial of your choice (the letter 'C' would be quite easy, 'B' rather more complex).

8 Place the shaped pastry, seam down on to a greased baking sheet. Brush the top of the pastry with the beaten egg to glaze, and sprinkle with the flaked almonds.

9 Bake in a hot oven, 230°C, for 20 minutes until golden brown.

Nutty savoury pasties

by The British Egg Information Service

Key learning points
» use ready-made puff pastry
» make a dish suitable for vegetarians
» glaze with nuts or sesame seeds

The filling for this dish can be used in place of sausage meat in the recipe for sausage rolls.

SERVES 4

1 × 200 g	packet frozen puff pastry, thawed	1 × 7 oz
50 g	Cheddar cheese, grated	2 oz
½	small onion, peeled and grated	½
3	eggs	3
1	slice bread, made into breadcrumbs	1
30 ml	fresh parsley, chopped	2 tbsp
	seasoning to taste	
	pinch cayenne pepper	
15 ml	chopped nuts or sesame seeds	1 tbsp

1 Roll out the pastry on a lightly floured surface large enough to cut out 4 × 18 cm (7 inch) rounds.

2 Mix together the cheese, onion, 2 eggs, parsley and seasoning.

3 Spoon the mixture evenly into the centre of each round of pastry. Brush round the edges of the pastry with the remaining beaten egg. Press together and seal.

4 Glaze the tops of the pasties with the remaining egg beaten lightly and sprinkle on the nuts or sesame seeds.

5 Place on a baking tray and bake at 200°C for 15 minutes or until light golden brown.

Fish plait
by McDougalls Catering Foods

Key learning points
» prepare short pastry from a convenience product
» combine fish and shellfish with white sauce to form a filling for a pastry case
» plait pastry

SERVES 10

450 g	short crust pastry mix	1 lb
125 ml	cold water	4 fl oz
100 g	smoked salmon	4 oz
100 g	prawns	4 oz
900 g	white fish, poached and flaked, e.g. cod, haddock	2 lb
600 ml	white sauce, cold	1 pt
25 g	fresh dill, chopped	1 oz
	beaten egg to glaze	

1 Make up the short pastry with water, as directed on the packet.

2 Roll out the pastry to form a long rectangle about 50 × 30 cm (20 × 12 inches).

3 Make two light cuts (as marks for cutting the plaits) along the length of the rectangle, to divide it into three equal bands each about 10 cm wide. The centre band will form the base for the fish mixture. The two outer bands are cut into plaits to fold up over the fish. To do this, cut parallel strips about 15 mm wide, working out from your marking lines.

4 Combine the fish with the sauce and dill. Place in the centre (uncut) band of the pastry.

5 Fold the side strips of pastry over alternately – one from the left, one from the right – to form a plait which covers the fish mixture (photograph on page 229).

6 Transfer to a baking tray. Brush with beaten egg and bake at 220°C for about 15 minutes until golden. Serve hot.

Quiche lorraine

Key learning points
» prepare fresh short pastry
» line a flan case
» use eggs to set a mixture
Alternatives:
a) omit the cheese for quiche lorraine
b) use cream in place of some or all the milk for a richer recipe
c) season with pinch of grated nutmeg

SERVES 8

450 g	short pastry	1 lb
10 g	butter, margarine or oil	½ oz
100 g	streaky bacon	4 oz
75 g	grated cheese (preferably Gruyère)	3 oz
350 ml	milk	12 fl oz
2	large eggs	2
1	clove garlic, crushed and peeled	1
	seasoning to taste	
	pinch cayenne pepper	

1 Line a 20 cm flan case with the pastry.

2 Cut the bacon into pieces roughly 7 mm square.

3 Heat the butter, margarine or oil in a frying pan, add the garlic and bacon and lightly cook without browning.

4 Sprinkle the garlic and bacon evenly across the base of the flan case. Layer the grated cheese on top of the garlic and bacon.

5 Whisk together the eggs and milk, and lightly season with the salt, pepper and cayenne pepper.

6 Pour most of this mixture into the flan case – it is best to do this by ladling it through a conical strainer – to cover the bacon, garlic and cheese. Top up with the remaining mixture after placing the flan on the oven shelf. This will avoid the risk of spilling.

7 Bake in a moderate oven at 190°C until cooked: about 40 minutes. The texture should feel just set when pressed lightly with a finger.

8 Allow the flan to cool slightly, then remove the flan ring:

for immediate service: transfer the flan to a warm serving dish, lined with a dish paper if required

in advance of service: place the flan on a clean tray or plate, cool quickly, and store in the refrigerator until required.

Potato spinach pie
by Mary Gwynn in BBC Vegetarian Good Food

Key learning points
» use puff or rough puff pastry for a vegetable pie
» make a dish suitable for vegetarians

SERVES 4 to 6

60 ml	olive oil	4 tbsp
1 kg	new potatoes, thinly sliced	2 lb
2	red onions, sliced	2
45 ml	fresh chives, chopped	3 tbsp
	freshly grated nutmeg	
25 g	toasted sesame seeds	1 oz
225 g	fresh spinach	8 oz
225 g	puff or rough puff pastry	8 oz
	seasoning to taste	
1	beaten egg	1

1 Boil the spinach for a minute or two. Cool quickly under running water and drain thoroughly.

2 Heat the oil in a large frying pan. Add the potatoes and onions, and cook over a medium heat for 5 minutes stirring frequently. Stir in the chives, nutmeg, sesame seeds and seasoning. Drain in a colander.

3 Roll out half the pastry and use to line a 20 cm (8 inch) deep pie plate. Layer the potato mixture with the spinach leaves over the pastry.

4 Brush the pastry rim with the beaten egg or water. Roll out the other half of pastry and use to cover the pie. Trim and seal edges. Re-roll pastry trimmings and use to decorate the pie.

5 Brush the pie with beaten egg, place on a baking sheet and cook for 35 to 40 minutes at 200°C. Serve hot.

Cornish pasties

Key learning points

» use preprepared fresh short pastry/ or a convenience product
» make a traditional dish

SERVES 10

750 g	short pastry	1 lb 14 oz
375 g	lean (or extra lean) coarse beef mince	15 oz
275 g	potato, finely diced	10 oz
125 g	onion, diced	5 oz
	seasoning to taste	
2 – 3 eggs, lightly beaten with a little water		2 – 3

1 Place the beef, potato and onion together in a bowl. Season and mix together thoroughly.

2 Roll out the pastry to a thickness of 3 to 4 mm, then cut it into 10 rounds using a plain round pastry cutter about 15 cm in diameter.

3 Divide the filling between the rounds of pastry (see photograph on page 215).

4 Brush with beaten egg a band about 15 mm wide round the edge. This will help stick the edges of the pastry together.

5 Fold the round in half, bringing both edges of the pastry upwards so that they meet over the top of the filling, then press together to seal.

6 Make a series of pinches in the tops to create an attractive wavy edge.

7 Transfer the pasties to a lightly greased and floured baking tray. Brush the tops evenly with the beaten egg to glaze.

8 Bake at 200°C until cooked and golden brown, about 40 minutes.

9 When the pasties are cooked, take them out of the oven. Serve immediately, or quickly cool, then store chilled until required for service.

Norfolk pie
by McDougalls Catering Foods

Key learning points

» prepare short pastry using a convenience product
» make a traditional dish suitable for vegetarians

SERVES 10

450 g	short pastry mix *frozen*	1 lb
125 ml	cold water	4 fl oz
225 g	onions, sliced	8 oz
4	celery sticks, sliced	4
225 g each	carrot, swede, parsnip, and potato, all sliced	8 oz each
225 g	broccoli, cut into small florets	8 oz
100 g	margarine	4 oz
1 litre	mornay sauce (see page 143, or use convenience product)	2 pts
	beaten egg to glaze	

1 Slightly cook all the vegetables (not broccoli) in the margarine in a covered saucepan: 5 to 8 minutes. They should still be firm.

2 Layer all the vegetables in a deep 10 portion dish, alternately with the cheese sauce.

3 Make up the short crust pastry with the water, as directed on the packet.

4 Roll out the pastry to form a lid for the pie dish. Seal and decorate the edges.

5 Brush with beaten egg, and bake at 220°C until golden, about 25 minutes.

6 Clean the edges of the pie dish. Serve hot.

Rainbow tart
by McDougalls Catering Foods

Key learning points

» prepare short pastry using a convenience product
» make and pipe a Viennese mixture, decorate with jams and lemon curd

SERVES 10

450 g	short pastry mix	1 lb
125 ml	cold water	4 fl oz
225 g	plain flour	8 oz
225 g	soft margarine	8 oz
50 g	caster sugar	2 oz
	vanilla essence	
100 g each	apricot jam, raspberry jam, lemon curd	4 oz each

1 Make up the short pastry with the water, following the directions on the packet.

2 Roll out pastry and line a 30 × 23 cm greased shallow tray (12 × 8 inches).

3 Beat together the flour, margarine, sugar and vanilla essence until smooth (Viennese mixture).

4 Pipe the Viennese mixture down each long edge of the tray. Then, at equal distances (about 15 mm) from each other, pipe 5 parallel rows down the centre of the pastry.

5 Pipe the jams and lemon curd between these rows, so that you form a repeating pattern of apricot, raspberry and lemon curd.

6 Bake at 170°C for about 20 minutes until the pastry and Viennese mixture are cooked.

7 Serve hot or cold.

Lemon curd tarts

by Ruth Watson, Fox and Goose,
Fressingfield, Suffolk. Published by
Caterer & Hotelkeeper, 30 January 1992

Key learning points
» prepare a variation on basic short
   pastry
» line individual tart cases and bake blind
» prepare a lemon curd thickened with
   eggs

SERVES 10

Lemon curd

8	eggs, size 2	8
8	lemons, large and juicy	8
625 g	caster sugar	22 oz
280 g	unsalted butter, soft	10 oz

Pastry

225 g	plain flour	8 oz
140 g	unsalted butter	5 oz
1	egg yolk	1
45 ml	cold water	3 tbsp
15 ml	caster sugar	1 tbsp
5 ml	icing sugar	1 tsp
	pinch of salt	

Lemon curd – prepare in advance if
required

1 Squeeze lemons, straining juice into
   a bowl. Before squeezing one of the
   lemons, grate the zest over the bowl,
   to collect all the volatile aromatic
   oils.

2 In a double saucepan over simmering
   water, or heavy bottomed pan over
   low heat, melt the butter. Add lemon
   juice, zest and sugar, whisk until the
   sugar has dissolved.

3 Beat eggs and slowly incorporate into
   the lemon/butter mixture. Keep
   stirring over heat until the mixture
   has thickened enough to form
   'ribbons' when lifted (see page 194).

4 Remove from the heat. Stir
   occasionally while the curd cools.

5 Use immediately. Or pour into
   sterilised jars and seal. Store in a
   cool room.

Pastry

1 Sift flour, sugars and salt together.
   Add butter (chopped). Mix until like
   rough breadcrumbs.

2 Beat egg yolk with the water. Mix
   quickly into other ingredients to make
   pastry. Cover and chill for 20 minutes.

   Roll out thinly, cut into circles and

line 10 tart cases (non-stick or well
greased). Allow to rest. Bake blind at
200°C for 10 to 15 minutes until
lightly coloured. (See page 225.)

4 When cool, fill each tart with lemon
   curd. It forms a more attractive finish
   if you swirl it in with a large spoon.
   Decorate with candied lemon peel.

Individual fruit tartlets

by McDougalls Catering Foods

Key learning points
» prepare short pastry using a
   convenience product
» whip and pipe cream, and combine with
   seasonal fresh fruits
» prepare pastry leaves and use to finish
   dish
Photograph on page 220 shows another
way of cutting the pastry.

SERVES 10

450 g	short pastry mix	1 lb
100 ml	cold water	4 fl oz
550 ml	whipping cream	1 pt
275 g	fresh fruit as available:	10 oz
	strawberries, cherries, redcurrants,	
	blackberries, etc.	

1 Make up pastry mix with the water,
   as directed on the packet.

2 Roll quite thin, and cut out into 20
   rounds (8 cm diameter). Make 10
   small leaves with remaining pastry.

3 Place pastry rounds and leaves on a
   greased baking tray. Bake at 220°C
   for 5 to 10 minutes until lightly
   browned.

4 When cool, divide the rounds into
   two groups, 10 for the base, and 10
   for the tops.

5 Whip the cream. Pipe a generous
   swirl of cream on to the base rounds.
   Decorate with fruit. Cover with the
   top rounds.

6 Decorate each fruit pastry 'sandwich'
   with a piped rosette of cream, a piece
   of fruit and pastry leaf. Dust with
   icing sugar. Chill until served.

Apple tart

by Redmond Hayward. Published by
Caterer & Hotelkeeper, 30 January 1992

Key learning points
» prepare a variation on the basic short
   pastry recipe
» prepare single-portion tarts
» glaze with icing sugar

SERVES 6

75 g	butter	3 oz
180 g	flour	6 oz
½	egg	½
	pinch of salt	
75 g	apple purée	3 oz
1 – 2	dessert apples, peeled, cored	1 – 2
	and cut into thin segments	

1 Sift the flour and salt. Rub the butter
   (chopped) into the flour to form light
   breadcrumb texture.

2 Make a well in the centre of the flour/
   butter mixture, add egg. Mix from
   the centre outwards to incorporate
   the flour/butter slowly. Cover and
   chill for about 20 minutes.

3 Roll out the pastry to a thickness of
   about 5 mm. With a 75 mm (3 inch)
   pastry cutter, press out 6 bases. Place
   on a greased baking sheet. Rest.

4 Place a dessertspoon of apple purée
   on each pastry base. Top with apple
   segments, fanned or overlapped in a
   circle.

5 Dust with icing sugar. Bake in a
   moderate oven (160°C to 180°C) for
   about 10 minutes.

6 Grill quickly to brown the surface.
   Dust again with icing sugar.

Baked pears in pastry

Key learning points
» use prepared sweet short pastry
» prepare pears for cooking
» bake fruit in a pastry case

SERVES 4

225 g	sweet short pastry	8 oz
4	pears, medium ripe	4
10 g	caster sugar	½ oz
1	egg, lightly beaten	1

1 Prepare the pears:

cut the stalks off

peel carefully, removing as little flesh as possible from the pears

using a corer or peeler, and working up from the base to the centre where the pips are located, remove the core

until required for cooking, leave in water with the juice of half a lemon added. This will stop the pears turning brown.

2 Roll out the pastry to a thickness of 3 mm, and cut into 4 triangles large enough to enclose the pears.

3 Drain the pears, wipe them, then, holding them upside down, spoon a little sugar into the hole cut in each pear. How much sugar you need to use will depend on the sweetness of the pears.

4 Place a pear at the centre of each triangle of pastry, taking care that the sugar does not fall out. Dampen the edges with the beaten egg, draw the corners upwards and seal to enclose the pears. Pinch the sides together and if required decorate the tops with pastry leaves (see page 220).

5 Brush with the beaten egg, then bake at 200°C until lightly browned, about 30 minutes.

6 Serve hot, accompanied with cream or custard.

Lemon meringue pie

Key learning points
» use sweet short pastry
» line a flan ring, and bake 'blind'
» make a lemon curd mixture
» make and pipe meringue

SERVES 6

275 g	sweet short pastry	10 oz
300 ml	water	12 fl oz
175 g	sugar	6½ – 7 oz
25 g	cornflour	1 oz
3	lemons	3
50 g	butter	2 oz
2	egg yolks	2
100 ml	egg white	4 fl oz
200 g	caster sugar	8 oz
	pinch of salt	

1 Line the flan case with pastry, and bake blind. (See page 225.)

2 Grate the zest from the lemons. Squeeze out the juice and strain.

3 Place the water and sugar into a saucepan and bring to the boil.

4 Dilute the cornflour with a little cold water and stir into the boiling water and sugar. Simmer for about 2 minutes, stirring occasionally to produce a thick, smooth paste.

5 Remove from the heat, add the butter, fruit juice and zest, stirring thoroughly. Mix in the egg yolks.

6 Pour the filling into the flan case.

7 Prepare the meringue:

scald the whisk and mixing bowl with boiling water to remove all traces of grease (see page 242)

whisk the egg whites with 25 g (1 oz) of the sugar, and a small pinch of salt to form a stiff mixture. Add two-thirds of the remaining sugar, a bit at a time

when a firm meringue has been produced, carefully fold through the remaining sugar.

8 Pipe the meringue neatly across the top of the flan. Bake at 200°C until the meringue is a good colour, about 5 minutes.

Fresh fruit shortcakes
by The Butter Council

Key learning points
» prepare a variation on sweet short pastry using butter
» make shortbread tartlets using patty tins as moulds
» use fromage frais as a base for fruit filling
» combine seasonal fruits to form an attractive presentation, and glaze with honey

SERVES 4

100 g	butter	4 oz
50 g	caster sugar	2 oz
175 g	plain flour	6 oz
	pinch salt	
275 g	fromage frais, plain or flavoured	10 oz
	fresh fruit as available: grapes, kiwi fruit, cherries, strawberries, bananas, apple, pineapple etc.	
30 ml	clear honey	2 tbsp

1 Beat butter and sugar together until evenly blended.

2 Add flour and salt, and work in until the mixture resembles breadcrumbs. Gather together to form a dough and knead quickly until smooth. Rest for 20 minutes.

3 Roll out carefully and cut out to line shallow patty tins, greased.

4 Prick each pastry case 3 or 4 times with a fork. Allow to rest.

5 Bake at 170°C for 10 to 15 minutes until lightly browned.

6 When cool, remove carefully from the patty tins.

7 Just before serving, place a little fromage frais in each tartlet, then top with the fresh fruit, neatly arranged. Brush with warmed honey to glaze.

Steak and kidney pudding

Key learning points
» prepare suet pastry
» steam a steak and kidney pudding

SERVES 10

1 kg	prepared stewing beef (e.g. thick flank) in 20 mm cubes (see page 55)	2 lb
275 g	prepared ox kidney, in 10 mm cubes	10 oz
275 g	onion, chopped	10 oz
25 g	plain flour	1 oz
15 ml	Worcestershire sauce	3 tsp
400 ml	brown stock	16 fl oz
1 kg	suet pastry	2 lb
	parsley, freshly chopped	
	seasoning to taste	
	white fat for greasing basin	

1 Mix together the beef, kidney, onions, parsley, seasoning and flour. Add the Worcestershire sauce and enough stock to cover the ingredients. Mix again.

2 Lightly grease two pudding basins, each with a capacity of 800 ml (about 32 fl oz).

3 Roll out three-quarters of the pastry and line the basins with it (see page 221).

4 Fill the basins with the beef and kidney mixture, leaving a small gap, about 15 mm between the filling and the top of the pastry.

5 Roll out the remaining pastry and use it to cover the puddings. Seal the edges and trim off excess pastry.

6 Cover each pudding with a circle of lightly greased greaseproof paper, pleating the paper in the middle to allow for expansion during cooking. Secure with a pudding cloth.

7 Place into an atmospheric or low-pressure steamer, or over boiling water in a saucepan and steam for 4 hours. Check this timing with workplace instructions for the particular equipment you are using.

8 When the puddings are cooked, remove the cloths and paper, and clean around the sides of the bowls. Wrap a folded napkin round each basin and serve on a dish or salver lined with a dishpaper. Just before service, a sprig of parsley can be placed in the centre of each pudding as decoration.

Huntingdon pie
by McDougalls Catering Foods

Key learning points
» prepare suet pastry using a convenience mix
» make and decorate a traditional pie

SERVES 10

1 kg	sliced bacon, rind trimmed off	2 lb
1 kg	cooking apples, peeled, cored and sliced	2 lb
450 g	onion, sliced	1 lb
½ litre	cider	1 pt
450 g	prepared suet pastry mix	1 lb
200 ml	water	7 fl oz
	seasoning to taste	
	beaten egg to glaze	

1 Layer the bacon, onion and apples in a 23 × 23 cm pie dish (9 × 9 inches.)

2 Pour over the cider. Season.

3 Make up the suet pastry mix as directed on the packet.

4 Roll out the pastry, and cover the top of the dish. Seal and decorate the edges. Brush with the beaten egg.

5 Bake in a moderate oven (160°C to 180°C) for 1 to 1½ hours.

6 Clean round the edge of the dish. Serve hot.

Chicken and mushroom pasties
by McDougalls (RHM Foods)

Key learning points
» prepare variation of short pastry with wholemeal flour
» prepare a variation of traditional pasties

SERVES 4

Pastry

225 g	wholemeal flour	8 oz
50 g	margarine	2 oz
50 g	lard	2 oz
	cold water to mix	
	beaten egg to glaze	

Filling

15 g	butter	½ oz
100 g	mushrooms, sliced	4 oz
25 g	plain flour	1 oz
150 ml	chicken stock	5 fl oz
45 ml	white wine	3 tbsp
175 g	chicken, cooked and diced	6 oz

1 Prepare filling: fry mushrooms in butter, stir in flour and cook for 1 minute. Gradually add the stock and wine, stirring continuously until the sauce boils and thickens. Add chicken and season. Cool.

2 Prepare pastry: rub margarine and lard into flour, stir in sufficient cold water to form a dough.

3 Roll out on a floured surface. Cut out 4 × 15 cm (6 inch) squares.

4 Divide filling between pastry squares, damp edges with a little stock or water, fold over and seal.

5 Place on a lightly greased baking sheet, glaze with beaten egg and bake for about 20 minutes at 200°C. Serve hot or cold.

Feta, olive and scorched pepper tartlets

by Richard Cawley in BBC Vegetarian Good Food

Key learning points
» prepare variation of fresh short pastry
» make tartlets
» make a dish suitable for vegetarians

It is easier to peel the peppers after step 3 if you leave them in a closed plastic bag for 30 minutes. Alternatively pierce the whole peppers with a skewer 2 or 3 times near the stem, then bake at 240°C for 34 to 45 minutes, turning half way through. They will become soft, blistered and dark.

SERVES 6

225 g	plain flour, sifted with ¾ tsp salt	8 oz
100 g	unsalted butter	4 oz
1	egg yolk, lightly beaten	1
4	large red peppers, quartered and deseeded	4
175 g	feta cheese, cut into small cubes	6 oz
175 g	black olives, stoned	6 oz
30 ml	extra virgin olive oil	2 tbsp

1 Rub the butter into the flour. Mix to a soft dough with the egg yolk and about 2 tbsp of iced water. Chill for 30 minutes.

2 Roll out and use to line six 10 cm (4 inch) loose-bottomed individual flan tins. Prick the bottoms with a fork and bake blind for 10 to 15 minutes at 220°C until pale golden. Do not allow to overcook.

3 Arrange the pepper quarters cut side down, on a lightly oiled baking sheet and grill until the skin is completely blackened. When cool, peel and cut the flesh into bite-sized pieces.

4 Mix the pepper pieces with the cheese and olives, and divide between the pastry cases. Drizzle with olive oil, season with black pepper and return to the oven to bake for 5 to 6 minutes. Serve hot.

NVQ SVQ RANGE CHECKLIST

LEVEL 1

1D8.1 Prepare pastry dishes

prepare preprepared or convenience pastry of 2 of these types

- [ ] short
- [ ] sweet
- [ ] puff

using 4 of these preparation methods

- [ ] rolling
- [ ] defrosting
- [ ] resting
- [ ] cutting
- [ ] shaping

for 3 of these products

- [ ] pies or pasties
- [ ] tarts or flans
- [ ] sausage or vegetarian rolls
- [ ] vol-au-vents or bouchées

1D8.2 Cook pastry dishes

using 2 of these preprepared or convenience pastries

- [ ] short
- [ ] sweet
- [ ] puff

to make 3 of these pastry dishes

- [ ] pies or pasties
- [ ] tarts or flans
- [ ] sausage or vegetarian rolls
- [ ] vol-au-vents or bouchées

and finishing by 1 of these methods

- [ ] dusting
- [ ] filling

LEVEL 2

2D8.1 Prepare fresh pastry

prepare 3 of these types of fresh pastry

- [ ] short
- [ ] sweet
- [ ] puff or rough puff
- [ ] suet

using 4 of these preparation methods

- [ ] mixing
- [ ] folding
- [ ] rolling
- [ ] relaxing
- [ ] kneading

2D8.2 Prepare and cook pastry dishes

from 3 of these types of prepared pastry

- [ ] short
- [ ] sweet
- [ ] puff or rough puff
- [ ] suet

using 3 of these preparation methods

- [ ] cutting
- [ ] shaping
- [ ] glazing
- [ ] rolling

and 2 of these finishing methods

- [ ] dusting
- [ ] piping
- [ ] filling

to make 3 of these pastry dishes

- [ ] pies or pasties
- [ ] sausage or vegetarian rolls
- [ ] tarts or flans
- [ ] suet puddings
- [ ] vol-au-vents or bouchées
- [ ] sweet pastries

Food Preparation and Cooking

Cakes and biscuits

Introduction

Perhaps the most important – and most enjoyable – feature of baked flour products, like cakes and biscuits, is the texture, whether it is delicate, crunchy, chewy or crumbly.

To get these textures exactly right, you need to work very precisely. The ingredients listed in a recipe have been carefully selected so that the different flours, fats, sugars, liquids and flavours all blend and react with each other correctly. This kind of recipe is so exactly formulated that if you use too much of one ingredient, too little of another, or substitute a different ingredient from the one given, you will almost certainly end up with a poor quality product, or perhaps a failure.

The method laid out in the recipe instructions will also have been worked out very carefully to make sure that the ingredients combine and bake properly. Any change to it can result in disaster, for example, if you:

- add an ingredient too soon
- do not beat the mixture enough
- use equipment which is too warm, or too cold, or work in an area of the kitchen which is too hot
- use mixing equipment which still has traces of grease on it from when it was last used
- set the oven at a temperature which is too high or too low.

Contents guide

 Units and elements covered in this section

1D9 Prepare, cook and decorate convenience cakes and biscuits `LEVEL 1`

- 1D9.1 Prepare convenience cake and biscuit mixtures
- 1D9.2 Cook convenience cakes and biscuits
- 1D9.3 Decorate convenience cakes and biscuits

2D9 Prepare, cook and decorate cakes and biscuits `LEVEL 2`

- 2D9.1 Prepare cake and biscuit mixtures
- 2D9.2 Cook cakes and biscuits
- 2D9.3 Decorate cakes and biscuits

Quality points

Baking products
- packaging in good condition
- correctly labelled
- not passed its use-by or best-before date

Storage of dairy products
1 Keep clean and covered.
2 Keep well apart from strong-smelling foods.
3 Rotate stocks, so that older stock is used first.
4 Do not use products which have passed their use-by or best-before date.

Cream will keep in a refrigerator unopened for up to 10 days. Double and whipping creams have a shorter shelf-life than single and half creams.

Once thawed, *frozen pasteurised cream* will keep fresh in a refrigerator for several days.

Unopened:

- *sterilised cream* (mainly sold in cans) will keep up to two years

- *UHT cream* (usually sold in cartons or plastic tubs) will keep for 2 to 4 months depending on the fat content. No need to refrigerate, but keep cool

- *UHT cream in aerosol cans* will keep for up to 3 months in a refrigerator.

Once opened, these products should be treated as fresh cream.

NUTRITION

Milk is an important source of:

calcium – a mineral, essential for growing children in forming strong teeth and bones, and throughout life for the maintenance of strong bones

riboflavin – helps the body to use protein, fat and carbohydrates to produce energy and build tissues

vitamin B12 – necessary for growth and blood cell formation. Required for the maintenance of a healthy nervous system.

The different types of milk are graded according to their *fat* content. The average for whole milk is 3.9% (of which 2.3% is saturated). For semi-skimmed milk a little over half the butterfat has been removed to give an average fat content of 1.6%. For skimmed milk almost all the fat has been removed to give an average of 0.1%.

Freezing cream and dishes containing cream

Do not attempt to freeze half, single or soured cream.

Double and whipping cream can be frozen in small quantities: up to 300 ml (½ pt). There will be some reduction in whipping properties (for this reason, it is usually better to buy commercially frozen cream, or purchase fresh).

For both whipping and double cream, best results are obtained by lightly whipping the cream before freezing. Thaw for 24 hours in a refrigerator. The semi-whipped cream may then be whipped to the desired consistency, but do not over-whip. (There is very little advantage in adding sugar to whipped cream before freezing.)

Whipping cream will whip satisfactorily after frozen storage for up to 2 months. But the longer the cream is frozen, the more buttery it becomes on thawing.

Double cream tends to become buttery more readily than whipping cream, so only 1 month freezer storage is recommended.

Clotted cream may be frozen but tends to become buttery after 1 month.

Most dishes containing cream will freeze successfully. Desserts with a high proportion of cream should be frozen for 1 month only, as longer storage leads to development of a granular texture.

Types of flour

Most cake recipes use *soft flours*. They are pure white, feel smooth and fine, and will stay in a lump if squeezed together. Soft flours develop far less gluten (see page 245) than strong or hard flours, which are mainly used for bread and other dough products.

General or *all-purpose flours* are a blend of hard and soft flours. They are designed to be used for a wide range of products, but do not produce the same quality cakes and pastries as the specialised products.

High-ratio flours are specially milled to a very fine particle size and heavily bleached so that they will absorb a lot of moisture. They are most effective when combined with a special high-ratio fat and quite economical for cakes because they can be used with fewer eggs than usual, and more liquid and sugar.

Self-raising flour is soft flour with a raising agent added. It should be used within 2 to 3 months of purchase, because the raising agent eventually loses its effectiveness.

Wholemeal flour consists of the whole of the wheat grain. Nothing is removed during the milling process, giving a flour which is high in dietary fibre and protein. Wholemeal flour absorbs more moisture than white flour, so it may be necessary to add more liquid when substituting wholemeal flour for white in recipes.

Wholemeal self-raising flour is a special soft cake flour. It gives a light texture, subtle nutty flavour and golden colour to the baked product.

Nuts

Nut is a term used to describe a seed that is covered with a hard shell.

Nuts in general are very nutritious, providing protein, vitamins, minerals and fibre. However they are also high in fat – brazils, for example, contain 66%.

Other varieties include: almonds, cashews, chestnuts, hazels (lower in fat than most other nuts), macadamia, peanuts, pecans, pine nuts, pistachios (more expensive than most other nuts) and walnuts.

Raising agents

These react with other ingredients in the mixture to produce bubbles of carbon dioxide and so help give the baked product volume and lightness. (Yeast, a raising agent used extensively in baking breads and other dough products, also creates carbon dioxide – see page 204.)

Sodium bicarbonate (commonly known as baking soda) is the simplest raising agent. However, it tends to leave a strong flavour and yellow colouration. It is used in some recipes for scones (where the after-flavour is not particularly noticeable).

Baking powder is a mixture of sodium bicarbonate (alkali) and an acid salt such as cream of tartar. It does not affect the colour or taste of the food. Some baking powders are double acting. This means that they release some gas bubbles immediately they come into contact with the recipe liquid, and then have a second stage of reaction when they are heated.

Sugar

Besides the obvious effect of making cakes and biscuits sweet, sugar also contributes to:

tenderness and moistness – this comes from sugar's ability to absorb liquid in the mixture, so preventing some of the proteins in the flour from forming gluten and reducing evaporation of moisture

lightness – when fat and sugar are creamed together, the sugar crystals cut air pockets in the fat

browning – this happens very effectively in high-temperature cooking when sugar is in the mixture.

Brown sugars give a richer colour and flavour than white and are particularly suitable for fruit cakes and gingerbreads.

For creamed mixtures, always choose caster or soft brown sugar, as this is easier to cream, ensuring a lighter texture.

Sometimes honey, golden syrup or treacle are used in place of all or some of the sugar.

CHEF'S TIPS

If you don't have self-raising flour, as specified in the recipe, use plain flour and add some baking powder. 400 g (1 lb) self-raising flour is equivalent to 450 g plain flour with 20 ml (4 tsp) baking powder.

Preparation methods

Using convenience products `LEVEL 1`

Always follow the instructions on the packet.

Before use, thaw *frozen cream pieces* (chips, sticks or cubes) at room temperature for 30 to 120 minutes. Pots of frozen cream may take longer.

Rapid thawing will spoil the appearance of frozen gâteaux. Remove any vacuum sealed packing before defrosting.

Thaw a large gâteau on the top shelf of the refrigerator for 12 hours. Never refreeze a frozen product which has been partially or fully thawed.

Portioning `LEVEL 1`

1 Before starting to cut cakes and gâteaux, check exactly what size portions you should be preparing. Customers will all expect to get the same size, and the price they pay is based on a particular portion size.

2 Plan how you are going to divide the cake, so that you get the required number of portions, all of the same size. For example, if it's 8 pieces per gâteau, cut the gâteau:

exactly into half

each half into half again, to get quarters

each quarter into half, to get eighths.

For frozen gâteaux, cheese cakes and similar products, the best portion can be obtained by cutting each slice when partially thawed. Use a long knife dipped briefly in very hot water. For easier handling, place a small square of greaseproof paper between each slice.

Victoria sandwich (see recipe on page 253) is prepared by the creaming method.

Cake making `LEVEL 2`

Drawn extensively from Better Baking *published by McDougalls*

Cakes can be classified according to the methods by which they are made.

Creaming

This method gives a light textured cake with good keeping qualities. (It is sometimes called the *sugar batter method*.)

1 Cut up the fat (softened but not melted). Beat until soft with a wooden spoon or spatula. Add the sugar and beat until light and fluffy.

2 Sieve or mix together the flour and any salt or spices which are used. Slowly add the eggs to the creamed mixture with a little of the flour. Stir, then beat thoroughly. Care must be taken when adding eggs – the mixture will separate and be ruined if too much is present.

3 Stir in milk and any syrup if used, and a little flour. Beat again. Add any additional ingredients such as fruit and flavourings, and the rest of the flour. Fold in lightly but thoroughly, and bake as directed.

Whisking

This method is used for very light sponges and Swiss rolls. Occasionally, oiled butter is added to give a special flavour and texture.

1 Have ready a large saucepan containing some boiling water (typically about 8 cm/3 inches deep), and a mixing bowl which fits over the pan without touching the water.

2 Break the eggs into the bowl, add sugar and whisk together over the boiling water until the mixture thickens and is luke warm. Take great care not to overheat the mixture.

3 Remove the bowl and whisk until the mixture is very thick and ropey. Add the flour or mixed flour and salt, using a metal spoon. Lightly cut and fold the flour into the mixture. Do this thoroughly but gently so that the air is not knocked out.

If using a machine, it is not necessary to place the bowl over hot water.

The one-stage method

The quickest and easiest of all.

1 Place flour, salt (if used), sugar, soft margarine and eggs in a bowl, together with any other ingredients.

2 Stir gently at first (so the flour does not fly out of the bowl).

Rubbing in

This method produces an open texture. Similar to the method used to make short pastry, the quantities are less critical than with other methods. This means the fat and sugar can be reduced to give a more economical or diet-conscious recipe. Block margarine or butter may be used – soft margarine will not give the correct texture or support the fruit used.

1 Sieve or mix together the flour, salt and spice (if used).

2 Rub fat and flour between fingertips until mixture resembles fine breadcrumbs. Then stir in the sugar, fruit and any flavourings.

3 Make a well in the centre, add beaten egg, any milk and water or syrup that may be included in the recipe. Mix well then bake as directed.

Melting

This method is used for some biscuits. It makes a product with good keeping qualities, but for best results the biscuits should be left to mature and soften for a day or so before serving.

1 Sieve flour, spices, any raising agents and salt into a bowl.

2 Place fat, sugar and syrup (if used) in a saucepan. Heat gently until the sugar has dissolved and fat melted.

3 Add this syrup mixture to the flour with milk and any eggs, and beat until smooth. Smooth into greased tin and bake as directed.

Some points to remember

1 Unless otherwise specified in the recipe, leave fat at room temperature for half an hour before using.

2 Remove eggs from refrigerator half an hour or so before use.

3 Do not over-cream butter and sugar (quite easy to do with a machine). The mixture should have a fluffy, creamy and pale consistency, but not be completely white.

4 If you need to wash dried fruit, use hot water if the fruit seems very dry. This will make it plumper. Otherwise use cold water. To dry, spread out on flat trays (loosely covered with a clean tea towel) and leave in a hot cupboard for 2 or 3 hours. Rinse sugared or glacé fruits in warm water and dry. Otherwise the sugary coating may cause the fruit to sink.

5 Cake mixtures made with baking powder can be allowed to stand for a short time before baking, if necessary, but should never be left for more than 20 minutes.

Preparing baking containers   **LEVELS 1 + 2**

Generally, baking tins should be greased before use. This is done with a white fat such as pastry margarine – not butter or yellow margarine (see page 222) – hence the rather unpleasant sounding term 'greased'.

Light cakes with little or no fat – grease base.

Other light cakes – grease base and sides, then sprinkle with flour. As an added precaution against sticking, many chefs also line the base of the cake tin with greased greaseproof paper or baking parchment. Sometimes this is called *base line*.

Medium to heavy cakes such as Madeira and light fruit cake – grease base and sides, then line base and sides with greased greaseproof paper.

Dense cakes, such as rich fruit cakes – grease base and sides, then line base with a cardboard circle and three or four thicknesses of greased paper.

Square and oblong tins

1 Place the tin on a sheet of greaseproof paper, and pencil around the base. Trim the size of the paper, so that it will cover the base and the sides of the tin.

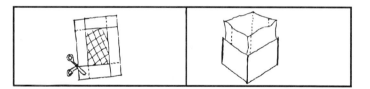

2 Cut along each corner, so that when the paper is placed in the tin, you can fold and overlap the sides.

Round tins

1 Cut a strip of paper about 6 cm (2 inches) wider than the depth of the tin, and long enough to wrap completely around the tin and overlap by about 2 cm.

2 Fold the paper along its length, so that the width of the wider strip equals the depth of the tin (therefore, the width of the shorter strip will be 6 cm). Cut a series of parallel cuts along the shorter strip, up to the fold. Place inside the greased tin, so that the cut edge fits around the base.

3 Place the tin on another sheet of paper, and pencil around the base. Cut out the circle, and fit into the tin.

How to separate eggs `LEVEL 2`

1 Holding the egg in one hand, hit the side of the egg on the edge of the bowl (or a firm, fairly sharp surface), so that the shell cracks open neatly.

2 Holding one end of the egg in each hand, and using your thumbs, prise it open carefully. Hold the egg above the bowl as you do this.

3 Keep the half with the yolk in it upright. Let the excess white drop into the bowl. Empty the white from the other half into the bowl.

4 Pour the yolk into the empty half shell, so that more egg white is released. Do this two or three times until you are just left with the yolk.

5 If you are separating several eggs, it is better to do them one at a time over a smaller bowl, transferring the white to the larger bowl after each egg. In this way, if there is a problem with one of the eggs, you will not spoil all the egg whites.

6 Scoop out any yolk or egg shell which spills into the white.

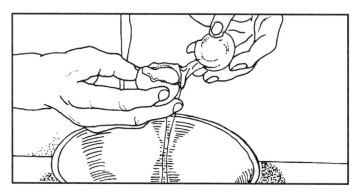

CHEF'S TIPS

Before whisking egg whites, scald the bowl and whisk in very hot water. Dry with a clean cloth or absorbent kitchen paper.

If you have one, use a copper bowl to whisk egg whites. Certain substances in the copper give the mixture greater stability. Otherwise add a pinch of cream of tartar.

ACTION

Make up a poster which might go by the mixing machine in a busy catering kitchen. The aim of the poster is to remind those using the machine of the various safety rules. (If you need to remind yourself what these are, see pages 7 and 224.)

If your supervisor agrees that the poster should go up, it will need to be laminated. Some photocopying shops will do this for you, or your training manager may have a machine.

What happens when egg white is beaten

When whipping begins, the egg white traps large pockets of air and the proteins begin to coagulate (start to attach to one another to form a sort of net).

The copper bowl on the left of the picture shows what happens:

- if whipping is stopped too soon – the liquid that contains uncoagulated protein will slowly drain way, causing the air pockets to burst and the foam to collapse

- if whipping goes on for too long – the coagulation will go so far that the liquid will start to seep out and the mixture will separate and lose volume.

If there is even a trace of fat in the mixing bowl or on the whisk, or any egg yolk (which contains fat) has got into the white by mistake, the effect is likely to be as disastrous as the mixture in the glass bowl on the right of the picture.

Once egg whites have been beaten to the right degree (and this is mainly judged from experience) they can stand the presence of fat. So beaten egg white can be used to give a light texture to sponge cakes, soufflés and similar products which contain fat.

Sugar is often added to egg white for flavour. While this can double the time it takes to whip the whites into a foam, the sugar strengthens the foam by absorbing some of the trouble-making water. To get the advantage without the hard work, add the sugar in stages:

- a small amount at the beginning

- up to two-thirds during whisking

- folding in the remainder after the whites have been whipped.

There are recipes for dishes with meringue on pages 17 and 234.

ACTION

Identify as many of the items in this photograph as you can, and note their name/main use below. You don't need to write a list of 54 items – many of them can be grouped. For example:

3, 4, 6, 7 mixing spoons   *2, 15, 16, 20, 38 mixing/storage bowls*

Now check your answer with page 246.

Cooking and finishing

`LEVELS 1 + 2`

How to get the best results in baking

1 Check in good time that the oven is at the temperature stated in the recipe.

2 Make sure that you use the correct size baking container. If the tin is too small, the mixture will continue rising, but without the support of the tin, it will collapse.

3 Place the filled baking tin in a suitable position in the oven. For a conventional oven this means for:

Swiss rolls: at the top

small cakes and sponges, scones: just above the centre

biscuits, Madeira cakes: centre

very rich fruit cakes: near the bottom.

4 If you open the oven door during the last few minutes of cooking to check progress, this will not usually cause a problem. (Before this stage, an influx of cold air will cause the cake to collapse.) Open the door by the minimum amount, and open and close it gently.

5 A cooked cake will:

feel firm when touched gently in the centre. A sponge cake will feel slightly spongy, and leave no imprint after being pressed

have shrunk slightly from the sides of the tin

have set throughout: a cocktail stick pushed in the centre comes out cleanly.

6 Follow recipe instructions for cooling the cooked product. Some dishes are turned out of the baking container after a couple of minutes, others have to be left for a while, or to cool completely. Place a rack over the top of the cake, turn upside down, and carefully lift off the cake tin. So that the cake top is not marked with indentations from the rack, invert it on to a second rack, or turn over very carefully by hand.

If the baking container has been well prepared, there should be no difficulty in turning the cake out.

Learning from your mistakes

Any of the specific problems described can also occur if you have used the:

– wrong sort of flour
– wrong position in the oven

Texture tough and chewy

– too much egg or flour used
– mixture has curdled (broken up into small lumps)

Texture coarse and open or uneven with large holes

– too much raising agent used
– undermixed
– oven too hot

Texture too solid and dense

– too much flour or fat used
– too little raising agent or liquid used
– cake dough overmixed
– scone dough over-handled, or liquid added too slowly
– too long a delay between mixing and cooking
– egg or fat has curdled
– oven not hot enough
– oven conditions too dry

Crust is too thick

– too much sugar
– oven not hot enough
– cooked for too long

Crust cracked

– oven too hot
– cake placed too high in the oven
– cake tin too small for recipe quantity
– too much flour or sugar used
– too little fat or liquid
– cake dough overmixed
– oven conditions too dry

Sunk in centre

– undercooked
– oven door opened during baking
– wrong quantity of liquid used

Crust too light in colour

– baking container too small
– oven temperature not hot enough
– not enough sugar

Crust too dark

– too much sugar
– oven temperature too high
– cooking time too long

Fruit in fruit cake sinks

– cake mixture too thin to support fruit
– pieces of fruit too big, or wet and syrupy

Biscuits spread too much on cooking

– too much liquid or egg used

Biscuits break when removed from the baking tray

– not enough time allowed to firm up (should be about 10 minutes)

What happens during baking

During baking, all flour products go through a similar sequence of events:

1 Air and/or gas in the mixture expands.

2 The mixture sets.

3 The surface browns and a crust forms.

Stages 1 and 2 are always closely linked. The recipe timing and cooking temperatures are designed to get the right balance for the ingredients used, so that the mixture sets at the moment that expansion has reached the right level.

How the mixture sets

Flours, eggs and milk all contain protein. When the proteins in the baking mixture reach a temperature of about 70°C they set (or *coagulate*). This is what gives structure to the final product.

There are many types of protein in flour, but it is the insoluble ones (called *gliadin* and *glutenin*) that are important in baking. When they are mixed with a liquid, they make a substance called *gluten*. (Wrap some flour in muslin and run it under the cold water tap. You will end up with the gluten.)

As well as coagulating when it is heated, gluten is extremely useful in baking because it is elastic enough to hold the bubbles of air and /or gases that are formed in the mixture and strong enough to stop them escaping (as they do in a very thick soup which is boiling, for instance).

As well as containing protein, flour is made up of starch, also important in baking. As soon as the flour is moistened with milk, for example, the starch granules start to absorb the moisture and swell, and the effect of this is that the mixture gets thicker. This helps to hold the structure until the proteins have set it. In a certain temperature range – 60°C to 65°C for wheat flours – the starch gelatinises and the cloudy appearance of the liquid changes to a clearer one. This is more obvious with cornflour than wheat flour.

How the surface browns

The things that contribute to browning are:

- high temperatures (above 150°C)

- sugar in the recipe and to some extent in the flour (which contains about 1% sugar)

- nitrogen compounds (milk is a good source)

- amino acids (eggs contain these).

Some products need help with browning. For example, items containing yeast (which uses up the sugar in the flour) sometimes need to be brushed with a little milk or beaten egg.

Although it is only the surface that is browned, the flavours that this creates spread through much of the product.

Crust formation

Crusts form easily on many baked products in the last stage of baking. What happens is that the water evaporates from the surface, leaving it dry.

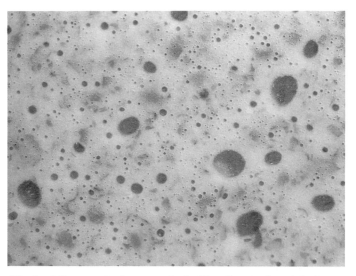

Much of the secret of success in baking has to do with the right amount of gas or air bubbles being created in the mixture while it is cooking (as in the picture above), and the mixture setting round them (as in the picture below) before they can escape.

Ovens do vary in their performance, so the first time you bake an item use the recommended temperature. Check the cooking progress and be prepared to adjust the temperature. Record any adjustments for future use of that particular oven.

Decoration methods

Using a piping bag

1 Select the nozzle you require. It should be the right size for the piping bag you are using, and have a plain or shaped end, as appropriate.

2 Push the nozzle right down to the pointed end of the piping bag. The nozzle should, of course, show through the opening. It should also make a tight fit with the bag, otherwise the mixture will ooze out, or the nozzle will shoot out of the bag.

3 If you are piping a rather soft mixture, there is a danger the mixture will run out of the bag while you are filling it. To avoid this, twist the bag a couple of times just above the nozzle, and firmly push the twisted part of the bag inside the nozzle. A clothes peg will do the job as well – but you might think it looks rather unprofessional!

4 Turn inside out the top one-third to half of the bag. This makes it easier to fill.

5 Holding the bag under the fold you have just made, spoon some of the mixture down into the bag. Do not fill more than halfway.

6 Unfold the top of the bag, then close it up neatly.

7 Take hold of the bag above the mixture. Pull the bag up between your thumb and forefinger until the palm of your hand is against the mixture.

8 Keep the top of the bag closed with your thumb and forefinger.

9 Exert pressure on the contents of the bag with the palm of your hand and the tips of your fingers. The other hand can be used a) to control the direction of the bag, or b) to hold the item being decorated.

10 Before starting a complicated decoration, make sure there is no air in the bag by squeezing some of the mixture out on to a plate or back into the bowl.

Opening the bag like this makes it easier to fill.

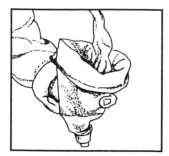

Try to drop the filling right down the bag, not on the sides.

Held properly, one hand is enough to squeeze out even firm mixtures.

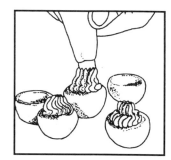

Using one hand to guide the direction of the nozzle.

This gâteau (see recipe on page 255) has been decorated with swirls of cream, pineapple pieces dipped in chocolate and piped chocolate motifs.

ANSWER ✓ ✓ ✓

ACTION page 243

Equipment often used in the mixing stage includes: *bowls made of glass, plastic, china (2) or stainless steel (15, 16, 20, 38); spoons made from wood (3, 4, 6, 7), plastic (33) or stainless steel (21) – sometimes perforated to help draining (23), whisks (5), rolling pins (17), flat tongs (24) and spatulas for lifting items, sieves for sifting flour (18), and straining (22), measuring jugs (53), scoops (54) and thermometers (25). For shaping mixtures: piping bags (9), and various nozzles (42), dough cutters (19), plain (36) and fluted (37), round cutters, as well as a variety of fancy shapes (41) for biscuits. For baking: some baking dishes are special shapes, as for horns (49), boats or barquettes (43); for individuals portions/cakes (12,13), pastry cases (8); for flans with plain (10) or fluted edges* (11), round cakes (50, 51, 52) or for particular purposes, such as deep cakes, e.g. fruit (1), square cakes (27, 28, 29), loaves (30), hollow circles or savarins (39), individual cakes, babas or crème caramels (35) called dariole moulds. China and porcelain dishes range from general-purpose pie dishes (32, 46, 47), to those used for soufflés (45) or individual soufflés or baked egg dishes (44), sur le plat dishes (34). Vitreous enamel dishes (48) are suitable for baking whole foods as well as made-up dishes. Baking trays come in many different sizes, many are made of black iron (see page 63), some of stainless steel (26, 40) or aluminium. Pastry brushes (14) are useful for producing a shiny, glazed surface, dredgers (31) for sprinkling flour or sugar over surfaces.

To make a paper piping bag

1 Cut a triangle from a sheet of greaseproof or waxed paper. To get the shape of the triangle and mark the cutting line, simply fold over one corner to meet the opposite edge.

2 With the longest side facing away from you, roll the paper up to form a cone, starting at one of the corners opposite you. If necessary, tighten the cone, so that the point is needle sharp.

3 Holding the cone firmly together with one hand, tuck the ends down inside to stop the cone unravelling.

4 Fill the piping bag – but not more than one-third full.

5 Flatten the cone above the filling. Fold over one side, then the other side. Finally, fold the centre over on to itself twice.

6 Cut off the tip of the piping bag with a sharp pair of scissors: the smaller the opening, the finer the decoration.

Step 1: cutting the paper.

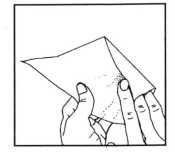

Step 2: in action.

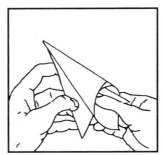

Step 2: Tightening the cone.

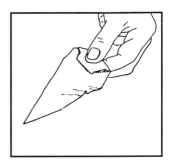

Step 5: with both sides folded in, and the centre folded over.

Using the bag

1 Keep the point of the bag a good distance above the surface (1 to 3 cm /½ to 1 inch), so that you can make a nice even decoration.

2 The faster you move the bag over the surface, the thinner the lines of decoration.

3 Try and work quickly. Don't leave a piping bag lying about with unused filling, otherwise the point will dry out, and you will have to start again with another bag.

The decoration in this illustration has been created by quickly drizzling chocolate over the surface, using a paper piping bag.

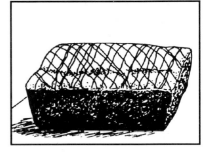

Feathered icing

Use fondant icing or glacé icing (adjust consistency so that it pipes easily – recipe on page 251).

1 Pipe parallel lines a short distance apart.

2 Turn the cake through 90° and run a long, thin bladed knife through the lines – the knife should barely touch the main surface – dragging the lines towards you. These lines should be quite well spaced, to allow for the series of lines made in the opposite direction (step 3). Wipe the knife blade clean after making each line.

3 Turn the cake through 180°, so that you pull the icing in the opposite direction. Drag the knife between each stroke in the same manner as before.

For a circular design, the first step is to draw a coil, starting from the centre of the cake. This can be difficult to do evenly, so practise drawing the coil on a work surface first.

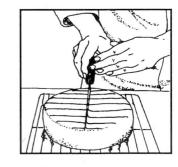

Points to remember when decorating

1 Start with the simplest ideas, until you gain the experience to be more ambitious. A simple decoration well done can be very effective. A complex decoration will be ruined by even a minor flaw.

2 Solid ingredients blended into piping mixtures should be ground fairly finely, otherwise they will clog the nozzle of the piping bag and spoil the smooth surface of the decoration.

3 When cutting a cake into two or more horizontal layers, keep the cake flat on the work surface. Use a long-bladed knife, sawing rather than pushing, as you keep the knife horizontal. Never stand the cake on its side.

4 If you are splitting a number of cakes, keep the layers of each cake together so that you can match them when you assemble the cake.

5 To decorate the sides of a cake:

if the cake can be picked up without risk of damaging it: spread the filling on a sheet of greaseproof paper, then holding the cake between the palms of your hands, gently roll it over the coating

for delicate cakes, press the coating against the side using a palette knife or your hands.

6 Allow almond paste to dry before coating with royal icing. Otherwise the oil is likely to discolour the icing. Brush the cake with jam or egg white before applying the almond paste, so that the paste sticks.

7 Allow icings to dry out before adding coloured icing as a decoration, otherwise the colours will mingle and spoil both the surface and the decoration.

8 Use colourings and essences sparingly. It is better to add a little at a time, until you have got the right effect.

9 When decorating fairly solid cakes, turn the cake over so that the flat base becomes the top. If what was the top is rounded, slice off so that it sits flat.

10 If you don't have access to a cake turntable, sit the cake on its board or on an upturned plate, on top of a basin. The basin acts as a turntable.

11 Practise piping decorations on a tray or board, before piping on to the cake. Scrape the icing off the tray before it hardens and return it to the bowl to use again.

Rolling a Swiss roll.

ACTION

In the space below devise a simple design that you could use for the top of a gâteau to be served as the sweet course at a dinner celebrating a friend's 18th birthday. List the toppings you would use.

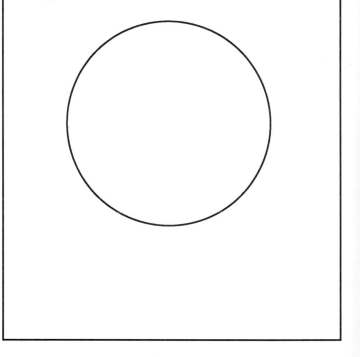

LEVEL 2

Spreading and rolling a Swiss roll

Swiss rolls have to be rolled within a short time of coming out of the oven, otherwise they will break up.

1 After cooking, loosen the sides and then turn out on to a lightly sugared sheet of greaseproof paper. Some chefs find it easier to use a cloth as well – as in illustration.

2 Peel off the lining paper used in the cooking.

3 Trim away the crisp edges from the long sides – if these are left on, the sponge may crack when rolled up.

4 If you are using a jam filling, spread the jam evenly over the sponge.

5 Roll up, with the longest side opposite you. Turn the edge of the warm sponge in fairly tightly to start with. Use the greaseproof paper (and cloth) to roll the sponge up.

6 Twist both ends of the paper, to prevent the roll loosening. Allow to cool.

If you are filling the sponge with whipped cream or buttercream, this should be done after the sponge has cooled:

• after removing the lining paper used for cooking, replace with a fresh sheet of greaseproof paper

• roll the sponge up

• allow to cool

• unroll carefully, remove paper

• add filling and roll up again.

Whipping cream

Cream should be whipped until it loses its sheen and takes on a matt finish. At this point the maximum number of stabilised air bubbles will have been incorporated into the cream. Fully whipped cream should stand in soft peaks, cling to the whisk and hold its shape.

1 Chill equipment, including piping bags and nozzles, and, if possible, work in a cool area of the kitchen. Use cream straight out of the refrigerator.

2 Only half fill the bowl in which the cream is to be whipped. Whip small amounts when you need them. This is easier than trying to whisk a large amount at once.

3 Whip quickly at first until cream takes on a matt finish.

4 Continue slowly until the cream stands in peaks.

5 Avoid overwhipping, as this will turn the cream into butter.

6 Whipped cream thickens with the pressure used to force it through a piping nozzle, so do not whip cream too stiffly for piping.

7 If cream is not required immediately, it should be covered and kept chilled.

8 The presence of sugar increases whipping time, and large amounts of sugar can reduce the stiffness and stability of cream. So it is best to add sugar after the cream has been whipped.

CHEF'S TIPS

For a pretty dusting, place a paper doily on top of the cake. Gently tap icing sugar from a sieve on to the cake. Very carefully remove the doily, lifting it straight upwards so that you do not spoil the pattern underneath.

When piping fresh cream on to frozen gâteaux or cheesecakes, do so while the cake is still frozen. This will keep the fresh cream well chilled during the process.

Aerosol whipping cream starts to collapse soon after applying. Dispense at the last possible moment before the dish is served.

By the National Dairy Council:

Fully whipped double cream may be piped into rosettes, open frozen on a tray and then carefully packed in layers with non-stick paper between each layer and sealed in a rigid container.

No cream?

A very acceptable cream containing about 47% butterfat can be made on a small scale using unsalted butter and milk. The following quantities make 250 ml (½ pt):

1 Melt 150 g (5 oz) unsalted butter in 150 ml (5 fl oz) milk over gentle heat.

2 Allow to cool slightly.

3 Blend the mixture in a liquidiser at top speed for 30 to 60 seconds.

4 Pour into a container and chill for 2 to 3 hours before use.

5 The cream may be whisked to give greater volume.

Double or whipping cream?

The optimum fat content for whipping is 35 to 40%. If the fat content is too low (e.g. single cream, 18%), there will not be enough fat to enclose air bubbles and form the foam. If the fat content is too high (e.g. clotted cream, 55%), the fat globules come into contact too easily and form butter granules before sufficient air can be incorporated.

Double cream (48% fat content) does not give as great an increase in volume (80% usually) as whipping cream (may be over 100%).

Add a little milk to double cream before whipping, to increase the volume and give a softer consistency: 60 ml (4 tbsp) milk to 600 ml (1 pt) of double cream.

SAFETY

Many of the safety risks involved in baking have to do with the high temperatures reached in the oven, and therefore by the baking tins and trays.

1 Always follow the correct procedure when lighting gas ovens.

2 Stand well back when opening the door of a hot oven.

3 Always use dry, thick oven cloths to handle hot tins and trays. Wet or greasy cloths will conduct heat.

4 When carrying trays of baked products from one part of the kitchen to another, always make sure that your way is clear. Take particular care going through doors, or around corners – a colleague might be rushing around from the other side.

5 If there is a trolley available for helping move things around, use it. It may take a few minutes to go and get it, but you will probably save time in the long run, and it will be much safer.

Choosing and using toppings

Where you can make or influence the decision, choose a topping that suits the:

- texture, flavour and colours of the cake or biscuit
- occasion on which it is to be served
- preferences of your customers.

For example:

- cream-based toppings are only suitable for products that can be kept chilled, and which will be eaten within a short time of preparation
- royal icing is traditional for wedding and celebration cakes, but there are quite acceptable alternatives for those who prefer softer coatings
- for customers who cannot eat dairy products, there are excellent cream-substitutes. Made from vegetable oils, these have a higher proportion of polyunsaturated fat, less saturated fat, and keep for longer
- gâteaux presented on buffets for customers to help themselves are normally pre-portioned: use a topping and decoration that will look good under these conditions.

Other points to remember

1   For a soft cake, use fillings and toppings that will spread easily, and not drag up the crumbs. Jam and butter cream are popular choices.

2   Jam fillings and toppings should be kept reasonably thin and even. Remove any large lumps of fruit before using and, if necessary, warm to get a better spreading consistency.

3   Butter creams tend to separate unless they are blended carefully. Flavourings which have to be heated, such as melted chocolate, should be cooled to room temperature before being added to the butter cream. Essences and other liquid ingredients should be whisked in a few drops at a time.

4   If the cake is to be covered with a thin coating, stand it on a wire rack resting on a tray. The tray will then catch the excess coating as it drips off the cake.

5   Because it sets hard, and has an attractive deep colour, plain chocolate is generally more suitable than milk chocolate for coatings and decorations.

6   Do not melt chocolate over direct heat as it scorches easily. Break into a bowl set over hot (not boiling) water and stir occasionally until the chocolate melts. Avoid drops of water getting into the chocolate, as this will cause it to become grainy.

ACTION

Against a list of each of the main toppings used in your workplace, state whether they are bought ready-prepared or made on the premises, what products they are used for, and one suggestion for an alternative topping which you think would have customer appeal. Discuss your suggestions with some of your colleagues before presenting them to your supervisor.

Topping	Source	Used for	Alternative

ACTION

Briefly describe how you dealt with an unexpected situation which occurred recently, concerning the preparation, cooking, or finishing of cakes and biscuits.

Kneaded fondant icing
by McDougalls (RHM Foods)

Key learning point
» prepare a variation on fondant icing for covering cakes

Covers 20 cm (8 inch) round or 8 cm (7 inch) square cake

450 g	icing sugar, sieved	1 lb
1	egg white, size 4	1
50 g	liquid glucose	2 oz
	colouring and flavouring	
	cornflour and icing sugar, for rolling	

1 Put the icing sugar into a bowl. Make a well in the centre. Add the egg white and glucose. Knead well until the fondant is smooth. Add colouring and flavouring as desired.

2 Roll out on a board dusted with equal quantities of icing sugar and cornflour.

Butter cream

Key learning point
» prepare butter cream

To fill/decorate 18 cm (7 inch) cake

50 g	butter (unsalted)	2 oz
100 g	icing sugar, sieved	4 oz
2–3 drops	food essence or flavouring	2–3 drops

Cream butter until soft. Gradually add icing sugar and cream together. Add flavouring to taste and beat well.

Variations

Lemon – add finely grated zest of 1 lemon and 1 tbsp lemon juice.

Orange – add finely grated zest of half an orange, and a few drops of orange colouring.

Mocha – add 1 tsp cocoa powder and 1 tsp coffee essence.

Ginger – add ½ tsp ground ginger.

Chocolate – add 25 g (1 oz) plain chocolate, grated and melted with 2 tsp of hot milk.

Glacé or water icing

Key learning point
» prepare basic icing

Covers 18 cm (7 inch) cake

100 g	icing sugar, sieved	4 oz
15 ml	water	1 tbsp
	few drops food colouring	

1 Mix icing sugar with water in a basin. Beat until smooth.

2 Colour as required.

Variations

Orange – replace water with strained orange juice or undiluted orange squash.

Chocolate – sieve 10 ml (2 tsp) cocoa powder with icing sugar before mixing with water.

Almond paste
by McDougalls (RHM Foods)

Key learning point
» prepare a basic covering for fruit cakes

Cakes coated with royal icing must have a base of almond paste, otherwise the cake will stain the white icing.

Covers 20 cm (8 inch) round or 18 cm (7 inch) square cake

150 g	icing sugar	5 oz
150 g	caster sugar	5 oz
275 g	ground almonds	10 oz
	1 egg (size 4) *or* 2 egg yolks	
15 ml	lemon juice	1 tbsp
	few drops almond essence	

1 Sieve the sugars into a bowl, add ground almonds and mix well.

2 Beat up egg in a basin. Add lemon juice and almond essence.

3 Gradually add egg mixture to the dry ingredients and mix to a pliable, smooth paste using a fork. If the paste is sticky, work in a little more sugar. If too stiff, work in a little more lemon juice.

4 Avoid handling the paste more than absolutely necessary or the warmth of your hands will draw the oil out of the almonds, making the paste very difficult to roll out.

5 To roll out, dust board and rolling pin with caster or icing sugar.

Chantilly cream

Key learning point
» prepare sweetened whipped cream

SERVES 4 to 6

150 ml	double or whipping cream	5 fl oz
25 g	caster sugar	1 oz
	few drops vanilla essence	

Place the ingredients in a cold basin (glass, stainless steel or china) and whisk until the cream stands in soft peaks. Set aside in the refrigerator (covered) until required for use.

Royal icing
by McDougalls (RHM Foods)

Key learning point
» prepare decorative icing

Lemon juice hardens the icing. Glycerine prevents it from becoming unduly hard if the cake is to be left for any length of time.

To decorate 23 cm (9 inch) round or 20 cm (8 inch) square cake

about 650 g	icing sugar	about 1½ lb
	2–3 drops lemon juice *or* 5 ml (1 tsp) glycerine	
4	egg whites, size 4	4

1 Sieve icing sugar through a fine sieve.

2 Break up egg whites in a mixing bowl using a fork, but do not beat. Add icing sugar gradually, beating well between each addition until the icing is a fairly thick cream.

3 Add lemon juice or glycerine. Continue beating until the icing is white, smooth, feels 'velvety' and is the consistency of thick cream. Vigorous beating is essential. If the icing is left to stand between beatings, or at any time during use, cover with a damp cloth to prevent a 'crust' forming on top.

4 If you are using an electric mixer, place egg white in bowl, and beat lightly with a fork. Add icing sugar gradually on speed 1 or 2, then beat at speed 2 or 3 for 5 to 8 minutes.

5 Allow icing to stand 1½ to 2 hours or overnight before use, covered with a well-dampened cloth to release the air bubbles.

Praline flan
by McDougalls Catering Foods

Key learning points
» make a sponge flan using a convenience sponge mix
» make praline and combine with whipped cream and gelatin to form flan filling

SERVES 10

450 g	sponge mix	1 lb
225 ml	cold water	8 fl oz
Praline		
125 g	whole almonds	5 oz
225 g	caster sugar	8 oz
50 ml	water	2 fl oz
Filling		
225 g	double cream, lightly whipped	8 fl oz
225 ml	milk	8 fl oz
	few drops of almond essence	
15 g	gelatin	½ oz

1 Make up sponge mix as directed on the packet. Pour into a 30 cm (12 inch) greased flan tin.

2 Bake at 200°C for 15 to 20 minutes (or follow directions on packet). Cool.

3 To make the praline, boil sugar and water until brown in colour. Stir in almonds. Remove 10 coated almonds, and set aside for decoration.

4 Pour praline on to an oiled marble slab or pastry board and leave to cool. When set, scrape off board, break into chunks. Liquidise into a powder.

5 Dissolve gelatin in a little of the milk. Stir into remainder of milk. Add almond essence. Fold in the whipped cream. Place in refrigerator.

6 When almost set, stir in three-quarters of the praline. Pour into flan case and leave to set.

7 Decorate with remaining praline and whole almonds.

Apple and cider cake
by McDougalls Catering Foods

Key learning points
» use convenience sponge mix
» decorate cake/flan with sliced apple
» glaze and flavour with cider-based sauce

SERVES 10

675 g	sponge mix	1½ lb
350 ml	water	12 fl oz
2	red apples, cored and sliced (skins on)	2
2	green apples, cored and sliced (skins on)	2
225 ml	sweet cider	8 fl oz
275 g	light soft brown sugar	10 oz

1 Make up sponge mix as directed on the packet.

2 Pour the sponge mixture into a greased and lined 30 cm (12 inch) round cake tin. Bake at 200°C for 25 to 30 minutes (or as directed on the packet).

3 Turn the sponge out and arrange the slices of red and green apples, alternately overlapping, around the top of the sponge.

4 Bring the cider and the sugar to the boil and simmer gently until the sugar has dissolved. Pour the hot sauce over the cake. Serve hot or cold.

Apricot and almond torte
by McDougalls Catering Foods

Key learning points
» use convenience scone mix
» combine convenience fruit pie filling with yogurt and cream to make torte topping
» whip cream with yogurt and pipe

SERVES 10

225 g	unsweetened scone mix	8 oz
100 g	dried apricots (chopped)	4 oz
5 ml	ginger	1 tsp
1	egg (beaten and made up to 125 ml/4 fl oz with water)	1
1 × 400 g	can apricot pie filling	1 × 14 oz
225 ml	double cream	8 fl oz
150 ml	thick set yogurt	5 fl oz
100 g	almonds (toasted)	4 oz
4	fresh apricots (optional)	4

1 Combine the unsweetened scone mix with the apricots, ginger and egg mixture and make up as directed on the packet.

2 Roll out the scone dough on a lightly floured board into a 25 cm (10 inch) circle, 15 mm (½ inch) thick.

3 Place the scone base on to a greased baking sheet and allow to rest for 15 minutes.

4 Bake at 220°C for approximately 15 minutes (or as directed on packet).

5 Place on a wire tray to cool.

To decorate

1 Pile the apricot pie filling on to the scone base.

2 Whip together the cream and yogurt, until it is of piping consistency. Spread a layer of the cream mixture over the scone base and press the almonds around the edge, reserving some for decoration.

3 Pipe the remaining cream on top of the torte, decorate with toasted almonds and fresh apricots.

Passion cake
by McDougalls   (RHM Foods)

Key learning points
» use wholemeal flour
» use bicarbonate of soda as raising agent
» make variation of butter cream

SERVES 10 to 12

450 g	plain 100% wholemeal flour	1 lb
2.5 ml	bicarbonate of soda	½ tsp
10 ml	mixed spice	2 tsp
60 ml	cooking oil	4 tbsp
60 ml	honey	4 tbsp
2	eggs	2
450 g	carrots, finely grated	1 lb
2	bananas, mashed	2
100 g	soft brown sugar	4 oz

Topping

100 g	cream cheese	4 oz
100 g	icing sugar	4 oz
5 ml	orange juice	1 tsp

1 Grease and line the base of a 20 cm (8 inch) round cake tin.

2 Place all the cake ingredients in a bowl and beat thoroughly to a stiff consistency.

3 Turn into the prepared tin, smooth level and bake for approximately 1¼ hours at 190°C. Cool.

4 Beat topping ingredients until smooth and creamy. Spread on top of cake and decorate with curls of orange peel.

Victoria sandwich

Key learning points
» make a sponge cake using the creaming method
» fill a sandwich cake with jam, and dust with icing sugar

This recipe is demonstrated by Danny Stevenson in the HCTC video *Foodcraft 6: Cakes*

SERVES 16

275 g	butter or margarine	10 oz
275 g	caster sugar	10 oz
10 ml	glycerine	2 tsp
275 ml	eggs (probably 6 or 7)	10 fl oz
275 g	plain flour	10 oz
5 ml	baking powder	1 tsp
100 g	raspberry jam	4 oz

icing or caster sugar to decorate

1 Lightly grease with white fat, two 25 cm diameter, 4 cm deep cake tins (9¾ inch by 1½ inch). Then coat with flour. Make sure the ingredients for the cake mixture are at room temperature (21°C to 22°C).

2 Sieve together the flour and baking powder, either on to a sheet of greaseproof paper or into a bowl.

3 Place the butter, sugar and glycerine into a mixing bowl and beat until light and creamy. Occasionally scrape down the sides of the bowl to ensure that all the mixture is beaten evenly.

4 Add the eggs a little at a time, thoroughly beating with each addition. From time to time, scrape the mixture down off the sides of the bowl.

5 Lightly mix in the flour with as gentle a movement as possible until it is evenly distributed.

6 Divide the mixture equally between the cake tins. Smooth the surface carefully with a spatula. Immediately place the tins on a baking tray and bake at 185°C until cooked – about 30 minutes.

7 Remove the cakes from the oven and allow to cool slightly. Carefully turn them the right way up on to a wire cooling tray and leave until cool.

8 Spread a good layer of jam on top of one cake, then place the other on top of it, flat side down.

9 Dredge over the surface with icing sugar and serve on a round dish or salver lined with a doily.

Whisked sponge
by The British Egg Information Service

Key learning point
» prepare a sponge cake using the whisking method

Filling suggestions: jam, cream or butter icing.

MAKES 15 cm (6 inch) SANDWICH CAKE

2	eggs	2
50 g	caster sugar	2 oz
50 g	plain flour, sieved twice	2 oz
¼ tsp	vanilla essence	¼ tsp

1 Very lightly grease and line base and sides of two 15 cm (6 inch) sandwich tins.

2 Place the eggs and sugar in a bowl over a pan of hot, not boiling, water. If using a table model electric mixer, do not whisk over hot water.

3 Whisk the mixture using a rotary or electric hand whisk for 5 to 10 minutes or until the mixture is light in colour and very thick. It increases in volume by about two-thirds. When the whisk is lifted up it should leave a trail in the mixture for at least 5 seconds.

4 Remove the bowl from the saucepan and continue to whisk for a further 3 minutes until cooled.

5 With a metal teaspoon, fold the flour and vanilla essence into the foam by cutting and folding the mixture until the flour is evenly mixed in.

6 Divide the mixture evenly into the sandwich tins.

7 Gently shake the tins to level the mixture before baking at 180°C for 20 to 25 minutes or until well risen and golden brown.

8 When cooled a little, turn out the cakes on to a wire cooling tray.

9 Just before filling, peel off the lining paper.

Rich Christmas or celebration cake
by McDougalls (RHM Foods)

Key learning point
» make rich fruit cake

This cake can be decorated with almond paste and royal or fondant icing (see page 251).

MAKES 20 cm (8 inch) cake

225 g	butter or margarine	8 oz
225 g	soft dark brown sugar	8 oz
15 ml	black treacle	1 tbsp
4	eggs, size 4	4
250 g	plain flour	9 oz
	pinch salt	
5 ml	mixed spice	1 tsp
	few drops vanilla essence	
225 g each	sultanas, currants and raisins	8 oz each
175 g each	mixed peel, chopped and glacé cherries	6 oz each
100 g	whole blanched almonds	4 oz
30 ml	brandy or sherry	2 tbsp
15 ml	lemon juice	1 tbsp

1. Grease and line a 20 cm (8 inch) round or 18 cm (7 inch) square tin.

2. Cut up the butter or margarine, add the sugar and beat until light and fluffy.

3. Add the egg to the creamed mixture a little at a time, thoroughly beating with each addition.

4. Sieve together the flour, salt and mixed spice. Fold into the creamed mixture with as little movement as possible until it is evenly distributed.

5. Add the rest of the ingredients carefully to the mixture.

6. Place the mixture into the cake tin. With a spatula, smooth the surface.

7. Bake for 3½ to 4 hours at 150°C. A thick collar of brown paper may be tied around the outside of the tin to prevent the cake becoming too dry during cooking (or see page 241).

Wholemeal Swiss roll
by McDougalls (RHM Foods)

Key learning points
» make sponge using whisking method and wholemeal flour
» roll Swiss roll and fill with jam and whipped cream, dust with icing sugar

MAKES 8 slices

2	eggs size 3	2
50 g	soft brown sugar	2 oz
50 g	100% wholemeal self-raising flour	2 oz

For decoration

	caster sugar
	apricot jam
	whipped cream
	icing sugar

1. Grease and line a Swiss roll tin measuring 30 × 20 cm (12 × 8 inches).

2. Prepare Swiss roll by whisking method (page 240), turn into tin and spread mixture evenly over the base. Bake for 8 to 10 minutes at 220°C until risen and golden. Do not overcook.

3. Sprinkle some caster sugar on to a sheet of greaseproof paper and turn the sponge upside down on to it.

4. Remove the lining paper and trim the edges of the sponge with a sharp knife. Roll up cake with paper still inside and leave to cool.

5. When cold, carefully unroll. Remove paper and spread with jam and cream. Roll up and dust with icing sugar.

Spicy chocolate loaf
by The Dutch Dairy Bureau

Key learning points
» make sponge using variation of creaming method
» use paper piping bag to decorate with melted chocolate

SERVES 4 to 6

3	eggs, size 3	3
175 g	caster sugar	6 oz
175 g	unsalted butter, melted	6 oz
175 g	self-raising flour	6 oz
15 ml	ground mixed spice	1 tbsp
	pinch salt	
75 ml	milk, heated	5 tbsp
75 ml	lemon juice	5 tbsp
	few drops vanilla essence	
75 g	plain chocolate, grated or roughly chopped in a food processor	3 oz

To decorate

	icing sugar, for dusting	
50 g	plain chocolate, melted	2 oz

1. Prepare a 1 kg (2 lb) loaf tin by greasing the inside and lining the base with greaseproof paper.

2. Beat the eggs in a mixing bowl with the caster sugar until pale. Add melted butter.

3. Sift the flour, mixed spice and salt into a bowl, stir into the mixture. Add lukewarm milk, lemon juice, vanilla essence and chocolate. Mix well and pour into the loaf tin.

4. Bake in the centre of the oven, at 180°C, for about 70 minutes. The cake will shrink slightly from the sides of the tin and should be firm to the touch when pressed lightly. Loosen the sides with a knife and turn on to a cooling rack.

5. To decorate: dust with icing sugar, then pipe thin lines of melted chocolate over the top of the cake. Can also be served with whipped cream.

Pineapple and chocolate gâteau
by McDougalls   (RHM Foods)

Key learning points
» make sponge cake using the one-stage method
» coat pineapple chunks with chocolate as decoration
» whip cream and pipe
» pipe chocolate using a greaseproof paper piping bag

SERVES 8

Cake

100 g	self-raising sponge flour	4 oz
100 g	soft margarine	4 oz
112 g	caster sugar	4½ oz
2	eggs	2
15 ml	water	1 tbsp

Filling

1 × 425 g	can pineapple chunks	1 × 15 oz
50 g	plain chocolate	2 oz
275 ml	double cream	½ pt
50 g	chopped mixed nuts	2 oz

1 Grease and line the base of a 20 cm (8 inch) cake tin.

2 Place all cake ingredients in a bowl and beat for 1 to 2 minutes until smooth and light. Turn into cake tin and bake for approximately 35 minutes at 180°C.

3 Let the cake cool, then cut in half and place on a wire rack.

4 Drain the pineapple chunks, reserving the juice. Reserve 8 of the chunks, and chop the remainder.

5 Place the chocolate in a small basin and put over a pan of hot water to melt.

6 Dry the reserved pineapple chunks thoroughly on kitchen paper, spear on a cocktail stick and half dip in chocolate. Place on a greaseproof paper until set.

7 Whip the cream until it stands in soft peaks. Mix one-third of the cream with the chopped pineapple.

8 Sprinkle both halves of the cake with pineapple juice, and sandwich with the pineapple and cream mixture.

9 Coat the top and sides of the cake with another third of the cream, and press the nuts on to the sides.

10 Use the remaining cream to pipe 8 large whirls around the outside edge of the cake. Place remaining chocolate in a greaseproof paper piping bag, and decorate the centre of the cake with 8 swirls (see page 246).

11 Place a chocolate coated pineapple chunk on each whirl of cream.

Demerara shortbread
by The Butter Council

Key learning point
» knead and shape shortbread mixture

MAKES 16

50 g	demerara sugar	2 oz
225 g	butter	8 oz
100 g	caster sugar	4 oz
350 g	plain flour	12 oz
	pinch salt	

1 Put butter and caster sugar in a bowl and beat together (thorough creaming is not required).

2 Add flour and salt, working into the mixture until it looks like crumbs. Gather mixture together and knead quickly until smooth. Avoid too much handling.

3 Form into a roll about 5 cm (2 inches) in diameter and roll in demerara sugar (sprinkled on to a large sheet of greaseproof paper). Cut off into 16 rounds and place on a baking sheet.

4 Bake for about 10 minutes at 180°C until lightly browned.

The best baked cheesecake
by The Butter Council

Key learning points
» make biscuit base suitable for cheese cake
» whip egg whites

Raisin cheesecake: add 2 oz (50 g) seedless raisins to the mixture after adding egg yolks.

Chocolate cheesecake: for the base, use 6 oz (175 g) crushed chocolate digestive biscuits, instead of plain. Swirl 4 oz (100 g) melted dark chocolate through the mixture before adding egg whites.

SERVES 4

75 g	butter	3 oz
175 g	digestive biscuits, crushed	6 oz
350 g	cream or curd cheese	12 oz
150 ml	natural set yogurt	5 fl oz
100 g	caster sugar	4 oz
5 ml	finely grated lemon rind	1 tsp
10 ml	vanilla essence	2 tsp
3	eggs, separated	3
	icing sugar, to serve	

1 Butter a 20 cm (8 inch) loose-bottomed cake tin.

2 Carefully melt the butter and stir in the biscuit crumbs. Press into the base of the tin.

3 Beat together the cheese, yogurt, sugar, lemon rind and essence until smooth. Beat in egg yolks.

4 Whisk egg whites until stiff and fold into cheese/yogurt mixture.

5 Pour into tin and bake at 170°C until set, approximately 1 hour. Cool and chill in tin.

6 Turn out and sift icing sugar on top before serving.

Banana teabread
by The Butter Council

Key learning point
» make sponge using creaming method and wholemeal flour

MAKES 18 cm (17 inch) sponge

350 g	wholemeal self-raising flour	12 oz
2.5 ml	salt	½ tsp
5 ml	cinnamon	1 tsp
175 g	sultanas or raisins	6 oz
175 g	soft brown sugar	6 oz
100 g	butter	4 oz
3	eggs, beaten	3
3	large bananas, mashed	3

1 Butter and line the base of 700 g (1½ lb) loaf tin, or 18 cm (7 inch) square cake tin.

2 Place the flour, salt, cinnamon and sultanas in a bowl and mix well.

3 Put the sugar in a large bowl. Melt the butter, being careful not to allow it to get too hot, then pour over the sugar and stir well.

4 Beat in the eggs gradually, then add the flour mixture and finally the bananas, mixing until thoroughly combined.

5 Transfer to cake tin and bake for 50 to 60 minutes at 190°C. Cool in tin for 10 minutes then turn out and cool completely.

Cheese and oregano twists
by McDougalls Catering Foods

Key learning points
» use convenience scone mix
» make decorative shape

MAKES 10

450 g	unsweetened scone mix	1 lb
225 ml	water	8 fl oz
175 g	Red Leicester cheese (grated)	6 oz
15 ml	dried oregano	3 tsp
	beaten egg to glaze	

1 Make up the unsweetened scone mix, as directed on the packet, adding ¾ of the cheese and ¾ of the oregano.

2 Roll out on a floured surface to 15 mm (½ inch) thickness. Cut into rounds with an 8.25 cm (3¼ inch) cutter. Using a 3.5 cm (1½ inch) cutter, cut out the scone centres and then twist over to form a figure of eight.

3 Put on to a greased baking sheet and allow to rest for 15 minutes.

4 Glaze with the beaten egg and sprinkle over the remaining cheese and oregano.

5 Bake at 220°C for 10 to 15 minutes.

6 Serve hot or cold.

Wholemeal yogurt scones
by The Flour Advisory Bureau

Key learning points
» make scones using wholemeal flour
» use bicarbonate of soda as raising agent

MAKES 12 to 15

225 g	wholemeal flour	8 oz
5 ml	salt	1 tsp
5 ml	bicarbonate of soda	1 tsp
25 g	margarine	1 oz
150 ml	natural yogurt	5 fl oz

1 Place flour, salt and bicarbonate of soda in bowl. Rub in margarine and stir in yogurt to make a soft dough.

2 Roll out to 1 cm (½ inch) thick and cut into rounds, using a 5 cm (2 inch) plain cutter.

3 Place on baking sheet and brush with a little milk. Bake at 220°C for 7 to 10 minutes until well risen and golden brown.

Muesli rock buns
by The Flour Advisory Bureau

Key learning point
» make high-fibre rock buns

MAKES 8

100 g	self-raising wholemeal flour	4 oz
2.5 ml	mixed spice	½ tsp
50 g	butter or margarine	2 oz
50 g	unsweetened muesli	2 oz
25 g	soft light brown sugar	1 oz
50 g	glacé cherries, roughly chopped	2 oz
30 ml	desiccated coconut	2 tbsp
1	egg, beaten	1
30 ml	skimmed milk	2 tbsp

1 Place flour and spice in a bowl and rub in fat until mixture resembles fine breadcrumbs.

2 Stir in muesli, sugar, cherries and coconut. Add egg and milk and mix to a soft consistency.

3 Place on a greased baking tray in eight rocky mounds. Bake at 200°C for about 20 minutes.

Quick-step sultana scones
by The Butter Council

Key learning points
» make scones using simple, quick recipe
» use milk to glaze

MAKES 12 to 15

225 g	self-raising flour	8 oz
	pinch salt	
50 g	caster sugar	2 oz
100 g	sultanas	4 oz
50 g	butter, at refrigerator temperature	2 oz
	milk to mix	

1 Place the flour, salt, sugar and sultanas in a large bowl.

2 Dice the butter and stir carefully through the flour mixture to leave the butter in pieces. Using a round bladed knife, add enough milk to mix to a firm dough. Roll out to a thickness of about 3 cm (1 inch) and cut into rounds.

3 Place on a baking sheet and brush with a little milk to glaze. Bake at 220°C for 10 to 15 minutes.

Honey triangles
by Mornflake Oats

Key learning point
» make biscuit using melting method

MAKES 16 to 20

40 g	walnuts, chopped	1½ oz
75 g	margarine	3 oz
30 ml	clear honey	2 tbsp
30 ml	golden syrup	2 tbsp
75 g	soft brown sugar	3 oz
125 g	oats	5 oz

1 Grease a shallow 17 cm (7 inch) square tin.

2 Melt the margarine, honey and syrup until blended. Do not boil. Stir in the sugar and oats. Spread evenly in the tin. Sprinkle with the walnuts and press in lightly.

3 Bake at 160°C for 25 to 30 minutes until golden brown and bubbling.

4 Allow to cool for a few minutes, then cut into triangles. Remove from tin when cold.

Grasmere gingerbread
by Mornflake Oats

Key learning points
» use rubbing in method
» use sodium bicarbonate and cream of tartar as a raising agent
» make biscuits with wholemeal flour and oats

MAKES 20

175 g	wholemeal flour	6 oz
50 g	oats	2 oz
2.5 ml	sodium bicarbonate	½ tsp
5 ml	cream of tartar	1 tsp
10 ml	ground ginger	2 tsp
175 g	margarine	6 oz
175 g	light soft brown sugar	6 oz

1 Grease a 30 × 18 cm (12 × 7 inch) Swiss roll tin.

2 Put flour, oats, sodium bicarbonate, cream of tartar and ginger in a bowl and mix well. Add margarine cut into small pieces, and rub in till mixture resembles breadcrumbs. Stir in sugar.

3 Press mixture into tin and bake at 150°C for 30 minutes.

4 Cool for 5 minutes, cut into 20 fingers. Cool in tin.

Date fingers
by McDougalls   (RHM Foods)

Key learning point
» make high-fibre biscuits using melting method

MAKES 14

75 g	margarine	3 oz
75 g	soft brown sugar	3 oz
30 ml	golden syrup	2 tbsp
100 g	plain 100% wholemeal flour	4 oz
50 g	porridge oats	2 oz
175 g	dates, chopped	6 oz
15 ml	lemon juice	1 tbsp

1 Grease an 18 cm (7 inch) square cake tin.

2 Gently melt margarine, sugar and syrup in a saucepan. Stir in flour and oats.

3 Press half the mixture into the tin.

4 Mix together the dates and lemon juice. Spread over the base.

5 Cover with remaining mixture and press firmly with a fork. Bake for 25 to 30 minutes at 180°C.

6 Cut into fingers while warm and cool in the tin.

Viennese fingers
by McDougalls   (RHM Foods)

Key learning points
» pipe biscuit mixture
» fill biscuits with jam or butter cream, decorate with chocolate

MAKES 16

175 g	margarine	6 oz
50 g	caster sugar	2 oz
175 g	self-raising flour	6 oz
	few drops vanilla essence	
	jam or butter cream and chocolate to finish	

1 Cream fat and sugar very thoroughly, stir in the flour and essence.

2 Place the mixture in a piping bag with a large star nozzle and pipe in 6.5 cm (2½ inch) lengths on greased baking trays.

3 Bake in a moderate oven at 160°C for about 20 minutes.

4 When cool, sandwich together with jam or butter cream and dip the ends in melted chocolate.

Fudge
by Nestlé

Key learning points
» cook sugar until soft ball stage is reached
» use a sugar thermometer

MAKES 775 g (1¾ lb)

400 g	sweetened condensed milk	14 oz
150 ml	milk	5 fl oz
450 g	demerara sugar	1 lb
100 g	butter	4 oz

1 Grease an 18 cm (7 inch) square tin.

2 Gently heat all the ingredients in a large, non-stick saucepan, stirring until the sugar dissolves.

3 Bring to the boil and simmer gently for 10 to 15 minutes, stirring continuously, until a temperature of 116°C is reached, using a sugar thermometer. *Alternatively*, test fudge by dropping a little of the mixture into cold water. If a soft ball is formed, the fudge is ready.

4 Remove from heat. Beat until thick and grainy (about 10 minutes). Pour into tin. When cold, cut into squares.

Nutty cookies
by Nestlé

Key learning point
» make biscuits using creaming method

MAKES 25 to 30 cookies

200 g	margarine	7 oz
125 g	light brown sugar	5 oz
15 ml	honey	1 tbsp
1	egg, size 3, beaten	1
175 g	self-raising flour, sifted	6 oz
50 g	cocoa, sifted	2oz
75 g	hazelnuts, chopped	3 oz

1 Cream together margarine and sugar until light and fluffy. Beat in honey and egg. Fold in flour and cocoa. Stir in half the nuts. Chill for 1 hour.

2 Divide mixture into heaped teaspoonfuls and roll into balls. Arrange on a greased baking tray about 30 mm (1¼ inch) apart.

3 Flatten with a fork and sprinkle with remaining nuts. Bake for 12 to 15 minutes at 190°C.

4 Stand for 2 minutes before transferring to a wire rack to cool.

1D9 Prepare, cook and decorate convenience cakes and biscuits

2D9 Prepare, cook and decorate cakes and biscuits

NVQ **SVQ** RANGE CHECKLIST

1D9.1 Prepare convenience cake and biscuit mixtures

these preparation methods
- [ ] reconstituting convenience mixtures
- [ ] portioning

involving at least 2 of these products
- [ ] cakes
- [ ] biscuits
- [ ] sponges

1D9.2 Cook convenience cakes and biscuits

cook at least 2 of these products
- [ ] cakes
- [ ] biscuits
- [ ] sponges

and finish them by
- [ ] turning out
- [ ] cooling

1D9.3 Decorate convenience cakes and biscuits

use at least 3 of these decoration products
- [ ] jams
- [ ] convenience icings or piping gels
- [ ] cream
- [ ] preprepared toppings

using at least 5 of these decoration methods
- [ ] trimming
- [ ] filling
- [ ] spreading and smoothing
- [ ] piping with cream
- [ ] dusting or dredging or sprinkling
- [ ] coating
- [ ] topping

for at least 2 of these products
- [ ] cakes
- [ ] sponges
- [ ] biscuits

2D9.1 Prepare cake and biscuit mixtures

prepare at least 2 of these products
- [ ] cakes
- [ ] biscuits
- [ ] sponges

by at least 4 of these preparation methods
- [ ] creaming or beating
- [ ] whisking
- [ ] folding
- [ ] rubbing in
- [ ] greasing
- [ ] melting

2D9.2 Cook cakes and biscuits

cook at least 2 of these products
- [ ] cakes
- [ ] sponges
- [ ] biscuits

and finish by at least 2 of the following methods
- [ ] turning out
- [ ] cooling
- [ ] spreading and rolling (Swiss roll)

2D9.3 Decorate cakes and biscuits

use at least 3 of these decoration products
- [ ] water icing
- [ ] royal icing
- [ ] butter cream
- [ ] whipped cream

and at least 6 of these decoration methods
- [ ] trimming
- [ ] filling
- [ ] spreading and smoothing
- [ ] piping with icing or chocolate
- [ ] piping with cream
- [ ] dusting or dredging or sprinkling
- [ ] coating
- [ ] topping

to decorate at least 2 of these products
- [ ] cakes
- [ ] sponges
- [ ] biscuits

Introduction

Cold food lends itself much more to decoration than does hot food. Decorative touches can range from simple slices of cucumber, leaves of lettuce or segments of orange, to stunning ice carvings or elaborate baskets made from sugar and adorned with flowers.

The flavour of the food – whether sweet or sharp, tangy or bland – will depend on what the functions of the dish are. This is usually decided by the dish's place on the menu. For example, whether it is supposed to stimulate the appetite, to refresh the palate, or to provide sweetness or contrast.

Variety of flavours and textures across a whole meal is the thing to aim at:

First course or starter – should stimulate the appetite without satisfying it. Light, crispy, tasty foods are appropriate, as are piquant dressings, sauces and dips.

Main course and accompaniments – should contain a variety of foods to give a balance of nutrients, and to satisfy the appetite. On the whole, very smooth-textured, sweet or bland foods should be avoided.

Refresher course – some meals include, after the main course, a green salad, a lightly dressed vegetable or a tart fruit salad. As such dishes are designed to refresh the appetite (this is sometimes referred to as cleansing the palate), they should be light and offer a good contrast to the previous course. Avoid rich, heavy dressings.

Contents guide

NVQ **SVQ** **Units and elements covered in this section**

2D13 Prepare food for cold presentation   **LEVEL 2**
- 2D13.1 Prepare and present cold canapés and open sandwiches
- 2D13.2 Present cooked, cured and prepared foods

With imagination and practice, you can make attractive garnishes out of most vegetables and fruit.

Preparation and presentation of cold foods

Creating visual appeal

Many chefs can arrange food attractively without being able to explain why it is that they are selecting particular colours and shapes, or why they are positioning items in one place rather than another.

But there are some basic rules which provide a starting point if you have not had much experience of doing this.

1 Choose different coloured foods, but do not use more than three as a rule, because too many colours can create a messy effect. Sometimes two or three shades of the same colour can be equally, or more, effective.

2 Make sure you have some variation in the heights of the different foods. Arrangements of food lying flat on the plate tend to look dull and lifeless. Piling up or overlapping some of the ingredients, or using one as a container for others (for example, a lettuce leaf containing finely sliced tomato), will provide the right kind of contrast.

3 Provide a focal point for the arrangement of food. This could be either the main ingredient, placed in a prominent position, or a related ingredient introduced because of its attractiveness (for example, an edible flower such as a nasturtium).

4 Take care to trim, prepare or cut the ingredients neatly. Ragged cuts and uneven edges or mixtures of shapes and sizes will create an overall impression of untidiness.

5 Use cuts and arrangements that make the food easy to recognise. Ingredients should not be chopped or minced so finely that they cannot be told apart (unless they are foods being used as a flavouring, such as garlic and onion).

6 Consider how the food is to be eaten. Open sandwich fillings, like chopped hard-boiled egg, for example, need to be mixed with a sauce or mayonnaise so that the filling does not fall off as the sandwich is raised to the mouth, and canapés should be small enough to be popped whole into the mouth. Salads may need to be prepared so that they can be eaten with a fork only, without pieces of lettuce falling over the side of the plate or bowl.

7 Keep arrangements simple. Elaborate designs are rarely worth the long time they take to prepare (often in conditions ideal for the growth of harmful bacteria).

The aim in presenting cold foods is that they should look appealing to your customers. What is right for a salad bar in a city centre health food restaurant (pictured above), is unlikely to be right for the cold food counter in a truckers stop, catering exclusively for long distance lorry drivers.

8 The garnish and arrangement of the food should take account of how the dish is to be served. In cold buffets, for example, dishes need to look good even when some portions have been taken from them. Sometimes a garnish is used to mark the extent of an individual serving, for example a slice of tomato, topped by an olive on each portion of a cold flan.

9 Make the most of the design and size of the service dish, so that the shape of the arrangement of food fits the shape of the dish. Select the right-sized dish – if it is too large, the food will look lost or too much will have to be used; if it is too small, the dish will be crowded. The rim should be left clear so that the dish can be handled without any danger of the food being touched, and the food is not likely to fall off.

10 When arranging food on the serving dish, plan the design you will be using in advance. A good idea is to sketch the effect you want on a piece of paper. A focal point in the centre, that the rest of the design leads into, is quite a good way of creating an interesting effect.

11 Try to keep everything roughly the same size, and don't overload the serving dish with so much that it looks crowded. Over-filled dishes are difficult to serve – some food may get spilt when the first portions are taken.

12 The flavour of the dish should not be interfered with by decorative additions, so check that their taste will not intrude.

HYGIENE

Cold food must look good, and it must be safe to eat. This means you should pay particular attention to:

timing – since the food is not cooked at all, or cooked then chilled and stored, the longer the delay before service, the greater the chance of bacteria multiplying to dangerous numbers. For this reason, cold foods should not be prepared too far in advance. Ideally, if cold foods are displayed for customers to help themselves to, or put on a trolley in the restaurant, then the equipment should keep the food chilled. If this is not possible, no more food should be displayed than is reasonably necessary, and then not for more than 4 hours

temperature – bacteria grow at temperatures above 4°C, and reproduce rapidly at temperatures between 38°C and 60°C (the range of most kitchens). Always keep cold foods properly chilled

preventing cross-contamination – don't let bacteria spread from uncooked to cooked food. Use knives and chopping boards that are specifically reserved (e.g. colour coded) for preparing cooked foods. Store cooked food well apart from raw food

personal hygiene – don't take any risks. Use a suitable implement, such as tongs, when handling food for service. In many kitchens, it is the rule that disposable gloves are worn when handling preprepared and cooked foods

cleanliness of equipment and work surfaces – wash equipment and work surfaces down regularly, and use an approved sanitising cloth or solution. It is best to use one surface for one purpose only. If workspace is limited, the working surfaces must be changed – i.e. by using a preparation board – and thoroughly cleaned and dried between each use. Wiping with a cloth is not enough.

Here are some other specific points:

1 Wash all fresh fruit, vegetables, salad items and garnishes such as parsley, in running cold water before use. In some workplaces, all such items must be left in chlorinated water for a specific period of time, then rinsed with fresh water before use.

2 Do not use cleaning cloths from raw food areas in cooked food areas. Where a colour-coding system is in operation, this rule will be easier to observe.

3 Where there is a choice, use the older stock first. Do not use items which have passed their use-by or best-before date.

4 Never process cooked meat (including canned or processed meat) on the same slicing or mincing machine that has been used for raw food – unless the machine has been dismantled and thoroughly cleaned and sanitised between operations.

5 Always make fresh aspic. Don't use left-overs from a previous day. The process of chilling and warming aspic many times over, so that its consistency is right for coating food, provides ideal conditions for the growth of harmful bacteria.

How to chop parsley:
1) Remove the larger stalks.
2) Roughly cut the bunches to reduce their bulk.
3) Holding the tip of the blade lightly against the board, use an up-and-down, backwards and forwards motion to chop until the parsley has been cut into tiny pieces.

On right: *judging the spacing and depth of the cut to get an attractive zig-zag finish gets easier with experience. Start by making very light marks or pin pricks around the circumference, at equal distances apart. You might also find it helpful to make guide marks to indicate the top and bottom of each cut.*

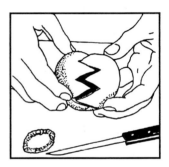

Lemons, oranges and tomatoes are often cut in this way. A variation (shown in the picture on page 259) is to leave part of the fruit intact, so that it forms a handle. In this case, you start by cutting down on each side of what will be the handle. Then move outwards, with the zig-zag cut. Finally, cut out the flesh under the handle.

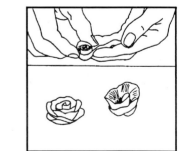

To cut a red rose. 1) Choose a firm, well coloured tomato. 2) Cut almost, but not quite through, the base of the tomato, then continue cutting a strip of the tomato skin, about 2 cm wide (¾ inch) and about 10 cm (4 inches) long. Use your knife like a jigsaw, in an up-and-down motion, so you get a wavy edge. 3) Cut a second strip, of similar length. 4) Fairly loosely curl the first strip up on to its base, to form the outer petals of the rose. 5) Place the second strip inside this, more tightly curled. Some chefs prefer to make the rose out of just one length of tomato skin.

Canapés

Canapés are usually eaten with the fingers, often lifted one at a time from a large serving dish on which a selection has been arranged. They should be:

- small enough to be popped into the mouth in one go
- firm enough to be lifted, yet easy to chew
- dips should not be so thick that they are difficult to scoop out, or so thin that they drip.

Many items are sufficiently firm to make a canapé on their own, or when combined with other ingredients. Examples are prawns, smoked oysters, stuffed hard-boiled eggs, a prune wrapped in bacon and stuffed with chutney, squares of firm cheese, asparagus rolled up in smoked trout, and cream cheese wrapped up in smoked ham.

Pastry, bread or biscuits are useful bases for other types of food, such as caviar, pâté, sliced meats and smoked fish. Bread is generally toasted and cut into shapes: rounds, squares, rectangles or triangles. There is no need to toast the bread if it has the support of its crust (as with French bread), or if it is quite dense in texture (as with pumpernickel or rye bread).

Vol-au-vents, bouchées and other pastry bases

Pastry provides a contrast in texture, as well as a means of holding various foods that are finely chopped, puréed or creamed. The size of the pastry case should be appropriate, so bouchées are better for a finger buffet than their larger cousins, vol-au-vents. If pastry horns are served as canapés, they should be small ones.

Pastry horns (see recipe on page 268). The strip of pastry is brushed with beaten egg along the edge that overlaps.

Squares, rectangles and triangles can be cut easily, and to the same size, from a loaf of bread that has been cut along its length to form 'planks'.

Note how an edge has been left on the bread, to give protection from the knife as the horizontal slices are cut.

Alternatively, bread can be sliced in this way using a slicing machine. On request, some bakers do this for you.

CHEF'S TIPS

by Michael Raffael, writing in The Bread Guide, *published in* Caterer & Hotelkeeper

The most useful tool for making canapés, apart from a long bladed serrated knife, is a rectangular *template*. Its size depends on the loaf you are slicing. It should be a little larger than the surface of the longer face and marked out with small squares or rectangles corresponding to your canapé size.

It is easier to work with bread which is recovering from the freezer. Once the outer crusts have been carved off, the loaf is sliced lengthwise. These 'planks' of bread are laid on the template one at a time, coated with the filling, and cut up, ready for use.

To keep them moist it helps to lay freshly-made canapés on a tray lined with a damp cloth.

To prepare *pin wheels* (bread Swiss rolls), cut out long sheets of bread, as for ordinary canapés, and lay them on a damp cloth, coat with filling and roll up. Leave them wrapped in the freezer for a short time before slicing.

You should take account of the filling when choosing the bread. *Rye breads* or *pumpernickel* can balance stronger, sharper flavours while *brown breads* are traditional with items such as smoked salmon, *brioche* with parfaits or foie gras, and *toasted bread* with scrambled eggs. *Country loaves*, although they may be more difficult to slice, suit charcuterie.

As for *spreadings*, in place of butter or margarine, try a favourite of the Victorian era: whipped cream, salt and mustard. It is easy to make and cheaper to use than modern low fat spreads, easy to spread and lower in cholesterol than ordinary butter.

Variations on this theme include shellfish butters, walnut butters, blue cheese butters and cress butters.

Open sandwiches

Open sandwiches can use the enormous range of fillings available for ordinary sandwiches (see page 32), with the additional advantage that the food can be arranged much more attractively:

- slices of meat or smoked fish can be rolled

- thick dressings like mayonnaise can be spooned or piped to form part of the final decoration, perhaps with a stuffed olive placed in the centre, or a little caviar

- fine, delicate vegetables like asparagus can add impact to the presentation, as well as contributing to the flavour

- provided the flavour is appropriate for the other items on the sandwich, there is almost no limit to the range of decorative touches.

The base of an open sandwich needs to be substantial enough to support the topping.

Some ideas

for garnishing open sandwiches

pineapple and apple – slices, rings

avocado, melon – slices, fanned

asparagus – tips

grapes and cherries – halved, pips removed

for fruit/vegetable canapés

squares or balls or other decorative shapes of pineapple, apple, melon, carrot, cucumber, courgette, etc., florets of cauliflower or broccoli – combined with another fruit/vegetable for contrast, or with cheese or meat or fish, or on. its own with a dip

asparagus – rolled in bread, sliced meat or smoked fish

for fruit/vegetable canapé bases

celery, cucumber and courgettes – cut into short lengths and stuffed

artichoke hearts – stuffed

To make (see photograph on page 259)

a radish rose – trim off root and stem end. Make 4 cuts nearly to the end, crossing in the centre of the root end. Leave in iced water for a short time, until they open out or 'bloom'

onion palm tree – trim spring onion root and leaves. Cut stem lengthwise 8 times. Leave in iced water to curl

gherkin fan – make 5 or 6 lengthwise cuts almost to the end of the gherkin from the thin end. Spread out to form an open fan

cucumber and lemon twist – take 2 slices of cucumber and place a lemon slice in the middle. Cut through to the centre, twist the cut edges in opposite directions and stand upright.

Cheese

Quality points

- skin or rind should not have spots of mildew
- soft cheeses should have a delicate, creamy consistency, not runny
- freshly cut cheese should not have dry areas or beads of fat on its surface
- cut, pre-wrapped cheese should have no evidence of mould, moisture or greasiness inside the packing
- when cut, no strong foreign smells or indication of ammonia should be present

Storing cheese

1 Cheese should be stored in the refrigerator at 5°C or below, well wrapped so it does not pick up the smells of other food, and to prevent drying out.

2 Wrap in greaseproof paper and/or kitchen foil, or clingfilm which is labelled suitable for fat-rich foods.

3 Cheese should be removed from the refrigerator about an hour before serving, to allow the flavour to develop.

4 Do not use beyond the use-by or best-before date on the packaging.

5 Unopened, vacuum-packed cheese usually has a storage life of several weeks. Stilton, Cheddar and Double Gloucester will keep well for as long as a month. Younger cheese, such as Caerphilly, should be eaten within a few days of purchase. Cream and cottage cheeses must be eaten when fresh.

Some soft cheeses

Cottage cheese is a low-fat cheese with a mild flavour and a grainy appearance. There are also flavoured varieties incorporating small pieces of fruit, vegetables, meat or fish. On its own, or mixed with other ingredients, cottage cheese is often used in salads.

Cream cheese has a soft, buttery texture with a rich, full and mildly acid flavour. It is ideal for spreads and dips.

Mozzarella is pure white, rindless, with a moist, elastic texture. With a creamy, delicate flavour, it is popular in recipes where other flavours need to be highlighted. It is available in two forms: left in its own whey, and in a drier form which is often vacuum-packed for longer life. The drier form is generally better suited to cooking.

Quark (pronounced 'kwark') is a type of soft cheese produced on a large scale in Europe. It has a smooth, white appearance, and a mild, clean, acid flavour. Good in low-fat dressings, and blended with other ingredients.

Fromage frais (literally meaning 'fresh cheese') is similar to quark, but tends to be used in sweet dishes rather than savoury.

Dressings

Dressings are used to:

- add flavour

- keep ingredients moist

- prevent discoloration

- help to bind or hold ingredients together

- make dishes look attractive

They are usually blended with the other ingredients before service, unless their role is simply to provide flavour, in which case they can be offered separately.

There are four groups of dressings:

1 Oil and vinegar – usually unthickened. These have to be shaken or stirred before use as the oil soon separates out and rises to the top.

2 Mayonnaise-based – creamy and thick.

3 Cooked – usually creamy and thick like mayonnaise, but more tart and often made without using any oil, and thickened with eggs or starch.

4 Unthickened liquids with a pronounced flavour. For example, yogurt, sour cream, acidulated cream (cream with a little lemon juice), lemon, lime or orange juice and rose water.

The only limit on the use of seasonings and flavouring liquids is that they should not dominate or swamp the flavour of the food or make it so strong-tasting that subsequent dishes cannot be enjoyed.

Flavourings that are quite widely used include mustard, Worcestershire sauce, Tabasco, chilli, coriander, chervil, chives, basil, tarragon, dill, parsley, mint and, of course, salt and pepper.

Garnishes added to dressings include finely chopped herbs, capers, gherkins, onion, shallots, cucumber, peppers and croûtons (small cubes of fried bread).

Vinaigrette

A mixture of oil and vinegar – a vinaigrette – is the most commonly used dressing on salads. Olive oil is considered by many to have the finest flavour, and is not considered unhealthy, but it is expensive. Alternative oils for salad dressings that are polyunsaturated and therefore do not involve health risks include sunflower, safflower, rapeseed, walnut and corn oils (one of the most economical).

There is also a wide range of vinegars including malt, wine and cider, as well as wine vinegars flavoured with various herbs, most commonly tarragon.

ACTION

Write down some of the different dressings used in your workplace, organised into the four groups suggested on this page. For each dressing, suggest alternative seasonings and/or flavouring liquids which might add interest to the dishes they are served with, and appeal to your customers.

Discuss your suggestions with your tutor or supervisor, and, if possible, try out some of them.

Oil and vinegar

Mayonnaise-based

Cooked

Unthickened liquids

Using dressings

1 Dressings which contain acids (lemon juice, vinegar, etc.) should not be put on green salads until half an hour or so before they are due to be eaten, otherwise the salad will go limp and lose colour and flavour.

2 Thin dressings are best for soft, delicate salads (thick dressings will turn them into a mush).

Vinaigrette

MAKES 100 ml (4 fl oz)

75 ml	salad oil	3 fl oz
25 ml	vinegar	1 fl oz
2.5 ml	French mustard	½ tsp
	seasoning to taste	

Place all the ingredients into a mixing bowl and whisk together thoroughly until combined.

Mayonnaise

MAKES 1 litre (2 pt)

125 ml	pasteurised egg yolks (equivalent to 5 yolks)	¼ pt
2.5 ml	mustard	½ tsp
75–125 ml	white vinegar	3–4 fl oz
1 litre	olive (or salad) oil	2 pt
	squeeze of lemon juice	
	seasoning to taste	

1 Place the egg yolks into a large mixing bowl.

2 Add the seasoning, and the mustard diluted in half the quantity of vinegar.

3 Whisk until thoroughly combined.

4 Add the oil (which should be at room temperature) in a thin stream, while whisking continuously. When the sauce becomes very thick, thin it as required using the remaining vinegar. The mayonnaise should be thick enough to hold its shape when placed on a serving spoon.

5 Finish with the lemon juice and check the seasoning.

When making mayonnaise, it is essential to add the oil very slowly at first. If you do not have a sufficiently steady hand to pour from a jug, use a small ladle.

Why vinaigrette separates and mayonnaise does not

Some liquids do not normally stay mixed, and even if they are shaken or mixed together, one liquid will soon separate out and rise to the top. This is what happens with the oil and vinegar in a vinaigrette. It is known as a *temporary* or *unstable emulsion*, which means that the droplets of oil stay suspended in the vinegar for only a short time.

It is worth remembering, though, that the longer the mixture is shaken or stirred, the smaller the droplets will become, and the longer the emulsion will last.

Unlike vinaigrette, mayonnaise (if it has been properly made) will stay mixed. This is because the egg yolks in it contain a substance called *lecithin* which forms a thin layer around the small droplets of oil so that they cannot join together and separate from the rest of the mixture – thus the emulsion is a stable one. The lecithin acts as an emulsifying agent.

The harder the mayonnaise is beaten to break up the small droplets, the more stable the mixture is. This is why it is so important to add the oil slowly, a drop at a time, during the first stage of making mayonnaise.

Vinaigrette is traditionally used to dress a salade niçoise. *Besides flavour, the dressing gives the salad an attractive shiny appearance, enhancing the colours of the various ingredients.*

The use of a creamy, thick dressing for this dish would result in a rather bland appearance. Where such a dressing is used, contrast of texture and colour can be provided by the use of lettuce and watercress, for example.

Slicing and filleting

The procedures for carving poultry and various joints of meat are described on pages 78–79. Filleting of fish is described on pages 100–101. To remind you of the main points:

- use the right knife for the job, and sharpen if necessary
- select a clean chopping board (colour-coded or labelled for cooked meat/fish), and wipe with a sanitising cloth or solution
- hold the joint firmly during carving
- cut across the grain of the meat
- let the knife do the work for you: use a gentle sawing action for carving, and a light stroking movement for filleting.

SAFETY ▲▲▲

Slicing machines are dangerous. There are some general safety points on page 7. As a reminder:

1 Never operate machines if the safety guards are not in place.
2 Use the carriage, never your hands, to push food against the cutting blade. Do not attempt to slice cucumber, tomatoes, onions and similar small, unevenly shaped or slippery items on a rotary blade slicing machine. The carriage will not hold the food firmly enough.

Note the effectiveness of a simple garnish when combined with attractive china, and with food that has an appetising appearance in its own right (gravlax and prawns) This photograph is used to help ensure consistently good presentation of this dish throughout the Metropole Hotels group.

Peeling hard-boiled eggs

1 When cooked (see page 192), immediately cool under running water.
2 Gently tap all sides of the egg against a firm surface to crack the shell. Or roll along a surface, pressing firmly.
3 Remove the shell carefully, so as to leave the white surface undamaged, if possible removing at the same time the skin that lies just beneath the shell.
4 If the eggs are difficult to peel – a welcome sign that they are very fresh – peel them under cold, running water. This gets between the membrane and the egg itself, so making it easier to shell.

Setting agents

A setting agent helps give blended foods a firmer texture that looks attractive and is more pleasant to eat.

Beaten egg white (pasteurised for reasons of hygiene) and/or *whipped cream* – to firm up mousses.

Butter or fat – sets as the mixture gets cold, as in pâtés and terrines.

Gelatin – available in powder or leaf form. Virtually colourless and flavourless. Before use, powdered gelatin should be softened for a few minutes in a little of the recipe liquid. Soak leaf gelatin in cold water for about 10 minutes before use. Follow recipe quantities for gelatin accurately. Too much will produce a rather rubbery result, too little and the structure may collapse.

Aspic – convenience product or freshly made with good quality stock, minced beef and finely chopped vegetables, clarified with egg white (see page 189). It should not overpower the flavour of the food it is being used with. When used as a garnish (cut into decorative shapes) or as a covering, it is essential that it forms a clear, glossy, unbroken layer.

Agar agar – made from seaweed and used in vegetarian cooking. Can be used in place of gelatin (the quantity required will not necessarily be the same), however it produces a slightly cloudy effect.

To unmould gelatin-thickened mixtures

1 Run a thin knife blade around the top edge of the mould to loosen it.
2 Dip the mould into hot water for one or two seconds.
3 Quickly wipe the outside of the mould dry, then place the serving dish upside down over the open end of the mould. The top surface of the serving dish should be in contact with the food's surface.
4 Hold mould and serving dish firmly together and turn over. Let the food slip gently on to the dish.
5 If the serving dish has been decorated, for example, you will not be able to turn it upside down. In this case the mould itself must be turned upside down. You will need to work quickly and accurately, so that the food slips out of the mould at the right time, and falls in the correct position on the serving dish. Sometimes it will help to keep your hand over the open base of the mould, until the mould is upside down and in position over the serving dish.
6 If it does not unmould, try shaking it gently. If this fails, then try wrapping a hot cloth around the mould – a tea towel dipped in hot water and wrung out.
7 Once the food is out of the mould, refrigerate it for a while so that it firms up again.

From left to right on each serving dish

Far left: *garlic sausage, luncheon sausage, Bierwurst, Danish salami, German salami, two types of Italian salami, Hungarian salami, and, at front, Polish salami.*

Left centre: *mortadella, smoked pork loin, ham.*

Right centre: *corned beef, boiled silverside of beef, ox tongue, brisket.*

Far right: *turkey breast, beef sirloin, leg of pork.*

ACTION

In cold presentation you will come across a great variety of different types of food. Test your knowledge of some of these by working through the simple – and hopefully entertaining – quiz that follows.

When you have completed the exercise, check your answers with your supervisor, tutor or assessor.

For each of the following statements, mark with a:

✔ those which are true/correct

X those which are untrue/incorrect

? those you are unsure about, or the answer depends on the circumstances

Nutrition

- [ ] vitamin C is not found in vegetables
- [ ] vitamin content reduces if the food is prepared too far in advance
- [ ] saturated fats help reduce cholesterol
- [ ] vegetarians only eat vegetables
- [ ] heat destroys some vitamins
- [ ] it is better to cut up vegetables well in advance to preserve vitamins
- [ ] wholemeal bread has a higher fibre content than white bread
- [ ] finely chopped vegetables retain more vitamins than larger cuts
- [ ] olive oil is the worst choice of oil, in terms of health, because of its very high saturated fat content

General knowledge

- [ ] canapés are eaten after a meal, with coffee
- [ ] pin wheels are like miniature Swiss rolls in shape
- [ ] open sandwiches are a single slice of bread with a topping

- [ ] colour coding is a system for distinguishing which equipment should be used to prepare certain types of food
- [ ] parsley is washed after chopping
- [ ] you can't get food poisoning from eating salads
- [ ] hard-boiled egg yolk, forced through a fine sieve, can be used in place of pasteurised egg yolk to make mayonnaise
- [ ] mayonnaise can't be made in a food processor
- [ ] those under the age of 18 are not allowed by law to clean dangerous machines (including slicing machines)
- [ ] hard-boiled eggs must be left to cool in the cooking water

Food commodities

- [ ] salting, pickling and smoking are methods of curing meat
- [ ] aspic can set too hard
- [ ] cooked ox tongue can make an attractive central display on a buffet
- [ ] cold roast sirloin of beef is one of the finest joints for a buffet
- [ ] salami consists of a mixture of lean pork and pork fat
- [ ] turkey is more popular than pork on a cold buffet
- [ ] smoked salmon is as good as smoked trout, but less expensive
- [ ] taramasalata is made from the roe of grey mullet or smoked cod, oil and garlic
- [ ] all taramasalata is bright pink in colour
- [ ] gravlax is a Swedish speciality. It is salmon pickled with dill, sugar, salt, peppercorns and sometimes brandy
- [ ] quark and fromage frais are not cheeses

- [ ] all salami is from Italy
- [ ] Parma ham is an Italian speciality
- [ ] Parma ham is sliced thickly and cooked before eating
- [ ] ham is always cooked before it is sold
- [ ] lobsters and whelks are both molluscs
- [ ] one of the most popular buffet dishes is braised salmon trout, served cold
- [ ] the only type of anchovies used in cold presentation is canned
- [ ] sevruga, osetrova and beluga are types of offal
- [ ] hot smoking (as in mackerel, trout and bucklings) means the fish is served hot
- [ ] cold-smoked fish has to be cooked before it is eaten
- [ ] salmonella bacteria are only found in eggs and bean sprouts
- [ ] shellfish are eaten uncooked

Storage

- [ ] joints of meat can be stored in a refrigerator for up to 6 days
- [ ] cooked fish should be stored no more than 2 days after preparation
- [ ] some types of ham are not stored in the refrigerator
- [ ] meat pies are exempt from the temperature control regulations provided nothing has been added to them after cooking, and they are consumed on the day of preparation or the next day
- [ ] the use of sweet trolleys has been banned under the Food Hygiene Regulations
- [ ] cooked shellfish can be stored in the same refrigerator as raw fish

Assorted cocktail wheels
by McDougalls (RHM Foods)

Key learning points
- » prepare canapés with short pastry base
- » pipe rosettes

MAKES 100 to 120 canapés

225 g	short pastry	8 oz

A) Savoury cheese wheels

15 ml	yeast extract	1 tbsp
50 g	cream cheese	2 oz
5 ml	sunflower seeds (to garnish)	1 tsp

B) Tomato and egg wheels

15 ml	tomato paste	1 tbsp
1	egg (size 4), hard boiled, mashed	1
15 ml	mayonnaise	1 tbsp
2	black olives (to garnish)	2

C) Bacon and liver pâté wheels

1 or 2	thin lean rashers bacon, de-rinded	1 or 2
25 g	liver pâté	1 oz
	red pepper, diced (to garnish)	

1 Roll pastry to a 30 × 20 cm (12 × 8 inch) rectangle. Divide into 3 strips (10 × 20 cm).

2 Spread strip A with yeast extract, strip B with tomato paste and lay bacon slices on strip C.

3 Roll up each pastry strip to enclose the spread (as you would a Swiss roll, see page 248). Cover and chill for 10 minutes (for the pastry to rest).

4 Slice pastry rolls about 0.5 cm (¼ inch) thick. Place on greased baking tray and bake for about 10 minutes at 200°C. Turn over and bake for 2 more minutes.

5 When cool, pipe with rosettes of the appropriate topping, then add garnish:

A – cream cheese – sunflower seeds

B – hard-boiled egg, mashed and blended with mayonnaise – olive

C – liver pâté – diced red pepper.

Crab horns
by McDougalls (RHM Foods)

Key learning points
- » prepare canapés made from rough puff pastry
- » make pastry horns
- » use gelatin

MAKES 24 horns

225 g	rough puff pastry	8 oz
1	egg (size 4) beaten	1
10 ml	gelatin	2 tsp
175 g	crabmeat	6 oz
1	spring onion, trimmed and finely chopped	1
1	stick celery, finely chopped	1
30 ml	mayonnaise	2 tbsp
10 ml	tomato ketchup	2 tsp
10 ml	lemon juice	2 tsp
2.5 ml	Worcestershire sauce	½ tsp

1 Roll pastry thinly to a 30 cm (12 inch) square. Cut in half. Cut each half into 12 strips about 2.5 cm wide and 15 cm long. Moisten down one edge.

2 Grease outside of pastry horn tins.

3 Starting at pointed end, wind strips half-way up, overlapping edges (see page 262).

4 Place on dampened baking sheets, pastry ends underneath. Brush with beaten egg.

5 Bake for 10 to 15 minutes at 230°C. Slide off tins. Leave to cool.

6 Dissolve gelatin in 2 tablespoons of hot water. Mix with the remaining ingredients: crabmeat, onion, mayonnaise, ketchup, lemon juice and Worcestershire sauce.

7 Spoon into pastry horns. Chill until served (the mixture will take 30 to 60 minutes to set).

Avocado with smoked mackerel and curried mayonnaise
by Dufrais

Key learning point
- » prepare a dish of smoked mackerel with mayonnaise-based dressing

SERVES 4

1	egg, size 3	1
2.5 ml	wholegrain mustard	½ tsp
2.5 ml	French mustard	½ tsp
10 ml	garlic wine vinegar	2 tsp
150 ml	grapeseed oil	5 fl oz
10 ml	mild curry paste	2 tsp
	seasoning to taste	
2	smoked mackerel fillets, skinned and flaked	2
2	ripe avocados	2
	lemon wedges (to garnish)	

1 In a blender or food processor, mix together egg, mustards and vinegar until smooth. Gradually add oil, drop by drop, until mixture begins to thicken, then add remainder of oil more quickly.

2 Transfer to a basin and mix in curry paste, seasoning and mackerel. For a smoother mayonnaise, blend in a food processor. Chill until ready to serve.

3 Cut avocados in half and remove skin. Cut into thin slices and fan out on to 4 plates. Spoon mackerel over avocado. (Pipe if you blended the mixture at step 2.) Garnish with lemon and serve immediately.

Potato and feta cheese salad
by Potato Marketing Board

Key learning point
» prepare dressed salad with cheese and pepperoni

SERVES 10

1 kg	new potatoes, well scrubbed, cooked and sliced	2 lb
350 g	feta cheese, diced	12 oz
24	black olives, stoned and halved	24
450 g	small cherry tomatoes	1 lb
150 g	pepperoni, sliced	5 oz
	seasoning to taste	

Dressing

150 ml	olive oil	5 fl oz
45 ml	white wine vinegar	3 tbsp
30 ml	fresh parsley, chopped	2 tbsp

1 Place all the salad ingredients into a bowl and season well.

2 Put the dressing ingredients into a suitable container, close tightly and shake vigorously.

3 Pour the dressing over the salad and toss gently until well coated.

Mixed bean salad
by Dufrais

Key learning points
» prepare salad with pulses
» make vinaigrette

SERVES 4

225 g	fine green beans, cut into short lengths	8 oz
1 × 397 g	can white cannellini beans or red kidney beans, drained and rinsed	1 × 14 oz
4	sticks celery, sliced	4
100 g	red /green grapes, halved, deseeded	4 oz

Dressing

30 ml	red wine vinegar	2 tbsp
	seasoning to taste	
	generous pinch of sugar and mustard powder	
60 ml	salad oil	4 tbsp

1 Cover the green beans with boiling water, bring back to a fast boil, drain and leave to cool. Mix together both types of beans, celery and grapes.

2 Shake together the dressing ingredients in a screw top jar, until evenly mixed. Pour over the salad, toss well and serve.

Caprese salad (*Capri style*)
by Galbani

Key learning point
» prepare a salad with cheese, dressed in olive oil

SERVES 4

400 g	fresh tomatoes (not too ripe), sliced	14 oz
225 g	Mozzarella cheese, sliced	8 oz
	sprigs of basil or dried oregano as preferred	
	seasoning to taste	
	olive oil	

1 Arrange alternately the tomato and cheese slices around the plate. Season.

2 Decorate with sprigs of basil, or sprinkle with oregano. Sprinkle with olive oil and serve.

Salade niçoise

Key learning point
» prepare a salad with cooked fish

SERVES 4

175 g	French beans, trimmed and cooked	6 oz
175 g	potatoes, cooked and cut into cubes or sliced	6 oz
2	small tomatoes, sliced	2
2	tomatoes, peeled, seeded and chopped	2
8	black olives, stoned	8
5 g	capers	¼ oz
8	anchovy fillets (canned)	8
75 g	tuna fish (canned or cooked)	3 oz
25 ml	vinaigrette	1 fl oz
	seasoning to taste	

1 Break the tuna fish into small pieces.

2 Place the potatoes, beans, chopped tomato and tuna into a bowl, lightly season and bind with the vinaigrette.

3 Pile the mixture neatly in the centre of the serving dish.

4 Arrange the sliced tomatoes in a ring around the salad mixture.

5 Wrap each olive with an anchovy fillet and place these on top of the tomato slices. Place a few capers between each slice of tomato (see photograph on page 265).

Greek salad
by The British Iceberg Growers' Association

Key learning point
» prepare salad with anchovies, feta cheese and oregano dressing

SERVES 6

1	iceberg lettuce	1
2	large tomatoes, sliced	2
100 g	feta cheese, sliced	4 oz
1 × 50 g	jar olives stuffed with anchovies	1 × 2 oz
6	spring onions, trimmed	6
60 ml	olive or corn oil	4 tbsp
30 ml	white wine vinegar	2 tbsp
	pinch dried crushed oregano	
	seasoning to taste	

1 Arrange outer leaves of lettuce round a salad bowl. Cube or shred the heart and place in the bowl. Arrange tomatoes, cheese, olives, spring onions and anchovies on top.

2 Put oil, vinegar, oregano and seasoning in a screw top jar and shake well. Pour dressing over salad and serve.

Pasta and frankfurter salad
by Herta

Key learning points
» prepare dressed salad with cooked sausages
Alternative: use cooked, diced potato or cooked rice.

SERVES 4

4	frankfurter sausages, thickly sliced	4
225 g	pasta shells, cooked	8 oz
50 g	red peppers, sliced	2 oz
50 g	spring onions, trimmed and sliced	2 oz
60 ml	mayonnaise	4 tbsp
10 ml	wholegrain mustard	2 tsp
10 ml	horseradish relish	2 tsp
15 ml	caraway seeds	1 tbsp
30 ml	single cream	2 tbsp
	seasoning to taste	

1 Mix together frankfurters, pasta, red pepper and onions.

2 Blend together mayonnaise, mustard, horseradish, caraway seeds and cream, and fold into salad. Chill.

Egg and bacon salad
by The Butter Council

Key learning point
» present a salad of eggs and bacon

SERVES 4

2	thick slices white bread, cut into cubes and fried in 50 g (2 oz) butter until golden brown (croûtons)	2
8	rashers streaky bacon	8
1	iceberg lettuce	1
4	eggs, hard-boiled, sliced	4
225 g	cherry tomatoes	8 oz
	seasoning to taste	
	few drops cider vinegar	
15 ml	sesame seeds	1 tbsp

1 Grill the bacon until crisp. Chop into small pieces.

2 On a layer of lettuce, arrange the egg, tomatoes, bacon and croûtons. Season, sprinkle with vinegar and sesame seeds, and serve.

Crunchy beef salad with warm orange dressing
by Meat and Livestock Commission

Key learning point
» present a salad of sliced cooked beef, with a hot dressing

SERVES 4

350 g	cooked beef, cut into strips	12 oz
45 ml	clear honey	3 tbsp
5 ml	ground ginger	1 tsp
90 ml	orange juice	6 tbsp
2	oranges, grated rind and segmented	2
2	sticks of celery, sliced	2
2	heads chicory, separated	2
50 g	hazelnuts, chopped	2 oz

1 Place the honey, ginger, orange juice and rind in a small saucepan. Bring to the boil, and simmer uncovered for 5 minutes, stirring occasionally until reduced. Allow to cool slightly.

2 Line the salad bowl with the leaves of chicory. Toss all the remaining ingredients gently in the warm dressing, pile in the centre of the chicory leaves and serve immediately.

Turkey salad with banana and cranberry dressing
by Ocean Spray Cranberry Sauce from RHM Foods

Key learning point
» present a salad of chopped turkey

SERVES 8 to 10

450 g	cooked turkey, cut into bite-size pieces	1 lb
4	bananas (medium-size)	4
60 ml	lemon juice	2 fl oz
150 ml	mayonnaise	5 fl oz
250 ml	natural yogurt	9 fl oz
50 ml	cranberry sauce	2 fl oz
	seasoning to taste	
2	green peppers, sliced	2
	black olives	

Mash bananas well, and beat in lemon juice, mayonnaise and yogurt. Stir in cranberry sauce and season. Mix this dressing with the turkey. Decorate with the peppers and olives.

Oriental chicken salad
by British Chicken Information Service

Key learning point
» present a sliced chicken salad

SERVES 4

4	chicken breast portions, cooked, skinned and sliced	4
175 g	Chinese-style beansprouts	6 oz
225 g	Chinese leaves, shredded	8 oz
2	carrots, cut into thin matchsticks	2
2	spring onions, trimmed and sliced	2
1	kiwi fruit, peeled and sliced	1

Dressing

2.5 cm	piece fresh ginger, peeled and finely chopped	1 inch
15 ml	light soy sauce	1 tbsp
15 ml	cider vinegar	1 tbsp
30 ml	soya oil	2 tbsp
	ground black pepper	

Gently combine the salad ingredients. Thoroughly blend the dressing, pour over the salad and serve at once.

NVQ **SVQ** RANGE CHECKLIST

LEVEL 2

2D13.1 Prepare and present cold canapés and open sandwiches

preparing
- [ ] canapés or vol-au-vents
- [ ] open sandwiches

from 2 of these product bases
- [ ] fresh toast or bread
- [ ] preprepared puff pastry
- [ ] preprepared short pastry

with 3 of these toppings and garnishes
- [ ] cooked or cured meats or poultry
- [ ] cooked or cured fish or shellfish
- [ ] fresh vegetables or fruit
- [ ] eggs
- [ ] cheese

2D13.2 Present cooked, cured and prepared foods

presenting 2 of these products
- [ ] cooked or cured meats or cooked poultry
- [ ] fish or shellfish
- [ ] preprepared pâtés or terrines

using 2 of these methods
- [ ] slicing or filleting
- [ ] dressing
- [ ] garnishing

Introduction

Definition Cook-chill is a complete catering system based on preparing food in bulk at one central point, and then using rapid chilling techniques and refrigeration to store the cooked food until it is needed for service.

At a central unit, the food is prepared and cooked to a safe temperature to kill any bacteria present. It is then placed in suitable containers and chilled immediately.

After chilling, the food is stored at just above freezing point – between 0°C and 3°C – for up to five days, including the day of cooking and the day of consumption (eating).

Immediately before service, the food is reheated. In some cases, the food will be reheated at the production unit, and possibly transported to a number of different service units using heated trolleys. Alternatively, the food will be transported in its chilled state, and reheated at the point of service.

Because of the risks involved (from food poisoning – see box on right), it would be wrong to think of cook-chill as a convenient way of preparing food, which can be introduced into any kitchen without the need for special equipment or procedures. In this respect, cook-chill has more in common with a manufacturing or industrial process than conventional catering.

Advantages of cook-chill

In any large catering set-up, menu planning has to take into account how the food is going to be prepared. A cold first and last course for a banquet for 500, for example, can be made in advance, so leaving the chefs free to concentrate on cooking the main course and vegetables.

In a hospital, it will take quite a time for the patients' meals to be plated, then taken to the wards. This means that some of the cooking may have to be staggered. Other dishes have to be able to stand the delay between cooking and arriving at the patients' bedsides.

Cook-chill overcomes many of these problems. The food can be prepared well before it is needed – for one meal, or for a number of meals, if this makes better use of staff time and equipment. A wider menu choice can be offered, because once customers have made their choice all that needs to be done is to reheat the food.

Better value can be offered, because food can be bought and prepared in bulk. If production schedules are planned carefully, equipment can be used to full capacity all the time.

Contents guide

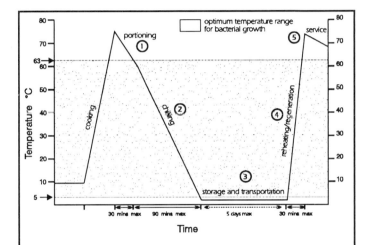

Bacteria which cause food poisoning grow at temperatures between 5°C and 63°C (see page 11). Below 5°C they grow very slowly, or not at all. Above 63°C, the bacteria start to die.

When the food is cooked it passes through this dangerous temperature range. When the food is chilled, as it is in cook-chill systems, it passes through the danger zone a second time. And when the food is reheated for service, conditions are again ideal for bacteria to reproduce.

To reduce these dangers as far as possible, there are strict controls over the maximum time allowed (see graph) for 1) portioning, 2) chilling, 3) storage and transportation, 4) reheating/regeneration and 5) service.

It is also a requirement that the temperature at the centre or core of the food reaches at least 70°C during cooking, and again when the food is reheated. This temperature will kill most harmful bacteria – but not all, hence the need for strict controls throughout the process.

	**Units and elements covered in this section**

2D15 Cook-chill foods	**LEVEL 2**
– 2D15.1 Portion, pack and blast-chill foods	
– 2D15.2 Store cook-chill foods	

Portioning and packing

The room temperature should be below 10°C. During portioning and packaging, staff handling uncooked food should not enter the area.

1   The work area should be prepared so that it is ready for operation, with a supply of the correct containers to hand.

2   The containers must be of the right depth and portion size, and checked to ensure they are clean and undamaged. If stainless steel, ceramic or similar re-usable containers are being used, they must be sterilised before use.

3   Equipment used for portioning and slicing should be clean and sterile. It should not be used for any other purpose – a system of colour-coding will help prevent confusion with equipment used for handling raw food.

4   Wear disposable gloves at all times. Change gloves regularly. Before putting on new gloves, thoroughly wash your hands using a suitable hand-cleaning agent, and dry them using disposable towelling or a warm-air dryer.

5   Follow your establishment's requirements regarding weight and portion size.

6   Complete the portioning process for each batch of food within 30 minutes of completion of cooking.

7   Meat and poultry which need carving or slicing should be sliced hot, and chilled within 30 minutes of leaving the oven. Alternatively, the joint should be sliced after it has been chilled to 10°C or below – and this temperature must be reached within 2½ hours of the food leaving the oven (some workplaces specify 1½ hours). It is mainly for this reason that whole poultry and joints of meat should not be more than 2½ kg (5½ lb) in weight before cooking, and not exceed 10 cm (4 inches) in thickness or height.

8   Fill the containers evenly, so the food is no more than 38 to 50 mm (1½ to 2 inches) deep at any point. If possible, keep the edges of the container free of food.

9   When packing sauces, avoid too much of the sauce flowing through to the base of the container. Otherwise, there is a risk it will overcook during reheating.

10   Generally, containers are closed prior to chilling. With some equipment and some dishes, however, the food must be left uncovered during chilling in order for it to reach the right temperature in the right time. Make sure you know the procedure at your workplace.

Staff in a cook-chill unit portioning food. Note the systematic way in which they are working: a) all the containers are lined up neatly, b) one person is adding the mushrooms, the other the onion.

HYGIENE   👣👣👣

Every effort must be made to avoid the risk of cross-contamination during all stages of the cook-chill process – see also *Hygiene*, pages 9–14.

1   Report any illness or infection before you come to work.

2   Maintain the highest standards of personal hygiene at all times.

3   Pay strict attention to instructions regarding time and temperature.

4   Make sure work surfaces and utensils are thoroughly cleaned before you start a particular task. Keep work areas uncluttered. Keep used items awaiting cleaning separate from clean equipment.

Cook-chill control profile – Catering and Allied Services						
DATE	FOOD	COOK	CHILLING			REHEATING
		CORE TEMP	TIME IN	TIME OUT	CHILL TEMP	FINAL TEMP

For every batch and menu item processed, records should be kept of the core or centre temperatures of the food during cooking, the time of the chilling or freezing process for portioned foods, and the centre temperature of the food at the completion of the chilling process.

This form, one of a number used by the contract catering firm, Catering and Allied Services, also records the final temperature at the time of reheating.

Labelling

1 Label each container as instructed. The label should clearly indicate what the contents are, the date of production, the use-by date, and any special reheating instructions. Sometimes a colour-coding system is used.

2 Attach the label firmly, in a position where it can be easily read during subsequent handling and storage.

Blast-chilling

Try to ensure that all batches of foods to be chilled are:

- of similar consistency or density
- packed in the same sort of container
- with lids on or lids off
- at more or less the same temperature before they go in the blast chiller.

All these factors affect the chilling time. If you have a mixed load, it will be necessary to open the chiller door part-way through the process to remove that food which has reached the right temperature (and before it freezes). This wastes your time, and increases your employer's electricity bill quite substantially.

1 Chilling must start within 30 minutes of the food being cooked.

2 Check the chiller is ready for use.

3 Stack containers so that the air can circulate around them (trolleys help ensure this).

4 The food must be chilled to between 0°C and 3°C within 90 minutes from start of chilling.

5 Check the temperature of the food with a clean temperature probe (which you have first dipped in a sanitising solution, or wiped with a sanitising wipe). Record the temperature and the time it has taken to chill the food.

6 If you are using chilling equipment with built-in probes, do not open the door of the chiller until the correct temperature has been reached. (An alarm or buzzer may sound at this point.)

7 If you are using equipment without built-in probes, check with your supervisor (or with workplace instructions) at what stage the chiller should be opened to check the temperature of the food. Opening the door too often increases chilling times and wastes energy.

8 Immediately after chilling is completed, transport the containers to the chilled store. The labels should still be firmly in place.

The cryogenic batch chiller *shown in this photograph uses liquid nitrogen or carbon dioxide. Both are capable of absorbing a massive amount of heat.*

Air blast chillers, *as the name suggests, use rapidly circulating cold air.* Conduction chillers *circulate ice-cold water around the containers of food, and are specially suitable for cooling bulky liquid dishes such as soup. They can be loaded with deep, lidded pans of up to 18 to 22 litres (4 to 5 gallons) capacity.*

Different types of container you may come across

Containers fall into two basic groups: *multi-portion* or *single-portion*. What is used very often depends on the menu choice, on the method of service being used, and on the equipment available. For example, when a choice of two main courses is available to customers in a self-service restaurant, multi-portion containers would usually be best. If patients in a private hospital have a choice of several dishes for each meal, then single-portion containers are the answer.

Multi-portion containers are usually made of heavy-gauge stainless steel, aluminium or ceramic material. Paper plastic laminates, aluminium foil or other flexible or semi-rigid containers are generally used for single-portion containers. The disadvantage of metal containers is that they cannot be used for reheating in a microwave oven.

Many refrigerators, storage racks, trolleys and reheating ovens are designed to take *gastronorm containers*. These are made to a standard international size. They hold about 3½ kg (8 lb) of food.

What is important, is that the container is sturdy and will not react with the food to cause discolouring or spoilage. The lid should be easy to remove without damaging the contents or causing spillage, and as airtight and watertight as possible, so that moisture, flavours and odours do not penetrate or escape during storage and transportation.

Storing

The food should be kept in a chilled storage compartment or cold room at 0°C to 3°C. Monitors outside the equipment should indicate exactly what this temperature is, and an alarm device should sound if the temperature goes outside the range.

1 The containers (covered and sealed, as appropriate) should be stored so that air can circulate.

2 Containers should be above floor level and away from the door, to keep them out of draughts which might cause temperature variation.

3 Stock rotation procedures must be maintained, with appropriate records. Food that has been stored longest should be used first on a first-in, first-out basis.

4 Chilled storage facilities should not be used for storing other food items.

5 No foods should be stored beyond the date of expiry – no longer than 5 days from the day of cooking.

6 Temperature variations outside the range 0°C to 3°C must be reported immediately. A variation of up to 2°C either side of this band will not usually cause a problem, provided it is promptly spotted and corrected straightaway. But this kind of variation should not happen more than twice in the period before reheating. If the temperature rises above 5°C, but remains below 10°C, the food must be consumed within 12 hours. If any other temperature variations occur, the food must be discarded.

Keeping samples of each food

When a food poisoning problem does occur, or a complaint is made about the quality of the food, it is important to be able to investigate the cause.

For this reason it is the usual practice to set aside a sample of each batch of food produced. It is labelled with the date of production and the name of the dish.

Samples are kept under the same refrigerated conditions as the other food from the batch. They are kept for two or three days beyond the date of consumption. This is because problems are not always reported immediately.

This section, like the NVQ/SVQ qualification in cook-chill, does not cover the preparation and cooking of the food. While this is done on a large scale, the principles are similar to those covered in the units dealing with meat, fish, vegetables, etc.

Nor does the section cover transportation of the food (usually carried out by transport technicians rather than catering staff), and its reheating (which is carried out at the point of service, often by different people from those who have prepared, packed, blast-chilled and stored the food).

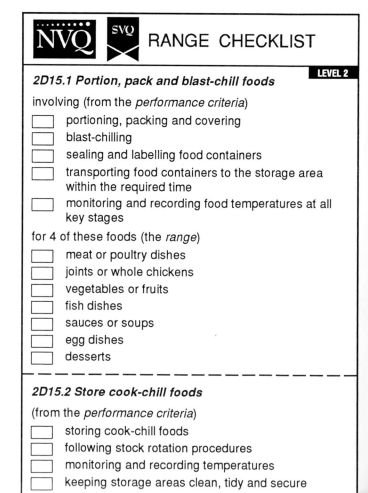

NVQ SVQ RANGE CHECKLIST

2D15.1 Portion, pack and blast-chill foods LEVEL 2

involving (from the *performance criteria*)

☐ portioning, packing and covering
☐ blast-chilling
☐ sealing and labelling food containers
☐ transporting food containers to the storage area within the required time
☐ monitoring and recording food temperatures at all key stages

for 4 of these foods (the *range*)

☐ meat or poultry dishes
☐ joints or whole chickens
☐ vegetables or fruits
☐ fish dishes
☐ sauces or soups
☐ egg dishes
☐ desserts

2D15.2 Store cook-chill foods

(from the *performance criteria*)

☐ storing cook-chill foods
☐ following stock rotation procedures
☐ monitoring and recording temperatures
☐ keeping storage areas clean, tidy and secure

Introduction

Definition Cook-freeze is a specialised food production and distribution system for prolonging the life of prepared and cooked food by rapid freezing, storage at very low temperatures and regenerating (reheating) at the time of service.

The process shares many of its advantages with cook-chill (see page 271). And because foods can be stored frozen for several weeks, rather than a few days, food can be bought in season when it is at its best and relatively inexpensive.

To take advantage of cook-freeze, some recipes need to be altered. Sauces, batters, thickened soups, stews and gravies will break down (or separate) unless a special type of flour is used.

Generally, precooked frozen food can be stored up to eight weeks without any significant loss of nutrients or eating quality. After that time, fish spoils quickly, and foods with a high fat content develop unpleasant flavours. Other foods can be satisfactorily stored for longer periods.

Under similar operating conditions, the running costs of a cook-freeze system are higher than they are for a cook-chill system. More energy is used at each of the following stages:

- freezing the food

- storing the frozen food at very low temperatures

- transporting the food from the central production unit to the points where it is required. To keep the temperature of the food constant, this has to be done in vehicles that are in effect mobile freezer rooms. For short distances, special insulated containers can be used

- reheating the food for service – because the process involves thawing the food and reheating it in one step, the term used for this stage is *regeneration*.

Perhaps the most important factor in the financial success of a cook-freeze system is making full use of the capacity of the equipment. A conventional kitchen, which costs tens of thousands of pounds to equip, can operate at half capacity, probably with fewer staff, and still keep going. But a cook-freeze production system, which costs hundreds of thousands of pounds, has to operate at almost maximum capacity to be cost-effective.

For these reasons, a lot of effort will go into planning such details as:

- what dishes are offered on the menu

- how far in advance they are prepared

- what staff and equipment will be needed for the preparation and cooking.

Contents guide

 Units and elements covered in this section

2D16 Cook-freeze foods **LEVEL 2**
- 2D16.1 Portion, pack and blast-freeze foods
- 2D16.2 Store cook-freeze foods.

This section, like the NVQ/SVQ qualification in cook-freeze, does not cover the preparation and cooking of the food. While this is done on a large scale, the principles are similar to those covered in the units dealing with meat, fish, vegetables, etc.

Nor does the section cover transportation of the food (usually carried out by transport technicians rather than catering staff), and its final regeneration (which is carried out at the point of service, often by different people from those who have prepared, packed, blast-frozen and stored the food).

Like cook-chill, cook-freeze systems mean that cooking can be done in batches, on a large scale. The pastry for these tarts was mixed, rolled, shaped in the aluminium foil pie base, and decorated by machine.

Portioning and packing

The room temperature should be below 10°C. During portioning and packaging, staff handling uncooked food should not enter the area.

1 Prepare your work area, ensure that it is absolutely clean and that you have the space you need to work in.

2 Ensure that the containers/packaging you require are ready to hand, of the right type and the right size, and that you have any equipment you will need.

3 Re-usable containers should have been cleaned and sterilised.

4 You should wear disposable gloves. Before beginning a new task, thoroughly wash and dry your hands and put on a fresh pair of gloves.

5 Do not touch the inside of the containers. Handle aluminium foil, paper and plastic containers carefully as they are not very rigid.

6 Joints of meat and poultry which need carving or slicing should be sliced hot, and put in the blast-freezer within 30 minutes of leaving the oven. Alternatively the joint should be sliced after it has been chilled to 10°C or below – and this temperature must be reached within 2½ hours of the food leaving the oven. (In some workplaces, this time limit is reduced to 1½ hours.) It is mainly for this reason that whole poultry and joints of meat should not be more than 2½ kg (5½ lb) in weight before cooking, and not exceed 10 cm (4 inches) in thickness or height.

7 Pack the food to an even depth, of not more than 50 mm (2 inches) at any point. If a microwave oven is being used to regenerate the food, the depth of the food in the container should not be more than 35 mm (1½ inches).

8 Keep the food free of the edges of the containers as far as possible.

9 Cover the food, sealing the container if necessary.

10 Check and record the temperature of the food.

11 Set aside a sample of each batch, labelling them and storing them as instructed.

The whole cook-freeze process – preparation, cooking, portioning, packaging, blast-freezing and storage – should operate to a carefully worked out timetable, so that equipment is available when required, yet kept working at maximum capacity. Serious delays at any point will usually mean that the food has to be destroyed.

HYGIENE 👣👣👣

The strictest standards of hygiene are necessary in cook-freeze systems. Harmful bacteria still present in the food after cooking, or introduced during the portioning and packing stage, will survive the freezing temperatures. And when the food is regenerated, there is a danger that these bacteria will multiply to dangerous levels.

Equipment and working areas must be regularly and thoroughly cleaned and sanitised.

Most large cook-freeze operations insist that all staff, before entering the work area:

- thoroughly wash and scrub forearms, hands and finger nails with a suitable sanitising soap
- take a shower before changing into clean uniform
- wear colour-coded uniform according to the area of the kitchen they are working in, and also rubber boots
- after changing, wash forearms and hands again in a sanitising solution and walk through a disinfectant footbath.

Labelling

1 Check that you have a good supply of the labels you will need.

2 Make sure that the labels have all the right information on them. This will normally include:

production and *use-by date*

name of dish/description of contents

number of portions

instructions for regenerating: type of oven to be used, temperature, timing, lid on or off, stirring before service, special finishing touches, etc.

3 Attach the label firmly in a position where it can be read during subsequent storage and handling.

Blast-freezing

Ordinary storage freezers cannot lower the temperature of food fast enough for the cook-freeze process, so specialist equipment has to be used.

Air blast-freezers take 75 to 90 minutes to freeze food, depending on how it is packaged. Very cold air (between $-32°C$ and $-40°C$) is blown by powerful fans over and around the food. The warmed air is constantly drawn out and recirculated through the heat exchange unit to lower its temperature.

In the larger models of freezer, the food is pushed in on a trolley at one end and the trolley is then wheeled out at the other. The largest models of all take the food automatically through a kind of freezing tunnel.

Cryogenic freezers are the fastest. Most models use liquid nitrogen and a typical freezing time is 25 minutes for uncovered food. Food covered by lids takes a little longer. Liquid nitrogen at $-196°C$ is sprayed through special nozzles into the freezing chamber. Fans circulate the cold nitrogen so that the food freezes evenly. The nitrogen absorbs heat from the food until it freezes, and the warmed gas is pumped out of the cabinet and more cold nitrogen is fed in.

Liquid carbon dioxide is a more expensive alternative to nitrogen. Time is longer, typically around 45 minutes.

1 Freezing should start as soon as possible after completion of cooking and portioning, and in any event within 30 minutes of the food being cooked.

2 There should be at least 20 mm (¾ inch) air space between layers of containers in the freezer.

3 In 90 minutes the food must be frozen to below $-5°C$.

4 Immediately after blast-freezing, transfer the food to the deep-freeze storage. As you do this, check that the labels are still clear and firmly attached.

This is the range of containers and labels used in one particular cook-freeze operation.

The benefit of disposable containers like these is that they are guaranteed to be clean (assuming, of course, that they have been stored correctly). Stainless steel containers which hold a number of portions (see page 273) are more durable, but they are too expensive to be left in the freezer for long periods. They also need to be cleaned very thoroughly.

Aluminium foil containers are not suitable for use in a microwave oven.

ACTION

Choose one or two of the safety rules in your workplace, and prepare a short talk which would be suitable for new staff. The idea is a) to put across clearly what the rule is, so that your audience will remember it, and b) to explain the reasoning behind the rule.

So, for example, if the rule is *Glass objects are not allowed in the kitchen*, you would point out that in a food production unit, where hundreds or thousands of meals are being prepared, the consequences of bits of broken glass getting into food are very serious.

The best way of guaranteeing that there won't be a problem is to ban the use of glass objects altogether.

Once you have prepared the notes and any visual aids which might help your talk, try it out on a friend. Afterwards, ask your friend to suggest ways in which your talk might be made even more powerful.

Storing

The food must be kept at the correct deep-freeze storage temperature. This is between –20°C and –30°C, and at least below –18°C.

Up-to-date and accurate records must be kept of deep-freeze performance temperatures. Some types of equipment automatically monitor and record temperatures.

The deep-freeze must have an alarm device which, should the temperature rise above the operating range, will alert the attention of someone in charge, no matter what the time of day or night.

1   Store the food (in covered or sealed containers according to the dish and freezing method) on shelves, trolleys or racks above floor level, away from the door, and with enough space around each item to allow the cold air to circulate.

2   Wear protective clothing and thick gloves when entering a deep-freeze store. These have to meet the hygiene requirements, so an anorak or gloves that you also wear outdoors will not be acceptable.

3   Do not stay inside the freezer for more than 2 minutes.

4   Maintain stock rotation on a first-in, first-out basis, and keep stock record systems accurately.

5   Report to your supervisor any foods that have passed their use-by date. On no account should these be used.

6   Food that has thawed either partially or completely should never be returned to the deep-freeze store.

The extent of drip and texture loss depends on the water content of the food. Strawberries, like tomatoes and other soft fruit, have a high water content and a fragile structure. They tend to get damaged easily during freezing and lose a great deal of liquid when defrosted.

Frozen storage and quality

Three conditions are important to maintain the quality of food during frozen storage:

1   Temperatures should be at least –18°C and preferably as low as –30°C. The lower the temperature, the less chance food spoilage organisms have.

2   Storage temperature must be kept as constant as possible. Even a few degrees' increase in temperature may cause some of the ice crystals in the food to melt. As the temperature drops again this liquid will re-freeze, usually forming bigger, more damaging crystals.

3   Food must be properly covered to prevent it losing moisture. Serious moisture loss causes freezer burn, and the food surface discolours (dark spots form on fresh meat, grey areas appear on cooked meat).

A second reason for keeping food covered is to protect it against frost. If warm air containing moisture enters the freezer, for example, when the door is opened, once the door is shut again the air will quickly cool and no longer be able to hold so much moisture. The moisture will then form frost on exposed food and food packaging.

NVQ SVQ RANGE CHECKLIST

LEVEL 2

2D16.1 Portion, pack and blast-freeze foods

involving (from the *performance criteria*)

- [ ] portioning, packing and covering
- [ ] blast-freezing
- [ ] sealing and labelling food containers
- [ ] transporting food containers to the storage area within the required time
- [ ] monitoring and recording food temperatures at all key stages

for 4 of these foods (the *range*)

- [ ] meat or poultry dishes
- [ ] joints or whole chickens
- [ ] vegetables or fruits
- [ ] fish dishes
- [ ] sauces or soups
- [ ] egg dishes
- [ ] desserts

2D16.2 Store cook-freeze foods

(from the *performance criteria*)

- [ ] storing cook-freeze foods
- [ ] following stock rotation procedures
- [ ] monitoring and recording temperatures
- [ ] keeping storage areas clean, tidy and secure

Accompaniments items served with particular dishes, e.g. horseradish sauce and Yorkshire pudding with roast beef.

Aerate incorporate air or gas into a mixture.

Al dente Italian expression – translates literally as 'to the tooth' – describes pasta, rice or vegetables that remain firm after being lightly cooked.

Aspic savoury jelly, usually based on meat or fish stock.

Au gratin sprinkled with cheese or breadcrumbs, and browned under the grill or in a hot oven.

Bacterium (single) **Bacteria** (plural) microscopic living organisms (micro-organisms). The harmful varieties are called pathogenic.

Bain-marie a) a utensil for gently cooking food while keeping it away from direct heat. One example is a double saucepan with hot water in the bottom section and food in the top. b) A type of hot cupboard which keeps food warm. The containers of food sit in the top, either in hot water or hot air.

Barding covering food with a layer of fat to protect and moisten its surface during roasting or braising.

Base sauce convenience sauce which can be combined with traditional ingredients or stock to make a range of classical sauces, e.g. lyonnaise, hollandaise.

Basting spooning fat, oil, marinade, sauce, etc. over food during cooking to prevent the surface from drying out.

Battening tenderising food, usually meat, by beating it with a heavy implement such as a cutlet bat.

Beating combining ingredients thoroughly. This is often done to incorporate air into the mixture.

Béchamel white sauce made with a roux and milk.

Bed of roots roughly cut vegetables used to protect the base of food in braising and roasting, and to add flavour to the dish. Also sometimes called matignon or mirepoix.

Beurre manié a paste made from blended butter and flour which is used to thicken liquids.

Blanching a method of pre-cooking or part-cooking food. Vegetables are blanched by being plunged briefly into boiling water before being cooled (refreshed) under cold water. Also a method of removing impurities from poor quality meats, by bringing them to the boil in cold water, discarding the water, using fresh water to complete cooking.

Blanquette type of stew. Meat is blanched to remove impurities, and then cooked in unthickened liquid, from which a sauce is made before service.

Blending thoroughly mixing two or more ingredients.

Bouquet garni collection of herbs used for flavouring in soups or stews. Traditionally, fresh herbs including a bay leaf, parsley stalks, thyme and rosemary are tied in a bunch. If dried herbs are used, they are placed in a small muslin bag or even wrapped in a stick of celery or leaf of leek which has been previously softened by blanching.

Bratt pan large item of floor-mounted cooking equipment that acts as a huge shallow saucepan. Used for large-scale catering, such as stewing in bulk.

Breaded coated in breadcrumbs before cooking.

Broiling American term for grilling.

Browning colouring food by heating it, usually quite fiercely.

Brunoise very fine dice, usually of vegetables.

Caramelise cooking sugar until it turns brown.

Carbohydrate one of the main classes of nutrients found in food. They include starches and sugars, and most of them are converted by the body into energy.

Carry-over cooking the cooking in roasting and microwaving which continues for a few minutes after the food has been removed from the oven.

Cartouche a piece of greased paper used to protect the surface of food (usually from drying out), which is shaped to fit inside the pot, tray or bowl.

Chinoise conical strainer.

Cholesterol substance produced in the body (by the liver) from fats, particularly saturated fats. Too much cholesterol causes heart disease.

Clarifying a) the stage in making consommé and aspic when the flavouring ingredients are separated out to leave a clear liquid. b) Making fat (especially butter) clear by gentle heating.

Clouté studded. For example, an onion pierced with a clove (usually holding a bay leaf in place) is called an onion clouté.

Coagulate setting or firming up of the proteins.

Combi ovens ovens that can provide more than one form of heating, e.g. convection and microwaving.

Concassé roughly chopped, usually tomato flesh.

Cooked out describes flour that has been cooked to the stage when it loses its starchy taste, as in a roux.

Coulis sauce made from a purée of fruit or vegetables.

Court-bouillon cooking liquid made of water and other ingredients such as stock, wine or vinegar, and vegetables, used to improve a food's flavour and sometimes to tenderise. An important use is in cooking fish and shellfish.

Covers cover means a place setting (at a table). Used as shorthand for the number of customers expected for, or served at a meal, e.g. 12 covers.

Creaming vigorously beating fat and sugar until mixture is creamy in colour and fluffy in texture.

Croquette minced or puréed food moulded in cylindrical shape, then often coated with breadcrumbs and deep fried.

Cross-contamination transfer of food-poisoning bacteria from an infected source (usually raw food) to previously uninfected food, for example, food that has been cooked.

Croûton shaped piece of fried bread.

Curdling separating of the mixture, e.g. a) in creamed fat and sugar, following the addition of egg, b) in mayonnaise or hollandaise sauce, when the oil floats to the top.

Decant pour off liquid after sediment has settled. For example, fat from a roasting tray once the meat juices and food particles have settled to the bottom.

Déglacer swilling out cooking pan with water after shallow frying or roasting to collect juices and food particles left from the cooking. The liquid can then be used as the basis for sauce or gravy.

Demi-glace a basic brown sauce.

Dice cut into cubes, as in diced vegetables.

Doily patterned dish paper.

Dry fried meat is placed in a cold frying pan and cooked over a low heat until some fat runs out. The heat is then increased and the meat fried for the recommended time.

Duxelles finely chopped mushrooms, shallow fried with finely chopped onion or shallots in a little oil or butter.

Egg wash beaten egg (sometimes mixed with a little water or milk). Used: a) in baking to join two pieces of pastry, b) in baking, to give a shiny golden appearance to the food when cooked, c) in shallow or deep frying to hold coatings on food.

Elastin a protein in connective tissue which remains fairly tough even after cooking.

Emulsion a mixture of two liquids, such as oil and vinegar. It may stay mixed for some time, e.g. mayonnaise, or separate quickly, e.g. some forms of vinaigrette.

Escalope thin slice of meat, poultry or game.

Espagnol basic brown sauce.

Farce stuffing, sometimes of minced poultry, meat, fish etc.

Fermentation the stage in baking doughs when yeast produces carbon dioxide.

Fibre parts of edible plants or seeds which cannot be digested by the body, but which are important in digestion because they provide bulk which helps food travel through the digestive system.

Filleting a) cutting and preparing fish by removing the bones to produce fillets (whole sides or lengths of flesh), b) used occasionally to describe certain methods of preparing meat.

Flake break food into pieces, e.g. canned tuna fish.

Flambé describes food that has had alcohol, such as brandy, poured on it and set alight so that it flames briefly and produces a distinctive flavour. Often done in the presence of the customer for dramatic effect.

Flan Open tart, with fruit, savoury filling etc.

Flash point temperature at which oil or fat bursts into flames.

Flash roasting placing food in a very hot oven to brown its surface.

Floured coated in flour.

Folding in carefully blending ingredients with a mixture (often already whisked) by gently turning or folding one part over the other with a spatula or spoon so that the mixture's lightness is retained.

Frappé served on a bed of crushed ice, e.g. melon frappé.

Fricassée type of stew, in which the meat is cooked in a thickened liquid.

Fumet very concentrated stock.

Garnish to make a dish look attractive, for example a twisted slice of lemon on a slice of smoked salmon.

Gelatin or **Gelatine** a virtually tasteless substance made from boiling animal hides and bones (or alternative sources), available in powdered or leaf form for thickening or setting cold foods, e.g. mousses, jellies, aspics.

Glazing giving food an attractive, shiny appearance: a) by repeated basting with the cooking liquid, b) by reducing with butter and sugar, c) by coating with a thickened fruit juice or thin jam.

Gratinate brown the surface of a cooked dish, usually under the grill or in a very hot oven.

Greasing rubbing baking utensil with fat to stop the food sticking.

Griddling shallow frying on a solid surface.

Gutting removing the intestines, heart, liver etc. from fish or poultry.

Hors d'oeuvre preliminary dish in a meal, designed to stimulate the appetite.

Jointing cutting up meat, poultry etc. into joints or at a joint.

Juliennes thin strips of food, as in juliennes of carrot.

Jus lié strong brown stock thickened with arrowroot.

Kneading working dough into a properly blended mixture.

Knocking back kneading dough after a period of fermentation to reduce its size and increase the effectiveness of the yeast.

Larding inserting strips of fat (or occasionally vegetables) into lean meat or fish to ensure that it remains moist during cooking.

Leaching leaking out of substances (e.g. vitamins) from food (e.g. vegetables) into the cooking liquid.

Liaison mixture of egg yolks and cream beaten together, then added to a cooking liquid (in a stew, for example) to thicken.

Macedoine fruit or vegetables (normally several types) cut into small dice.

Marinating or **marinading** soaking food in a flavouring (and sometimes tenderising) liquid.

Mask to cover with a smooth, thick sauce.

Matignon see *Bed of roots*.

Microorganism any organism such as a bacterium or virus which is microscopic in size.

Minerals a group of essential nutrients that occur naturally in many foods and help control the body's functions and maintain health.

Mirepoix see *Bed of roots*

Mise en place collecting together all the ingredients and equipment necessary for a particular dish or range of dishes.

Nutrients chemicals in food which provide essential substances for the health and proper functioning of the body. They include carbohydrates, fats, minerals and vitamins.

Offal edible internal organs of animals such as the heart, tongue and liver, and also the parts of the animal that are left after the meat has been removed, such as the feet and tail.

Ovenproof able to withstand the high temperatures reached in an oven.

Oxidisation the effect that oxygen (and therefore air, which contains oxygen) has on certain substances. Many foods are affected, e.g. fats turn rancid.

Pané coated in breadcrumbs.

Parboiling boiling food until it is partly cooked, usually for a very short time.

Pass strain food such as a soup or sauce through a sieve.

Pathogenic harmful, as in pathogenic bacteria.

Paupiette thin slice or fillet of meat or fish, stuffed and rolled into a cylindrical shape.

Piping forcing whipped cream, icing stuffing etc. through a small nozzle: a) as a decoration for the food, b) as a convenient way of stuffing a small object e.g. a length of celery stick.

Piquant sharply flavoured.

Glossary

Plat à sauter shallow frying pan with vertical sides.

Poêler see *Pot roasting*.

Polyunsaturated fat type of fat. Better for healthy eating than saturated fat.

Pot roasting or **poêler** cooking food in the oven in a sealed pot on a bed of vegetables with butter.

Protein one of the groups of nutrients that are essential for the body to function properly and remain healthy. Proteins are especially important for the body's growth and are present in a wide range of animal and vegetable foods, especially meat and dairy products.

Proving allow a yeast dough to rest in a warm place to rise and expand.

Purée smooth mixture or pulp, obtained by: a) cooking the food until it breaks up, b) mashing or beating or mixing the food vigorously, c) forcing the food through a sieve, d) blending it in a liquidiser.

Quenelles food formed into small cigar shapes, e.g. finely minced meat, fish or vegetables.

Rancid fats or fatty foods which have gone bad and taste or smell unpleasant because of oxidisation.

Reconstituting another word for regenerating.

Reducing boiling a liquid, e.g. sauce or stock, so that it reduces in volume, becoming more flavoured and, if appropriate, thicker.

Refreshing plunging food into cold water to lower the temperature rapidly and so stop the cooking process.

Regenerating controlled reheating of food which has already been fully cooked and then chilled or frozen.

Rendering melting suet or other hard fat to become dripping or lard.

Ribbon stage in thickening an egg-based sauce, when some is lifted up on a spoon and allowed to run back into the mixture, a visible trail mark is formed on the surface of the mixture.

Roux paste of flour and fat that is cooked for a short time before being used to thicken liquid, e.g. in sauce or soup making.

Rubbing in (in baking) incorporating fat into flour by rubbing between fingertips, until the mixture resembles breadcrumbs.

Sabayon egg yolks mixed with a liquid and then heated until the mixture thickens.

Salamander overhead grill.

Sanitise to use chemical disinfectant to kill harmful bacteria.

Saturated fats type of fat found most commonly in dairy products and meat. A less healthy alternative than polyunsaturated fats.

Sautéing a shallow frying process: cooking food quickly in very hot oil or fat so that it browns.

Sauteuse shallow cooking vessel with sloping sides.

Scoring cutting just through the surface of food, to: a) stop the skin bursting in grilled fish, b) allow food to take in the flavour of a marinade, c) give a decorative effect.

Sealing an old-fashioned term for searing.

Searing using high temperatures to brown the surface of food.

Seasoned flour flour seasoned with salt and pepper.

Seasoning adding salt, pepper and other savoury flavourings to food to improve its flavour.

Shortening term for fats used in baking.

Shredded very finely sliced.

Simmering gentle boiling when the surface of the liquid is only just broken by small bubbles.

Skimming removing surface fat, scum and impurities that rise to the top of a liquid, especially during boiling and simmering.

Smoke point temperature at which oil gives off a visible smoke.

Soft flour flour which does not form much gluten (important in cake making, for example).

Standing time the short period of time when food is deliberately allowed to rest: a) after roasting meat and before carving (so that the meat can set), b) after microwaving (to allow carry-over cooking).

Starch a type of carbohydrate, and therefore an important nutrient. It occurs naturally in many vegetables and grains, e.g. potatoes and rice, and is converted by the body into energy.

Sterilise to make free of living microorganisms, especially harmful bacteria. Normally refers to use of heat (as opposed to sanitise).

Stir frying cooking very quickly in a wok, over a high heat, constantly stirring the food.

Straining passing liquid through a sieve or cloth to separate off any solids.

Strong flour flour that is capable of forming a lot of gluten (important in bread making, for example).

Suprêmes a) cut of poultry which includes one side of the breast and sometimes the first part of the wing bone, b) a piece cut on the slant from a large fillet of fish.

Sweating shallow frying food gently without allowing it to brown.

Temperature probe instrument which is inserted into food to measure the internal temperature.

Tenderising making food tender and therefore easy to chew.

Thermostat instrument usually incorporated into equipment like an oven, which adjusts the temperature to keep it constant.

Topping and tailing trimming off the tough extremities of foods such as French beans or gooseberries.

Trail stage when a whisked mixture becomes thick enough for the whisk to leave trail marks behind it.

Trussing securing food (usually a joint of meat) with string so that it keeps a neat shape during cooking.

Turning shaping pieces of food, e.g. potatoes, often in an oval or barrel form.

Velouté a sauce made with a roux and white stock.

Vitamins group of essential nutrients that help the body to function properly and remain healthy. Different vitamins occur naturally in different foods, e.g. vitamin A in carrots and egg yolk.

White fats fats produced specifically for baking.

Wok metal cooking pot with a bowl shape, for stir frying.